Herencia

The Anthology of
Hispanic Literature
of the United States

Recovering the U.S. Hispanic Literary Heritage

HERENCIA

The Anthology of HISPANIC LITERATURE *of the United States*

EDITOR

NICOLÁS KANELLOS — University of Houston

CO-EDITORS

KENYA DWORKIN Y MÉNDEZ	Carnegie-Mellon University
JOSÉ B. FERNÁNDEZ	University of Central Florida
ERLINDA GONZÁLEZ-BERRY	Oregon State University
AGNES LUGO-ORTIZ	Dartmouth College
CHARLES TATUM	University of Arizona

COORDINATOR

ALEJANDRA BALESTRA — University of Houston

OXFORD
UNIVERSITY PRESS

OXFORD
UNIVERSITY PRESS

Oxford New York
Auckland Bangkok Buenos Aires Cape Town Chennai
Dar es Salaam Delhi Hong Kong Istanbul Karachi Kolkata
Kuala Lumpur Madrid Melbourne Mexico City Mumbai
Nairobi São Paulo Shanghai Taipei Tokyo Toronto

First published by Oxford University Press, Inc., 2002
First issued as an Oxford University Press paperback, 2003
198 Madison Avenue, New York, New York 10016
www.oup.com

Library of Congress Cataloging-in-Publication Data
Herencia: the anthology of Hispanic literature of the United States /
editor, Nicolás Kanellos; co-editors, Kenya Dworkin y Mendez . . .
[et al.]; coordinator, Alejandra Balestra.
p. cm.
Includes bibliographical references.
ISBN 0-19-513824-4 (cloth) ISBN 0-19-513825-2 (pbk.)
1. American literature—Hispanic American authors.
2. Hispanic American literature (Spanish)—Translations into English.
3. Hispanic Americans—Literary collections.
I. Kanellos, Nicolás. II. Dworkin y Méndez, Kenya.
III. Balestra, Alejandra.
PS508.H57 H48 2001
810.8'0868—dc21 2001033131

9 8 7 6 5 4 3 2 1

Printed in the United States of America on acid-free paper

ACKNOWLEDGMENTS

The editors express their sincerest thanks to the Rockefeller Foundation for underwriting the research as well as the organizational planning that went into the compilation of this anthology. In particular, we are forever indebted to Tomás Ybarra-Frausto and Lynn Szwaja. We are also grateful for the support rendered by the Ford Foundation, the Meadows Foundation, the Mellon Foundation, and the National Endowment for the Humanities for their support of research that went into the preparation of this anthology. Many thanks to Elda Rotor at Oxford University Press, who believed in this project from the beginning and has given us invaluable guidance. And, of course, mil gracias to all of the scholars around the country and abroad who have participated directly or indirectly in the Recovering the U.S. Hispanic Literary Heritage project.

CONTENTS

An Overview of Hispanic Literature of the United States

Introduction

In recent years, more and more Hispanic surnames have been appearing on the pages of book reviews and on college syllabi throughout the United States. One tends to associate this rather sudden appearance of a body of work with the growing Hispanic presence within the borders of the United States, as well as with the seemingly ubiquitous Hispanic influence on popular culture in the country. In fact, due to the lack of available texts, most scholars have limited the study and teaching of Chicano, Puerto Rican, and Cuban literatures in the United States to works published within the last forty years, furthering the impression that U.S. Hispanic literature is new, young, and exclusively related to the immigrant experience. A systematic and thorough examination of Hispanic life in the United States, however, reveals a greater and richer contribution to literature and culture than has been understood up to the present. Historically, the diverse ethnic groups that we conveniently lump together as "Hispanics" or "Latinos" created a literature in North America even before the founding of the United States. The sheer volume of their writing over 400 years is so overwhelming that it would take thousands of scholars researching for many years to fully recover, analyze, and make accessible all that is worthy of study and memorializing. And, in its variety and multiple perspectives, what we will call "U.S. Hispanic" literature is far more complex than the mere sampling of the last forty years would lead us to believe. This literature incorporates the voices of the conqueror and the conquered, the revolutionary and the reactionary, the native and the uprooted or landless. It is a literature that proclaims a sense of place in the United States while it also erases borders; it is transnational in the most postmodern sense possible. It is a literature that transcends ethnicity and race, while striving for a Chicano, Nuyorican, Cuban American, or just Hispanic or Latino identity. *Herencia: The Anthology of Hispanic Literature of the United States* is a first effort to recover interesting artifacts selected from the historical development of this literature and the first to attempt to interpret and understand this diverse and at times contradictory cultural past. Included are many texts that until now have been hidden from view, even as Hispanic culture in the United States has been hidden in the shadows of history.

The Literature of Exploration and Colonization

The introduction of Western culture to the lands that eventually would belong to the United States was accomplished by Hispanic peoples: Spaniards, Hispanicized Africans and Amerindians, mestizos, and mulattos. For better or worse, Spain was the first country to introduce a written European language into an area that would become the mainland United States. Beginning in 1513 with Juan Ponce de León's diaries of travel in Florida, the keeping of civil, military, and ecclesiastical records eventually became commonplace in what would become the Hispanic South and Southwest of the United States. Written culture not only facilitated these records, but it also gave birth to the first written descriptions and studies of the fauna and flora of these lands new to the Europeans, mestizos, and mulattos. It made possible the writing of laws for their governance and commercial exploitation and for writing and maintaining a history—an official story and tradition—of Hispanic culture.

Ponce de León was followed by numerous other explorers, missionaries, and colonists. Among the most important was Alvar Núñez Cabeza de Vaca, whose *La relación* (The Account), published in Spain in 1542, may be considered the first anthropological and ethnographic book in what became the United States, documenting his eight years of observations and experiences among the Indians. Some scholars have treated his memoir as the first book of "American" literature written in a European language. Other chroniclers, memoirists, playwrights, and poets followed in the Floridas and the area that would become the southwestern United States.

This introduction of writing in the Spanish language was followed by a literate culture that spread northward through New Spain and into the lands that by the mid-nineteenth century would become part of the United States through conquest, annexation, and purchase.

All of the institutions of literacy—schools, universities, libraries, government archives, courts, and others—were first introduced by Hispanic peoples to North America by the mid-sixteenth century. The importation of books to Mexico was authorized in 1525; the printing press was introduced in 1539; and newspapers began publishing in 1541. As for communications and publishing, the populations on the northern frontier of New Spain fared better after independence from Spain, during the Mexican period of government, when the missions were secularized and the responsibility for education shifted into the hands of a liberal government struggling to establish a democracy. During the Mexican period, printing presses were finally introduced into these frontier areas, with both California and New Mexico housing operating presses by 1834. The California press was a government press, while the New Mexican press was held in private hands, by Father

Antonio José Martínez, who printed catechisms and other books as well as New Mexico's first newspaper, *El Crepúsculo*, beginning in 1835. The printing press had already made its way into Texas in 1813 as part of the movement for Mexico's independence from Spain. Thus, considerable progress had been made toward the establishment of a literate population before Northern Mexico became part of the United States.

Hispanics settling in the thirteen British colonies had immediate access to printing. In the mid-seventeenth century, the first Spanish-speaking communities were established by Sephardic Jews in the Northeast of what would become the United States. They were followed by other Hispanics from Spain and the Caribbean who, by the 1800s, were issuing through early American printers and their own presses hundreds of political and commercial books, as well as many works of creative literature written principally by Hispanic immigrants and political refugees. In Louisiana and later in the Southwest and to some extent the Northeast, bilingual publications often became a necessity for communicating, first with the Hispano- and Francophone populations and later the Hispano- and Anglophone populations, as publications reflected bicultural life in the United States.

Hispanic literate culture in the United States, however, has existed quite beyond the need to communicate with non-Spanish speakers and non-Hispanics. By the beginning of the nineteenth century, Hispanic communities in the Northeast, South, and Southwest were substantial enough to support trade among themselves and, thus, to require written and printed communications in the Spanish language. Spanish-language newspapers date from the beginning of the nineteenth century. *El Misisipi* was published in 1808 and *El Mensagero Luisianés* in 1809, both in New Orleans; *La Gaceta de Texas* and *El Mexicano* were issued in 1813 in Nacogdoches, Texas, and Natchitoshes, Louisiana. These were followed by numerous others in Florida, Louisiana, Texas, and the Northeast. It is estimated that some 2500 periodicals were issued between 1808 and 1960, to carry news of commerce and politics as well as poetry, serialized novels, stories, essays, and commentary both from the pens of local writers as well as reprints of the works of the most highly regarded writers and intellectuals of the entire Hispanic world, from Spain to Argentina. When northern Mexico and Louisiana were incorporated into the United States, this journalistic, literary, and intellectual production, rather than abate, intensified. The newspapers took on the task of preserving the Spanish language and Hispanic culture where Hispanic residents were becoming rapidly and vastly outnumbered by Anglo and European migrants—or "pioneers," if one prefers, although they were hardly pioneers if Hispanics, Amerindians, and mestizos had already lived in those areas and had established institutions there. The newspapers became forums for discussions of rights, both cultural and civil; they became the libraries and memories of the small towns in New Mexico and the *defensores de la raza* (defenders of Hispanics) in the large cities. Quite often they were the only Spanish-language textbooks for learning to read and write Spanish in rural areas—and they were excellent textbooks at that in providing the best examples of written language drawn from the greatest writers in the Hispanic world, past and present. Many of the more successful newspapers grew into publishing houses by the end of the nineteenth and beginning of the twentieth centuries.

Newspapers in immigrant communities reinforced the culture of the homeland and its relationship with the United States; newspapers that saw their communities as minorities in the United States reinforced a native identity, protected the civil rights of their communities, and monitored the community's economic, educational, and cultural development. Whether serving the interests of immigrants or an ethnic minority community, it was always incumbent on the press to exemplify the best writing in the Spanish language, to uphold high cultural and moral values, and, of course, to maintain and preserve Hispanic culture. Quite often, too, Hispanic-owned newspapers and the literature they published took on the role of contestation, challenging and offering alternative views to those published in the English-language press, especially as concerned their own communities and homelands.

From the beginning of the nineteenth century, the literary culture of Hispanics began assuming the expressive functions that have characterized it to the present day. These have been predominantly three distinctive types of expression: that of natives, immigrants, and exiles. Not only do these categories reveal the three general identities of Hispanics in the United States across history, but they also allow us to understand the literary expression of Hispanics. For this reason, the present anthology has been organized to reflect the distinct realities and expressive culture of native, immigrant, and exiled Hispanics. On the foundation of the written and oral legacy of Hispanic exploration and colonization of vast regions that became the United States, these three historical processes and patterns of expression planted firm roots. This foundational base of exploration and settlement included descriptions of the flora and fauna, encounters with the Amerindians and their evangelization, and daily life on the frontier as perceived by the Spanish and Hispanicized peoples (including Africans, Amerindians, mestizos, and mulattos) in chronicles, journals, ethnographies, letters, and oral lore. The first texts were written by the explorers who charted this territory and its peoples, such as Alvar Núñez Cabeza de Vaca and Fray Marcos de Niza; epic poems were composed by soldiers, such as Gaspar Pérez de Villagrá in his *History of New Mexico,* and missionaries, such as Alonso Gregorio de Escobedo in his *La Florida.* Later, settlers and missionaries, such as Fray Gerónimo Boscana and the anonymous authors of the folk dramas *The Texans* and *The Comanches* and the *indita* and *alabado* songs, developed a distinctive mestizo literature, exhibiting many of the cultural patterns that persist to the present.

All of this literary ferment, whether written or oral, took place in the northern territories of New Spain and Mexico that did not have access to the printing press. Although the world of books, libraries, and education had been introduced by the Spanish to North America, the strict banning of the printing press by the Royal Crown in its frontier territories impeded the development of printing and publishing among the native Hispanic population, the strongest base of Hispanic native culture in what would become the Southwest of the United States. Instead, there is a strong legacy that persists to this date of oral or folk expression in these lands, reinforced as well by the overwhelmingly working-class nature of Hispanics over the last two centuries. Ironically, the earliest widespread use of printing and publishing by Hispanics in the United States took place in an English-speaking environment. In the Northeastern United States at the turn of the nineteenth century, it was the Spanish-speaking exiles and immigrants who were the first to have access to the printing press.

Native Hispanic Literature

Native Hispanic literature develops first out of the experience of colonialism and racial oppression. Hispanics were subjected to more than a century of "racialization" through doctrines such as the Spanish Black Legend and Manifest Destiny (racist doctrines which justified the appropriation of lands and resources by the English and Anglo-Americans). The Hispanics were subsequently conquered and/or incorporated into the United States through territorial purchase and then treated as colonial subjects—as were the Mexicans of the Southwest, the Hispanics in Florida and Louisiana, the Panamanians in the Canal Zone and in Panama itself, and the Puerto Ricans in the Caribbean. (I could also make a case that in many ways Cubans and Dominicans also developed as peoples under U.S. colonial rule during the early twentieth century.) Added to the base of Hispanics already residing within the United States was the subsequent immigration of large numbers of people from the Spanish-speaking countries to the continental United States over a period of 100 years. Their waves of immigration were directly related to the colonial administration of their homelands by the United States. Their children's subsequent U.S. citizenship created hundreds of thousands of new natives with cultural perspectives on life in the United States that have differed substantially from those of immigrants and exiles.

Hispanic native literature developed as an ethnic minority literature first among Hispanics already residing in the Southwest when the United States appropriated it from Mexico. Very few extant Hispanic texts from Louisiana and Florida from U.S. colonial and early statehood days have survived. Native Hispanic literature has specifically manifested itself in an attitude of entitlement to civil, political, and cultural rights. From its very origins in the nineteenth-century editorials of Francisco Ramírez and the novels of María Amparo Ruiz de Burton, Hispanic native literature in general has been cognizant of the racial, ethnic, and/or minority status of its readers. Making use of both Spanish and English, Hispanic native literature has also included immigrants in its readership and among its interests; and it has maintained a relationship with the various "homelands," such as Cuba, Mexico, Puerto Rico, or Spain. But the fundamental reason for existence of this literature and its point of reference has been and continues to be the lives and conditions of Latinos in the United States. Unlike immigrant literature, it does not have one foot in the homeland and one in the United States. For native Hispanic peoples of the United States, the homeland *is* the United States; there is no question of a return to their ancestors' Mexico, Puerto Rico, or Cuba.

Thus, this literature exhibits a firm sense of place, often elevated to a mythic status. Chicanos in the 1960s and 1970s, for example, referenced Aztlán, the legendary place of origin of the Aztecs supposedly in today's Southwest, and which gave them—as mestizo people—priority over Euro-Americans. This sense of place, which for the immigrants often was the "Trópico en Manhattan" or the "Little Havana," in the 1960s and 1970s became transformed into a place where new, synthetic, or syncretic cultures reigned supreme, as in the Nuyoricans' "Loisaida" (the Lower East Side of New York), so eulogized by poet-playwright Miguel Piñero in *A Lower East Side Poem* and other works, and "El Bronx," as in Nicholasa Mohr's *El Bronx Remembered.* This sense of belonging to a region or place where their culture has transformed the social and physical environment is only one manifestation of the general feeling of newness, derived from the synthesis of the old Hispanic and Anglo cultures that had initially opposed each other.

The "Chicanos" and "Nuyoricans" appeared in the 1960s along with the civil rights movement to claim a new and separate identity from that of Mexicans (even from Mexican Americans) and Puerto Ricans on the island. They proclaimed their bilingualism and biculturalism, and mixed and blended the English and Spanish in their speech and writing to create a new aesthetic that was interlingual and transcultural—one that to outsiders at times seemed inscrutable because of the outsiders' own linguistic limitations. The construction of this new identity was often explored in literary works that examined the psychology of characters caught between cultures, pondering the proverbial existential questions, as in four foundational works on coming of age: Piri Thomas's autobiography *Down These Mean Streets* (1967), Tomás Rivera's novel (in Spanish) . . . *And the Earth Did Not Devour Him* (1971), Rudolfo Anaya's *Bless, Me Ultima* (1972), and Nicholasa Mohr's *Nilda* (1973). But the process of sorting out identity and creating a positive place for themselves in an antagonistic society was at times facilitated only by a cultural nationalism that, as in immigrant literature, promoted a strict code of ethnic loyalty. The *vendido* (sellout) stereotype replaced those of the *pocho, agringado,* and *renegado* as negative models. No other artist explored the question of image and identity more than playwright Luis Valdez throughout his career, but most certainly in his allegory of stereotypes *Los Vendidos* (1976), in which he revisited the history of Mexican stereotypes, the products of discrimination, and the culture clash.

Many of the Hispanic newspapers, books, and other publications which appeared in the Southwest after the Mexican War (1846–48) laid the basis for U.S. Hispanics shaping themselves as an ethnic minority within this country. While the origins of their literature date to a time well before the crucial signing of the peace treaty between the United States and Mexico, it was the immediate conversion to colonial status of the Mexican population in the newly acquired territories, such as California, New Mexico, and Texas, that first made their literature a sounding board for their rights as colonized and later as "racialized" citizens of the United States. There was a nascent native Spanish-language literature in Florida and Louisiana, but the Hispanic population was not large enough to sustain it at the time of their takeover by the United States; only later in the twentieth century does one emerge again in Florida authors such as José Rivero Muñiz, Jose Yglesias, and Evelio Grillo.

While the printing press was not introduced to California and New Mexico until 1834, the society there, as in Texas (where the press appeared in 1813), was sufficiently literate to sustain a wide range of printing and publishing once the press was allowed. And when Anglos migrated to these new territories after 1848, they made printing and publishing more widespread. Later they also introduced the telegraph, the railroads, and improved communications, thus facilitating the ability of the native populations to associate with each other over distances and solidify their cultures. Despite attempts to form public opinion and exert social control over the Hispanics through bilingual newspapers and publications, the Anglo-American colonial establishment ironically brought the means for Hispanics to effect their own self-expression and creativity, which led to development of alternative identities and ideologies. Subsequently, Hispanic intellectuals founded an increasing number of Spanish-language newspapers to serve the native Hispanic populations. By the 1880s and 1890s, books were also issuing from these presses, although it should be noted that books written in Spanish were printed from the very inception of the printing press in 1834. A native oral literature and a literature in manuscript form had existed since the colonial period as a prenative base for later expression, and when the printing press became available, this literature made the transition to print. The last third of the century saw an explosion of independent Spanish-language publishing by Hispanics in the Southwest. Autobiographies, memoirs, and novels appeared, specifically treating the sense of dislocation and uprootedness, the sense of loss of patrimony, and, given their status as a racial minority in the United States, the fear of persecution and discrimination.

In 1858, Juan Nepomuceno Seguín published his *Personal Memoirs of John N. Seguín*, the first memoir written by a Mexican American in the English language. Seguín was the embattled and disenchanted political figure of the Texas Republic, who ultimately experienced great disillusionment in the transformation of his Texas by Anglo-Americans. In 1872, the first novel written in English by an Hispanic of the United States was published by María Amparo Ruiz de Burton. Her romance *Who Would Have Thought It?* reconstructed antebellum and Civil War society in the North and engaged the dominant U.S. myths of American exceptionalism, egalitarianism, and consensus, offering an acerbic critique of Northern racism and U.S. imperialism. In 1885, Ruiz de Burton published another novel—this from the perspective of the conquered Mexican population of the Southwest—*The Squatter and the Don,* which documents the loss of lands to squatters, banking, and railroad interests in Southern California shortly after statehood. Even Californios, such as Platón Vallejo and Angustias de la Guerra de Ord, who tended to romanticize the Hispanic past in their writings and dictations, were ambivalent and circumspect about the American takeover. In 1881, the first Spanish-language novel written in the Southwest was Manuel M. Salazar's romantic adventure novel, *La historia de un caminante; o, Gervacio y Aurora* (*The History of a Traveler on Foot; or, Gervasio and Aurora*), which created a colorful picture of pastoral life in New Mexico at that time, perhaps as a means of contrasting this idyllic past with the colonial present. During this territorial and early statehood period in the Southwest, there were also various oral expressions of not only resistance but outright rebellion. Examples are to be found in the proclamations of Juan Nepomuceno Cortina and in the *corridos fronterizos,* or border ballads, about social rebels such as Joaquín Murieta and Catarino Garza. Cortina, himself the leader of a massive rebellion known as the "Cortina War," was also a subject of these ballads.

But the real forum in which an Hispanic ethnic-minority consciousness developed was the Spanish-language newspaper. When Francisco P. Ramírez founded *El Clamor Público* (*The Public Clamor,* 1855–59), he created a landmark in awareness that Hispanics in California had been and were being treated as a race apart from the Euro-Americans who had immigrated into the area. Even the wealthy Californios who had collaborated in the Yankee takeover saw their wealth and power diminish under statehood. In addition to covering California and U.S. news, *El Clamor Público* also maintained contact with the Hispanic world outside California and attempted to present an image of refinement and education that demonstrated the high level of civilization achieved throughout the Hispanic world. This, in part, was a defensive reaction to the negative propaganda of Manifest Destiny which had cast Mexicans and other Hispanics as unintelligent and uneducated barbarians incapable of developing their lands and the natural resources of the West. Ramírez and his paper were staunch supporters of learning English; it was important not only for business, but also for protecting the Californios' rights. Ramírez from the outset assumed an editorial stance in defense of the native population; on June 14, 1856, he wrote: ". . . it has been our intent to serve as an organ for the general perspective of the Spanish race as a means of manifesting the atrocious injuries of which they have been victims in this country where they were born and in which they now live in a state inferior to the poorest of their persecutors." In his editorials, Ramírez laid the basis for the development of an Hispanic ethnic minority consciousness in the United States; his influence in disseminating that point of view in the native population and raising their consciousness as a people cannot be underestimated. Ramírez seems to have been the first Mexican-American journalist of the West and Southwest to consistently use the press to establish a Hispanic native perspective and to pursue civil rights for his people.

In the years to come, there were many successors to *El Clamor Público* and Ramírez who insisted on integration into the American education and political system and promoted learning the English language for survival. In doing so, they created a firm basis for the development not only of an ethnic minority identity, but also of biculturation, that is, a bicultural and bilingual citizenry for Mexican Americans—precisely what Hispanics advocate today in the United States.

In Texas, at the turn of the century, the Idar family of journalists and labor organizers concentrated on the consistent year-in, year-out power of editorials and political organizing. Laredo's *La Crónica* (*The Chronicle*, 1909–?), written and published by Nicasio Idar and his eight children, became one of the most influential Spanish-language periodicals in Texas. Like many Hispanic newspaper publishers and editors who spearheaded social and political causes for their communities, Idar and his eight children led many liberal causes. His daughter Jovita Idar was at the forefront of women's issues and collaborated in a number of women's periodicals. *La Crónica* editorials decried everything from racism and segregation in public institutions to negative stereotypes in tent theaters and movie houses. Of a working-class and union-organizing background, Nicasio Idar's overriding theme was that man in general and specifically Mexicans in Texas needed to educate themselves; only through education would social and political progress come about; and it was the special role of the newspapers to guide the way and facilitate that education. Mexican families were exhorted to keep their children in school so that gradually the situation of Mexicans in the state would improve from one generation to the next (October 11, 1910). The Idar family headed up a successful statewide drive to import Mexican teachers, find them places in which to teach children, and support them financially. Through this strategy, two social ills began to be addressed: nonadmittance of Mexican children to many schools and the stemming of the loss of the Spanish language and Mexican culture among the young.

In New Mexico, which received far fewer immigrants than California and Texas, a native press flourished. Because of drawing comparably fewer Anglo settlers and entrepreneurs than California and Texas and because of its proportionately larger Hispanic population—only in New Mexico did Hispanics maintain a demographic superiority in the late nineteenth and early twentieth centuries—New Mexico was the territory that first developed a widespread independent native Hispanic press and sustained it well into the twentieth century. Not only did more Hispanics than Anglos live there, but they resided in a more compact area and with comparably less competition and violence from Anglo newcomers. The Nuevomexicanos were able to hold onto more lands, property, and institutions than did the Hispanics of California and Texas. Control of their own newspapers and publications became essential in the eyes of Hispanic intellectuals and community leaders in the development of Nuevomexicano identity and self-determination in the face of adjusting to the new culture that was foisted upon them during the territorial period. Nuevomexicanos were living under a double-edged sword. On the one hand, they wanted to control their own destiny and preserve their own language and culture while enjoying the benefits and rights of what they considered the advanced civilization the United States had to offer through statehood. On the other hand, the Nuevomexicanos immediately became aware of the dangers of Anglo-American cultural, economic, and political encroachment. Nuevomexicanos felt the urgency of empowering themselves in the new system—and/or retaining some of the power they had under Mexico—while Washington was delaying statehood for more than fifty years, in expectation, most historians agree, of Anglos achieving a numerical and voting superiority in the territory (Gómez-Quiñones, 232–38).

In the decade following the arrival of the railroad in 1879, native Hispanic journalism and publishing increased dramatically in New Mexico. Nuevomexicano journalists set about taking control of their social and cultural destiny by constructing what they saw as a "national" culture for themselves, which consisted of using and preserving the Spanish language and formulating their own version of history and their own literature, all of which would ensure their self-confident and proud entrance as a state of the Union. From within the group of newspaper publishers and editors, in fact, sprung a cohesive and identifiable corps of native creative writers, historians, and publishers who were elaborating a native and indigenous intellectual tradition, which is the basis of much of the intellectual and literary work of Mexican Americans today. The development of the New Mexican Hispanic press, thus, at that time followed a pattern very different from that of New York's Hispanic press, which received publishers, writers, and journalists who had been trained in their homelands and who saw themselves as exiles or immigrants.

The cultural nationalism of these native journalists, of course, sprang from the necessity to defend their community from the cultural, economic, and political onslaught of the "outsiders." To counter the American myth of "civilizing the West," the Nuevomexicano writers began elaborating a myth of their own, that of the glorious introduction of European civilization and its institutions by the Spanish during the colonial period. Prior achievement legitimized their claims to land as well as to the protection and preservation of their language and culture. In their rhetoric the Nuevomexicano editorialists were able to turn the tables on the Anglo-American settlers and businessmen who had "invaded" the territory. The Nuevomexicanos claimed their own higher breeding and Catholic religion over the low morality, vicious opportunism, and hypocrisy of the Anglo-Protestant interlopers and adventurers. In the construction of their history, the editors included historical and biographical materials regularly, even in weekly columns, covering the full gamut of Hispanic history, from the exploration and colonization of Mexico, including what became the U.S. Southwest, to the life histories of important historical figures, such as Miguel de Hidalgo y Costilla, Simón Bolívar, and José de San Martín. They also began to publish history books and biographies documenting their own evolution as a people. Even in their newspapers, biographies became standard fare as they documented the contributions of their own forebears and even their contemporaries in New Mexico and the Southwest.

This "fantasy heritage" of Spanish superiority was carried on long into the twentieth century by essayists, storytellers, poets, and cadres of women writers who sought to remember and preserve the culture and folkways of their Hispanic ancestors. When English became the language of widespread publication in the twentieth century, Nina Otero Warren, Fabiola Cabeza de Vaca, and Cleofas Jaramillo cultivated this idealized heritage in attempts at retaining a grandiose past that reminded them, and supposedly their Anglo readers as well, of the high culture and privilege that anteceded the transformations brought on by the migrants from the East. Even the religious poet and historian Fray Angelico Chavez memorialized the Hispanic past and previously unaltered landscape of New Mexico. In Texas, too, Adina de Zavala and Jovita González plumbed history and folklore in an effort to preserve the Hispanic heritage. Despite the emphasis on validating, some would say romanticizing, life on ranches and missions, their study and preservation of folklore translated to respect for the culture of common men and women. This perspective differed from that of the nineteenth-century Californios, such as Platón Vallejo, Brígida Briones, Angustias de la Guerra Ord, and María Amparo Ruiz de Burton, who had elevated the pastoral and mannered life on ranches and missions to an elite status superior to that of the rough and rowdy Forty-Niners and "pioneers" who purportedly had civilized the West.

Ironically, during the early twentieth century, while a number of immigrant authors and refugees—such as María Cristina Mena, Salomón de la Selva, and Louis Pérez—found their way into the mainstream English-language publishing houses in the United States, most of the works of these native writers were issued by small, regional presses or they remained unpublished. While Miguel Antonio Otero, Adina De Zavala, and Amparo Ruiz de Burton had the resources to self-publish and underwrite their books, Américo Paredes was unsuccessful in placing his early works in English (he had previously published in Spanish in Texas newspapers). His 1936 novel *George Washington Gómez* did not make it into print until 1990. Even as late as 1953, when his manuscript novel *The Shadow* won a national contest, Paredes was unsuccessful in locating a publisher. Similarly, Jovita González in her lifetime never saw her two novels in print: *Caballero* and *Dew on the Thorn*, novels that sought to preserve the Hispanic cultural past of Texas. It was not until the 1960s that Puerto Ricans Piri Thomas and Nicholasa Mohr, Cuban American José Yglesias, and Chicanos José Antonio Villarreal and Floyd Salas, a descendant of the original Hispanic settlers in Colorado, saw their works issued by the large commercial houses in New York (actually Doubleday issued Antonio Villarreal's *Pocho* in 1959). Most of these fit into that melting-pot genre par excellence: ethnic autobiography. The Hispanics civil rights movement and the entrance of a broad sector of Hispanics into universities helped to usher in a period of flourishing of Hispanics literature in the English language that began in the 1970s and persists today.

The Hispanic civil rights movement that emerged in the 1960s had inherited a legacy of resistance against colonialism, segregation, and exploitation; this legacy was expressed in the writings of editorialists, union organizers, and defenders of the culture in the early twentieth century. At the turn of the century, Nicasio and Jovita Idar used their Laredo newspaper *La Crónica* to raise the level of consciousness about the cultural and political struggles, as well as to organize communities of both natives and immigrants. From the 1920s through the 1940s, Alonso Perales published hundreds of letters and editorials in newspapers in defense of civil rights of Mexicans in the Southwest long before he came together with others to found the League of United Latin American Citizens (LULAC), which is still fighting civil rights battles today. New Mexico's Aurora Lucero and Eusebio Chacón delivered an untold number of speeches in defense of the Spanish language and cultural rights. In San Antonio, the firebrand of the 1938 pecan shellers' strike, Emma Tenayuca, moved thousands with her passionate speeches in the first large, successful strike in that industry. Tenayuca and another activist, Isabel González, created in their essays a firm, ideological base for the civil rights struggles of Mexican Americans. But it was Américo Paredes, writing in English in the mid-1930s, who best articulated the cultural and economic devastation felt by his generation of bilingual-bicultural natives of the Southwest. In poems, novels, and short stories, this native of Brownsville, Texas, was able to capture the nuances of language and the ethos of an oppressed people that he would transmit during the Chicano movement of the 1960s and 1970s through his leadership as a scholar and teacher at the University of Texas. Indeed, a broad range of writers, scholars, and even singer-songwriters, such as Tish Hinojosa and Linda Rondstat, continue to cite Paredes as their cultural mentor.

Since the late nineteenth century, New York, as the principal port of entry for immigrants from Europe and the Caribbean, has always harbored and nurtured a culture of immigration that facilitated the integration of immigrants into the economy and overall culture. Numerous immigrant newspapers flourished, some of which reflected the awareness of their communities' evolution toward citizenship status or American naturalization, and pronounced the demands for the entitlements and guarantees of citizenship. Even *Gráfico*—which in most respects was a typical immigrant newspaper—began to recognize the American citizenship of its readers, mostly Puerto Ricans and Cubans residing in East Harlem. And while the editors of *Gráfico* often compared their community to those of other immigrant groups, the editors were leveraging the U.S. citizenship of many Hispanics residing in East Harlem. Because of the Jones Act of 1917 extending citizenship to Puerto Ricans, these former islanders did not have to learn English, acculturate, or assimilate to become citizens; citizenship was automatic. Since 1917, this line between immigrant and citizen for Puerto Ricans in New York has been blurred, accounting for highly complex modes of expression that exhibit the confidence and entitlement to the expressive rights of natives, but nevertheless maintaining that dual perspective characteristic of immigrant culture.

With the advent of the Depression, New York did not experience the massive repatriation of Hispanics that occurred in the Southwest. Instead, the opposite was true. Hard economic times on the island brought even more Puerto Ricans to the city, a trend that would intensify during World War II as Northeastern manufacturing and services industries experienced labor shortages and recruited heavily in Puerto Rico. The massive return of Puerto Ricans from serving in the war further intensified the community's identity as a native citizenry. Community members were appealed to as citizens by their local newspapers to organize politically and vote. In 1941, a new newspaper, *La Defensa* (*The Defense*), appeared in East Harlem specifically to further the interests of the Hispanics of the area who were there to *stay* ("*no somos aves de paso*"—we are not here as passing birds).

In 1927, a league was formed in New York City to increase the power of the Hispanic community by unifying its diverse organizations. Among the very specific goals of the Liga Puertorriqueña e Hispana (The Puerto Rican and Hispanic League) were representing the community to the "authorities," working for the economic and social betterment of the Puerto Ricans, and propagating the vote among Puerto Ricans. The league founded a periodical in 1927 entitled the *Boletín Oficial de la Liga Puertorriqueña e Hispana* to keep its member organizations and their constituents informed of community concerns. However, the *Boletín* evolved into much more than a newsletter, functioning more like a community newspaper and including essays and cultural items as well as news items in its pages. Later, under the directorship of Jesús Colón, coverage of working-class issues and ideology became more emphasized. Like Américo Paredes in the Southwest, Jesús Colón was a figure who made the transition from Spanish to English and laid the basis for a more militant literature during the 1960s and 1970s among Nuyoricans. In fact, Colón must be considered one of the most important immigrant writers in the early twentieth century, but by the time he was writing in English for the *Daily Worker* and had published his first collection of essays, *A Puerto Rican in New York*, in 1963, he had already articulated many of the perspectives on race, class, and aesthetics that Nuyoricans would soon adopt.

The Chicano and Nuyorican generations were fortunate to have these models of working-class aesthetics available, not only from educators like Paredes and journalists like Colón, but from community poets and activists raised in the oral tradition. Historians date the beginning of the Chicano movement to the mid-1960s' effort to organize the United Farm Workers Union, led by César Chávez. The farm-worker struggle served as a catalyst for a generation of Mexican Americans inspired by the African American civil rights movement and the protest against the Vietnam War. This was the first generation of U.S. Hispanics to have greater access to college, largely due to the Kennedy–Johnson initiatives to democratize education. For Chicano literature, the decade of the 1960s was a time of questioning all the commonly accepted truths in the society, foremost of which was the question of equality. The first writers of Chicano literature committed their literary voices to the political, economic, and educational development of their communities. Their works were frequently used to inspire social and political action, quite often with poets reading their verses at organizing meetings, boycotts, and before and after protest marches. Of necessity, many of the first writers to gain prominence in the movement were the poets who could tap into the Hispanic oral tradition of recitation and declamation. Rodolfo "Corky" Gonzales, Abelardo Delgado, Ricardo Sánchez, and Alurista stand out in this period. They created works to be performed orally before groups of students and workers in order to inspire them and raise their level of consciousness. The two most important literary milestones in kicking off the movement were both related to grass-roots activism. In 1965, actor-playwright Luis Valdez organized farm workers from the nascent union into an improvisational agit-prop theater company, El Teatro Campesino. In 1967, the epic poem *I Am Joaquín* was written and self-published by "Corky" Gonzales, the founder of the militant Chicano civil rights and social service organization, the Crusade for Justice.

Under the leadership of Valdez and the powerful example of El Teatro Campesino, a full-blown grass-roots theater movement emerged and lasted for almost two decades, with hundreds of community and student theater companies dramatizing the political and cultural concerns of the communities while crisscrossing the nation on tours. The movement, largely student- and worker-based, eventually became professionalized, producing works for Broadway and Hollywood and fostering the creation of the field of Chicano theater at universities. By 1968, Valdez and El Teatro Campesino had left the vineyards and lettuce fields in a conscious effort to create a theater for the Chicano nation, a people which Valdez and other Chicano organizers and ideologues envisioned as exclusively working-class, Spanish-speaking or bilingual, rurally oriented, and with a strong heritage of pre-Columbian culture. Indeed, the word "Chicano" was a working-class derivation and abbreviation of the indigenous-based pronunciation of the name of the Aztec tribes, "Mechicano," from which the name of Mexico is also derived. Through extensive touring of El Teatro Campesino, the creation of a national Chicano theatrical organization, and publication of a *teatro* magazine and the company's *Actos*, Valdez was able to broadcast and solidify the movement. Eventually, a generation grew of not only theaters and actors but also bilingual-bicultural playwrights, directors, producers, and theater educators who are still very active today.

Gonzales's *I Am Joaquín* followed a similar trajectory not only in disseminating a similar nationalist aesthetic, but also in providing a model for poets, whether at the grass-roots level or at universities. The poem, which summarized Mexican and Mexican American history, shaped a nationalist ideological base for activism, using the model of the nineteenth-century social rebel Joaquín Murieta (see the Murieta entry in this anthology). The short bilingual pamphlet edition of the poem was literally passed from hand to hand in communities, read aloud at rallies, dramatized by Chicano theaters, and even produced as a slide show on a film with a dramatic reading by none other than Luis Valdez. The influence and social impact of *I Am Joaquín*, and of works of the other poets who wrote for and from the grass roots in the militant stage of the Chicano movement, is inestimable. This period was one of euphoria, power, and influence for the Chicano poet, who was sought after, almost as a priest, to give his or her blessings in the form of readings at all Chicano cultural and movement events.

The grass-roots movement was soon joined by one in academe, with university-based magazines and publishing houses and Chicano studies and bilingual education departments. Sharing a nationalist aesthetic similar to that of Valdez and Gonzales were scholars Octavio Romano and Herminio Ríos, the publishers of the most successful magazine, *El Grito* (*The Shout*—a title harking back to the Mexican declaration of independence from Spain), and its affiliate publishing house, Quinto Sol (Fifth Sun—a title based on the renascence of Aztec culture). Besides introducing Alurista's bilingual poetry and Miguel Méndez's trilingual (English, Spanish, and Yaqui) prose to a broad audience through its magazine and its first anthology, Quinto Sol consciously set about constructing a Chicano canon with its publication of the first three award-winning literary works, all of which have become foundational for Chicano prose fiction: Tomás Rivera's *. . . y no sel tragó la terra/ . . . And the Earth Did Not Devour Him* (1971), Rudolfo Anaya's *Bless Me, Ultima* (1972), and Rolando Hinojosa's *Estampas del valle y otras obras/Sketches of the Valley and Other Works* (1973). This predominantly male canon belatedly admitted a feminist writer of stories and plays in 1975, with the publication of Estela Portillo Trambley's *Rain of Scorpions*. Her influence, however, has not been as lasting as that of other women writing from the mid-1970s and who by the 1980s had taken the reins of Chicano literature, making up the first generation of writers to cross over to mainstream publishing in English. Most of these writers—including Ana Castillo, Lorna Dee Cervantes, Denise Chávez, Sandra Cisneros, Pat Mora, Helena María Viramontes, and Evangelina Vigil—had received their first national exposure through the literary magazine *Revista Chicano-Riqueña*, founded in 1973, and Arte Público Press, founded in 1979, both published at the University of Houston. In addition to picking up the pieces after the demise of Quinto Sol by publishing Alurista, Tomás Rivera, Rolando Hinojosa, and Luis Valdez, Arte Público Press continues to bring newer writers to the fore. In its pan-Hispanism, the press has also been the major publisher of Nuyorican and Cuban American literature. In fact, Arte Público Press and *Revista Chicano-Riqueña* have been the major and longest-lived promoters of a national Latino culture and literature; they were the first publishing enterprises to open their doors to writers of all of the Hispanic ethnic groups in the United States. Arte Público Press itself has launched the current project to recover the Hispanic literary past and to publish this anthology.

Nuyorican writing made its appearance in the United States with a definite proletarian identity, emerging from the working-class, urbanized culture of the children of the migrants. It arose as a dynamic literature of oral performance based on the folklore and popular culture within the neighborhoods of the most cosmopolitan and postmodern city in the United States: New York ("Nuyorican" was derived from "New York Rican"). Piri Thomas's multivolume autobiography in the poetic language of the streets, Victor Hernández Cruz's urban jazz poetry, and Nicholasa Mohr's developmental novel *Nilda*—all issued by mainstream commercial presses—led the way toward the establishment of a new cultural and literary Nuyorican identity that was as hip as salsa music and as alienated and seethingly revolutionary as shouts from urban labor camps and from prisons—the prisons in which many of the first practitioners of Nuyorican poetry and drama learned their craft. Ex-con and ex-gang leader Miguel Piñero and the Nuyorican group of poets, some of whom were outlaws in the literal as well as figurative sense, embellished on the theme of urban marginalization and repression, and made it the threatening dynamic of their bilingual poetry and drama. Piñero was successful at taking it even to the stages of Broadway and to Hollywood films. Their works threatened the very concept of literature cultivated by the academy as highly crafted art based on literate models selected from the classical repertoire of Western civilization.

The Nuyorican writers created a style and ideology that still dominates urban Hispanic writing today: working-class, unapologetic, and proud of its lack of schooling and polish—a threat not only to mainstream literature and the academy, but also, with its insistence on its outlaw and street culture elements, to mainstream society. Poets such as Tato Laviera, Victor Hernández Cruz, Sandra María Esteves, and Pedro Pietri did not seek written models for their work. They were far more attuned to and inspired by the salsa lyrics and the recitations of bards and folk poets who had always performed works about news, history, and love in the public plazas and festivals of small-town Puerto Rico—often in the form of *décimas* and the refrains of *bombas* and *plenas*, the prevalent folk-song frameworks on the island. In capturing the sights and sounds of their "urban pastoral," it was an easy and natural step to cultivating bilingual poetry, capturing the bilingual-bicultural reality that surrounded them, and reintroducing their works into their communities through the virtuosity that live performance demands in folk culture. El Barrio, the Bronx, and Loisaida neighborhood audiences, accustomed to the technical sophistication of salsa records and performance, as well as television and film, demanded authenticity, artistic virtuosity, and philosophical and political insight. And Laviera, Hernández Cruz, Esteves, and Pietri reigned as masters for almost two decades. That they are accessible to far more people through oral performance than publication is not an accident nor is it a sign of lack of sophistication; it was their literary mission, their political and economic stance. In fact, it was Miguel Algarín, a university-educated poet and Rutgers University professor also raised in the Puerto Rican barrios, who stimulated through example and entrepreneurial insight the publication of Nuyorican poetry in anthologies, magazines, and through Arte Público Press books. He further showcased Nuyorican performance art at his Nuyorican Poets Cafe in Loisaida and took troupes of writers on national tours of poetry slams. Besides authoring outstanding avant-garde poetry himself, Algarín helped to solidify the Nuyorican literary identity and foster its entrance into the larger world of contemporary American avant-garde poetics.

During the 1980s and to the present, with the assistance of publishing houses such as Arte Público and Bilingual Review Press, a new wave of Hispanic writers has emerged, not from the barrios, fields, prisons, and student movements but from university creative writing programs. Almost all are monolingual English-speaking and -writing: Julia Alvarez, Denise Chávez, Sandra Cisneros, Judith Ortiz Cofer, Cristina García, Oscar Hijuelos, Alberto Ríos, Gary Soto, and Helena María Viramontes. (The outstanding Chicana poet Lorna Dee Cervantes is a transitional figure who arose in the mid-1970s as part of the Chicano movement, but after becoming a recognized poet, she returned to the university in the 1980s in pursuit of a Ph.D.) Most of them are natives of the United States, but some arrived as children from Puerto Rico, Cuba, and the Dominican Republic. They cultivate coming-of-age novels and novels of immigrant adjustment to American society, akin to the ethnic autobiography written in the United States by a variety of minorities and ethnic groups—to be distinguished from the literature of immigration that is written in Spanish and promotes a return to the homeland. They and many others continue to explore their identity in U.S. society. Some authors, such as Gloria Anzaldúa, Cherríe Moraga, and Aurora Levins Morales, have furthered feminist positions in their literature, exploring the relationship between gender and ethnic identity and entering realms considered taboo by earlier generations of Hispanic writers, such as those concerning sexual identity. And from the ranks of the new wave, Hispanic literature in the United States produced its first Pulitzer Prize–winner, Oscar Hijuelos, for *The Mambo Kings Play Songs of Love.*

The literature of this generation is the one that is most familiar to a broad segment of readers in the United States today and has the greatest possibility of entering and influencing mainstream culture. However, this is also the Hispanic literature which has emerged from and been influenced most by mainstream culture and its institutions. On the other hand, this literature is the literature of a minority of Hispanic writers and the very tip of an iceberg whose body is made up of writing in Spanish from the three traditions identified in this anthology: native, immigrant, and exile.

The Literature of Immigration

While the roots of immigrant literature were planted in nineteenth-century newspapers in California and New York, it was not until the turn of the century that a well-defined immigrant expression emerged from New York to the Southwest. Although New York had been the port of entry, major cities in the Southwest received an outpouring of approximately one million dislocated working-class Mexicans during the Mexican Revolution of 1910. And it was Los Angeles and San Antonio that received the largest number of Mexican immigrants and consequently supported most writing and publication efforts. San Antonio became home to more than a dozen Spanish-language publishing houses, more than any other city in the United States. In New York, Los Angeles, and San Antonio, an entrepreneurial class of refugees and immigrants came with sufficient cultural and financial capital to establish businesses of all types to serve the rapidly growing Hispanic enclaves. They constructed everything from tortilla factories to Hispanic theaters and movie houses, and through their cultural leadership in mutual aid societies, churches, theaters, newspapers, and publishing houses, they were able to disseminate a nationalistic ideology that ensured the solidarity and isolation of their communities, or market, if you will. In addition to the obvious reason of being the location of important preexisting Hispanic communities, these cities were chosen by both the economic and political refugees because their urban industrial bases were expanding, undergoing rapid industrialization and modernization. New York offered numerous opportunities in manufacturing and service industries, while Los Angeles and San Antonio were also good bases for recruitment of agricultural and railroad workers.

Since their arrival in the United States, Hispanic immigrants have used the press and literature in their native language to maintain a connection with the homeland while attempting to adjust to a new society and culture here. Hispanic immigrant literature shares many of the distinctions that Park identified in 1922 in a study on the immigrant press as a whole. Included among these distinctions were: (1) the predominant use of the language of the homeland, in (2) serving a population united by that language, irrespective of national origin, and (3) solidifying and furthering nationalism (9–13). The literature of immigration serves a population in transition from the land of origin to the United States by reflecting the reasons for emigrating, recording the trials and tribulations of immigration, and facilitating adjustment to the new society, all the while maintaining a link with the old society.

Underlying Park's distinctions and those of other students of immigration are the myths of the American dream and the melting pot: the belief that the immigrants came to find a better life and thus, implicitly, a better culture, and that soon they or their descendants would become Americans and there would no longer be a need for literature in the language of the "old country." These myths and many of Park's opinions and observations about European immigrants do not hold true for the literature of Hispanic immigration, which was *not* about assimilating or "melting" into a generalized American identity. In fact, the history of Hispanic groups in the United States has shown an unmeltable ethnicity, and, as there has been a steady flow of immigrants from Spanish-speaking countries since the founding of the United States to the present, there seems to be no end to the phenomenon.

In general, the literature of Hispanic immigration displays a double-gaze perspective: forever comparing the past and the present, the homeland and the new country, and seeing the resolution of these double, conflicting points of reference only when the author, characters, and/or the audience can return to the *la patria*, home soil. The literature of immigration reinforces the culture of the homeland while facilitating the accommodation to the new land. While fervently nationalistic, this literature seeks to represent and protect the rights of immigrants by protesting discrimination, human rights abuses, and racism. As much of this literature arises from or is pitched to the working class, it adopts the working-class and rural dialects of the immigrants. Today, earlier immigrant literature may be seen as a museum of orality during the time period of its writing. Among the predominant themes in the literature of immigration are the description of the metropolis, often in satirical or critical terms, as seen in essays by José Martí, Pachín Marín, and Nicanor Bolet Peraza; the description of the trials and tribulations of immigrants, especially in their journey here and, once here, in their being subjected to exploitation as workers and to discrimination as foreigners and racial others, as in novels by Daniel Venegas and Conrado Espinosa; the conflict between Anglo and Hispanic cultures, ubiquitous in this literature; and the expression of gender anxieties in nationalist reaction against assimilation. Highly politicized authors, including those of the working class, often cast their literary discourse in the framework of an imminent return to the homeland or a warning to those back home not to come to the United States and face similar disillusionment. In actuality they were speaking to their immigrant enclave or community here in the "belly of the beast," to use Martí's term, which helped authors to find common cause and solidarity with their audiences. Almost invariably, the narratives of immigration end with the main characters returning to the *la patria*. Failure to do so resulted in death, the severest poetic justice, as illustrated in the first novel of immigration, Alirio Díaz Guerra's *Lucas Guevara* (1914) and, almost half a century later, in René Marqués's play *La carreta* (*The Oxcart*, 1953). Because of the massive migrations of working-class

Mexicans and Puerto Ricans during the first half of the twentieth century, much of immigrant literature is to be found in oral expression, folk songs, vaudeville, and other working-class literary and artistic expression. The anonymous Mexican corrido *El lavaplatos* (The Dishwasher) reproduces the same cycle as Daniel Venegas's working-class novel *Las aventuras de Don Chipote; o, Cuando los pericos mamen (The Adventures of Don Quixote;* or, *When Parrots Breast Feed,* 1928), of leaving home to find work in the United States, disillusionment in laboring like a beast of burden here, and eventual return home. The immigrants' songs of uprootedness and longing for the homeland can be heard in the *décima* (a song with ten-line stanzas and a sonnet-like rhyme scheme) *Lamento de un jíbaro* (*Lament of the Highlander*). But the ultimate disillusionment and disgrace for the immigrant was being deported, as documented in the plaintive refrains of the *corrido Los deportados* (*The Deportees*) and the outraged newspaper editorial by Rodolfo Uranga. Quite often the setting for this literature is the workplace, be that on the streets walked by Wen Gálvez's door-to-door salesman, in the factory of Gustavo Alemán Bolaños's *La Factoría* (1925), or under the burning sun in the agricultural fields, as in Conrado Espinosa's *El sol de Texas* (1926). But domestic settings are also frequent, even in contemporary plays, such as René Marqués's *La carreta* and Iván Acosta's *El super* (1977), both depicting the intergenerational conflict splitting U.S.-acculturated children from their immigrant parents.

In fact, culture conflict of all sorts typifies this work, and from this conflict arise some of its most typical characters, such as the *agringados* (gringoized), *renegados* (renegades) and *pitiyanquis* (petit Yankees), who deny their own culture to adopt "American" ways. But more than any other archetype of American culture, the predominantly male authors chose the American female to personify the eroticism and immorality, greed, and materialism that they perceived in American society. What was an amoral Eve in a metropolis identified as Sodom for Alirio Díaz Guerra evolved into the 1920s flapper in Jesús Colón, Daniel Venegas, and Julio B. Arce ("Jorge Ulica"). This enticing but treacherous Eve led unassuming Hispanic Adams into perdition. These authors placed the responsibility for preserving Hispanic customs and language, for protecting identity, in the hands of *their* women, and subsequently levied severe criticism at those who adopted more liberal American customs or even dared to behave like flappers themselves.

Despite this conservative, even misogynist propaganda, from these very same communities emerged a cadre of Hispanic women journalists and labor leaders who rejected circumscribed social roles even if fashioned in the mordant satire of Jorge Ulica's *La estenógrafa* (*The Stenographer,* 1925). Leonor Villegas de Magnón and Sara Estela Ramírez inspired social action through their speeches, poems, and journalism. Teacher Ramírez was renowned for inspiring predominantly male workers to unionize through her eloquently passionate speeches; sister teacher in Laredo, Villegas organized Anglo and Mexican/Mexican-American women to enter the Mexican Revolution as nurses, and then sought to record their contributions for posterity in her memoir, *The Rebel.* María Luisa Garza, as a *cronista* (editorial columnist) writing under the pseudonym of Loreley, took on the defense of women in numerous unflinching and elegantly well-reasoned articles. They did this despite their having to negotiate the hostile environment of an all-male editorial staff. Consuelo Lee Tapia sought to document the history of activism and contributions to Puerto Rican nationhood by women. On the same pages of Tapia's *Pueblos Hispanos* (Hispanic Peoples), one of the greatest lyric poets of the Americas, Julia de Burgos, wed her intimate verses to the movement for Puerto Rican nationhood. And on the very grass-roots but subtle level of vaudeville tent performances, Netty Rodríguez through her *agringada* persona vigorously resisted her mate's exhortations to conform to the feminine role as prescribed by working-class Mexican culture. But the clearest example of Hispanic feminism dates back to the beginning of the twentieth century, when again in deed and practice Puerto Rican labor organizer Luisa Capetillo disseminated her spirited break with all social constraints on women in her treatises, plays, and poems. All of these women writer-activists would present powerful models of thought and expression that would inspire their spiritual descendants today.

For the Hispanic immigrant communities, defense of civil and human rights extended to protecting their enclaves from the influence of Anglo-American culture and the very real dangers present in the workplace, in the schools, and in public policy. Editorial discontent has dominated the publications of Hispanic immigrants in the major cities since the beginning of the century. Joaquín Colón, president of the Puerto Rican and Latin League and brother to Jesús Colón, used the bully pulpit in the league's newspaper during the 1930s to chastise the Hispanic community for its failings. In the Southwest, Rodolfo Uranga decried one of the greatest injustices perpetrated on Mexican immigrants (and on numerous natives, as well): widespead deportations during the Depression. Today's Spanish-language newspapers continue in the same tradition, repeatedly criticizing discrimination and deportations by the Immigration and Naturalization Service. However, because Puerto Ricans have been citizens since 1917, deportation for their political or labor-organizing activities as well as for being "burdensome" to the welfare system has not been part of their imaginary. Thus, once again, there is a clear distinction between the "immigrant" legal status and the "immigrant" cultural experience. Puerto Ricans in the continental United States have immigration and migration deeply imbedded in their collective experience, but the fear of deportation as a form of discrimination and oppression has for the most part been absent.

Since the beginning of Hispanic immigrant literature, authors have felt it their duty to insulate the community from the influence of Anglo-American culture and the Protestant religion. This explains in part Díaz Guerra's moralistic attack on the big city (New York) and his depiction of the American Eve as representing all of the ills of American society. Mexican publishers and writers in the Southwest, moreover, were almost unanimous in developing and promoting the idea of a *México de afuera*, or Mexican colony existing outside of Mexico, in which it was the duty of individuals to maintain the Spanish language, keep the Catholic faith, and insulate their children from what community leaders perceived as the low moral standards practiced by Anglo-Americans. The ideology was expressed and disseminated by immigrant and exile writers alike, some of whom were political and religious refugees from the Mexican Revolution. They represented the most conservative segment of Mexican society in the homeland; in the United States, their cultural leadership was exerted in all phases of life in the *colonia*, solidifying a conservative substratum for Mexican-American culture for decades to come. While many of the writers were educated and came from middle- to upper-class backgrounds, the largest audiences for the plays, novels, and poems were made up of the working-class immigrants crowded in urban barrios who, thanks to the expanding American economy, could afford these cultural representations of their lives.

There was a genre that was more traditionally identified with and central to Hispanic newspapers everywhere and essential in forming and reinforcing community attitudes. It was the *crónica*, a short, weekly column that humorously and satirically commented on current topics and social habits in the local community. Rife with local color and inspired by oral lore of the immigrants, the *crónica* was narrated in the first person from the masked perspective of a pseudonym. *Cronistas* surveyed life in the enclave and served as witnesses to the customs and behavior of the colony whose very existence was seen as threatened by the dominant Anglo-Saxon culture. Influenced by popular jokes, anecdotes, and speech, their columns registered the surrounding social environment. It was the *cronista*'s job to fan the flames of nationalism and to sustain *México de afuera* and *Trópico en Manhattan* ideologies, the latter signifying the transformation of the metropolitan landscape into home by Caribbean Latinos as proclaimed by writers such as Bernardo Vega and Guillermo Cotto-Thorner. *Cronistas* harped on the influence of Anglo-Saxon "immorality" and worried about the erosion of the Spanish language and Hispanic culture with equally religious fervor. Sometimes their messages were deliveed from the bully pulpit through direct preaching, as in *crónicas* signed by Jesús Colón as "Miquis Tiquis." But Alberto O'Farrill, under the guise of "O'Fa," and Julio B. Arce, under the mask of "Jorge Ulica," often employed a self-deprecating humor and a burlesque of characters in the community to represent general ignorance or adoption of what their characters believed to be superior Anglo ways. While these two writers entertained their audiences with the misadventures of working-class immigrants, the autodidact Colón seriously set about elevating the level of education and culture in the Hispanic community. Colón became one of the most important Hispanic columnists and intellectuals in the New York Hispanic community for more than fifty years.

Although since 1917 Puerto Ricans were citizens of the United States and legally and politically not immigrants (at least not in the traditional sense), the texts of most of the working-class writers who had migrated to the city during the twentieth century exhibit many of the classic patterns of Hispanic immigrant literature, including the emphasis on returning to the island. Even non-working-class artists whose residence in New York was not as prolonged as Vega's or Colón's nevertheless employed the double gaze and culture conflict in their works. The whole object of René Marqués's *La carreta* was to construct an argument for the return of the Puerto Rican working classes to the island. And while José Luis González and Pedro Juan Soto identified themselves politically and sympathized with the uprooted working-class Puerto Ricans, their texts nevertheless depicted the metropolis as an inhuman, inhospitable place for Latinos. Even the title of González's book, *En Nueva York y otras desgracias* (*In New York and Other Disgraces*, 1973), echoes the sentiment that has persisted since Díaz Guerra's writing at the turn of the last century.

But whether the immigrant texts stress a return to the homeland or concentrate on registering life in the immigrant enclaves, contact and conflict with other cultures in the metropolis is the stuff of immigrant literature, from the texts of Alirio Díaz Guerra and Daniel Venegas to those of more contemporary writers, such Ernesto Galarza,

Guillermo Cotto-Thorner, Wilfredo Baschi, Roberto Fernández, and Mario Bencastro. While Bencastro focuses on the interaction of Central American immigrants with their foremen, bosses, and authority figures today in Washington, D.C., Roberto Fernández satirizes the residents in Miami's Little Havana: their obsession with reproducing and continuing life as it once was for them in Cuba while not realizing how they are truly living culturally hybrid lives. In fact, because of the political status of Cuban refugees in the United States, return to Cuba is for the near future—and has been more than for forty years—impossible. Thus writers such as Iván Acosta, Roberto Fernández, Dolores Prida, Cristina García, Virgil Suárez, and Gustavo Pérez Firmat find ways for the community to accommodate here in the United States. For Acosta in *El super*, it is accepting Miami as an imperfect copy of the homeland. For Dolores Prida in *Botánica* (*The Herb Shop*, 1991) and Pérez Firmat, the secret lies in accepting and sustaining hybridization. For others, it lies in tropicalizing the environment or otherwise transforming the urban landscape, as had been done earlier in the *México de afuera* and *Trópico en Manhattan* generations. But even in today's writers there are cries of desperation, as in Suárez's protagonist who at the end of his novel *Going Under* (1996) jumps into the ocean to swim back to Cuba.

Another trend that began in the early twentieth century was the sporadic and intermittent acceptance of works by Hispanic authors in English-language mainstream publications. Mexican immigrant author María Cristina Mena saw her old-country-based stories published in *Century* and *Harper's*, among others. Louis Pérez, another Mexican immigrant, saw his novel *Coyote* published by Holt in 1947 (Pérez's other literary works remain unpublished to date). Today, there is a notable cadre of immigrant writers who, like Mena, relocated as children to the United States and have been able to write and publish their works in English, quite often in mainstream, commercial houses: Cristina García, Virgil Suárez, Julia Alvarez, Judith Ortiz Cofer, Junot Díaz, Gustavo Pérez Firmat, and a handful of others. Each of these is part of a generation educated in American colleges and, for the most part, embarked on professional writing careers. Indeed, Ortiz Cofer, Suárez, and Alvarez were trained in university creative writing programs. But each has made the immigrant experience the grist of their well-crafted literary art. Their audience is not the immigrant enclave, but the general English-speaking reader more likely to purchase their works in a chain bookstore than through a mail-order catalog advertisement in a Spanish-language newspaper. Acculturated in the United States from youth and preferring to write in English for a broad general public, these authors assume many of the stances of native writers, but their predominant theme and their double gaze are distinctly immigrant in nature.

The Literature of Exile

The study of Hispanic exile literature in the United States is the examination of the great moments in the political history of the Hispanic world, from the beginning of the nineteenth century on: the Napoleonic intervention in Spain, the movements of the Spanish American colonies for independence from Spain, the French intervention in Mexico, the War of 1898, the Mexican Revolution, the Spanish Civil War, the Cuban

Revolution, the recent wars in Central America, and the numerous struggles in Spanish America against autocratic regimes and foreign interventions, including the many incursions into the domestic affairs of these countries by the United States. The very act of U.S. partisanship in the internal politics of the Spanish American republics at times directed the expatriate streams to these shores. All of these struggles contributed hundreds of thousands of political refugees to the United States throughout its history. Because of U.S. territorial expansion and Hispanic immigration, the United States gradually became home to large communities of Spanish speakers which continually received the expatriates. Thus, the refugees found familiar societies where they could conduct business and eke out a living while they hoped for and abetted change in the lands that would someday welcome their return. Much of the literary expression of the exiles has traditionally emerged from their hopes and desires for the political and cultural independence of their homelands, be that from the Spanish empire or from U.S. imperialism. Much of this literature, particularly that of the nineteenth century, is highly lyrical and idealistic in its poetry and often elegant in its prose. However, it is also characterized by its aggressive and argumentative tone because of its commitment to political change in the homeland.

Printing and publication by Hispanics began at the turn of the nineteenth century in three cities: New Orleans, Philadelphia, and New York. Judging from the number of political books published at the beginning of the nineteenth century, the overwhelming motive for the Spaniards, Cubans, Puerto Ricans, and other Spanish Americans in the United States to bear the cost of printing and distribution of their written matter was their desire to influence the politics in their homelands. Spanish-speaking political refugees from both Spain and the Spanish American countries have as part of their political culture repeatedly taken up exile in the United States to gain access to a free press and thus offer their compatriots uncensored news and political ideology, even if their writings had to be smuggled on and off ships and passed surreptitiously hand-to-hand back home. In many cases, the exile press also engaged in political fund raising, community organizing, and revolutionary plotting to overthrow regimes in their countries of origin. The raison d'être of the exile press has always been to influence life and politics in the homeland: by providing information and opinion about the homeland, changing or solidifying opinion about politics and policy in the *patria*, assisting in raising funds to overthrow the current regime.

The freedom of expression available in exile was highly desirable in light of the repression that existed in the homelands. The historical record is rife with examples of the prison terms, torture, and executions of writers, journalists, publishers, and editors during the struggles to establish democracies in Spanish America in the wake of Spain's colonialism. Numerous exile authors represented in this anthology suffered torture in prisons and death on battlefields in the Americas. Many authors, viewing themselves as patriots without a country, were forced to live in exile and/or wander from country to country creating their literary works and spreading their political doctrines. This ever-present base for the culture and literature of Hispanic communities in the United States exemplifies how U.S. Hispanic literature is transnational and can never be truly understood solely from within the geographical and political confines of the United States. Hispanic communities in the United States have never really been cut off from the rest of the Americas and the world of Hispanic culture and the Spanish language, nor have they been just limited to their immediate ethnogeographic communities. And certainly, the literature written on U.S. soil, even if written by exiles, is part of the U.S. Hispanic literary heritage.

The first political books printed in exile by Hispanics were written by Spanish citizens who were protesting the installation of a puppet government in Spain by Napoleon. These exiled writers published poetry and novels in addition to their political treatises. Typical of these titles was the attack on Napoleon in *España ensangrentada por el horrendo corso, tyrano de la Europa . . .* (*Spain Bloodied by the Horrendous Corsican, Tyrant of Europe . . .*) published in 1808 in New Orleans by an anonymous author. Shortly thereafter, the wars for independence of the Spanish colonies from Spain were supported by numerous ideologues who had assimilated the teachings of Thomas Paine, Thomas Jefferson, and John Quincy Adams and adopted them to the Hispanic world. Cuban filibusterer José Alvarez de Toledo, in his *Mexicanos: Ilegado es el tiempo* (*Mexicans: Signaled by Providence*), included here, militated from Baltimore as early as 1812 for Caribbean and Mexican independence. In 1813 he was one of the founders of the first newspaper in Texas, *La gaceta de Texas* (*The Texas Gazette*), as part of the revolutionary movement led by Miguel de Hidalgo for independence from Spain. By 1822, Hispanics began operating their own presses and publishing houses. One of the first to print his revolutionary tracts on his own press was Ecuadorian Vicente Rocafuerte, who issued his *Ideas necesarias a todo pueblo . . .* (*Ideas Necessary for All Peoples . . .*) in Philadelphia in 1821 as part of an effort to export the liberal ideas of the newly founded American Republic in support of the South American wars of independence against Spain. By 1825, Carlos Lanuza's press (Lanuza, Mendía and Co.) was operating in New York, printing and publishing political tracts as well as creative literature. In the 1830s, they were joined by the Imprenta Española of Juan de la Granja and the press of José Desnoues, both in New York, but it bears repeating that New York and Philadelphia newspapers, such as *El Mensagero* (*The Messenger*), *El Reflector* (*The Reflector*), and *El Mundo Nuevo* (*The New World*), were also printing and publishing books. Most of these Hispanic printers and publishers were rather short-lived, but eventually two enterprises appeared with strong enough financial bases and business acumen to last for decades and provide some of the most important books by Hispanics in the nineteenth century: the houses of Cubans Néstor Ponce de León and Enrique Trujillo, from whose presses were issued some of the renowned classics of the Spanish-speaking world, authored by exiled authors José María Heredia, José Martí, Lola Rodríguez de Tió, and Pachín Marín, among many others.

The longest-lasting independence movement in the hemisphere was that of Spain's Caribbean colonies, Cuba and Puerto Rico, and many of their independence struggles were plotted, funded, and written about from U.S. shores. One of Cuba's first and most illustrious exiles was the philosopher-priest Félix Varela, who founded the newspaper *El Habanero* in Philadelphia in 1824 and moved it to New York in 1825. Subtitled "*papel político, científico y literario*" (political, scientific, and literary paper), *El Habanero* openly militated for Cuban independence from Spain. Varela set the precedent for Cubans and Puerto Ricans of printing and publishing in exile and having their works circulating in their home islands. In fact, Varela's books on philosophy and education, most of which were published in the United States, were said to be the only "best sellers" in Cuba, and Varela himself was the most popular author there in the first third of the nineteenth century—this despite there being in effect a "conspiracy of silence" in which his name could never even be brought up in public on the island (Fornet, 73–74). While still residing in Philadelphia, Varela also authored the first historical novel ever written in the Spanish language, *Jicoténcal* (named after the protagonist), which illustrated the Spanish abuses of the Native Americans in Mexico and thus bolstered the arguments for independence of the Spanish colonies, which now were made up of people who saw themselves as creatures of the New World.

For the most part, the expatriate journalists and writers founded and wrote for Spanish-language or bilingual periodicals. (Some politically oriented newspapers were bilingual because they aspired to influencing Anglo-American public opinion and U.S. government policy regarding Cuba and Puerto Rico.) Very few of the exiled intellectuals found work in the English-language press, except as translators. One notable exception was Miguel Teurbe Tolón, who in the 1850s worked as an editor for Latin America on the New York *Herald*. Teurbe Tolón had been an editor of *La Guirnalda* (*The Garland*) newspaper in Cuba, where he also had launched his literary career as a poet. In the United States, besides working for the *Herald*, he published poems and commentary in both Spanish- and English-language periodicals, and translated Thomas Paine's *Common Sense* and Emma Willard's *History of the United States* into Spanish. One of the most important pioneers of Hispanic journalism in the United States, Tolón was also one of the founders of the literature of Hispanic exile, not only because of the exile theme in many of his poems, but also because his works figure most prominently in the first anthology of exile literature ever published in the United States, *El laúd del desterrado* (*The Exile's Lute*, 1856), issued a year after his death.

Since the writings of Heredia, Varela, Teurbe Tolón, and their colleagues, exile literature has been one of the continuing currents in Hispanic letters and culture in the United States. Many of the writers to follow in the next century and a half became steeped in that tradition, building on the work of their predecessors who used their literary art to promote their political causes. Exile writers also influenced immigrant and native writers. To this date, some of the commonplaces of exile literature remain, even among the most recent exile writers from Central America and Cuba. In general, the literature of exile is centered on the homeland, *la patria*, rather than on the fate of the exile community in the United States. Always implicit is its premise of return to *la patria*, and thus there is no question of assimilating into the culture during the temporary sojourn in the States. Despite this desire, the historical fact is that throughout history many exiles and their families have taken up permanent residence, never to return. As return is always impending, there is a static vision of the homeland culture that often does not reflect the evolution during the exiles' absence. This literature is nostalgic for *la patria*, and on foreign soil these authors seek to preserve the language and culture in order to facilitate an easy return home. The writing does not support the mixing of Spanish and English; the stories tend to be epic in nature and heroes larger than life, even in their tragic downfalls. Often, the metaphors that characterize their lives far from home relate to the Babylonian captivity and to "paradise lost." Their fiction and nonfiction writings emphasize the strangeness of the new social environment and the dangers it poses for cultural survival. The nineteenth century authors engaged in the movements for independence from Spain, often cultivating the "Spanish Black Legend" (propaganda about the Spanish abuses of the Amerindians spread by the English and Dutch in their competition with Spain for New World colonies) and identifying themselves with the Native Americans suffering the inhuman abuses of the Spanish conquistadors as they sought to construct their own New World identity. Thus, the literature was nationalistic not only culturally but often politically as well, and affected by the fact that many of these writers were actually engaged in armed revolutionary and political struggles. The creative and publishing activity of exiled Cubans and Puerto Ricans rivaled the productivity of writers in the homeland. Many of the leading writers and intellectuals of both islands produced a substantial corpus of their works in exile rather than in the repressive environment of Spanish colonial rule. Their substantial legacy includes political thought not only in a remarkable corpus of elegant and exquisite essays, such as those of José Varona and José Martí, but also in books on pedagogy, natural sciences, technology, and, of course, history. Some of the most important Cuban and Puerto Rican literary figures were to follow the examples of Heredia, Varela, and Teurbe Tolón, writing, publishing, and militating from exile in Philadelphia, New York, Tampa, Key West, and New Orleans until the outbreak of the Spanish-American War in 1898. Many of them were journalists and publishers as well as prolific poets of exile: Bonifacio Byrne, Pedro Santacilia, Juan Clemente Zenea, and later, but most important, José Martí. They all studied the works of their model, José María Heredia, whose wanderlust far from his native soil is recorded in some of the most evocative romantic verse of the nineteenth century. In fact, in *El laúd del desterrado,* homage is paid to Heredia by opening with his poems.

Puerto Rican intellectuals joined the expatriate Cubans who established revolutionary clubs and supported book and newspaper publication. In clubs such as Las Dos Antillas (The Two Antilles), cofounded by the Afro-Puerto Rican bibliographer Arturo Alfonso Schomberg, they pronounced the eloquent speeches that would be printed in the newspapers that circulated throughout the exile communities and were smuggled into Puerto Rico. Serving as an important convener of the group at her home in New York was the thrice-exiled Doña Lola Rodríguez de Tió, whose nationalistic verse appeared frequently in local periodicals. In addition to the illustrious philosophers, essayists, and poets who made up this group of expatriate Puerto Ricans, there were two craftsmen whose work was essential to the revolutionary cause and to the literature of exile: typesetters Francisco Gonzalo "Pachín" Marín and Sotero Figueroa, who were also exponents of exile poetry.

Marín brought his revolutionary newspaper *El Postillón* (*The Courier*) from Puerto Rico, where it had been suppressed by the Spanish authorities, to New York in 1889. In the print shop he set up in New York, Marín published his paper, as well as books and broadsides for the Cuban and Puerto Rican expatriate communities. His shop became a meeting place for intellectuals, literary figures, and political leaders. In New York, Marín published two volumes of his own verse that are foundational for Puerto Rican letters: *Romances* (1892) and *En la arena* (c. 1895). Sotero Figueroa was the president of the Club Borinquen and owner of the print shop Imprenta América, which provided the composition and printing for various revolutionary newspapers and other publications, including *Borinquen* (the indigenous name of the island of Puerto Rico), a bimonthly newspaper issued by the Puerto Rican section of Cuban Revolutionary Party. But more important, Figueroa worked closely with José Martí on both his political organizing (Figueroa was the board secretary for the Cuban Revolutionary Party) and his publishing projects. Figueroa printed one of the most important organs of the revolutionary and literary movements, New York's *Patria*, which after being founded by Martí became the official organ of the Cuban Revolutionary Party and in which Martí and Figueroa published essays, poems, and speeches.

Writers such as Sotero Figueroa and Cuban Francisco Sellén were not only attacking Spaniards in their prose and poetry, but also laying down a mythic and ideological background on which to construct their nation's culture. In his published play *Hatuey* (1891), Sellén (like Varela in *Jicoténcal*) identified Cubans with the indigenous past by writing about the last rebel Amerindian chief in Cuba and glossing on Bartolomé de Las Casas's documentation of Spanish inhumanity during the Conquest. This work not only attempted to create a mythological base for Cuban nationhood, but also indicted the immorality of the Spanish colonialists.

While Cubans and Puerto Rican expatriates had to endure passage by ship and inspections by customs authorities to enter as refugees into the United States, Mexican exiles crossed the border with relative ease in order to establish their press in exile. Given that there was no Border Patrol until 1925, they simply walked across what was an open border for Hispanics—as opposed to Asians who were barred by various exclusionary laws—and installed themselves in the long-standing Mexican-origin communities of the Southwest. In fact, the relatively open border had served as an escape route for numerous criminal and/or political refugees from both the northern and southern sides of the dividing line for decades. The Mexican exile press began around 1885, when the Porfirio Díaz regime in Mexico became so repressive that scores of publishers, editors, and writers were forced north into exile. Publishers such as Adolfo Carrillo, who had opposed Díaz with his *El correo del lunes* (*The Monday Mail*), crossed the border, hoping to smuggle their papers back into Mexico. Carrillo ended up in San Francisco, where he established *La República* in 1885, and remained there for the rest of his life. Carrillo became so identified with the Hispanic tradition in California that he set his short stories in California's Hispanic past. Notwithstanding Carrillo's example, most of the exiled Mexican literati of the late nineteenth and early twentieth centuries eventually returned to Mexico when the environment was once again safe for their respective political ideologies.

By 1904, the most important Mexican revolutionary journalist and ideologue, Ricardo Flores Magón, had gone into exile in the United States and begun publishing *Regeneración* in San Antonio, in St. Louis in 1905, and in Canada in 1906. In 1907, he founded *Revolución* in Los Angeles, and in 1908 revived *Regeneración* there. Throughout these years, Flores Magón and his brothers employed any and every subterfuge possible to smuggle their writings from the United States into Mexico, even stuffing them into cans or wrapping them in other newspapers sent to San Luis Potosí, where they were then distributed to sympathizers throughout the country. They also became leaders of labor union and anarchist movements among minorities in the

United States, for their revolutionary efforts, they were persistently repressed and persecuted by both the Mexican and U.S. governments.

Numerous Spanish-language periodicals in the Southwest echoed the ideas of Flores Magón and were affiliated with his Mexican Liberal Party (PML), which was promoting revolution. Among the most interesting newspapers were those involved in articulating labor and women's issues as part of the social change that should be implemented with the triumph of the revolution. Notable among the early writers and editors associated with the PML and Flores Magón was schoolteacher Sara Estela Ramírez, who immigrated from Mexico to teach in Laredo, Texas, in 1898. With her passionate and eloquent speeches and poetry performed at meetings of laborers and community people, she spread the ideas of labor organizing and social reform in both Mexico and Texas. Ramírez wrote for two important Laredo newspapers, *La crónica* (*The Chronicle*) and *El demócrata fronterizo* (*The Border Democrat*), and in 1901 began editing and publishing her own newspaper, *La corregidora* (*The Corrector*). Other periodicals under the direction of women not only furthered the revolutionary cause, but also articulated gender issues within that cause: Teresa Villarreal's *El obrero* (*The Worker*, 1909), Isidra T. de Cárdenas' *La voz de la mujer* (*The Woman's Voice*, 1907), Blanca de Moncaleano's *Pluma roja* (*Red Pen*, 1913–15), and Teresa and Andrea Villarreal's *La mujer moderna* (*The Modern Woman*).

The Mexican exile press flourished into the 1930s, with weekly newspapers siding with one faction or another, and publishing houses, often affiliated with newspapers, issuing political tracts as well as novels of the revolution. In fact, more than any other literary genre published in book form, the novel of the Mexican Revolution flourished. Through the novel of the revolution, expatriate authors such as Teodoro Torres and Manuel Arce sought to come to terms with that cataclysm that had disrupted their lives and had caused so many of their readers to relocate to the southwestern United States. The authors represented the full gamut of the revolutionary factions in their loyalties and ideologies, but for the most part the genre was characterized by a conservative reaction to the socialistic change in government and community organization that the revolution had wrought. One of the first to establish this genre was the now classic work of Latin American literature, Mariano Azuela's *Los de abajo* (*The Underdogs*), which was not counterrevolutionary. *Los de abajo* appeared as a serialized novel in an El Paso Spanish-language newspaper and was later published in book form in that city in 1915. From that time on, literally scores of these novels were published from San Diego to San Antonio. By no means was the press and the publishing enterprise as liberal as the exile press prior to the outbreak of the Revolution. To the contrary, many of these novels were typical of the exile culture promoted by conservatives dislodged from Mexico by the socialist revolution; they came with resources in hand to well-established Mexican American communities and became entrepreneurs in cultural as well as business enterprises. Some of them founded newspapers, magazines, and publishing houses to serve the rapidly expanding community of economic refugees, and their newspapers eventually became the backbone of an *immigrant* rather than an *exile* press, as their entrepreneurial spirit overtook their political commitment to change in the homeland. Indeed, the large Hispanic communities in the United States could reproduce the culture of the homeland for enclaves of working people who had the financial resources to sustain business and culture. Most of these people were economic refugees, that is, immigrants, whose ethos differed from that of the political exiles.

The next large wave of Hispanic political refugees to reach these shores came from across the Atlantic: the liberals defeated by Spanish fascism. Hispanic communities across the United States embraced the refugees and sympathized with their cause. Many Cuban, Mexican, and Puerto Rican organizations held fundraisers for the Republicans during the Spanish Civil War. The Spanish expatriates themselves were fast to establish their own exile press. Their efforts hit fertile soil in Depression-era communities that were hotbeds for union and socialist organizing. During this period and the years of the Franco regime that followed, some of Spain's most famous writers took up refuge in the United States and Puerto Rico. Among their number were novelist Ramón Sender and poet Jorge Guillén, as well as poet Juan Ramón Jiménez, who while living in Puerto Rico would win the Nobel Prize.

The focus of protest writing shifted somewhat during the twentieth century to attacking modern dictatorships and authoritarian regimes, as well as to criticizing the repeated intervention of the United States in the Latin republics' domestic politics, quite often on the side of dictators and their repressive regimes. The pseudonymous writer Lirón was one of the most outrageously graphic in his attacks on Spanish dictator Francisco Franco, while Salvadoran Gustavo Solano, who used the pseudonym of "El Conde Gris" (The Grey Count), consigned Manuel Estrada Cabrera, the Guatemalan dictator, to Hell in his play *Sangre* (*Blood*, 1919). Before residing for many years in exile in the United States, Solano had been incarcerated for his revolutionary activities in Mexico and had become persona non grata in almost all of the Central American republics for his pursuit of a united and democratic Central America.

From their distant perspective in the United States, other Central American writers in particular, such as Nicaraguan Santiago Argüello, reinvigorated Simón Bolívar's ignored vision of a united Spanish America, not only to stave off the imperialist threats of the United States, but also to fully integrate the economies and cultures of Central and South America. Puerto Ricans Juan Antonio Corretjer and his wife Consuelo Lee Tapia militated through their newspaper *Pueblos Hispanos* (*Hispanic Peoples*) and their individual writings for Puerto Rican independence from the United States. Corretjer, who had been imprisoned in an Atlanta federal penitentiary for his nationalist activities on the island, took up residence in New York after he was prohibited by federal authorities from returning to Puerto Rico. The U.S. military administration of the island colony was far more repressive than authorities in New York and other cities on the continent. The Puerto Rican dissidents enjoyed greater freedom of association and were less noticed writing in Spanish and organizing in the Hispanic communities of New York, Tampa, and Chicago than in full view of their vigilant government at home. Corretjer and Tapia were at the center of a cadre of Puerto Rican nationalist writers in New York, while many of their compatriots, even the more radical ones, such as Jesús Colón also writing in *Pueblos Hispanos*, were staking out claims on New York as their rightful home. But while Corretjer and Tapia indicted the U.S. military government of Puerto Rico, Dominican journalist Carmita Landestoy eloquently unmasked the Rafael Trujillo regime in her homeland, a regime that was also supported by the United States, which had administered a military government in the Dominican Republic for most of the early twentieth century. Thus the ironic situation in which the Caribbean and Central American writers found themselves was that of being exiled in the belly of the beast that they accused of causing many of the ills in their homeland.

With the Cuban Revolution and the United States fighting much of the Cold War through involvement in the civil wars in Central America and Chile, large-scale immigration of political refugees has continued to the present day, and the dictatorships in these countries and Argentina have arisen as themes in the literature of Hispanic exile. Beginning in 1959, a new wave of refugees from the Cuban revolution established a widespread exile press as well as a more informal network of hundreds of newsletters. Chileans, Salvadorans, Nicaraguans, and other Spanish American expatriates have all contributed to a literature of exile. What is different today is that many of these exiled voices have been readily translated into English, and the works of liberal writers such as Argentines Luisa Valenzuela, Manuel Puig, and Jacobo Timmerman; Chileans Emma Sepúlveda and Ariel Dorfman; and Guatemala's Arturo Arias are published alongside the more conservative voices of Cuban exiles, such as those of Heberto Padilla and Reinaldo Arenas. As the Hispanic population of the United States continues to grow—estimated to be one-fourth of the total population by 2050—and as the economy of the United States becomes more integrated with those south of the border through agreements such as the North American Free Trade Agreement (NAFTA), United States culture will become even more directly linked to the internal politics of Spanish America. The culture of Hispanic exile will continue to be part of the overall culture of the United States into the foreseeable future; the United States will continue to be a preferred base from which political refugees will use the press, the electronic media, and U.S. popular culture, such as the recent film hits *Death and the Maiden* and *The Kiss of the Spider Woman,* to express their opposition to governments in their homelands.

But more than that, Hispanic political refugees, through their use of the press and their leadership in community organizations and churches, have left indelible marks on the ethos and philosophy of Hispanic communities within the United States. Their knowledge and perspectives live on in Hispanic culture today, regardless of whether particular refugees have returned or not to their homelands. And many of those that remained here, and their children, intermarried with other Hispanic natives and immigrants; many of them and their children eventually blended into the grand community that is recognizable today as a national ethnic minority.

Sin Frontera: Beyond Boundaries

Hispanic literature of the United States is transnational in nature; it emerges from and remains intimately related to the crossing of political, geographic, cultural, linguistic, and racial boundaries. Hispanic peoples in the United States are the result of the United States expanding its borders, of conquering and incorporating and importing peoples from the Hispanic world, which has existed not only immediately outside but within the United States. Hispanic peoples in the United States have never severed nor felt the need to sever their ties to the rest of the Hispanic world. Likewise, U.S. Hispanics have created their own cultural patterns, which in turn have influenced the rest of the Hispanic world through travel and communications.

Our paradigm of native, immigrant, and exile cultures and literatures is meant to be dynamic: It allows for the ebbs and flows of new cultural inputs and for culture change from one generation to another. It allows for entrances and exits from Hispanic U.S.A. and for evolving cultural stances, language preferences, and identities of individuals, such as Jesús Colón, Américo Paredes, and Adolfo Carrillo, who in one moment saw themselves as immigrants or exiles and in another as naturalized citizens or natives identifying strongly with the long history of Hispanic culture in the United States. Given that immigration and exile are still very much a part of the daily life and promise to remain so for a long time, the transnational and borderless nature of Hispanic culture will become only more apparent and characteristic as media also continue to cement the relationship of Latinos in the United States to the rest of the Spanish-speaking world. The three U.S. Spanish television networks function hemispherically by satellite; Spanish-language book and magazine distribution is every day more hemispheric. Some forty years of bilingual education in the United States, often imparted by immigrant teachers, has solidified cultural bonds with nearby Spanish American countries. Moves toward the economic integration of the Americas through agreements such as NAFTA will further consolidate the interdependence of the nation-states of the Americas and of the Spanish-speaking populations. Air travel is cheaper and more accessible to all populations and will continue to contribute to a borderless America/*América.*

Among the many writers who have been able to identify the transnational and borderless nature of Latino culture are the visionaries Luis Rafael Sánchez and Guillermo Gómez Peña. Sánchez, responding to the cultural circumstances of Puerto Ricans being defined by their colonial status on the island and migrant-citizen status on the continent, chose "*la guagua aérea*" (*the airbus*) as the symbol of Puerto Rican culture. It does not abandon Puerto Rican ethnicity but acknowledges its dynamism, its ability to evolve and incorporate but, most of all, to survive. Writer and performance artist Gómez Peña sees the cultural dynamism of borders—that is, hybridity, fluidity, synchretism, and synthesis—overtaking and becoming the common communication style not only for the United States and Spanish America but for the entire world. In fact, this may be the overriding lesson and example of Hispanic literature of the United States.

About the Anthology

Herencia: The Anthology of Hispanic Literature of the United States is the result of ten years of work by scholars and graduate students from throughout the United States, Cuba, Mexico, and Puerto Rico collaborating in Recovering the U.S. Hispanic Literary Heritage, a project to research, preserve, and make accessible the literature created by Hispanics in all areas that came to be part of the United States, from the colonial period up to 1960. The project's goals are to compile the master bibliography of all works written and published (some 18,000 entries to date); to locate, preserve, index, and digitize portions of all the newspapers published by Hispanics (some 1700 located to date);

to examine, index, and create access to important archives containing Hispanic materials; to fund scholars to research and write about works long forgotten; and to sponsor biannual international conferences on recovery. The editorial team for this anthology was able to access thousands of texts, study them, and select some of the most noteworthy and representative in this initial edition of the first historical compilation of Hispanic literature of the United States. Thus, this anthology results from the assiduous work of hundreds of scholars working through the Recovery Project, whose textual contributions and insights are reflected not only in the selections themselves, but also in some of the introductory texts for the individual works. As such, this anthology is a collective effort emerging from a very active and diligent field of investigators and teachers who have created a new subdiscipline in American literature and Hispanic literature studies. To make the material more intelligible and accessible to general readers and students, the work has been organized to respond to the three cultural processes that have shaped Hispanic life in the United States: exile, immigration, and the development of a native culture in the United States. The works grouped in these three categories are arranged in loose chronological patterns, which allow for the highlighting of the subthemes listed in the table of contents. In addition, more specific themes are identified in the thematic index available on the Recovery website: www.arte.uh.edu. Because Hispanic literature is interlingual and bilingual, we have translated much of the original Spanish-language material—before 1960, some 90 percent of Hispanic literature was written in Spanish—in order to make the material accessible to English speakers. Most of the documents written before 1960, included in this anthology, have never been anthologized nor have they been available to students, scholars, or the general public.

The work of the Recovering the U.S. Hispanic Literary Heritage project, however, is not done. There are still thousands of documents that are missing or, at least, have not been accessed due to the ravages of time, inattention, and/or lack of funding for research. The project has estimated that as many as 500 newspapers published by Hispanics before 1960 are still missing; that is, not one page has been found of these periodicals. Much of the legacy is contained in books that were printed on acid paper, but important repositories at universities and other institutions have not identified these books as rare or as even belonging to the cultural heritage of the United States. And thus they have not been targeted for deacidification, microfilming, or safeguarding in rare books collections. There is also a dearth of historical and literary scholars trained to research and critically evaluate this material, much less incorporate it into curriculum at every level of education and actually teach it. Thus, this anthology is, in addition to all the other purposes we have designed for it, a call for action by scholars and cultural institutions to preserve, make accessible, and incorporate this material into their representations of American cultural identity.

As one peruses the selections in this anthology, it will become immediately evident that this is not a collection of strictly "literary" expressions but also an assemblage of documents which contribute to the construction of the historical legacy of Hispanics in the United States. For the first time, the editors have gone beyond just sampling the works of poets, novelists, and playwrights to survey the varied expression of journalists, political and labor activists, and common everyday people through their folklore and testimony, to compose a broad vision of how Hispanics have used language to define themselves and their culture. The premise of the scholars working in recovery is that the literature of a people transcends not only class and educational boundaries but also the limits of literacy. Indeed, a people's culture and identity are generated and expressed at every level of the society in a wide spectrum of genres and for various audiences, including the self in society. Here, then, is the literary legacy of Hispanics in the United States, as broadly defined as the people themselves have been across time.

Neither this anthology nor the rest of the work conducted by the Recovering the U.S. Hispanic Literary Heritage project would have been possible without the confidence and generous financial commitment made by the Rockefeller Foundation to this whole endeavor. While the Rockefeller Foundation underwrote the core work conducted nationally and at the program's center at the University of Houston, other foundations awarded specific project support over the course of research that contributed to the making of this anthology: the Andrew Mellon Foundation, the Meadows Foundation, the Ford Foundation, the AT&T Foundation, the A. H. Belo Foundation, the Summerlee Foundation, the National Endowment for the Arts, the Department of the Interior, and the National Endowment for the Humanities. The editor, coeditors, coordinator, and affiliated scholars throughout the country are deeply indebted to these wonderful supporters of our efforts and to Oxford University Press for making this volume a reality.

NICOLÁS KANELLOS, General Editor

Works cited: Ambrosio Fornet, *El libro en Cuba* (Havana: Editorial Letras Cubanas, 1994); Juan Gómez-Quiñones, *Roots of Chicano Politics, 1600–1940* (Albuquerque: University of New Mexico Press, 1994); Nicolás Kanellos, with Helvetia Martell, *Hispanic Periodicals in the United States, Origins to 1960: A Brief History and Comprehensive Bibliography* (Houston: Arte Público Press, 2000); Gabriel Meléndez, *So All Is Not Lost: The Poetics of Print in Nuevo Mexicano Communities* (Albuquerque: University of New Mexico Press, 1997); Doris Meyer, *Speaking for Themselves: Neo-Mexicano Cultural Identity and the Spanish-Language Press, 1880–1920* (Albuquerque: University of New Mexico Press, 1996); and Robert E. Park, *The Immigrant Press and Its Control* (New York: Harper and Brothers, 1922). See also www.arte.uh.edu.

PART I

The Literature of Exploration and Colonization

Alvar Núñez Cabeza de Vaca (1490–1564?)

The Account (excerpt)

During Spain's process of exploration and conquest in the Western Hemisphere, the chronicle, a traditional genre in Spanish literature, recorded much of this enterprise. Many of these men were neither learned scholars nor did they have aesthetic concerns in mind, yet their chronicles are filled with creative power as well as valuable information. Among these men was Alvar Núñez Cabeza de Vaca, the first European to traverse—on foot—a large portion of the recently discovered territory of North America. His journey (1528–36) of hardship and misfortune is one of the most remarkable in the history of the New World. A product of this odyssey was *La Relación* (*The Account*). Published in Zamora, Spain, in 1542, *The Account* is one of the earliest reports of Spanish explorations in North America, and a document of inestimable value for students of history and literature, ethnographers, anthropologists, and the general reader. It contains many first descriptions of the lands and their inhabitants. Furthermore, it is one of the first Spanish accounts that calls for a compassionate and tolerant policy toward the natives of the Western Hemisphere. Born in Jerez de la Frontera, Spain, in 1490, Cabeza de Vaca distinguished himself as an officer in the Spanish army. Appointed as royal treasurer of the ill-fated expedition of Pánfilo de Narváez to Florida in 1528, Cabeza de Vaca became only one of four survivors. Finally, after eight years of wandering as slaves and faith healers, they were able to reach Mexico. After his return to Spain in 1537, he was appointed Governor and Captain General of the South American Province of the Río de la Plata in 1540. Known for his humane views and liberal policies toward the natives, Cabeza de Vaca was overthrown by his subjects and sent to Spain in chains. Acquitted of charges, he was named Chief Justice of the Tribunal of Seville. It is believed he died in 1564. The selection from chapter 7 of his narrative offers the first description in Spanish letters of the flora and fauna of Florida. Chapter 12 narrates, in a most powerful and moving manner, the Spaniard's predicament after being cast ashore at Galveston Island. The selection from chapter 15 offers us an interesting account of how the survivors became faith healers. (JBF)

Further reading: Alvar Núñez Cabeza de Vaca, *The Account*, trans. Martin A. Favata and José B. Fernández (Houston: Arte Público Press, 1993).

Trans.: MAF and JBF

Chapter Seven: What the Land Is Like

From the place where we landed to this village and land of Apalachee, the country is mostly flat, the soil sandy and firm. Throughout it there are many large trees and open woodlands in which there are walnut trees and laurels and others called sweet-gums, cedars, junipers, live oaks, pines, oaks and low-growing palmettos like those in Castile. Throughout it there are many large and small lakes, some of them very difficult to cross, partly because they are so deep and partly because there are so many fallen trees in them. They have sandy bottoms, and the ones we found in Apalachee are much larger than any we had encountered on the way. There are many cornfields in this province, and the houses are as spread out through the countryside as those of the Gelves.

The animals that we saw in those lands were three kinds of deer, rabbits and hares, bears and lions and other wild animals, among which we saw one which carries its young in a pouch on its belly. While they are small they carry them in that manner until they can get their own food. If they happen to be out of the pouch searching for food when people approach, the mother does not flee until she has gathered them all in her pouch. The country there is very cold and has good pastures for livestock. There are many kinds of birds: very many geese, ducks, large ducks, royal ducks, ibises, egrets and herons and quail. We saw many falcons, marsh hawks, sparrow hawks, goshawks and many other birds.

Two hours after we arrived in Apalachee, the Indians that had fled from there returned peacefully to us, asking us for their women and children. And we returned them, except that the Governor held one of their chiefs, which angered them. The following day they came back ready for battle and attacked us so boldly and swiftly that they were able to set fire to the lodges we were in. But as we sallied they fled and took refuge in some lakes very close by. For this reason and because of the large cornfields there, we could do little harm to them, except for one that we killed.

The following day Indians from a village on the other side came and attacked us just as the first group had done. They escaped in the same manner, and one of them died too. We stayed in this village twenty-five days, during which we went into the countryside three times. We found the country sparsely inhabited and hard to cross because of its difficult terrain, its forests and lakes.

Chapter Twelve: How the Indians Brought Us Food

The following day at sunrise, at the time the Indians had indicated, they came to us as promised, bringing us much fish, some roots which they eat, the size of walnuts, some larger or smaller. Most of these are pulled with great difficulty from under the water. In the evening they returned to bring us more fish and the same kind of roots. They had their women and children come to see us and they considered themselves rich with little bells and beads that we gave them. The following days they returned to visit with the same things as before.

Seeing that we were provisioned with fish, roots, water and the other things we requested, we agreed to embark on our voyage once again. We dug up the boat from the sand. We had to strip naked and struggle mightily to launch it, because we were so weak that lesser tasks would have been enough to exhaust us. Once we were out from the shore the distance of two crossbow shots, a wave struck us quite a blow and got us all wet. Since we were naked and it was very cold, we let go of the oars. Another strong wave caused the boat to capsize. The Inspector and two other men held on to it to survive, but quite the opposite occurred because the boat pulled them under and they drowned. Since the surf was very rough, the sea wrapped all the men in its waves, except the three that had been pulled under by the boat, and cast them on the shore of the same island. Those of us who survived were as naked as the day we were born and had lost everything we had. Although the few things we had were of little value, they meant a lot to us.

It was November then and the weather was very cold. We were in such a state that our bones could easily be counted and we looked like the picture of death. I can say for myself that I had not eaten anything but parched corn since the previous May, and sometimes I had to eat it raw. Although the horses were slaughtered while we were building the boats, I was never able to eat them, and I had eaten fish fewer than ten times. This is but a brief comment, since anyone can imagine what shape we were in. On top of all this, the north wind began to blow, and so we were closer to death than to life. It pleased our Lord to let us find some embers among the coals of the fire we had made, and we made large fires. In this way we asked our Lord's mercy and the forgiveness of our sins, shedding many tears, with each man pitying not only himself but all the others who were in the same condition.

At sunset the Indians, thinking that we had not gone, looked for us again and brought us food. When they saw us in such a different state of attire and looking so strange, they were so frightened that they drew back. I went out to them and called them and they returned very frightened. I let them know through sign language that one of our boats had sunk and that three of our men had drowned. And there before their very eyes they saw two of the dead men, and those of us who were alive seemed as if we would soon join them.

The Indians, seeing the disaster that had come upon us and brought so much misfortune and misery, sat down with us. They felt such great pain and pity at seeing us in such a state that they all began to cry so loudly and sincerely that they could be heard from afar. This went on for more than half an hour. In fact, seeing that these crude and untutored people, who were like brutes, grieved so much for us, caused me and the others in my company to suffer more and think more about our misfortune. When their crying ceased, I told the Christians that, if they agreed, I would ask those Indians to take us to their lodges. And some who had been in New Spain responded that we should not even think about it, because if they took us to their lodges they would sacrifice us to their idols. But seeing that we had no other recourse and that any other action would certainly bring us closer to death, I did not pay attention to what they were saying and I asked the Indians to take us to their lodges. They indicated that they would be very pleased to do this. They asked us to wait a bit and then they would do what we wanted. Then thirty of them loaded themselves with firewood and went to their lodges, which were far from there. We stayed with the others until nearly nightfall, when they held on to us and took us hastily to their lodges. Since it was so cold and they feared that someone might faint or die on the way, they had provided for four or five large fires to be placed at intervals, and they warmed us at each one. Once they saw that we had gained some strength and gotten warmer, they took us to the next one so rapidly that our feet scarcely touched the ground. In this way we went to their lodges and found that they had one ready for us with many fires lighted in it. Within an hour of our arrival they began to dance and have a great celebration that lasted all night. For us there was no pleasure nor celebration nor sleep because we were waiting to see when they would sacrifice us. In the morning they again gave us fish and roots and treated us so well that we were a little reassured and lost some of our fear of being sacrificed.

Chapter Fifteen: What Happened to Us in the Village of Misfortune

On that island I have spoken of, they wanted to make us physicians, without testing us or asking for any degrees, because they cure illnesses by blowing on the sick person and cast out the illness with their breath and their hands. So they told us to be useful and do the same. We laughed at the idea, saying they were mocking us and that we did not know how to heal. They in turn deprived us of our food until we did as they ordered. Seeing our reluctance, an Indian told me that I did not know what I was talking about when I said that all that was useless. He knew that even rocks and other things found in the fields have beneficial properties, for he healed and took away pain by passing a hot rock across the stomach. And since, he said, we were powerful men, we were certain to have greater powers and properties. In brief, we were in such need that we had to do it, putting aside our fear that anyone would be punished for it.

Their manner of healing is as follows: When they are sick, they call a medicine man, and after they are cured they give him not only all their possessions, but also seek things from their relatives to give him. What the medicine man does is to make a cut where the pain is and suck around it. They cauterize with fire, a practice they consider very beneficial. I tried it and found that it gave good results. Afterward they blow on the painful area, believing that their illness goes away in this manner.

We did our healing by making the sign of the cross on the sick persons, breathing on them, saying the Lord's Prayer and a Hail Mary over them, and asking God our Lord, as best we could, to heal them and inspire them to treat us well. God our Lord in his mercy deigned to heal all those for whom we prayed. Once we made the sign of the cross on them, they told the others that they were well and healthy. For this reason they treated us well, and refrained from eating to give us food. They also gave us hides and other small things.

Everyone's hunger was so great there were times that I went three days without eating anything, and they did too. It seemed impossible for me to survive, although I found myself in greater want and hunger afterward, as I shall relate later on.

The Indians that were keeping Alonso del Castillo and Andrés Dorantes and the other survivors were of another language and lineage. They went to another part of the mainland to eat oysters and stayed there until the first day of April. Then they returned to the island which was up to two leagues away across the widest part of the water. The island is half a league wide and five leagues long.

All the people of this land go about naked. Only the women cover part of their bodies with a kind of wool that grows on the trees. Young women cover themselves with deer-skins. These people share all that they have with one another. There is no chief among them, and all the people of one lineage live together. Two language groups live there: one group is called the Capoques and the other the Han. They have the following custom: When they know each other and see each other from time to time, before speaking they cry for half an hour. When this is finished, the one who is visited rises first and gives the other everything he owns. The other one accepts and in a short while leaves with it. Sometimes they leave without saying a word after accepting the gifts. They have other strange customs, but I have described only the principal and most noteworthy ones so that I can go on and tell more of what happened to us.

Fray Marcos de Niza (1495–1558)

Discovery of the Seven Cities of Cibola (excerpt)

We know very little about Fray Marcos de Niza's early life except that he was born in Italy and joined the Spanish missionary effort to come to the New World in 1531. He began his missionary work in Guatemala and Peru where he became proficient in Spanish, after which he came to the Viceroyalty of New Spain (Mexico). He was uniquely qualified as a cartographer, expertise that attracted the attention of the Bishop of New Spain, who asked him to embark on an expedition to explore and chart the northern territories of New Spain. In 1538, Fray Marcos set out from Mexico City with a group of soldiers and other personnel that included Esteban (popularly known as Estevanico and as Stephen in translation), the Moor who had accompanied Cabeza de Vaca on his earlier trek across the southwest. Fray Marcos selected Esteban as the expedition's official guide due to his knowledge of the territory that was to be explored. As is apparent in the following selection, Fray Marcos became increasingly more interested—perhaps even obsessed—with the prospect of discovering the fabled Seven Cities of Cibola as different northern Indian tribes he encountered shared supposedly reliable information about their location and wealth. Esteban's account of his sighting of one of the cities further stimulated Fray Marcos's curiosity and belief that he was on the right track. Finally, Fray Marcos himself became convinced that he had seen one of the cities of which he gives a much embellished description. Later explorers and historians concluded that he had transformed in his imagination a simple Zuni Indian village into a beautiful city. (ChT)

Further reading: Fray Marcos de Niza, *Discovery of the Seven Cities of Cibola* (Albuquerque, N.M.: El Palacio Press, 1926).

Trans.: PMB

Before arriving at the desert, I came to a green, well-watered settlement, where there came to meet me a crowd of people, men and women, clothed in cotton and some covered with cowhides, which in general they consider a better dress material than cotton. All the people of this town wear turquoise hanging from their noses and ears; these ornaments are called cacona. Among them came the chief of the town and his two brothers, very well dressed in cotton, encaconados, and each with a necklace of turquoises around his neck. They brought to me a quantity of game—venison, rabbits and quail—also maize and meal, all in great abundance. They offered me many turquoise, cowhides, very pretty cups and other things, of which I accepted none, for such was my custom since entering the country where we were not known. And here I had the same account as before of the seven cities and the kingdoms and provinces as I have related above. I was wearing a garment of dark woolen cloth, of the kind called Saragosa, which was given to me by Franscisco Vasquez de Coronado, governor of New Galicia. The chief of the village and other Indians touched it with their hands and told me there was plenty of that fabric in Totonteac, and that the natives of that place were clothed with it. At this I laughed and said it could not be so, that it must be garments of cotton which those people wore. Then they said to me: "Do you think that we do not know that what you wear and what we wear is different? Know that in Cibola the houses are full of that material which we are wearing, but in Totonteac there are some small animals from which they obtain that with which they make a fabric like yours." This astonished me, as I had not heard of any such thing previously, and I desired to inform myself more particularly about it. They told me that the animals are the size of the Castilian greyhounds which Stephen had with him; they said there were many of them in Totonteac. I could not guess what species of animals they might be.

The next day I entered into the desert and at the place where I had to go for dinner I found huts and food enough by the side of a watercourse. At night I found cabins and food again and so it was for the four days that I traveled through this desert. At the end of them, I entered a very well-populated valley and at the first town many men and women came with food to meet me. They all wore many turquoises suspended from their noses and ears, and some wore necklaces of turquoises, like those which I said were worn by the chief of the town on the other side of the desert, and his brothers, except that they only wore one string, while these Indians wore three or four. They were dressed in very good cloaks of ox leather. The women likewise wore turquoises in their noses and ears and very good petticoats and blouses. Here they had as much information of Cibola, as in New Spain they have of Mexico and in Peru of Cuzco. They described in detail the houses, streets and squares of the town, like people who had been there many times, and they were wearing various objects brought from there, which they had obtained by their services, like the Indians I had previously met. I said to them that it was not possible that the houses should be in the manner which they described to me, so to make me understand they took earth and ashes and mixed them with water, and showed how the stone is placed and the edifice reared, placing stone and mortar till the required height is reached. I asked them if the men of that country had wings to climb those stories; they laughed and explained to me a ladder as well as I could do, and they took a stick and placed it over their heads and said it was that height from story to story. Here I was also given an account of the woolen cloth of Totonteac, where they say the houses are like those at Cibola, but better and bigger, and that it is a very great place and has no limit.

Here I learned that the coast turns to the west, almost at a right angle, because until I reached the entrance of the first desert which I passed, the coast always trended toward the north. As it was very important to know the direction of the coast, I wished to assure myself and so went to look out and I saw clearly that in latitude 35 degrees it turns to the west. I was not less pleased at this discovery than at the good news I had of the country.

So I turned to follow my route and was in that valley five days. It is so thickly populated with fine people and so provided with food that there would be enough to supply more than three hundred horses. It is all watered and is like a garden. There are villages at every half or quarter league or so. In each of them I had a very long account of Cibola, and they spoke to me in detail about it, as people would who went there each year to earn their living. Here I found a man who was a native of Cibola. He told me he had fled from the governor whom the lord had placed there in Cibola, for the lord of these seven cities lives and has his residence in one of them, which is called Ahacus, and in the others he has placed persons who command for him. This citizen of Cibola is a man of good disposition, somewhat old and much more intelligent than the native of the valley and those I had formerly met; he told me that he wished to go with me so that I might procure his pardon. I interrogated him carefully and he told me that Cibola is a big city, that it has a large population and many streets and squares, and that in some parts of the city there are very great houses, ten stories high, in which the chiefs meet on certain days of the year. He corroborated what I had already been told, that the houses are constructed out of stone and lime, and he said that the doors and fronts of the principal houses are of turquoise; he added that the others of the seven cities are similar, though some are bigger, and that the most important is Ahacus. He told me that toward the southeast lay a kingdom called Marata, in which there used to be many very large towns, having the same kind of houses built of stone and with several stories; that this kingdom had been, and still was, at war with the lord of the seven cities; that by this war Marata had been greatly reduced in power, although it was still independent and continued the war.

He likewise told me that to the southeast there is a kingdom named Totonteac, which he said was the biggest, most populous, and the richest in the world, and that there they wore clothes made of the same stuff as mine, and others of a more delicate material obtained from the animals of which I had already had a description; the people were highly cultured and different from those I had hitherto seen. He further informed me that there is another province and very great kingdom, which is called Acus—for there are Ahacus and Acus, Ahacus, with the aspiration, is one of the seven cities, the most important one, and Acus, without the aspiration, is a kingdom and province by itself.

He corroborated what I had been told concerning the clothes worn in Cibola and added that all the people of that city sleep in beds raised above the floor, with fabrics and with tilts above to cover the beds. He said that he would go with me to Cibola and beyond, if I desired to take him along. I was given the same account in this town by many other persons, though not in such great detail.

I traveled in this valley three days and the natives made for me all the feasts and rejoicings that they could. Here in this valley I saw more than two thousand oxhides, extremely well cured; I saw a very large quantity of turquoises and necklaces thereof, as in the places I had left behind, and all said that they came from the city of Cibola. They know this place as well as I would know what I hold in my hands, and they are similarly acquainted with the kingdoms of Marata, Acus and Totonteac. Here in this valley they brought to me a skin, half as big again as that of a large cow, and told me that it was from an animal which has only one horn on its forehead and that this horn is curved toward its chest and then there sticks out a straight point, in which they said there was so much strength, that no object, no matter how hard, could fail to break when struck with it. They averred that there were many of these animals in that country. The color of the skin is like that of the goat and the hair is as long as one's finger.

Here I had messengers from Stephen, who told me on his behalf that he was then entering the last desert, and the more cheerfully, as he was going more assured of the country; and he sent to me to say that, since departing from me, he had never found the Indians out in any lie, but up to that point had found everything as they had told him and so he thought to find that beyond. And so I held it for certain, because it is true, that from the first day I had news of the city of Cibola, the Indians had told me of everything that till then I had seen, telling me always what towns I would find along the road and the numbers of them and, in the parts where there was no population, showing me where I would eat and sleep, without erring in one point. I had then marched, from the first place where I had news of the country, one hundred twelve leagues, so it appears to me not unworthy to note the great truthfulness of these people. Here in this valley, as in the other towns before, I erected crosses and performed the appropriate acts and ceremonies, according to my instructions. The natives of this town asked me to stay with them three or four days, because there was a desert four leagues thence, and from the beginning of it the city of Cibola would be a march of fifteen days and they wished to put up food for me and to make the necessary arrangements for it. They told me that with the negro Stephen there had gone more than three hundred men to accompany him and carry food, and that many wished to go with me also, to serve me and because they expected to return rich. I acknowledged their kindness and asked that they should get ready speedily, because each day seemed to me a year, so much I desired to see Cibola. And so I remained three days without going forward, during which I continually informed myself concerning Cibola and all other places. In doing so I took the Indians aside and questioned each one by himself, and all agreed in their account and told me the number of the people, the order of the streets, the size of the houses and the fashion of the doorways, just as I had been told by those before.

After the three days were past, many people assembled to go with me, of whom I chose thirty chiefs, who were very well supplied with necklaces of turquoises, some of them wearing as many as five or six strings. With these I took the retinue necessary to carry food for them and me and started on my way. I entered the desert on the ninth day of May. On the first day, by a very wide and well-traveled road, we arrived for dinner at a place where there was water, which the Indians showed to me, and in the evening we came again to water, and there I found shelter which the Indians had just constructed for me and another which had been made for Stephen to sleep in when he passed. There were some old huts and many signs of fire, made by people passing to Cibola over this road. In this fashion I journeyed twelve days, always very well supplied with victuals of venison, hares, and partridges of the same color and flavor as those of Spain, although rather smaller.

At this juncture I met an Indian, the son of one of the chiefs who were journeying with me, who had gone in company with the negro Stephen. This man showed fatigue in his countenance, had his body covered with sweat, and manifested the deepest sadness in his whole person. He told me that, at a day's march before coming to Cibola, Stephen, according to his custom, sent ahead messages with his calabash, that they might know he was coming. The calabash was adorned with some rows of rattles and two feathers, one white and one red. When they arrived at Cibola, before the person of the lord's representative in that place, and gave him the calabash, as soon as he took it in his hands and saw the rattles, with great anger he flung it on the ground and told the messengers to be gone forthwith, that he knew what sort of people these were, and that the messengers should tell them not to enter the city, as if they did so he would put them to death. The messengers went back, told Stephen what had passed. He said to them that that was nothing, that those who showed themselves irritated received him better. So he continued his journey till he arrived at the city of Cibola, where he found people who would not consent to let him enter, who put him in a big house which was outside the city, and who at once took away from him all that he carried, his articles of barter and the turquoises and other things which he had received on the road from the Indians. They left him that night without giving anything to eat or drink either to him or to those that were with him. The following morning my informant was thirsty and went out of the house to drink from a nearby stream. When he had been there a few moments he saw Stephen fleeing away, pursued by the people of the city and they killed some of those who were with him. When this Indian saw this he concealed himself and made his way up the stream, then crossed over and regained the road of the desert.

At these tidings, some of the Indians who were with me commenced to weep. As for myself, the wretched news made me fear I should be lost. I feared not much to lose my life as not to be able to return to give a report of the greatness of the country, where God, Our Lord, might be so well served and his holy faith exalted and the royal domains of H.M. extended. In these circumstances I consoled them as best I could and told them that one ought not to give entire credence to that Indian, but they said to me with many tears that the Indian only related what he had seen. So I drew apart from the Indians to commend myself to Our Lord and to pray Him to guide this matter as He might best be served and to enlighten my mind. This done, I returned to the Indians and, with a knife, cut the cords of the packages of dry goods and articles of barter which I was carrying with me and which till then I had not touched nor given away any of the contents. I divided up the goods among all those chiefs and told them not to fear and to go along with me, which they did.

Continuing our journey, at a day's march from Cibola, we met two other Indians, of those who had gone with Stephen, who appeared bloody and with many wounds. At this meeting, they and those that were with me set up such a crying, that out of pity and fear they also made me cry. So great was the noise that I could not ask about Stephen nor of what had happened to them, so I begged them to be quiet that we might learn what had passed. They said to me: "How can we be quiet, when we know that our fathers, sons, and brothers who were with Stephen, to the number of more than three hundred men, are dead? And we no more dare go to Cibola, as we have been accustomed." Nevertheless, as well as I could, I endeavored to pacify them and to put off their fear, although I myself was not without need of someone to calm me. I asked the wounded Indians concerning Stephen and as to what happened. They remained a short time without speaking a word, weeping along with those of their towns. At last they told me that when Stephen arrived at a day's march from Cibola, he sent his messengers with his calabash to the lord of Cibola to announce his arrival and that he was coming peacefully and to cure them. When the messengers gave him the calabash and he saw the rattles, he flung it furiously on the floor and said: "I know these people; these rattles are not of our style of workmanship; tell them to go back immediately or not a man of them will remain alive." Thus he remained very angry. The messengers went back sad, and hardly dared to tell Stephen of the reception they had met. Nevertheless they told him and he said they should not fear, that he desired to go on, because, although they answered him badly, they would receive him well. So he went and arrived at the city of Cibola just before sunset, with all his company, which would be more than three hundred men, besides women. The inhabitants would not permit them to enter the city. They at once took away from Stephen all that he carried, telling him that the lord so ordered. "All that night," said the Indians, "they gave us nothing to eat or drink. The next day, when the sun was a lance-length high, Stephen went out of the house and some of the chiefs with him. Straightway many people came out of the city and, as soon as he saw them, he began to flee and we with him. Then they gave us these arrow-strokes and cuts and we fell and some dead men fell on top of us. Thus we lay till night-fall, without daring to stir. We heard loud voices in the city and we saw many men and women watching on the terraces. We saw no more of Stephen and we concluded that they had shot him with arrows as they had the rest that were with him, of whom there escaped only us."

In view of what the Indians had related and the bad outlook for continuing my journey as I desired, I could not help but feel their loss and mine. God is witness of how much I desired to have someone of whom I could take counsel, for I confess I was at a loss what to do. I told them that Our Lord would chastize Cibola and that when the Emperor knew what had happened he would send many Christians to punish its people. They did not believe me, because they say that no one can withstand the power of Cibola. I begged them to be comforted and not to weep and consoled them with the best word I could muster, which would be too long to set down here. With this I left them and withdrew a stone's throw or two apart, to commend myself to God, and remained thus an hour and a half. When I went back to them, I found one of my Indians, named Mark, who had come from Mexico, and he said to me: "Father, these men have plotted to kill you, because they say that on account of you and Stephen their kinsfolk have been murdered, and that there will not remain a man or woman among them all who will not be killed." I then divided among them all that remained of dry stuffs and other articles, in order to pacify them. I told them to observe that if they killed me they would do me no harm, because I would die a Christian and would go to heaven, and that those who killed me would suffer for it, because the Christians would come in search of me, and, against my will, would kill them all. With these and many other words I pacified them somewhat, although there was still high feeling on account of the people killed. I asked that some of them should go to Cíbola, to see if any other Indian had escaped and to obtain some news of Stephen, but I could not persuade them to do so. Seeing this, I told them that, in any case, I must see the city of Cíbola, and they said that no one would go with me. Finally, seeing me determined, two chiefs said that they would go with me.

With these and with my own Indians and interpreters, I continued my journey till I came within sight of Cíbola. It is situated on a level stretch on the brow of a roundish hill. It appears to be a very beautiful city, the best that I have seen in these parts; the houses are of the type that the Indians described to me, all of stone, with their stories and terraces, as it appeared to me from a hill whence I could see it. The town is bigger than the city of Mexico. At times I was tempted to go to it, because I knew that I risked nothing but my life, which I had offered to God the day I commenced the journey; finally I feared to do so, considering my danger and that if I died, I would not be able to give an account of this country, which seems to me to be the greatest and best of the discoveries. When I said to the chiefs who were with me, how beautiful Cíbola appeared to me, they told me that it was the least of the seven cities, and that Totonteac is much bigger and better than all the seven, and that it has so many houses and people that there is no end to it. Viewing the situation of the city, it occurred to me to call that country the new kingdom of St. Francis, and there, with the aid of the Indians, I made a big heap of stones and on top of it I placed a small slender cross, not having the materials to construct a bigger one. I declared that I placed that cross and landmark in the name of Don Antonio de Mendoza, viceroy and governor of New Spain for the Emperor, our lord, in sign of possession, in conformity with my instructions. I declared that I took possession there of all the seven cities and of the kingdom of Tontoneac and Acus and Marata, and that I did not go to them, in order that I might return to give an account of what I had done and seen.

Then I started back, with much more fear than food, and went to meet the people whom I had left behind, with the greatest haste I could make. I overtook them after two days' march and went with them till we had passed the desert and arrived at their home. Here I was not made welcome, as previously, because the men, as well as the women, indulged in much weeping for the persons killed at Cíbola. Without tarrying, I hastened in fear from that people and that valley. The first day I went ten leagues, then I went eight and again ten leagues, without stopping till I had passed the second desert.

On my return, although I was not without fear, I determined to approach the open tract, situated at the end of the mountain ranges, of which I said above that I had some account. As I came near, I was informed that it is peopled for many days' journey toward the east, but I dared not enter it, because it seemed to me that we must go to colonize and to rule that other country of the seven cities and the kingdoms I have spoken of, and that then one could see it better. So I forebore to risk my person and left it alone to give an account of what I had seen. However, I saw from the mouth of the tract seven moderate-sized towns at some distance, and further a very fresh valley of very good land, whence rose much smoke. I was informed that there is much gold in it and that the natives of it deal in vessels and jewels for the ears and little plates with which they scrape themselves to relieve themselves themselves of sweat, and that these people will not consent to trade with those of the other part of the valley; but I was able to learn the cause for this. Here I placed two crosses and took possession of all this plain and valley in the same manner as I had done with the other possessions, according to my instructions. From there I continued my return journey, with all the haste I could, till I arrived at the town of San Miguel, in the province of Culiacan, expecting to find there Francisco Vazquez de Coronado, governor of New Galicia. As I did not find him there,

I continued my journey to the city of Compostella, where I found him. From there I immediately wrote word of my coming to the most illustrious lord, the viceroy of New Spain, and to our father provincial, Friar Antonio, of Ciudad-Rodrigo, asking him to send me orders what to do.

I omit here many particulars which are not pertinent; I simply tell what I saw and what was told me concerning the countries where I went and those of which I was given information, in order to make a report to our father provincial, that he may show it to the father of our order, who may advise him, or the council of the order, at whose command I went, that they may give it to the most illustrious lord, the viceroy of New Spain, at whose request they sent me on this journey.

Alonso Gregorio de Escobedo, O.F.M. (dates unknown)

La Florida (excerpt)

La Florida is a narrative, historical poem comprising more than 22,000 verses. Begun at the end of the sixteenth century, it details the history and conquest of the Timucuan natives of Florida by the Spanish conquistadors and their ultimate conversion by the Franciscan missionaries. Written by Franciscan friar Alonso de Escobedo, its format, context, and theme justify characterization as Florida's first epic poem. Some consider it to be the first epic poem composed in a European language in territory that would became part of the United States, while others cast doubt on the claim. In his narrative, Escobedo presents a complex view of the indigenous people. He praises their virtues and is amazed at their physical and athletic strengths. Nevertheless, the text also conveys the particular apprehensions shared by many Spaniards at the time regarding cultures unknown to them. In the following passages, Escobedo narrates the fiercely competitive ballgames of the natives of Florida. (AS) The Spanish text of this excerpt can be found in Nicolas Kanellos et al., eds. *En otra voz: antologia de la literatura hispana de los Estados Unidos* (Houston: Arte Publico Press, 2002), pp. 17–19, or visit the Arte Publico Press website, at www.artepublicopress.com.

Further reading: James W. Covington, ed., *Pirates, Indians and Spaniards: Father Escobedo's "La Florida"* (St. Petersburg, Fla.: Great Outdoors, 1963).

They play a game of ball. It will be a pleasure to tell you exactly how it is done. They arrange themselves twenty on a side and play the game in a brisk, athletic manner. The ball carrier handles it smartly and he plays such an effective game with his sure shots that we can state that he scores on each shot. They erect goal posts made from pine trees about seven feet tall and on top of this goal they place a figure. Suddenly the forty players dash to the field, commence playing, and the game had begun with a rush. It is a rough game which many times proves to be costly to some unfortunate player who gets seriously injured. These seasonal games last one month.

Even if the one carrying the ball returns to the game on the following day, he will try to move in a different direction. His adversary, however, will be just as fast, attempting to intercept him with his hands and feet and throw him to the ground. While the other thirty-eight struggle among themselves, these two carry on the fight between themselves. Each one attacks his opponent and tries to cast him to the ground. If some persons assist the one who is carrying the ball because he is their friend, they are disqualified and never again will be allowed to play. The two teams fight as if they were in a real battle and each one tries to get a good grip on his adversary. The arms of the Indians in the game are as valuable as the net was to the gladiators.

In Castile the hands are used in playing ball, but these Indians play ball with their feet. They propel the ball with their feet directly at the goal. I have seen fifteen; then fifty direct shots, until the player gave up because he was exhausted. That number was the maximum allowed by the rules of the game. The Indian who is lucky and has good control over the ball plays eagerly but rather blindly like an inspired man. If he is playing against a strong opponent, he tries to overcome him and sometimes is full of tricks for the opponent. I have observed him in action when his intentions are not fair.

Those assisting the one who propels the ball carry on such a quarrel that they do not respect brother, or even father or son. The opponent tries to break up the locking of arms. If one loses his grip, another will come to the rescue and clasp the arm. So it is a continuous war until time is called. The one holding the ball with his foot will kick the ball straight at the goal. If he makes the mark, his friends go wild because the reward is worth the struggle and it is considered an act of great skill to hit the mark. The other team remains quiet and disappointed. Their eyes will be downcast throughout the day for their opponent won the game and they are depressed.

Gaspar Pérez de Villagrá (1555–1620)

History of New Mexico

Little is known about Gaspar Pérez de Villagrá. He was born in Puebla, Mexico, and studied at the prestigious University of Salamanca, Spain. After completing his studies, he returned to Mexico. In 1596, he was appointed captain and legal officer of Juan de Oñate's colonizing expedition to New Mexico. The *History of New Mexico* is the title Villagrá gave his epic poem, published in Alcalá de Henares, Spain, in 1610, where he was living as a result of his forced exile from Mexico, after being found guilty of the death of two of the expedition's deserters. The poem in thirty-four cantos of hendecasyllabic verse and one prose passage is a detailed account of that expedition. In spite of the poetic form, Villagra's work is a simple narrative in verse, with occasional lyrical passages, especially at the beginning of each canto. It is important in the literary history of the Southwest because it describes the landscapes of New Mexico and gives information about its people, thus creating a literary image of the region. Of importance also is Villagrá's account of the staging, in 1598, of a play by Marcos Farfán de los Godos, the first theatrical presentation in the Southwest. In the last eight cantos Villagrá describes the fall of the native village of Acoma to the Spanish conquistadors. Canto 31 narrates the storming of Acoma by the conquistadors under the command of Vicente de Zaldívar and the heroic defense undertaken by the natives. In the canto there are references to classical literature, a common practice in Spanish Golden Age epics. (LL)

Further reading: Gaspar Pérez de Villagrá, *Historia de la Nueva Mexico*, trans. and eds. Miguel Encinias, Alfred Rodriguez, and Joseph P. Sánchez (Albuquerque: University of New Mexico Press, 1992).

Trans.: ME, AR, and JPS

Canto 31

How the battle was carried forward until gaining victory and how fire was set to all the pueblo, and of other things that happened.

Always astute prevision, diligence,
A careful watchfulness and care
Never to lose a single point,
This, for a warrior in fight,
5 Is what most elevates and raises up
The clear resplendency and the greatness
Of deeds heroic and adventurous
That we see him embark upon.
With such qualities, the Sergeant,
10 Pedro Sánchez Monrroi, Marcos García,
Martín Ramírez, Cristóbal López,
Juan Lucas, Juan de Olague, Cabanillas,
Juan Catalán, Zapata, Andrés Pérez,
Francisco de Ledesma, and the good
Márquez,
15 No skillful reapers do more swiftly wield
Their curving sickles, flashing rapidly,
When they do quickly knot within their
arms
One handful after other and do so
Set up their sheaves in a thousand places,
20 As these brave, haughty combatants
Who, stumbling upon a lofty mound
Of bodies now dead, never ceased
To shed space a mighty sum
Of fresh red blood, by which the wall
25 Was everywhere, upon all sides,
Bathed and ensanguined, and nothing
Remained that was not sprent with it.
Yet not for this the furious barbarians
Would yield or surrender, but as we see
30 Fierce flames increase and tower high
Combated by the powerful winds,
And the more that they blow and fight
The greater is their force and their power,
So they, ferocious, all roaring,
35 Did charge the very musket's mouth
Without fear or caution before the storm
Of deadly balls which struck them down

Canto Treinta Y Vno

Como se fve prosigviendo la batalla hasta alcanzar la victoria y como se pegó fuego a todo el pueblo, y de otras cosas que fueron sucediendo.

Siempre la prevención y diligencia,
Hastuta vigilancia y el cuidado
De no perder jamás vn sólo punto,
Estando en la batalla el buen guerrero
Es lo que más encumbra y más lebanta
El claro resplandor y la grandeza
De los heroicos hechos hazañosos
Que assí vemos emprende y acomete.
Con cuias buenas partes el Sargento,
Pedro Sánchez Monrroi, Marcos García,
Martín Ramírez y Christóbal López,
Iuan Lucas, Iuan de Olague y Cabanillas,
Iuan Catalán, Zapata y Andrés Pérez,
Francisco de Ledesma y el buen
Márquez,
No tienden, apañando, con más ayre
La corba hoz los diestros segadores
Quando apriessa añudan sobre el brazo
Vna y otra manada y assí, juntos,
Lebantan por mil partes sus gavillas,
Como estos bravos y altos combatientes,
Que, en vn grande ribazo tropezando
De cuerpos ya difuntos, no cessaban
De derramar apriessa grande suma
De fresca y roja sangre, con que estaba
Por vna y otra parte todo el muro
Bañado y sangrentado, sin que cosa
Quedase que teñida no estuviesse.
Mas no por esto amainan y se rinden
Los bárbaros furiosos; mas, qual vemos
Crecer y lebantar las bravas llamas
De poderosos vientos combatidas,
Que mientras más las soplan y combaten
Más es su brava fuerza y gran pujanza,
Assí, feroces, todos rebramando,
A boca de cañón arremetían
Sin miedo ni rezelo de la fuerza
De las soberbias balas que, a barrisco,

Unto that dust and killed them all.
He of Zaldívar, seeing such ferocity,
40 Was like the valiant tiger which beholds
Itself pressed closely by huntsmen and, mad,
Turns on the spears and the fierce dogs
That follow it so close and, scourging them
By dint of teeth and claws, it drives
45 Them back and scatters and wounds them,
And so your Spaniard, furious in wrath,
Did lay about him with his good right arm.
And round him, then, the battle raged so fierce
And was so bloody upon both the sides
50 That only immense God was there enough
For them to hold against the savage force.
Because of their great fury the astute
Sergeant did order that there be brought up
Two fieldpieces, and, in the interim,
55 Addressing his men, he thus spoke to them:
"Ye founders of manorial houses,
Ye columns of the Church invincible,
Ye mirrors for brave men, whose breasts
Deserve with reason to be honored
60 With crosses red and white and green,
Today your deeds attain the highest point
And to the highest homage that Spaniards
Have ever yet raised them on high.
Let them not fall, sustain the scale
65 That thus sustains and weights the true greatness
Of the most honorable, gallant deed
That noble arms were ever seen to do."
Just then the two pieces came up
And were set at the place and spot
70 Where an attack, by chance, was being made
By three hundred brave, furious barbarians,
All delivering terrible shouts.
And as they made their charge, at last,
The two pieces did suddenly belch forth
75 Two hundred spikes from each, at which,
Just as we see the magpies, terrorized,
Suspend their chirping and their cackling
At the charge of powder which scatters

A todos los llevaban y acababan.
Y viendo el de Zaldívar tal fiereza,
Como valiente tigre que acosado
Se ve de los monteros y rabioso
Contra los hierros buelve y perros bravos
Que assí le van siguiendo y hostigando,
Y a fuerza de los dientes y los brazos
A todos los retira, esparce y hiere,
Assí, vuestro Español furioso, ayrado,
La poderosa diestra allí rebuelve.
Y anduvo la batalla en sí tan fuerte
Y de ambas partes tanto ensangrentada
Que sólo Dios inmenso allí les era
Bastante a reprimir su fuerza brava,
Por cuia gran braveza, luego quiso
El hastuto Sargento se guindasen
Dos piezas de campaña. Y en el inter,
Hablando con los suyos, les dezía:
"Fundamento de casas solariegas,
Columnas de la Iglesia no vencida,
Espejo de esforzadas, cuios pechos
Merecen con razón estar honrrados
Con rojas cruzes, blancas y con verdes,
Oy suben vuestras obras a la cumbre
Y más alto omenage que Epañoles
Nunca jamás assí las lebantaron.
No las dexéis caer, tened el peso
Que assí sustenta y pesa le grandeza
Del hecho más honrroso y más gallardo
Que jamás nunca vieron brazos nobles."
En esto, las dos piezas se subieron,
Y assentadas al puesto y a la parte
Por donde a caso fueron embistiendo
Trecientos bravos bárbaros furiosos,
Terribles gritos todos lebantando,
Y assí come de hecho arremetieron,
De presto las dos piezas regoldaron,
Cada, dozientos clavos y, con esto,
Qual suelen las hurracas que, espantadas,
Suspenden los chirridos y grasnidos
Con la fuerza de pólvora que arroja

	Great store of small shot, and we see	De munición gran copia, con que vemos
80	A few escaping and others	Escapar a las vnas y a las otras
	Remain with shattered limbs, and others dead,	Quedar perniquebradas y otras muertas
	And others beating their wings on the ground,	Y otras barriendo el suelo con las alas,
	Their black beaks gaping and their bowels	El negro pico abierto y con las tripas
	Pouring from out their torn bellies,	Arrastrando, rasgadas las entrañas,
85	We then beheld, not otherwise than this,	No de otra suerte, juntos todos vimos,
	A sudden great heap of the dead,	De s˙bito, gran suma de difuntos,
	Mangled, without hands, legs, shattered,	Tullidos, mancos, cojos, destroncados.
	Deep wounds opened into their breasts,	Abiertos por los pechos, mal heridos,
	Their heads laid open and their arms,	Rasgadas las cabezas y los brazos,
90	Pierced a thousand times, their flesh	Abiertos por mil partes y las carnes
	Pouring out blood in mortal agony,	Vertiendo viva sangre, agonizando
	Took leave of their immortal souls,	Las inmortales almas despedían,
	Leaving the bodies quivering there.	Dexando allí los cuerpos palpitando.
	Upon this slaughter brave Qualco,	Con cuias muertes Qualco, corajoso,
95	As does the swordfish, which in midst	Qual suele el espadarte que en la fuerza
	Of shoals of fish doth charge and strike	Del espeso cardume embiste y rasga
	The meshes of the net and so break them	Las mallas de las redes y las rompe
	And renders safe the fish captured in them	Y a los opressos pezes assegura
	And gallantly and freely gives them liberty,	Y libre libertad les da, y gallardo,
100	Writhing his mighty sides and his strong sword,	Blandiendo el ancho lomo y fuerte espada,
	And goes away, cleaving the crystal deep,	Las cristalinas aguas va hendiendo,
	Contented, happy, free, and gay,	Desempachado, alegre, suelto y ledo,
	So he, the strong, invincible, barbarian,	Assí, el fuerte bárbaro inbencible,
	Depending on his valiant strength,	En sus valientes fuerzas sustentado,
105	And justly, for two stalwart bulls	Y con razón, pues dos valientes toros
	Upon the plains of Zibola had been	En los llanos de Zíbola rendidos
	Subdued by his own valiant arm,	A sus valientes brazos vieron tuvo,
	Having dispersed our men somewhat	Abiendo derramado allí a los nuestros
	And made a wide space, like a bull	Y hecho vna ancha plaza, como vn toro,
110	Did charge on Diego Robledo	Para Diego Robledo fue embistiendo
	With a short mace. And as he came	Con vna corta maza, y en llegando
	Upon the valiant Roble, the Spaniard	Para el valiente Roble, fue largando
	Thrust with his sword; the mace came down	La hoja el Español y fue bajando
	And all by which the sword was longer	La maza poderosa, y todo aquello
115	Did glide onward and so did pass	Que la espada excedía fue colando
	Its deadly point through the barbarian,	Por el bárbaro pecho y ancha espalda
	Through breast and back, in such a sort	La rigurosa punta, de manera
	That powerful Qualco, pierced through	Que, de vna y otra vanda atravesado,
	From one side to the other, wounded sore,	El poderoso Qualco, mal herido,

120 Then dropped his mace, and with his fist,
Though run through once again before he
struck,
Did deal him such a blow upon the side
As struck him down open-mouthed
Upon the earth, near dead. And rapidly,
125 Before he could recover any breath,
He seized him by the leg and, as we see
The rustic man when he places
A massive stone in the broad part
Of whirling sling and, with his arm
130 Whirling it round, lets it go
Humming into the empty air,
Not otherwise, strong Qualco whirling
round
Brave Roble in a series of circles
At full arm's length above his head
135 Had hardly hurled him two men's lengths
When the barbarian, dead, soulless,
Fell down upon the earth. And after this
The Spaniard, seeing himself stretched out,
By such noble action thus defeated,
140 Recovering himself, charged furiously,
Like snarling cat which on offal
Doth prey from ravening hunger
And in it sets its teeth and grapples it
With its sharp claws, and raises high
145 Its swelling tail and bristling back,
And, stumbling upon the dead corpse,
He stood there trembling, hesitant,
Noting the great strength it possessed
And how narrowly he 'scaped death.
150 Then great Zapata and good Cordero,
Cortés, Francisco Sánchez, Pedraza,
Ribera, Juan Medel, Alonso Sánchez, too,
Juan López, Naranjo, and noble Ayarde,
Simón de Paz, Guillén, Villaviciosa,
155 Carabajal, Montero, and Villalba,
Did set on fire some of the houses there
To frighten them, but not for this
Did they abate a whit or slack
The power of the arms they swung.
160 The Sergeant, then, seeing the bravery,
Endurance and persistence with which all
Of the barbarians yet fought furiously,

Allí largó la maza y con el puño,
Abiéndole otra vez atrabesado,

Le dio tan grande golpe en el costado
Que dio con él, hipando y boqui abierto,
Casi por muerto en tierra. Y con presteza,
Antes que recobrase algún aliento,
Assiole por la pierna y, como vemos
Al rústico villano quando assienta
El mazizo guijarro en lo más ancho
De la rebuelta Honda y sobre el brazo
Dándole en torno vueltas, le despide,
Zumbando, por el Cóncabo del ayre,
No de otra suerte Qualco, rebolviendo

Con vna y otra buelta al bravo Roble
Por encima del brazo y la cabeza,
No bien le despedió dos largas hrazas
Quando sin alma el bárbaro difunto
Caió tendido en tierra. Y tras desto,
Viéndose el Español allí arrastrado,
De generosa afrenta ya vencido,
Cobrándose, furioso fue embistiendo,
Qual regañado gato que a los bofes
Con la maganta hambre se abalanza
Y allí los dientes clava y se afierna
Con las agudas vñas, lebantando
La cola regordida y pelo hierto,
Y en el difunto cuerpo tropezando
Suspenso se quedó allí temblando,
Notando la gran fuerza que alcanzaba
Y la poca que muerto allí tenía.
En esto, el gran Zapata y buen Cordero,
Cortés, Francisco Sánchez y Pedraza,
Ribera, Iuan Medel y Alonso Sánchez,
Iuan López y Naranjo y noble Ayarde,
Simón de Paz, Guillén, Villaviciosa,
Carbajal, Montero, con Villalba,
Dieron en pegar fuego por las casas
Por ponerles temor, mas no por esto
Algún tanto amainaban, o temían,
La fuerza de las armas que cargaban.
Viendo, pues, el Sargento la braveza,
Dureza y pertinacia con que a vna
Los bárbaros furiosos combatían,

That he might see no more of butchery,
Just as the clever, cautious pruner does
165 Who judges well the vine and looks and runs
His careful glance over each spreading bough,
And when he has surveyed, doth act and prune
The ill-shaped branches and the withered ones,
With all superfluous and useless ones,
170 And leaves with skill and good judgment
The stems with runners and new shoots
Which are considered fruitful ones,
That great soldier, surveying all the field,
Withdrawing all the soldiery
175 From their appointed stations,
He ordered that from him the foe be told
They should observe the slaughter, the destruction
Of all the miserable wretches that there were
Stretched out upon the ground and they should grieve
180 At such corpses and blood, and he gave them
The word and faith of noble gentleman
To do them justice and with clemency
To hear their case as if he were
Their own true father. And immediately
185 Loosing a great flight of arrows,
Like to mad dogs, they made reply
They would not speak of this, but they would take
Their arms and teeth and fists, as well,
Because they, their wives and children
190 Perforce would die and would give up
Their lives and souls and their honor
In this struggle. And, upon this,
They, fighting furiously, did charge
To die or conquer with such force
195 That they caused fear and terror to us all.
Now at this time, turned cowardly
And thinking to find safety here,
Zutacapán did come and beg for peace

Por no ver ya tan gran carnizería,
Qual suele el podador hastuto y cauto
Que juzga bien la cepa, tiende y pone
La vista cuidadosa en cada rama
Y, luego que ha visto, corta y tala
Los mal compuestos brazos y rebiejos,
Con todo lo superfluo, mal trazado,
Y dexa con destreza y buen acuerdo
Las varas con las uvas y pulgares
Que dicen esquilmenas, provechosas,
Assí, mirando el campo, el gran guerrero
La soldadesca toda entresacando
De sus debidos puestos señalados,
Mandó que de su parte les dixessen
Mirasen el estrago y el destrozo
De tantos miserables como estaban
Tendidos por el suelo y se doliessen
De aquella sangre y cuerpos, que él les daba
Palabra y fee de noble caballero
De guardarles justicia y con clemencia
Mirar todas sus causas qual si fuera
Su verdadero padre. Y luego al punto,
Arrojando de flechas grande suma,
Como rabiosos perros respondieron
No les tratasen desto y que apretasen
Las armas y los dientes con los puños
Porque ellos y sus hijos y mugeres
Era fuerza acabasen y rindiessen
Sus vidas y sus almas y sus honrras
En las lides presentes. Y con esto,
Combatiendo furiosos, embestían,
A morir o vencer, con tanta fuerza
Que pasmo y grima a todos nos causaba.
Por cuia causa luego, acobardado,
Pensando por aquí tener salida,
Zutacapán se vino y pidío pazes

Before the gallant Sergeant; he, content,
200 Not knowing who that traitor was,
Told him that he should give and hand
over
Only the chief ones who had caused
The recent mutiny and that with this
He would do all that he well could.
205 The tender cinquefoil was never seen
To tremble so at single gentle touch
Of a soft hand as he then shook,
That brutal savage, at the word.
And so, hesitant, sad, suspicious,
210 Hardly had there driven to his settling,
In mighty and precipitous course,
The sun his beauteous chariot and hid
The light with which he lighted us,
When in the sorry town all was
215 Divided and set off in two parties,
Both one and the other being timorous
About the Spaniards' strength and their
courage.
And when the light did grow once more
The barbarians, having discussed
220 All the grave matters of this peace,
Seeing Zutacapán had been the chief
Who had brought on the recent mutiny,
With all his friends and all his followers,
Like leafed forests that are rustled
225 By powerful Boreas, shaken,
So in a confused mass they move
Hither and thither, shaking off
Their dust, raising and altering
Their lofty tops, and all about
230 Are all moved to and fro and everywhere,
These poor barbarians, ruined,
Took refuge in their arms to such effect
That for three whole days the soldiers
Nor ate nor slept nor drank a drop,
235 Nor sat down nor laid aside
Their strong weapons from out their
hands,
Shedding such store of blood they now
Were flooded, tired out with shedding it.
And now the fire kept sending up

Al gallardo Sargento, y él, contento,
Sin conocer quién fuesse aquel aleve,
Luego li dixo diesse y entregase
Solós los principales que causaron
El passado motín, y que, con esto,
Haría todo aquello que pudiese.
Nunca se vio jamás que assí temblase,
De vn sólo toque manso y blanda mano,
La tierna argentería qual temblaba
Aqueste bruto bárbaro, del dicho.
Y assí, suspenso, triste y rezeloso,
No bien por el ocaso derribaba,
Con poderoso curso arrebatado,
El Sol su bello carro y trasponía
La lumber con que a todos alumbraba,
Quando el triste poblacho todo estaba
En dos partes diviso y apartado,
Los vnos y los otros temerosos
De la fuerza de España y su braveza.
Y luego que la luz salió encendida,
Después de aber los bárbaros tratado
Sobre estas pazes todos grandes cosas,
Viendo Zutacapán ser el primero
Que el passado motín abía causado
Con todos sus amigos y sequaces,
Quales hojosos bosques, sacudidos
Del poderoso boreas y alterados,
Que assí, en montón confusso, se
rebuelven
Por vna y otra parte y se sacuden
Las pajas, lebantando y alterando
Sus lebantadas cimas, y en contorno
Todos por todas partes se remecen,
Assí estos pobres bárbaros, perdidos,
Bolvieron a las armas, de manera
Que tres días en peso los soldados
No comieron, durmieron ni bebieron,
Ni se sentaron ni las fuertes armas
Dexaron de los puños, derramando
Tanta suma de sangre que anegados
Estaban ya y cansados de verterla.
En esto, ya yba el fuego lebantando

240	A ruddy vapor, bit by bit,	Vn vapor inflamado, poco a poco
	Attacking all the sad houses,	Todas las tristes casas calentando.
	And then in a short time it mustered up	Y luego, en breve rato, fue cobrando
	Sufficient vigor and in the dry pine	Vigor bastante, y por el seco pino
	Of the resinous houses and dwellings	De las teosas casas y aposentos
245	It crackled in the roofs and in a thousand spots,	Restallando los techos por mil partes,
	A very thick and dense and sluggish smoke,	Vn muy espeso, denso y tardo humo,
	Like great fleeces, was puffing out thickly	Como gruessos vellones, las ventanas
	From windows here, there, and everywhere,	Por vna y otra parte respiraban
	And like the most ardent of volcanoes	Y como fogosíssimos bolcanes
250	They poured out, whirling toward the sky	Bolando hazia el Cielo despedían
	Great store of embers and of sparks.	Gran suma de centellas y de chispas.
	And thus, those wild and mad barbarians,	Y assí, los brutos bárbaros, furiosos,
	Seeing themselves now conquered, 'gan to kill	Viéndose ya vencidos, se mataban
	Each other, and did so in such fashion	Los vnos a los otros, de manera
255	That sons from fathers, fathers from their loved children,	Que el hijo al padre y padre al caro hijo
	Took life away, and further, more than this,	La vida le quitaba, y , demás desto,
	Others in groups did give aid to the fire	Al fuego, juntos, otros ayudaban
	So that it might leap up with more vigor,	Porque con más vigor se lebantase
	Consume the pueblo and destroy it all.	Y el pueblo consumiese y abrasase.
260	Only Zutacapán and they his friends,	Sólo Zutacapán y sus amigos,
	Fleeing as cowards lest they see themselves	Huiendo de cobardes por no verse
	Within Gicombo's hands, did hide themselves	En manos de Gicombo, se escondieron
	Within the caves and hollows which there were	En las cuevas y senos que tenía
	Upon the fortress rock, whose great extent	La fuerza del peñol, cuia grandeza
265	Did show itself a second Labyrinth	Segundo labirinto se mostraba
	Because of many caves and hiding holes,	Según eran sus cuevas y escondrijos,
	Their entrances and exits and chambers.	Sus salidas y entradas y aposentos.
	The General and brave Bempol, seeing	Y viendo el General y bravo Bempol
	That all did kill themselves and seal	Que todos se mataban y cumplían
270	Truly the pact which all had sworn	La fuerza de aquel pacto que jurado
	To suicide if they as conquered should	Estaba de matarse si vencidos
	Come from the struggle with the Castilians,	Saliessen de los brazos Castellanos,
	Determined jointly they would kill themselves.	Junto determinaron de matarse.
	And so, fearful, because of this,	Y assí, por esta causa, temerosos
275	Of such incurable evil, not to see all	De mal tan incurable, por no verse
	In death's own arms, some of their friends,	En brazos de la muerte, les hablaron
	Sad, much dismayed, did speak to them,	Ciertos amigos, tristes, encogidos,
	Begging sincerely they would surrender	Pidiéndoles con veras se rindiessen

	And so, together, they might save their lives.	Y que las vidas, juntos, rescatasen.
280	At this appeal they instantly replied,	Por cuia causa luego replicaron
	Those furious, obstinate barbarians:	Los pertinaces bárbaros, furiosos:
	"Tell us, ye Acomans unfortunate,	"Dezidnos, Acomeses desdichados,
	What state is this of Acoma today	¿Qué estado es el que Acoma y tiene
	To undertake so infamous a thing	Para emprender vn caso tan infame
285	As this you ask us? Tell us now	Qual éste que pedis ? Decid agora,
	What refuge you do think that fate doth leave	¿Qué refugio pensáis que os dexa el hado
	As soon as peace might be secured	Luego que aquestas pazes celebradas
	All firmly with these Castilians?	Estén con los Castillas con firmeza?
	Do you not see that we have now arrived	¿No hecháis de ver que abemos ya llegado
290	At that last sorrow and that final point	Al vltimo dolor y postrer punto,
	Where we all must, without our liberty,	Donde sin libertad es fuerza todos
	Live out our sorry life as infamous wretches?	Vivamos, como infames, triste vida?
	Acoma was once, and upon the peak	Acoma vn tiempo fue, y en alta cumbre
	We saw her name, heroic, lifted high,	Vimos su heroico nombre lebantado,
295	And now the very gods who gave	Y agora aquellos dioses que la mano
	Their hands to her, to raise and honor her,	Le dieron por honrrarla y lebantarla
	We see only did so that her ruin	Vemos que la subieron porque fuesse
	Might be more miserably felt	Su mísera ruina más sentida
	By those poor wretches who did hope	De aquellos miserables que esperamos
300	For such firmness in such feeble weakness.	En tan débil flaqueza tal firmeza,
	For this reason, we, all of us, agreed,	Por cuia causa juntos acordamos,
	If you are, as we two do feel you are,	Si estáis, como nostros entendemos,
	Firm in the promise which we swore	Firmes en la promesa que juramos,
	That we would give our throats to happy death	Que a la felice muerte las gargantas
305	And submit them since there remaineth not	Las demos y entreguemos, pues no queda,
	Another greater remedy for this our health	Para nuestra salud, mayor remedio
	Than to give up the hope that yet remains	Que perder la esperanza que nos queda
	For us to gain it and to secure it."	De poder alcanzarle y conseguirle.
	And when, with this, the haughty General	Y luego que con esto otras razones
310	Had also told them other arguments,	El bravo General les fue diziendo,
	Maximian, Macrinus, Maxentius,	Maximino, Macrino ni Maxencio,
	Procrustes, Diocletian, nor Tiberius,	Procrustes, Diocleciano ni Tiberio,
	Nero, nor all the rest of cruel men,	Nerón ni todo el resto de crueles
	Displayed upon no one ferocity	Con ninguno mostraron su braveza
315	More harsh, atrocious, nor more terrible	Más brava, más atroz ni más terrible
	Than these displayed upon their very selves,	Que éstos consigo mismos se mostraron,
	Not only men, but the women as well.	No sólo los varones, mas las hembras.
	Some, like to Dido, took leave of	Las vnas, como Dido, abandonaron
	Their bodies and did perish in the flames,	Sus cuerpos y en las llamas perecieron.

320	And, like the Spartans, they also	Y assí, como espartanos, sus hijuelos
	Gave up their tender babes unto harsh death.	También a dura muerte se entregaron.
	Others did hurl and cast their babes	Otras los arrojaban y lanzaban
	Into the burning flames, and others, sad,	En las ardientes llamas, y otras, tristes,
	With them held tight, from off the wall	Con ellos abrazadas desde el muro
325	Hurled themselves dashing down, as we could see.	Las vimos con esfuerzo despeñarse.
	Others, like Portia, quickly satisfied	Otras, qual Porcia, apriessa satisfecha
	With living coals, did end their lives.	De brasas encendidas acababan.
	Others, like Lucrece, with a keen dagger	Otras el tierno pecho, qual Lucrecia,
	Piercing their tender breasts, did thus speed forth	Con dura punta roto, despedían
330	Their miserable souls, and many more	Las almas miserables, y otras muchas
	By very many other sorts of death	Con otros muchos géneros de muertes
	Did end and render up their lives.	Sus vidas acababan y rendían.
	In the meantime, the fair sisters	En este medio tiempo, las hermanas
	Of Zutancalpo brave, in great distress	Del bravo Zutancalpo, desvalidas,
335	Beside themselves, went out to seek	Fuera de sí, salieron a buscarle
	Their brother, to end their sad lives with his.	Por acabar con él la triste vida,
	Their bitter grief, their sad weeping,	Cuio dolor acerbo y triste llanto
	I wish, lord, in a canto new to sing.	Quiero cantar, señor, en nuevo canto.

Fray Francisco de Escobar

The Account (excerpt)

A Franciscan friar, Fray Francisco de Escobar was sent by the Count of Monterrey in 1603 to help Juan de Oñate consolidate his colonization of New Mexico. Oñate entrusted the friar, who was known for his mastery of Indian languages, to appease the Acoma natives. A year later, Father Escobar accompanied Oñate in search of the Mar del Sur. While Escobar's *The Account* purports to be a report on Oñate's expeditionary ventures in the Southwest, it is more reminiscent of a fairy tale than a historical document. Almost comical in nature and bordering on the absurd, the friar spins a fantastic story concerning the natives of the Southwest. (JBF)

Further reading: Fray Francisco de Escobar, "Relación," *Missionalia Hispánica* 43, no. 126 (1986): 377–93; Herbert Eugene Bolton, *Father Escobar's Relation of the Oñate Expedition to California* (Washington, 1919).

Trans.: HEB

This Indian Otata also told us of all the people who live on the Buena Esperanza River, clear up to its source, showing this to be close to the sea, toward the northwest, as did many others likewise, all asserting that the Gulf of California makes this complete turn. He told us also of the people who live between the Buena Esperanza River and the sea, making a drawing of the country on a piece of paper, on which he indicated many nations of people so monstrous that I will make to affirm them with no little fear of being discredited through not having seen them, which I was unable to do, on account of the lack of horses, and particularly of supplies, which the Governor experienced, and on account of the little or no grass which the country promised, so that for horses so weak and worn out as were most of those which we had, the enterprise appeared almost impossible, and that to hope to achieve it with such lack of appeared no little temerity; and although to some it must appear temerity to me to recount things so monstrous and never seen in our times (nor even in the past if it is remembered that they have been seen always by witnesses so far away that the door is always left open for each one to believe what he pleased), nevertheless, I make bold to relate what I have heard stated to a great multitude of Indians in my presence, for since I affirm as true only what I saw with my eyes, I may dare affirm it.

The Indian Otata told us in the presence of many others, who corroborated his story, of a nation of people who had ears so large that they dragged on the ground, and big enough to shelter five or six persons under each one. This nation was called in its own language Esmaleatatanaaha, and in the language of this Bahacocha nation Esmalca, which means "ear," the etymology of the word indicating the characteristic of the nation.

Not far from this nation, he said, there was another whose men had their members so long, they wrapped them four times around the waist, and that by the act of generation the man and woman were far apart. This Nation was called Modara Qualchoquata.

Likewise, we learned from this Indian and the others that near the foregoing people there was another nation with only one foot, who were called Niquetata people.

They told us of another nation, not far from the last, who lived on the banks of a lake in which they slept every night, entirely under the water. These people, they said, were the ones who wore handcuffs and bracelets of yellow metal, which they called anpacha. This nation was called Zinoes, which with more propriety we might call Hamaca Coemacha Fish. We learned from all these Indians that near this last nation there is another which always sleeps in trees. The reason we could not ascertain, whether it was for fear of wild beasts or insects or from some natural characteristic or custom of theirs. This nation they called Ahalcos Macha.

The monstrosities of another nation, which they said was near this one, did not stop here, for they sustained themselves solely on the odor of their food, prepared for this purpose, not eating it at all, since they lacked the natural means to eliminate the excrements of the body. This nation they called Xamexo Macha.

They told of another nation not far from this one which did not lie down to sleep but always slept standing up, bearing some burden on the land. This nation they called Tascano Paycos Macha.

Here we learned from all these Indians what we had observed many days before from many others, great and small, that the principal person obeyed by the people who lived on the island was a woman called Cinoca Cohota, which signifies or means "principal woman" or "chieftainess." From all these Indians we learned that she was a giantess, and that on the island she had only a sister and no other person of her race, which must have died out with them. We learned that the men of this island were bald, and that with them the racial line ended.

It appears to me doubtful that therc should be so many monstrosities in as short a distance, and so near us, for the Indians asserted that they were all over river, which it was necessary to cross in order to go to the island, that was only five days' journey away (this would be twenty-five or thirty miles). But, even though there might be still greater doubt of all these things, it seemed yet more doubtful to remain silent about things which, if themselves would result, I believe, in glory to God and in service to the King our Lord and although the things in themselves may be so rare and may never before have been seen, to any one who will consider the wonders which God constantly performs in the world, it will be easy to believe that since He is able to create them, He may have done so, and that since so many and different people, in a distance of two hundred leagues testify to them, they cannot lack foundation, about things of which these Indians are not the first inventors, for there are more books which tell of them, and of others even more monstrous and more wonderful.

And if they do cause wonderment, but I do not have any doubt that such monstrous things exist at such a short distance from us, so close that the Indians affirm that on crossing a river to get to an island, where five of those women could be seen asleep from a distance of some twenty-five or thirty leagues away. And although there may be great doubt about these things, it seemed wrong to me not to mention them, which when discovered would be credited to the glory of God and a service to our Lord the King. Because, although these things in and of themselves may be so rare and never before seen, for anyone who marvels at what God has wrought in the world, it will be easy to believe that He has created them, just as He has created other marvels; and, because they have been corroborated by such a wide and diverse group of people, and some from a distance of more the two hundreed leagues, their existence must not be baseless, being that these Indians are not the first to mention them, given that there are many books in which they are treated, and even more monstrous things that cause great surprise. If perchance they do communicate, by the love of heaven, with less than one hundred men it will be possible to verify the truth of all these things, both of the silver and the tin, or whatever metal it is on the island: of the gold, copper, or brass bracelets or handcuffs worn by the Indians of the Laguna; of the coral; of the pearls which the Indians declare are contained in the shells which we found, and which the Governor and so many Spaniards declare there are in the Gulf of California; and of the turn which the Indians say the Gulf makes toward the north and northeast, not a person being found that knew its terminus; as well as of the monstrosities reported by so many Indians of ten different nations, scattered through more than two hundred leagues, and saying that they had seen them and others that they had heard of them.

Fray Matías Sáenz de San Antonio (dates unknown)

Lord, if the shepherd does not hear the sheep's complaint . . .

Franciscan friars were among the first missionaries that came to the New World to convert the natives to the Catholic faith. Among these friars was Fray Matías Sáenz de Antonio. Believed to be from Zacatecas, Mexico, Fray Matías came to present-day northeastern Texas in 1716 to preach the gospel to the natives and establish a buffer zone against French encroachments in the area. The reading selection is a salient example of the seventeenth-century epistolary genre. Although the letter is not a model of stylistic perfection, it nevertheless is a witty and most exhilarating plea to the Spanish Crown to send colonists to present-day northeastern Texas. Although the author portrays the territory as an Arcadia, he chastises Spanish officials for exploiting the soldiers and abusing the natives. (JBF)

Further reading: Thomas P. O'Rourke, *The Franciscan Missions in Texas 1690–1793* (Washington: Catholic University of America Press, 1927).

Trans.: HA

Lord,
If the shepherd does not hear the sheep's complaint, if the father does not hear his children's cries, if the Lord does not heed his vassals' lament, he will not feel a loving duty to fill these needs. As Saint Bernard said in the vernacular, eyes that not see, heart that does not break.

Today urgent needs are placed before the royal and pious Catholic Majesties, needs of the inhabitants of the newly conquered New Philippines in the Province of Texas, in the time of capable government of the Marqués de Valero in New Spain, so that our Majesty, as Shepherd, may hear them, as Father, may give encouragement, and, as King and Lord by right, may protect them and provide for them. Understand, Your Majesty, that in their need they come to you with the love and the gratitude that Your Majesty has for this assistance.

So that Your Majesty will better understand the core of these difficulties, I should first set before you, for your Royal consideration, what the Province is, its location, and who its inhabitants are, in a few words, but so that you may acquire an understanding of it.

For a hundred years before seventeen-sixty, we did not gain even an inch of land in these territories. Then divine Providence decided that, at great risk, with twenty-five men, forty fellow Brothers from the Apostolic college of Our Lady of Guadalupe and Zacatecas, and five other brothers from Santa Cruz de Querétaro, with great travail we make our way three hundred leagues, from the last Christian Garrison into said Province of Texas, in the hills of whose district innumerable Barbarian Nations live. In that selfsame Texas we established six Missions that exist to this day, the last one within sight of a French Garrison. Upon becoming aware of it, I went to scout perimeter, so that the French could not advance until I could notify the Crown.

This Province, my Lord, is so rich in minerals that every mound is a treasure trove. It is so lush with flowers and plants, rivers and springs, that it is a paradise. It is so fertile in fruits, that it is a wonder. In fact, everything one puts into it, it returns a hundredfold or more. It is overrun with wild fruit, such as grapes, plums, pomegranates, medlars, walnuts, and chestnuts, and many other fruit in abundance. It includes indigo plants, and diverse medicines, and substantial foodstuffs. The meadows are wondrous for all manner of meat, turkey, pigeon and other birds, of which there are a great many. The rivers and springs are rich with many different kinds of succulent fish. Its inhabitants are Barbaric gentiles, idol-worshippers, without discipline nor government, whose houses are little shacks and a few caves. They often move in search of the wild fruits and roots they live on and to hunt the bear, deer, wild boar, and buffalo on which they survive. They go naked from head to toe. They wear animal skins to stave off the rigors of winter, but have no style in their dress. They live on no more than what the natural world of animals has given them. Nevertheless, they are by nature docile and well disposed to the Spanish, who treat them well, because with the Spanish they feel protected and defended against their enemies.

These lands are situated at about 32 degrees north. The climate is healthy, similar to that of Castile. From the center of the Province, looking north, one can see New Mexico at a distance of leagues, prudently speaking; to the south is the Province of Tampico, at more or less 200 leagues; toward the east, one finds the Port of Santa Maria de Galvez, which is on the edge of Central Mexico. Its neighbor is the port of Movila [Mobile], which the French occupy and which stretches 200 or more leagues, from the Nachittoos border, next to our Texas, to the aforementioned Movila, whose district the French have settled with small towns and Garrisons, and whose capital is New Orleans, on the Palisade river, which empties into the sea there. This river is very lush, being composed of the Missouri, Mississipi, and Red rivers, all of which are large. To the northeast are the English and the Picaroons [pirates], whom we have not wanted to have contact with because of these nations' and their Indian friends' opposition to us. To the west is the Kingdom of New Leon, whose border we crossed to come here. The Barbarian Nations, who occupy these areas, are innumerable and many.

Now that we have given you a brief picture of the Province, its location, and inhabitants, I place before the pious eyes of Your Majesty the needs of your new children and vassals, which they offer to you, as Shepherd, Father, King, and Lord, for remedy and assistance.

First, they need financial support and doctrinal guidance. For this they need settlers of Christian habits, and workers like Galicians or [Canary] islanders, who will teach them, inspire them, and stimulate them to the beneficial use of the land, the making of houses and cloth, and other tasks that comprise a well-ordered Republic, for which the Creoles of America are no good. The creoles are for the most part feeble workers, some because of their constitution. Some are lazy, others are idlers because their land is so fertile and abundant. The rest are no good because of habits born of similar principles. Because the Infidels are rough and uncultured, they receive the holy Faith and Christian Doctrine through their eyes more than their ears. They need upstanding models if they are to follow this Doctrine and the Holy Sacrifice of the Mass and acquire obedience and reverence to priests and evangelical ministers, as the primitives of those other territories have had. In this way Christianity will succeed here, as it has done there.

If this is provided, the lost and scattered sheep of Christ will gather together in life's needed pasture, rejecting the death grip in which the devil blindly holds them. In such company they will be able to defend themselves and secure themselves against this enemy, by whose hand they live a divided existence. When they have such peace, they will be able to free themselves from sudden, warlike assaults when they gather together at differing times and places, only to die like ants, with the devil reaping an abundant harvest. It is a shame that Catholic hearts cannot respond to such feelings of so many souls lost, a situation so different from that of most precious blood of our Redeemer, whose representative is Your Majesty, to whom, as a pious Father, these wretched people, these forsaken children, set forth their needs.

To you, their King and Lord, they would like to make clear that the loss of not only these lands and provinces is threatened but that of all the kingdoms of New Spain, in view of the fact that the French, English, and Picaroons come ever nearer. The power of these nations is increased by the addition of a multitude of Indians, who are already skilled in the use of firearms, pikes, broadswords, lances, and half-moons, which have been provided to them, and if, may God forbid, peace cannot be maintained or the European Powers take up arms, any of them could run through our land and reach as far as Mexico as easily as if they were walking through their own homes, since the land is solid and clear, free of obstacles. The 300 men that Your Majesty keeps on the Bay of Espiritu Santo on the San Antonio River and in Texas itself, stationed over a distance of greater than 200 leagues, serve more to maintain your dominations than to defend them in an emergency.

This, in particular, is what demands Your Majesty's attention. The French, English and Picaroons are composed of Huguenots and other heretics who, wherever they go, declare freedom of conscience, a powerful attraction for the peasants, who are able to retain their habits and false religions, to which, aided by the devil, they give themselves over voluntarily, their safety satisfied by armed protection. If such a misfortune were to occur, it would be very serious, even cruel. In the heart and the Kingdom of our Mexican Provinces, our Holy Faith is ailing and the palates of most inhabitants are so ill-favored to the sweetness and tenderness of the Laws of Christ that if they become accustomed to this pestilential freedom of conscience they will run breathless to the enemy, who outnumber us. If you take away Your Majesty's faithful, committed vassals, the great body of our people is composed of Negros, Mulattoes, Lobos, Indians, and Mestizos, so much so that for every Spaniard they number 500. This, my Lord, weighs heavy upon us. And this fact is so well known to the public that you will not find anyone who has been in these territories who will not support it. As an upstanding witness, the Marqués of Valero can substantiate this. This situation must be attended to without delay and the path to its remedy cleared, before more damage is done. If such a remedy is brought about promptly, it will be easy and not expensive to the Royal House. If well thought out, it can result in increases to Your Majesty's fortunes (as good a reason as any to carry it out). In this way, our Holy Faith will be spread, preserved, and increased in Your Majesty's dominions, as I will hereafter make clear.

If Your Majesty sends, as indeed you should, 500 families, if possible Galicians and Islanders, and distributes 150 of them in the Bay of Espíritu Santo and the outpost at San Antonio, and 250 in appropriate parishes, the free passage of these foreign nations will be impeded. The year after they settle in these areas, 200 soldiers of the 300 Your Majesty currently maintains in Texas, the outpost at San Antonio, and the Bay of Espíritu Santo could be eliminated. The 135 pesos that these 300 soldiers cost per year will be reduced by 90 pesos a year. If you take into account the many subsequent years, the Royal Exchequer will save millions. These eliminated soldiers can stay in the area with the financial support of settlers. All in all, these lands will continue to flourish, the nation will expand, duties, tributes and other Royal Prerogatives will increase, and

Christianity will grow here. We have seen an example of this in the production of fruit and tobacco on the island of Havana, as it has been in all the other provinces of the American Empire, which have supported and continue to support the Spanish peninsula and have enriched all the European powers.

With these grants, my Lord, you will contain these foreign nations. Your Majesty's domains and the Empire of Jesus Christ will expand among many nations, which will seek Spanish protection. Your Majesty will achieve the same glory as his ancestors, from the invincible Carlos V, Hercules I of the New World, to Your Majesty, every one of whom tried to spread Catholic devotion, in the interests of God. Your Majesty father the King manifested this so clearly in the Golden Charter, which Your Majesty's has reiterated during your invaluable and exemplary reign, whose tenderness would melt stone.

Finally, my Lord, what is requested is very little; what it means is great. Not doing this would put everything at risk, because the way such a Monarchy as this is constituted, its preservation is like that of a body, composed of flesh and blood. The blood of this body is that of the mineral veins of the American kingdom. And if, may God forbid, we fail, it will mean complete ruin. In that ruination, and the inexplicable misfortune of such an outrage to God's Faith and the Mansion of Jesus Christ, the devil will take the throne, and our God will be badly served. To this end, my Lord, God has brought me to these vast regions, for Your Majesty's Royal projects, under the protection of the Marqués de Valero, who can testify to and support these truths with more elegant and convincing reasons and who has himself looked into these difficulties.

I must also put forth for Your Majesty's consideration the grave need for spiritual guidance in the things experienced by your vassals in the two kingdoms of New Leon and New Vizcaya, one of which borders Texas and the other New Mexico. These provinces suffer from a lack of ecclesiastical assistance since their governors overemphasize politic and the military. The governors tend to their own interests, to the detriment of Your Majesty's vassals and to the detriment of both Your Majesties. In both kingdoms of New Leon and New Vizcaya, most people die without the Blessed Sacrament of Confirmation, because their bishops never reach most of these kingdoms. This is not the Bishops' fault. The See of Durango and that of Guadalajara to which they belong are more than 350 leagues long and are for the most part uninhabited, with no house for 40 or 50 leagues. Much of the time there is danger from hostile, heathen Indians who have threatened many travelers in the past and continue to threaten them today. The Bishops take steps to learn about their parishioners and send inspectors, who are usually young men since they need to be robust. Of these, none can perform confirmations. Many of them, instead of cleansing the ailments and infections of the sheep and dressing them in holy instruction, undress them, and promote these selfsame ailments, by introducing new ailments that I will not mention. In New Mexico and its environs, where until now no Bishop has come, not even an inspector, they live like sheep without a shepherd, even though they have Curates. I feel the influence of the sun will never bear ripe fruit. Your Catholic Majesty is the firmament of that light, and must provide it.

Added to this, motivated by their own whims and desires, the governors exalt their own power which they obtain more from their own tyranny than from the Crown or the Papacy and suppress the ecclesiasts and lay brothers more than they should, contrary to the laws of God and Your Majesty. Even the Viceroys of Mexico cannot solve this problem, since their patients are scattered over more than 500 leagues. Nor have these poor people recourse in the courts since they have little means and because those who express their complaints are later strongly oppressed. If someone had the strength to do so, going as an Inquiry, he could not win a judgment, either, because everyone, to avoid persecution or because of self-interested friendship, bears false witness, contrary to the truth and in favor of the governors. In such remote regions, someone or other will always supply false testimony. All this is why the land is so little inhabited, because so many of these poor people leave and go elsewhere.

These governors use soldiers to serve their household needs, and sometimes as mail carriers in Your Majesty's service, taking for themselves the money the soldiers are owed, which is the reason that, being few, and busy with task, they don't patrol the borders, nor do they attend to dangerous areas. Because of this, hostile Indians have places to steal livestock and kill ranchers and unforewarned travelers, whose troubles also force them to leave. This, my Lord, is a fact that, even if a trial judge should find out about it, nothing will happen, because of the reasons already mentioned. I have seen this and felt it personally, as I go about these parishes on my apostolic rounds. As your loyal vassal and evangelical minister, I must tell this to Your Majesty, affirming it (as I do affirm) that I am not motivated by anything more than the service to both Majesties and the discharging of my conscience to Your Majesty, as God is my witness.

To this I should add that the soldiers go hungry, half-naked, and many unarmed because the governors and captains collect their salaries and pay them with merchandise from shops they themselves own, at very high prices. The soldiers end up being given what is worth six for twenty, so that two thirds of the soldiers' pay is lost. They go about perennially in debt, their basic needs unmet. What happens is that some of them run away, some because they cannot pay their debts. When others die, those who replace them are often charged with debts of the dead ones. No one is willing to take the position under such conditions, they are left vacant, until these obligations, which are not really due them, are satisfied. With fewer soldiers, the Royal Service becomes less effective.

I have no idea what the solution is for this. But if we go back to the experiences of the past, it seems to me that the best way is for Your Majesty to provide persons of great enthusiasm in the service of God and of souls, and service of Your Majesty, to the Sees of El Parral de New Vizcaya and New Mexico, and the Kingdom of New Leon, naming Apostolic and unselfish men, as those lands have requested, so that they might apply themselves enthusiastically to their work, adapting themselves to the meagerness or mediocrity offered in the current state of these Jurisdictions, and get along decently. And if Your Majesties decide to confer on them the payments the Governors and Military Captains receive today, they will have even more relief, and many other benefits will result. First, because they will look upon their parishioners and the soldiers as do Fathers. The latter will be assisted with charity and will not be tyrannized, because having to assist them with alms for their needs, they will not take these poor peoples' work away from them. Second, because they will be in the shadow and company of such Prelates, these lands will be settled, as the See of Durango was settled, which, until a Bishop was installed there, had found itself with the same needs. Third, the Holy Gospel will shine more brightly, Christian Doctrine will be more widely practiced and the Curates and Judges will find themselves more closely overseen. Fourth, in all cases Your Majesty and the Viceroys of Mexico will have witnesses of great integrity for news and emergencies. Fifth, and most remarkable, one particular evil will be suppressed, a huge obstacle to the propagation of our Holy Faith. This is that, until now, the Governors and Captains, in the name of patrolling the land, have gone into heathen territory to kidnap children and women in order to give them to their friends, relatives and colleagues and often to sell them as slaves, contrary to all rights and royal and divine laws. When they commit these atrocities, they injure some people and kill others. The poor, terrified Indians flee from our Holy Faith and, in pain, like lions whose cubs have been taken away, they run wildly through the hills, ridges, and passes, bringing nations together for the purpose of revenge. In such a way they roam the land enraged. With a Bishop, a charitable and zealous Apostolic Governor, these troubles will disappear. The Indians will seek the Bishops out, and with tenderness and affection they will bestow on them things of little value, like glass beads, coral, ribbons, little mirrors, combs, knives, tobacco leaves, sackcloth, flannel, and other things to which they are drawn like a flock of sheep. All of this my experience with the Indians of Texas has taught me: When beginning to seek them out and to attract them, how to attract them is to find this type of gift, because this is the only powder with which these innocents are defeated, these are the swords and arms for which they give themselves up. It is not much, because, being children of these rocky hills, even such small gifts break their resolve.

If Your Majesty wants more direct and broader notice of proof of these truths, the Marquis de Valero can give it to you. He is aware of it from his time as governor of Mexico for Your Majesty's father the King, and today he finds himself with paper, minutes and instruction for the said Bishops, with all the information needed for their elevation, with the reasons for their fitness and how fitting they are. Your Majesty can find out from the aforementioned Marquis about the most prudent resolution. If for a judicious accord it seems appropriate to Your Majesty to inform a Minister of Intelligence in these parts to give me a hearing and put these difficulties before him, I will give him these reasons that, according to God, I will reach. I stand ready to do whatever Your Majesty decides, for the great service that I place in God, the people, and Your Majesty. May you live for many years.

PART II

Native Literature

CHAPTER 1

Toward a Mestizo Culture

Anonymous

By Our Father Jesus, Nuestro Padre Jesús

The *alabados* are a repertory of hymns of praise sung by the Hermandad de Nuestro Padre Jesús Nazareno (Brotherhood of Our Father Jesus the Nazarene), a lay Catholic penitential brotherhood credited with the maintenance of religion, culture, and community welfare in northern New Mexico since their appearance in the late eighteenth century. Conserved in oral tradition and in hand-copied notebooks, several date to seventeenth-century Spain. Musically, some are related to even older Gregorian chants, their modal melodies being indicators of their antiquity. Their poetics indicate that some are of erudite origins and were undoubtedly introduced by Franciscan priests. But the eight-syllable quatrain structure of the majority is an indication of humble, more recent local origins in northern Mexico. Like medieval plainsong, these hymns are sung a cappella in unison, without measure or steady beat, and proceed only as the words and themes progress. Occasionally, the trill of the pito or vertical fipple flute is heard, not to carry melody, but to evoke the tears of Mary and the cries of the souls in Purgatory. Lead singers alternate verses with group responses, an antiphonal feature with distinct pedagogical value for missionary priests teaching the stories of the church. The singing style is highly melismatic, with a quavering voice reminiscent of Arabic and Jewish music, as well as Flamenco. The dominant themes of the *alabados* are the Passion of Jesus and the suffering of Mary. In performance, the *alabados* are kind of triple meditation, whose power lies in their poetry, their music, and the specific services and devotions with which they are used. *By This Divine Light* is a profession of faith in the Brotherhood itself, and is used in initiations as well as in other services. (EL)

Further reading: William H. González, *Alabados, alabanzas y oraciones de la Nueva México (1598–1998)* (Madrid: Eypasa, 1999).

By this Divine Light,	Por ser mi divina luz
O Jesus of my soul,	¡Ay! Jesús de l'alma mía,

I take in my brotherhood
Our Father Jesus.

Listen well, sinners,
All ye slaves of Jesus,
And comply with your oath
To our Father Jesus.

Listen well, sinners,
To the glories of Jesus,
And contemplate this Light
Of our Father Jesus.

Listen well, sinners,
And contemplate this Light
Which is the Divine Crown
Of our Father Jesus.

Acclaiming these brothers,
Acclaiming this Light,
That you may take in your heart
Our Father Jesus.

Sinners, sinners,
Who suffer for Jesus
And who will feel the nails
Of our Father Jesus.

In these arms outstretched,
Here is the Divine Light!
In His brotherhood we take
Our Father Jesus.

The nails we shall suffer,
And this Divine Light,
And in His brotherhood take
Our Father Jesus.

Brothers who truly
Accompany Jesus,
Do not break the mystery
Of our Father Jesus.

This painful passion
Jesus suffered for you,

Llevando en mi compañía
A nuestro Padre Jesús.

Escuchen bien, pecadores,
Los esclavos de Jesús,
Cumplan con el juramento
De nuestro Padre Jesús.

Escuchen bien, pecadores,
Alabanzas de Jesús,
Y contemplen esta luz
De nuestro Padre Jesús.

¡Óiganme bien pecadores,
Y contemplen esta luz
Que es la divina corona
De nuestro Padre Jesús.

Aclamarán los cofrados
Aclamarán esta luz
Para llevar en su pecho
A nuestro Padre Jesús.

Pecadores, pecadores,
Que padecen por Jesús,
Que veneran a los clavos
De nuestro Padre Jesús.

En los brazos estrechados
Aquí esta divina luz,
En su compañía lleva
A nuestro Padre Jesús.

Los clavos que veneramos
Aquí esta divina luz
En su compañía lleva
A nuestro Padre Jesús.

Hermanos verdaderos
Que acompañan a Jesús
No quiebren el misterio
De nuestro Padre Jesús.

La dolorosa pasión
Que Jesús pasó por vos,

Comply with your oath
And be thankful to Jesus.

Happy those who serve God
In His Sacred Passion
And in their breasts receive Him
In the Holy Communion.

Brothers who in this Light
Are suffering for God,
You will be in His kingdom
With our Father Jesus.

Those who believe in this Church
And in this Divine Light
Are the slaves truly
Of our Father Jesus.

Let us all go on our knees,
Worshiping this Light,
With a *Credo* and a *Salve*
To our Father Jesus.

Cumplan con el juramento
En agradecimiento á Dios.

Felices los que a Dios sirven
En su Sagrada pasión
Y que reciben en su pecho
En la Santa comunión.

Hermanos que con su luz
Van padeciendo por Dios
Allá estarán en su reino
Con nuestro Padre Jesús.

Los que creen en la iglesia
Y en esta divina luz
Son esclavos verdaderos
De nuestro Padre Jesús.

Vamos todos de rodillas
Alabando aquí esta luz
Con un credo y un salve
A nuestro Padre Jesús.

Anonymous

The Comanches (Los comanches)

Scholars speculate that the probable author of this spectacular equestrian play is Pedro Bautista Pino, a prominent militiaman and rancher from Galisteo, New Mexico. The play is an ambivalent celebration of the defeat in August 1779 of the great chief Cuerno Verde in the final campaign of the devastating Comanche wars of the eighteenth century. He and his Spanish Mexican opponents can be found on the pages of chronicles and letters from the period. Notably missing from the action is Governor Juan Bautista de Anza, probably due to popular discontent with his brash military policies. On the field of battle, the cast of mounted braves and soldiers meet to taunt each other and exchange fierce *arengas,* or military harangues, in a dazzling verbal display. Two captive children are rescued in a skirmish. A messenger from another group of Comanches arrives at the last minute with an offer of peace, but the conflict is already at hand, ending in a rout of Comanches. In some versions, Cuerno Verde dies, and in others he remains alive. A clownish character named Barriga Dulce watches the captives, robs the dead on the battlefield, and ridicules the entire spectacle. Across a performance tradition of more than two centuries, the text has evolved to express the changing cultural and political aspirations of the Nuevomexicanos. (EL)

Further reading: Aurelio M. Espinosa, "Los Comanches, a Spanish Heroic Play of the Year Seventeen Hundred and Eighty," *University of New Mexico Bulletin* 1, no. 1 (December 1907);

Arthur L. Campa, "Los Comanches: A New Mexican Folk Drama," *University of New Mexico Bulletin* 7, no. 1 (April 1, 1942).

Trans.: LT

Sweet Belly:
I have come with haste to warn thee,
Don Fernández, on this field,
That I saw close to that mesa
A bold Indian with a shield.
They did really want to seize me
But I, with my sling and mace,
Quickly caused them to forsake me;
So effective was my pace
That I've come hither to tell thee.

Captain:
If 'tis true what you are telling
I, with campaign shall then fight,
And triumphant, with joy swelling,
Shall tomorrow each unite.
Let the morning reveille herald.
Let each general attend,
And shall I, with sword unfurled,
Lead all to that crucial end.

(The trumpet sounds.)

Don Carlos:
What blast is that I am hearing
Which surprised me with its surge?

Captain:
Near that mesa, I am fearing,
The Comanches have emerged.

Don Carlos:
Quickly please, my captain hasten.
Hold your soldiers readily.
Meet the Indians at that basin
When you well-prepared shall be.
Here you hold the solemn banner
Which the sargeant shall beflout,
Since, despite pretense and manner
Our religion shall win out.

Barriga Dulce:
Vengo a avisaros de prisa
Fernández, mi capitán,
Que allá al pie de aquella mesa
Vi un indio con chimal.
Ellos me querían llevar,
Pero yo con mi honda y maza
Los hice pronto arrancar;
Y fué tan buena mi traza
Que os he venido a avisar.

Capitán:
Si es cierto lo que dices
Pronto me pondré en campaña,
Y triunfantes y felices
Nos reuniremos mañana.
El clarín que toque diana,
Y que venga el general,
Y con mi espada el la vaina
Los saldremos a encontrar.

(Toca el clarín.)

Don Carlos:
¿Qué toque llamado es ese,
Que me tiene sorprendido?

Capitán:
Que allá al pie de aquella mesa
Los comanches han salido.

Don Carlos:
Pronto pues, mi capitán,
Prepare vuestros soldados,
Y al indio hostil encontrar
Cuando estéis bien preparado.
Aquí tenéis la bandera
Que el sargento llevará
Porque de cualquier manera
La religión triunfará.

Captain: (Seizing the banner)
Oh, thou flag amongst all pennants;
Spanish emblem passing fair
The clouds hide the sun in tenants
From the world, sire, ruling there.
I adore thee for thou wert here
All the glory of my dreams.
My unbridled fantasy near,
And now with delightful schemes
I shall leave thee, banner now, dear.
With my hand to hoist thy gleams.
(To the sargeant)
Sargeant, take and guard securely
The bespangled army tent,
And kill the Comanches surely
In fame of this kingdom spent.

Capitán: (Agarrando la bandera)
Bandera entre mil banderas;
Hermosa emblema español,
De nubes se pone el sol
Del mundo señor, empero.
Yo te adoro porque eras
La gloria que en sueños ví.
Mi entusiasta fantasía,
Y hora que quisiera ufano
Enarbolarte en mi mano.
Te dejo, bandera mía.
(Al sargento)
Tomad, sargento y cuidad
Del pabellón estrellado,
Y a los comanches matar
¡En gloria de este reinado!

(The Indians make a slight skirmish and advance toward the fortress while the trumpet sounds.)

(Los indios hacen escaramuzas y se adelantan al castillo mientras suena el clarín.)

Green Horn:
From the east to west horizons
From the south to northern cold
Rings the blast of that bright trumpet
Where doth reign my steel so bold.
Among all the varied nations
I do battle daring, last,
And such is the valor reigning
Here within my breast held fast.
Increased flags to wind unfurl
Turning round and round about
More than those I did attribute.
I, the daring, stop and flout,
I devour the most intrepid;
With my bravery admire
There be no rock nor no mountain
Which does not yield to my fire,
Every youth scorned and rejected,
Everyone that's thus abased,
To this end is brought by fortune
To this wretched state effaced.
There be no township nor place name
Undefeated verily
By my proud and haughty nation

Cuerno Verde:
Desde el oriente al poniente,
Desde el sur al norte frío
Suena el brillante clarín
Y reina el acero mío.
Entre todas las naciones
Campeo osado, atrevido,
Y es tanta la valentía
Que reina en el pecho mío.
Se levantan más banderas
Por el viento giro a giro
Que de las que he atributado.
Refreno al más atrevido,
Devoro al más arrojado;
Pues con mi bravura admiro
Que no hay roca ni montaña
Que de éste no haiga rendido,
Al más despreciado joven,
Aquel que más abatido
Se ve porque su fortuna
A tal desdicha lo ha traído.
Pues no hay villa ni lugar
Que no se vea combatido
De mi nación arrogante

At this time you all can see,
You shall see this all too shortly.
This imposing fortress here
All this I'll reduce to rubble.
Full-abased and beaten clear.
With its stones and bulwarks slanted
Although in preparedness,
And with all the inconvenience
Of a sudden heedlessness,
All the more stalwart the courage
Which our fighters do possess
I can certify and witness
As their own fame doth express,
With full shouts from their headquarters.
Let the Caslana Apaches,
As so many nations claim
Whose own sovereignty I've taken.
Now, by slow degrees the same
Pueblos shiver at my prowess,
When they find themselves engaged
And then fleeing from my fury.
Dwindling their courage waged.
They withdraw from such a fortune
Which 'til now we hadn't seen.
But, why should I ever weary
In recounting what has been
Since I now reign in their province,
Where all Christianity
I removed from every nation
Untold arithmetically?
All alone the Spanish reverence
My great valor which doth shine.
But today shall swell the bloodlines
Of this vengeful heart of mine.
It recalls to mind and memory
Of a daring Spanish wit
Who, full-proud and filled with valor,
And with unsurpassing grit
Dressed the bodies as with flowers
Crimson and with scarlet red,
Of the men, women and children
Killed at distance, fully-dead.
We could not begin to number
Nor to count the captives claimed.
Well then, let's see, noble captains,

Que hoy con el tiempo se ha visto,
Y como ahora lo veréis.
Este soberbio castillo
Hoy lo he de ver en pavezas.
Lo he de postrar y abatirlo
Con sus rocas y baluartes
Aunque se hallen prevenidos,
Y con la incomodidad
De un repentino descuido,
Seá más osado el brío
Que tienen nuestras personas
Que certifico y he visto,
Como lo canta la fama,
Y un cuartelejo de gritos.
Diga la nación Caslana,
Díganlo tantas naciones
A quien quité el señorío.
Hoy se ven combatidos
Huyendo de mi furor.
Se les ha acabado el brío,
Se remontan de tal suerte
Que hasta hora no lo hemos visto.
Pero, ¿para qué me canso
En referir lo que han visto
Que este reino en sus lugares,
Cuando todo el Cristianismo
Traje de tantas naciones
Que no le alcanza el guarismo?
Y sólo los españoles
Refieren el valor mío,
Pero hoy ha de recorrer sangre
Del corazón vengativo.
Me recuerda la memoria
De un español atrevido
Que, ufano y con valentía,
Y con tanto osado brío
El cuerpo vistió de flores
En sangre de colorido,
De los muertos la distancia
Hombres, mujeres y niños
No pudimos numerarse
Ni contarse los cautivos.
Ea, nobles capitanes,
Que se pregone mi edicto,
Que yo, como general,

That my edict be proclaimed.
That I, as your general speaking
Must be well-prepared and seize;
For a general who reposes
Within sight of enemies
Very well could be called haughty,
And might daring be indeed.
But I shall not be contented
With these fickle destinies
And so, start the war chant ever.
Beat the drum and play the fife!
Hoof the dance and launch the battle!
Through the district, full of life
Let us march that all may see us
Armed and ready for a fight.
And I tell you, this allegiance
Which you've promised me so far
I shall safeguard well and prudent,
For such is the fame in war
Of our fathers and our offspring.
Since I, for impious pass,
I shall show my fearceness ever
With this black obsidian lance.
I defy the most disdainful
Bear or tiger as I do
Even the resplendant Helen,
And likewise, this brute shall too.
I find none to fear nor cower.
Such is my own strength and might
That I enter, bold and haughty,
Seek their general with my sight
Who, with senseless rant and raving
And his own ferociousness
Destroyed all, as I have stated.
Him, I summon with duress,
To the battlefield and challenge
Him to state his name, confess!

Don Carlos:
You must stop, desist, wait ever
For I am of noble heart,
That I come without your summons
To safeguard this fort apart.
No need to exchange agreements;
I've heard of your prowess here.

He de estar prevenido;
Que general que descansa
En vista del enemigo
Bien puede ser arrogante,
Bien puede ser atrevido.
Yo no me he de conformar
Con estos vagos destinos
Y así, comienzen un canto.
¡Qué suene el tambor y pito!
¡Al baile, y punto de guerra!
Pasaremos al distrito
Para que en vista de todos
Estemos aprevenidos.
Y advierto que con la unión
Que me tienen prometida
Obraré como prudente,
Que tal renombre ha tenido
Toda nuestra descendencia.
Y así, como el más impío,
He de mostrar mi fiereza
Con esta lanza de vidrio.
Al oso más arrogante
Y al fiero tíguero rindo,
La más elevada Elena.
Este bruto salto a un brinco,
Pues ya no hallo a quién temer.
Es tanta mi fuerza y brío
Que entrando osado y altivo
Buscando a ese general
Que con locos desvaríos
Usó de tanta fiereza,
Destruyó como he dicho.
Lo llamo en campal batalla,
Lo reto y lo desafío
¿Quién es, y cómo se llama?

Don Carlos:
Aguarda, detén, espera
Que soy de tan noble brío
Que vengo sin que me llames
A cuidar este castillo.
Pues no es menester carteles;
Ya tus valentías he oído.

State your name for I would have it
Knowing all without that fear.
But I'll save us both discussion
What you've said's enough and clear.

Green Horn:
I am that selfsame, great captain.
No sire, few words I've devised.
Of all tribes I am the leader,
And by all am recognized.
I am, by this headdress, noticed,
And this horn which you did laud
Green and gold as now you see it.
All kneel to me as to God.
And not just by my own nation
Which my lordship undertakes,
But by every other nation
That the northern cold lays waste.
Blindly they pledge me obedience.
Kiowas, Cuampis, Quechuas, too,
Pánanas, Jumanos, Ampáricas.
Countless others also do.
But so as to not belabor,
I'll cease talking now to you.

Don Carlos:
You must stop, desist, wait ever
For my chains around your craw
Shall soon crush your self-importance.
Don't you know, in Spain by law
The most Sovereign Lord of Heaven
And of all the Earth right here
By the four poles thus enclosèd
Within this unending sphere
Shines in majesty and splendor?
And when His name's heard withall,
Tremble Portuguese and Germans,
Turkey, as does England all,
At the mention of us Spaniards,
Every single nation quakes.
You have yet to face our rigor,
And the fury to partake,
Of our Catholic arms when brandished.
That is why you brave so much.
If you'd know my appellation,

Dime tu nombre, porque
Del todo quede entendido.
Para ahorrarme de palabras
Basta con lo que me has dicho.

Cuerno Verde:
Yo soy aquel capitán.
No capitán, poco he dicho.
De todos soy gran señor,
De todos soy conocido.
Yo soy, y por el turbante,
Este cuerno que ha aplaudido
Verde y dorado que ves.
Hoy se me postran rendidos.
No sólo de mi nación
Que emprende mi señoría,
Sino todas las naciones
Que coloca el norte frío.
Ciegos me dan la obedencia.
Caiguas, y Cuampis, Quichuas,
Pánanas, Jumanos, Ampáricas,
Y otras muchas infinitas.
Y por no cansarme, callo.
Basta con lo que he dicho.

Don Carlos:
Aguarda, detén, espera
Que he de anular tu cerviz
Y quebrantar tu soberbia.
¿Que no sabes que en la España
El Señor Soberano
De los cielos y la tierra
Y todos los cuatros polos
Que este gran círculo encierra,
Brilla su soberanía?
Y al oír su nombre tiemblan
Alamanes, portugueses,
Turquía, y la Inglaterra,
Porque en diciendo españoles,
Todas las naciones tiemblan.
Tú no has topado el rigor,
No has visto lo que es fiereza
De las católicas armas.
Por eso tanto bravas.
Si quieres saber quién soy,

I'll reveal it to you such.
This is not the first engagement
On the battlefield for us.
The campaigns I've fought are many,
Carlos Fernández am I thus.
O'er the sea and land I'll challenge
Your stout mettle and your pride
I am wont to give you battle.

Te lo diré porque sepas.
Que no es la primera batalla
Ésta que tú me demuestras.
Las que he hecho son infinitas,
Siempre soy Carlos Fernández,
Por el mar y por la tierra,
Y para probar tu brío
Voy a hacer junta de guerra.

Green Horn:
I shall do the same outside.
The sun is our only sovereign.

Cuerno Verde:
Pues yo voy a hacer lo mismo.
El sol es quien no gobierna.

(The trumpet sounds the call to battle.)

(Toca el clarín a junta de guerra.)

Don Carlos:
To the death, captain, with pride!
Have the battle cry be sounded
So that with dexterity
From your never ending vigil
You might, with agility
Hearten to the undertaking
Every great heart anxiously.
Let us witness, loyal captains,
Who be vassals of the king,
Cause each one in your own homeland,
And that Highest Ruler mine,
Who bestows on us the vict'ry
By His conception divine,
Take the field and shield us ever!
For if you, great champion be,
You'll prepare yourself for battle.
Show Comanches bravery.
I address you in this manner,
So that all may come to know
How Comanches, ever-daring
Like a wild beast do show
Themselves quite aghast when facing
Saint James! Slayer of them all.
Smite to death this mob ignoble.
Let us break our swords withall;
Cause the death of this brute creature.
Destroy all since few they be,
And break down their heroism!

Don Carlos:
¡Guerra a muerte, capitán!
A guerra mande tocar
Para que con la destreza
De vuestra gran vigilancia
Use usted con gran presteza
Y concurran a la empresa
De los grandes corazones.
¡Ea, leales capitanes,
Cuyos vasallos del rey,
Hacen que vuestra patria,
Y el Altímiso Patriarca,
Que nos ha de dar victoria
Por su concepción divina,
Marche al campos y no prevenga!
Si tú eres grande campeón,
Te prepararás a la guerra.
Muestra al comanche, el valor.
Yo te hablo de esta manera,
Pues para que todos sepan
Cómo el comanche atrevido
Como una bárbara fiera
Se arroja despavorido
¡Santiago! Y darle a esta infame
Canalla hasta que mueran.
Vamos a romper por acero;
Hacer que muera esa fiera.
¡A destruirlos que son pocos,
Y a quebrantar su braveza!

Asking thin disguisedly
If I were dextrous in battle,
Or the captain of the field
Who would trample down their region,
Or to meet them I should yield
Well, most clearly did I show them
Our great fortress with no peer.
My own breast heaves now with trembling.
But I'll say no more right here,
Let my tongue be stilled in silence.
Let us sally forthwith now
For this day be ruled by battle.
Tell me your thoughts anyhow
As those who are versed in battle.
Don Tomás Madril are you,
And Don José de la Peña,
Soldiers, chiefs, and sargeants too.
And Don Salvador Ribera,
In whose sight and presence shall
We procede forthwith to battle.
Having brought an end to all,
We shall see what is ordained.

(The trumpet sounds. The march begins.)

Don José de la Peña:
I must answer for 'tis needed,
For your valor does compel.
Valiant commandant your courage
Bolsters me and heartens well.
For you see, my life is yours now
And command it, well you may.
I have promised you obedience
And I'm soon to join the fray,
And will shortly give credentials.
Though the number be dire high;
Be they hundred men in battle
There, unvanquished shall be I
I have always known this truly
And my heart beats very fast
Knowing I shall not be captured
By this savage nation cast.
To retake the land is best now;
It's what we can do; 'tis fate
To safeguard our kingdom here

Preguntando con disfraz
Si yo era diestro en la guerra,
O si yo era el capitán
Que le pisaba sus tierras,
Y saliéndole al encuentro
Con claridad le di muestra
De aquel castillo sin par.
De decirlo el pecho tiembla.
Pero mejor es callar,
Y que enmudezca la lengua.
Pero vamos adelante,
Que hoy se trata de la guerra.
Dadme vuestro parecer
Como diestros en la guerra.
Usted, Don Tomás Madril,
Y Don José de la Peña,
Soldados, cabos, sargentos,
Y Don Salvador Ribera,
Y en vista de su presencia
Se procederá a la guerra.
Y estando todo concluído,
Se verá lo que se ordena.

(Toca el clarín. Sigue la marcha.)

Don José de la Peña:
Respondo porque es preciso,
Porque tu valor me esfuerza.
Esforzado comandante,
Así tu valor me alienta.
Viendo que esta vida es vuestra
Y que me podéis mandar.
Yo os prometo la obedencia
Y es para pronto pelear,
Y breve daré la prueba.
En un número crecido;
Siendo cien hombres de guerra
No me daré por vencido
Pues tengo bien conocido
Y me late el corazón
Que jamás seré cautivo
De esta bárbara nación.
A ganarles el terreno
Es lo mejor que se puede
Para salvar nuestro reino

Since our homeland venerates
Blessed Michael of nine choirs;
The hierarchies he allays.
He will be our intercessor
In the war these dreary days.
Sire, this is the truth I've spoken
'Tis my proposition true,
That we should discharge our weapons
So that they repent and rue.

The Lieutenant:
Oh, illustrious General Peña,
To whom all obedience I
Must set forth and do so freely
With my loyalty held nigh,
This distinguished seat of power
Which doth flout itself for thee,
Shall we now reduce with bullets
'Til they repent verily.

Don Salvador Ribera:
My lord, Don Carlos Fernández
This, your reasoning gives to me
Strength to see that you can order
And I yield my will to thee.
I'm content to be as stated
Our lieutenant solemnly,
And Don José de la Peña,
To defeat Green Horn you see
Who's the most courageous Indian
In each combat and each strife.
Who does flout his valor ever
To the world and to my life.
Seems to me that I perceive him
With the courage that refines
The Comanche, but what is it
That Dark Hair wants at this time?

Dark Hair:
Desist now, sire, ever valiant,
For such is my fierceness here,
That I would, with my alertness
Tell thee my decree right here.
Well, I would that thou shouldst know me,
Witness all my strength that be,

Que nuestra patria venera
Aquel Príncipe Miguel,
De las nuevas jerarquías.
Será nuestro gran sostén
En la guerra de estos días.
Señor, ésta es mi verdad,
Ésta es toda mi propuesta,
Con nuestras armas tirar
Para que así se arrepientan.

El Teniente:
Oh, ilustre general,
A quien toda la obediencia
Debo dar, y se la doy
Con mi lealtad dando muestras
Esa insigne capital
Que de por sí se demuestra,
¡Pólvora y balas con ellos
Para que así se arrepientan!

Don Salvador Ribera:
Señor Don Carlos Fernández,
Esta razón me hace fuerza
De ver que podéis mandar,
Y yo os daré la obediencia.
Me conformo con que sea
Como lo ha dicho el teniente,
Y Don José de la Peña,
En rendir a Cuerno Verde
Que es el indio más valiente
Que se esfuerza en la pelea.
Así su valor me esnseña,
Que todo el mundo lo vea.
Me parece que ya veo
Con todo el valor que medra
Al Comanche ¿qué desea
El indio Cabeza Negra?

Cabeza Negra:
Détente, insigne señor,
Porque es tanta mi fiereza,
Que quiero con mi destreza
Daros mi resoulción.
Pues, quiero que me conozcan,
Y que ustedes vean mis fuerzas,

So thou'd know whom thou'rt addressing	Que sepas con quién conversas
And who's speaking back to thee.	Y quién te habla en la ocasión;
So that thou would know the courage	Y que sepas mi fiereza
That my valiant heart has taught,	Y mi valiente corazón.
It was I who from the Christians	Yo saqué de los Cristianos
Took two children that I caught,	Dos niños que cautivé,
And with all my might I showed thee	Y con mis fuerzas mostré
And thy countrymen quite fair	El valor a tus paisanos.
That I did not ever harm them	Sin hacerlos ningún daño
But sustained them with my wares.	Los mantuve con mis bienes,
They're the two youth which thou hast now	Y son los dos que tú tienes
In this land where thou intrude	Hoy transitando esta tierra
For which the Comanche hasten	Por quien el Comanche viene
To do battle ever crude.	A formarte cruda guerra.
And I am that selfsame captain,	Yo soy aquel capitán,
Who does never budge right there	Soy aquel que nunca medra
Be in war or be in peacetime;	En la guerra y en la paz;
Always known as Lord Dark Hair.	Siempre soy Cabeza Negra.
My great fame remains unbroken,	Mi fama jamás quiebra,
And with strong resistance tense	Y con fuerte reisitencia
Everyone who sees me, trembles.	Todo el mundo al verme, tiembla.
Now, thou'll witness my defense.	Hoy verás tú mi defensa.
Brown Bear:	*Oso Pardo:*
There's no need to sue for favor	No hay que detenerse un punto,
Since, I'd do what to a beast,	Que, como bárbara fiera,
With my great, blood thirsty lancet	Con esta lanza animosa,
I would lop the head at least	Le he de cortar la cabeza
Of that Christian who's so haughty,	A aquel Cristiano arrogante,
Swift and with agility.	Al punto y con ligereza.
If one should transgress the limits;	Si alguno se propasare;
Not remember who I be,	Sin hacer reminiscencia,
That I am without an equal	De que soy el sin segundo
Both in valor and in might,	En brío y en fortaleza,
And if one be so foolhardy	Y si alguno en su arrogancia
As to test them, with delight	Quisiera tocar mis fuerzas,
I would challenge to pitched battle,	Lo reto a campal batalla,
Hand to hand we then would fight.	De cuerpo a cuerpo a la empreza.
Green Horn:	*Cuerno Verde:*
See to it now, noble captains,	Ea, nobles capitanes,
That assured be the defense;	Aseguren la defensa;
That your arms be sharp and ready	Todos preparen sus armas
From this very moment hence	A punto fijo a que sea
Honed with courage and with valor.	Con esfuerzo y con valor.

Gladly sing, for it is time
That we start the planned for battle.
Let our fifes and drums beat rhyme
That the hour is fast upon us.
If their captain sounds alarms,
Your response on this occasion:
Place your hand upon your arms.
No uncertainty must ever
Hold you back for just a trace.
I shall calm all wrath and fury,
Putting prudence in its place.
Everything must be well measured
Work in harmony and too,
As we now hear from our elder,
Our advisor, Beaded Shoe.

Beaded Shoe:
I must answer as it's needed,
For, although each offer be,
Which our captain did propose now,
Executed carelessly,
As one body move toward battle
Showing full conformity
Focus on the very subject;
For the rest is fantasy.
Let our leaders step forth boldly
To destroy the savage beast
Terrorizing all the mountain
Which, in forests, makes its feast.
E'en the tiger in the mountains
Can be made to hide and flee.
Who opposes my own valor?
Who'll entrap my pride that be?
Who'll undo the bonds that hold back
That unending loyalty
In my breast where it's enclosèd?
Who'll divide it verily?

Don José de la Peña:
I shall shatter all his fury,
As my last name indicates.
I am Rock in might and valor,
Which my strengh ne'er moderates.
Your exalted gallantries are
Born and bred of foolish pride.

Cantos alegres, que ya
Se va a comenzar la guerra.
Los pífanos y tambores
Suenen, que la hora se llega.
Y si sale el capitán
No se admite más respuesta
Que poner mano a sus armas,
Sin que tenga resistencia
Ninguno. No se detengan.
Yo haré que sosiegue la ira,
Y que use de prudencia.
Porque todo en un compás
Sean conjunto; la propuesta
Salga, porque ya es preciso
Un señor Zapato Cuenta.

Zapato Cuenta:
Respondo porque es preciso,
Que aunque todas las propuestas
Que había dado el capitán
Se cumplen con negligencia,
Quiero de conformidad
Que vayamos a la guerra
De la que así se platica;
Que lo demás es quimera.
Y que salga un capitán
A destrozar esta fiera
Que horroriza la montaña
Y que hace sufrir las selvas.
El tíguere en las montanñas
Huye en la oculta sierra.
¿Quién se opone a mi valor?
¿Quién cautiva mi soberbia?
¿Quién habrá que desbarate
Tanta lealtad que se encierra
En lo altivo de mi pecho?
¿Quién hay que lo desvanezca?

Don José de la Peña:
Yo quebrantaré la furia,
Que soy la más alta peña.
Soy peñasco en valentía,
En bríos y en fortaleza.
Esas locas valentías
Son criadas de la soberbia.

Spurred and infused is your valor
From that lard you have inside
Gleaned from buffalo and eaten
With such healthy appetite
To engender strengh within you
By your labor made just right.
The sun rises and it sets then,
And you've never, hand to hand,
Fought with any force behind you.
In a skirmish on this land,
Although you were hundred warriors,
With that sum increasèdly,
Within your barbaric nation,
You could not win victory.
Yours are naught but boasts outstretching
History as it should work,
Which outstrip by far the prowess
Of the German and the Turk.
Further still from being equal
To those great Twelve Peers of France;
I would place them far above you
Just to watch you squirm and dance.

Don Toribio Ortiz:
I am Don Toribio Ortiz
General like all the rest;
At my cost the king I'm serving
With a special mindfulness.
Of both troops and the militia
The core principal I be.
See if there be one among you
Who does not answer to me.
Which of one thinks he's my equal?
Let him step forth instantly
For I'll smite the life force from him!
Chief Green Horn, they're telling me
Is the man of greatest courage;
Please don't start that tale with me.
I can't stand him and his people.
With my troops they all shall see,
Soldiers, chieftains, sargeants also
All in perfect harmony.
Be alert to what I'm saying:
As the sun shall run its course
All shall see a mighty portent

Que tanto infunde el valor
En vosotros la manteca
Que coméis con tanta gula
Y con ella criáis la fuerza
De vuestras disposiciones
Por vuestra industria compuestas.
Nace el sol y luego muere,
Porque nunca cuerpo a cuerpo
Habéis hecho resistencia.
En un choque tuvimos,
Siendo cien hombres de guerra,
Siendo el número crecido
De tu bárbara nación,
La victoria no fué vuestra.
Esa sí que es arrogancia
De historia verdadera,
Que exceden en valentía
Al alemán y a Turquía.
Los doce pares de Francia
Lejos quedan de tu tierra;
Yo te los pondré delante
Que te tiemble la corteza.

Don Toribio Ortiz:
Yo soy Don Toribio Ortiz
Que en todo soy general;
Al rey le sirvo a mi costa
Con un esmero especial.
De las tropas y milicia
Soy la vase principal.
Vean si hay entre vosotros
Quien me pueda contestar.
¿Quién de éstos me cabe en suerte?
¡Salga luego, que al instante
Verá si le doy la muerte!
El Cuerno Verde, me dicen
Que es el hombre más valiente;
No tengo para empezar
Con él y toda su gente.
De mis tropas arregladas,
Soldados, cabos, sargentos
Ninguno se descomponga.
Esténme todos atentos:
Que hoy el sol en su carrera
Ha de verse algún portento,

Of a satisfactory force
And an opportune, apt casting.
All shall render their lives here
Lest there not be one among them.
Saint James and the Virgin pure
Shall be our north star and compass
Among these people of fear.

(Some Indians and soldiers meet in battle. The other Indians are trading with Sweet Belly and Tobacco Smoking Janchi. After a few shots, the Spaniards turn back. The Indians retake the two Indians that were held in the fort. Afterward, Tobacco Smoking Janchi returns with a white flag.)

Tobacco Smoking Janchi:
All of you as noble chieftains
Have thus ordered things put straight
All against the Christian weapons.
And now I am here to state
That I too am such a leader,
With no equal among peers.
For my valor knows no second,
Since no one can match my years;
The whole world does quake in terror
To behold my embassy.
I, to Taos, was emissary,
Sued for peace and as you see.
Not a single one dared follow
For they lacked my manliness.
All I sought for was then given
In attest of my success.
All nobility does truly
Reign within the Spanish breast
And so I'll lay down my weapons
And surrender like the rest.
I don't want to be a rival;
Nor a traitor want to be.
I just want to relish ever
My own proper embassy.
Sound the fife, begin the drumbeat
And the war prepare to start

En caso tan adecuado
Y lance tan oportuno.
Todos rendirán sus vidas
O de éstos no queda ni uno.
Santiago y la Virgen María
Serán nuestro norte y guía
Entre esta gente cobarde.

(Se revuelven en batalla algunos soldados y algunos indios. Los demás de los indios están tratando con Barriga Dulce y Tabaco Janchí. Después de algunos tiros, retroceden Los españoles. Los indios se llevan A los dos indios que están en el castillo. Después, vuelve Tabaco Janchí Con bandera de paz.)

Tabaco Chupa Janchí:
Como nobles capitanes
Han mandado disponer
Contra las cristianas armas.
Ahora os hago saber
Que también soy capitán,
Y falta mi parecer.
Mi valor es sin segundo,
Porque ninguno me iguala;
Tiembla de pavor el mundo
Sólo de ver mi embajador
Yo a Taos fuí de embajador
A solicitar la paz,
Y ninguno me siguió
Porque no se halló capaz.
Se me concedió al momento,
En virtud de mi valor.
Porque toda la nobleza
Reina en el pecho español
Y así mis armas están
Rendidas por la ocasión.
No quiero ser enemigo;
Ya no quiero ser traidor.
Gozar quiero del empleo
Que tenga de embajador.
Suene el pífano y tambor
Y apercíbase la guerra

With great force and full of valor,
Winning honor in your heart.
I shall go and bring a message
To the Spanish Captain there.
(He approaches the Spanish fortress.)
Stand still oh most worthy martyr!
Halt, commendable lord fair!
You shall hear what Green Horn's doing,
He, and all his men, of course.
They have raised the battle standard
All against the Spanish force.
From the great Arkansan River
I've come but to tell you this.
You shall learn how Brown Bear started
With Dark Hair, that friend of his,
A campaign against all Spaniards
To do battle close at hand,
So you must now start preparing,
I'm returning to my land.

Don Carlos:
Go back now and take this message
That I am fully prepared
To accept their latest challenge
Such as they have sent me, scared.
If they've swayed my other Indians,
I shall quickly this avenge.
I shall win them back or finish
With their nation in revenge.
My ambition is for battle
From the north come sweeping down.
(The Indian leaves and the Captain addresses his men.)
Our own state of things you'll witness
And my answer of renown
Which, on your behalf I've given,
By accepting the request
Wrapped up in a word I sent it.
Ending thus, I may attest
From your loyal hearts it echoes
The illustrious champion who
Is but our own valiant courage
Speaking in this way for you.
Let us see now, noble captains,
Servile to our own homestead!

Con esfuerzo y con valor,
Y adquirir algún honor.
Que yo me voy a avisar
Al Capitán español.
(Se acerca al castillo de los españoles.)
¡Paraos, valeroso martir!
¡Détente, insigne señor!
Verás como Cuerno Verde;
Él, y toda su nación.
Han levantado bandera
En contra del español.
Yo de Napeiste he venido
Sólo a traerte esta razón.
Sabrás cómo el Oso Pardo,
Y también Cabeza Negra,
Han compuesto esta campaña
Para darte cruda guerra,
Y así vete apreviniendo,
Que yo me voy a mi tierra.

Don Carlos:
Anda y lleva la contesta
De que yo estoy preparado,
Y que acepto la propuesta
Como ellos me la han enviado.
Si a mis indios se han llevado,
Pronto me podré vengar.
Se los volveré a quitar
O acabaré su nación
Pues mi ambición es pelear
Desde el norte al sentirrón.
(Se va el indio, y el capitán se dirige al los suyos.)
Veréis nuestro parecer
Y conozco la contesta
Que le he dado por los míos,
Aceptando la propuesta
Que doy yo en una palabra.
Concluída de esta manera
De los leales corazones
Que siendo ilustre campeón
Nuestro esforzado valor
El hablar de esta manera.
¡Ea, nobles capitanes,
Obedientes a la grey!

For our God and for our country
And the crown on our king's head,
For I put my trust in Mary
And in Joseph, master mine,
That they both will grant us victory.
Mercy, Conception divine.
Thou, conceived without a blemish;
Pure and clean and full of grace.
The archangel, blessed Gabriel
Leads the troops in Heaven's place,
We must put our hand to blade now.
We must take the battlefield
And prepare the field completely
Wearing down and letting yield
Even the resplendant Helen.
Let us break the fence at will
Hastening the beast's own downfall.
By destroying those few still,
Splitting all their heads wide open.
Saint James the apostle blessèd
And Mary's Conception too
Serve as north star and as compass
'Gainst this faint and craven crew.

(The trumpet blasts and they return to the fort.)

Green Horn: (Addressing his men)
They are coming wholly ready.
It bespeaks much, you can bet
For this vile, unworthy captain
Who won't let me rest just yet.
(He beats the drum.)
Sound the instrument of battle
To begin the war, I say!
Valiant sons of dual nations
Valor shines from you today.
Sing the war chant to begin now
Since this be not the first time
That against a foolish people
I have raised my standard high.
Hasten all ye full of valor
And break down their baseless pride,
That I may gather Don Carlos
As with compass to my side.

Por Dios y por nuestra patria
Y la corona del rey,
Porque confío en María
Y en el patriarca José,
Que nos han de dar victoria.
Piedad, Concepción divina.
Concebida sin pecado;
Tan limpia y de gracia llena.
El arcángel San Gabriel
De aquellas tropas excelsas,
Preciso es tocar el arma.
Marche el campo a la batalla
Y todo el campo aprevenga.
Yo haré que se desborone
La más elevada Elena
Vamos a romper el cerco
Y hacer que muera esta fiera.
A destruirlos, que son pocos,
Y a quebrantar su cabeza.
El apóstol Santiago
Y Concepción de María
Contra esta gente cobarde
Me sirva de norte y guía.

(Toca el clarín y dan vuelta al castillo.)

Cuerno Verde: (A los suyos)
Ya vienen apericibidos.
Ya el encuentro me da muestra
De este indigno capitán
Que desahogar no me deja.
(Toca el tambor.)
¡Qué suenen el instrumento
Para comenzar la guerra!
Genízaros valerosos
Hoy vuestro
Valor se muestra.
Canten para dar principio
Que no esl a primera vez
Qué con esta gente necia
Levantaré mis banderas.
Acomented valerosos,
Y quebrantad su soberbia,
Porque junto en un compás

(The trumpet sounds the attack.)

Captain:
Death to Indians at my hands now,
Ceasing all their valiantry.
Push on, countrymen of courage,
May God be a guide to thee!

(Shots)

Sweet Belly:
Let them all die, for to me then
All the spoils will then stay!
Store rooms, skins and bedrolls also
For my kids to sleep away.
And the meat, my wife, I'd ask her
To prepare it nice for me,
And to season it with chile
As a dish most heavenly.
Push on forward, dear companions,
For it warms my heart and soul!
We shall soon reach the great throne room
Where doth rule my dear bread whole.
I shall enter through that doorway,
Lest an arrow pierce me clean.
That is not good for my body.
I'll go vitalize the scene
Of that gem that costs me dearly.
I'll usurp it all for me,
And I'd do so 'til I perish.
As when in woods totally
I was lost upon the mountain
At great peril of my life
Having to escape or forfeit.
Are you not in that same strife,
Cartridge box and all you soldiers?
From the Pecas, are you free?
Why then, are your hands still tied thus?
We are not exempt, you see
If we still must come to seek them.
Don't you know that I'm the sweet,
Carameled milk, and tasty medley,
Sugar coned and sugar treat,

Don Carlos en mi presencia.

(Toca el clarín Guerra Fuerte.)

Capitán:
Mueran indios a mis manos,
Y cese vuestra osadía.
¡Seguid, valientes paisanos,
Que Dios sea vuestra guía!

(Tiros)

Barriga Dulce:
¡Qué mueran, que para mí,
Todos los despojos quedan!
Tiendas, antas, y conchelles
Para que mis hijos duerman.
Y la carne, a mi mujer
He de hacer que me la cuesa
Y me la guise con chile
Que es una comida buena.
¡Apriétenles compañeros!
Que de eso mi alma se alegra.
Hemos de llegar al trono
Donde está mi panadera.
Yo entraré por esta puerta,
No me ofenda una saeta
Que esto no gusta a mi cuerpo.
Vaya yo de animador
De esa prenda que me cuesta.
Lo he de apropiar para mí,
Y lo he de hacer hasta que muera,
Pues me hallaba yo en la selva
Encima de la montaña
Puesto en la contingencia
De escapar o de pagarla.
¿No están despuestos lo mismo
Los soldados y la caja?
¿No estaban libres las Pecas?
¿Por qué ahora están amarradas?
No podemos estar zafos
Si venimos a buscarlos.
No saben que soy el dulce,
La cajeta, la ensalada,
L'azúcar y el piloncillo

Too am I anise and gracious.
For in all I ever do,
You will always find my valor
And my honor in arms too.
Always at my waist I carry
My own sling securely tied.
And if one should argue with me
I'd convince his foolish pride.
Do you think my staff and slingshot
Really do not matter more?
With what do you think I vanquished
The vile shepherd and the Moor
Who would boast of his own greatness
Hammering at Heaven's door?
Well, for now I'll stop my yapping
For it's time to start the war.
Push on forward, bold companions!
Long live Don Carlos and too,
Long live José de la Peña,
And the mayordomos who
Dedicate their souls most surely
To the Virgin up above
Who is Mother full of graces
And the jewel of such love,
Who in us infuses valor.
Saint James! Jesus be right there
As I go back to my home to
See my Catalina fair
And an old hen with her chickens
Left there brooding when I came.
Push on forward, bold companions
Doing dance and songs of praise,
Comanches and maricuetas
Try to do as best you can
With your churlishness and limits.
Good news, captains, off they ran!
All flee and not one is staying
Guarapé and Comanche,
And Green Horn is also leaving.

*(The war trumpet sounds.
Sweet Belly runs out to where
Las Pecas are and returns with them.
The Indians run off with the
Spaniards behind them.)*

Los anices y la gracia.
Porque en todas mis funciones,
Siempre se halla mi valor
Y mi nobleza en las armas.
Tengo siempre en mi cintura
Mi honda muy bien fajada.
Y si alguno me replica
Le convenceré con pruebas.
¿Piensan que el báculo mío
Y mi honda no valen nada?
¿Con qué vencí al pastorcillo
Y al moro que levantaba
Hasta el cielo su grandeza
De la gloria que llamaba?
Pues, callo, porque ya es tiempo
De comenzar la batalla.
¡Apriétenles companeros!
¡Viva el Señor Don Carlos,
Y Don José de la Peña,
Y vivan los mayordomos!
Que toda su alma le entriegan
A la Santísima Virgen
Que es Madre de gracia llena,
Que como prenda estimada
Es la que nos da valor.
¡Santiago! Jesús nos valga,
Ahora sí voy a mi tierra
A ver a mi Catalina,
Y a una gallina con los pollos
Que dejé cuando me vine.
Apriétenles, compañeros,
Haciendo danzas y loas,
Comanches y maricuetas
Al modo que se permite
La limitada rudeza.
¡Albricias, que se nos van!
Huyen y ninguno queda
El guarapé en el comanche
Cuerno Verde ya se va.

*(Suena el clarín de guerra.
Sale corriendo Barriga Dulce a donde
Están la Pecas, y se las trae.
Los indios salen huyendo con
los españoles tras de ellos.)*

Captain:
You cannot hide from my vision,
Traitorous Indian inhumane.
By my own hand you shall perish;
Death to Green Horn and his name!

(They shoot and Green Horn falls.
They pursue the others and return
with their prisoners.)

Sweet Belly:
Lash them, lash them, brave companions,
Because they had fled from me.
Follow ever, dear bread bakers
For I crave both debts from thee.
You shall have your shield most trusty
I shall have my guavas sweet,
Pumpkin seeds and cactus candy,
And that sprouted flour treat;
Money, chile and sweet onions
Laced with aromatic herbs,
Marinated in a skillet
We shall make some fine preserves.
Run away, you sorry orphans.
To your captain make your wail.
If you have no real feelings,
Knock your heads to no avail.

(He whips them and they cry and dance.)

Captain:
Come to me, my fairest banner,
Riddled crudely by grape-shot.
Ever you shall be in battle
My companion, constant sought.

(The trumpet sounds the Retreat.)

Capitán:
Ya mi vista no te pierde,
Indio traidor, inhumano.
Serás muerto por mis manos;
¡Muera, muera Cuerno Verde!

(Le tiran y cae Cuerno Verde.
Siguen a los demás y los
traen prisioneros.)

Barriga Duce:
Muelan, muelan, compañeros,
Porque se me habían ido.
Sigan, buenos panaderos,
Que yo los dos pagos pido.
Para ustedes el chimal
Y para mí los guayabes,
Las semillas y el nopal,
La panocha y estos reales;
También el chile y cebolla
Con toditas estas hierbas,
Que cosiéndolas en una olla
Haremos buenas conservas.
Anden ustedes, mostrencos.
Lloren a su capitán.
Si no tienen sentimientos,
a golpes han de llorar.

(Les pega y lloran, y le bailan cabellera.)

Capitán:
Venid, hermosa bandera,
Rota por cruda metralla.
Tú serás en la batalla
Mi constante compañera.

(Toca el clarín Retirado.)

Anonymous

Little Indian Ballad of Plácida Romero (La Indita de Plácida Romero)

Plácida Romero was a New Mexican woman who was taken captive by the Gileño Apaches, the easternmost band of Chiricahuas, in their last war with the United States in 1881. She endured nine months of captivity until her escape in northern Mexico. When she returned to her native village of Cubero (1881), a poet composed this haunting *indita* ballad, which is still performed by her great-granddaughters in commemoration of her pain and her faith. The *inditas* of the latter nineteenth century are New Mexico's unique contribution to the history of Hispanic balladry in the Southwest. Like the Iberian romances and the greater Mexican corrido ballads to which they are closely related, the inditas share a thematic fascination with disasters, natural and historical, and the personal dimensions of human tragedy. The powerful devices of first-person narration, plus a reflective chorus, distinguish the *indita* (translated as "little Indian girl" or "little Indian song"). The latter is a folk term applied to a variety of musical and poetic forms, including a large corpus of historical narrative ballads, a smaller corpus of burlesque love songs, a few intercultural religious song/dances, and even a popular social dance performed to the instrumental music of the previous forms. As the term *indita* implies, there is usually some connection to Indians or Native American culture in the songs, both thematically and musically. The historical ballads appear only in the New Mexican repertory, but the burlesque and religious *inditas* are also occasionally performed in the Indian Pueblos. (EL)

Further reading: Enrique Lamadrid, "History, Faith, and Inter-Cultural Relations in Two New Mexican 'Inditas': 'Plácida Romero' and 'San Luis Gonzaga,'" in *Treasures of the Spirit: A Portrait in Sound of Hispanic New Mexico,* ed. Genaro Padilla (Alburquerque: Academia/El Norte Publications, 1994).

Trans.: EL

The day of Saint Lawrence
was a powerful day,
when they took me captive
and killed my husband.
In the year of eighty one,
close to ten in the morning,
that was when it was I think
when this happened to us,
when they killed my husband
and the man named Jesús María.

Farewell, I'll be gone, *[chorus]*
gone into suffering.
Farewell, my beloved daughters,
when will I see you again?

Farewell, La Cebolla Ranch,
why have you turned away?
The trees, the rocks are weeping
to see me go into captivity.
Farewell, my famous Cubero,
your bravery was finished.
Maybe your ammunition was gone,
or your people failed you.

El día de San Lorenzo
era un día poderoso,
que me llevaron cautiva
y mataron a mi esposo.
El año de ochenta y uno,
cerca de las diez del día,
así sería yo pienso
cuando esto nos sucedía,
que mataron a mi esposo
y al hombre Jesus María.

Adiós, ya me voy, *[refrán]*
voy a padecer.
Adiós, mis queridas hijas,
¿cuándo las volveré a ver?

Adiós, Rancho de la Cebolla,
¿por qué te muestras esquiva?
Los palos, las piedras lloran
de verme salir cautiva.
Adiós, Cubero afamado,
se te acabó lo valiente.
Quizá no tenías parque,
o te ha faltado la gente.

-chorus-

Manuelita the oldest,
take care of your little sisters
they have lost all our warmth,
they were left orphans.
Farewell, town of Cubero,
farewell, my house and my home,
farewell, walls and corners,
farewell, mother Marucasia.
Farewell, finest little mother,
may you remember my grief.

-chorus-

Farewell, Domingo Gallegos,
farewell, fine companion,
perhaps you had no brothers,
nor relatives there in Cubero,
since your bones remained
in a sad chicken house.

In the mountains of Galeana,
there my days [of captivity] ended.
What I realized,
was that what I saw were people.
I said to my little companion,
"don't stray from me,
do you hear, Procopio García."
I got to Ojito Salado [Salt Spring]
and started looking,
to see if I could see
my father or brother coming.
Also to see if my brother
Cayetano was coming.

My Lady of Light
was the one who reigns in Cubero,
asking of the Holy Child
my escape from captivity.

-chorus-

-refrán-

Manuelita la mayor,
cuida a tus hermanitas
que ya les faltó el calor,
se quedaron huerfanitas.
Adiós, plaza de Cubero,
adiós, mi hogar y mi casa,
adiós, paredes y esquinas,
adiós, madre Marucasia.
Adiós, madrecita fina,
duélete de mi desgracia.

-refrán-

Adiós, Domingo Gallegos,
adiós, fino compañero,
quizá no tenías hermanos,
ni parientes allí en Cubero,
que se quedaron tus huesos
en un triste gallinero.

En la sierra de Galeana,
allí terminaron mis días.
Lo que reconocí,
que era gente la que venía.
Le dije a mi compañero,
"no te retires de mí,
oyes, Procopio García."
Llegué al Ojito Salado
y me puse a devisar
a ver si veía venir
a mi padre o a mi hermano.
También si veía venir
a mi hermano Cayetano.

Mi Señora de la Luz
fue la que reina en Cubero,
pidiéndole al Santo Niño
que salga del cautiverio.

-refrán-

Anonymous

The Contest of Coffee and Corn Gruel (Trovo del café y el atole)

Once popular throughout northern Mexico and the Southwest, the *trovo* is a musical contest in which two *trovadores,* or troubadors, face off to debate in song any number of themes including love, philosophy, and politics. Often improvised on the spot, the response of the audience would determine the winner. The nineteenth century yielded several master *trovadores* whose reputations extended throughout the Southwest. Chicoria, El Pelón, Gracia, and El Viejo Vilmas were among the most famous, and their poetic encounters were commemorated in verse. In this satirical *trovo*, Café and Atole (Mr. Coffee and Ms. Corn Gruel) represent the competition between the native and the foreign. Mr. Coffee is sophisticated, stimulating, and worldly, but he costs the people money. Ms. Atole finally wins the duel, because not only is she a popular beverage, but she nourishes the people, who use the sweat of their brow and not money to enjoy her. (EL)

Further reading: Enrique R. Lamadrid, with Jack Loeffler, *Treasures of the Spirit: A Portrait in Sound of Hispanic New Mexico,* ed. Genaro Padilla (Albuquerque: Academia/El Norte Publications, 1994).

Trans.: EL

Coffee:
How is it going, friend Atole,
how have you passed your time?
From my country I have come
to make you an argument.

Atole:
Well, and how goes it for you?
And now I will ask you
by your grace and your name
tell me, who are you?

Coffee:
By my grace and my name
I call myself Mr. Coffee.
In the most beautiful stores
there you will find me.
I have come to America
and it is clear and evident,
I have come from my country
to conquer your people.

Atole:
It is true I am Corn Gruel

Café:
¿Cómo te va, amigo Atole,
cómo has pasado tu tiempo?
Desde mi país he venido
a formarte un argumento.

Atole:
Bien, y a ti ¿cómo te va?
Y ahora te preguntaré
por tu gracia y por tu nombre,
dígame, ¿quién es usted?

Café:
Por mi gracia y por mi nombre
yo me llamo Don Café.
En las tiendas más hermosas
allí me hallará usted.
A la América he venido
y es claro y evidente,
desde mi país he venido
a conquistar a tu gente.

Atole:
Verdad yo soy el Atole

and I ask peace from God,
Coffee, you are going strong.
I will also tell you
that many in the stirrup
end up later on foot.

Coffee:
I am coffee.
With sugar I am delicious
also with fried meat
and with fried bread generous
with rolls victorious,
and in well-arranged points,
I look great on tables
with fried eggs.

Atole:
I am also Corn Gruel
and I will give you my points.
How well I maintain my people
with tortillas and chile,
with corn well toasted!
Now I will give you news,
Coffee in order to buy you
nothing is left for shirts.

Coffee:
I am Coffee
known to all
in North America
of everyone I am preferred.
In the world I'm distinguished
with complete satisfaction
people use me in little cups
drinking my dark water.

Atole:
I am also Corn Gruel
and here I give you battle.
How well I maintain my people
only for working the land!
And you, proud Coffee,
may the whole world know,
you sacrifice my people
from buying you with money.

y a Dios le pido la paz,
Café que recio vas.
También yo te diré
que muchos en el estribo
se suelen quedar a pie.

Café:
Yo soy el Café.
Con azúcar soy sabroso,
también con carnes fritas
y con sopaipilla generoso,
con bollitos victorioso,
y en puntos bien arreglados,
bien parezco en las mesas
con huevos estrellados.

Atole:
Yo también soy el Atole
y te pondré mis paradas.
¡Qué bien mantengo a mi gente
con tortillas enchiladas,
con esquite bien tostado!
Ahora te daré noticias,
Café, por comprarte a ti
ya no se alcanzan pa' camisas.

Café:
Yo soy el Café
y de todos conocido
en la América del Norte
de todos soy preferido.
En el mundo soy distinguido
con satisfacción completa
en tacitas todos me usan
bebiendo mi agüita prieta.

Atole:
Yo también yo soy el Atole
y aquí te hago la guerra.
¡Qué bien mantengo a mi gente
con sólo labrar la tierra!
Y tú, Café orgulloso,
que sepa el mundo entero,
sacrificas a mi gente
de comprarte con dinero.

. . .

Coffee:
Even though I am Coffee,
friend Corn Gruel I tell you,
by way of friendship
I don't wish to fight you.

. . .

Atole:
You know I am Corn Gruel
with this I take my leave,
I submit my pure labor
as does Coffee,
as this duel closes
and may everyone know
that Corn Gruel has won.

. . .

Café:
Aunque yo sea Café,
amigo Atole te digo,
por vía de la amistad
no quiero pelear contigo.

. . .

Atole:
Sabes que soy el Atole,
con esto ya me despido,
ya mi trabajo puro
como también el Café,
a carga cerrada entrego
y todos queden entendidos
que ya el Atole ganó.

CHAPTER 2

Memories of Things Past

José Francisco Palomares

Testimony Recounted by José Francisco Palomares (excerpt)

In this first-person narrative by José Francisco Palomares, we have an account of one of the many military campaigns he launched in California during the 1800s against indigenous people. This text forms part of a longer *testimonio*—a dictation of Palomares's memories to an interviewer. The narration tells of the adventurous life on the frontier in a way that affirms the popular, romantic notion of a Wild West. This text has unique historical value insofar as in it, a traditionally mute voice, that of a Mexican Californio, can be heard. Palomares, by his own account, was born in Santa Barbara in Alta California in 1808. At the age of twenty-five he married and settled in San Jose, where he eventually became a lieutenant in the cavalry. This testimonio was recorded in 1877 by Emilio Peña, an agent of Hubert Howe Bancroft, a rich businessman interested in the Californios' recollections as raw material for the history of California he was writing. It is to this larger history that Palomares's testimony contributes through the portrayal of the conflict between "men of reason" and the Indians. Moreover, the Californios in general were unlikely informants with a unique perspective: They had moved from a more privileged space as pioneering settlers in the northern Mexican territories to the disenchanting experience of living during the U.S. appropriation of their lands. It is through this newly assigned role as an outsider that Palomares affords us an intimate snapshot of reality as perceived by the Californios in the first half of the 1800s. (TEW)

Further reading: Rosaura Sánchez, *Telling Identities: The Californio Testimonios* (Minneapolis: University of Minnesota Press, 1995).

Trans.: TEW

The story of the campaign against the savages of the Gollima settlement, who were led by a commander named Gollima, and the miraculous healing with the *jarazo* herb performed by a savage prisoner

Fifteen days after the second campaign, I had to prepare another expedition against the tribe of Chief Gollima, who, with his band of infidels, had lain siege upon the neighboring ranches and had taken around 60 animals. I organized this expedition with 10 well-armed and well-equipped men, whose names I don't remember, except for Francisco Altamirano and his brother, Rafael. These were very brave men who loved to fight with the Indians and were always interested in accompanying me on my battles against them. From San Jose, we traveled for two days in order to get to the ranch. It was about 8 a.m. when we attacked them. There must have been 200 in the tribe, including warriors, the elderly, women and children. Even though there were so many, we soon had the advantage because of our superior weapons. We cleared the ranch of Indians and succeeded in taking the horses without much resistance. After several hours of a very bloody battle, the infidels fled and in the settlement we were left with fifteen of their dead, a Christian prisoner named Pedro, and everything that they had stolen. Of our men, Ignacio Acedo, Francisco and Rafael Altamirano, and somebody else whose name I don't remember, were all seriously wounded, as was I. An arrow had hit me in between the ribs on the left side, with the tip reaching the area around my heart and the pain of this wound was so great that it made it impossible to move from one side to another. At one point, I remembered that the Indians knew of an herb that was very good for treating all types of wounds and injuries and that the prisoner we had could cure me and my friends. I sent someone to bring him to me and told him that if he treated us, I'd not only free him, but would also give him the best horse that we had. He promised that he'd do it, but asked if I'd first let him go to find the *jarazo* herb. I told one of the healthy men to take his rifle and accompany the Indian, and if he tried to escape, to kill him. The infidel, who understood Spanish quite well, laughed at my words and said that he'd never return to his tribe because they'd kill him if they found out that he'd treated some of those "men with reason." They returned soon after and the Indian carried in his hands the herb that he had mentioned before. I wanted him to treat me right then and there, but he made it known that it would be better if we descended to the sierra and camped somewhere near water. I gave the order and, step-by-step, we slowly made the trip, with the injured suffering from fever and a vicious thirst. We all begged for water upon arriving, but our doctor informed us that we'd die if we drank it.

After we rested for several hours, he had us drink a few sips of *atole de pinole*, which he had made, and then he began the cure. He began with me, as I was the leader of the group and, as a matter of fact, the one in the worst condition. He gave me the *jarazo* to chew and had me drink its juice. Then he chewed some also and, covering my wound with his mouth, he bathed it in his saliva mixed with the liquid produced from chewing the herb. He began to suck the wound to remove the blood that had coagulated around it and, when his mouth was full, he'd spit and begin sucking again. He continued in this way until he was sure that the inside of the wound was clean. Next, with great skill, he extracted the piece of the arrow that still was inside of me, arrowhead and all. He had me chew more of the herb and drink more of the juice, then he washed the inside of the wound with more of the liquid and covered the outside of it with the chewed pieces of *jarazo*. In this way, more or less, he cured the injured.

We remained there for six days, during which time we were on a strict diet. He took such good care of us and the cure was so successful that in that short time I began to feel well and, after consulting with the other wounded, found that they were feeling the same way. With this in mind, I gave the order to leave and we did. I told the Indian, upon departing, that I had to fulfill my word and that he should take a horse and go, that his life was spared, and if we should meet again, I wouldn't harm him. He answered that he'd take the horse, but said that he wouldn't be leaving for any Indian settlement because, wherever he might go, they would know that he'd healed some of the "men with reason" and they'd kill him. With that, he came to the mission with us, and there he stayed. He gave me back the horse and despite my insistence, refused to take it back.

This Indian served me faithfully for six years: harvesting for me, taking care of my corn, and doing other types of farm work, without receiving any compensation other than the seeds he needed for subsistence. When I'd give him money, he didn't want to take it, as he felt contented and sufficiently compensated with having had his life spared. As it turns out, during one of the attacks against the infamous, savage bandit Góscolo, poor Pedro, who had been so loyal to me, was killed by an arrow through the heart. When they brought his body to the mission, they told me that Góscolo's men had killed him. But I have reason to believe that it was one of Pedro's relatives who took advantage of this opportunity to seek revenge on him because he had cured us. It was common among the Indians to consider other Indians traitors if they provided services to the Whites, their mortal enemies. It didn't matter whether they were forced to do so or not. Further, the traitors' relatives thought themselves to be the most obligated to enact the revenge and kill when given the opportunity.

Brígida Briones (dates unknown)

A Glimpse of Domestic Life in 1827

Other than what can be gleaned from the two articles Briones published in the *Century Illustrated Monthly Magazine* in 1891, very little is known about this native of California, who was born early enough to have lived when the state belonged to Mexico, perhaps early enough to have seen Spanish dominion. What is certain is that Briones belonged to the landed gentry and, in her *Glimpse* furthered the romanticization of the past which so many Californios cultivated in their writings during the late nineteenth and early twentieth centuries. From references in her evocation of the pastoral and benign life of Mexican California, we can infer that Briones was born in Monterey, the daughter of a large landholder, probably an owner of a Spanish or Mexican land grant. What is also clear is her posturing as a child of the upper classes, manners, and civility that Eastern readers of the magazine might not have expected from a resident of the "wild and wooly West." But the Californios were actively engaged in reclaiming and rewriting the "official" history that had cast them as semibarbarous and had justified the appropriation of their lands by the "pioneers." (NK)

Further reading: Brígida Briones, "A Carnival Ball at Monterey in 1829," *Century Illustrated Monthly Magazine* 41 (1891): 470; Donald De Nevi, *Sketches of Early California: A Collection of Personal Adventures* (San Francisco: Chronicle Books, 1971).

The ladies of Monterey in 1827 were rarely seen in the street, except very early in the morning on their way to church. We used to go there attended by our servants, who carried small mats for us to kneel upon, as there were no seats. A tasteful little rug was considered an indispensable part of our belongings, and every young lady embroidered her own. The church floors were cold, hard, and damp, and even the poorer classes managed to use mats of some kind, usually of tule woven by the Indians.

The dress worn in the mornings at church was not very becoming; the *rebozo* and the petticoat being black, always of cheap stuff, and made up in much the same way. All classes wore the same; the padres told us that we must never forget that all ranks of men and women were equal in the presence of the Creator, and so at the morning service it was the custom to wear no finery whatever. One mass was celebrated before sunrise, for those whose duties compelled them to be at work early; later masses took place every hour of the morning. Every woman in Monterey went daily to church, but the men were content to go once a week.

For home wear and for company we had many expensive dresses, some of silk, or of velvet, others of laces, often of our own making, which were much liked. In some families were imported laces that were very old and valuable. The rivalry between beauties of high rank was as great as it could be in any country, and much of it turned upon attire, so that those who had small means often underwent many privations in order to equal the splendor of the rich.

Owing to the unsettled state of affairs for a generation in Mexico and in all the provinces, and the great difficulty of obtaining teachers, most of the girls of the time had scanty educations. Some of my playmates could speak English well, and quite a number knew something of French. One of the gallants of the time said that "dancing, music, religion, and amiability" were the orthodox occupations of the ladies of Alta California. Visitors from other countries have said many charming things about the manners, good health, and comeliness of these ladies, but it is hardly right for any of us to praise ourselves. The ladies of the province were born and educated here; here they lived and died, in complete ignorance of the world outside. We were in many ways like grown-up children.

Our servants were faithful, agreeable, and easy to manage. They often slept on mats on the earthen floor, or, in the summer time, in the courtyards. When they waited on us at meals we often let them hold conversations with us, and laugh without restraint. As we used to say, a good servant knew when to be silent and when to put in his *cuchara* (or spoon).

María de las Angustias de la Guerra de Ord (1815–1880)

Occurrences in Hispanic California (excerpt)

Occurrences in Hispanic California is one of more than 100 testimonials that Hubert Howe Bancroft collected for the *History of California*, the historiographic project that he published from 1884 to 1890. In 1878, Angustias de la Guerra de Ord dictated her reminiscences to Thomas Savage, one of Bancroft's agents. Her narrative is a record of the colonial history of California, documenting the numerous revolts by Native Americans and the military invasions by the Mexican and the United States governments. Born to an influential rancher and presidial family, Angustias de la Guerra de Ord chronicles the ways in which the Californios resisted both Mexican and Anglo-American aggression. On one occasion, Angustias de la Guerra de Ord delivered messages from her father to Padre Luis Antonio Martínez, who was being imprisoned for conspiracy against the Mexican government. On another occasion, she concealed José Antonio Chávez, a lieutenant in the resistance movement who was accused of spying against the United States. Nevertheless, it is important to note that her second marriage was to an Anglo-American, James L. Ord, a surgeon in the occupation army. Several critics have referred to her as the first *historiadora* of Hispanic California. (SZP)

Further reading: Angustias de la Guerra de Ord, *Occurrences in Hispanic California*, trans. and ed. Francis Price and William H. Ellison (Washington, D.C.: Academy of American Franciscan History, 1956); Rosaura Sánchez, Beatrice Pita, and Bárbara Reyes, eds., *Nineteenth Century California Testimonials*, San Diego Crítica Monograph Series (La Jolla, Calif.: University of California at San Diego, 1994).

Trans.: FP and WHE

Bouchard Episode, 1818: Indian Revolt, 1824

I, María de las Angustias de la Guerra, was born in San Diego on the 11th of June, 1815. My parents were Lieut. (later Captain) Dn José de la Guerra y Noriega, who was then on duty there, and Da María Antonia Carrillo, daughter of Captain Dn Raimundo Carrillo and Da Tomasa de Lugo.

I was about 40 days old when my parents moved to Santa Barbara, taking me with them. My father came here to take command of the presidio, because Capt. Dn José Argüello had left, or was about to leave, for Baja California to assume the duty of governor.

About the end of 1818 (in October) there arrived at Santa Barbara an American ship, commanded by one Don Enrique, who informed my father that an expedition of privateers was arming in the Sandwich Islands to come to attack California, which then was under the rule of the King of Spain.

This Don Enrique had been detained by the government some time before, I do not know whether for smuggling or seal hunting, which was prohibited to aliens. During his detention he lived in my father's house, who treated him very well, and for this reason, Don Enrique held him in high regard. It was for this reason that when he learned what was being prepared in the Sandwich Islands, he hurried back to California and brought to my father, whom he considered his best friend, the news so that he could make preparations against the invaders.

My father brought the news immediately to the knowledge of the governor, Dn Pablo Vicente de Solá (my baptismal godfather), and that gentleman immediately gave orders for the defense of the country and for the protection of the mission properties. As the ships were delayed a month or more in arriving, Sr. Solá wrote a very insulting letter to my father, accusing him of telling tall stories. After the mail carrying this letter left Monterey, the two insurgent frigates arrived at Monterey flying the flag of Buenos Aires, under the command of Hipólito Bouchard. There was considerable exchange of shots, and José de Jesús Vallejo, corporal of militia artillery who had charge of a cannon, had the luck to hit the larger frigate several times, as I learned. The final outcome was that Bouchard landed a formidable force at the town, and everything was burned after removing what was useful to the invaders. The governor, all the troops and their families had gone, most of them on foot, fleeing to the woods and retiring to the Missions.

I heard said that the governor was fearful that the invaders would go to the Mission of Santa Cruz and ordered the evacuation of all the goods and the padres and neophytes, so that the invaders could not seize anything. Though the insurgents did not go there, the Mission was well looted by Indians and even by others who were not Indians.

Bouchard's ships remained some days at Monterey before weighing anchors. On reaching Refugio (the ranch of the Ortegas), they landed a force which looted the storehouses, burned the buildings and then embarked. Some soldiers went from here under the command of my uncle, the distinguished Sgt. Dn Carlos Anta Carrillo, who managed to capture an officer, one Joseph Chapman, as well as some others. I do not remember the number of the captives.

After committing these acts of piracy against defenseless people, the insurgents moved on.

The prisoners were taken to Santa Barbara where the officer was offered to Bouchard in exchange for one Molina.

When my father, Capt. de la Guerra, learned of the arrival of the insurgents at Monterey, he ordered the families of the presidio to leave for a place of safety. Many of them including the de la Guerra family had made ready on receipt of the first news. My father remained with his troops at the presidio. The families left under the care of the Mission Indians (vaqueros) and also of some old and infirm white men. Some families left on foot. I recall that Padre Antonio Ripoll, pastor of Santa Barbara Mission, went on horseback, but dismounted to give his horse to a sick woman. Some of the families took off for San Buenaventura, but the majority went to Santa Inés, some by way of Refugio and the Ortega ranch, and others by San Marcos Pass. My family went by the latter way. I remember that the day of departure was very rainy. I rode in a cart, into which the rain poured from every side.

The insurgents did not commit any outrages in Santa Barbara. A boat came in under a flag of truce, and a man leaped from it to the beach and left there a paper and departed immediately. I do not know what the paper contained, but I have an idea that Bouchard proposed an exchange of prisoners. The one who was put ashore was the said Molina, a Peruvian whom they had captured at Monterey. Molina, years later, was a servant to my father and died in his service. This man was much addicted to drinking, and it seems that drunk, he mingled with the insurgents who took him aboard.

My family went on to Santa Inés and remained there a time until all danger of the return of the enemy passed. The latter continued on to San Juan Capistrano where they also did great damage, spilling out the wine they did not drink. They carried off the olive oil and other things. There some of the insurgents who did not want to go on surrendered to our troops with their arms.

When the ships were sighted here, my father posted his troops and some citizens from here and from Los Angeles, the total number of which was not more than 50, besides Indians, on the seashore in a willow thicket at the shore. This thicket no longer exists but I knew it well. There he had the men perform evolutions [*sic*] to make the enemy believe that he had a much greater force. As I said, the enemy did not disembark.

I learned that from Capistrano the insurgents went to San Diego and did damage there. Later they went to Loreto in Baja California, stealing the magnificent pearl jewelry which adorned the image of the Virgin of Loreto.

In 1824, when I was about 9 years old, while Capt. Dn Luis Anto Argüello was acting governor of California, then under the flag of Mexico, there occurred an uprising of the Indians of the Missions of La Purísima, Santa Inés, and Santa Barbara. A soldier came flying from one of those Missions to notify my father, at the time Comandante at Santa Barbara, that the Indians were in revolt and threatening the white families. This was on a Saturday between noon and 2:00 p.m. Immediately my father ordered my uncle, Dn Antonio Anastasio Carrillo, with 15 men to aid the Missions and the families. That night my uncle Dn Carlos Antonio Carrillo prepared to leave by the next day with a somewhat larger force. As it was Sunday, Padre Antonio Ripoll, one of the fathers of the Mission, came here to say Mass for us. My father directed that he should say his Mass without loss of time because when the troop was ready it should march. The padre was very sad and my father asked him what was the matter. He said the Indians did not want to go to Mass. Then my father asked if this was something new. The padre answered that the Indians were alarmed because troops had been sent to Santa Inés and La Purísima. Then my father begged that he speak the truth—had the Indians risen? Padre Ripoll replied that it was so. My father then arranged that the missionary could not give warning, and that the troops should remain in the presidio and for him to go with them to Santa Barbara [Mission] and attack the Indians.

Padre Ripoll got to his feet crying like a woman, and said, "My God! Don't kill my children. I will go to see them first. The troops need not go." My father did not want him to go, fearing they would attack him. But he went. As soon as the Indians saw him they said they were going to kill him. But some of the Indians were opposed and they advised him to return to the presidio, because the others had no intention of sparing him, but were bent on killing as many white people as they could, and then retire to the mountains. This about killing the white people, Padre Ripoll did not tell us but the Indian who accompanied him did.

The associate of Padre Ripoll at the Mission was Padre Anto Jayme, a man of advanced age who walked with difficulty. When the Indians forced Padre Ripoll to return to the presidio, he begged his associate to go with him, but the Indians refused to allow it and gave assurance that they would do no harm to Padre Jayme.

When Padre Ripoll arrived at the house my father asked him what result he had had with the Indians, and the answer was, crying, that they would do nothing to Padre Jayme.

My father went at once to the Mission with the troops and there saw no Indians except those who were in the corridor who had put Padre Jayme on the parapet and were firing their arrows from behind him.

There was at the Mission a Russian called José who was a servant there. He was among the Indians shooting a firearm. The troops from here killed some Indians who exposed themselves darting from behind the rocks to shoot their arrows. A few attracted the attention of the troops while the bulk of the Indians went from the Mission toward the mountains. Already during the previous afternoon and night, the Indian women and children had left for the Tular. The troop was from 8:00 a.m. to 1:00

p.m. doing what they could in attacking the Indians. By 1 o'clock the Mission was almost abandoned by the Indians, but the troops did not know it then. At that hour they retired to the presidio to get food, carrying 2 wounded companions. All this while Padre Ripoll was in a room which had a window toward the Mission. He had nothing to drink. My mother sent him a little broth. I went in with the servant and told him "they have killed some Indians." The padre began to cry and would not take even one drop of broth. I ran out overwhelmed for having given to him news that had saddened him so.

A little later the Indian sacristan of the Mission arrived with the keys of the church and he told the padre that the Indian alcaldes were saying they would take away everything in the Mission because it was theirs, but of that which was in the church they would take nothing because it was God's; that the revolting Indians had now gone to the Tular.

Padre Ripoll loved his neophytes as a devoted mother. His emotions were so great that he became ill, though not seriously so.

That same afternoon 2 Indians came bringing Padre Jayme to my father's house. During the whole day in the Mission the Indians did not forget to give him his food. The priests stayed on at our house. This outbreak was on February 27, 1824.

When my uncle Don Anastasio Carrillo arrived at Santa Inés the Indians had already set fire to the Mission. The priest in charge of the Mission was Father Francisco Uría, a Vizcayan and a prime husbandman.

When the Indians started to fire the Mission on one side the men, some 6 or 7 in number (including the missionaries and the guard) had taken refuge in the padre's quarters. From there they kept firing at the Indians until nightfall, because the Indians were trying to kill them. My uncle Don Anastasio arrived at sunrise. He seized the ringleaders after a short battle (the rebel Indians losing some dead in this combat and from the firing of the day before).

Padre Uría came to live in my father's house. The families were settled in the presidio.

The Indians of Purísima seized all of the white families, but did them no harm. They ordered them to say that if troops came against the Indians, they would kill the families. If no troops came, they would be released. The Indians complied with this promise, bringing the families to Santa Barbara without harm.

On the day of the uprising at La Purísima, two residents of Los Angeles reached there returning from Monterey. One of these was Dolores Sepúlveda.

The slayers of these persons were caught (except one), tried before a board of officers of the army, sentenced to death and shot on the spot. From Monterey came troops under the command of Lieut. Don José Estrada.

I forgot to say that the Indians of Santa Barbara killed 2 white people at a ranch named San Emigdio. One of these was a North American named Daniel (his surname I do not remember). The other was a Californian named José Antonio Félix. Both were good men. About 3 years before, Sr. Félix was attacked by an Indian and he struck him and knocked him down dead. At first he thought the Indian was merely stunned from the blow, but he soon realized that he had killed him.

When the Indians had been secured, they first cut off the right hand and then they killed them.

Later troops went in pursuit of the Indians who had gone to the Tular. Those from Santa Barbara were commanded by Lieut. Narciso Fabregat, a Catalan, and my uncle Carlos Antonio Carrillo. The troops from Monterey, I believe, were commanded by Don José Estrada. But the expedition did not accomplish its object. The Indians engaged in skirmishes and then disappeared. The troops returned. A little later troops returned to find the Indians. On this occasion Padres Vicente Francisco de Sarría, Prefect of the Missions, and Antonio Ripoll, Minister of Santa Barbara, went along. The troops were more of an escort for the padres. The force of these padres obtained a final result. They were authorized by the governor to offer safe conduct to the insurgent Indians. The latter listened to the words of the padres and returned to their Missions. Thus was concluded the revolution which threatened the destruction of all the advances made in behalf of religion.

These Indians fortunately were at odds with those of San Buenaventura. But for this circumstance the Indians of the latter Mission would have risen, and they would have been followed by those of San Fernando, San Gabriel, and of others.

Platón Vallejo (1841–1925)

Letter to William Heath Davis

The only college-educated child of Mariano Guadalupe Vallejo and Francisca Carrillo de Vallejo, parents from distinguished old-line Californio families, Vallejo became a medical doctor and served with honor as a surgeon in the Union Army during the Civil War. After receiving his medical degree from Columbia University in New York, he settled down with a medical practice in Vallejo, California, and devoted himself to intellectual pursuits, including writing sketches of pre-statehood Alta California. In his recollection of the golden years of California's past, Vallejo credited the Hispanic past for the development of California's resources; he also attempted to elevate the status of the Californios by emphasizing the accomplishments of their Spanish ancestors, countering the ethnocentrism of the Easterners who had overwhelmed the native population. He did recognize and, somewhat paternalistically, defend the Indians, but often cast them as "noble savages." Both his letters and his dictated "Memoirs of the Vallejos" reveal his efforts to counter official history of California and the West. In the letter below to a writer of California history, Vallejo protested the treatment of the Californians by historians. (NK)

Further reading: Platón Mariano Guadalupe Vallejo, "From Memoirs of the Vallejos," in *Nineteenth Century Californio Testimonials,* San Diego Crítica Monograph Series (La Jolla, Calif: University of California at San Diego, 1994), 106–22.

Vallejo July 9th '93

Mr. Wm. Heath Davis

Dear Sir,
Your letter of the 7th instant came to hand in due time and I am pleased to tell you that I have read it over and over again. Why? Because as in your work "50 years in California"

you are not occupied in slandering and throwing mud at everything Californian that was not a '49er or who did not count among his ancestors some anglo-saxon stock. And as for throwing mud we are acquainted with the history and topography of my native land well enough to know where are the muddiest holes and who are the biggest cranks that ever tramped hitherward—! but I forbear. I would not stain this white sheet of paper nor waste my ink telling it. I consign all that business to the filthy slums of the bay among the rule lands to be purified by the salt waters of the great pacific ocean. I wish to be forgiving though often I cannot help remembering!—

There are many beautiful episodes in the course of our grand history that it were a pity to lose our precious time pointing out the thistles whilst we could be gathering the wild flowers and placing them amidst our admirable domestic plants in the literary gardens of California. In telling the story of our country let us not neglect to preserve the precious stones and the more worthy metals and let the mud slide away to the bottom of the seas.

"Seize upon truth where'er tis found on Christian or on heathen ground. The flower's divine where'er it grows. Neglect the prickles—assume the rose."

In my last letter I merely mentioned the article about the census taker as a unique joke as one of the straws showing which way the wind blows. All the census takers in the world could not make me believe that I was a foreigner in a land that my ancestors found despite the sneers of the whole civilized or uncivilized nations of Europe, Asia and Africa combined. Why, my own people after a war of 800 years sent forth Don Cristoval Colon a navigator in the Spanish service to circumnavigate the earth and prove that the world was round. Whilst Columbus was nearly lost at sea Divine providence disclosed before his eyes the greatest gem ever known to have been found by intelligent men, *one half of the world.* Al Rey infinitis tierras, a Dios infinitis almas, dio Colon (Columbus has brought boundless land to the King and innumerable souls to God.)

The name of Vallejo figures also honorably in those days of chivalry and discovery. I believe I could trace my people back to Adam and Eve. Among the Conquerors of the vast Empire of Mexico Don Pedro Vallejo was one of the leaders with Cortez. The renowned Franciscan Fray Junipero Serra had for his companions the excellent Don Gaspar de Portola and the Distinguished Don Ignacio Vicente Ferrer Vallejo.

In the acquisition of this lovely California by the grandest of all nations of modern times my father (que en Dios descanse) may and can be truthfully said to have placed the diadem among the galaxy of stars that now adorn the fair brow of Columbia. And after this can I believe that anyone would or should have the amiability to call me a foreigner?—Why I am an American by right of discovery, by right of conquest, by right of possession and by act of the *will* and not by accident or coercion. My people were heroes in the old country. These heroes discovered America. America has revolutionized the world. To land in America is to become a freeman. To set foot on the golden shores of California is equivalent to seeing the World's Fair all your life. What a pity it would be if California were separated from the rest of the world! Where would you find another country like it! The beautiful hills and mountains. The bays and the grand ocean. And our glorious climate! If we could send these to Chicago—we'd never get them back again I fear.

But I fear that someone might read my letter and imagine that I was *"romancing."* I have not said one word about the big pumpkins, nor the big trees, nor the treasures stored away in the vaults of the Sierras, and I do not wish to be thought to exaggerate. Let the World's Fair people come to our California, prove and establish the fact so as to exclude possibility of doubt to them who can appreciate.

When a rooster has by his natural superior capacity found a bug does he not at once pick it up and call all the chickens to come and help him eat up the big bug? Well the Californians, proverbially generous, invite all good people here to share with them the products of our generous soil. Perhaps they will come to see and perhaps they may or *will* come to stay. From Victoria to Cape St. Lucas may be found room enough for thousands of families. Let those who now possess the land continue to be generous to others and make it easy for them to acquire a lot or a piece of ground; quit moving, settle down and live in peace and plenty. I am going to close now without apologizing for this long chat.

Yours truly

Dr. P. Vallejo

José Policarpo Rodríguez (1829–1914)

"The Old Guide": Surveyor, Scout, Hunter, Indian Fighter, Ranchman, Preacher: His Life in His Own Words

The Old Guide is one of the earliest autobiographical accounts of a Mexican immigrant to the United States, published in Nashville in 1898. Like other nineteenth-century Mexican American autobiographies, *The Old Guide* is a transcription of the author's dictations to an amanuensis. Rodríguez was born in Zaragoza, Mexico. At the age of twelve, he emmigrated to San Antonio, where he was apprenticed to a gunsmith. When the apprenticeship ended abruptly, young José joined a team of surveyors. He spent the next thirty-eight years as a guide for the Republic of Texas and the United States Army, establishing roads and settlements throughout Texas. Along the way, he had numerous encounters on the frontier, many of which are memorialized in *The Old Guide*. Perhaps the most significant encounter was his refusal to fight in either the Mexican-American War or the Civil War. In both cases, he chose instead to return home and enlist in the San Antonio Home Guard. Nevertheless, the book is more than the memoir of a frontiersman. In 1872, Rodríguez became a Methodist minister. The final chapters of *The Old Guide* narrate his religious conversion, which was condemned by other Mexican Americans, who believed that Rodríguez was renouncing his cultural heritage. In the end, *The Old Guide* is a spiritual confession in the Augustinian tradition. At that time, Protestant ministers were often expected to give public accounts of their conversion experiences to qualify for church membership. (TK)

Further reading: José Policarpo Rodríguez, *Jose Policarpo Rodríguez, "The Old Guide": Surveyor, Scout, Hunter, Indian Fighter, Ranchman, Preacher: His Life in His Own Words* (Nashville, Tenn.: Publishing House of the Methodist Episcopal Church, South, Smith and Lamar, Agents, 1898).

Chapter Thirteen: Bears, Indians, and a Night Ride

After General Smith left Texas, I remained again in the employ of the quartermaster department with Major Belga. It was decided to establish a camp on the San Antonio River at a crossing in Wilson County, where the Indians crossed whenever they came into the country on their horse-stealing raids. It was about fifty miles below San Antonio, and was called Conquista Crossing. We were there in all about six months. No Indians came that way while we were there. By some mysterious means they knew of our presence there, and avoided the place. I contracted chills at Conquista Crossing, and was ordered to go to Camp Verde with Captain Palmore, of the Second Cavalry. Camp Verde was about sixty miles northwest of San Antonio on a branch of the Guadalupe. This was in 1856. While there a man (Dr. Nowlin), came into camp and said that his horses had been stolen. A party was detached to go after the Indians. I went as guide. The doctor and his brother went along. We followed close after the Indians for several days.

We were out of fresh meat, and one day I saw a fat bear in the open plain, and I said: "Sergeant, let me go and kill that bear. We've got no fresh meat."

"All right," he said.

"Let me have your horse, won't you? Mine is jaded and run down by hunting this trail back and forth."

He had a fine, fresh horse, and he let me have him. I started after the bear. I came up near him, but that horse flew back and started as hard as he could run, and I could not control him. He made a great circle round and I brought him again toward the bear, but he broke again and made another circuit with me. The sergeant had no rope on his saddle, or I would have tied the horse and followed the bear on foot; but I could do nothing with that fool horse, and the bear got into the brush and got away from me, and I had to go back without him. O, I was so mad at that horse!

We saw a party of Indians ahead of us one day, and thought they were the Indians we were after. I went ahead with another man, and the men followed on. When near enough I called to the sergeant to charge into them. They were cooking, and had not yet seen us. They broke and ran, leaving their arms and everything they had. For some reason our men did not come up, and one of the Indians—the chief, I suppose—called the others back and they came slipping back and picked up their arms and aimed at me. I was calling to the man with me to keep moving about so they could not get aim at him and shoot him, and hallooing to the sergeant to pitch into them. He and his men commenced firing from their horses. The sergeant had never been in an Indian fight before. I said: "Sergeant, dismount the men and fight on foot, and I will go after the Indians' horses and pack mules."

I started after the horses and got them while the men were shooting at the Indians. When I got back I saw one of the soldiers, a man named MacDonell, a big man and a bully, always fussing and bullying among the men, standing behind a tree, and not fighting at all. I said: "Sergeant, look at MacDonell behind that tree. Make him come out from there and go to fighting."

The sergeant ordered him out, and abused him for being a coward; but that man never moved: he stayed right behind that tree, the coward! Our men moved around a little to get at the Indians, and left our horses exposed, and two Indians on foot started after them. I said: "Sergeant, those Indians will get our horses if we don't stop them."

The bugler, Jim Tafolla, saw the Indians after our horses, and started to meet them. I called to him that he would get killed, but he went galloping right after those two Indians, shooting at them with his pistol. The Indian in front had a shield on his arm, and I could see when the bullets hit the shield that they knocked up the dust close around him as they glanced off. These shields are made of several thicknesses of rawhide, and get so tough and hard that unless a bullet strikes them very square and solid it will glance off. Tafolla kept advancing and shooting. The Indian kept his shield whirling from side to side, and the bullets glanced off. When close up, Tafolla's pistol refused to fire; a cap had caught, and the cylinder would not revolve. The Indian shot with his bow and Tafolla struck at his head with his pistol. The Indian dodged down and escaped. Tafolla had an overcoat rolled up and tied on the front of his saddle. The arrow struck it and cut about fifty holes in it, and the arrowhead entered Tafolla's body just inside of the hip bone. The Indian started back, but kept turning his head and watching to see if Tafolla, whom he evidently thought he had killed, would fall. The other Indian must have been wounded; he went back first, but did not hop so lively as when he came. The main body of the Indians had got behind some ledges of rocks right on the bank of the little lake, and it was hard to get at them. The sergeant said to me: "Polly, do you think we can get those Indians? What do you think we'd better do?"

I said: "Sergeant, you'll lose two or three men before you get them."

"Well, we'll let them alone; we've got their horses and the things they left in camp. Come on, men; let 'em go."

Just before we drew off from them, Dr. Nowlin, who had been shooting at the Indians, had his horse shot down while standing very near it loading his gun. He and the others then moved farther away. The doctor was anxious to get his saddle, bridle, and rope off the dead horse. No one would volunteer to go with him. I said: "I will go, Doctor, but let some one come out here and take care of these horses."

We started. I said: "You understand the fastening of your saddle, so you take it off, and I will get the bridle and rope."

We stooped as low as we could, and made quick work of it, the Indians firing at us all the time, but none of them hit us. In this encounter we got five horses besides some pack mules, a number of buffalo robes, belts, moccasins, and other accouterments. One of our men, Martin, was pretty badly wounded by a gunshot. When I came up, the lower part of his lungs were hanging from the wound. He said: "Polly, do you think I am very badly wounded?"

I tried to encourage him, and said: "O no, Martin, I hope not; sit down here and we will do something for you.' "

The sergeant decided to go to Fort McCabet (still standing), in San Saba County, about forty miles away. I had never been there, nor had I ever been in the country just where we then were. The sergeant said that he would fasten a buffalo robe between two horses and let it swing and place Martin on it, to carry him to the fort. The robe was fixed and Martin was placed on it, but after two or three miles he said he could not stand it to travel that way; it shook and jolted him so the pain was very great. I said:

"Sergeant, the best way to fix him will be to let him ride and put the lightest man we've got up behind him to hold him."

It was so arranged, and Tafolla, whose wound did not hurt him much and who was a very small man, got up behind, and we carried him that way to the fort. It was late in the evening when we started. I knew the direction, and took the lead. When night came on it was very dark and cloudy; we could see nothing, but the southeast breeze was blowing, and while it lasts it keeps the same course. So I guided myself after dark by the breeze. I kept my course so that the breeze was all the time on my right cheek. This took me in a northeast course. It was a long, dark ride, and the men kept asking me how far it was and bothering me with no end of questions, till I said: "Sergeant, you must make the men stop talking to me. I don't know this country. I am traveling by the wind. I can see nothing, and they are bothering me so that I shall soon know nothing."

The sergeant said: "Men, don't another man speak to Polly. You bother him so he'll never get us out of here. If another man speaks to him, I'll tie him to his horse's tail and make him walk to the fort. Let Polly alone."

Not another man spoke to me after that threat. About one o'clock the moon rose. A little later we saw some large, white object far ahead of us. The sergeant said: "What's that, Polly?"

"I don't know, but I think that's the fort."

An hour later we saw it was the fort, and were soon there. The men were so glad they hugged me and lifted me and carried me around. I had kept my course exactly, and come straight to the fort. But in spite of our relief, poor Martin died an hour after we got there. The doctors at the fort held a post-mortem, and found that he could not possibly have lived even with the best of care. He was shot through the top of the stomach, the alimentary canal being cut.

CHAPTER 3

Roots of Resistance

Juan Nepomuceno Seguín (1806–1890)

Personal Memoirs of John N. Seguín, from the Year 1834 to the Retreat of General Woll from the City of San Antonio 1842

Born into a prominent ranching and political family, Seguín watched what has become Texas go through five governments, four wars, and numerous political upheavals. Seguín was one of several Mexican Texans who joined with Anglos to revolt against the Mexican government. In 1836, he was commissioned as a captain in the army with orders to report to the Alamo. He escaped Santa Anna's final attack only because he was sent through the Mexican lines to request reinforcements. Afterward, Seguín served for a short time as a senator in the Republic of Texas. He was later elected mayor of San Antonio. Seguín also served as a land speculator, until Anglos began to cast doubt on his loyalty to the Republic. In 1842, he resigned as mayor and sought exile in Mexico. Upon arrival, he was arrested and compelled to serve in the Mexican army. After the Mexican-American War, Seguín returned to Texas and published his memoirs in an attempt to restore his political reputation. *Personal Memoirs* is the earliest autobiographical account written by a Mexican American in the English language, published in San Antonio in 1858. In the text, Seguín used the English translation of his name in passionately defending his actions in the years surrounding the Texas rebellion. In many ways, the account prefigures the Chicano experience of cultural conflict in the U.S.–Mexico borderlands. Neither Mexican nor American, he was an originary trace of an emergent consciousness produced by the cultural *mestizaje* of the Americas. Nine years later, Seguín returned to Mexico, where he died at eighty-four. (TK)

Further reading: Juan Nepomuceno Seguín, *Personal Memoirs of John N. Seguín, from the Year 1834 to the Retreat of General Woll from the City of San Antonio 1842* (San Antonio: Ledger Book and Job Office, 1858); Jesús F. de la Teja, ed., *A Revolution Remembered: The Memoirs and Selected Correspondence of Juan N. Seguín* (Austin: State House, 1991).

A native of the City of San Antonio de Bexar, I embraced the cause of Texas at the report of the first cannon which foretold her liberty; filled an honorable situation in the ranks of the conquerors of San Jacinto, and was a member of the legislative body of the Republic. I now find myself, in the very land, which in other times bestowed on me such bright and repeated evidences of trust and esteem, exposed to the attacks of scribblers and personal enemies, who, to serve *political purposes*, and engender strife, falsify historical facts, with which they are but imperfectly acquainted. I owe it to myself, my children and friends, to answer them with a short, but true exposition of my acts, from the beginning of my public career, to the time of the return of General Woll from the Rio Grande, with the Mexican forces, amongst which I was then serving.

I have been the object of the hatred and passionate attacks of some few disorganizers, who, for a time, ruled, as masters, over the poor and oppressed population of San Antonio. Harpy-like, ready to pounce on everything that attracted the notice of their rapacious avarice, I was an obstacle to the execution of their vile designs. They, therefore, leagued together to exasperate and ruin me; spread against me malignant calumnies, and made use of odious machinations to sully my honor and tarnish my well-earned reputation.

A victim to the wickedness of a few men, whose imposture was favored by their origin, and recent domination over the country, a foreigner in my native land, could I be expected stoically to endure their outrages and insults? Crushed by sorrow, convinced that my death alone would satisfy my enemies, I sought for a shelter amongst those against whom I had fought; I separated from my country, parents, family, relatives and friends, and what was more, from the institutions, on behalf of which I had drawn my sword, with an earnest wish to see Texas free and happy.

Ere the tomb closes over me and my contemporaries, I wish to lay open to publicity this stormy period of my life; I do it for friends as well as for my enemies, I challenge the latter to contest, with facts, the statements I am about to make, and I leave the decision unhesitatingly to the witnesses of the events.

The tokens of esteem, and evidences of trust and confidence, repeatedly bestowed upon me by the Supreme Magistrate, General Rusk, and other dignitaries of the Republic, could not fail to arouse against me much invidious and malignant feeling. The jealousy envinced against me by several officers of the companies recently arrived at San Antonio, from the United States, soon spread amongst the American straggling adventurers, who were already beginning to work their dark intrigues against the native families, whose only crime was, that they owned large tracts of land and desirable property.

. . . In those evil days, San Antonio was swarming with adventurers from every quarter of the globe. Many a noble heart grasped the sword in the defense of the liberty of Texas, cheerfully pouring out their blood for our cause, and to them everlasting public gratitude is due; but there were also many bad men, fugitives from their country, who found in this land an open field for their criminal designs.

San Antonio claimed then, as it claims now, to be the first city of Texas; it was also the receptacle of the scum of society. My political and social situation brought me into continual contact with that class of people. At every hour of the day and night, my countrymen ran to me for protection against the assaults or exactions of those adventurers. Sometimes, by persuasion, I prevailed on them to desist; sometimes, also, force had to be resorted to. How could I have done otherwise? Were not the victims my own countrymen, friends and associates? Could I leave them defenseless, exposed to the assaults of foreigners, who, on the pretext that they were Mexicans, treated them worse than brutes? Sound reason and the dictates of humanity would have precluded a different conduct on my part.

On my return to San Antonio [in 1842], several persons told me that the Mexican officers had declared that I was in their favor. This rumor, and some threats uttered against me by Goodman, left me but little doubt that my enemies would try to ruin me. . . . Reports were widely spreading about my pretended treason. Captain Manuel Flores, Lieutenant Ambrosio Rodriguez, Matias Curbier, and five or six other Mexicans, dismounted with me to find out the origin of the imposture. I went out with several friends, leaving Curbier in my house. I had reached the Main Plaza, when several persons came running to inform me, that some Americans were murdering Curbier. We ran back to the house, where we found poor Curbier covered with blood. On being asked who assaulted him, he answered, that the gunsmith Goodman, in company with several Americans, had struck him with a rifle. A few minutes afterwards, Goodman returned to my house, with about thirty volunteers, but, observing that we were prepared to meet them, they did not attempt to attack us. We went out of the house and then to Mr. Guilbeau's, who offered me his protection. He went out into the street, pistol in hand, and succeeded in dispersing the mob, which had formed in front of my house. Mr. John Twohig [*sic*] offered me a shelter for that night; on the next morning, I went under disguise to Mr. Van Ness' house; Twohig, who recognized me in the street, warned me to "open my eyes." I remained one day at Mr. Van Ness'; next day General Burleson arrived in San Antonio, commanding a respectable force of volunteers. I presented myself to him, asking for a Court of Inquiry; he answered, that there were no grounds for such proceedings. . . .

I remained, hiding from rancho to rancho, for over fifteen days. Every party of volunteers en route to San Antonio, declared, "they wanted to kill Seguin." I could no longer go from farm to farm, and determined to go on to my own farm and raise fortifications.

Several of my relatives and friends joined me. Hardly a day elapsed without receiving notice that a party was preparing to attack me; we were constantly kept under arms. Several parties came in sight, but, probably seeing that we were prepared to receive them, refrained from attacking. On the 30th of April, a friend from San Antonio sent me word that Captain Scott, and his company, were coming down by the river, burning the ranchos on their way. The inhabitants of the lower ranchos called on us for aid against Scott. With those in my house, and others to the number of about 100, I started to lend them aid. I proceeded, observing the movements of Scott, from the junction of the Medina to Pajaritos. At that place we dispersed, and I returned to my wretched life. In those days I could not go to San Antonio without peril of my life.

Matters being in this state, I saw that it was necessary to take some step which would place me in security, and save my family from constant wretchedness. I had to leave Texas, abandon all, for which had fought and spent my fortune, to become a wanderer. The ingratitude of those, who had assumed to themselves the right on convicting me, their credulity in declaring me a traitor, on mere rumors, when I had to plead in my favor the loyal patriotism with which I had always served Texas, wounded me deeply.

Seeing that all these plans were impracticable, I resolved to see a refuge amongst my enemies, braving all dangers. But before taking this step, I sent in my resignation to the

Corporation of San Antonio as Mayor of the city, stating to them, that, unable any longer to suffer the persecutions of some ungrateful Americans, who strove to murder me, I had determined to free my family and friends from their continual misery on my account, and go and live peaceably in Mexico. That for these reasons I resigned my office, with all my privileges and honors as a Texan.

I left Bexar without any engagements towards Texas; my service paid by persecutions, exiled and deprived of my privileges as a Texas citizen, I was in this country a being out of the pale of society, and when she could not protect the rights of her citizens, they were privileged to seek protection elsewhere. I had been tried by a rabble condemned without a hearing, and consequently was at liberty to provide for my own safety.

After the expedition of General Woll, I did not return to Texas till the treaty of Guadalupe Hidalgo. During my absence nothing appeared that could stamp me as a traitor. My enemies had accomplished their object; they had killed me politically in Texas and the less they spoke of me, the less risk they incurred of being exposed in the infamous means they had used to accomplish my ruin.

. . . The rumor, that I was a traitor, was seized with avidity by my enemies in San Antonio. Some envied my military position, as held by a *Mexican*; others found in me an obstacle to the accomplishment of their villainous plans. The number of land suits which still encumber the docket of Bexar County, would indicate the nature of these plans and any one, who has listened to the evidence elicited in cases of this description, will readily discover the base means adopted to deprived rightful owners of their property.

I have finished my memoirs; I neither have the capacity nor the desire to adorn my acts with literary phrases. I have attempted a short and clear narrative of my public life, in relation to Texas. I give it publicity, without omitting or suppressing anything that I thought of the least interest, and confidently I submit to the public verdict.

Several of those who witnessed the facts which I have related, are still alive and amongst us; they can state whether I have in any way falsified the record.

Francisco P. Ramírez (1837–?)

Editorials

Ramírez was only seventeen years old when he began editing *El Clamor Público*, but despite his young age, he was very successful in creating a voice for the Mexican citizens of California. Ramírez in the beginning was an ardent supporter of Mexicans assimilating into U.S. culture, which is evident by his support for Mexicans learning English, California statehood, and his belief in the U.S. Constitution. However, as time passed, his indignation grew as he realized that equality under U.S. law did not exist for Mexicans. Ramírez's editorials can be seen as precursors to the Chicano movement as every week he set out to denounce the wrongdoings afflicted upon Mexicans. Ramírez argues that in a country where slavery is permitted, Manifest Destiny is institutionalized, and its newly found citizens are denounced as "greasers," it is impossible for liberties to exist despite their guarantee by the U.S. Constitution. In the editorial "Inquisition," Ramírez reproves the hypocrisy of the justice system that prevails in the United States and how it is implemented by vigilantism and even the lynching of Mexicans. Ramírez uses his newspaper as a catalyst for political involvement of his fellow

Mexicans and, more important, to defend the legal rights of his compatriots, rights that were not being protected by the U.S. government. (SH)

Further reading: Francisco Ramírez, Editorial, *El Clamor Público* [Los Angeles], July 24, 1855, p. 22; "Inquisición," *El Clamor Público* [Los Angeles], Aug. 28, 1855, p. 42; Nicolás Kanellos, *Hispanic Periodicals in the United States: A Brief History and Comprehensive Bibliography* (Houston: Arte Público Press, 2000).

Trans.: PP

Editorial, July 24, 1855

The United States' conception of freedom is truly curious. This much-lauded freedom is imaginary. We think that a man is not truly free when he is obligated to pay a tax for so many doors and windows, even for the air he breathes. In our opinion, freedom is what all rational creation has a right to make use of as it sees fit, conforming to reason and justice. There are three species of freedom: natural, civil, and political, or rather, freedom of man, freedom of the citizen, and freedom of the nation. Natural freedom is the right man enjoys by nature to make use of it according to his free will, in keeping with the purpose for which he was raised. Civil freedom is the right that links all citizens to society so that they can do as they please when it is not to the contrary of the established laws. And lastly, political or national freedom is the right that all nations have to work for themselves independently of another nation, to be subject or servile to no tyrant. But here in this fabulous country, he who robs and assassinates the most is he who enjoys freedom. Certain people have no kind of freedom—this freedom, we say, is that which the courts deny to all individuals of color. To buy a man for money, to hang or burn him alive arbitrarily, is another great liberty which any individual has here, according to his likes. This happens in the United States, where slavery is tolerated, where the most vile despotism reigns unchecked—in the middle of a nation that they call the "Model Republic." It is enough that these institutions are unique in a country that tries to consume everything due to its "Manifest Destiny." Ultimately, we here in California have been favored by our "Model Legislature," with two laws so original that they have no equal in the annals of any civilized nation. These are the Sunday law and the famous vagrant law. The former prohibits dances and other innocent diversions on Sunday, on pain of incarceration and fine for all those who infringe on the decree, as if to force people to stay at home to fast and pray to the Almighty for our welfare. (Wouldn't it be better to pray so that he would free us from such legislatures?) The supposition that people are made more moral by taking away their past-times and diversions is truly ridiculous. The latter is that which affects our Californian and Mexican population directly. They particularly distinguish us by the title of Greasers. This law has served to widen the gap that has existed for some time between the foreigners and the natives.

Inquisition

On our first page we published the resolutions adopted by the good people of the county of Amador, immediately after they hung three Mexicans arbitrarily and without any justice. This proceeding on the part of the American public has filled with indignation all the descendents of the Spanish race. The authorities of a country should look after the safety of its citizens, and it is incumbent on them to judge and punish the criminal; but an infuriated mob does not have the right to take the life of a man without being certain that he has committed the crime charged. To expel all Mexican inhabitants for a crime in which they had no part, and if they were allied, as they say, with various Americans and Chileans in committing it, then their comrades should also pay the same penalty the Mexicans do. Why don't they do the same with the Americans that took part in this crime? It is true that in Mexico, as in all other parts of the world, there are bad men, but it must be also admitted that there are many good men that earn their subsistence through honorable methods, and who revere the laws of this country.

We read in the *Sacramento State Tribune*: "We know that the people of Ranchería and their neighbors, exasperated by the brutal assassinations committed recently in this area, are indiscriminately killing all the Spanish and Greasers that they find."

Since the year of 1849 a certain animosity (so contrary to a magnanimous and free people) has existed between the Mexicans and Americans, to such an extent that the Americans have wished with all their heart that all the Mexicans put together had no more than one head to cut off (to do away with them all at once). They have suffered many injustices, and primarily in the mines they have been abused and mistreated with impunity. If a Mexican is unfortunate enough to have a case in the state courts, he will lose for sure. It is impossible to negate these assertions because we know many unhappy people that this has happened to after the efforts they have made to obtain their rights and impartial justice.

Pablo de la Guerra (1819–1874)

The Californios (Editorial, April 25, 1856 [?])

The scion of an important Californio family from Santa Barbara, de la Guerra was one of the few natives to take part in the constitutional convention to create the state of California in 1850. In addition to protesting policy before the legislature as it affected the Hispanics, de la Guerra also assumed the responsibility of defending the Amerindians through numerous speeches. In his 1860 speech *The Californios*, published in Spanish in Los Angeles's *El Clamor Público* newspaper, de la Guerra attacked the practices by which land rights were adjudicated under U.S. and California law. In this heart-rending description of the disenfranchisement of the Californios, de la Guerra used one of the phrases that best characterized the condition of the native peoples: "foreigners in their own land." The same year, 1860, that de la Guerra delivered this speech, he decided to leave the legislature and run for a position as judge in Santa Barbara, a position that he won and held until his death. (EA)

Further reading: Joseph E. Cassidy, "Life and Times of Pablo de la Guerra," Ph.D. diss., University of California at Santa Barbara, 1977.

Trans.: PP

Who are the defendants? They are the conquered, prostrated in front of the conquerors, asking for protection in their enjoyment of the little their bad luck has left them. They are those who have been sold like sheep; they are those who were abandoned and sold by

Mexico. They don't understand the prevalent tongue of their land of birth. They are foreigners in their own country. They have no voice in this Senate, excepting that which is now speaking so weakly in their favor. I do not blame anyone who doesn't think over this question closely; they haven't closely examined both sides. But I have. I have seen elders of sixty and seventy years cry like children because they have been thrown out of the home of their parents. They have been humiliated and insulted. They have been denied the privilege of using their own well. They have been denied the privilege of cutting their own firewood. Yet still the individuals who committed these outrages have come here to look for protection, and, to my great surprise, the Senate has sympathized with them. You, Senators, did not listen to the complaints of the Spanish class. You did not sufficiently consider the fairness of their land deeds and their just rights to their possessions.

The Senators have said that the residents have fair rights; that they have worked in good faith; that they have occupied lands without proof, demarcations, limits, or paper to distinguish them from the public domain; and that having worked in good faith, they should be paid for their improvements. Well, if the object was simply to protect the rights of those who had established themselves with good faith, the compensation would have been adopted immediately; but the Senators of Sonoma and Sacramento have told us that this would destroy the bill. For this reason, I think that your object is to protect those settlers in *bad faith*. Any impartial man who examines the law would see that it protects the squatter, and that law, for better or worse, dispossesses the owner of the land of his just rights—inviolable rights, by human or divine laws. . . .

Let us consider the fairness of the situation. The owner possessed large portions of lands, which, in many cases, have belonged to the same family for more than half a century. By the law passed by the Land Commission, they were obligated to present their deed. In my county we have calculated that what has gone to pay just the lawyers to defend the deeds before the commission is greater than a third part of the value of the property. In all the cases decided in favor of the owner, they appealed to the District Court, and even after this they make another appeal to the high tribunal of the nation—the Supreme Court of the United States. To complete the extraordinary litigations, they took another third part of our property. So what was left to the owner?

We should demonstrate a little consideration. Aside from these unjust and illegal costs, we are obligated to pay contributions that are greater than one million pesos, and to pay those expenses we have found ourselves compelled to sell our personal property and part of our lands to save the remaining—to save this land sacredly and solemnly guaranteed us by means of a treaty with the Mexican nation. And when, after suffering all these injustices and surviving all types of injuries, now we find a Legislature hungry to rob us of our last centavo simply because the squatters are more numerous than the natives of California.

Juan Nepomuceno Cortina (1824–1892)

Proclamation

The 1848 Treaty of Guadalupe Hidalgo that ended the U.S.-Mexican War supposedly protected the rights of Mexicans who became naturalized U.S. citizens in the newly acquired territories. These were rights guaranteed under the provisions of the U.S. Constitution. However, with the exception of the free exercise of religion, the constitutional rights and guarantees of U.S. citizens of Mexican descent were systematically violated well into the twentieth century. Municipal, state, and federal officials frequently conspired with wealthy landowners, politicians, and lawyers to deprive these newly naturalized citizens of their properties and land grants through illegal means. The Mexican-American population frequently resisted these and other injustices committed against them. So-called social bandits spearheaded guerrilla warfare against Anglo authorities during much of the nineteenth and early twentieth centuries. One such social bandit, Juan Nepomuceno Cortina, popularly known as the "Red Robber of the Rio Grande," led a band of men united by resistance to Anglo injustices. He and his men made many successful raids against Anglo military and quasimilitary forces in the Brownsville, Texas-Matamoros, and Tamaulipas area from about 1859 to 1875. Cortina issued the following 1859 *Proclamation* to the citizens of Texas—especially the population of Brownsville—declaring the right of Mexican Americans to defend themselves against Anglo injustices by pursuing and punishing the perpetrators of crimes including assassinations and the theft of land. Cortina and sixty of his men occupied Brownsville until the Mexican consul persuaded them to leave the city. (ChT)

Further reading: Carlos E. Cortés, ed., *Juan Nepomuceno Cortina: Two Interpretations* (New York: Arno Press, 1974).

Trans.: TEW

Fellow citizens: An issue of grave importance, in which luck has it I have had the opportunity to participate as a principal actor since the morning of the 28th day of this month [September], has you anxious and afraid, perhaps of its consequences and progress. You do not have to fear, because orderly people and upright citizens and their interests are inviolable to us. Our objective, as you are aware, and whose record you cannot deny, has been to punish our enemies' shameless behavior, which thus far has gone unpunished. They have plotted amongst themselves and, so to speak, form a perfidious, inquisitorial lodge to persecute and rob us without reason and for no other motive or crime than that of being of Mexican origin; they deem us, without a doubt, lacking in the leadership qualities that they themselves do not have.

In order to defend ourselves, and making use of the sacred right of self-preservation, we have gathered together in a mass meeting to discuss putting an end to our ills.

The combination of origin, parentage and commonality of injury has been, so to speak, the cause for which we, exhibiting our most obvious exasperation, have directly embraced the proposed objective upon setting foot in our pretty city.

With the meeting organized and presided over by me, by the grace of the trust that I inspire in you as one of those most aggrieved, we have gone through the streets of the city in search of our antagonists, wanting to punish them, as the authority of the law as administered by their own hands, unfortunately, has not had the desired effect. Some of them, as afraid as they are remiss to respect our demands, have perished for having wanted to carry their malevolence beyond the limits permitted by their fragile situation. Three of them, all criminals and notorious among the people for their transgressions, have died. The others, still more unworthy and miserable, dragged themselves through the mud to elude our anger and now, perhaps, with their boasting, intend to be the cause of infinite evils through cowardice. They hid themselves, and we knew where they were; but we refused to attack them in the enclosure of other people's quarters so as to not bear the burden of seeing respectable people confused in their cause, as has actually occurred in the end.

Moreover, we should reject as unjust the alarmist motive and the character that they have wanted to give to the affair. Some of them have even taken their short-sightedness to the point of imploring the protection of Mexico and alleging as a reason that their goods and persons were exposed to vandalism. So what? Were any outrages committed during the time that we took possession of the city which allowed us to be the arbiters of their destiny? Could our enemies be so blind, petty, or incensed that they would refuse to accept the truth of the events? Is there anyone who will say they were robbed, hurt, or that his house was set on fire?

The unfortunate D. Viviano García was a victim of his own generous behavior. Faced with such an unfortunate example, we gave up on our objective, horrified perhaps to have to spill the blood of the innocent without the assurance, in the least, that the villains, if they were less cowardly, would have accepted our challenge.

As we have said, these men, along with a multitude of lawyers, constitute a conspiracy and its branches to dispossess the Mexicans of their lands and to usurp them immediately. Proof is in the conduct of one Adolfo Giavecke, who, entrusted as a deputy, and in accord with the above-mentioned lawyers, has spread terror among the gullible, making them believe that he will hang Mexicans using whichever accusation possible, or that he will burn their ranches, etc., so as to obligate them, in this way, to abandon the territory and thus, achieve his goal. This is not a supposition, it is the truth, and in the absence of another scenario, when this threat is no longer pervasive, everyone will be convinced of what some men, who are as criminal as Marshal, the Warden, Morris, Neale, etc., are capable of.

The first of these, in his history and behavior, always has been infamous and treacherous. He is the assassin of the unfortunate Colonel Cross, of Captain Woolsey, of Antonio Mireles, who was assassinated at the "Las Prietas" Ranch, the scene of these murders. In short, the traitor, instigating some and helping others, has supervised a thousand transgressions and, to vindicate himself and make the witnesses of his deprivations disappear, has been the first to pursue us to the death. The others, more or less, have the same pattern of ignominy, and we no longer will tolerate them in our bosom because they are deleterious to tranquility and our own well-being.

There can be no truce between us and them because of the circumstance of our having interests and property in this territory. Nor can there be a truce with the misfortunes weighing upon the unfortunate Republic of Mexico having obligated us, for political reasons, to abandon her and to relinquish our possessions there; she was a victim of our feelings, or of the indignities to which her own position reduced us, since the period of the treaty of Guadalupe. Then the laborious, enthusiasts—savoring the appetizing goodness of liberty in the classic country of their origin—induced us to naturalize ourselves and to be part of the confederative society here. We were promised the most luxurious and calm future living here and the chance to inculcate in our children the feeling of gratitude toward a country under whose shadow we would have cultivated their happiness. Our contribution would have been our good conduct, testimony to the whole world that all the aspirations of the Mexicans can be reduced to one, which is to be free. And having attained this, these villains would have no other end to their misfortune than to lament having lost a piece of land. They would have the satisfaction that their old citizens live peacefully, as if Providence were affording them an example of the benefits of serenity and public tranquility. In reality, all of this has been nothing more than a dream, and our hopes defrauded in the most cruel way misfortune can wound. What is left is for us to make an effort—there could not be, scrupulously, any other solution to our problem—and with one fatal blow destroy the obstacle to our prosperity.

It is necessary: the time has come, there are no more than six or seven oppressors. Hospitality and some other noble feelings protect them, for now, from our rage, and the laws of humanity are to us inviolable, as you have seen.

No more innocent people will die. No. Moreover, if need be, we will live itinerantly and await the opportunity to seek revenge and purge society of some people who are so low that they debase it with their shameful conduct. Our families have turned into strangers, begging for a haven in their former homeland. Our property, if it has to be the prey of the miserly greed of our enemies, then it shall be, which is better than if it were victim of our own vicissitudes. In terms of the land, Nature concedes to us whatever is needed to support ourselves, and we accept all of the associated consequences. Our personal enemies will not possess our land, except by paying for it with their own blood.

Even so, we are left with the hope that the government, by its own dignity and justice, accedes to our demand, pursuing and passing judgment on those men or allowing them to be subjected to the consequences of our immutable resolution.

The only thing left for me to say is that accidentally segregated from the other neighbors of the city by being outside of it, but not renouncing our rights as North American citizens, we energetically condemn and protest the action of the Mexican National Guard having crossed the border to interfere in a question so foreign to that country, that there is no way to forgive such weakness by those who requested it.

Anonymous

Joaquín Murieta; The Ballad of Gregorio Cortez (Joaquín Murieta; Ballade de Gregorio Cortez)

The following two selections come from the corrido (ballad) tradition. The corrido evolved from the *romance corrido*, a narrative song form that the Spanish brought to the New World in the sixteenth century. The corrido along the Texas–Mexico border often reflects the heightened tension associated with intercultural conflict between Anglos and Texans of Mexican descent from about 1848 through the Second World War. Border corridos typically feature an epic Mexican-American hero who, through his acts of defying Anglo authority, expresses the collective resistance to oppression and injustice. Today, corridos composed and sung in Mexico as well as throughout the southwestern United States may vary musically and formally from tradtional corridos but they have retained their narrative quality. They relate in song a wide variety of themes, including migration, political figures and happenings, assassinations, incidents related to smuggling and drug trafficking, and sports events and figures. *Joaquín Murieta* is an example of a corrido that features an epic hero. Unlike the typical border corrido that takes place along the Texas–Mexico border, this one is about the exploits of a California hero who according to legendary history was an honest Mexican miner in northern California in the early 1850s. Most corridos, as well as prose fiction versions of Murieta's exploits, paint him as a simple man who turns to social banditry in order to defend against the injustices perpetrated by Anglos. This particular version contains a heavy dose of boasting and self-aggrandizement. *Gregorio Cortez*, on the other hand, is a prototypical epic hero corrido that thrived along the Texas–Mexico border. It focuses on a tragic misunderstanding between a Texas-Mexican rancher and Anglo lawmen that resulted in two shootings and Cortez's flight from prosecution. Local balladeers wrote many versions of these events. (ChT)

Further reading: Américo Paredes, *El Corrido de Gregorio Cortez, a Ballad of Border Conflict* (Austin: University of Texas Press, 1956), *A Texas-Mexican Cancionero* (Urbana: University of Illinois Press, 1975).

Trans.: MAT, MFO

Joaquín Murieta

I am not an American
But I understand English.
I learned it with my brother
Forwards and backwards
And any American
I make tremble at my feet.

When I was barely a child
I was left an orphan.
No one gave me any love,
They killed my brother,
And my wife Carmelita,
The cowards murdered her.

I came from Hermosillo
In search of gold and riches.
The Indian poor and simple
I defended with fierceness,
And a good price the sheriffs
Would pay for my head.

From the greedy rich,
I took away their money.
With the humble and poor,

Joaquín Murieta

Yo no soy americano
pero comprendo el inglés.
Yo lo aprendí con mi hermano
al derecho y al revés.
A cualquier americano
lo hago temblar a mis pies.

Cuando apenas era niño
huérfano a mí me dejaron.
Nadie me hizo ni un cariño,
a mi hermano lo mataron,
Y a mi esposa Carmelita
Cobardes la asesinaron.

Yo me vine de hermosillo
en busca de oro y riqueza.
Al indio pobre y sencillo
lo defendí con fiereza
Y a buen precio los sherifes
pagaban por mi cabeza.

A los ricos avarientos
yo les quité su dinero.
Con los humildes y pobres

I took off my hat.
Oh, what laws so unjust
To call me a highwayman.

Murieta does not like
To be falsely accused.
I come to avenge my wife,
And again I repeat it,
Carmelita so lovely
How they made her suffer.

Through bars I went
Punishing Americans.
"You must be the captain
Who killed my brother,
You grabbed him defenseless,
You stuck-up American."

My career began
Because of terrible scene.
When I got to seven hundred [killed]
Then my name was dreaded.
When I got to twelve hundred
Then my name was terrible.

I am the one who dominates
Even African lions.
That's why I go out on the road
To kill Americans.
Now my destiny is no other
Watch out, you people!

Pistols and daggers
Are playthings for me.
Bullets and stabbings
Big laughs for me.
With their means cut off
They're afraid around here.

I'm neither a Chilean nor a stranger
On this soil which I tread
California is Mexico's
Because God wanted it that way,
And in my stitched serape,
I carry my baptismal certificate.

yo me quité mi sombrero.
Ay, qué leyes tan injustas
fue llamarme bandolero.

A Murieta no le gusta
lo que hace no es desmentir.
Vengo a vengar a mi esposa,
y lo vuelvo a repetir,
Carmelita tan hermosa,
cómo la hicieron sufrir.

Por cantinas me metí,
castigando americanos.
"Tú serás el capitán
que mataste a mi hermano.
Lo agarraste indefenso,
orgulloso americano."

Mi carrera comenzó
por una escena terrible.
Cuando llegué a setecientos
ya mi nombre era temible.
Cuando llegué a mil doscientos
ya mi nombre era terrible.

Yo soy aquél que dominó
hasta leones africanos.
Por eso salgo al camino
a matar americanos.
Ya no es otro mi destino
¡pon cuidado, parroquianos!

Las pistolas y las dagas
son juguetes para mí.
Balazos y puñaladas,
carcajadas para mí.
Ahora con medios cortados
ya se asustan por aquí.

No soy chileno ni extraño
en este suelo que piso.
De México es California,
porque Dios así lo quiso,
Y en mi sarape cosido
traigo mi fe de bautismo.

How pretty is California
With her well-laid-out streets,
Where Murieta passed by
With his troops,
With his loaded pistol,
And his silver-plated saddle.

I've had a good time in California
Through the year of '50 [1850]
With my silver-plated saddle
And my pistol loaded
I am that Mexican
By the name of Joaquín Murieta.

Qué bonito es California
con sus calles alineadas,
donde paseaba Murieta
con su tropa bien formada,
con su pistola repleta
y su montura plateada.

Me he paseado en California
por el año del cincuenta,
Con mi montura plateada
y mi pistola repleta.
Y soy ese mexicano
de nombre Joaquín Murieta.

The Ballad of Gregorio Cortez

In the county of El Carmen
Look what has occurred,
The Major Sheriff is dead,
And Ramón lies gravely hurt.

The very next morning
When the people had arrived,
They said to one another:
"No one knows who committed the crime."

They went about asking questions,
And after a three-hour quest,
They discovered that the wrongdoer
Had been Gregorio Cortez.

Now Cortez is outlawed,
In the whole state he is banned,
Let him be taken dead or alive,
Several have died at his hands.

Then said Gregorio Cortez,
With his pistol in his hand:
"I'm not sorry that I killed him,
My brother's death I would not stand."

Then said Gregorio Cortez,
With his soul all aflame:
"I'm not sorry that I killed him,
Self-defense is my rightful claim."

Ballade de Gregorio Cortez

En el condado del Carmen
miren lo que ha sucedido.
Murió el sherife mayor
quedando Román herido.

Otro día por la mañana
cuando la gente llegó
Unos a los otros dicen
no saben quién lo mató.

Se anduvieron informando
como tres horas después
Supieron que el malhechor
era Gregorio Cortez.

Insortaron a Cortez
por toditito el estado.
Vivo o muerto que se aprenda
porque a varios ha matado.

Decía Gregorio Cortez
con su pistola en la mano,
"No siento haberlo matado,
al que siento es a mi hermano."

Decía Gregorio Cortez
con su alma muy encendida
"No siento haberlo matado
la defensa es permitida."

The Americans started coming,
Their horses seemed to soar,
Because they were all after
The three-thousand-dollar reward.

Venían los americanos
que por el viento volaban,
porque se iban a ganar
tres mil pesos que les daban.

He set out for González,
Several sheriffs saw him go,
They decided not to follow
As they all feared him so.

Siguió con rumbo a González,
varios sherifes lo vieron,
no lo quisieron seguir
porque le tuvieron miedo.

The bloodhounds began coming,
His trail took them afar,
But tracking down Cortez
Was like following a star.

Venían los perros jaundes
venían sobre la huella
Pero alcanzar a Cortez
era alcanzar a una estrella.

Then said Gregorio Cortez:
"Why bother scheming around,
When you can't even catch me
With all of your bloodhounds?"

Decía Gregorio Cortez
"Pa' qué se valen de planes,
si no pueden agarrarme
ni con esos perros jaundes."

Then said the Americans:
"If we catch him, what should we do?
If we fight him man to man,
The survivors will be few."

Decían los americanos
"Si lo vemos qué le haremos
si le entramos por derecho
muy poquitos volveremos."

He left Brownsville for the ranch,
Some three hundred in that locale
Succeeded in surrounding him,
But he jolted their corral.

En el redondel del rancho
le alcanzaron a rodear.
Poquitos más de trescientos
y allí les brincó el corral.

Over by El Encinal,
According to what is said,
They got into a gunfight,
And he shot another sheriff dead.

Allá por el Encinal
a según por lo que dicen
Se agarraron a balazos
y les mató otro sherife.

Then said Gregorio Cortez,
With his pistol in his hand:
"Don't run off, cowardly rangers,
From one sole Mexican man."

Decía Gregorio Cortez
con su pistola en la mano,
"No corran rinches cobardes
con un solo mexicano."

He struck out for Laredo,
With no fear in his breast:
"Follow me, spineless rangers,
For I am Gregorio Cortez."

Giró con rumbo a Laredo
sin ninguna timidez.
"Síganme rinches cobardes,
yo soy Gregorio Cortez."

Gregorio says to Juan
At the ranch they call Cypress:
"Tell me all the news,
For I am Gregorio Cortez."

Gregorio says to Juan:
"Now you just wait and see,
Go and call the sheriffs,
Tell them to arrest me."

When the sheriffs got there
Gregorio gave himself up to go:
"You can take me because I'm willing.
If you force me, the answer's no."

They've finally caught Cortez,
It's over now, they claim,
And his poor sad family
In their hearts must bear the pain.

With this I bid farewell
In the shade of a cypress,
And thus are sung the final notes
Of the ballad of Gregorio Cortez.

Gregorio le dice a Juan
en el rancho del Ciprés,
"Platícame qué hay de nuevo,
yo soy Gregorio Cortez."

Gregorio le dice a Juan,
"Muy pronto lo vas a ver,
anda háblale a los sherifes
que me vengan a aprender."

Cuando llegan los sherifes
Gregorio se presentó
"Por la buena sí me llevan
porque de otro modo, no."

Ya agarraron a Cortez
ya terminó la cuestión,
la pobre de su familia
la lleva en el corazón.

Ya con esta me despido
con la sombra de un ciprés
Aquí se acaba cantando
la tragedia de Cortez.

Miguel Antonio Otero, Jr. (1859–1944)

The Real Billy the Kid (excerpt)

Miguel Antonio Otero lived his life as a privileged member of New Mexico's landed gentry and was appointed governor of the territory during the period it was striving for statehood. Otero was a public figure whose life mirrored the transformation of New Mexico—his father descended from an old, distinguished New Mexican family dating back to colonial days and his mother from an Anglo family representing the new order. The beneficiary of an elite college education back east, Otero was not only a politician but an intellectual, and was one of the first Nuevomexicanos to publish his memoirs in English: a nostalgic autobiography, *My Life on the Frontier*, 1864–1882 (1935); two additional volumes followed, *My Life on the Frontier, 1882–1897*, and *My Nine Years as Governor of the Territory of New Mexico, 1897–1906*. The latter two titles of his autobiographical trilogy were not finished until 1940. Between publication of the first and second volumes of his trilogy, Otero became one of the first Nuevomexicanos to write an English-language biography, *The Real Billy the Kid, with New Light on the Lincoln County War* (1936), published twenty-nine years after his life as a politician had ended. In it, Otero recounts his personal experiences with Billy the Kid and the Lincoln County War, a conflict of natives versus newcomers that would greatly affect Nuevomexicano and Anglo political culture. One can sense the ambivalence about the old and new ways that characterized Otero's life, as well as his effort to challenge the civilizing myths that justified Anglo dominance in the Southwest. Otero's historical biography is also the first to transcribe various oral histories of Billy the Kid that existed among the native Nuevomexicanos from the geographic areas that involved the war in Lincoln. (JMR)

Further reading: Miguel Antonio Otero, Jr., *The Real Billy the Kid, with New Light on the Lincoln County War*, ed. and introduced by John-Michael Rivera (Houston: Arte Público Press, 1998).

Chapter Thirteen: When the Author Met the Kid

My own meeting with Billy the Kid was coincidental. On the morning of December 23, 1880, Pat Garrett, Frank Stewart, Lon Chambers, Lee Hall, Louis Bozeman, alias "The Animal," James East, Barney Mason, Tom Emory, alias "Poker Tom," and Bob Williams killed Charlie Bowdre and captured Billy the Kid, Dave Rudabaugh, Billy Wilson and Tom Pickett.

Shortly after The Kid and his companions had taken refuge in a little rock house, Pat Garrett closed around them. The posse besieged the little house all night, and when Charlie Bowdre appeared at the door early next morning, Garrett, giving unmistakable indication of the nature of his quest, shot and killed Bowdre. It may be true, as Garrett claimed, that he mistook Bowdre for The Kid because of the hat he was wearing—a hat which supposedly resembled The Kid's. However, the act was a manifestation of the Garrett spirit. The Kid and the remaining three of his company proposed terms of surrender with promise of protection of their lives until they could be tried, to which Garrett agreed.

In seeking a jail secure enough to hold the four outlaws, Garrett turned toward Santa Fé. Since the nearest railroad station was East Las Vegas, he carried his prisoners thither, heavily shackled, and with an escort of mounted deputies. The news that the noted desperadoes were coming through Las Vegas brought together large numbers of people curious to see them.

Albert E. Hyde was in Las Vegas at the time, a guest at the Grand View Hotel, where I also happened to be stopping. Years later, Hyde wrote a magazine article giving a graphic account of the entry of Garrett's party into Las Vegas:

"It was a beautiful afternoon, the elevation of the hotel affording a wide vision across the plains. As the hours passed waiting for their arrival, the crowds became impatient and skeptical when, from our point of vantage, we suddenly discerned a cloud of dust in the southwest. When it advanced closely enough and the people saw a wagon outfit accompanied by mounted men, a mighty shout went up. The news was true! Billy the Kid was a prisoner and Pat Garrett was a hero."

As the wagon approached, we saw four men sitting in the bed, two on either side, facing each other. The Kid, whom Dr. Sutfin had known in his cowboy days and instantly recognized, was on the side nearest us, chained to a fierce-looking, dark bearded man who kept his slouch hat pulled down over his eyes, looking neither to the right nor to the left. He was the daring and dangerous Dave Rudabaugh who had killed the Mexican jailer at Las Vegas a short time before. He feared recognition because he knew the Mexican population thirsted for his blood. The other two prisoners were Pickett and Wilson, prominent members of The Kid's gang.

Billy the Kid was in a joyous mood. He was a short, slender, beardless young man. The marked peculiarity of his face was a pointed chin and a short upper lip which exposed his large front teeth, giving a chronic grin to his expression. He wore his hat pushed far back, and jocularly greeted the crowd. Recognizing Dr. Sutfin, he called, "Hello, Doc! Thought I'd drop in to see how you fellows in Vegas are behavin' yourselves."

Heavily armed deputies rode on each side of the wagon, with two bringing up the rear. Garrett rode in front and was obviously annoyed as well as surprised at the large crowds. Fearing for the safety of Rudabaugh, he turned and ordered the mule driver to run across the plaza to the jail.

Garrett heard during the next few hours that an attempt was about to be made to lynch Rudabaugh. He promptly increased his force to thirty men, who guarded the jail that night. He proposed to take the prisoners to Santa Fé for safe-keeping the following morning, but his plans were kept secret.

The next morning he began preparations to move them to Santa Fé by railroad, but he had great difficulty in getting the San Miguel County officials to allow him to take Rudabaugh along. Local sentiment was strongly against it now that he was back at the scene of his crime. Garrett protested that he held his prisoners under a United States warrant and that he had precedence over the local officials. Despite the crowd's protests, Garrett placed his prisoners in a closed carriage and got them to the railroad station, where a group of Las Vegas officials had already assembled. Again Garrett had to put up an argument for taking Dave Rudabaugh.

Under heavy guard he succeeded in getting his prisoners aboard the train. A mob had collected and was surrounding the train. Garrett stood on the platform calmly awaiting developments and said: "I promised these men I would deliver them to the Sheriff of Santa Fé County or to the United States Marshal at Santa Fé. If you people insist on trying to take them away from me, I will arm every one of them and turn them loose to defend themselves as best they can. What's more, all my officers and I will assist in protecting them."

When Pat Garrett finished talking, my father, Miguel A. Otero, mounted the platform and stood beside him. He shook Garrett's hand, and turning to the mob, speaking first in Spanish and then in English, he said: "Gentlemen, these prisoners are in the custody of Mr. Garrett and he has given his word that he will turn them over to the proper authorities at Santa Fé. It is a very serious thing for you men to hold up the United States mail as you are doing. I appeal to you to retire at once because the consequences may be severe. Let Mr. Garrett fulfil his promise. The judge of this judicial district lives in Santa Fé, and on their arrival he will take full charge."

My father's speech had the desired effect. The officers and the mob withdrew, and the train which had been held up for about an hour pulled out on its way to Santa Fé.

The Kid was disappointed that the mob did not attack the car since it would have unquestionably resulted in his escape. He was on the friendliest of terms with the native element of the country; he had protected and helped them in every possible way. The natives would have done all in their power to have been of assistance to him. If there had been an attack, the chances were that Garrett and his companions would have been killed; Rudabaugh would have fallen into the hands of the mob and been lynched on the spot. The Kid would probably have lost himself in the crowd and disappeared from the scene.

My brother and I were so much interested that Father permitted us to go along on the train to Santa Fé. On the way we talked with Billy the Kid and Dave Rudabaugh. We knew Rudabaugh well; he had been on the police force in East Las Vegas. Though we had never seen The Kid before, we were familiar with his part in the Lincoln County War and in the reign of terror he had created.

In Santa Fé we were allowed to visit The Kid in jail, taking him cigarette papers, tobacco, chewing gum, candy, pies and nuts. He was very fond of sweets and asked us to bring him all we could. The Kid's general appearance was the same as most boys of his age. I was just one month older than Billy. I liked The Kid very much, and long before we even reached Santa Fé, nothing would have pleased me more than to have witnessed his escape. He had his share of good qualities and was very pleasant. He had a reputation for being considerate of the old, the young and the poor; he was loyal to his friends and above all, loved his mother devotedly. He was unfortunate in starting life, and became a victim of circumstances. I had been told that Billy had an ungovernable temper; however I never saw evidences of it. He was always in a pleasant humor when I saw him—laughing, sprightly and good natured.

Mrs. Jaramillo, at Fort Sumner, said of him: "Billy was a good boy, but he was hounded by men who wanted to kill him because they feared him. He was always on the defensive."

Don Martin Chavez, of Santa Fé, said of him: "Billy was a perfect gentleman and a man with a noble heart. He never killed a native citizen of New Mexico in all his career; the men he did kill, he had to in defense of his own life. He had plenty of courage. He was a brave man and did not know what fear meant. They had to sneak up on him in the dead of night to murder him."

I have known Mrs. Jaramillo for many years. She is a lovely woman—kind and gentle, honest and truthful in expressing her opinion of Billy the Kid. Martin Chavez is a quiet, unassuming and kindly gentleman. He has always been highly esteemed by the residents of his community. The testimonies of these two regarding the real character of The Kid carry weight. My own personal impressions corroborate those of other people. In looking back to my first meeting with Billy the Kid, my impressions were most favorable and I can honestly say that he was "a man more sinned against than sinning."

María Amparo Ruiz de Burton (1831–1895)

The Squatter and the Don

An extraordinarily talented writer whose powerful voice addressed crucial issues concerning ethnicity, power, gender, class, and race, Ruiz de Burton crafted her two novels in English from the vantage point of an acculturated Californio. Being born in Loreto, Baja California, to a cash-poor but socially privileged family, Ruiz de Burton moved to California at the end of the U.S.-Mexican War, a relocation that afforded her a certain critical distance from which to view and critique the transformations taking place in the United States. Her time on the East Coast as the wife of an U.S. Army officer provided her an opportunity for first-hand assessment of the U.S. government and culture. While living in San Diego in the early 1850s, Ruiz de Burton wrote, produced, and later published a five-act comedy based on *Don Quixote*. In 1872, she published her first novel, *Who Would Have Thought It?*, a bitingly satirical text that parodies the United States during the period of the Civil War. *The Squatter and the Don* (1885) is the first published narrative—written in English—giving the perspective of the conquered Mexican population that, despite being promised full rights of citizenship under the provisions of the 1848 Treaty of Guadalupe Hidalgo that ended the U.S.-Mexican War, was, already by 1860, a subordinated and marginalized national minority. The work reconstructs the misfortunes of many Californio families and the legal problems they faced in retaining their lands, but centers on the trials and tribulations of two "star-crossed lovers" from the Alamar and Darrell families, building on the tension between the romantic and the historical. (BP)

Further reading: *The Squatter and the Don: A Novel Descriptive of Contemporary Occurrences in California*, ed. and introduced by Rosaura Sánchez and Beatrice Pita (Houston: Arte Público Press, 1992); *Who Would Have Thought It?*, ed. and introduced by Rosaura Sánchez and Beatrice Pita (Houston: Arte Público Press, 1995).

Chapter Two: The Don's View of the Treaty of Guadalupe Hidalgo

If there had been such a thing as communicating by telephone in the days of '72, and there had been those magic wires spanning the distance between William Darrell's house in Alameda County and that of Don Mariano Alamar in San Diego County, with power to transmit the human voice for five hundred miles, a listener at either end would have heard various discussions upon the same subject, differentiated only by circumstances. No magic wires crossed San Francisco bay to bring the sound of voices to San Diego, but the law of necessity made the Squatter and the Don, distant as they were—distant in every way, without reckoning the miles between them—talk quite warmly of the same matter. The point of view was of course different, for how could it be otherwise? Darrell thought himself justified, and *authorized*, to "take up lands," as he had done before. He had had more than half of California's population on his side, and though the "*Squatter's Sovereignty*" was now rather on the wane and the "*squatter vote*" was no longer the power, still the squatters would not abdicate, having yet much to say about election times.

But Darrell was no longer the active squatter that he had been. He controlled many votes yet, but in his heart he felt the weight which his wife's sad eyes invariably put there when the talk was of litigating against a Mexican land title.

This time, however, Darrell honestly meant to take no land but what belonged to the United States. His promise to his wife was sincere, yet his coming to Southern California had already brought trouble to the Alamar rancho.

Don Mariano Alamar was silently walking up and down the front piazza of his house at the rancho; his hands listlessly clasped behind and his head slightly bent forward in deep thought. He had pushed away to one side the many armchairs and wicker rockers with which the piazza was furnished. He wanted a long space to walk. That his meditations were far from agreeable could easily be seen by the compressed lips, slight frown, and sad gaze of his mild and beautiful blue eyes. Sounds of laughter, music and dancing came from the parlor, the young people were entertaining friends from town with their usual gay hospitality, and enjoying themselves heartily. Don Mariano, though already in his fiftieth year, was as fond of dancing as his sons and daughters, and not to see him come in and join the quadrille was so singular that his wife thought she must come out and inquire what could detain him. He was so absorbed in his thoughts that he did not hear her voice calling him—"What keeps you away? Lizzie has been looking for you; she wants you for a partner in the lancers," said Doña Josefa, putting her arm under that of her husband, bending her head forward and turning it up to look into his eyes.

"What is the matter?" she asked, stopping short, thus making her husband come to a sudden halt. "I am sure something has happened. Tell me."

"Nothing, dear wife. Nothing has happened. That is to say, nothing new."

"More squatters?" she asked. Señor Alamar bent his head slightly in affirmative reply.

"More coming, you mean?"

"Yes, wife; more. Those two friends of squatters Mathews and Hagar, who were here last year to locate claims and went away, did not abandon their claims, but only went away to bring proselytes and their families, and a large invoice of them will arrive on tomorrow's steamer. The worst of it all is, that among the new comers is that terrible and most dangerous squatter William Darrell, who some years ago gave so much trouble to the Spanish people in Napa and Sonoma Counties by locating claims there. John Gasbang wrote to Hogsden that besides Darrell, there will be six or seven other men bringing their families, so that there will be more rifles for my cattle."

"But, didn't we hear that Darrell was no longer a squatter, that he is rich and living quietly in Alameda?"

"Yes, we heard that, and it is true. He is quite well off, but Gasbang and Miller and Mathews went and told him that my rancho had been rejected, and that it is near enough to town to become valuable, as soon as we have a railroad. Darrell believed it, and is coming to locate here."

"Strange that Darrell should believe such men; I suppose he does not know how low they are."

"He ought to know them, for they were his teamsters when he crossed the plains in '48. That is, Miller, Mathews, Hughes and Hager were his teamsters, and Gasbang was their cook—the cook for the hired men. Mrs. Darrell had a colored woman who cooked for the Darrell family; she despised Gasbang's cooking as we despise his character, I suppose."

Doña Josefa was silent and, holding on to her husband's arm, took a turn with him up and down the piazza.

"Is it possible that there is no law to protect us; to protect our property; what does your lawyer say about obtaining redress or protection; is there no hope?" she asked, with a sigh.

"Protection for our land, or for our cattle, you mean?"

"For both, as we get it for neither," she said.

"In the matter of our land, we have to await for the attorney general, at Washington, to decide."

"Lizzie was telling Elvira, yesterday, that her uncle Lawrence is a friend of several influential people in Washington, and that George can get him to interest himself in having your title decided."

"But, as George is to marry my daughter, he would be the last man from whom I would ask a favor."

"What is that I hear about not asking a favor from me?" said George Mechlin, coming out on the piazza with Elvira on his arm, having just finished a waltz—"I am interested to know why you would not ask it." "You know why, my dear boy. It isn't exactly the thing to bother you with my disagreeable business."

"And why not? And who has a better right? And why should it be a bother to me to help you in any way I can? My father spoke to me about a dismissal of an appeal, and I made a note of it. Let me see, I think I have it in my pocket now"—said George, feeling in his breast pocket for his memorandum book—"yes, here it is—'For uncle to write to the attorney general about dismissing the appeal taken by the squatters in the Alamar grant, against Don Mariano's title, which was approved.' Is that the correct idea? I only made this note to ask you for further particulars."

"You have it exactly. When I give you the number of the case, it is all that you need say to your uncle. What I want is to have the appeal dismissed, of course, but if the attorney general does not see fit to do so, he can, at least, remand back the case for a new trial. Anything rather than this killing suspense. Killing literally, for while we are waiting to have my title settled, the *settlers* (I don't mean to make puns) are killing my cattle by the hundred head, and I cannot stop them."

"But are there no laws to protect property in California?" George asked.

"Yes, some sort of laws, which in my case seem more intended to help the lawbreakers than to protect the law-abiding," Don Mariano replied.

"How so? Is there no law to punish the thieves who kill your cattle?"

"There are some enactments so obviously intended to favor one class of citizens against another class that to call them laws is an insult to law, but such as they are, we must submit to them. By those laws any man can come to my land, for instance, plant ten acres of grain, without any fence, and then catch my cattle which, seeing the green grass without a fence, will go to eat it. Then he puts them in a '*corral*' and makes me pay damages and so much per head for keeping them, and costs of legal proceedings and many other trumped up expenses, until for such little fields of grain I may be obliged to pay thousands of dollars. Or, if the grain fields are large enough to bring more money by keeping the cattle away, then the settler shoots the cattle at any time without the least hesitation, only taking care that no one sees him in the act of firing upon the cattle. He might stand behind a bush or tree and fire, but then he is not seen. No one can swear that they saw him actually kill the cattle, and no jury can convict him, for although the dead animals may be there, lying on the ground shot, still no one saw the settler kill them. And so it is all the time. I must pay damages and expenses of litigation, or my cattle get killed almost every day."

"But this is infamous. Haven't you—the cattle owners—tried to have some law enacted that will protect your property?" George asked. "It seems to me that could be done."

"It could be done, perhaps, if our positions were reversed, and the Spanish people—'*the natives*'—were the planters of the grain fields, and the Americans were the owners of the cattle. But as we, the Spaniards, are the owners of the Spanish—or Mexican—land grants and also the owners of the cattle ranchos, our State legislators will not make any law to protect cattle. They make laws '*to protect agriculture*' (they say proudly), which means to drive to the wall all owners of cattle ranchos. I am told that at this session of the legislature a law more strict yet will be passed, which will be ostensibly '*to protect agriculture*' but in reality to destroy cattle and ruin the native Californians. The agriculture of this State does not require legislative protection. Such pretext is absurd."

"I thought that the rights of the Spanish people were protected by our treaty with Mexico," George said.

"Mexico did not pay much attention to the future welfare of the children she left to their fate in the hands of a nation which had no sympathies for us," said Doña Josefa, feelingly.

"I remember," calmly said Don Mariano, "that when I first read the text of the treaty of Guadalupe Hidalgo, I felt a bitter resentment against my people; against Mexico, the mother country, who abandoned us—her children—with so slight a provision of obligatory stipulations for protection. But afterwards, upon mature reflection, I saw that Mexico did as much as could have been reasonably expected at the time. In the very preamble of the treaty the spirit of peace and friendship, which animated both nations, was carefully made manifest. That spirit was to be the *foundation* of the relations between the conqueror and conquered. How could Mexico have foreseen then that when scarcely half a dozen years should have elapsed the trusted conquerors would, *In Congress Assembled*,' pass laws which were to be retroactive upon the defenseless, helpless, conquered people, in order to despoil them? The treaty said that our rights would be the same as those enjoyed by all other American citizens. But, you see, Congress takes very good care not to enact retroactive laws for Americans, laws to take away from American citizens the property which they hold now, already, with a recognized legal title. No, indeed. But they do so quickly enough with us—with us, the Spano-Americans, who were to enjoy equal rights, mind you, according to the treaty of peace. This is what seems to me a breach of faith, which Mexico could neither presuppose nor prevent."

"It is nothing else, I am sorry and ashamed to say," George said. "I never knew much about the treaty with Mexico, but I never imagined we had acted so badly."

"I think but few Americans know or believe to what extent we have been wronged by Congressional action. And truly, I believe that Congress itself did not anticipate the effect of its laws upon us and how we would be despoiled, we, the conquered people," said Don Mariano, sadly.

"It is the duty of law-givers to foresee the effect of the laws they impose upon people," said Doña Josefa.

"That I don't deny, but I fear that the conquered have always but a weak voice, which nobody hears," said Don Mariano.

"We have had no one to speak for us. By the treaty of Guadalupe Hidalgo the American nation pledged its honor to respect our land titles just the same as Mexico would have done. Unfortunately, however, the discovery of gold brought to California the riff-raff of the world, and with it a horde of land-sharks, all possessing the privilege of voting, and most of them coveting our lands, for which they very quickly began to clamor. There was, and still is, plenty of good government land, which anyone can take. But no. The forbidden fruit is the sweetest. They do not want government land. They want the land of the Spanish people, because we 'have too much,' they say. So, to win their votes, the votes of the squatters, our representatives in Congress helped to pass laws declaring all lands in California open to preemption, as in Louisiana, for instance. Then, as a coating of whitewash to the stain on the nation's honor, a 'land commission' was established to examine land titles. Because, having pledged the national word to respect our rights, it would be an act of despoliation, besides an open violation of pledged honor, to take the lands without some pretext of a legal process. So then, we became obliged to present our titles before the said land commission to be examined and approved or rejected. While these legal proceedings are going on, the squatters locate their claims and raise crops on our lands, which they convert into money to fight our titles. But don't let me, with my disagreeable subject, spoil your dance. Go back to your lancers, and tell Lizzie to excuse me," said Don Mariano.

Lizzie would not excuse him. With the privilege of a future daughter-in-law, she insisted that Don Mariano should be her partner in the lancers, which would be a far pleasanter occupation than to be walking up and down the porch thinking about squatters.

Don Mariano therefore followed Lizzie to their place in the dance. Mercedes sat at the piano to play for them. The other couples took their respective positions.

The well-balanced mind and kindly spirit of Don Mariano soon yielded to the genial influences surrounding him. He would not bring his trouble to mar the pleasure of others. He danced with his children as gaily as the gayest. He insisted that Mr. Mechlin, too, should dance, and this gentleman graciously yielded and led Elvira through a quadrille, protesting that he had not danced for twenty years.

"You have not danced because you were sick, but now you are well. Don't be lazy," said Mrs. Mechlin.

"You would be paying to San Diego climate a very poor compliment by refusing to dance now," George added.

"That is so, Papa. Show us how well you feel," Lizzie said.

"I shall have to dance a hornpipe to do that," Mr. Mechlin answered, laughing.

To understand this remark better, the reader must know that Mr. James Mechlin had come to San Diego, four years previously, a living skeleton, not expected to last another winter. He had lost his health by a too close application to business, and when he sought rest and relaxation his constitution seemed permanently undermined. He tried the climate of Florida. He spent several years in Italy and in the south of France, but he felt no better. At last, believing his malady incurable, he returned to his New York home to die. In New York a friend, who also had been an invalid, but whose health had been restored in Southern California, advised him to try the salubrious air of San Diego. With but little hope and only to please his family, Mr. Mechlin came to San Diego, and his health improved so rapidly that he made up his mind to buy a country place and make San Diego his home. William Mathews heard of this and offered to sell his place on what Mr. Mechlin thought very moderate terms. A lawyer was employed to pass upon the title, and on his recommendation the purchase was made. Mr. Mechlin had the Mathews house moved back near the barn and a new and much larger one built.

Mr. Mechlin devoted himself to cultivating trees and flowers, and his health was bettered every day. This was the compensation to his wife and two daughters for exiling themselves from New York, for it was exile to Caroline and Lizzie to give up their fine house in New York City to come and live on a California rancho.

Soon, however, these two young ladies passed their time more pleasantly, after making the acquaintance of the Alamar family, and soon their acquaintance ripened into friendship, to be made closer by the intended marriage of Gabriel—Don Mariano's eldest son—to Lizzie. Shortly after, George—Mr. Mechlin's only son—came on a visit, and when he returned to New York he was already engaged to Elvira, third daughter of Señor Alamar.

Now, George Mechlin was making his second visit to his family. He had found New York so very dull and stupid on his return from California that when Christmas was approaching he told his uncle and aunt—with whom he lived—that he wanted to go and spend Christmas and New Year's Day with his family in California.

"Very well; I wish I could go with you. Give my love to James, and tell him I am delighted at his getting so well," Mr. Lawrence Mechlin said, and George had his leave of absence. Mr. Lawrence Mechlin was president of the bank of which George was cashier, so it was not difficult for him to get the assistant cashier to attend to his duties when he was away, particularly as the assistant cashier himself was George's most devoted friend. George could have only twelve days in California, but to see Elvira for even so short a time he would have traveled a much longer distance.

CHAPTER 4

Defending Cultural and Civil Rights

Eusebio Chacón (1870–1948)

A Protest Rally, 1901

Oratorical skills have always been valued in Hispanic culture and deemed a prerequisite for leadership. Eusebio Chacón was a highly respected orator, journalist, and civic leader in New Mexico and Colorado during the first half of the twentieth century. The piece included below was a speech Chacón delivered at a town meeting called "La Junta de Indignación" (The Indignation Meeting), held in Las Vegas, New Mexico, in 1901. Subsequently published in *La Voz del Pueblo* (November 12, 1901), the speech was written as a rebuttal to an article by Protestant missionary Nellie Snider published in *The Review* of Las Vegas. Born in Peñasco, New Mexico, Chacón moved with his family to Trinidad, Colorado, where he received his early education. He returned to New Mexico to study at the Jesuit Las Vegas College and received his law degree from Notre Dame in 1889. In 1892 *El Boletin Popular* in Santa Fe published, under one cover, two short novellas written by Chacón: *Hijo de la tempestad* and *Tras la tormenta la calma* (*Son of the Tempest* and *Calm After the Storm*). They stand as the first examples of fiction published in New Mexico in a venue other than a newspaper. (EGB)

Further reading: Eusebio Chacón, *Hijo de la tempestad; Tras la tormenta la calma: Dos novelitas originales* (Santa Fe, N.M.: El Boletín Popular, 1982), "Descubrimiento y conquista de Nuevo Mexico en 1540 por los españoles," *Las Dos Repúblicas,* March 7, May 23, 1896.

Gentlemen:

The commission entrusted with conducting this meeting has assigned me the difficult task of addressing the issue which has motivated this manifestation of popular indignation. Fearing that I could not carry out this task properly, I have decided against depending on the inspirations of the moment, and I prefer to read the observations which I have to present on this subject.

In these times when so much is said about morality, about liberal ideas and what else, the entire population of New Mexico has seen the degradable sight of an English newspaper from this city flinging handfuls of vile insults at the native people of the Territory. I refer to the article which was published in *The Review* of Las Vegas under the title of "The Spanish American."

It appears that this production was not written by the editor, and it was inserted in his newspaper while he was away at the Albuquerque Fair; it is the production, from what can be seen, of a sectarian missionary, who thought of doing us a favor by repeating—her pretext being to take us out of the grasp of superstition—what has so often been said of us by envious tourists and journalists, more or less with acrimony. From what can be seen, the editor has been victim of an overly precarious situation, and when he returned from his trip, he was confronted by the people of Las Vegas in serious uproar. But, having heard his explanation, we are satisfied enough to respect his apology, and we intend to place the blame where it belongs.

The things which have been said about us in the cited article do not contain as such the elements to constitute a libel suit, due to the imperfect state of our present laws; but the spirit in which they have been said, and the manner and occasion employed, can serve no other purpose than to set us in ridicule, and degrade us in the eyes of the government and the good American populous which does not know us yet.

But so that no one can say that we are unjustly attacking persons who disagree with us, it is necessary to point out here, although hurriedly, the things in the said article to which we take exception. The meaning of the said writing is that we the Spanish Americans are a dirty, ignorant and degraded people, a mixture of Indians and Iberians, whom the lack of evangelical light always has in retrocession, and whom the sectarian fever reclaims for spiritualization with its dogmas. If the manner in which it has been written would not hurt our susceptibilities, we would banish it from our consideration as a childish thing; but there is a need to rectify a gratuitous and ungrounded slander through the severity of disapproval; there is a need to conjure the malice with which this slander has been given to the press to frustrate our political hopes.

The author of the article, whoever she is, produces a sick tribute to the magnificent land of New Mexico; perhaps tuberculosis brought her to these parts. And as she takes a shot at being lyrical, she burdens us with a verbose prelude, in which the pale stars come out to play in the blue of the sky, with the rivulets murmuring and the breezes sighing through the branches. Finally, the first part of the article is an extravagant waste of fantasy, that is, as Carlyle would say, a verbal diarrhea. But since this does not appeal to us, let us overlook these extravagances and concentrate on subject matter.

With the vulgar curiosity of one who possesses great animal instinct and does not know the most basic rules of human life, the writer seems to have gone through one of the many small villages which there are in the area, and there, she even stuck her nose inside the ovens and chickencoops. I do not like to exaggerate, so let us go to the proof. The said writer begins to amaze us by saying that the Spanish American or Mexican is part Spanish and part Indian; that he resembles his Spanish and Indian ancestors in language, customs, appearance and habits. How she has twisted linguistic canons to combine the Spanish and Indian tongues is a mystery to us. What molds she has used to dress the Spanish and confuse them with the Indians, still needs to be debated. But to avoid digressions, the writer continues, saying that the Mexican lives in an adobe house in which there is generally but a single room which is ten by twelve feet; that the floor is earthen, adorned by some animal pelts, and that the bed is a pile of old rags, pieces of rug, etc., in a corner. Their seats are broken chairs, and that in effect the Mexican prefers to squat on the ground like a Bedouin. She pays great attention to an eighty-year-old woman who, blind and bent with age, went every day to the author's house, to sew some evangelical skirts with the needle of Christianity; and from all appearance, since the said writer does not know the Spanish American matron—serious, proud and reserved—even from afar, she believes that she has found the prototype of the old women among our people in the ragged beggar. Some flowers, she claims, struggle for life on a small window ten by twelve inches; the door is low and one has to lower one's head to enter. The Mexican has no idea about ventilating his house, nor does he try to secure that "luxury" for himself. The floor is swept with a broom made from native thick-stalked grass; the houses are plastered on the outside with mud, and the inside is whitewashed with gypsum, with borders of yellow dirt. As many as seven persons live in these habitations; the children are born and reared in poverty, ignorance, superstition and degradation.

Let us stop for a moment to regain our spirit after so much raving. I am Spanish American as are those who hear me. No other blood circulates through my veins but that which was brought by Don Juan de Oñate, and which was borne afterwards by the illustrious ancestors of my name. If in any part of the Spanish Americas, or what were Spanish domains before that, there has been a preservation of pure physiognomical characteristics of the conquering race, it has been in New Mexico. There has been some mixture, it is true, but so slight and in such rare cases, that to say that we are, as a community, a mixed race, is neither verifiable by historical fact, nor resistant to scientific analysis. But if it were true that we are a mixed race, there is nothing in that which is dishonorable or degrading. If this were true, instead of degenerating, our race would have received new vigor, as did the Romans from the Goths, as did the Normans from the inhabitants of Albion in feudal times. And one must note that the so-called Germanic or Saxon races, in the period of human development which amalgamated the European peoples, had nothing in either temperament or intellectual gifts which was superior to the indigenous race of America when our forefathers conquered it.

Regarding the interesting description of our homes, I confess that mine, although part adobe, does not resemble that seen by our ecstatic writer. Yours do not resemble that house either, and throughout my many travels in this territory, those parched flowers which agonize on the small windows which the author describes, have seemed to be strong and robust plants to me—a sure index of artistic and delicate temperament in those persons who cultivate them. There might be such cases as the lady describes; perhaps in some hidden mountain valley some bear hunter has settled with his wares and constructed a hovel which meets the description; perhaps there the lady has seen the piles of old rags which she points out. When it comes to my house, and those of my many friends and fellow countrymen, the sound of an evangelical missionary's footsteps is unknown and for the same reason she is unable to give a competent description of its interior. Thanks to our good fortune there has not yet been one of these evangelists going around, yardstick in hand, inside our homes, measuring the doors and windows or scraping the walls and tasting the dirt to show that we fix our homes with mud. But if this lady had truly seen our homes inside, she would have noticed that we have good beds and tables; that our children grow up surrounded by all the amenities which love can lavish. In country homes, where the necessities of life are simpler than in the cities, there are no alabaster lamps nor white velvet sofas which make our houses miniature palaces. But there is a plentiful table, where hospitality sweetens the traveler's troubles, where Christian charity never denies the weary traveler a bed on which he can rest his forehead. And, oh, what soft and gentle beds those are which the poor peasant prepares with his meager savings, and for which he never accepts even the tribute of gratitude! It is a lie that his beds are filthy rags. I have stayed at these humble huts many times; I have spent long nights listening to their simple tales; I have descended from the spheres of my ideals to be a man with them, and to be human and be happy. I have rested my forehead on their poor pillows—poor, but white like the ermine of their souls, perfumed with the mystical aroma of goodness.

But returning to the raving of our author, after measuring doors and windows with her yardstick she steps inside our kitchens, and there with evangelical intuition she penetrates even the mysteries of chile and tortillas. She finds the tortillas indigestible; that is to say, the lady has attacked a theological proposition which is more abstract than those which kept the apostle St. Paul from sleeping. And it must be suspected that the lady forgot that many mornings she herself had eaten American tortillas, that is to say, those terrible chamois skins from the pan which they call "pan cakes." The lady's tender and delicate palate receives a painful "shock" from the fiery chile, and to douse those pagan flames which burn the tongue, she takes Mexican coffee; but oh, that coffee sickens her, because it is black and has no sugar. But these trivialities do not cool her Christian love, and she follows her evangelical road up to the corral. There her quick sight spies an oven; she wants to know what that round thing in the form of a beehive is, and let us listen to what she herself says: "This is made of adobe too; it has two levels. The top level is used for cooking, and the bottom one for a chickencoop. When the oven has only one level, during the summer it serves for baking bread, and during the winter it is converted into a chickencoop." The lady does not tell us where the tortillas are made during those winters when this item is set to such vile uses. But this was a *lapsus linguae.* And this good creature, who tries to follow the footsteps of the tame Lamb from Bethlehem, who aspires to shed Christian truth, although it might be upon Mexican ovens, lies with the coolness of a Pharisee, and with the shamelessness of a scribe. Where, in the whole expanse of this Territory, has anyone seen those combinations of oven and incubator which she describes? If such a marvelous invention existed, it would already be displayed at the Exposition in Buffalo to show the world the rare New Mexican ingenuity; they would already have one of those ovens there, and its maternal hen with its many chicks, warming a nest of tortillas. Poor New Mexico! Poor sons of those who, defying the ferocities of the ocean in a poorly secured craft, searched for a new home in the New World! Here the overly Christian evangelical fever has us raising chickens in ovens. And beware that the inventor of incubators might find out, because if he should hear about it he would slap us with a lawsuit. Oh, how great was our downfall! And little remains for this famous historian of what she has not seen to discover the Castilian shields on the table serving as bowls for the barbarous feast of chile and black coffee.

Continuing her inquisitive mission, our lady passes suddenly to the place where the Spanish American women wash their clothes. And here one sees that the instinct of washerwoman always overwhelms this outsider, and it embelishes her with those things which more skilled authors would overlook altogether. By means of a marvelous process she brings all our women to the Hot Springs of Las Vegas, to wash the clothes from their homes in a certain spring of thermal waters. There, of course, is repeated the immortal scene of the washerwoman in Homer or L'Assomoir.

But there is no need to tire out this audience any longer with the repetition of so much slander. The task is vexatious; and from what has been said, it remains evident that the author of that article has mingled with the most infamous people of our community, and that, committing the grave error of every superficial writer, she attempts to reach general conclusions from particular premises. This person does not know us; if she did, she would not speak that way. She knows, it is true, some sad beggar who goes to her house with the pretense of sewing, but in reality looking for a bite to eat; she knows, it is true, some wretch who has forsaken his origin and his self-respect as a man, and seeks support for himself and his family, even changing his faith; she knows, it is true, some poor young woman here and there who, receiving her education in the sectarian schools which the reformed religion has brought among us, is prepared to graduate as a chambermaid or a servant at the home of some American lady. But she does not know the Mexican woman; she does not know the spiritual youth and dreamer from our race; and she does not know, nor will she ever know, the true Spanish American—proud, imprudent, rash, but protective of his home and loving of his family. Her foot will never step on the rug where our tots play with their toys; she will never know the moral side of our existence, because she does not sit down to read with us, next to the warm lamplight, those sweet and profound works with which the Dantes, the Victor Hugos and the Walter Scotts have ennobled the world. Her voice will never desecrate the place where we go every evening to deposit our griefs, that place where the rhythm of song awaits us, when the sweet companions of our existence conjure melodies of love on the piano keyboard. No, those angular and hypocritical faces; those people with yardstick in hand and numbers in mind; those who measure religion with the merchant's scale—those shall never penetrate our homes.

As was already pointed out, this is not the first time that the people of New Mexico grow pale from attacks which are gratuitous as well as unjustified; and in vain we do try to find any rational causes for that; the fact remains always veiled in the mystery that since our forefathers came from Spain, we have lived on this soil, claiming it through our labors and populating it with our posterity. Without resources, far from the metropolitan center, and surrounded by brave and warring tribes, the existence of the people of the Territory, during the Spanish and Mexican domination, was a continuous struggle. Under those circumstances, teaching institutions would have fared poorly among us, provided that there would have been any. But there were none; and this seems to be our crime, along with having come to populate the New World. If for this crime she attacks us with gross acrimony, one must lower one's head and admit our guilt. But times have changed since then. The immense buffalo herds have disappeared and where once the heavy cart was dragged with difficulty, today the train crosses bellowing and speeding. The entire face of the Territory has changed, but our fortune, if we eliminate the Indian threat, has not changed much. The government which boasts so much nowadays about educating the Cubans, Puerto Ricans and Filipinos, has done nothing to spread education among us. The few educational institutions which there are among us are the fruits of our own labor, resulting from our savings, and maintained at our expense. There, you will not see a single cent from our national government. And if this is certain, why should we be surprised that among us there are no profound writers, erudite statesmen or learned economists? But this notwithstanding, and although no New Mexican has yet achieved world renown, we are not so God-forsaken around here as we are depicted by some writers who pass among us like apocalyptic horsemen, with the cup of wrath in one hand and the scythe of hatred in the other. We have suffered, it is true; we have patiently awaited the hour of our redemption; but that redemption is not borne, for sure, by those who insult our homes and our beliefs. We return today, with the zeal of those who know no other homeland nor banner than the American, to petition, perhaps for the twentieth time, that overly desired admission to the sovereignty of Statehood to prove that we are worthy of republican liberties, and capable of assuming the responsibilities which they bring with them. And while, everywhere and from all the political parties, all that one hears is the popular voice which calls for this change, here in this city, in our midst, there rises an unknown, asphixiating, and troublesome voice which denounces our native people. Could this be with the hope that our petition be ignored, and that we continue in the precarious state of national tribute as acknowledgement of superiority?

People of New Mexico, if your destiny is but to be a beast of burden; if you must remain forever in this sad tutelage of government which you have had until now; if you must never participate in the public affairs of this nation, which is yours; if your Anglo-American brothers view you with distrust, and they begrudge you the minor happiness of being able to govern yourselves; it is time that you pick up your household goods, and that you take them, along with the remains of your forefathers, to a more hospitable country. You are not lacking in talent, you are not lacking in energy. The same stars which illuminated the path of Cabral and Alarcón shine forth every night exactly where they saw them; the same breezes which pushed Magellan's ships around the world still blow upon the seas which he furrowed. Men who think like you, who speak like you do, and who embrace the same beliefs, have raised stupendous cities at the foot of Chimborazo on the shores of the Paraná. If the country where your Diego de Vargas sleeps no longer has any hopes for your sons, observe that the world is large, the world is good, the world is generous. Look for a country where you can determine your own destiny.

Aurora Lucero White Lea (1894–?)

Plea for the Spanish Language

Many factors contributed to the denial of statehood to New Mexico for sixty-four years. However, the fact that its population did not speak English, and Spanish was used as a language of instruction in its public schools, almost always appeared on the list of objections. When Congress finally agreed to grant statehood to New Mexico, it forwarded to the territorial legislature an enabling act that was to serve as a model constitution. Two articles were of special concern to the Nuevomexicano population. One demanded knowledge of English for members of juries and candidates for state offices, and the other stipulated that English was to be the sole language of instruction in public schools. Aurora Lucero delivered the following critique of these articles at the Territorial Intercollegiate Language Competition while she was a student at the teacher's college in Las Vegas. This speech, originally delivered in English, was subsequently translated and published in both Spanish- and English-language newspapers. Her piece was instrumental in mobilizing New Mexicans against those articles of the enabling act inimical to the Spanish language. The actual state constitution subsequently included articles that protected Spanish and guarded against the disenfranchisement of New Mexico's Spanish-speaking population. Lucero White Lea, the daughter of the first Secretary of State in New Mexico, Antonio Lucero, was a teacher for thirty years in the public schools of New Mexico and also served as Superintendent of Schools in San Miguel County and Assistant State Superintendent of Schools. While we do not have extant copies of her literary works, the record shows that she wrote several historical plays. She also published three volumes of folkloric material gathered in New Mexico. (EGB)

Further reading: *The Shepards* (Rochester, N. Y.: 1941); *Literary Folklore of the Hispanic Southwest* (San Antonio: Naylor Co., 1953).

The territory of New Mexico has undergone many changes, politically and socially, it has solved many problems; and now, upon the eve of statehood, a new problem is being discussed in every hamlet, village and city:

"Shall the Spanish language continue to be taught in our public schools?"

It seems beyond all doubt that New Mexico is soon to take her place as one of the states, in the grand sisterhood of commonwealths of this mighty union. That boon which for 60 long years she has sought in vain seems now within her reach, and to all appearances she has but to extend her hand in order to gain it; yet in her enthusiasm and eagerness to obtain it, she must not forget that she has problems to meet and solve such as no other state ever had.

In order to understand this problem thoroughly, let us state the peculiarities of our achievement. There is to the south of this rich and vast domain a population of more than 60,000,000 people, all descended from the Spanish Conquistadores. To the north, are found the homes of at least 90,000,000 of another people, nearly all of Anglo-Saxon blood, speaking an entirely different language. New Mexico is the meeting ground of these representatives of the Romanic and Germanic races, and no one can fail to see, even now, that their amalgamation is but a question of time. What the final outcome of such a union will be, of course no one can predict with absolute certainty, but if it be true that history repeats itself under analogous conditions, then we may venture the prediction that a new race will spring from such a union that will far surpass either of its factors in all those traits and characteristics that make man better fitted for high responsibilities. The past history of these two races is a record of glorious deeds and notable achievements. Both have in their natures elements of greatness, and the union of the calm, business like spirit of the Anglo-Saxon with the sanguine, chivalrous enthusiasm of the Castilian will be such a blending of all that is best in human nature that we fail to see how anything better for the wealth of humanity could possibly happen.

A difficulty presents itself at the very beginning; no matter how eager one may be that a new race should people these plains and hills, his hopes will be blasted if the essential means are ignored, means efficacious to the desired end. One of these is the cultivation of a thorough acquaintance, one with the other—the Anglo-Saxon with Castilian—the Anglo-American with the Spanish-American. How can this be done unless each understands the other's language?

In New Mexico, English and Spanish are the leading languages of the territory. The English language is the language in which the great bulk of the business of the country is transacted. The Spanish language, the language of the Spanish-Americans, the language of the Cortezes, the De Sotos and the Coronados, has been for more than three centuries the home language of the territory. Now, however, it has been proposed by the president and the congress of the United States to deprive the territory of this language; that is, they seem to wish to break into fragments at a single blow this strong and marvelous link in the chain of events, which has connected and held together the history of the old and new work; for this is exactly what the Spanish language has done, is doing, and will continue to do as long as it is not eliminated from the public schools and driven out of the territory.

In the act enabling New Mexico to become a state, passed by congress, it was provided that none except those who speak, read and write the English language with sufficient correctness shall be eligible to the legislature of the new state, or to any of the state public offices. It is claimed by some of those who passed this act that the Spanish-American will become a better citizen by depriving him of the use of his vernacular. In resorting to such a course, it would seem that the contrary effect might be produced in him by the unwarranted interference of congress with his natural rights, and instead of becoming a better, he might be made a worse citizen. Yet the Spanish-Americans of New Mexico have never been bad citizens. They have more than once proved their loyalty to the government and their love for the "Stars and Stripes," as their conduct in the Civil and the Spanish-American wars, and in many of the Indian wars, abundantly testifies.

It is impossible to understand why, in view of such a record, the people of New Mexico should be so unceremoniously deprived of a right which flows from the very essence of their manhood, for the right of language in man is a God-given right, and as such it is guaranteed and secured to him by the federal constitution when it declares that the natural rights of all men are inalienable. To single out New Mexico, then, for such unprecedented treatment, at the very moment that she is welcomed into sisterhood, is not only a gratuitous insult to the intelligence of her people, but it is also a proceeding as untenable in principle as it seems to be outrageous in its intent.

Man is by nature fond of distinction in anything that is praiseworthy. Everyone loves the praise of others, and to obtain it tries to become as accomplished as he can. We are accustomed to recognize the superiority of the person who has a command of one or more foreign languages. Consequently, as an accomplishment in the individual, the study of languages should be encouraged in its citizens. Why, then, should this most enlightened nation prevent the study of the Spanish language in the schools of New Mexico, where that language is even now the language of the majority of the people, and especially since it is as cultured and refined as any of the modern languages and far surpasses them in dignity, beauty and majesty?

A few Spanish words are sufficient to set in motion all the finer and nobler sentiments of our nature. Take, for instance, the entrancing and patriotic image pictured by Espronceda when, in appealing to the Spanish people to rescue their country from the regime of the pusilanimous Charles IV, who was absolutely dominated by France:

Del cetro de sus Reyes los pedazos
Del suelo ensangrentados recogía,
Y nuevo trono en sus robustos brazos
Levantado, a su Príncipe ofrecía.

This passage from Espronceda is but a single, isolated instance of the richness of Spanish poetry. Pathos, tragedy, indomitable courage, patriotism, and the passionate appeal to action—all are eloquently and sublimely compressed into four short lines.

There is a host of Spanish writers who have beautified and ennobled Spanish literature to at least as high a degree as have the Chaucers, Drydens, Miltons, Byrons and Websters, uplifted the English language. We have our De Vegas, Calderons, Escriches, Castellars, Bellos and Arboledas, whose talents make them fully the compeers of the best Saxon bards and prose writers and whose pens have made Spanish literature the delight of scholars in every age and clime; while towering above them all stands the colossal genius, the author of "Don Quixote," whose superb merit is universally acknowledged and whose fame is rivaled but not surpassed by that of the great bard of Avon.

Yet this grand array of illustrious scholars, not to mention a vast number of others not less brilliant, will be lost to the youth of New Mexico when the Spanish language ceases to be taught in her schools.

Then consider the great commercial importance of this language. Besides being spoken in Spain and the Philippines, it is spoken in all countries south of the United States. These countries offer an unlimited field for the investment of American energy and enterprise. The advice of Horace Greeley to the young men of our country: "Go West" was heeded and the West became a blooming garden and a mighty empire: But the West is now filling up rapidly and those young men must soon turn south to these Spanish-American countries. If then we would cultivate their friendship and good will, get them to do business with us, admit us into their society, we should be able to greet them with a "Cómo está Usted?" as well as that they should be able to greet us with a "How do you do?"

Our public schools must have the Spanish language for the same reason that other modern languages are taught in them; they must have it as the inseparable companion of her sister, the English; they must have it if we wish that our youth shall be fully prepared to meet the duties which are awaiting them in all the Spanish-American countries—duties which they will in vain try to perform, without a thorough knowledge of the Spanish language.

The Spanish language is the language of our fathers, it is our own language, and must be now and hereafter the language of our children and our children's children. It is the language handed down to us by the discoverers of this New World. We are American citizens, it is true, and our conduct places our loyalty and patriotism above reproach.

We want to learn the language of our country, and we are doing so; but we do not need, on that account, to deny our origin or our race or our language or our traditions or our history or our ancestry, because we are not ashamed of them; and we will not do it, because we are proud of them.

The Spanish, next to the English, is the language most widely spread throughout the world; and though now the sun sets on the dominions of the actual successor of Charles V, it does not set, nor will it ever, on the dominion of the Spanish language. It is spoken in the far-off Philippines, and far along, from frozen mountain peaks to blooming valleys, it leaps with ever-increasing echo from Mexico and Central America down to the Straits of Magellan. All the islands cradled in the bosom of the Atlantic rejoice in its grandeur and its majesty. Lastly, it is spoken, written and sung in Spain—romantic Spain—the land of knighthood and the mother of heroes, the power that saved Europe from the fate of the Roman Empire, the hand that first unraveled the mystery of the sea, to give a New World to civilization, and to hoist the ensigns of Christianity on the Teocalis of the Incas and the Montezumas.

Such is the language against which it is proposed to close the doors of the public schools of this territory. A language with such a record, such a history, such traditions and backed, as in the Spanish by the moral influence of so many civilized countries, deserves a place not only in the public schools of New Mexico where it belongs by inheritance and the right which three centuries of permanency therein give it, but in the best colleges of the United States in the proudest seats of learning in the world.

Therefore, in the name of all that is noble, grand and beautiful in the literature of the world; in the name of the broadening of the fields of our business interests, and in the expansion of trade relations with our immediate neighbors; in the name of the Anglo-Saxon youth of this territory who are everywhere endeavoring, with an earnestness fully worthy of the excellent cause to learn the Spanish; in the name of the rights which the people of New Mexico have as citizens of this great republic; in the name of its duty to them, as contracted most solemnly before the world at Guadalupe Hidalgo; in the name of honesty and justice, let us by all means see to it that the Spanish language is not driven from the public schools of New Mexico.

"P.G."

The Spanish Language: A Plea to the Hispanic Legislators/La Lengua Española: Plegaria a los Legisdores Hispanos

Protections included in the state constitution notwithstanding, Spanish as a language of instruction in the public schools of New Mexico came under fire in 1914. The customary ethnic solidarity gave way to partisan politics, and the Nuevomexicano community split on the issue. Some believed that the use of Spanish impeded the learning of English. Others argued that in addition to learning English, Hispanic children in New Mexico had every right to become literate in their mother tongue through appropriate public instruction. In the poem below, "P.G." exhorts Hispanic legislators to act in unison in order to preserve native language rights, reminding them of the literary and utilitarian value of Spanish, as well its important historical legacy for the people of New Mexico. "P.G." is the abbreviated form of the pen name "Pero Grullo" (a traditional satirical pen name meaning nonsense), a regular but unidentified contributor to the weekly *La Revista de Taos* (*The Taos Journal*, November 20, 1914). (EGB)

Further reading: Gabriel Meléndez, *So All Is Not Lost: The Poetics of Print in Nuevo Mexicano Communities* (Albuquerque: University of New Mexico Press, 1997).

Trans.: EGB

Oh! Peregrine lawmakers!
Oh! dawning makers of the law!
Truly you are able and wise,
Therefore, please pay heed
To this my early mourn verse.

You say you have been chosen
To act for our welfare
And that to offer your very best
Avoiding all form of grievance
Is your collective aim.

I, simple mortal that I am,
All of that and more believe,
As such I dare now to speak
Of a matter most essential
And I shall state it plainly!

Know that the native language
Suckled at my mother's breast,
The revered language
Spoken in modern Spain,
Is here banished and condemned.

And with heavy handed artifice
To our fair Hispanic youth
Its instruction is forbidden
Through the hate or vengeance
Of treacherous engineers.

It has no place in our schools
This language of my people
As it soundly is rejected
With a lamentable rigor
That beyond injustice goes.

¡Oh! legistas peregrinos!
¡Oh! Licurgos en envión!
Que sois listos y ladinos,
Escuchad con atención
Estos versos matutinos.

Decís que sois elegidos
Para hacernos beneficio,
Y que a prestar buen servicio
Estáis todos decididos,
Y a evitar todo perjuicio.

Yo como simple mortal
Todo eso y más creeré,
Y por esto os hablaré
De lo que es más esencial
Y aquí mismo os lo diré.

Sabed que el idioma natal
Que en los pechos he mamado,
El idioma celebrado
Que se habla en la España actual
Es proscrito y desterrado

Y con artera asechanza
Se ha privado su enseñanza
Entre los niños hispanos
Por el odio o la venganza
De pérfidos artejianos.

No tiene entrada en la escuela
El idioma de mi raza
Y su uso se rechaza
Con rigor que desconsuela
Y de injusto se propasa.

Cervantes' very Language
That of Lope and Calderón
That then and now has flourished
In lands and nations hither and yon.

El idioma de Cervantes
De Lope y de Calderón
De tanto ilustre varón
Que ha florecido hoy y antes
En tanta tierra y nación.

The language of Isabel the Catholic
Who succored the discovery
And with noble fervor
With singular faith
Moved Columbus' arduous feat.

El de Isabel la Católica
Que ayudó al descubrimiento
Y con tan noble ardimiento
Animó con su fe insólita
A Colón en su arduo intento.

The language spoken now
In more than twenty nations
And for which the future holds
Fame beyond compare
For its resounding urbanity.

La lengua que hablan ahora
Naciones aun más que veinte,
Y a que el futuro atesora
Renombre tan eminente
Por su suavidad sonora.

The language always used
By the settlers of this land
Who with unequaled heroism
To their progeny left a legacy
Without fear of impending harm.

La lengua que siempre usaron
Los que esta tierra poblaron
Con heroísmo sin igual,
Y que a sus hijos legaron
Sin temor a ningún mal.

This our banished language
Through the ingratitude
And hapless adulation
Of unworthy native sons
Finds itself betrayed.

Esta lengua desterrada
Se halla por la ingratitud
Y adulación desgraciada
De unos hijos sin virtud
Por quienes fue traicionada.

This the Spanish language
Fell prey to the contempt
and senseless pride
Of slothful legislators
Who slumber without care.

Esta lengua es la española
Que por un orgullo necio
Contemplaron con desprecio
Legistas que a la bartola
Dormitan con sueño recio.

Now this enslaved language
Begs you for its freedom
Hoping that compassion move you
To remove all shackles
Of slavery and evil.

Ahora esta lengua esclava
Os pide la libertad
Y espera en vuestra piedad
Que remováis toda traba
De servidumbre y maldad.

This time that all Hispanos
Their native tongue study

Pues justo es que los hispanos
Estudien su lengua propia

For 'tis a treasure and reminder
Of the proud recollections
Of which our history is composed.

Discharge, therefore, your duty
Illustrious makers of the law
Then and only then
Will you deserve
Our absolute applause

Yours shall be the honor
Bright as the radiant sun
If you guarantee that Spanish
With fervor and devotion
Be studied in this land.

Porque es el tesoro y copia
De recuerdos tan ufanos
De que está llena su historia.

Cumplid, pues, vuestro deber
Ilustres legisladores,
Y os haréis acreedores
A obtener y merecer
Nuestros aplausos mayores.

Recibiréis grande honor
Que brillará como el sol
Si hiciereis que el español
Se enseñe en nuestro redor
Con celo y con devoción.

Jovita Idar (1885–1942)

For Our Race: Preservation of Nationalism; We Should Work

Jovita Idar was at the forefront of women's issues and collaborated in a number of women's periodicals, in addition to writing a good portion of the Idar family's weekly *La Crónica* and later directing her own newspaper in Corpus Christi, Texas. In the January 8, 1910, issue of *La Crónica*, Nicasio Idar explained that he was the author of the paper's editorials, while his children, Clemente, Eduardo, and Jovita, wrote the entire newspaper. It is presumed that Jovita was the author of numerous progressive articles and essays on topics such as women, youth, and education. She particularly advocated women obtaining an education and becoming economically independent of men, which is reflected in her article *We Should Work*, reprinted from the 1911 issue of *La Crónica*. In 1910, the Idar family spearheaded the organization of the first Mexicanist Congress in Texas, the goal of which was to form an association to protect the rights of Mexicans. The congress promoted a nationalist ethos of "Por la Raza y para la Raza" (By the People and for the People), which is echoed in Jovita Idar's *For Our Race*, reprinted below from a 1911 issue of *La Crónica*. The congress also founded the women's association of the movement, the Liga Femenil Mexicana (League of Mexican Women), in which Jovita Idar took a leadership role. (NK)

Further reading: Nicolás Kanellos, with Helvetia Martell, *Hispanic Periodicals in the United States: A Brief History and Comprehensive Bibliography* (Houston: Arte Público Press, 2000).

Trans.: TEW

For Our Race: Preservation of Nationalism

In our previous article we stated that "most regrettably, we have seen Mexican teachers teaching students of their race English without taking into consideration, at all, their mother tongue." With that we did not intend to imply—not in the least—that the language of the land they inhabit should not be taught, as it is the medium available for direct contact with their neighbors, and that which will allow them to ensure that their rights are respected. What we wanted to suggest, simply, is that the national language should not be ignored, because it is the stamp that characterizes races and nations. Nations disappear and races sink when they forget their national language. For that reason, nations, like the Aztecs, no longer exist. Rome, through her language, profoundly influenced the people she had conquered. If the Jews today do not comprise a nation, it is because each one speaks the language of the land they inhabit.

We are not saying that English should not be taught to Mexican Texan children, but, whether appropriate or not, we are saying you should not forget to teach them Spanish. In the same way that arithmetic and grammar are useful to them, English is useful to those people who live among English speakers.

We are all creatures of our environment: we love things that we have seen since our infancy, and we believe in that which has permeated our souls since the first years of our lives. Therefore, if in the American school our children attend they teach Washington's biography and not Hidalgo's, and instead of the glorious accomplishments of Juárez they refer to the exploits of Lincoln, no matter how noble and fair these men were, that child will not know the glories of his homeland. He will not love his homeland, and will even view his parents' compatriots with indifference.

There was not one Mexican Texan who, with the best intentions in the world, did not adorn his jacket with a picture of the heroic Juarez on September 16, 1910. This uplifts any person who loves his race. Good and honorable Mexicans, who are so patriotic and worthy, why do you ignore the noble actions of those who have sacrificed their lives to give us freedom?

It is true that we are in the country of business, and that time is money, but while history and geography are not indispensable for earning a living, they are good for the preservation of patriotism.

Mexican-Texan youngsters need instruction to gain the esteem and sympathy of those around them; they need it to obtain a livelihood with greater ease and to be more influential.

We Should Work

The modern woman, cognizant of and recognizing the need to contribute her quota to aid in the development of erudition among the masses, prepares herself valiantly and invades every field of industry, at all levels, without fear and without laziness. She abandons idleness and inactivity, since in the present age, so full of life opportunities and replete with energy and hope, there is no room for the socially indolent.

Inactivity and laziness are seen as contemptible today and, as such, are undone by all of those things that are considered factors in the development and progress of the people.

The modern woman does not spend her days lounging in a comfortable chair. This, not even the rich woman does, since those flattered by fortune also dedicate themselves to the practice of generosity or other philanthropic work, or to the organization of charitable or recreational clubs. What is desirable is to do something useful for yourself or for your fellow man.

The working-class woman, recognizing her rights, raises her head with pride and confronts the struggle; her period of degradation has passed. She is no longer the slave sold for a few coins, no longer the servant. She is an equal to man, his companion; he is her natural protector and not her master and lord.

Much has dealt with and been written about the feminist movement, but despite the opposition, already in California women can cast their vote as jury and occupy public office.

Those fastidious, superficial and unworthy souls make many mistakes in criticizing this type of woman who, brushing aside social convention, dedicates her energies to work for something beneficial and charitable; these critics do not realize the moral influence that this exerts, because a person dedicated to certain jobs or tasks does not have time to be bothered with futile and prejudicial things. She does more, the steadfast working woman, behind a counter and seated in front of her sewing machine or already an office worker, than the young lady with time to spare who occupies herself with making daily social calls or in going through, one by one, every store, which is a life filled with gossip and vulgar stories.

The single woman, decent and hardworking, does not demand a living at the expense of the head of her family, whether or not it be a father, brother or relative. No. A healthy woman, valiant and strong, dedicates her energy and her intelligence to helping her family, or at least, to providing for her own sustenance.

Just as decent and hardworking men regard unemployed and vagrant men with disdain, so too do working women disparage good-for-nothing and unemployed women.

LA DEFENSA

Greetings and Aims (Editorial)

In general, Hispanic community papers took very seriously their function as a vanguard of antidefamation and protector of the civil and human rights of their communities. In New York, one newspaper even chose to announce this defensive function in its title. The first editorial in its inaugural edition not only emphasized its defense against racism and exploitation but also announced proudly that Hispanics were here to stay. For the most part a periodical that arose from and targeted the Puerto Rican community, *La Defensa* marked the transition from an immigrant ethos to one of native entitlement and rights. (NK)

Further reading: Nicolás Kanellos, *Hispanic Periodicals in the United States: A Brief History and Comprehensive Bibliography* (Houston: Arte Público Press, 2000).

Trans.: TEW

The principal purpose of this editorial is to put in writing—in a precise and clear manner—the goals that inspire us and the plan of action that we must follow in the execution of the mission entrusted to us. But before moving ahead, let us pause to extend our most cordial greeting to the Hispanic community of New York. In particular, we would like to salute the Hispanic societies, fraternities and religious congregations that fight and endeavor to sustain, at the highest possible level, the spirit of cohesion, the morale and the culture of the citizens of Hispanic heritage who reside in the great Metropolis. We also would like to extend our greeting to all the people of America who speak the sacrosanct and harmonious language of Eugenio María de Hostos and Andrés Bello.

Let us consider the fact that this publication comes to light in the middle of the most abject misery in the heart of our humble quarter of Harlem, where vice and pain inexorably contend for the squalid victims of ignorance, racial prejudice and the current defective system of political economy. Under such circumstances, in defense of our legitimate rights as citizens we can do nothing less than consecrate this weekly and confirm the belief that a free press is the most efficient defender of human rights and the firmest guarantee that justice will function properly.

Despite the many evils, real or imaginary, that are associated with our neighborhood, a greater part of its residents are morally upright, love order, and possess all the attributes necessary to comply with the obligations of good citizens. Therefore, one of the fundamental objectives of *La Defensa* is to prove the fact that there are individuals in the neighborhood who, with their intelligence and willpower, can influence and impact the course of civic events in our Hispanic community. If it were not for this, we would stop condemning, with the vigor of all our strength, the evils that actually exist and that are the cause of our collective denigration.

It is time for us to realize that we are not migratory birds, that we are here to stay, and that it is necessary to prepare the way for those who will come after us. It is imperative that we establish our society on a foundation that is more solid and realistic, in accordance with our social conditions, and without an insistence upon conserving class differences inherited from another age and other circumstances. Our present economic conditions do not justify such distinctions. On the contrary, they become termites that destroy the foundation of our social structure.

It will not be possible for us to put in motion the aims that motivate us unless we receive the trust and cooperation of the Hispanic public that reads. Accordingly, to deserve this trust and cooperation, we commit ourselves to working assiduously so that *La Defensa* becomes a genuine instrument of Puerto Rican and Hispanic views. We will make space in its columns for writings and articles of collective interest that tend, in all cases, to reflect the slogan of this publication: Justice, Culture and Dignity.

Lorenzo Piñeiro Rivera, Ruperto Udenburgh, Gerardo Peña, Carlos Carcel, and Ramón Rodríguez

Open Letter to a Libelist

This open letter, published in an undated issue of the Bronx periodical *Brújula* sometime in the 1940s, responds to attacks made on Puerto Ricans by Charles E. Hewitt, Jr., in *Commentator* magazine, in which he proposed ways to curtail Puerto Rican migration to the mainland. The writers, following the time-tested role for community periodicals, defend the honor of the immigrant community by tracing the economic and political causes of the emigration from Puerto Rico. The letter takes Hewitt to task for blaming the victims themselves for the dislocation resulting from

American colonialism in Puerto Rico. Following this explanation, the authors proceed to outline the contributions of Puerto Ricans to the struggle for freedom in the world and to defend the honor, sense of morality, and cleanliness of Puerto Ricans which Hewitt had questioned. (NK)

Further reading: Nicolás Kanellos, *Hispanic Periodicals in the United States: A Brief History and Comprehensive Bibliography* (Houston: Arte Público Press, 2000).

Trans.: TEW

Mr. Charles E. Hewitt, Jr., City.

Dearest Sir:

With surprise and indignation we have read your article published in the March edition of the magazine Commentator, issued by the Scribner publishing house. Our surprise stems from the fact that there is a magazine in the United States, whose government claims to be the banner in the fight for human rights, that has published an article in which an entire people, whose history would be cause for pride in all civilized individuals, was seriously wronged, both morally and intellectually, without regard for the millennial norms that regulate relations among men.

The taunts and insults that you freely inflict upon our nationality are the motivation for our indignation. And, that indignation has increased with our profound conviction that the facts or information cited as the foundation for such serious insults are untruthful and evidence a crass ignorance on your part about the real Puerto Rican nation and what it has meant to the history and culture of all the nations of the New World, including the United States.

By way of this medium, we wish to respond to your insults with all the vigor of our collective spirit and strength of understanding, without consideration for, certainly, those imponderable economic forces shielded in your name that back this campaign of defamation and ignominy. They are attentive only to your bastard interests, and for being so, are necessarily at odds with the supreme aspirations of the most perfect political, social and moral unit in our hemisphere: the Puerto Rican nation.

We begin by challenging the authenticity of your statistics cited in the shameful lampoon. And lacking any other means to clarify the truth—your supposed truth and our genuine truth—we invite you to discuss in public, wherever you choose, the contents of your article. We guarantee before hand that you will be treated with due respect by our compatriots. There, we will discuss the truthfulness of your statistics, the intelligence of your generalizations and finally, the human and social implications of the solutions you proposed to that which you have termed, irresponsibly, the Puerto Rican problem.

In the meantime, and stemming from the fact that you will not dare accept our challenge, we will proceed by shedding light on the real Puerto Rico, as well as the significance of Puerto Rican emigration to this country. Before continuing, as we are the children of a generous and uncovetous nation, it is necessary for us to recognize that there are some truths in your article. However, unfortunately, they are only half truths, which are always worse than the most crooked lies, as the source of the Puerto Rican problem (we do not deny its existence) is considered, but in a cowardly and selfish way. This is the most reprehensible attitude with which to confront the tragedy of a country or human conglomerate.

Puerto Rico is a nation of definite characteristics, possessing a culture, tradition, history and, with regard to life, a collective attitude informed in the principles of Christianity. It was so in 1898, and continues to be so today, despite the cruel process of denaturalization suffered over the past 42 years, a denaturalization carried out by the most resourceful and powerful on earth. As you will see shortly, the idea of nationality—which is equal to saying the maintenance of a dignity, of generosity and excellence in the noblest fields of human civilization—has remained alive in the depths of the Puerto Rican soul.

The day arrived in which this nationality, which was still poor and humble but happy because it could achieve the fulfillment of its vital needs while shaping its patriotic destiny, was invaded forcibly by the Army. Thus began that which you referred to in paragraph 7, page 15 of the magazine in question. The powerful economic interests that followed the United States flag in the invasion deposited their money in Puerto Rico to transform the economy of that nation. This task was facilitated by a political regime that represented the new interests and, to that end, began by changing the Puerto Rican currency in circulation at the time. This was the first blow to the jugular of the economic body of the Puerto Rican nation. The reactionary economists who supported the North American invasion have calculated that Puerto Rico lost no less than 40 percent of its hard cash by virtue of the currency change. At the same time, there were two other causes, and together with the first represent the introductory trilogy of the Puerto Rican tragedy. In the first place, Puerto Rico immediately lost the markets for the sale of its agricultural production, which were France, Germany, Italy, Spain, England, etc., while at the same time felt obligated to buy in the most expensive market in the world.

These three facts, of incontrovertible historical truth, created the financial crisis and economic impoverishment that made it possible for our lands, 90 percent of which were in the hands of Puerto Ricans, to pass to absentee hands over a short period of time, as you assert. Thus an enormous factory was created where more than 80 percent of the population has been subjected to indignity under the guidance of huge corporate interests that are in no way accountable to Puerto Rican public opinion for the dispossession and misery they cause.

Along with this crisis, mass Puerto Rican emigration began. And the crisis was not only of an economic nature, because it was accompanied by the subjugation of the highest values of the native culture by those who served as the banner for the invading culture; and it also was accompanied by the crowning of a mediocre regime in the task of directing the nation's destiny, since it was the mediocre people there who were ready to serve the foreign will. They were found there in the same way they have always been found in all corners of the planet during all ages.

The Puerto Rican is not a man who emigrates. That is to say, he is of the type who abandons his native shores only when imponderable events deny him access to daily sustenance. Moreover, already emigrated, he continues to think of his emigration as a transitory thing and continues to dream of the longed-for return. For that reason, he does not renounce his rural personality but keeps the defining contours of his culture alive. In regard to the issue that concerns us here, he keeps these contours alive for the good of the people who accept them, as this contributes a new note or different tone to the vital rhythm of this people. This is why we affirm, contrary to your opinion, that the

American people should feel grateful for Puerto Rican emigration. It has contributed to life in North America through music, a dreamy and profoundly humane attitude, a transcendental understanding of the noblest realities, a sacrificial and generous spirit, a note of excelling as high as the day in which this same note will be incorporated into the essence of Americanism—in the Anglo-Saxon sense—on that day your nation will be saved in the eyes of the highest spirits of our time, as the researchers and historians and historiographers in the centuries to come will record for posterity the performance of the United States on the stage of humanity.

Once the emigre arrives, men like yourself present themselves and affirm that Puerto Ricans are degenerate. Suffice it to ask: Do they become degenerate because they live here? The question is logically deduced from your affirmations. And even though we do not accept the premise you proposed as true, we are responding because, if Puerto Ricans become degenerate in New York, it is because the environment of New York is degenerating. Assuming this, it should be a problem that concerns all the higher beings of our times, since New York is not only the mosaic where true United States citizenship is taking shape, but now it is also the place where all men on the planet converge, equal to the crossroads of all worldly paths. But, it is obvious we do not accept that New York is a center of degeneration or that, once arrived here, Puerto Ricans become degenerate.

We are not denying that there are prostitutes in New York who were born in Puerto Rico, as you also will not deny that there are American prostitutes of pure Aryan blood walking the streets of New York. As in the case of one or the other, these unhappy women who find themselves obliged to search for daily sustenance in vice are not to blame for that situation. The only thing responsible for prostitutes is the existence of that which we have come to call prostitution. And yes, it is clear that the existence of prostitution as a way of life and a business, where that which is most costly to human dignity is that which is sold, is the fault of the social and political order that, with its enormous contradictions and terrible injustices, makes this evil possible and permits its existence.

We deny, yes indeed, that Puerto Rican girls prostitute themselves as a way to earn money with which to pay the passage of their husbands who have stayed back home. This affirmation of yours we have to necessarily qualify as one of the most despicable and dastardly things we have ever heard. In declaring this, we are relying on our so called freedom of speech, which is so often proclaimed in the United States and which you have abused, but the difference is that you speak to insult an entire people, while we speak to tell you the truth.

Our women possess a deep sense of dignity that is a tradition inherited from those who advanced Puerto Rican nationhood. An important part of this legacy, also attributable to our men, is considering honor as the supreme virtue, a value like no other value, and possessing a deep sacrificial spirit, the same one that makes it possible today for a single Puerto Rican man or a solitary Puerto Rican women to resist, serenely and peacefully, the wrath of the most powerful empire on earth. Part of this legacy is a sacrificial and fertile spirit that made it possible in the past for thousands of Puerto Ricans—which included the most celebrated voices of our culture in this epoch—to give their lives for the Independence of Cuba. It is the same legacy that made it possible for a Puerto Rican, Marshall Antonio Valero of Bernabé, to be the hero of Zaragosa in Spain, facing Napoleon's troops, who were defeated; for however late it came to be, together with the liberating swords of Iturbide in Mexico and Bolivar in South America, he was one of the greatest heroes of the liberating epic in the New World.

This same sacrificial spirit made it possible for us to send the apostolic figure Eugenio María de Hostos, with a Socratic mentality and Nazarene heart, to all parts of the Americas to preach the gospel of culture and of love as the salvational norm for the new nations that sprang to life out of liberty. Many other great Puerto Rican spirits, informed in that same sense of sacrifice, crossed the paths of the Americas and even of the Old World, motivated by the high ideals of humanity and service.

Now you can see that you do not know the history of Puerto Rico. This does not surprise us, as it is clearly documented in a recent editorial in the New York Hispanic daily, La Prensa: that well known vice of your North Americans of going to some specific geographic location, living there any number of weeks, and returning to the United States to write a book about that region. You do so transformed magically into authorities on the history, culture and miracles of the geographic area visited. You show us your ignorance of Puerto Rican history when you affirm that Ponce de León, our first governor under Spanish domination and the person who discovered Florida close to one century before the arrival of the Cabots on the northern coasts of the New Hemisphere, and, accordingly, the real discoverer of North America, today occupied by the ethnic element of Anglo-Saxon origin, baptized our country with the name of Puerto Rico. For your information, we must inform you that our country was discovered and baptized by Christopher Columbus, the remarkable sailor, and he named it San Juan Bautista.

Puerto Rico has not caused the United States any affliction. If there is anything frightful in the tragic panorama that our country represents these days, it is that which the United States has offered to humanity as a magnificent example of its "civilizing" work in the only Indo-Hispanic nation subjected to the protection of North American governmental despotism. If we accept for a moment the authenticity of the picture painted by you, with Machiavellian ends no doubt, it would represent the most serious accusation against the government of the United States, since this is the only party responsible for all that has happened in Puerto Rico over the past 42 years. It was that same government which, without consulting the Puerto Rican will, imposed American citizenship upon the people, a factor of juridical and constitutional character which is the cause of that which has alarmed you, and against which you cry out: unrestrained entry by Puerto Ricans into the United States.

To justify your outcries and indignation against unrestrained entry by Puerto Ricans into the United States, you invoke, cunningly, the tragedy of the European refugees. We cannot believe you are sincere in trying to manifest sympathy for the men and women who are victims of racial prejudice and political persecution today in the old continent, and who try to find refuge for themselves and their ideals in new American lands. Yes, we can speak with sincerity about that tragedy because we have felt it in our own bones. By the way, it is fair to say that one of the few truths in your article is based upon wanting to allude to those people pursued in Europe in relation to the Puerto Ricans living in New York and you call them, "you refugee friends." It is true that the Europeans who have fled totalitarian persecution, just like the Puerto Ricans who emigrated, faced with sudden attacks of democratic tyranny, are fellow refugees. As much the ones as the others are victims of regimes that, even though they can distinguish themselves in purely external aspects, respond, despite this, to identical economic and political factors.

If the statistics you cite about Puerto Ricans who are victims of diverse illnesses are as correct and exact as your affirmation that it is these people who "have brought with them to America the habit of using narcotics," or that "they have brought to the blacks all the foreign corruption of the Indies," we have to necessarily affirm that both are a product of a sick mind, blinded by prejudice or hatred, and lacking in all relation to reality. Several Puerto Ricans, at least as educated as you, will tell you it was not until mass emigration of Puerto Ricans to the United States began that they heard for the first time of marihuana. These people also could tell you the true origin of these vices.

Making use of isolated cases like the ones you cite to prove such absurd generalizations as those made in your article is neither intelligent nor honorable. With all certainty, we affirm that Francisco F. is not the only Puerto Rican with his mouth open. Nor will you deny that we have seen dozens like Francisco with blonde hair and Saxon diction in the United States. Jose V. is certainly not the only idiot Puerto Rico child. You affirm that in Puerto Rico there are no institutions for idiot children and display such ignorance by denying that the philanthropic organizations of the United States, like hundreds of North American households, are full of idiot children. More so, the households and philanthropic organizations of the United States, and even the streets of this country, are not only full of idiot children but of idiot men as well. The case of Maria L. does not surprise us either, who, judging from what you say, will never recover her sight. The homes for the blind in the United States, just like the households and streets of this country, are full of many like Maria L., with blonde hair and a decidedly English accent.

It is not true that our people live in such a state of abandonment and of poor hygiene to merit the common example of "four occupants is the minimum amount per night per bed"; or that dozens of them live in one room together; or that now, "eighty people use the same outhouse each day." Nor does your affirmation that the apartments in which our people live keep them in the state of desolation and misery that you presume to illustrate as responding to reality. Accepting, for one moment, that this were certainly and undeniably the cause of the state of affairs, the responsibility for it would fall upon the irresponsible government that allows such a level of poverty. To deny that in Puerto Rico running water is not known, proves once more your ignorance about, and prejudice against, our country.

You tell a partial truth when you affirm that Blanton Winship, the recently deposed governor, "had 60 million dollars in assistance after 1935, and it was very liberal assistance from the Department of Insular Affairs" to resolve Puerto Rico's economic problems. Besides the fact that it is debatable whether the amount sent by the Roosevelt Administration to solve the country's problems was that high, the full truth is that a large part of the money allocated by Congress for that reason was used in the militarization of the police force, with the purpose of destroying the Puerto Rican freedom movement; was used for lining the pockets of the past general, with the goal of making his native lackeys happy and of creating another vast bureaucratic agency in our country. In an outstanding eulogy of the colonial regime that Puerto Rico endures, Mr. Filipo de Hostos, President of the Chamber of Commerce, has demonstrated that Puerto Rico has paid back with interest each dollar that the New Deal has invested in our country during the past seven years of its existence.

The terrible increase in the cost of living, that has come as a consequence of the literacy agencies of the new administration, devalued any dollars our people would receive.

Because of all of this, it does not surprise us that the Admiral Leahy, the new governor, has by the grace of the imperial North American will affirmed that "the situation of the impoverished natives is so desperate that it cannot be expected that they will be any help to America in case of war." That is not due, simplistically, as you want to have us believe, to entirely economic reasons. Underneath that attitude is manifest all of the pain of a people who have seen how their institutions have been destroyed, how their economic base has been undermined, and lastly, how their elevated historical destiny has been disposed of without having their collective will consulted, even indirectly. Because of these affirmations, which you attribute to the Admiral Leahy, we ask: Why does Puerto Rico have to be of any use to America in case of war? What right does the United States have to order the construction of naval bases in Puerto Rico without first consulting the Puerto Rican people and without respecting the eternal and eminent principle of sovereignty of nations? In defense of whom, and against the attack of whom, have they constructed those naval, military and air force bases on Puerto Rican land?

It is clear that the solution you suggest or advance to the supposed problem of emigration in the United States demonstrates as much ignorance of the fundamental questions involved as the same exposition made by you of our actual problems. An elementary knowledge of American Constitutional Law should be sufficient to know that that is not the legal solution to end Puerto Rican emigration; besides the fact that it would not be the decent or just solution, either. If the American people and their government want to stop Puerto Rican emigration to this country, they have to begin with recognizing the right of the Puerto Rican people to control their own destiny, so that we can then resolve, in accordance with our will, in our best interest, and with our indisputable capacity, the problems that lead to that emigration. That is not the only thing the United States has to do, even though it has to be the first step. The United States also has to legally repair all the wrongs it has occasioned upon Puerto Rico over the past 42 years of mismanagement.

Allow us to finish by paraphrasing in part the last paragraph of your shameful article. As long as the United States does not do that which we signaled in our last paragraph, it will be laughable for the United States to continue telling the rest of the world which is the perfect type of government, boasting its democracy and sense of justice. As long as it is not done, it will be laughable for the United States to become indignant before the continued assaults that in the Old World are made against small nations. And, in addition, the protest cries, not only of the American people will be laughable, but also of her highest rulers before the persecution of minority groups in different parts of the planet. In summary, it has been laughable until now that the United States has not fulfilled its responsibility in the case of Puerto Rico, with all the preaching about the politics of being a good neighbor and the well-known aspirations on the part of this country of assuming world dominance in defense of rights and justice.

Hoping never to direct ourselves to you again for this same reason, the below signatories enlist themselves in hope for the happiness of the Puerto Rican people:

Lorenzo Piñeiro Rivera, Ruperto Udenburgh, Gerardo Peña, Carlos Carcel, Ramón Rodríquez.

Alonso S. Perales (1899–1960)

Ignorance: The Cause of Racial Discrimination; The Evolution of Mexican-Americans

One of the most persistent, outspoken civic leaders among Mexican Americans, Alonso S. Perales became sensitive to the issue of equity and the need to organize while serving in the Army in World War I, after which he began organizing Texas Mexicans politically. He was a founding member of the Order of the Sons of America in 1921 and, in 1929, of the League of United Latin American Citizens (LULAC), the longest-lasting Mexican American civil rights organization. A native of tiny Alice, Texas, and a lawyer, Perales was at the forefront of defining the identity and rights of Mexican Americans through the scores of letters to the editor, essays, and speeches that he wrote over some four decades of activism. Perales collected many of his writings in the two books that he published in 1931 and 1937 when he was serving the United States in the diplomatic corps. Many of the pieces written before the founding of LULAC and his diplomatic career were much more militant than the moderate identity that LULAC came to embody later. In the essays below, written to be delivered as speeches in 1923 and 1924, Perales continues the practice of elevating the accomplishment of the Spaniards and Spanish Americans in the past in order to substantiate the high degree of "civilization" in the Mexican populations of the Southwest prior to the coming of the Anglo and against Anglo racism. Perales also included the Native Americans as illustrious ancestors of Mexican Americans. Also evident in his writing is the underlying pride in *mestizaje* and the belief in the Mexican American as a mestizo race apart from whites. (NK)

Further reading: Alonso S. Perales, *El méxico americano y la política del sur de Texas: Comentarios* (San Antonio, 1931), *En defensa de mi raza* (San Antonio: Artes Gráficas, 1937).

Trans.: TEW

Ignorance: The Cause of Racial Discrimination

A careful analysis of the situation leads us to the conclusion that the existent racial prejudice against Mexicans, and Hispanics in general, partly is due to the ignorance of certain people who—unfortunately for those of us who live here—are abundant in the state of Texas. The fact that Mexicans are considered inferior, without exception, reflects the lack of culture and education that is pervasive here.

It is not my intention to become an apostle for socialism, but moreover to support and petition so that all people get what they deserve. Mexicans should be judged for what they are individually, and not for what other individuals of the same national origin seem to be, for "a cup is not the same as a jug, just because they both are made from the same clay."

In the North and East of this country, Mexicans, and Hispanics in general, are welcome and respected. Of course, there are also some ignorant "children" there, as no rules are without exception, and there are some people who, no matter how white their skin is, still exist on the fringes of civilized society and culture. In the North and East there are several schools, colleges and universities where the Anglos learn the history and psychology of the honorable Hispanic race. Culture is accessible to everyone, both the rich and the poor. And what is the result? When the Anglos leave their classrooms, abreast of the merits and virtues of our race, they know that they should not deride and denigrate Spaniards or Hispanic-Americans when they encounter them. Instead, they should greet them politely, at least out of respect and in recognition of the founders of this Continent and the illustrious heroes that figured in Hispanic-American history. These people who study us to better understand us do not ignore the level of civilization achieved by the Indians who, prior to the arrival of the Spanish conquest, inhabited the major part of this Continent for centuries. They know about the conditions under which America was discovered and do not deny that the apostles who harvested the first seeds of knowledge in the New World were not Anglo-Saxons, but Hispanics. They know who Bolívar, Juárez, Hidalgo and Cuauhtémoc were, and are not unfamiliar with the names of Ramón y Cajal, Francisco León de la Barra, and many others who have elevated the Hispanic race.

The situation is quite different in the state of Texas. Here, education is not a given. The attitude of many Anglo-Texans leads us to this conclusion and, slowly but surely, they are destroying the unwritten laws by which we deserve to live.

In addition to the frequent humiliations that our fellow Mexicans endure, there are several residential districts in San Antonio, and elsewhere, in which Mexicans of all social classes find it difficult to settle down. Accordingly, although we try to be optimistic, we cannot. If truth be told, our situation is completely unsatisfactory.

Not long ago, I had the pleasure of hearing a prominent Anglo-American lawyer present an eloquent speech about this city to a Mexican audience. This gentleman said, among other things, more or less the following:

"My friends, I respect and admire the Mexican race because I know your history. You should feel proud to be the descendants of Hidalgo and Juárez."

When I had the floor a minute later, while alluding to the words of the illustrious lawyer, I commented that it had been a lovely allocution and we appreciated it. I added that the only regrettable thing was that the talk was not directed at an Anglo-American audience, seeing that we already know our political and ethnic history, and so forth. Now, what we would like is that those Anglos who do not understand us make the effort to study us in order to know us better, instead of hating us without reason. In the name of self-improvement and equity for our race, we would like them to decide "to give each one his due," or better said, to recognize the merits and virtues of the worthy and noble Mexican race.

The Evolution of Mexican-Americans

Sixty-six years have passed since Texas came to be part of the American Union and we Mexican-Americans still are considered outsiders even today. The problem we have before us, gentlemen, is that of improving our condition, and it is our responsibility to find a way to resolve this. In my humble opinion, the solution to the problem is based on three factors: Education, Unity and Politics. Allow me to consider the first one.

It is a known fact that Education is one of the basic factors in human progress. It is also known that intellectual advancement will bring with it economic progress, and that economic development will result in social evolution. Therefore, it is urgent that we force ourselves to educate our children, so that instead of perpetuating the production of migrant, day-laborers, we shall produce men of duty, destiny or profession. The other peoples that make up this cosmopolitan nation do this. Why is it that we do not do the same thing? The day that our earning power is equal to that of our compatriots from other nations will be the day that our "standard of living" will be equal to theirs. If even then they insist on seeing us as nothing more than Mexicans, it will not matter at all, for in calling us Mexicans, they honor us, and this should make every enlightened Mexican American proud.

The second issue is Unity. Everyone knows that unity equals power. We Mexican-Americans who live in the United States should organize ourselves. However, for our organization to be a reality, it is absolutely indispensable that we be able to count on a number of leaders born in our country, and should be intelligent, active, sincere and honorable men. They should be people who, for the good of our people and our country, work with genuine faith and enthusiasm. We do not need any more leaders that simply talk and talk. As long as men with all of these qualities do not emerge, all efforts toward unity will be in vain. Why do I propose such high standards? Allow me to explain myself. It is necessary for our leaders to be intelligent and sincere people so that they understand profoundly what the phrase "Consistency of Principles" means and, thus, accommodate their conduct to these principles. Upon returning from Washington, I have had the occasion to observe individuals in Texas who seem to be capable of serving as leaders, but who, despite professing to be enthusiastic fighters in support of the well-being of our race, once given the opportunity to enter into politics (the most effective weapon that we have to fight for our rights), they have ended up supporting the so-called candidates of an organization extremely hostile to the concerns of Mexicans. These same individuals pretend to be our leaders and defenders of our people! Where is the consistency of principles? Something is wrong with those people: they pursue bastardly ends under the guise of a pro-Mexican campaign or they misinterpret the phrase consistency of principles. To prove that the secret organization to which I am referring is an enemy of our people, I am going to take the liberty to quote the following declarations that appeared in the official publication of this organization in San Antonio, Texas, on December 15, 1923:

"Even though the city of San Antonio has always been run by White American men, our officials never have been elected by a majority of White votes. For that reason the city perenially has been under the influence of foreign voters who pay no attention to who occupies the administrative positions. (The ignorant fools call us foreigners, not understanding that if we vote, clearly we are as American as they are!)

"As such, San Antonio, supposedly an American city, and one of the largest in the state, has always been dominated by foreign influences, or at least by those who are against the principles upon which our state and national governments are based. We are sure that what we say will never be denied, except by those individuals who are more interested in their own personal gains than in the well-being of the state, the county, or the municipality.

"In San Antonio, the Mexican vote is always a deciding factor in every election . . . and the White man who gets this Mexican vote benefits, of course, and once again the newspapers appear with the news of 'the battle that was just won by White, patriotic Americans . . . . ' As you would expect, in all of the local elections, every candidate, regardless of his background, receives some American support. Notwithstanding, the man from San Antonio who wins is elevated to his post by the votes of the foreigners (Mexicans!) and the Blacks!

"One of these days, things are going to change in San Antonio. The Battle of the Alamo was a victory and a symbol for its defendors, despite the fact that the heroes of this bloody conflict died in combat. San Antonio was a scratch on the surface, but in the battle of San Jacinto, Sam Houston and his small group of valiant Texans deepened the wound. This famous battle will be repeated in San Antonio when, for the good of the population and of this district, this city sends the foreign element on a 'Marathon for tall timber.' That day will come. It is as sure as the sky itself. So let us prepare ourselves for the job and success, though slow in coming, will be ours."

Here we have some of the popular opinions about our people. Despite those declarations, there were many enthusiastic "defenders of our people" who, not satisfied with just contributing their votes to the cause, dedicated themselves during the campaign to openly persuading the Mexican community to vote for the so-called candidates of this organization . . . perhaps to better ensure our political and social improvement!

There you have it, gentlemen, the reason why it is absolutely indispensable that our leaders be intelligent, patriotic, sincere and honorable men, whose racial pride surpasses their personal ambitions. The man who is proud of his racial origin, almost certainly will never abandon a noble cause, like ours, to join the ranks of the enemy. We should, then, join together. It is urgent that we study and investigate those men who pretend to be our leaders, for the banner of our desperately needed unity should be nothing less than patriotism and justice.

The third factor in the solution of our problem is Political activity. We Mexican-Americans of this nation should take more of an interest in our government. Ours is a Republican government, and, in the words of the great President Lincoln, "a government of the people, by the people and for the people." Accordingly, those of us who are citizens of this country are as American as the best American. Not one person in whose veins flows blood from some other race that makes up this nation has the right—even if he does have the audacity—to tell us that we are not "one hundred percent American." As I have already said, based on ethnicity, history and geography, nobody—except for the pure American Indian—has more right than we, the descendents of Hidalgo and Cuauhtémoc, to call themselves one hundred percent American. I challenge anyone to refute my assertion.

Politics, I repeat, are the most powerful weapon that we have to fight for our rights and to improve our situation in every sense. Accordingly, during elections we should study the candidates for public office, be they municipal, state or national elections, as we are giving the men we elect the responsibility to govern us. Thus, it is imperative that these men be educated, sincere, fair and honorable. They should be people who, once in power, are ready to demand justice for our race. We Mexicans, regardless of our citizenship, ask neither for favor nor beg for sympathy—but we do ask for JUSTICE. This is our goal and our dream.

To demonstrate why it is that we should study the candidates for government positions, I am going to mention the case of the ex-Governor, James E. Ferguson. In 1921 this man unjustifiably made some denigrating and inflammatory comments about our race. These were comments that I did not hesitate to energetically deny from Washington, D.C., once I found out about them. In my letter, I made him see the injustice in his attacks as well as his ignorance about the real merits of Mexicans as a race. In August of this year, he stated that he stood by his statements from 1921, and added that his wife did not, *in the least*, need the Mexican vote to win.

Well, when this man was promoted to the position of Governor, how many Mexicans do you think completely ignored his feelings about our race and supported him? With men like Ferguson in power, there is no doubt that our chances of improving, in any and every sense of the word, are absolutely tremendous. Right? Well, now I wonder how many Mexican-Americans will support Mrs. Ferguson next month, despite her husband's attacks on our race?

Here we have, gentlemen, the answer to the question of why it is that we need to study the candidates for government positions. And here we have an opportunity to demonstrate, with facts, that we are proud to have Mexican blood in our veins.

Next month in November, we conscientious Mexican-Americans will have an opportunity to register a protest against the unjustifiable attacks that Mr. Ferguson made against our race. All Mexican-Americans that are truly proud of their ethnic roots should go to the polls on November 4th and vote against Mrs. Ferguson. That is the best way to fight our enemies!

So then, gentlemen, when we have educated, enlightened and organized ourselves, and taken more interest in our government, we will have evolved and, furthermore, we will have salvaged the good name of our worthy and noble Mexican Race.

Emma Tenayuca (?–1999) and Homer Brooks (1905–?)

The Mexican Question in the Southwest

A native of San Antonio, Texas, Emma Tenayuca is best known as a political activist who led the 1938 pecan shellers strike. This essay makes explicit the beliefs that underlined many of her political practices. *The Mexican Question in the Southwest*, which she co-authored with her husband Homer Brooks, was originally published in *The Communist* in 1939. Tenayuca's essay marks one of the first political treatises written by a Mexican American in English to argue for the rights and status of Mexicans in the United States. Written at the height of the pecan strike, Tenayuca expands upon Marxist theories of nationalism, emancipation, and citizenship. It is important to remember that the "Mexican Question" was originally a national "Anglo" inquiry into the rights, lands, and status of Mexicans that became critical with the signing of the Treaty of Guadalupe Hidalgo in 1848, which is the historical point from which Tenayuca begins her essay. Tenayuca argues that the Mexicans of the Southwest do not constitute a separate nation; they are inextricably connected not only to each other by race and land, but also to Anglo Americans and U.S. institutions. (JMR)

Further reading: Zaragosa Vargas. "Tejana Radical: Emma Tenayuca and the San Antonio Labor Movement During the Great Depression," *Pacific Historical Review* (Nov. 1997): 553–580.

The war of the United States with Mexico, in 1846, following the annexation of Texas, resulted in the conquest of the territory which now makes up the states of California, New Mexico, Arizona, Colorado and part of Utah and Nevada. From the historical point of view the forcible incorporation of these areas in the United States was progressive, in that it opened up for development these territories which until then had stagnated under the inefficient, tyrannical, and semi-feudal control of Mexico. The predominant influence of the Spanish in the Southwest, particularly in California, New Mexico, Arizona, Colorado and Texas, can be seen in the names of such cities as Los Angeles, Santa Fe, San Antonio, San Diego and San Francisco.

The acquisition of these lands brought into the Union a population originally Spanish and later Mexican, whose customs, language, traditions and culture were essentially different from those of the rest of the country. In the border area of the Southwest the Mexicans have always constituted a majority, both before and after the war with Mexico.

The expansion and industrialization that followed the Civil War, lasting until a relatively late period in the Southwest, saw the importation of thousands of Mexican workers into Texas, California, Colorado and Arizona. (To a lesser degree this was true of New Mexico, for geographical reasons. Deserts and mountains bordering Mexico prevented free interrelation with old Mexico; at the same time this border region has not made for the development of large-scale capitalist farming.) Railroad companies alone were responsible for a great number of those imported. It is safe to say that most of the railroads of these five states were built by Mexican labor.

With the development of capitalist farming in these states, and particularly in California and Texas, Mexico was again a source of cheap labor. Early figures on the number of Mexicans immigrating into the United States are not available, since until a relatively late period entrance into the United States was comparatively simple. Complete figures as to the number of Mexicans in the United States are today not available, since until 1930 Mexicans living here were not classified separately.

However, between 1925 and 1929 the heaviest immigration from Mexico took place. In the course of these five years, 283,738 Mexicans entered the United States, as follows:

1925	50,602
1926	58,017
1927	77,162
1928	58,456
1929	39,501

Source: The World Almanac, 1937.

The 1930 census showed 1,500,000 Mexicans residing in the United States. Of these, all but 150,000 were found to be living in the states of California, Texas, New Mexico,

Colorado and Arizona. However, these figures include only the foreign-born and first-generation Mexicans. They exclude the large Spanish-speaking population of New Mexico, which, according to H. T. Manuel of the University of Texas, numbers over 250,000, or approximately half the state population. These figures also exclude Mexicans of the third, fourth and fifth generations and those descendants of the early Spanish colonists of any of the other four states. Therefore, we can readily state that the Mexican population of the Southwest numbers approximately 2,000,000.

Thus, we can see that the present Mexican population in the Southwest is made up of two groups: descendants of those living in the territory at the time of annexation, and immigrant Mexicans and first- or second-generation native-born drawn from the impoverished peasantry of Northern Mexico to work as superexploited wage workers in railroad and building construction and in highly developed (capitalist) agriculture in the border area.

However, there is no sharp distinction between these two groups, either in their social conditions or in their treatment at the hands of the Anglo-American bourgeoisie. Assimilation among those groups which were here before the conquest of these territories by the United States has been slow, and the Spanish language remains today the language of both groups.

The distinction has been sharpened somewhat in New Mexico, since a lack of direct contact with Mexico led the majority of Mexicans to regard themselves as Spanish-Americans or Latin Americans, and consequently to regard Spain rather than Mexico as the mother country. However, this distinction is being done away with more and more by the social conditions under which the Mexicans or Spanish-Americans are suffering, which are breaking down barriers and leading to unification. The pro-Mexico sentiment among the people in New Mexico was seen when the Spanish-speaking population rallied to support Mexico during the recent oil expropriations and even raised funds to be sent to Mexico.

Those Spanish-speaking people of Texas whose ancestors were in the state prior to its annexation from Mexico today regard themselves as Mexicans. We can thus state that the Spanish-speaking population of the Southwest, both the American-born and the foreign-born, are one people. The Mexican population of the Southwest is closely bound together by historical, political and cultural ties.

The treatment meted out to the Mexicans as a whole has from the earliest days of the sovereignty of the United States been that of a conquered people. From the very beginning they were robbed of their land, a process that has continued even up to the present time. In 1916, immediately following the abortive De la Rosa movement in the Texas lower Rio Grande Valley for an autonomous Mexican regime, Texas Rangers, in cooperation with land speculators, came into small Mexican villages in the border country, massacred hundreds of unarmed, peaceful Mexican villagers and seized their lands. Sometimes the seizures were accompanied by the formality of signing bills of sale—at the point of a gun. So that, where, until 1916, virtually all of the land was the property of Mexicans, today almost none of it is Mexican-owned. In many cases farmers who were well-to-do landowners today barely eke out a living employed as irregular wage workers at 60¢ to 75¢ a day on the very lands they once owned. This land-grabbing has continued under one guise or another throughout the Southwest. In

New Mexico fewer than one half of the Mexican or Spanish American farmers retain any of their ancestral lands.

The Present Social Status of the Mexican People

With the penetration of Anglo-Americans into these states, the Mexicans have been practically segregated into colonies. This is particularly true of Colorado. Disease, low wages, discrimination and lack of educational facilities are typical of these communities.

Mexican labor imported into the United States has uniformly received lower wages than those paid Anglo-American workers. The vast majority of the Southwest are today found doing only the most menial work, the bulk of them having been excluded from skilled crafts. In the cities, although Mexicans are found in the garment industry and laundries and as laborers in building construction, the overwhelming majority are also seasonal agricultural workers. This is true of the Mexicans in all states except the Spanish-Americans of New Mexico, where instead of being agricultural workers, the majority are small farmers, tenants or sharecroppers.

In Texas, in the area of Corpus Christi, few if any Mexicans are found working in the extensive oil field discovered there several years ago. Corpus Christi, we may add, is one of the cities that lies within the belt where the Mexicans form the majority of the population. An example of the kind of industry that Mexicans are not excluded from is the pecan industry in San Antonio, which until recently employed 12,000 Mexican workers, with wages averaging two to three dollars a week.

Near-starvation faces thousands of Mexican agricultural workers who must live part of the year in the cities and try to get work on W.P.A. A special clause in the relief appropriation act of 1937, which excludes foreign-born workers who have not taken out citizenship papers, resulted in dismissals of thousands from W.P.A. In El Paso, for example, 600 out of 1800 on W.P.A. were so dismissed.

The reaction of most of the Mexican W.P.A. workers to these dismissals could not lead to acquiring citizenship papers due to language, cost, and other burdensome obstacles. Their resentment was expressed by demanding the opportunity to work on all jobs, regardless of citizenship, a demand which by virtue of their historical rights in this territory is unchallengeable.

Discrimination against the Mexican people can also be seen in regard to relief appropriations. The Relief Commission of Los Angeles presents a special budget for Mexicans, claiming that diet and living expenses are lower among the Mexicans than among other sections of the population. Since the Mexicans live in houses without electricity or natural gas, they are subject to smaller relief portions in every state in the Southwest.

The conditions of the Mexican agricultural workers can be compared only to those of the Negro sharecroppers in the South. According to the United Cannery, Agricultural, Packing and Allied Workers of America, the average wage of the Mexican beet worker in Colorado is from $100 to $200 per year. The average wage of the Texas cotton picker is considerably less; in 1938 it ranged from 35c to 75¢ per 100 lbs. In those places where the U.C.A.P.A.W.A. carried on struggles, the prices were raised.

In New Mexico, where the Mexicans or Spanish-Americans have been engaged in small farming, fully one half of the farmers have lost their land. Individuals such as

John T. Raskob and large corporations have taken over ownership, and sharecropping is rapidly taking the place of small independent farming. Another factor which threatens the existence of the farmers of New Mexico and the agricultural workers of the Southwest has been the large migration of Anglo-American farmers from the dust bowl.

The crisis has intensified the competition for jobs; a fact that is resulting more and more in displacing Mexican workers in the cities. For example, the Sun-Tex canneries in Texas, located in a city with an overwhelming majority of Mexicans, hires only Anglo-American workers.

The Mexicans are not only subject to wage differentials and discrimination, but a view of their political status in the five states referred to, reveals conditions in many ways comparable to the political status of the Negro people in the South. Denial of voting rights to the foreign born means disfranchisement of nearly half the adult Mexican population. Secondly, the semi-migratory character of the work of most of the Mexican workers disfranchises in addition many of those who are citizens. Finally, in Texas the poll tax disfranchises many of those who would otherwise be able to vote. Thus, due to one or another of the three causes, in San Antonio, a city of 250,000, nearly half of whom are Mexicans, only 8,000 Mexicans were eligible to vote in 1938.

This disfranchisement has resulted in nearly complete Anglo-American domination politically in most of the communities where the Mexican people are a majority. In only two or three countries in Texas do the Mexicans hold the decisive elective positions. (In New Mexico the situation is otherwise, since there the majority are Spanish-American, non-migratory, and no poll tax is in force.) The 800,000 Mexicans in Texas have only two representatives in the State Legislature.

Lack of representation in local or state politics and low economic standards have resulted in poor health conditions and lack of educational facilities. An example of this is Texas, where the death rate among Mexicans is decidedly higher than among Anglo-Americans, and even higher than the rate among Negroes. The following statistics well illustrate this fact:

	Percent of illiteracy	*Deaths per 10,000*
Countries with a heavy Mexican population	15.5	98
Countries with a heavy Negro population	6.7	86
Countries with Anglo-American population	1.7	58.5

Actually, the relative difference in the death and illiteracy rates is higher, since the statistics refer to country averages which include considerable Anglo-American and some Negro populations in all of the countries having a heavy Mexican population. Health conditions among the Mexicans are evidently worse than among any other section of the population in the Southwest, or even in the United States. San Antonio has the highest infant mortality rate of any large city in the United States. It likewise has a higher rate of deaths from tuberculosis than any other city in the country.

The unequal treatment that the Mexican people suffer is manifested in all phases of life. The practice of excluding Mexicans from hotels and restaurants is prevalent in all these five states. A few years ago an international incident took place in Victoria, Texas, when an official delegation of students from Mexico was excluded from a restaurant. Signs bar Mexicans from dance halls in Los Angeles. In Colorado small town restaurants display signs: "White Trade Only."

Segregation of Mexican children in small town public schools in Texas is a common practice. Several years ago a group of Mexican tax-payers in San Antonio, by threatening to withhold the payment of school taxes, successfully fought this issue. A few months ago Dr. Juan Del Rio, a resident of San Marcos, had to bring suit against the school board of that city to win the right of his children to attend the school established for Anglo-American children.

The suppression of the Spanish language, of the native culture of the Mexicans, is one of the reasons for the high rate of illiteracy. The most important reason is, of course, the semi-migratory life of the agricultural worker, which forces the children out of school at an early age, and makes school attendance irregular for many.

The social conditions of the Mexicans can well be summed up by the following statistics based on the census of 1930:

Percentage of Illiteracy

	New Mexico	*Arizona*	*Colorado*
Native white	7.7	0.5	0.8
Mexicans	36.4	28.5	22.0
Negroes	. . .	. . .	3.9

Source: The World Almanac, 1937.

To summarize, the Mexican people of the Southwest have a common historical background and are bound by a common culture, language and communal life. It should be noted, however, that the Mexican communities exist side by side with Anglo-American communities within a territory where the populated districts are separated by large but thinly populated mountainous and arid regions.

Should the conclusion, therefore, be drawn that the Mexican people in the Southwest constitute a nation—or that they form a segment of the Mexican nation (South of the Rio Grande)? Our view is no. Historically the Mexican people in the Southwest have evolved in a series of bordering, though separated, communities, their economic life inextricably connecting them, not only with one another, but with the Anglo-American population in each of these separated Mexican communities. Therefore, their economic (and hence, their political) interests are welded to those of the Anglo-American people of the Southwest.

We must accordingly regard the Mexican people in the Southwest as part of the American nation, who, however, have not been so accepted heretofore by the American bourgeoisie; the latter has continued to hinder the process of national unification of the American people by treating the Mexican and Spanish-Americans as a conquered people.

Comrade Stalin's classic definition of a nation states: "*A nation is a historically evolved, stable community of language, territory, economic life and psychological make-up manifested in a community of culture*" [*Marxism and the National and Colonial Question*]. We see, therefore, that the Mexicans in the United States lack two of the important characteristics of a nation, namely, territorial and economic community.

Isabel González (dates unknown)

Step-Children of a Nation

Civil rights activist Isabel González of Denver, Colorado, spoke out about the unjust conditions Mexican American and Mexican people faced in the United States in the postwar era. Active in local and national organizations to defend the democratic, constitutional, and human rights of people of Mexican descent, González was Executive Secretary of the Committee to Organize the Mexican People (COMP) of Denver. She presented her essay *Stepchildren of a Nation* at the Annual Conference of the American Committee for the Protection of the Foreign Born in Cleveland, Ohio, on October 25–26, 1947. In this work, González draws on educator George I. Sanchez's metaphor to analyze, theorize, and interpret the history of Mexican American and Mexican people in the United States since the end of the U.S. Mexican War in 1848 as a history of conquest and marginalization. González's writings, like those of Jovita Idar, Emma Tenayuca, and other Chicana/Mexicana political activists of the first half of the twentieth century, established a legacy that Chicana feminists and other scholars continue to uncover and reclaim. (AC)

Further reading: Clara Lomas, "In Search of an Autobiography: On Mapping Women's Intellectual History of the Borderlands," introduction to Leonor Villegas de Magnón, *The Rebel* (Houston: Arte Público Press, 1994); Roberto Calderón and Emilio Zamora, "Manuela Solís Ager and Emma Tenayuca: A Tribute," in Teresa Córdova et al., eds., *Chicana Voices: Intersections of Class, Race, and Gender* (Austin: Center for Mexican American Studies, 1986), 30–41.

There are approximately five million people of Mexican origin in the United States. Of these some three and one-half million are American citizens who live principally in the West and Southwest. The other million and a half are non-citizens, and constitute the largest group of non-citizens in the country. These are also concentrated in the Southwest and the West, with the exception of centers like Chicago, Kansas City, St. Paul, Detroit and New York City.

Why is it that so many Mexicans in the United States have failed to become citizens? Is it because they do not wish to enjoy the privileges of citizenship; or is it because they do not feel a loyalty to the United States; or is it because, as some say, the Mexican people are too ignorant to meet the qualifications for citizenship?

Could it be, however, that obstacles are placed in the way of Mexicans who seek citizenship; or could it be because the depressed status of the Mexican people as non-citizens bears profits for certain economic interests? Could it be also that the U.S. Government has helped some economic interests in their search for cheap labor to lure Mexicans into this country only to suppress and terrorize them once they are here?

The answer to the first series of questions as to why the Mexicans have failed to become American citizens is an emphatic "*no.*" The Mexicans, like any other group, prefer equality. As to their loyalty, the first World War, as well as the last one provide ample evidence. In the first World War, New Mexico had more volunteers per capita than any other state in the Union. As a matter of fact, New Mexico, as well as Mexican centers all over the Southwest, had so many volunteers, there were not enough able-bodied men left to fill the draft quotas. In the list of "conscientious objectors" in the last war, one does not find a single Spanish name, but the list of outstanding American heroes contains names like Joe Martinez, Arturo Musquiz, Maestas and many others like them. It is a well known fact that the number of war casualties among the Mexican-American soldiers was very high in proportion to the population.

There might be more validity to the question of ignorance, since the Mexican people, whether citizen or non-citizen, as George I. Sanchez puts it in his book, *Forgotten People*, have remained the "step-children of a nation," especially insofar as educational facilities and opportunities are concerned.

This government never made due recognition of its responsibilities to the native people of the region it took from Mexico. It failed to take note of the fact that those people were, in effect, subject peoples of a culture and of a way of life radically different from that into which they were suddenly and unwittingly thrust by the Treaty of Guadalupe Hidalgo.

Poverty, segregation, poorly paid teachers and inferior educational facilities are conditions which have not been conducive to the acquiring of an education by the Mexican people, or to even afford them the opportunity to learn a minimum amount of English. Their condition is aggravated, as Dr. Joaquin Ortega, of the University of New Mexico, states,

> by intolerance on that part of some members of the dominant Anglo-Saxon group, and the concomitant resistance on the part of the dominated to lose their identity to an unkind people. When a so-called "superior" culture wants to superimpose itself upon another, it must do so persuasively, for otherwise the "attacked" culture in a natural move of self-assertion and self-preservation (which is, by the way, the measure of its strength) instead of acceding to assimilation maintains stubbornly its own practices.

An Inferior Status

Perhaps, by looking a little deeper into the history of the development of the West and Southwest, we will be able to find the answers to the last series of questions. With the raising of the American flag over the Southwest in 1848, the Mexican people were reduced to an inferior status. A mold of inferiority was cast, into which all later arrivals were forced to fit. Not only did the Mexican population lose political control, but it also lost control of the economy which it had begun to build. The large landed estates were taken from their owners, and false claims of newcomers were validated by the courts. The Spanish language was replaced by English as the official tongue and equal civil rights were abolished in practice. Submergence of the Mexican culture and influence became a systematic program. Mexicans had their mining claims jumped, and could find no legal protection.

At the first session of the California Legislature in 1850, a Foreign Miners' Tax Law was adopted, the purpose being to drive out "foreigners," meaning Mexicans and Chinese, from their mines. Using the Act as a spearhead, a systematic campaign was launched to oust Mexicans from their claims. In the same year, a mob of 2,000 American miners descended on the Mexican mining camp of Sonora and, "firing at every Mexican in sight," proceeded to raze the town. The rioting lasted a week, with scores of murders and lynchings.

As more Anglo-Americans entered the territory, the conquest became more firmly established. Gradually, the equality of the Spanish language, the right to equal justice in the courts, and early political privileges, namely, participation in local governments, state legislatures, etc., were taken away. By the 1900's the Mexican immigrants who poured across the border in response to thousands of handbills and posters distributed by railroad companies, mining, lumbering and agricultural interests, found their lot quite different from the rosy picture of high wages and resplendent opportunities painted by the leaflets. The demand for cheap labor was so great in the Imperial Valley of California, the cotton-raising regions of Arizona, and the sugar beet fields of Colorado, that the railroads offered free transportation into the country, until freight and broken-down passenger trains loaded with hundreds of Mexicans from Central Mexico became a familiar sight in all the railway centers of the Southwest.

In 1930, due largely to the depression and governmental restrictions, the rate of legal entrants from Mexico dropped from a six-year average of 58,000 per year to approximately 16,000. When the economic crisis of the United States created an over-abundant supply of cheap labor, Mexican workers were the first to become surplus; the same big interests which once encouraged immigration now loudly demanded deportation. From 1928 to 1933, 160,000 Mexicans from California either left or were "repatriated"—a term covering everything from voluntary departure to nocturnal kidnapping by immigration authorities. Beginning with 1931, "repatriation" was in excess of 75,000 from Los Angeles alone. Scores of thousands more left from Texas and Arizona. During the depression, Mexican families on relief had no choice; either they agreed to repatriation, or were cut off the relief rolls.

The economic situation of the Mexican family in the Southwest has always been very bad, particularly among the agricultural workers. In the years 1920 to 1930, three-fourths of California's 200,000 agricultural workers were Mexican. Being unorganized, they received low wages, faced long periods of unemployment, lived under horrifying conditions. Their children, changing from school to school as the family followed the crops in "their caravans of sorrow" (as a Colorado beet worker described them) received only the most deficient education and practically no health care. Thus the real purpose of the deportations and "repatriations" was not to fit the labor supply to the number of jobs, but to further intimidate, oppress and force the Mexican workers to accept an even lower standard of living and to be used in a competitive sense against the other workers in the area.

Health

Tuberculosis is the first cause of death among Mexicans precisely because of the economic conditions under which they live. In Los Angeles, a report given by a representative of the Tuberculosis Association in 1945 stated that, of the total number of deaths from this disease, 17 per cent were Mexicans; from diptheria 33 per cent. In Texas, the 1944 statistics of the Texas State Department of Health indicate a tuberculosis death rate among Anglo-Americans of 31 per 100,000 population; among Negroes of 95 per 100,000; and among Mexicans of 209 per 100,000. In other words, in Texas, the Mexican death rate from tuberculosis is seven times that of the Anglo population. It is estimated by Tuberculosis Associations and Public Health Departments that this same ratio of T.B. deaths also applies to New Mexico and Arizona. In 1939 the Saginaw Tuberculosis Hospital in Michigan reported that of 100 beds, 25 were occupied by Mexican sugar beet workers who migrated from Texas.

The statistical picture of infant deaths among the Mexican people from poverty and filth-borne diseases, such as diarrhea and enteritis, is just as appalling. Because it is impossible to find figures for the whole region, key cities or states in the West and Southwest, which can serve as barometers for the whole region, are referred to. According to statistics furnished by Dr. Lewis C. Robbins, of the San Antonio Health Department, the number of live births among the Mexican and Anglo populations during the five-year period from 1940 to 1944 were about equally divided (totals: 21,556 Anglo and 21,436 Mexican), despite the fact that the city's residents of Mexican descent comprise only 33 to 40 per cent of the population. However, the number of infant deaths were far from equally divided. The total number of Anglo infant deaths for the five-year period was 781, while the total Mexican infant deaths was 2,295. In Denver, Colorado, the infant death rate in 1940 among Mexican-Americans, according to a study made by the Denver Unity Council on Housing, Employment, Health, Recreation and Education of the Spanish-speaking Population, was three times as high as that of the Anglos.

Housing

Since health and housing are intimately related, it is only natural that we take a look at the housing conditions of the Mexican people. A newspaper man, Allen Quinn, in a series of articles which he wrote for the *Dallas Morning News* during the city's slum clearance campaign, on December 15, 1944 stated:

> No one who will take a close look at the Dallas slums can doubt they should be cleaned out immediately. Just take a good look at that area known as little Mexico, which lies directly north of the business district to the west of Cedar Springs. Thousands of persons who live in comfortable homes in some of Dallas' best residential districts pass by there daily without knowing what lies behind the scenes.
>
> Squalor is the lot of many of those who live in that area where almost 100 per cent of the houses are substandard and many in a condition hardly fit for housing livestock on a farm. Most of them have had no repairs for years; they are not worth the expense to the owners, but bring a rental income far beyond their value. Many

> of the places that people call home appear on the verge of collapse. Most have no plumbing. Water is obtained from outside community hydrants, frequently close beside a filthy, disease-breeding outside dry toilet. Unpaved streets are quagmires when it rains and filth abounds despite the efforts and desires of many residents to try to put up a better front.

These conditions, far from being peculiar to Dallas, prevail in all towns and cities where any sizeable Mexican population lives. It is the usual pattern for the Mexicans to live in one section of town, not because they are a *gregarious* people and like to live close to one another, as some would have you believe, but because they are not permitted to rent or own property anywhere except in the "Mexican districts," regardless of their social, educational, or economic status. In smaller towns, this section is usually set apart from other residential sections by railroad tracks, a highway, or perhaps a river, or even a combination of these, like in Denver, Colorado. As a rule, the "Mexican district" is devoid of paved streets, sewer lines, and frequently even electric power, gas mains, garbage disposal service and public transportation.

For housing, like health, wages and employment, or any other phase of Mexican life in the United States, no regional surveys can be found, but statistics for one key city can serve not only as an indicator for the region but can almost be duplicated in practically any other town or city. A housing survey of Denver made by the University of Denver in 1940 shows that "nine out of every ten of Denver's Spanish-speaking people live in houses that are substandard. And almost half of these houses (41%) are both physically and occupancy sub-standard." The survey also shows that not only do most of Denver's Spanish-speaking people live in sub-standard houses, but they also live in the oldest houses in town. The median age for a house in Denver is 29.8 years, and the median age of the houses in the census tracts where the Mexican people are concentrated from 10 to 19 years older than the city median.

As a rule, the Mexicans not only live in slums in the cities, but also live in slums in the rural areas, and if you think their housing conditions in the cities are wretched and appalling, consider the 70,000 workers, most of them Mexicans and a few Filipinos, required to harvest the sugar beet and potato crops in Colorado, Montana and Wyoming. From sample studies made of the living conditions, a Government specialist in the field worked out the following conclusions: 60,000 live in houses that have no sanitary sewage disposal; 67,000 have no garbage disposal facilities; 10,000 use ditch water for drinking; 34,000 have a questionable water supply; 33,000 have no bathing facilities; 70 per cent of the houses have no screens or very poor ones. The average "house" consists of two and a half rooms and the average-size family consists of five persons. The housing includes converted railroad cars, sheds, granaries, chicken sheds, barns, and tent camps.

Studies conducted by the Children's Bureau in the agricultural areas of Texas give the same picture of squalor, shacks, overcrowding and disease. These are the conditions under which, generally speaking, the Mexican population (whether citizen or non-citizen) has to live throughout the Southwest. I have no figures on Chicago, Detroit, and New York City, but I have seen the districts where the Mexican people live and even by casual observation one can see that their living conditions are not any great improvement over those of their brothers in the Southwest.

Let me repeat that no distinction is made between citizen and non-citizen when it comes to the treatment accorded to the Mexican people. As a matter of fact, even among migratory workers, who are, generally speaking, the latest arrivals from Mexico, more than 90 per cent of the children are, by birth, citizens of the United States; yet they too are regarded as "foreigners." The word "Mexican" is often even applied as a term of opprobrium. Is it any wonder that the Mexicans, even though they have lived in this country for many, many years, and do not intend to go back to Mexico, remain non-citizens? The conditions cited offer very little incentive for them to become naturalized.

A Conquered People

But why are conditions especially severe for the Mexican people in the United States? Perhaps, if we again delve into the historic background of the millions of Spanish-speaking people living in the Southwest, we can find the answer. This huge group of people are not just another minority in the same sense that the Italians or Irish or Jews constitute a minority group in this country. We have already referred to them as a conquered people, and it is this peculiar historic background, shared only by the Indians and, to some degree, by the Louisiana French, that makes the difference. They were long-established residents taken over, or rather conquered outright, by the military forces of the United States. Their background, history, culture and economic contributions are part and parcel of the background, history, culture and economic development of the states of the Southwest which at one time constituted two-thirds of the area of the Republic of Mexico, namely, California, Arizona, New Mexico, Utah, Texas, and Colorado.

The Mexican problem has an important international aspect. Although the United States at the time of the Mexican War was not yet developed to the point of economic imperialism, an aggressive, expansionist policy had already been adopted in the interests of both northern industrialists and southern slave-owners, who wished to arrest the wide abolitionist movement that had swept the newly-liberated Hispanic-American countries. American armies penetrated as far as Vera Cruz and Mexico City, forcing Mexico to cede the territory mentioned.

Economic Exploitation

History has made economic exploitation by American interests the lot of the Mexican people both north and south of the border. Powerful interests, like the Great Western Sugar Company, the greatest importer of Mexican labor, the railroads, the mining and lumbering industries, the cotton and fruit growers, and the cattle and sheep industries have succeeded in keeping the Mexican the most underpaid and most oppressed worker so that they will always have a surplus of cheap labor. This is amply demonstrated by the constant demand for importation of Mexican nationals by the sugar industries and the railways, supported by the powerful lobbies maintained by these interests in Washington.

The demand for importation of Mexican labor is based on the theory that the native American worker would not "work for the wages paid to the Mexicans." In this way not only is cheap labor obtained, but, equally as important, the standard of living of the native worker is dragged down. And so we find our government acting as procuror and solicitor for the big sugar, cotton and the rest of the interests mentioned, exploiting our neighbors and breaking the standard of living in our own country. A Texan testifying before the House Committee on Immigration and Naturalization in 1926 is quoted by Carey McWilliams in *Ill Fares the Land* as saying:

> Mr. Chairman, here is the whole situation in a nutshell. Farming is not a profitable industry in this country, and in order to make money out of it, you have to have cheap labor. In order to allow landowners now to make a profit off their farms, they want to get the cheapest labor they can find, and if they get the Mexican labor, it enables them to make a profit. That is the way it is along the border, and I imagine that is the way it is anywhere else.

What does this mean in round figures for the Mexican worker? Pauline Kibbe in her book, *Latin Americans in Texas*, gives the following figures which she takes from a study made by the Children's Bureau on agricultural workers in Hidalgo County, Texas: " . . . . the weekly family income for two-thirds of the 342 families was $7.69; the median earnings per week were only $6.54; and one out of every eight families earned less than $3.85 per week in 1940." Carey McWilliams found that seasonal agricultural workers in Arizona earn about $6.00 per week and their annual earnings per family do not exceed an average of $250. He also found that a Mexican family of 5.6 members working in the beet fields of Colorado, Montana, Wyoming or Nebraska, the domain of the Great Western Sugar Company, earns an average of $259 per year from their labors.

In Texas, Pauline Kibbe says: "The fable that migrants 'get rich' in the beet fields is effectively exploded by the earnings reported by the Crystal City laborers. Of the total of 188 families who engaged in beet work, 13 per cent earned less than $200.00 per family; 23 per cent earned less than $300.00 per family; while only 9 per cent earned $1,000.00 or more. For individual workers, weekly earnings during the seven-month period averaged $6.33 for forty-nine hours of work per week."

Mexican cotton pickers in Texas have been known to earn an average of 80 cents per day and other agricultural or truck farm workers to make 60 cents per day. Entire families of pecan shellers have averaged 75 to 90 cents per day per family. In California in the late 30's migratory Mexican families earned an average of $254 per year.

You might feel that these figures do not reflect the complete wage picture for the Mexican worker because they are only for agricultural work. The fact remains that a very small portion of Mexicans are employed in industry, and that no matter what field of employment you choose, you still find them in the lowest paid jobs with little or no chance of promotion or up-grading. In petroleum, the biggest industry in Texas, only three per cent of those hired during the war were Mexicans, and then they received 91 cents per hour, while the Anglo worker got $1.06 for the same kind of work. The wage pattern for Mexicans is the same everywhere, even in the states of Michigan, Wisconsin and Minnesota.

You might ask how these special interests have been successful in keeping such a large mass of workers in a constant state of impoverishment, hunger and misery. Obviously, such a condition is not voluntarily agreed to by the Mexican people. The answer is: only through terror and oppression. One of their chief weapons has been and still is the threat of deportation and the refusal to grant to the Mexican people the citizenship which they so richly deserve. This can be understood if we get a picture of the conditions of immigration.

Immigration from Mexico

Immigration quotas do not apply to Mexicans. They are permitted to enter this country either upon being recruited by American commercial interests, or upon the whim of American consular officials. It is next to impossible for a Mexican to enter this country to stay and become a citizen.

Most of the Mexicans living in this country entered from 1910 to 1930. Up until 1910 immigration from Mexico had been a mere trickle, compared to that coming from Europe. For most of these Mexicans, even though they have lived in this country many years, it is very difficult to establish proof of legal residence. Either they have lost their papers or are incapable of wading through all the red tape necessary because of their inadequate command of the English language. In fact, for the Mexican immigrant who entered the U.S. prior to 1924, the process of proving that he ever got here at all is complicated, expensive and loaded with potential danger. He may very well succeed in proving only that he was an illegal entrant and find himself holding, instead of first papers, a one-way deportee's ticket to the border. It is a recurring nightmare for him every time he has to fill out an application for public assistance, a job, as well as for citizenship. Even when he decides to steel himself to the possibility of being deported, the process of proving continuous residence in the United States since he entered, and/or the legal nature of any subsequent return and re-entry, no matter how brief, is a herculean undertaking. For persons who have been excessively migrant, as most of the agricultural workers have been of necessity, or for those who were brought to the U.S. at an early age by their parents, proof may be simply impossible. At best, it is likely to involve fees for expert assistance running as high as several hundred dollars.

Naturalization Difficulties

Anyone who has tried to assist a Mexican immigrant in the preliminaries to citizenship is well aware of the difficulties involved. It is no accident that the bulk of naturalized citizens in the U.S. are those who entered after 1924, when regulations for entry were enforced and some sort of orderly accounting maintained. A large number of quasi-immigrants who remain unnaturalized, even though they have spent their lives in the U.S., and speak perfect English, quite frankly admit that they remain aliens because they have neither the finances nor the courage to tackle the job of proving that they entered legally. Even the older immigrant, after he has given you all the customary reasons about having a "hard head" for the learning of English and history, is likely to settle on the difficulty of proving entry as the main deterrent. They often remember some "paisano" who tried to become a citizen and will tell you: "Look at Juan Martinez. He was going to be a citizen. And where is he now? Back in Juarez and his wife and children starving here."

In view of the fact that slipshod entry was largely the result of American greed for cheap labor, it might seem as though some of the unholy punctiliousness after the act might be relaxed. A reasonable construing of facts of entry prior to 1924, combined with some conveniently located and resourcefully taught adult education classes might result in a veritable rush of Mexican applicants for citizenship. As it is now, even the inducement of old age pensions, so desperately needed by the older folks, are [*sic*] insufficient to entice them into the perilous and costly business of applying for citizenship. Besides, as a number of them rightfully ask, "What added status or privileges can citizenship confer on me, as long as the tenet is held by the dominant group that 'once a Mexican, always a Mexican'?" He knows that the position of the naturalized citizen is little different from that of his alien neighbor. In some respects, it may by worse, because the protection of the consulate is thereby withdrawn.

Nevertheless, the threat of deportation has served as a very effective weapon to keep the Mexican people as a whole in bondage because, as soon as a leader arises among them, deportation proceedings are immediately used to remove him from such leadership—witness the case of Humberto Silex, whose defense your Committee has already taken up. The case of Refugio Ramon Martinez, of Chicago, a leader of the United Packinghouse Workers of America, is another example. This is why COMP (Committee to Organize the Mexican People) regards the work of the American Committee for Protection of Foreign Born as a very important contribution toward making democracy work in this country of ours. This is also why COMP proposes to fight for the following program and hopes to enlist your support.

We propose:

1—Since the Mexicans who entered this county prior to 1924 are not responsible for the slipshod methods of immigration practiced then, that the burden of proof be put on the shoulders of the Immigration and Naturalization Service and that requirements be relaxed to make it possible for this group to get citizenship papers.

2—The Mexican applicant for citizenship be permitted to meet the literacy requirement either in English or Spanish and not be forced to meet it in English only.

3—The Immigration and Naturalization Service establish strict regulations on the sugar companies, the railroads, cotton farmers, citrus fruit growers, and others in regard to illegal importation of Mexican workers, and provide for the prosecution of these interests for violation of such regulations.

4—An interpreter be provided at all hearings on matters of immigration and naturalization.

5—That the proper government agencies concern themselves with the enforcement of payment of prevailing wages to imported labor.

6—A congressional investigation be held where true representatives of the Mexican people are allowed to testify on the conditions under which the Mexicans are forced to live and work.

Américo Paredes (1915–1999)

The Mexico-Texan; The Hammon and the Beans

Américo Paredes is considered one of the pioneers of Chicano literature. In the late 1930s he began cultivating many of the themes and expressed much of the sensibility that would typify many works that appeared during the Chicano movement of the 1960s and 1970s. In reality, Paredes, born and raised in Brownsville, Texas, is a transitional figure who went from publishing poems in Spanish in immigrant newspapers such as San Antonio's *La Prensa* to writing novels in English for mainstream publication and distribution; he even penned the types of bilingual poems that would become a staple of Chicano literature of the younger generations. After working at a variety of jobs, including as a journalist, and serving in the armed forces during the Korean War, Paredes received an advanced education and went on to become one of the most respected Hispanic scholars in the United States. He was instrumental in the development of the academic field of folklore as well as the field of Mexican American studies; he served as the president of the American Folklore Society and won numerous national and international awards for his scholarship. But as a writer, Paredes was so much a visionary that his works went unrecognized and unpublished. His first and greatest novel, *George Washington Gomez*, written in 1936, was not accepted for publication until 1990. Likewise, his novel *The Shadow*, the winner of a national award in 1953, was not accepted for publication until 1998. His many poems and stories also took decades to see the light of day in book form. As the selections below aptly illustrate, Paredes openly dealt with culture conflict, poverty, and oppression at times through satire, as in *The Mexico-Texan* and *Between Two Worlds*, and other times through gritty realism, as in *The Hammon and the Beans*. The latter provides a vivid portrait of changing times and political challenges during the increasing dispossession of Mexicans in Texas. (NK)

Further reading: Américo Paredes, *Between Two Worlds* (Houston: Arte Público Press, 1990), *George Washington Gómez* (Houston: Arte Público Press, 1990), *The Hammon and the Beans* (Houston: Arte Público Press, 1994).

The Mexico-Texan [1935]

The Mexico-Texan he's one fonny man
Who leeves in the region that's north of the Gran',
Of Mexican father he born in these part,
And sometimes he rues it dip down in he's heart.

For the Mexico-Texan he no gotta lan',
He stomped on the neck on both sides of the Gran',
The dam gringo lingo he no cannot spik,
It twisters the tong and it make you fill sick.
A cit'zen of Texas they say that he ees,
But then, why they call him the Mexican Grease?
Soft talk and hard action, he can't understan',
The Mexico-Texan he no gotta lan'.

If he cross the reever, eet ees just as bad,
On high poleeshed Spanish he break up his had,
American customs those people no like,
They hate that Miguel they should call him El Mike,
And Mexican-born, why they jeer and they hoot,

"Go back to the gringo! Go lick at hees boot!"
In Texas he's Johnny, in Mexico Juan,
But the Mexico-Texan he no gotta lan'.

Elactions come round and the gringos are loud,
They pat on he's back and they make him so proud,
They give him mezcal and the barbacue meat,
They tell him, "Amigo, we can't be defeat."
But efter elaction he no gotta fran',
The Mexico-Texan he no gotta lan'.

Except for a few with their cunning and craft
He count just as much as a nought to the laft,
And they say everywhere, "He's a burden and drag,
He no gotta country, he no gotta flag."
He no gotta voice, all he got is the han'
To work like the burro; he no gotta lan'.

And only one way can his sorrows all drown,
He'll get drank as hell when next payday come roun',
For he has one advantage of all other man,
Though the Mexico-Texan he no gotta lan',
He can get him so drank that he think he will fly
Both September the Sixteen and Fourth of July.

The Hammon and the Beans

Once we lived in one of my grandfather's houses near Fort Jones. It was just a block from the parade grounds, a big frame house painted a dirty yellow. My mother hated it, especially because of the pigeons that cooed all day about the eaves. They had fleas, she said. But it was a quiet neighborhood at least, too far from the center of town for automobiles and too near for musical, night-roaming drunks.

At this time Jonesville-on-the-Grande was not the thriving little city that it is today. We told off our days by the routine on the post. At six sharp the flag was raised on the parade grounds to the cackling of the bugles, and a field piece thundered out a salute. The sound of the shot bounced away through the morning mist until its echoes worked their way into every corner of town. Jonesville-on-the-Grande woke to the cannon's roar, as if to battle, and the day began.

At eight the whistle from the post laundry sent us children off to school. The whole town stopped for lunch with the noon whistle, and after lunch everybody went back to work when the post laundry said that it was one o'clock, except for those who could afford to be old-fashioned and took the siesta. The post was the town's clock, you might have said, or like some insistent elder person who was always there to tell you it was time.

At six the flag came down, and we went to watch through the high wire fence that divided the post from the town. Sometimes we joined in the ceremony, standing at salute until the sound of the cannon made us jump. That must have been when we had just studied about George Washington in school, or recited "The Song of Marion's Men" about Marion the Fox and the British cavalry that chased him up and down the broad Santee. But at other times we stuck out our tongues and jeered at the soldiers. Perhaps the night before we had hung at the edges of a group of old men and listened to tales about Aniceto Pizaña and the "border troubles," as the local paper still called them when it referred to them gingerly in passing.

It was because of the border troubles, ten years or so before, that the soldiers had come back to old Fort Jones. But we did not hate them for that; we admired them even, at least sometimes. But when we were thinking about the border troubles instead of Marion the Fox, we hooted them and the flag they were lowering, which for the moment was theirs alone, just as we would have jeered an opposing ball team, in a friendly sort of way. On these occasions even Chonita would join in the mockery, though she usually ran home at the stroke of six. But whether we taunted or saluted, the distant men in khaki uniforms went about their motions without noticing us at all.

The last word from the post came in the night when a distant bugle blew. At nine it was all right because all the lights were on. But sometimes I heard it at eleven when everything was dark and still, and it made me feel that I was all alone in the world. I would even doubt that I was me, and that put me in such a fright that I felt like yelling out just to make sure I was really there. But next morning the sun shone and life began all over again, with its whistles and cannon shots and bugles blowing. And so we lived, we and the post, side by side with the wire fence in between.

The wandering soldiers whom the bugle called home at night did not wander in our neighborhood, and none of us ever went into Fort Jones. None except Chonita. Every evening when the flag came down she would leave off playing and go down towards what was known as the "lower" gate of the post, the one that opened not on main street but against the poorest part of town. She went into the grounds and to the mess halls and pressed her nose against the screens and watched the soldiers eat. They sat at long tables calling to each other through food-stuffed mouths.

"Hey bud, pass the coffee!"

"Give me the ham!"

"Yeah, give me the beans!"

After the soldiers were through, the cooks came out and scolded Chonita, and then they gave her packages with things to eat.

Chonita's mother did our washing, in gratefulness—as my mother put it—for the use of a vacant lot of my grandfather's which was a couple of blocks down the street. On the lot was an old one-room shack which had been a shed long ago, and this Chonita's father had patched up with flattened-out pieces of tin. He was a laborer. Ever since the end of the border troubles there had been a development boom in the Valley, and Chonita's father was getting his share of the good times. Clearing brush and building irrigation ditches, he sometimes pulled down as much as six dollars a week. He drank a good deal of it up, it was true. But corn was just a few cents a bushel in those days. He was the breadwinner, you might say, while Chonita furnished the luxuries.

Chonita was a poet too. I had just moved into the neighborhood when a boy came up to me and said, "Come on! Let's go hear Chonita make a speech."

She was already on top of the alley fence when we got there, a scrawny little girl of about nine, her bare dirty feet clinging to the fence almost like hands. A dozen other kids were there below her, waiting. Some were boys I knew at school; five or six were her younger brothers and sisters.

"Speech! Speech!" they all cried. "Let Chonita make a speech! Talk in English, Chonita!"

They were grinning and nudging each other except for her brothers and sisters, who looked up at her with proud serious faces. She gazed out beyond us all with a grand, distant air and then she spoke.

"Give me the hammon and the beans!" she yelled. "Give me the hammon and the beans!"

She leaped off the fence and everybody cheered and told her how good it was and how she could talk English better than the teachers at the grammar school.

I thought it was a pretty poor joke. Every evening almost, they would make her get up on the fence and yell, "Give me the hammon and the beans!" And everybody would cheer and make her think she was talking English. As for me, I would wait there until she got it over with so we could play at something else. I wondered how long it would be before they got tired of it all. I never did find out because just about that time I got the chills and fever, and when I got up and around, Chonita wasn't there anymore.

In later years I thought of her a lot, especially during the thirties when I was growing up. Those years would have been just made for her. Many's the time I have seen her in my mind's eye, in the picket lines demanding not bread, not cake, but the hammon and the beans. But it didn't work out that way.

One night Doctor Zapata came into our kitchen through the back door. He set his bag on the table and said to my father, who had opened the door for him, "Well, she is dead."

My father flinched. "What was it?" he asked.

The doctor had gone to the window and he stood with his back to us, looking out toward the lights of Fort Jones. "Pneumonia, flu, malnutrition, worms, the evil eye," he said without turning around. "What the hell difference does it make?"

"I wish I had known how sick she was," my father said in a very mild tone. "Not that it's really my affair, but I wish I had."

The doctor snorted and shook his head.

My mother came in and I asked her who was dead. She told me. It made me feel strange but I did not cry. My mother put her arm around my shoulders. "She is in Heaven now," she said. "She is happy."

I shrugged her arm away and sat down in one of the kitchen chairs.

"They're like animals," the doctor was saying. He turned round suddenly and his eyes glistened in the light. "Do you know what that brute of a father was doing when I left? He was laughing! Drinking and laughing with his friends."

"There's no telling what the poor man feels," my mother said.

My father made a deprecatory gesture. "It wasn't his daughter, anyway."

"No?" the doctor said. He sounded interested.

"This is the woman's second husband," my father explained. "First one died before the girl was born, shot and hanged from a mesquite limb. He was working too close to the tracks the day the Olmito train was derailed."

"You know what?" the doctor said. "In classical times they did things better. Take Troy, for instance. After they stormed the city they grabbed the babies by the heels and dashed them against the wall. That was more humane."

My father smiled. "You sound very radical. You sound just like your relative down there in Morelos."

"No relative of mine," the doctor said. "I'm a conservative, the son of a conservative, and you know that I wouldn't be here except for that little detail."

"Habit," my father said. "Pure habit, pure tradition. You're a radical at heart."

"It depends on how you define radicalism," the doctor answered. "People tend to use words too loosely. A dentist could be called a radical, I suppose. He pulls up things by the roots."

My father chuckled.

"Any bandit in Mexico nowadays can give himself a political label," the doctor went on, "and that makes him respectable. He's a leader of the people."

"Take Villa, now . . ." my father began.

"Villa was a different type of man," the doctor broke in.

"I don't see any difference."

The doctor came over to the table and sat down. "Now look at it this way," he began, his finger in front of my father's face. My father threw back his head and laughed.

"You'd better go to bed and rest," my mother told me. "You're not completely well, you know."

So I went to bed, but I didn't go to sleep, not right away. I lay there for a long time while behind my darkened eyelids Emiliano Zapata's cavalry charged down to the broad Santee, where there were grave men with hoary hairs. I was still awake at eleven when the cold voice of the bugle went gliding in and out of the dark like something that couldn't find its way back to wherever it had been. I thought of Chonita in Heaven, and I saw her in her torn and dirty dress, with a pair of bright wings attached, flying round and round like a butterfly shouting, "Give me the hammon and the beans!"

Then I cried. And whether it was the bugle, or whether it was Chonita or what, to this day I do not know. But cry I did, and I felt much better after that.

CHAPTER 5

Preserving Cultural Traditions

Adina De Zavala (1861–1955)

The Courteous and Kindly Child and the "Good People" on the Underground Passageway

History and Legends of the Alamo and Other Missions in and Around San Antonio is a compilation of personally recovered historical documents, folk narratives, and legends concerning the Alamo and the Spanish Missions in San Antonio and other areas of Texas. The author, Adina De Zavala, was the granddaughter of Lorenzo De Zavala, a Mexican statesman who also became the first unofficial Vice-President of the Republic of Texas. *History and Legends of the Alamo* is a work at once original, romantic, and embedded in layers of factual and fictional stories. De Zavala, until recently, was the unrecognized heroine of the Alamo who worked incessantly to recover it from capitalist entrepreneurs in the 1890s and then have it recognized by the State of Texas in 1905. An early member of the Daughters of the Republic of Texas, De Zavala was voted out of this organization for working to preserve an understanding of the Alamo that included its history as a Spanish Mission and a more factual view of the 1836 battle. (RF)

Further reading: Adina De Zavala, *History and Legends of the Alamo and Other Missions in and Around San Antonio,* ed. and introduced by Richard R. Flores (Houston: Arte Público Press, 1996); Richard R. Flores, "Private Visions, Public Culture: The Making of the Alamo," *Cultural Anthropology* 10 (1995): 99–115.

The Alamo has always been credited with being the abode of ghosts—and some of them marvelous ghosts. Every one knows the story of the ghosts with the flaming swords who are forever stationed to protect the Alamo fortress. This old Fort also boasts of a number of ghosts who have a predilection for stormy weather and who do not confine their sphere of action to any special apartment, but who manifest themselves in all parts of the Fort. At the time that part of the Fort was used as a prison for detention of city prisoners—many of the inmates—prisoners and officers alike, bore testimony to the strange and unaccountable noises—the rattling of chains, the distinct military tread of ghostly sentinels, the clank of sword and spur being heard, especially on rainy or stormy nights. Other singular and fascinating tales refer to the "good people" who are believed to inhabit the vast underground passageways leading from the old fortress and connecting with all the other missions of the San Antonio Valley and the Ancient Government Palace. One of the more modern of these tales follows:

A beautiful and cultivated gentlewoman lived on the east side of the San Antonio River in a strongly built rock house. Everything in the place betokened refinement and culture. One afternoon she sat alone sewing; looking up from her sewing, she sighed, as gazing toward the town she watched the slow and painful progress of her husband on his return from a trip for the mail. He had been injured in one of the early Indian fights and had been incapacitated ever since. He was up and down continually, but never seemingly making any headway toward health, and this had continued for seven years—soon after the first anniversary of his little girl's birth. There was almost no way for women to make money in those days, and speculation as to the future caused the brave little woman much anxiety. When he came in she said, "O Joseph, I was just praying that some time Ursula might meet the good woman of the underground passage! There might still be hope for you! Ursula is so kind and gentle and loving that she could not fail to win the good will of these good people. I am living in that hope. You know the good fortune that befell Mrs. Ramón's little Mary!" "Dear Ann, I know the good fortune that befell Mary and her mother, but you know I do not believe in any 'underground people' or 'the good woman of the underground passage'! I still think that some friend chose this method—of helping them. I am really surprised that you repeat the oldfolk tales current here about—but I think, dear, that in your case the wish is father to the desire to believe, for your heart is set on my visiting the celebrated Doctor———." The couple then became engrossed in the bundle of mail which had arrived and some business matters were discussed at length. It was quite late before they thought of the time, and the continued absence of little Ursula, who had gone over to the old Alamo Fort to play with some of her little friends and pick wild flowers in the fields. The mother decided to go to look, for the children should have been at home long before. As she neared the Alamo Fort, and all was still, she became nervous, for in those days there was still the possibility of Indian raids. She passed around the Fort and called, but everything was quiet; there were no children to be found anywhere. Much alarmed, she visited the nearest house and the people said that the children had returned to the town long ago. Not wishing needlessly to distress her husband, she went around the place and on into San Antonio to the homes of some of the children, hoping, but not believing that her child had followed one of her friends to her home. But none of them had seen her since they had separated to pluck the wild flowers, or, play hide-and-seek. They thought it strange that she had gone home without telling them; however, they had reconciled it to themselves by saying that she may have gone too far, and become tired.

The mother, now almost frantic, called upon the men to take up the search while she went back home to try if possible to divert her husband who was powerless to render aid.

All thought of Indians, and the men started out to examine the vicinity of the Alamo, where the children had been at play, for signs of them, but no trace of Indians could be found. A number carried lanterns, and it occurred to some to examine the ruins, thinking that it may have been possible for her to have fallen among the rocks from the housetops in such a way as to render her unconscious. They had about abandoned all hope when some of them entered the arched room fronting the *baluarte* [buttress] on the south side of the courtyard adjoining the Church. They were about to leave when they caught a gleam of something white in the shadow, and there was little Ursula fast asleep with her lap full of wild flowers. These she carefully gathered up, when the happy women in the party kissed her awake, and she was soon restored to the arms of her distracted parents.

When questioned, Ursula explained that the children were playing "hide-and-seek" and while she was hiding, a dear old lady who had entered the Alamo, caught her dress on a thorn bush and had fallen down. Ursula had helped her up and had given her some of her flowers. After she had rested, Ursula had carried her bundles and assisted her out of the Alamo. Just then, she saw the children dart about, and thinking they were looking for her, she dashed back to her hiding place. She did not know how she came to fall asleep. The old lady gave her something small wrapped up and motioned her to put it in her pocket. And there it was in her pocket. With suppressed excitement, the mother held out her hand for the package. It suddenly flashed upon her that her little girl had really met the "good woman" of the underground way. In the package were several very old Spanish gold coins, two diamonds and three pearls. Without doubt she had met the "good woman of the underground passage," and her first thought was that now, Joseph, her husband, could go to consult and secure the services of the eminent specialist so long looked forward to. She fell on her knees in thanksgiving, and then, pulling the child to her side, covered her with kisses.

Adolfo Carrillo (1865–1926)

The Phantoms at San Luis Rey

A political refugee from persecution by the government of Mexican dictator Porfirio Díaz, Adolfo Carrillo settled in San Francisco, California, where he continued working in his profession as a journalist for Spanish-language newspapers. Besides working as newspaperman, Carrillo also ran his own printing establishment and wrote books. His book *Cuentos californianos*, first published in the early 1920s, indicates the degree to which he identified with the Hispanic background of California and the Southwest. In his story from that book, *The Phantoms of San Luis Rey*, Carrillo evokes the pastoral life on the large haciendas, the adventure and ever-present danger of pirate and bandit incursions and contrasts it with the rowdy, cosmopolitan atmosphere of California during early statehood. His irreverent sketch of the padre depicts a Don Juan-type libertine whose sins are even more egregious because they are committed during the sacred season of Christmas. (NK)

Further reading: Adolfo Carrillo, *Cuentos californianos* (San Antonio: Lozano, c. 1922).

Trans.: NK

I

Friar Pedro Somera, Prior of the San Luis Rey Mission, was leaving the Refectory, where he had just enjoyed a large breakfast, and proceeded to make his way along the broad arches that bordered the vegetable garden. With one hand, he held his Breviary, and with the other, he patted his belly, as if to tell it, "Look how stuffed you are! If you keep that up, we'll have to roll around instead of walk." Later, feeling tired, he stretched out in his favorite hammock, drawing in great whiffs of the fragrant air that wafted through the flower gardens. As he began to read his Breviary, the vibrating ring of the large bell in the squat tower announced its presence: One! Two! Three! "Holy Mother of God!" murmured Friar Somera, hopping up from his swing all at once. "Someone needs Communion urgently! Is it possible that Doña Claudina is still sick?" At that moment, Gervasio, the neophyte, appeared. After kissing the Prior's hand reverently, he said that Don Cirilo Zárate's wife was in agony and was begging for his presence at her deathbed.

"I have a saddled horse outside awaiting your Reverence. It is tame, but fast, and we'll arrive in Encinitas within a half hour." This transpired one morning in June, 1815. After a half hour of riding their horses at a loping trot, the Prior and his aide were crossing the Estero Valley, which was thickly vegetated around sand dunes and white oaks, and inhabited by meadow larks and aquatic fowl. In the distance, Lake Piedras Blancas appeared in a silvery ribbon, which reflected on its surface the branches of the weeping willows along its banks. It was enthrallingly beautiful day, with the chiaroscuro of woods and mountains and reds and blues in the distance.

"Finally, we're here!" Friar Somera exclaimed with impatience upon seeing the estate house of the large Encinitas Ranch, with its white walls, wide portals and reddish roofs.

Don Cirilo came out running to greet the illustrious prelate who, after dismounting, made his way to the patio between two rows of servants competing with each other for the honor of kissing his habit. He followed the hacienda owner into a large living room whose windows faced the threatening outline of the San Isidro Hills.

I

In a room of feudal dimensions, with natural light entering in golden cascades, could be seen a generously proportioned bed in whose center lay the emaciated figure of Doña Claudina, almost lost amid quilts of purple silk. On the wall over the bed hung a tormented ivory crucifix inclining its divine head, radiating from its wounded body sublime hope and spiritual motivation. In one of the corners was erected a small altar lighted by candles and covered with flowers. On seeing the priest, the sick woman extended a hand glittering with precious stones.

"Glory be to God!" she murmured.

She gestured for her husband to leave them, and was soon left alone with her conscience and the missionary. After her husband had exited and the door closed, the agonizing woman gave a tender glance at the crucifix and moved her lips in silent prayer. Then she turned from the altar and, propping herself up on pillows, began to speak. "Did your Reverence ever meet Juan José de la Serna, who was prior of San Luis Rey for many years? When he arrived in California from Spain, I was a young woman of marrying age considered to be very beautiful. My father, Don Juan Regil, was the owner of Rancho Escondido, about a league from the mission. Of course, I would come into contact with José . . . I mean, Friar Serna . . ."

"Continue, Doña Claudina, continue. As sinners, we are all the same, even at the time of death!" interjected Somera, kissing the golden cross that hung from his gray habit.

The dying woman continued: "Serna was a young, gallant-looking man, with shining dark eyes, and his Franciscan habit fit him beautifully. What happened was that he fell in love with me and I with him. And, with my eyes wide open, I fell head over heels, right into his arms . . . We would see each other every night in the basement of the mission, only able to see each other in the dim light shed by a lantern. The fruit of that sacrilegious love affair was a little girl . . ."

"How can this be possible, Doña Claudina? Isn't what you've said the product of feverish hallucinations?" asked the priest, growing pale. "Father, I am confessing what I did, and not what I imagine I did!" the sick woman blurted out, lowering herself into the bed sheets.

Slowly and painfully, the confession grew, passing from the idyllic to the dramatic, from the dramatic to the tragic. Before wedding Don Cirilo, Claudina was already the mother of two little children, both of whom had been entombed by Friar Serna in fear that his secret and that of his lover would be discovered. Crazy and furious on the very same day of her wedding, attired in her shimmering wedding gown, Claudina lifted her veil and, before the entire devout wedding assembly, cursed the Prior with these infamous words:

"May God grant that your black blood stain the steps of this altar! May the heavens ordain that you die the agony of the damned and that your unburied cadaver be food for buzzards and wolves!"

Seeing that the penitent woman was failing as she gripped her bed sheets, Friar Somera prostrated himself by the bed and with a sympathetic and solemn voice said, "In the name of the Father, the son and the Holy Ghost, I absolve you and bless you."

And turning his saddened face toward the ivory crucifix, which seemed to move its angelic blue eyes, he began singing the "Veni Creator Spiritus" hymn in a vibrant voice.

III

In 1816, Prior Serna had been transferred from San Luis Rey to San Juan Capistrano, and in 1818, he was still there scandalizing the region with his binges and loud orgies. It was at this time that he was interrupted by the sudden invasion of that ferocious pirate René Bouchard, who had been commissioned as a corsair by one of the nascent Spanish-American republics involved in a war to the death with Spain and its possessions in the Americas.

Bouchard was about thirty years old, a giant of a man with Herculean strength. It is said that he could kill a man with just one blow of his fist and that he could bend a horseshoe with just two fingers. On the night before Christmas Eve of that same year, 1818, Bouchard disembarked in San Diego, followed by three hundred of his men, all armed to the teeth, each one with a cutlass, two pistols and a combat knife. Captain Bouchard wore a short red jacket, short pants of the same color and knee-high boots. A skull cap covered his unruly black mane and from his waist hung a cutlass with a silver hilt, a knife with a gold handle and dragoon pistols. His face was fiery red with a condor's eyes, a curved nose, a large black, twisted mustache that reached back to his ears. When his boats had been spied along the Pacific Coast, flying the skull and crossbones, all the fearful people headed for the hills, leaving behind their homes and possessions. Bouchard would drink the strongest liquor without ever getting drunk, as he entertained himself sacking, killing and raping virgins, many of whom he would pass on to his soulless crewmen after he had had first rights.

Bouchard disembarked as evening fell, and without wasting time headed straight for Vista Linda, crossing through La Luz Ranch and San Onofre Ranch, setting them on fire as he went by. The owner of the latter got it into his head to mount a horse and gallop off to San Juan Capistrano Mission in order to warn the missionaries and save the holy reliquaries housed there.

While this was happening in the countryside, where everything was ablaze, lighting up the landscape with an infernal glow, the prior of San Juan Capistrano was using the pretext of Christmas to host a feast of imperial proportions, so much so that the large oak table was squeaking from the weight of the wines and exquisite cuts of meat it had to support. Half a dozen women of the night brought from Monterey, which was at that time a nest of smugglers, were attending to the erotic desires of the missionaries, many of them perched on the ample laps of the friars. Friar Serna poured one cup after another of amontillado sherry, and from time to time, he rolled up his habit to dance, singing verses so profane that they made the statues of the Virgin tremble in their niches.

Suddenly, there was a furious knocking at the door, and Don Serafin Roquena entered with a distorted look on his face. He had witnessed the advance of the pirate hordes of Bouchard.

"Save the holy relics and, if possible, yourselves as well! In less than fifteen minutes, the enemies of the King and of God will arrive at Capistrano!" And, without answering all the questions that were flying at him from every direction, he remounted his horse and headed for Los Angeles. With the scare, the drunkenness evaporated in a second; the fallen women cried while grabbing on to the Franciscans' habits, and Serna, taking advantage of all the confusion, ran out to the stables, bridled a mare and balanced himself on its back. But it was too late! The pirates had surrounded the mission and were already sacking and pillaging it. Captain Bouchard, who without a doubt had heard of Prior Serna, ordered that the reverend be brought to him. Facing the prior, Bouchard stated, "So you're the one who walled up and killed your own children? Ah, this Ferdinand VII has created the best disciples! But he cannot beat me in devilry. By killing I serve God better than he does praying."

What followed that night was a saturnalia. The mission cellar was emptied of all its wines, the orgy lasting until four in the morning, when the pirates decided to head for the San Luis Rey Mission. They arrived there as the first rays of the morning sun shone on the Coyuco Hills. Prior Serna, who had been tied to a mule, with his habit stained with blood and wine, was taken by the pirates to a place called Aguaje. Swearing and laughing the whole time, they strung him up to the branches of a stout birch tree, which still exists today and the campesinos call the "Friar's Tree." They say that every bird that perches on its branches immediately falls dead as if struck by lightning. And every time they try to burn it down, it grows back even stronger. And they say that on moonlit nights, you can see the silhouette of a lynched man swinging in the nocturnal breeze, causing the coyotes foraging in that deserted thicket to howl.

IV

One winter night, some travelers were warming themselves by the stove of the Grant Hotel in the city of San . . . Among the guests, mostly Americans, there was a Hollywood photographer who had been searching for phantasmagoric images, that is, images of specters and ghosts for one of Ibsen's dramas that was being produced.

"My camera lenses," he was saying to the group, "were ground in Berlin by the famous lens maker, Dr. Urbach. Nothing escapes those lenses, not even intangible and invisible objects. I've heard that at the San Luis Rey Mission there are apparitions, and this very night I'm going to see if that's true or not. Can any of you give me any details?"

After a few seconds of silence, a corpulent old-timer, a Californio from his appearance and diction, responded in a slow and even tone, "Well, they've been telling you true. Night after night, ghosts are seen at the mission. First there are two girls who appear dressed in white; then, there's a young woman; and lastly, there's a missionary priest who is really terrifying. I've seen them myself on various occasions." The listeners were so interested in the conversation that they crowded around the young photographer and the old Californio.

After a minute, the photographer broke the silence and said, "Very well, would you accompany me there? If what you say is true, I'll give you a check for one thousand dollars. But if it's a lie, you'll have to pay the bill." Then, addressing everyone at once and nobody in particular, he exclaimed, "Gentlemen, would you all like to accompany me?"

So, some out of curiosity and others out of love for art, left the hotel and headed for San Luis Rey.

It was raining on and off, and a threatening sky cloaked the evening. Mr. Link, the Hollywood photographer, loaded his camera and prepared his lenses on arriving. He told his companions to keep silent and to keep searching through the ruins. How many hours did they spend in their vigil? No one knows. But all of a sudden from the cracked walls of the mission appeared two girls dressed in white, one holding the hand of the other, both shadowy profiles in the halo of light. Click, click! went the photographer's camera, and the apparition disappeared among the crumbling colonnades. By the light of an electric bulb Mr. Link examined the negative and shouted in excitement, "Gentlemen, the world of the spirits is an undeniable reality! Wonderful! Let's continue!"

Fifteen minutes later, lightning erupted in the countryside and bathed the colonnades with a livid radiance. A woman dressed in mourning was wandering through the ruins, bending over here and there in search of something or someone. On the click-clicking of the camera, the mysterious silhouette was swallowed by the shadows, leaving the impression among the observers that it had not been anything but an optical illusion caused by the midnight shadows.

The proud and sharp voice of the Hollywood artist soon was heard to remove their doubt, as he held up another negative and exclaimed, "By jingo, splendid! We have stolen heaven's secret!"

Later, he looked at his time piece and, guided by the old Californio, he started walking to the southeast of San Luis Rey, while pushing his equipment on wheels. It was about two in the morning; the thick drizzle had ceased and a thick fog had come in from the nearby ocean. His companions followed Mr. Link to the banks of a small stream in whose curve the white oak tree was standing, a grey skeleton profiled against the pulsing clouds. The group stopped in front of the tree and crowded around the camera. During a few moments, the hooting of owls and croaking of swamp frogs were the only beats to be heard in the dead of night. But then the click-click of the camera was heard again and, on raising their eyes, not without fear, they perceived the figure of a lynched man swinging in the tree while trying to untie with fleshless hands the knot and the hangman's noose. As the apparition extinguished itself, flocks of carrion flew back and forth like blind bats in search of their lairs. The illusion had completely disappeared!

The next day by breakfast time, Mr. Link had developed his negatives. There they were, without the shadow of a doubt, the details of the somber drama, the phantasmagoric transformed into positive images, suffering souls surprised by science, dramatic episodes right out of Aeschylus, emerging briefly in life as a weird phenomenon.

"And why not?" Mr. Link was saying on being congratulated by his friends. "In England, the modern camera has captured the silhouettes of King Lear and Banquo entering the banquette hall, thus demonstrating that the Bard of Avon's creations were reality and not fantasy.

"Ladies and gentlemen," concluded the quicksilver photographer as he put on his coat and tied up his suitcase with a nervous hand, "the train for Los Angeles leaves in ten minutes. Very soon people will applaud the showing on screen of the tragedy without music that you have just witnessed. So long!" And in two hops he was at the station, improvising a way to take a slug of liquor from a whiskey flask without being seen, because the spirited enjoy the privilege of communicating with spirits.

Herminia Chacón

Samuel's Christmas Eve

From the noted family of New Mexico (later El Paso) journalists and writers, Herminia Chacón began her literary career publishing poetry and short stories in her father's Albuquerque newspaper *La Bandera Americana*. In the December 21, 1923, issue of the paper appeared this well-wrought Christmas tale. (NK)

Further reading: A. Gabriel Meléndez, *So That All Is Not Lost: The Poetics of Print in Nuevomexicano Communities, 1834–1958* (Albuquerque: University of New Mexico Press, 1997).

Trans.: NK

It was December 24th, and it seemed that each and every soul on earth was busy and content. Except, that is, for Samuel. He just could not find a job, and he was so tired of roaming the streets, suffering hunger and freezing from the cold.

What's worse, the landlady running the boarding house where he rented a room—who always charged him on time and to the penny—at last announced that he either pay up or get out. Samuel answered that he'd be leaving, he just did have a penny to his name. Just one favor was all he asked her: that she let him stay one more night, that being Christmas Eve. But the landlady was not in the mood for charity. She needed money, and it was hard for her to earn it, too. The poor woman had been abandoned for a time by her beloved husband, who had taken off all of a sudden and was not to be found. So, poor Samuel left the house with all his earthly possessions tied up in a red silk neckerchief.

As he passed a large toy store, a boy called out for him to enter. There Samuel found the owner: a short and fat but greedy man.

"Would you like to earn five *pesos*?" he asked Samuel. "Yes? Well, I need a Santa Claus. That boy, there, will give you a suit and you'll go outside with a sack of toys and do all you can to get people to come into the store. You understand?"

Samuel did not understand him all that well, but he nevertheless followed the boy, who helped him dress up.

After awhile, Samuel appeared in the happy garb of good old St. Nick. He picked up his sack of toys and a bell, went out and started calling for passersby to enter the store. As the day was quite cold and Samuel was shivering and coughing, prospects did not look too good. Children surrounded him, laughing and shouting, "That's not Santa Claus!" All that noise and carrying on at last caught the attention of the store owner, who came out and yelled at Samuel in a furor: "Take your five *pesos* and get out of here. You're nothing but a laughingstock!"

Samuel took the five pesos and, forgetting to take off his Santa suit and leave the sack of toys, he headed through some of the poorest neighborhood in town.

Samuel walked as if in a dream. He headed for the boarding house he had left behind that morning and went in. He stopped for a moment to rest at the foot of the stairway, when all of a sudden he was surrounded by poor children from the neighborhood. For these miserable and needy children, Samuel was not an object of ridicule but St. Nicholas himself.

Among the joyous shouts of "Saint Nicholas" and "Santa Claus," Samuel gave out the gifts to all of the children, even to the landlady's kids.

"God bless you," she told Samuel. "If it weren't for you, my poor children would have had a vary sad Christmas Eve. But, come on in, my husband is here too."

Samuel entered the house to the greetings of a tall, strong-looking man. "Are you Samuel?" he asked. "Well, cheer up, I have work for the both of us in a new factory." Samuel was so choked up, he couldn't speak. He had five dollars in his pocket, and outside children were shouting, "Hurrah for Santa Claus!" and "Wow, that was Santa Claus!" And now, his friend was telling him that there was work for the both of them! Samuel was happy. It was Christmas Eve and church bells were ringing: "Peace on earth, goodwill to men."

Jovita González (1904–1983)

The First Cactus Blossom

Jovita González was a teacher, folklorist, and writer who was the first Mexican American woman to graduate with a master's degree in the state of Texas. As a disciple of the eminent "Father of Texas Folklore," J. Frank Dobie, she became president of the Texas Folklore Society.

After graduating, González was unsuccessful in getting a university teaching position, and returned to Corpus Christi, Texas, and dedicated the rest of her life to teaching high school Spanish and to writing textbooks, novels, and literary adaptations of oral lore. González's two novels, *Dew on the Thorn* and *Caballero,* remained unpublished while she was alive. *The First Cactus Blossom*, one of the many tales she collected and elaborated, is an Amerindian folk legend that she published in 1932 in a Texas Folklore Society anthology titled *Tales and Songs of the Texas-Mexicans*. In the tale, the beliefs of Hispanics concerning Amerindian customs and religion are illustrated poetically. (SR)

Further reading: Jovita González, *Caballero* (College Station: Texas A&M Press, 1996), *Dew on the Thorn* (Houston: Arte Público Press, 1997).

For some unknown crime that had been committed, a thing of evil had been sent to punish the Indians. It was a black shapeless beast that walked over the land, flew through the air, burning with his breath all vegetation and living things and blasting all hopes. Sometimes in the shape of an Indian warrior, gloomy and forbidden, he was a forerunner of wars, pestilence, and famine. He spoke to no one and no one dared to address him as he passed through the villages, leaving panic behind him. Like all evil things, he was most unhappy and he longed for the companionship of man, for the touch of a little child and the smile of a maiden.

Tired of his solitary life, he went to the medicine men. The solution to his problem was difficult indeed. He would cease to be evil and become a mortal being when a maiden with hair like the rays of the sun, eyes like a royal emerald, and face like a magnolia blossom would allow him to kiss her. And because of this dim hope he grew more restless, trapped over the earth, and brought more death and destruction upon the people.

Now on the hill beyond was the city of the chief who was mighty and brave like the mountain lion. But a strange thing happened in the household of the king. A child was born to him, not bronzed like all people, but fair, with hair like the Sun god's and eyes like the emerald. All the soothsayers and witches were called to a council to interpret the meaning of it all.

"Oh, king," said the oldest of all, "a great joy and sorrow awaits thee. The child will bring happiness to your people but only though her death."

Then the king commanded the building of a big house in the heart of a deserted island. A thick cactus wall was built all around it and a double one of maguey. In this island the child and the wisest witch that could be found were placed. In the time the cactus grew so tall that the leaves reached the sky and the thorns were so sharp and pointed that not even a bird could fly through the fence.

And the king, seeing that his child was free from harm, was happy.

In the meantime the baby had grown into a lovely maiden. She sang all day and no lover robbed her of her dreams of peace. One night the old witch was awakened by the princess's screams. In her dreams she had been pursued by a black something with huge bat-like wings that filled her with terror. The witch knew that the time appointed by the prophesy was come and she began to study the means of saving her charge. Every night the princess had the same dream and each time the monster came nearer and nearer and scorched her with his fiery breath.

One evening, as the princess was walking by the wall, she was attracted by a waning plume black as night. It reminded her of the dreams she had had, but the voice that called her was sweet like the playing of a reed flute. She approached him and there heard the most wonderful things of the outside world and the people who lived beyond the cactus fence. That night she had the most dreadful dream of all, for the black monster took her in his arms and flew away to unknown regions. The old witch knew then that nothing could now save the princess. She told her good-bye and gave her a cactus thorn, with this admonition, "When in trouble, prick your hand with the thorn and you will be safe."

Next morning the princess heard the song of the unknown warrior. and she came out to meet him. Forgetting himself, forgetting to be gentle, he pressed her into his breast. With a cry of fear she broke loose, for the touch burned like the touch of the black beast in her dreams. She, remembering the cactus thorn, pricked her hand with it as the witch had advised her. To the warrior's antonishment, the princess at once flew into space, getting smaller and smaller, and finally settled in a cactus leaf. But even then she was beautiful, golden and pale. The cactus blossoms had been so ever since.

And then he wept and, kneeling, kissed the little flower that she had loved so well. As he did so something was born within him—a good heart.

Marcelina

Midwife (Collected by Annette Hesch Thorp, February 15 and March 11, 1941, New Mexico Federal Writers' Project)

Midwife is part of the oral histories collected from elderly Hispanas in New Mexico for the Works Progress Administration under President Franklin D. Roosevelt during the 1930s and 1940. The project was established to gather cultural and historical information to be published in a series of state guides. One of several collectors, Annette Hesch Thorp, interviewed many women about their lives and about local beliefs and customs. The wide range of stories included tales of local history, women and their work, beliefs in witches and other supernatural tales, as well as details about ordinary lives. The use of local herbal remedies and methods of curing were of great interest. The story included here tells not only of the remedies used and the way the midwives helped deliver babies, but also of beliefs about children born in leap year, the effects of the moon on a woman about to have her first child, and stories illustrating these beliefs. (TDR)

Further reading: Tey Diana Rebolledo and Teresa Márquez, eds., *Women's Tales from the New Mexico WPA: La diabla a pie* (Houston: Arte Público Press, 2000).

Juana Romero had been a *partera* (midwife) in the days when Lina was married. She had attended when Lina's children were born. In those days, the *partera* had a *tenedor* (holder) who always went with her to help at the births.

The *tenedor* was usually some old man who was still strong. He was taken to help the *partera* in case the birth should turn out to be a difficult one.

When a woman labored two or three days, which they sometimes did, the *tenedor* had plenty to do. A woman in labor was kept on her feet until the child was born. If she were not so very ill, she walked up and down by herself, but in bad cases, when the mother was too weak to stand alone, the *tenedor* had to hold her up and keep her walking, sometimes dragging her back and forth for hours. If she fainted or showed signs of fainting, the *partera* placed coals in a *barro* (dish) and sprinkled ground horse hair and *trementina* (resin or hard pitch from pinon trees) then held this smoke to the patient's nostrils until she revived. When she did, she was again made to walk, while the *tenedor* held her up. When a birth was easy, the *tenedor* had nothing to do, but was always taken along in case he should be needed.

Parteras learned their profession from their mothers or grandmothers, who had been midwives before them, and sometimes they started by helping at a delivery.

The *partera* often was the *curandera* also, but not always. The *curandera* treated all, men, women, and children, while the *partera* cared only for women.

Sometimes the *partera*'s husband was the *tenedor*—that was if he was strong. In that case both were gone most of the time. Their children and relatives attended their work, such as planting and wood hauling; for a good *partera* and *tenedor* not only cared for the sick women in their own village, but received calls from others. They never charged for their services, but left it to the patient's family to give what they thought their services were worth. Some were generous, and gave corn, beans, chili, goats, and sometimes money if they had it; but usually the pay was in grain. And if someone did not have very much and could not pay with grain, the father of the child helped the *partera's* husband with his planting or gathered his crops for him; or sometimes the women would go in the fall and plaster the *partera*'s house. All tried to pay, for they never knew how often they would need her.

The *partera* was called or sent for at all hours. Some came in wagons, others on horses or burros. If it were a burro or horse, the *partera* and *tenedor* rode the same animal, she in front holding her bag of *remedios* and the *tenedor* behind. Then there were times when she had to walk, for some were so poor that they were unable to provide any method of transportation.

There were two things that the old midwives dreaded, a first birth and births in the last quarter of the moon. They believed the moon had much to do with childbirths. The first quarter meant that the moon was weak, and it could not do much harm. A full moon meant that the moon was happy. In the last quarter it was dying and would try to do all the harm it could before being succeeded by another moon.

When a *partera* felt that she was getting old, and needed help, she looked around among her family and friends for someone to take her place. The one she picked had to be married, and close to middle age, for then she was through having children. A young woman with small children never became a midwife, for she was either raising a baby or expecting one, and had no time to spare. If one of her married daughters was strong and fearless, she would take her; but if her own daughter was not considered sufficiently courageous or intelligent, a friend or relative, who was suitable, was chosen.

The *partera* first taught her helper about *remedios*, what each one was good for, and how to use them. After the pupil knew about these *remedios*, she was taken along with the midwife to help a birth. If it were an easy one, the helper did all the work under the direction of the *partera*; but if a difficult one, she helped only. After going to four or five cases, she was considered a midwife; she did not compete with her tutor, however, but only attended cases when the *partera* sent her as her substitute.

These old *parteras* were jealous of their position, never giving up their calling except for sickness or some disability. If this were the case, she would send the new one in her place. But as long as she lived, she expected to be consulted and told about everything when the helper got back.

Two *parteras* in the same village—and sometimes there were—never were friends. They were rivals and envious of each other. If one *partera* was called, the other felt aggrieved, and when called by some member of the family, who had summoned the other *partera*, she would refuse to go. The only ones approved were those they themselves had trained.

It often happened that a *partera* delivered a child, she was asked to be its *madrina* [godmother]. The midwives did not like this, because then they received nothing for their work; moreover, the *madrina* had to get the *ropón* (christening robe) and go to some expense for the baptismal. This often occurred because the parents were so poor, they did not have much to give the *partera*, and were ashamed to give too little. They knew that the *partera* told her family and friends what and how much was given by each, who tried to outdo the other in presents of food, work and grain.

Año bisiesto (leap year) was considered a very unlucky year. More women died in the childbirth in these years than in any other. Why this was thought unlucky, no one seems to know; but the old midwives used to say it was a very bad year.

When a baby was born dead, the *partera* had it buried next to the house under a canal waterspout so it could have water whenever it rained. This was done because the child had died before it could be baptized. These children were called *niños de limbo*, a place or region assigned to unbaptized children.

When someone came to call the *partera*, she was sure to ask if it was a *primeriza* (first child), if she did not know the woman. If it was and the moon was full she would feel no anxiety; but if it was a first child, and the moon was in the last quarter, she would be very fearful, saying, "I will do all I can, I will leave the rest to God."

Lina had been told by old Juana that the moon did not like women, and would try to hurt them when the were expecting children; that expectant mothers had to be very careful, especially when there was an eclipse of the moon, for that was a sign that the moon was angry, and would do as much harm as it could. Also, women who were expecting a child were told to hang the door or padlock keys at their waists. This was the only thing that could prevent the moon from hurting the unborn child. And on moonlit nights windows were covered over, doors closed, and keys taken to bed with them. The reason for this was that in case there should be an eclipse late at night, the moon would not see and harm them while asleep.

Nina Otero-Warren (1882–1965)

The Clown of San Cristóbal

Old Spain in Our Southwest, published in 1936, is a series of reminiscences by educator and writer Nina Otero-Warren. Among them are stories influenced by folkloric material gathered by the Federal Writers Project during the 1930s. These stories reveal a sense of urgency that stems from the perception that the traditions and values of her Hispanic heritage were disappearing. Otero-Warren felt the isolation and alienation of this disappearance as she mourned an idealized Spanish past while trying to survive the transition to an Anglicized world. In *The Clown of San Cristóbal*, we have a tale describing a power struggle between the arrogant secular governor and the beloved priest of the town. The lowly sacristan saves the priest's job by answering cleverly (as well as philosophically) three questions the governor asks. The tale celebrates the intelligence of the common people. Otero, who was born into an old and distinguished family in New Mexico, was active in politics and in 1917 chaired New Mexico's suffragettes' chapter. She served as Santa Fe County school superintendent, held a position in President Franklin D. Roosevelt's Works Progress Administration, and was a candidate for the U.S. Senate, but was not elected. (TDR)

Further reading: Nina Otero, *Old Spain in Our Southwest* (New York: Harcourt Brace, and Company, 1936).

Midnight Mass was being celebrated in the village of San Cristóbal. Already most of the women and children had entered the church. In the plaza outside stood horses hitched to wagons, saddled horses with reins tied to wagon wheels, burros with coats thrown over their heads to prevent their straying, while their owners warmed themselves before the small fires which surrounded the church. All were awaiting the sound of the last bell which would announce the beginning of Mass. Candles in paper sacks, placed on the flat roof of the building, gave a pleasant illumination to the Mission church and to the *plaza.* A coach, drawn by four horses, arrived, and from it, with his family, stepped the Governor of the Province—a man more violent than kind, whose subjects were cowed but not subdued.

The arrival of the Governor was the signal for the last bell, for which the sacristan had been waiting. The Bald One was the nickname by which the sacristan was known. He served the people of the community as he did the priests of the parish; for on feast days he disguised himself as a clown, and with his laughter and his verses made up to suit the occasion he brought joy to the whole community, children and grown-ups. On this occasion the sacristan, attending to his religious duties with equal eagerness, seized the bell-rope and swung with it as the stroke of the copper bell announced the arrival of the Governor and the beginning of the services.

The church was lighted by wax candles, on the walls and before the altar. And, as this was the Mass of the Cock-crow on Christmas Eve, a miniature statue of Christ in the Crib was placed on the altar, with a plate for offerings from the faithfully devout who, after Mass, would come to kiss the hand and kneel at the tiny foot of the image of the new-born Saviour.

At the altar, dressing himself in the church vestments preparatory to saying Mass, the Priest, a most pious man, was praying aloud as he put on his vestments one by one. There was no adjoining room or sacristy, so the robes must be put on in the presence of the congregation. When he was ready, the Priest went to the foot of the altar where the sacristan was kneeling. He rang a tiny bell, and began the Mass of the Cock-crow. After the gospel, the people dropped their coins on the plate which the sacristan passed among them and then passed to the altar, with gifts for the Holy Child.

This annoyed the Governor. Here were his subjects, who had refused to contribute to his government, contributing generously to the Church! After Mass he and his family hurriedly left without stopping to wish the people Happy Christmas. On his way home the Governor determined that this Priest must be done away with, for it was evident he was too much loved by the people. The Governor must have an excuse to give to his subjects, lest they turn on him and destroy his government. After some deliberation, he determined to put an unanswerable riddle to the Priest.

On Christmas afternoon he sent for the Priest who arrived bewildered but hopeful of favors for his parish. On entering the presence of the Governor, the Priest said: "May God bless Your Excellency on this the birthday of the King of Kings."

"Yes, yes," said the Governor. "Be seated and listen well. I feel it my duty to test your ability to instruct the people of this province. Now, I will put three questions to you and give you three days to meditate on them. On Wednesday noon, present yourself here ready to make answer. If you cannot do this to my satisfaction, it will be evident that you are not fit to instruct the people, and I shall see that you are removed from this Mission. If, however, my questions are correctly answered, even I will believe in your superior knowledge and you may continue undisturbed in your religious work. My questions are:

"How deep is the ocean?

"How much is the Governor of this Province worth?

"What is the Governor thinking?"

The Priest made his departure. He went through the narrow streets with bowed head, blessing those who knelt and asked for his benediction, for he was beloved by all. For two days he said little, going about his duties as though in a daze. The sacristan, respecting his silence, waited on him until the beginning of the third morning when, after Mass, he went to him and said:

"Little Father, what makes you sad? Have I offended you? Maybe the food I have prepared has not been to your liking. Tell your humble servant that he may make reparation."

"My sadness," said the Priest, "is of another nature. I must appear before the Governor of the Province this day at the noon hour, and answer three questions correctly or be sent away. As the questions are unanswerable, I fear I shall never see you again or be able to serve the people of the Río Grande."

"May I presume on your silence and ask you to tell me, your ignorant servant, what the questions are that could make a Holy Man such as you, so sad?"

The Priest repeated the questions to the sacristan.

"Oh," said the sacristan, "those are not difficult. I will go and make answer for you."

"What!" said the Priest. "You! Why, it is impossible, he will recognize you even in my clothes. Your bald head would make you known even with a mask."

The sacristan hurriedly left the house and soon returned with a bundle under his arm.

"Little Father," he said, "I am not now the sacristan who serves you, but the clown who makes the world laugh and who soon will make the Governor think."

The sacristan hurried away and made up his face cleverly to look like the Priest.

"I must make myself look saintly," said the sacristan, addressing the Priest, "for, Padre, you have never looked into a mirror; you know not your resemblance to San Cristóbal. Not even San Pedro would recognize me now."

"But your baldness," said the Priest, "is not so easy to disguise. There is nothing to hold your wig on."

"I will attach it to my ears," said the sacristan, "and even fool the burros who will not then bray when they see me."

The sacristan worked until he put hair on a wig which he then slipped on his head.

"Now, Little Father, the benediction"—as he knelt for the Priest's blessing.

The sacristan hurriedly passed through the village, not noticing the people who called to him, thinking he was the Priest.

As the mid-day bells were ringing, the sacristan was admitted to the presence of the Governor. His Excellency was gleeful, for, certain that his questions could not be answered, he could now dispose of the Priest as he chose.

"Well, Father," said the Governor, "you have had time to meditate, but so learned a man needs not to reflect in answer to such simple questions. Let us proceed to the business which brings you here. My first question is: How deep is the ocean?"

The sacristan reflected for a moment, then slowly answered:

"The ocean is as deep as the fall of a stone thrown into it."

The Governor raised his eyebrows to his attendants, laughed aloud and exclaimed: "You are right. Listen, all of you! The Priest has correctly answered my first question; but, my good man, the second is not so easy! How much is the Governor worth?"

Again the sacristan seemed to reflect and meditatively answered: "The Governor is worth twenty-nine pieces of silver."

The Governor murmured in anger, but the sacristan continued: "Christ was sold for thirty pieces of silver."

The Governor was now the one who meditated. Greatly annoyed, and more serious, he gruffly said: "Now for my third question, one that no one but my God and I can answer correctly: What is the Governor thinking?"

The sacristan deliberated, then said: "The Governor is thinking I am the Priest. But," removing his wig and bowing, "I am only the Clown of San Cristóbal."

Fray Angelico Chavez (1910–1998)

The Fiddler and the Angelito

Angelico Chavez was fourteen when he left his home in New Mexico to join a Christian Brothers seminary in Cincinnati, Ohio. As his studies progressed, he developed an interest in New Mexico history, and would over the course of his life become a prolific contributor to New Mexican historiography. But his talents were not merely academic; Fray Angelico was also a painter and a creative writer. The twenty-three books of history, biography, genealogy, philology, poetry, and fiction, which he left to posterity, indeed make him one of the most important figures of the Hispanic cultural legacy. Fray Angelico also drew on his experiences as a Christian Brother to capture the ethos of the rural villages and Native American pueblos he ministered. In *The Fiddler and the Angelito*, Fray Angelico draws on the wellspring of communal beliefs and lore to give us a delightful story with a supernatural twist. (EGB)

Further reading: Angelico Chavez, *New Mexico Triptych: Being Three Panels and Three Accounts* (Paterson, N.J.: St. Anthony Guild Press, 1940), *My Penitente Land* (Albuquerque: University of New Mexico Press, 1974), *La Conquistadora: The Autobiography of an Ancient Statue* (Santa Fe: Sunstone Press, 1975), *Cantares: Canticles and Poems of Youth 1925–1932* (Houston: Arte Público Press, 2000).

From his father Facundo had inherited a creaky old violin and a paunchy female burro, together with a log *jacal*, plastered with the clay from which adobes are made, and which sheltered both the heir and the heirlooms.

With these he had also received enough skill to fiddle a few squeaky tunes and to arrange a cord of neatly-chopped firewood in the shape of a turkey's spread fan around the low sides and back of the donkey. With the pardonable pride of a specialist, Facundo would drive his load to some kitchen door and, having made a sale, would deftly pull a rip-cord which allowed the wood to roll gently into two neat piles on the ground.

For years and years Facundo had plied his trade of *leñero*, chopping and splitting piñon and juniper branches as evenly matched as matchsticks, then goading his seemingly overladen burro down the steep slopes of the mountain to the housewives in the valley who knew him as an old man when they were girls. His beast of burden, of course, was the same one only in the sense that one generation followed another from the original stock on the maternal side.

The violin, since it consisted of barren dead wood and the dried entrails of sheep, was the very same one his father had used. Like his father before him, Facundo was never known to play it at home, nor would he consent to fiddle at dances, even those given on the eve of the valley's patron saint.

Only when a child died did he take out the instrument from an adze-hewn chest in the corner of his *jacal*.

Incidentally, it was the only occasion, outside of Sundays and fiestas, that the donkey dam got a rest or the leisurely chance to wander off and possibly assure herself of a successor.

Facundo played long and heartily beside the little white coffin at the home. The melodies were the same *seguidillas* played at dances, half-sad and half-joyful as are old Spanish airs, and nobody wondered about this, possibly because disappointment stalks the dance floor and happiness surrounds a child, even a dead one. How the old fellow kept his flowing beard from tangling in the bow or the strings was more a source of wonder to the many children who hovered about undismayed by death. He then accompanied the body, sawing away all the while, from the home to the mission chapel and from the chapel to the *campo santo*, which lay tilted with its broken crosses and half-sunken graves upon the long bare slope between the village and his own mountain slope.

Such a monotonous life, bleak like a surrealist painter's limitless plain with hunched dark figures in the foreground, had to have a break, a highlight—either a bright pink seashell or a figure in unadulterated zinc white, to give finality to that maddeningly endless plain.

So here is one of those tales which change in name and locale with each telling; in truth, the various narrators in widely-scattered parts of New Mexico will say that it happened to a long-dead relative, or that the said relative knew the old woodcutter and fiddler, whose name was Miguel or Juan or Benito, and who had a tiff one day with an angel.

One summer day Facundo (which is the name I give him) was summoned to play for a little boy who had just died. He had expected the call because that very morning the mission bells down in the valley had chimed wildly and long for pure joy.

For New Mexico folks in those hard times long ago had their Faith for undertaker: a child in his innocence, was he not made part of God's singing Court? Indeed, it was only with regard to children that they were certain of salvation. The complex interior workings of adults, God knows, were for no man to judge, no matter how virtuous a person or how wicked. A grown individual was not even sure of himself in this matter, hence the grim necessity that some men felt for bloody penances at the *morada* during Lent; and one had to beg God's mercy on the most sincere and fervent *Penitente* after he was dead.

But for children who died, reaching Heaven was as simple as passing from one room to another. And so they called them *angelitos*, little angels. And no matter how painful, how bitter, a young mother's parting with the life of her life may be, still the church bells must rejoice that there was another being joined with the angels to praise God forever and pray for his own here below.

In this particular valley, besides the joyous ringing of bells observed elsewhere, there was this custom of long standing which Facundo and his fiddle was carrying on. But this time he received the news with a bit of impatience. Howsoever even the tenor of his ways and his calling, the old man had a mind of his own, which balked occasionally, and for no reason that he might have given, just as his burro sometimes chose to halt with its load on a steep mountain trail, or shook off the wood before her master had finished his turkey-fan arrangement. Most likely he had contracted this quirk from the animal, wooden stubbornness being an inborn trait peculiar to the species.

Briefly, Facundo told the messenger to be off, that he had decided to fetch wood from a certain cedar clump that day, and that no dead baby was going to keep him from it.

With more than his usual slow purpose he placed the criblike wooden saddle on the burro's back, cinched it tightly under the somewhat swollen belly, and ended this bit of harnessing by buckling the wide strap which passed loosely around the animal's buttocks under the tail. Then, with the authority of a bearded mahout, he gave the word to proceed.

No sooner were they among the pine trees and beyond sight of the *jacal* than the beast halted dead in her tracks. There was a steep wall of granite on the right side of the narrow path, and on the left a deep arroyo. Facundo stopped to venture a thought, for this donkey had never balked before when not loaded—none of his dynasty of donkeys ever had through the years. When almost buried beneath the fan of faggots, yes; often they halted stubbornly and he was forced to use his stout stick of scruboak without mercy.

He now applied the goad from all angles. Repeatedly the cudgel fell on one side of the rump, then the other. He vainly tried to reach the overlarge bulk of head in front where the great ears were spread meekly outward.

But in his anger Facundo had failed to take note of their position; for in a true orgy of stubbornness those ears either stood up straight like a jackrabbit's, or collapsed stiffly like a pair of scissors against the wooden neck. More blows fell on the end nearest him, accompanied by hoarse threats that echoed through the narrow defile.

Facundo stopped at last; to catch his breath, it is true, and also to find a way of getting past the gray woolly hulk to where the head was attached. For he knew that burros, like more rational creatures, are more amenable to persuasion when the matter is brought before their nose.

At this moment the sound of a thin clear voice gave him a start. He listened, and the ever-soughing pines seemed to hold their breath also.

"You cannot make her go, Facundo," he heard the voice say once more. "I have her tightly by the nose!"

A red cave appeared in the middle of the woodcutter's matted whiskers as his toothless jaw fell. He tried to look over the donkey's head between the massive cars, but it was too far forward. Then he threw his rheumy gaze over either side of the bulging gray flanks, but it was impossible to see around curves.

"You will have to make her back out," said the voice. It was a child's voice.

"Facundo, pull her back off the trail and then go to your house and get your violin!"

Facundo squatted down slowly and peered through the animal's thin legs. Peering back at him stood a beautiful little boy who did not have to bend much in order to look between the forelegs. He still had his little fingers clamped in the burro's nostrils, which as a rule never hung too far off the ground.

His slow mind still unaware of the truth, Facundo began to threaten the boy.

"You ill-reared brat!" he said angrily. "Let go of that nose."

The lad smiled back and did not move.

"If you do not let go of that nose, I will come over and break this stick on your legs," Facundo threatened.

The boy looked at the cliff on one side, then at the gully on the other, and then peeked back beneath the burro with a bigger smile.

"Very well. If you do not let go, I will go and tell your mother."

This time the child's answering smile was absolutely beatific.

"All right, you little *bribón* [brazen one]! Who is your mother?"

"My mother was that woman whose little boy died this morning!"

Slowly it all dawned on Facundo. But when the full truth finally lighted up his brain it was like a sunburst. Still blinded by it, he made the burro back out of the narrow trail by hauling on the loose strap under her tail, and quite smoothly, for presumably the little lad in white was applying his influence at the front end.

When the donkey turned around on wider ground Facundo did not see the child any more, nor did he expect to. But he did recognize the little face in the white coffin down in the valley as he falteringly rubbed the pine-resin on his bowstrings.

And never again did he miss a child's wake or burial; after that, no one had to be sent to call him from the mountain. The joyous peal of the bells below were summons enough.

CHAPTER 6

Militant Aesthetics

Rodolfo "Corky" Gonzales (1928–)

I Am Joaquín (Yo soy Joaquín)

Gonzales was born in Denver, Colorado, to migrant worker parents. He took up boxing at age fifteen in order to escape the despair and unpromising future of growing up poor and Chicano in an urban barrio. He became a very successful professional boxer after World War II and retired in 1953 to launch a political career, first in organized politics and later as a Chicano activist. He held several important Democratic Party positions, including his role as the party's first Mexican American district captain in Denver. Gonzales eventually became disillusioned with the political process and the inability and unwillingness of established Democratic Party officials to deal meaningfully with minority rights. He left the party as his stance against discrimination became more radical. In 1966, he founded the Crusade for Justice, a service-oriented cultural center that began to challenge the Denver city government and the Democratic Party to become more committed to eradicating poverty and to dealing effectively with racial injustice. The Crusade for Justice sponsored the First Annual Chicano Youth Conference in 1969, attended by Chicano community and university activists from throughout the Southwest. Through his organization and its sponsored events, Gonzales encouraged young Chicanos to join the struggle to claim their rights as American citizens. He currently lives in Denver. Gonzales's most famous literary work, *I Am Joaquín*, must be considered within the context of his social activism. Gonzales urges his readers to recognize and embrace with pride their Indo-Mexican cultural heritage and to join in the struggle against racial prejudice and social injustice in order to claim their rights as citizens. The following selection is both an invocation of this heritage and a call to action. (ChT)

Further reading: Rodolfo "Corky" Gonzales, *Message to Aztlán: Selected Writings* (Houston: Arte Público Press, 2001).

I am Joaquín,
lost in a world of confusion,
caught up in the whirl of a

Yo soy Joaquín,
perdido en un mundo de confusión,
enganchado en el remolino de una

gringo society,
confused by the rules,
scorned by attitudes,
suppressed by manipulation,
and destroyed by modern society.
My fathers
have lost the economic battle
and won
the struggle of cultural survival.

And now!
I must choose
between
the paradox of
victory of the spirit,
despite physical hunger,
or
to exist in the grasp
of American social neurosis,
sterilization of the soul
and a full stomach.

Yes,
I have come a long way to nowhere,
unwillingly dragged by that
monstrous, technical,
industrial giant called
Progress
and Anglo success . . . .

I look at myself.
I watch my brothers.
I shed tears of sorrow.
I sow seeds of hate.
I withdraw to the safety within the
circle of life—
MY OWN PEOPLE.

I am Cuauhtémoc,
proud and noble,
leader of men,
king of an empire
civilized beyond the dreams
of the gachupín Cortés,
who also is the blood,

sociedad gringa,
confundido por las reglas,
despreciado por las actitudes,
sofocado por manipulaciones,
y destrozado por la sociedad moderna.
Mis padres
perdieron la batalla económica
y conquistaron
la lucha de supervivencia cultural.

Y ¡ahora!
yo tengo que escojer
en medio
de la paradoja de
triunfo del espíritu,
a despecho de hambre física,
o
existir en la empuñada
de la neurosis social americana,
esterilización del alma
y un estómago repleto.

Sí,
vine de muy lejos a ninguna parte,
desinclinadamente arrastrado por ese
gigante, monstruoso, técnico, e
industrial llamado
Progreso
y éxito angloamericano . . . .

Yo mismo me miro.
Observo a mis hermanos.
Lloro lágrimas de desgracia.
Siembro semillas de odio.
Me retiro a la seguridad dentro del
círculo de vida—
MI RAZA.

Yo soy Cuauhtémoc,
majestuoso y noble,
guía de hombres,
rey de un imperio civilizado
incomparablemente a los sueños
del gachupín Cortés,
quien igualmente es la sangre,

the image of myself.
I am the Maya prince.
I am Nezahualcóyotl,
great leader of the Chichimecas.
I am the sword and flame of Cortés
the despot.
And
I am the eagle and serpent of
the Aztec civilization.

I owned the land as far as the eye
could see under the crown of Spain,
and I toiled on my earth
and gave my Indian sweat and blood
for the Spanish master
who ruled with tyranny over man and
beast and all that he could trample.
But . . .
THE GROUND WAS MINE.
I was both tyrant and slave.

I am Joaquín.
I rode with Pancho Villa,
crude and warm,
a tornado at full strength,
nourished and inspired
by the passion and the fire
of all his earthy people.
I am Emiliano Zapata.
"This land,
this earth
is
OURS."

The villages
the mountains
the streams
belong to Zapatistas.
Our life
or yours
is the only trade for soft brown earth
and maize.
All of which is our reward,
a creed that formed a constitution
for all who dare live free!

la imagen de mi mismo.
Yo soy el príncipe de los mayas.
Yo soy Netzahualcóyotl,
líder famoso de los chichimecas.
Yo soy la espada y llama de Cortés
el déspota.
Y
yo soy el águila y la serpiente
de la civilización azteca.

Fui dueño de la tierra hasta donde veían
los ojos bajo la corona española,
y trabajé en mi tierra
y di mi sudor y sangre india
por el amo español
que gobernó con tiranía sobre hombre y
bestia y todo los que él podía pisotear.
Pero . . .
EL TERRENO ERA MÍO.
Yo era ambos tirano y esclavo.

Yo soy Joaquín.
Cabalgué con Pancho Villa,
tosco y simpático,
un tornado a toda fuerza,
alimentado e inspirado
por la pasión y la lumbre
de su gente mundana.
Soy Emiliano Zapata.
"Este terreno,
esta tierra
es
NUESTRA."

Los pueblos
las montañas
los arroyos
pertenecen a los Zapatistas.
Nuestra vida
o las vuestras
es el único cambio por tierra blanda y
morena y por maíz.
Todo lo que es nuestro regalo,
un credo que formó una constitución
para todos los que se atreven a vivir libres!

"This land is ours . . .
Father, I give it back to you.
Mexico must be free . . . ."

I ride with revolutionists
against myself.
I am the Rurales,
coarse and brutal,
I am the mountain Indian,
superior over all.
The thundering hoof beats are my horses.
The chattering machine guns
are death to all of me:
Yaqui
Tarahumara
Chamula
Zapotec
Mestizo
Español.

I have been the bloody revolution,
the victor,
the vanquished.
I have killed
and been killed.

I am the despots Díaz
and Huerta
and the apostle of democracy,
Francisco Madero.

And now the trumpet sounds,
the music of the people stirs the
revolution.
Like a sleeping giant it slowly
rears its head
to the sound of
    tramping feet
    clamoring voices
    mariachi strains
    fiery tequila explosions
    the smell of chile verde and
    soft brown eyes of expectation for a
better life.

"Esta tierra es nuestra . . .
Padre, yo te la doy de vuelta.
Méjico debe ser libre . . . ."

Peleo con revolucionarios
contra mí mismo.
Yo soy Rural
ordinario y bruto,
yo soy el indio montañero,
superior a todos.
El galope truenoroso son mis caballos.
El chirrido de ametralladoras
es muerte para todos que son yo:
yaqui
tarahumara
chamula
zapoteca
mestizo
español.

Yo he sido la revolución sangrienta,
el vencedor,
el vencido.
Yo he matado
y he sido matado.

Yo soy los déspotas Díaz
y Huerta
y el apóstol de democracia,
Francisco Madero.

Y ahora suena la trompeta,
la música de la gente incita la
revolución.
Como un gigantón soñoliento lentamente
alza su cabeza
al sonido de
    patulladas
    voces clamorosas
    tañido de mariachis
    explosiones ardientes de tequila
    el aroma de chile verde y
    ojos morenos, esperanzosos de una
vida mejor.

And in all the fertile farmlands,
the barren plains,
the mountain villages,
smoke-smeared cities,
we start to MOVE.

La Raza!
Méjicano!
Español!
Latino!
Hispano!
Chicano!
or whatever I call myself,
I look the same
I feel the same
I cry
and
sing the same.

I am the masses of my people and
I refuse to be absorbed.
I am Joaquín.
The odds are great
but my spirit is strong,
my faith unbreakable,
my blood is pure.
I am Aztec prince and Christian Christ.
I SHALL ENDURE!
I WILL ENDURE!

Y en todos los terrenos fértiles,
los llanos áridos,
los pueblos montañeros.
ciudades ahumadas,
empezamos a AVANZAR.

¡La Raza!
¡Méjicano!
¡Español!
¡Latino!
¡Hispano!
¡Chicano!
o lo que me llame yo,
yo parezco lo mismo
yo siento lo mismo
yo lloro
y
canto lo mismo.

Yo soy el bulto de mi gente y
yo renuncio ser absorbido.
Yo soy Joaquín.
Las desigualdades son grandes
pero mi espíritu es firme,
mi fé impenetrable,
mi sangre pura.
Soy príncipe azteca y Cristo cristiano.
¡YO PERDURARÉ!
¡YO PERDURARÉ!

Miguel Méndez (1930–)

Pilgrims in Aztlán (excerpt)

Originally published in 1974 in Spanish as *Peregrinos de Aztlán*, the English translation was published in 1992. Because Miguel Méndez writes exclusively in Spanish, he is not as well known among English-speaking readers as many other contemporary Chicano writers. He has, however, received much critical acclaim in both Mexico and Spain. The original Spanish version of *Pilgrims* has proven difficult to understand even for educated native speakers of Spanish due to the writer's use of several different linguistic registers, including highly baroque cultured Spanish, idiomatic northwest Mexican rural Spanish, and the almost impenetrable speech of lower-class urban youth. In the following selection, which captures—albeit inadequately in English translation—some of this linguistic complexity, the reader is introduced to the never-ending cycle of farm labor along the border. Méndez portrays working-class culture from within and shows how many of the other poor and dispossessed inhabitants of the U.S.–Mexico border disappear silently and are forgotten. The novelist's task is to record their histories in order to keep memory of them alive for later generations. Méndez, a retired professor of Spanish at the University of Arizona where he taught for many years, continues to write and give readings in the United States, Mexico, and Europe. (ChT)

Further reading: Miguel Méndez, *Pilgrims in Aztlán* (Tempe: Bilingual Press/Editorial Bilingüe, 1992), *From Labor to Letters: A Novel Autobiography* (Tempe: Bilingual Press/Editorial Bilingüe, 1997).

Trans.: DWF

How beautiful the cotton fields looked! In the middle of the day it looked just like a night maiden showing off a dress adorned with stars. The soft tufts looked lavish, soft, white to the eyes and touch, spongy and warm like loving hands, laughing like brides on their wedding day. The earth looked like it had grown old contentedly with gray hair, or that the quartz had transmuted its flinty consistency into a glow nestled in the endless threads of the skein.

Ol' Chuco knew a lot about cotton. In the mornings before beginning to pick, he would stand looking at the tufts covered with dew. As though his eyes had wheels, he would send them roaming over the furrows. With a long harvest bag tied to his waist, dragging along the ground, he cast a look that was half-rancorous and half-defiant toward the sun; bending over, he began pulling at the tufts, which little by little started to fill up the hungry maw of the snaking bag.

"You, pal, where are you from, huh? Are you from the States or are you from south of the border?"

"I don't follow you."

"Hell, what kind of guy are you! I mean, are you from Mexico, guy?"

"That's right, I'm from Mexico."

"Well, now. Well, now. What do you know about that, the guy's a real square, sure enough. Right? Is this the first time they got you to do the picking?"

"Yes, it's the first time for me to pick cotton."

"Well, watch your step, buddy. Look, here's how you strip these babes."

The babes ol' Chuco was stripping clean were the cotton bushes. He was a real sight, skinny and on the tiny side, moving around with an agility so prodigious that it made you think of a dancer or boxer or some feline who would synchronize his movements by combining his elasticity with tremendous energy. In just a few seconds he could pluck dozens of cotton tufts, and he did that hour after hour until he had the incredible quantity of 500 pounds in a single day.

We picked cotton in the fields of Marana, in Arizona. There ol' Chuco was the real champ, but there were others who dogged his heels. We would camp out in the fields themselves, in a hut that provided no protection from the wind, which made it roar like a sick animal. Ol' Chuco went about his business with a certain air of superiority, because, after all, he was the best. Later we found out from others that he had been the star in cutting watermelons in Yuma. In the harvesting of grapes, tomatoes, and eggplants he had also been number one. Ol' Chuco was all of 35 and, according to his own story, he had been in the fields since beginning his career at twelve. Twenty-three years breaking records! If the work in the farm fields had been classified as an Olympic sport, how many gold medals ol' Chuco would have won!

"Listen here, Chuco my friend. All that money you earn picking, do you spend it?"

"Well, not really. You know what? I help my mother out—there's a bunch of us kids. My dad, damn him, kicked the bucket. And as for what's left, I don't give a damn. You know how it is."

"Ah, my friend Chuco, how you like a good blast!"

"You know what, at night we go to the cathouse and dance with the girls. You know who the bastards are, so don't go squealing on me. Put'er there!"

That night we went to the dance. That devil Chuco turned into a dancing demon with a real cute chick. Too bad she already had a lover. He said to Chuco, "Come on, let's fight to the death over her."

"Come on, ol' Chuco, this is a foreign land, don't be a jerk."

"Nah, you know I don't shirk anything. I'm a guy you can count on. Only guys who're married get scared. I'm gonna take care of what my old lady gave birth to."

I carried what ol' Chuco's mother had given birth to on my back. His rival had left him all bruised where he wasn't bleeding. Ol' Chuco continued on his way to California and the grapes, and I stayed behind in Phoenix working construction.

Rolling stones find each other. Ten years later, just by chance, I bumped into Chuco in downtown Los Angeles, Aztlán. Boy, was he a mess! All wrinkled like a raisin, even littler and all bent over. I recognized him because he was making a couple of pedestrians mad. He had squatted down in the middle of the sidewalk in a fetal position, with a straw hat plunked on his head. Ol' Chuco was carrying on by himself. He was studying a lighted panel in front of him that showed a Mexican sleeping sitting down, his arms around his knees, leaning against a saguaro with his hat down around his nose and wearing huaraches.

"Damned lazy people!"

"All they think of is booze and sleep!"

"Yes, drink and do something . . . mañana!"

"By the way, has someone called the cops?"

"Ol' Chuco, old friend. How are you?"

Chuco turned around. His aged face was lined with cares. He smelled like cheap wine.

"You know what, pal? You see that pal there, leaning against the cactus? These people, pal, say that he's lazy, that he doesn't work, you know, but that guy's there, really, because he's all beat and all sad. The fellow was the harvest champion, you know. He's there because he's all tired out with no one to help him, not even anyone to respect him, just like a shovel or a worn pick that's not worth a damn anymore . . . ."

Up close I could see that tears were rolling down ol' Chuco's cheeks. The others thought he was laughing, but I knew he was really crying out of deep bitterness.

They braked loudly. Two burly guys made of steel got out, looking like iguanodons. They picked ol' Chuco up by the neck like he was an old piece of twine.

"Don't yank. You'll rip my clothes, stupid fucking police!"

They struck him and shoved him around mercilessly. His head must have cracked from the shove they gave him.

Everybody was happy to see them carting the drunken Chicano off, real decent people, most of them wearing nice ties, the sign of well-being and good jobs.

"So that pachuco was in a hurry to work."

"He was a real good worker and a real stoic, but the poor guy is now old. But just take a look at how he can dance up a storm."

"Well, I was never impressed, if you want to know the truth, although now that you've told me all this, I see him in a different light."

"He's really a great guy, I told you, but he's a pain when he drinks. By the way, he's been sleeping it off for two hours now."

"Tell me more adventures about ol' Chuco, you can see they really entertain me."

"Well, it happened more or less during the first days I knew ol' Chuco . . . ."

"Hey, guy, do you think the work'll be over by summer? Nah, Chaleco! You know what, pal? With the money I've saved, I'm going to get hitched with a real cool chick."

"I sweat like it's poison coming out, and my shirt and pants rot real fast. Where does so much sweat come from, huh?"

"I saw this dame over at the cathouse, and this guy sure wowed her. Hey, let's grab a cup'a coffee."

"Naw, I don't dig coffee."

"Then let's eat. And you know what that chick said to me?"

"Cut the shit, kid, or you're going to get into trouble."

"I can't hack the winter, brother. I sure don't like it, with the frost you end up like an old rooster, buddy. You know, right? Are you gonna go do lettuce in Wilcox?"

"Well, that chick was looking at me and smiling. She sure thought I was cool. Let's go! Let's dance, come on. I'll be right back, fellows. I'm gonna go weigh this cotton and pick up my pay."

"Hey, to pay for the beer, right?"

"Sure."

"That guy's real drunk."

"Hah, buddy, that guy works for his parents. If he's got any money left over, he'll put up, like everybody else."

"That's great, pal. I don't have a mother. She died last year. I'd say to her: Calm down, little momma, I'll get you one of those houses like the gringos got, with a nice car, the whole bit. But you work your butt off, and no matter what, it always turns out the same way. You know what I mean."

"Here comes that guy. He's sure off his rocker."

"Yeh, no question about it."

"What does the old geezer who does the weighing have to say, guy? He didn't catch on you had rocks in your bag of cotton?"

"Nah, the guy's nuts. He gets all upset because of the green leaves, and he didn't catch on about the other load."

"He doesn't give you a break. How come Chicanos who work as foremen are worse than the bosses themselves?"

"Because the bastards're sellouts. It's worse in construction, pal. They try to do you in in just one day. These guys are real nuts and before you know it, they're talking to you in English."

"If I can save up a hundred bucks, I'm gonna go make time with that chick."

"This guy's all hot for the chick."

"Didn't you say she's treating you like a dog?"

"Like I was saying, I danced with her, cheek to cheek. See? She says she liked me from the moment she set eyes on me, but us guys who work back and forth in the fields on both sides are bad news."

"We all have to pay for a few bad ones, guy. Bunch of bastards that go from one crop to the next. Shit! They go after the chicks and then just leave them hot and hungry. You know what? These guys're something like professional fuckers, you know?"

"Yuma doesn't bother me, pal, even with all the heat that toasts you like a peanut. But the frost really stops up the pipes in my chest. A real drag. In the winter I go work in the canneries."

"Heh, Chuco! It's your turn to cook. Ok?"

"Shit! I cooked this morning. It's ol' Fairo's turn."

"Come on! I'll give you doughnuts and coffee with milk. That's real great!"

"Get out of here with your doughnuts, pal, let this guy put up the beans."

"You know what, good buddies? Better cut the gab and get to work. If we spend too much time talking, we won't earn a cent."

"You said it!"

"Get going!"

God dresses the lilies very finely and makes the birds happy every morning. Fortunate is the man made in His image.

The city awoke with an invasion of shoeless children, defenseless old people, and all those who are forced to seek their survival with despair. They went in search of a happy mortal who might want to be a millionaire. They ran through the downtown streets in search of the bossman. They would jump in front of him, pull at his arm, his jacket, and beg at him with persuasive voices.

"Win a million, sir."

"No! I'm not interested."

"Half a million, sir."

"I just said no, and I'll repeat it a hundred times. No!"

"Come on, sir, a quarter of a million for you. So I can have a meal, don't be mean. Yes?"

"Give me a share, then. Damn it. You guys are real pests."

When the day was already well along, they would go over to where the whores were sunning themselves with their legs spread apart and their faces vinegary, and there they passed out millions right and left. They tangled with the pedestrians on the sidewalk, offering them riches.

"Here are pesos by the millions, sir."

"Mister, mister. Look, money, money."

They wandered among the cars when the traffic slowed with congestion, shouting in the windows.

"Get rich, sir, buy a lottery ticket from me."

Doña Candelita got up early to sell shares of lottery tickets. She wasn't sure exactly how old she was. She just knew that by the time the new century was born she was already a young lady who danced and had a boyfriend. When Porfirio Díaz was overthrown, she'd already given birth to her first child. One morning she related the happy news that she knew she had a boyfriend because he squeezed her hand when they danced. Not like today, where in broad daylight in the middle of the street youngsters from the best families fall all over each other kissing each other's ears and going kissy kissy as if they were in heat. In those days, no sir, you danced far apart, either the polka or the waltz. "Ah! What business." She was answered by a young Indian woman who sold lottery shares. "Just go see the spiders fight." The old woman got angry, and answered the young woman back, that in her day people had shame and covered their bodies. She ended up telling her accusingly that now everybody goes around with their rears hanging out. Another woman selling shares, wearing a miniskirt, blind in one eye, and the other all runny, chimed in that in the old days they didn't show their feet because they were all crooked and covered with bunions from wearing shoes that were too small, or they didn't even have enough money to buy shoes. Doña Candelita told the young woman that the skirt she was wearing was so short she could see her underpants. "Of course. That way they'll look." She slapped her, furious. "Well, I've got something to show, not like you, you old hag." Candelita had to move off to another corner with her tickets because the competition was getting out of hand there. Before moving off, she shouted to the one who had something to show. "What you're showing, you tramp, are underpants full of yellow stains. You probably think it's gold embroidery, but it's pure pee soup."

Doña Candelita extended the folds of the lottery shares for all the tourists and pedestrians, making sad eyes at them and speaking in a thin pleading voice. Buy some shares from me, sir, come on. I don't have a crumb to eat. Nothing. They looked at her as though asking for an accounting. "Well, just what are you doing here in the world, old woman? You should be good and dead." Doña Candelita returned to her hovel. An adobe room without plastering, but with cockroaches and rats, a symphony of crickets, in addition to other bugs that usually won't show their faces. She took a piece of hard bread out of a hole, dunked it in a glass of water and begin to gnaw at it with her gums. A sort of bloodish liquid oozed down her wrinkles from her tiny eyes sunk in the smog of the years. Doña Candelita got crafty the next day. That was it, she wasn't going to die of hunger. That day she sold all the shares she set out to. She put a soccer ball she found down the back of her dress, and the clients stopped to look at the hunchback. A spark of greed ordered them to buy from the old hunchback. Some could not resist it, and they touched her hump. The little old lady smiled condescendingly. Her rivals choked with rage.

Listen, Cloudy, look at the crafty old bitch. She's really selling those shares.

And Cartucho saw her. Damn it, she's so old she knows more than the devil's own grandmother.

Alurista (1947–)

must be the season of the witch; mis ojos hinchados

Born in 1947 in Mexico City as Alberto Baltazar Urista, Alurista (his penname) emigrated with his family to the United States when he was thirteen. His family settled in California where he received a public school education and earned a doctorate in literature. Alurista started writing poetry in Spanish as an elementary school student in Mexico, a practice that would become a lifelong passion. He is completely comfortable in both English and Spanish both as spoken and as written languages. He also studied the Mexican indigenous languages of Náhuatl and Maya and uses all four languages in his poetry, often alternating between them in the same poem. Alurista's early interest in religion led him to explore Catholicism (his family religion) as well as Protestantism, Buddhism, Hinduism, Islam, and eventually pre-Columbian religions. His knowledge of religions is amply reflected in the frequent use of indigenous and Christian motifs, imagery, and traditions. Alurista became focused as a poet in the mid-1960s when he began preparing his poetry for publication. At the same time, he became committed to social activism and often recited his poetry in support of causes such as the César Chávez–led farmworker union struggle. Through his poetry publications and frequent recitations at public events, he made an important contribution to advancing the concept of a Chicano homeland known as Aztlán. (ChT)

Further reading: Alurista, *Floricanto en Aztlán* (Los Angeles: UCLA Chicano Cultural Center, 1971), *Return: Poems Collected and New* (Ypsilanti: Bilingual Review/Press, 1982).

must be the season of the witch

must be the season of the witch
  la bruja
  la llorona
she lost her children
  and she cries
en las barrancas of industry
  her children
devoured by computers
and the gears
must be the season of the witch
  i hear huesos crack
in pain
  y lloros
la bruja pangs
  sus hijos han olvidado
la magia de durango
  y la de moctezuma
  —el ilhuicamina
must be the season of the witch
la bruja llora
sus hijos sufren; sin ella

mis ojos hinchados

mis ojos hinchados
  flooded with lágrimas
de bronze
melting on the cheek bones
of my concern
  razgos indígenas
the scars of history on my face
  and the veins of my body
that aches
  vomita sangre
y lloro libertad
  i do not ask for freedom
i am freedom
  no one
not even yahweh
  and his thunder
can pronounce
  and on a stone
la ley del hombre esculpir
  no puede
mi libertad
and the round tables
  of ice cream
   hot dog
  meat ball lovers meet
to rap
  and rap
and i hunger
  y mi boca está seca
el agua cristalina
  y la verdad
transparent
in a jarro
  is never poured
dust gathers on the shoulders
  of dignataries
y de dignidad
  no saben nada
muertos en el polvo
  they bite the earth
and return
  to dust

Rolando Hinojosa (1929–)

Dear Rafe

Rolando Hinojosa, a prolific writer born and raised in the Lower Rio Grande Valley, is one of a handful of contemporary Chicano writers who have published in Spanish. His first formal education was at a Spanish-speaking private school taught by Mexican exiles. Before completing his B.A. in Spanish at the University of Texas at Austin, he served in the Army in Korea, an experience that is amply reflected in most of his works. He completed a Ph.D. in Spanish literature from the University of Illinois in 1968, and currently occupies an endowed chair in the Department of English at the University of Texas at Austin. His first novel, *Estampas del valle y otras obras*, won the third annual Quinto Sol prize in 1973, and his second novel, *Klail City y sus alrededores*, won the prestigious Cuban Casa de las Américas literary prize for 1976. Originally published in Spanish as *Mi querido Rafa* (1981), the revised and translated version, *Dear Rafe*, was published in 1985. The novel forms a part of Hinojosa's Klail City Death Trip series, which consists of several novels and a long narrative poem that take place in and around the fictious town of Klail City in Belken County, located somewhere in the Lower Rio Grande Valley. The novel is divided into two parts, the first consisting of twenty-two letters that Jehú Malacara writes to his cousin Rafa Buenrostro, who is recovering from wounds suffered in Korea. Most of the second part of the novel concerns speculation about Malacara's mysterious departure from the Klail Savings and Loan, where he was serving as loan officer. Both sections are representative of Hinojosa's technique of creating multiple perspectives about a wide range of personal, social, and political occurrences in his fictitious locale. Tensions between Anglos and the Mexican origin population form the nexus of this and his other works. (ChT)

Further reading: Rolando Hinojosa, *The Valley* (Ypsilanti: Bilingual Review/Press, 1983), *Dear Rafe* (Houston: Arte Público Press, 1985), *Klail City: A Novel* (Houston: Arte Público Press, 1987), *Ask a Policeman: A Rafe Buenrostro Novel* (Houston: Arte Público Press, 1998).

1

Dear Rafe:
Here's wishing you a hale and hearty and hoping to hear that you're doing better, much better. According to Aaron, he claims you look as thin and pale as a whooping crane, and all I can say is "Fatten up, cousin," and you'll be up and out of that hosp. before you know it.

Not much to tell about the Valley right now, but things'll pick up when the primaries come around. The job at the Bank is a job at the Bank, and you'd be surprised (most prob. not) about how some people run their lives in Klail and in Belken County. Not a matter of a three-alarmer, no, but their accounts reveal that all is not well with some of the citizens in our tip of the L.S. State.

The trial for those killers you uncovered has been set for next Jan. 8. You're safe to be up and around by then; will you then be asked to testify?

Since you'll be in exile in Wm. Barrett for a while, I'll keep you up-to-date, as far as I can, on the doings here. For now, then, the primaries which are just around the corner.

Yesterday, and what follows is rumor, gossip, and hearsay, my boss, Noddy Perkins, called Ira Escobar into his office; it's soundproof, of course, and late that afternoon, Ira called on the interoffice phone: "Got to see you, Jehu." I initialed the tellers' accounts, popped my head in Noddy's office, and said good-night to him. On my way to the back lot, there's Ira again.

He could hardly stand it, whatever it was, and then, in a rush, he said that Noddy "and some very important persons, Jehu" had talked to him seriously and on a high level. It happens that our Fellow Texans want Ira to stand for County Commissioner Place Four. And, what did I think a-that?

My heart didn't miss a beat, needless to s., and poor Ira felt a bit deflated. Neither of us said a word for a second or more until I hit him for a light after having first accepted one of his cigarettes. (Ira's dumb, but not *that* dumb.) He saw that, far from envy, it was plain disinterestedness on my part, but he still wasn't sure about my reaction or lack of it.

He looked at me again and asked if I didn't have any earthly I-de-ah what THAT meant: Noddy and the very imp. pers. wanted and had *asked* him to run, and that they were ready (and standing in line, I supposed) to help him all the way.

Wherever that may happen to lead, say I. But, who am I to go around breaking hearts and illusions? By now you're prob. way ahead of me here since the only thing Ira was interested in was to let me know the Good News, and that was it.

Forward! Maaarch! The last thing he'd want from me would be some advice, and I'm not good at that either. There we were, two lonely people in a treeless parking lot, at 6 p.m., with 97 degrees F staring us in the face, and Ira saying: "Jay, Jay, don't you see? County Commissioner Place Four, the *fat* one, Jay." (Yes, he calls me Jay). About all I could think of was to wonder what Noddy, the Ranch, the Bank, etc. were up to this time; I mean, they already own most of the land 'in these here parts' and they have ALL THAT MONEY, SON; so it's prob. something else in that woodpile aside from the wood, right? I finally shook his hand, or the other way round, and then he went straight home to give his wife the second surprise of her life.

Ira and his wife were new to Klail, and I'm fairly certain you don't know her, her name's Rebecca Caldwell (we who know and love her, call her *Becky*) and she's from Jonesville-on-the-Rio. Her father's Caldwell, but a Mexican for a'that. Her mother's a Navarrete, and enough said. I've seen her a couple of times at a Bank party and other Bank doings and what-not.

The phone! A call from one of the relatives in Relámpago; Auntie Enriqueta says she's coming along nicely; nothing serious. (Remember when we used to hit Relámpago fairly often? I wonder whatever-happened-to-those-baldheaded-tattooed-twins, Doro and Thea, right?) Anyway, getting back to Becky, she's a bit of a looker. We get along, and we do look each other in the eye when we've said 'hello' and such. Nice looking face to go with a well-rounded little *bod*. We'll see.

Now, it could be it's a false alarm, and it may be that the Central Powers are merely testing our boy here. You never know. If Noddy *were* testing the waters, and Ira's enthusiasm showed through, Noddy could read that as our boy's willingness to serve the public.

Old Man Vielma sends his best; ran into him at the Blue Bar. In re his daughter who now shares a house with your former sister-in-law, Delfina, our illuminated friends are up in arms about 'those two shameless women who live together.' Why go on? As you can see with that one good eye you've got left, we're still as nice and as sweet and understanding in Klail City as ever.

Well, cuz, take care, eat well, and I'm sure that before either one of us knows it, you'll be back hard at work at the Court House. (Thought I'd make your day: Sheriff Parkinson, he of the big feet, is taking much of the credit for solving those murders you and Culley and Sam Cleared up. Big Foot's no fool; he says it was his *office* that solved them, and since he is the sheriff . . .)

Best,
Jehu

Dear Rafe:

First off: kindly excuse the delay in answering your latest; it has to do with the work here, a rush on time, and then, before I know it, two weeks have come and gone, and I haven't dropped you line one. Second excuse: attended and participated in a sad funeral: don Pedro Zamudio's, that old Oblate of Mary Immaculate, who graced the fair city of Flora long and well.

It happens that he had two older brothers (yes, *older*), and they came down from God only knows what aerie of His. Black hats, hooked-noses, and as bald as Father Pedro himself. Half the world and most of Belken County showed up, and I almost broke up thinking on that grand and glorious burial we gave Bruno Cano that bright Spring morning years ago. It's rained here and snowed elsewhere since that time, son. And now, sic transit.

On the way back to Klail, I stopped off at the old mexicano cemetery near Bascom. One of those things, I guess: I walked around reading the stones and markers, looking over the old and loved names. As you know, we're all one day nearer the grace.

Public Notice: The offer to Ira appears to be on the level. Noddy Perkins' sister (more on her in a minute) came by the Bank *eins-zwei-drei* times, and where there's smoke, there's a political barbecue, right?

Tidy-up time: you're wrong on the Escobar familial relationships, and I'll explain why in short order. Ira's an Escobar on his father's side (old don Nemesio Escobar, who's related to the Prado families from Barrones, Tamaulipas. Got that?) But, Ira also happens to be a Leguizamón, sad to say, and it comes from the maternal end of things: A Leguizamón-Leyva for a mother who's from Uncle Julian's generation. Of course, if you were to see Ira, you'd pick him out in a crowd, straight off. It's the nose and jaw that gives the Leguizamón's away every time. And, as far as the Bank job's concerned, he got *that* because of his Leguizamón connections (this from Noddy, by the way). That aside, if I were Ira, I'd watch Noddy P. NP's not a lost babe, and our boy Ira is, in a word, blinded by the goal that glitters. To sum up, then, he looks as easy a prey as a jackass flats bunny, wide-eyed (and blind), ears pointed up (and deaf as a door), and ready for someone to pick him off with a .22 long. He seems to love it, though. It's God's truth that there's always someone who's willing to do anything in this world.

Ira himself told me that he'll pay the filing fee at the Court House this p.m. I've no proofs, of course, but I'm dead sure Noddy's got something up that sleeve of his'n. Yes, he do. I've been here three now, and I've barely scratched three or four layers in that man's make-up. And he goes much deeper'n that, believe me.

A S F G & don't look at the key.

Q W E R T & keep your eyes on me!

Yep! Powerhouse Kirkpatrck is Noddy Perkins' sib. (The first time she saw me at the bank, must be going on three years now, she spotted me in my office & said, "Are you the Buenrostro boy?")

Well! I knew *she* knew who I was (it's their bank, dammit, and they know who they hire) but I went along, & we both wound up laughing and what-all. Getting up in years is Old Powerhouse, and widowed all these twenty years, Jehu, but I've got all my teeth, she says. (And all that money Tinker Kirkpatrick left her, too, sez I). Her main interests these days revolve around the Klail City Woman's Club & the Music Club. If she rules there the way she did at Klail High, God help 'em.

By the by, Ira's not to run for a Place Four, as he'd been told. (There's a note of sadness to that 'as he'd been told,' isn't there?)

This is what I think the play will be:

Ira's to run v. Morse Terry (Place Three) in the Democratic Primary. Do you recall MT? He was up at Austin with us; speaks Spanish (natch), and he's a friend of the mexicano. Sure he is. (Same old lyrics to Love's Old Sweet Song.)

Here's the story, Your Honor: Looks like some toes were stepped on; or maybe a double cross or two, not sure, but *something* happened. Big, too. Soooo, Noddy's lining up some of our Fellow Texans against Morse Terry, and backing Ira Escobar.

Talk about your strange bedfellows. The rundown: Ira v. Terry with Bank backing, and our fair-haired boy's on his way to the victory circle. I can imagine Ira at night, alone, and softly, in the bathroom, facing the mirror, that Ira sees himself as a future Congressman in Washington; how's *that* for a dream? Still, stranger things have happened, mirabile visu et dictu.

There *is* one problem, however, and thus Powerhouse's comings and goings: Noddy wants Ira's wife's admission to the Woman's Club, and that's a tall order, Chief. More on this later as soon as the news develops.

Next week this here cousin a-yours is off to the Big House for a kickoff Bar-B-Q; Ira's announcement, most prob. One of the girls at the Bank says that a lot of people (she put the stress on *people*) have been invited out there; I'll keep you posted.

And, too, word of honor and, as a relative, I'll say more in re Noddy and his antecedents although this may just be repeating something you already know. Correct me if I'm wrong.

Gotta go. Am enclosing a pix; the girl on the left is a current one.

Best,
Jehu

3

Dear Rafe:

Well, sir, you take the cake *and* the icing; the words 'excuse me' are still a part of the lexicon, & I'll wait for them. And, furthermore, erase, expunge, and take away all of your *feelthy* thoughts, you cad. Strange as it may seem, to you, I *have* been known to have the very best honorable intentions, at times. Well, enough said & amen. Keep the picture and apologize to it.

What I'd promised in re Noddy:

Noddy Perkins is a man just short of his mid-sixties; his parents were fruit tramps who showed up in the Valley just before the times of the Seditious Ones; that puts it around 1915 or so. His old man was killed by a freight truck & cut up in halves or thirds, depending on who's telling the story. Some of the those who say they remember, attest that 1) the old man had been drinking; 2) that he merely stumbled on the tracks on his way home. Noddy's no souse, by the way; a daily highball or two, but that's about it. He likes to be in control, you see.

Echevarría (a long time ago) told me that Noddy didn't have a pot or a down payment for one when he married Blanche Cooke; a head of business, yes, then and now. (He speaks Spanish, oh, yes, & he likes for his mexicano hands to call him *Norberto* when he dresses up like a Laredo cowboy on weekends. I keep telling you: it takes all sorts to populate Belken County. Pay attention.)

He hired me (personally) some three years ago; he knew me from Klail Savings, of course (which the Ranch also owns); of course. That piece of information must come as a first-class shock to you. As you may know, we've no branch banking in Texas; not yet, anyway.

His wife, Blanche, aka Miz Noddy, Mrs. Perkins, etc. has been slightly burned by both the sun and the Oso Negro gin. She's got a natural enough tan, and her voice is a bit mushy with a touch of hoarseness. The martinis get a goodly share of the blame for that, I suspect. Doesn't show up here much, but when she does or whenever she's back from her 'periodic drying out' as her dearest friends call it, she and Noddy go over to the Camelot Club or maybe to the beach to celebrate her return.

One of the V.P.'s here, he's also the Cashier, is a full-fledged member of the Cooke-Blanchard clan. Of course, of course. His name's E.B. Cooke (he's called Ibby) and he thinks Texas mexicanos were put in the Valley for the family's absolute convenience. We get along, neither well nor badly; we just get. In other words, it's 'good morning' in the a.m., and 'good evening' at closing time. Noddy hired me, so I work for him is Ibby's thinking; but he's up front about it which is a blessing.

Noddy's wife gets along with Powerhouse; prob. has no option or say so in the matter. At any rate, they share different interests, as Powerhouse says. But make no mistake: they *all* get along & more so when it's family v. anybody else. The spoiled darling here is Sammie Jo; two marriages, as you know, no kids, but this and that you already know. *We* still get along just fine, thank you.

Back to Noddy's father: he was called Old Man Raymond; Raymond was the fort name, and the old mexicanos remember him as that. In English, too: Olmén Reymon.

Old Man Raymond died not only mangled but broke as well, and Noddy must've have had a hard time of it for a while. (No one talks about Noddy's mother; not a word.) Now, how he came to marry someone like Blanche Cooke is a mystery to me; one thing, I don't think he caused the alcohol problem, although one never knows. As you know, Sammie Jo's our age, and so NP must have married kinda late, right?

Noddy has 1) few illusions &, 2) less friends. It could be that he has the type of friend that rich have, BUT! in Klail, who's rich, besides them?

One more thing, he won't rattle. To be sure, he's got more than half the deck on his hand at all times; still, you've got to see him in action. Nota Bene: you've got to watch him every second; don't turn your back on him. He's the type that'll watch your hide dry.

And that's about the book on NP.

Must close, cuz.

Best,

Jehu

Pedro Pietri (1944–)

Puerto Rican Obituary

Pedro Pietri is one of the best known "Nuyorican" poets of his time. Born in Puerto Rico, he moved to New York City at age three, and in the late 1960s became one of the central figures of a cultural movement that—under the influence of contemporary African American poetry and the aesthetics of the Beat generation—revolutionized the terms of Puerto Rican migrant literature, proclaiming a permanence and entitlement in New York. Nuyorican literature thus became formally (although not thematically) freed from the fears of cultural contamination that had so dominated Puerto Rican literature of the previous decades. Instead, Pietri and other Nuyorican poets valorized the switching of linguistic codes between English and Spanish. They made it a privileged means of poetic signification and cultural critique rather than simply an object of scorn or grammatical moralizations. Pietri's first book, *Puerto Rican Obituary* (1973), was a watershed event in this regard. Poetry of belligerent and uncompromising social protest, it is characterized by experimental and defiant language and by relentless repetition and flowing raps. The *Obituary* is not to be read in comfortable solitude and silence. Strident and high-pitched, this ironic elegy demands emphatic public performance. (ALO)

Further reading: Pedro Pietri, *Puerto Rican Obituary* (New York: Monthly Review Press, 1973), *Traffic Violations* (Maplewood, N.J.: Waterfront Press, 1983), *The Masses Are Asses* (Maplewood, N.J.: Waterfront Press, 1984).

They worked
They were always on time
They were never late
They never spoke back
when they were insulted
They worked
They never took days off
that were not on the calendar
They never went on strike
without permission
They worked
ten days a week
and were only paid for five

They worked
They worked
They worked
and they died
They died broke
They died owing
They died never knowing
what the front entrance
of the first national city bank looks like

Juan
Miguel
Milagros
Olga
Manuel
All died yesterday today
and will die again tomorrow
passing their bill collectors
on to the next of kin
All died
waiting for the garden of eden
to open up again
under a new management
All died
dreaming about america
waking them up in the middle of the night
screaming: Mira Mira
your name is on the winning lottery ticket
for one hundred thousand dollars
All died
hating the grocery stores
that sold them make-believe steak
and bullet-proof rice and beans
All died waiting dreaming and hating

Dead Puerto Ricans
Who never knew they were Puerto Ricans
Who never took a coffee break
from the ten commandments
to KILL KILL KILL
the landlords of their cracked skulls
and communicate with their latino souls

Juan
Miguel

Milagros
Olga
Manuel
From the nervous breakdown streets
where the mice live like millionaires
and the people do not live at all
are dead and were never alive

Juan
died waiting for his number to hit
Miguel
died waiting for the welfare check
to come and go and come again
Milagros
died waiting for her ten children
to grow up and work
so she could quit working
Olga
died waiting for a five dollar raise
Manuel
died waiting for his supervisor to drop dead
so he could get a promotion

Is a long ride
from Spanish Harlem
to long island cemetery
where they were buried
First the train
and then the bus
and the cold cuts for lunch
and the flowers
that will be stolen
when visiting hours are over
Is very expensive
Is very expensive
But they understand
Their parents understood
Is a long non-profit ride
from Spanish Harlem
to long island cemetery

Juan
Miguel
Milagros
Olga

Manuel
All died yesterday today
and will die again tomorrow
Dreaming
Dreaming about queens
Clean-cut lily-white neighborhood
Puerto Ricanless scene
Thirty-thousand-dollar home
The first spics on the block
Proud to belong to a community
of gringos who want them lynched
Proud to be a long distance away
from the sacred phrase: Qué Pasa

These dreams
These empty dreams
from the make-believe bedrooms
their parents left them
are the after-effects
of television programs
about the ideal
white american family
with black maids
and latino janitors
who are well trained
to make everyone
and their bill collectors
laugh at them
and the people they represent

Juan
died dreaming about a new car
Miguel
died dreaming about new anti-poverty programs
Milagros
died dreaming about a trip to Puerto Rico
Olga
died dreaming about real jewelry
Manuel
died dreaming about the irish sweepstakes

They all died
like a hero sandwich dies
in the garment district
at twelve o'clock in the afternoon

social security number to ashes
union dues to dust

They knew
they were born to weep
and keep the morticians employed
as long as they pledge allegiance
to the flag that wants them destroyed
They saw their names listed
in the telephone directory of destruction
They were trained to turn
the other cheek by newspapers
that mispelled mispronounced
and misunderstood their names
and celebrated when death came
and stole their final laundry ticket

They were born dead
and they died dead

Is time
to visit sister lopez again
the number one healer
and fortune card dealer
in Spanish Harlem
She can communicate
with your late relatives
for a reasonable fee
Good news is guaranteed

Rise Table Rise Table
death is not dumb and disable
Those who love you want to know
the correct number to play
Let them know this right away
Rise Table Rise Table
death is not dumb and disable
Now that your problems are over
and the world is off your shoulders
help those who you left behind
find financial peace of mind
Rise Table Rise Table
death is not dumb and disable
If the right number we hit
all our problems will split

and we will visit your grave
on every legal holiday
Those who love you want to know
the correct number to play
Let them know this right away
We know your spirit is able
Death is not dumb and disable
RISE TABLE RISE TABLE

Juan
Miguel
Milagros
Olga
Manuel
All died yesterday today
and will die again tomorrow
Hating fighting and stealing
broken windows from each other
Practicing a religion without a roof
The old testament
The new testament
according to the gospel
of the internal revenue
the judge and jury and executioner
protector and eternal bill collector

Secondhand shit for sale
Learn how to say Como Esta Usted
and you will make a fortune
They are dead
They are dead
and will not return from the dead
until they stop neglecting
the art of their dialogue
for broken english lessons
to impress the mister goldsteins
who keep them employed
as lavaplatos porters messenger boys
factory workers maids stock clerks
shipping clerks assistant mailroom
assistant, assistant assistant
to the assistant's assistant
assistant lavaplatos and automatic
artificial smiling doormen
for the lowest wages of the ages

and rages when you demand a raise
because is against the company policy
to promote SPICS SPICS SPICS

Juan
died hating Miguel because Miguel's
used car was in better running condition
than his used car
Miguel
died hating Milagros because Milagros
had a color television set
and he could not afford one yet
Milagros
died hating Olga because Olga
made five dollars more on the same job
Olga
died hating Manuel because Manuel
had hit the numbers more times
than she had hit the numbers
Manuel
died hating all of them
Juan
Miguel
Milagros
and Olga
because they all spoke broken english
more fluently than he did

And now they are together
in the main lobby of the void
Addicted to silence
Off limits to the wind
Confined to worm supremacy
in long island cemetery
This is the groovy hereafter
the protestant collection box
was talking so loud and proud about

Here lies Juan
Here lies Miguel
Here lies Milagros
Here lies Olga
Here lies Manuel
who died yesterday today
and will die again tomorrow

Always broke
Always owing
Never knowing
that they are beautiful people
Never knowing
the geography of their complexion

PUERTO RICO IS A BEAUTIFUL PLACE
PUERTORRIQUENOS ARE A BEAUTIFUL RACE

If only they
had turned off the television
and tuned into their own imaginations
If only they
had used the white supremacy bibles
for toilet paper purpose
and make their latino souls
the only religion of their race
If only they
had returned to the definition of the sun
after the first mental snowstorm
on the summer of their senses
If only they
had kept their eyes open
at the funeral of their fellow employees
who came to this country to make a fortune
and were buried without underwears

Juan
Miguel
Milagros
Olga
Manuel
will right now be doing their own thing
where beautiful people sing
and dance and work together
where the wind is a stranger
to miserable weather conditions
where you do not need a dictionary
to communicate with your people
Aquí Se Habla Español all the time
Aquí you salute your flag first
Aquí there are no dial soap commericals
Aquí everybody smells good
Aquí tv dinners do not have a future

Aquí the men and women admire desire
and never get tired of each other
Aquí Que Pasa Power is what's happening
Aquí to be called negrito
means to be called LOVE

Miguel Algarín (1941–)

Saliendo; Light after Blackout

Miguel Algarín is one of the founders and leaders of the Nuyorican literary movement, both as a writer and as owner-administrator of the Nuyorican Poets' Cafe, which since the 1970s, taking the model of the beat-generation cafe, has been dedicated to the oral performance of literature. Born in Santurce, Puerto Rico, Algarín moved with his family to New York City in the early 1950s. Algarín obtained advanced degrees in literature from the University of Wisconsin and Pennsylvania State University, after which he worked as a professor at Rutgers University. A writer of plays and prose, Algarín is mainly known as the creator of bilingual poetry which runs the gamut from jazz-salsa poetry to mystical, avant-garde verse. The author of some five books of poetry, he is also important for his work as a translator of Pablo Neruda and for his anthology, with Miguel Piñero, *Nuyorican Poetry: An Anthology of Puerto Rican Words and Feelings* (1976), introducing the world of the Nuyorican to a broad audience. From *On Call* (1980), can one appreciate the pace and rhythm of jazz poetry, the paeans to "Loisaida" (Lower East Side) and the incorporation of bombarded media messages and popular culture that are so important to Nuyorican poetry. (NK)

Further reading: Miguel Algarín, *On Call* (Houston; Arte Público Press, 1980), *Time's Now/Ya es tiempo* (Houston: Arte Público Press, 1985); Miguel Algarín and Miguel Piñero, *Nuyorican Poetry: An Anthology of Puerto Rican Words and Feelings* (New York: William Morrow, 1976).

Saliendo

Moving out on the sidewalk, leaving my inner cranium
living room space to regenerate while external living
keeps energy flow becoming muscular volcanic eruptions,
saliendo, coming out, moving out, looking around,
shaping, responding to children screeching their love
at Kojack as he leaves "Paco's Antique Tienda" wearing
his navy blue cashmere overcoat, dark blue velvet hat
and gold-rimmed shades,
Kojack's down on sixth street! stepped right out of the boob-tube,
settling crime on New York streets, arriving just in time to catch
the punk by the collar and make him pay for wrongs he's done,
children screech when they see Kojack,
they move out of inner-livingroom
space to shout arrows of joy at Kojack, to touch him,

to feel illusion harden into fact in their presence,
Kojack in the living room of actual space and time,
illusion become reality, hero become matter,
touchable, sensual time, Kojack's here! same as T.V.
Saliendo, coming out of myself, out of my T.V. image of self,
out of my inner self, out, out, out of myself,
out, out onto the sidewalks of my astral projections
where I'm Kojack with a Flash Gordon electronic gun
that shoots arrows of art through villainous hearts
saliendo . . . . .saliendo . . . . .saliendo,
leaving my inner cranium living room space to regenerate.

Light after Blackout

Badillo was being honored by a group of educators
when mild mannered Juan Soler announced that
"there's going to be a blackout, stand still, all will be well"
Juan was right, all electric clocks
still stand at 9:39 P.M.
when it's 2:10 P.M. next day my Seiko self-wind,
the light after the blackout escapes
without waiting for night to come,
Con Edison promises electricity by Thursday
but when I asked if the National Guard was coming
the gap-toothed officer sitting in the back of the squad car said
"no, we've got some paratroopers from Kentucky coming out,"
Wednesday 13, 1977, July,
the month where air-conditioning
and the cool it craze take over cause a blow out,
plunging into darkness the educators gathered to raise
funds and workers for Badillo who's running
in the Democratic Primary against seven candidates,
plunged into darkness Nellie and I scamper onto a narrow railed walk
from which we see eager buses and taxis transporting people,
keeping people afloat, the sidewalks are full,
the moon lights the city generously
as if to counteract hysteria,
we talked gaping down at people filled sidewalks
pleased to see the moles of city apartments out at night,
Nellie stretches out
in the absence of Con Edison pink lamp post light,
she stretches fine, finer yet when she slips off
her black slipover shirt with a mandala knitted in the center
and dances topless in the middle of Lexington Avenue,
two Germans approach at the same time that a Mercedes-Benz
pulls up and two out on the town Irish Americans offer Nellie

thirty dollars to get in the car and party
but she dances some more before they go away,
ten blocks south on Lexington a prostitute
rescued from the lamp post light sells "quickies"
right on the street corner while a cheering crowd
moves round her to shield her and her customers
from a squad car cop
who's shining his flashlight into the crowd,
fearing we're looting he jumps out,
she sensually lifts her buttocks,
the customer slurps out,
the crowd wildly applauds,
the squad car moves on,
another hearty client unzips,
the crowd thickens and here and there
a wandering hand gropes uninhibited groins,
New Yorkers growing sensual in the humid rains of
a blacked out night.

Luis Valdez (1940–)

Los Vendidos

Luis Valdez is considered the father of Chicano theater. He has distinguished himself as an actor, director, playwright, and filmmaker. However, it is in his role as the founding director of El Teatro Campesino, a theater of farm workers in California, that his efforts inspired young Chicano activists across the country to use theater as a means of organizing students, communities, and labor unions. Luis Valdez was born into a family of migrant farm workers in Delano, California. The second of ten children, he began to work the fields at the age of six. Valdez's education was continuously interrupted because of migrant work, but he managed to earn not only a college degree but an M.A. in English from San Jose State College in 1964, presenting his play *The Shrunken Head of Pancho Villa* as his master's thesis. He went on to work with the San Francisco Mime Troupe and, in 1965, joined César Chávez in the effort to organize farm workers. By 1968, he had left the fields with his troupe and began to explore broader issues and investigate the historical forms of theater in the Mexican American community. (NK)

Further reading: Luis Valdez, *Luis Valdez: Early Works* (Houston: Arte Público Press, 1990), *Zoot Suit and Other Plays* (Houston: Arte Público Press, 1992).

Characters:
Honest Sancho
Secretary
Farmworker
Pachuco

Revolucionario
Mexican-American

Scene: HONEST SANCHO's *Used Mexican Lot and Mexican Curio Shop. Three models are on display in* HONEST SANCHO's *shop. To the right, there is a* REVOLUCIONARIO, *complete with sombrero, carrilleras and carabina 30-30. At center, on the floor, there is the* FARMWORKER, *under a broad straw sombrero. At stage left is the* PACHUCO, *filero in hand.* HONEST SANCHO *is moving among his models, dusting them off and preparing for another day of business.*

SANCHO: Bueno, bueno, mis monos, vamos a ver a quién vendemos ahora, ¿no? (*To audience.*) ¡Quihubo! I'm Honest Sancho and this is my shop. Antes fui contratista, pero ahora logré tener mi negocito. All I need now is a costumer. (*A bell rings offstage.*) Ay, a costumer!
SECRETARY: (*Entering.*) Good morning, I'm Miss Jimenez from . . .
SANCHO: Ah, una chicana! Welcome, welcome Señorita Jiménez.
SECRETARY: (*Anglo pronunciation.*) JIM-enez.
SANCHO: ¿Qué?
SECRETARY: My name is Miss JIM-enez. Don't you speak English? What's wrong with you?
SANCHO: Oh, nothing, Señorita JIM-enez. I'm here to help you.
SECRETARY: That's better. As I was starting to say, I'm a secretary from Governor Reagan's office, and we're looking for a Mexican type for the administration.
SANCHO: Well, you come to the right place, lady. This is Honest Sancho's Used Mexican Lot, and we got all types here. Any particular type you want?
SECRETARY: Yes, we were looking for somebody suave . . .
SANCHO: Suave.
SECRETARY: Debonaire.
SANCHO: De buen aire.
SECRETARY: Dark.
SANCHO: Prieto.
SECRETARY: But of course, not too dark.
SANCHO: No muy prieto.
SECRETARY: Perhaps, beige.
SANCHO: Beige, just the tone. Así como cafecito con leche, ¿no?
SECRETARY: One more thing. He must be hard-working.
SANCHO: That could only be one model. Step right over here to the center of the shop, lady. (*They cross to the* FARMWORKER.) This is our standard farmworker model. As you can see, in the words of our beloved Senator George Murphy, he is "built close to the ground." Also, take special notice of his 4-ply Goodyear huaraches, made from the rain tire. This wide-brimmed sombrero is an extra added feature; keeps off the sun, rain and dust.
SECRETARY: Yes, it does look durable.
SANCHO: And our farmworker model is friendly. Muy amable. Watch. (*Snaps his fingers.*)
FARMWORKER: (*Lifts his head.*) Buenos días, señorita. (*His head drops.*)

SECRETARY: My, he is friendly.

SANCHO: Didn't I tell you? Loves his patrones! But his most attractive feature is that he's hard-working. Let me show you. (*Snaps fingers.* FARMWORKER *stands.*)

FARMWORKER: ¡El jale! (*He begins to work.*)

SANCHO: As you can see he is cutting grapes.

SECRETARY: Oh, I wouldn't know.

SANCHO: He also picks cotton. (*Snaps.* FARMWORKER *begins to pick cotton.*)

SECRETARY: Versatile, isn't he?

SANCHO: He also picks melons. (*Snaps.* FARMWORKER *picks melons.*) That's his slow speed for late in the season. Here's his fast speed. (*Snap.* FARMWORKER *picks faster.*)

SECRETARY: Chihuahua . . . I mean, goodness, he sure is a hard worker.

SANCHO: (*Pulls the* FARMWORKER *to his feet.*) And that isn't half of it. Do you see these little holes in his arms that appear to be pores? During those hot sluggish days in the field when the vines or the branches get so entangled, it's almost impossible to move, these holes emit a certain grease that allows our model to slip and slide right through the crop with no trouble at all.

SECRETARY: Wonderful. But is he economical?

SANCHO: Economical? Señorita, you are looking at the Volkswagen of Mexicans. Pennies a day is all it takes. One plate of beans and tortillas will keep him going all day. That, and chile. Plenty of chile. Chile jalapeños, chile verde, chile colorado. But, of course, if you do give him chile, (*Snap.* FARMWORKER *turns left face. Snap.* FARMWORKER *bends over.*) then you have to change his oil filter once a week.

SECRETARY: What about storage?

SANCHO: No problem. You know these new farm labor camps our Honorable Governor Reagan has built out by Palier or Raisin City? They were designed with our model in mind. Five, six, seven, even ten in one of those shacks will give you no trouble at all. You can also put him in old barns, old cars, riverbanks. You can even leave him out in the field over night with no worry!

SECRETARY: Remarkable.

SANCHO: And here's an added feature: every year at the end of the season, this model goes back to Mexico and doesn't return, automatically, until next Spring.

SECRETARY: How about that. But tell me, does he speak English?

SANCHO: Another outstanding feature is that last year this model was programmed to go out on STRIKE! (*Snap.*)

FARMWORKER: ¡Huelga! ¡Huelga! Hermanos, sálganse de esos files. (*Snaps. He stops.*)

SECRETARY: NO! Oh no, we can't strike in the State Capitol.

SANCHO: Well, he also scabs. (*Snap.*)

FARMWORKER: Me vendo barato, ¿y qué? (*Snap.*)

SECRETARY: That's much better, but you didn't answer my question. Does he speak English?

SANCHO: Bueno . . . no, pero he has other . . .

SECRETARY: No.

SANCHO: Other features.

SECRETARY: No! He just won't do!

SANCHO: Okay, okay, pues. We have other models.

SECRETARY: I hope so. What we need is something a little more sophisticated.

SANCHO: Sophiti-qué?

SECRETARY: An urban model.

SANCHO: Ah, from the city! Step right back. Over here in this corner of the shop is exactly what you're looking for. Introducing our new 1969 JOHNNY PACHUCO model! This is our fast-back model. Streamlined. Built for speed, low-riding, city life. Take a look at some of these features. Mag shoes, dual exhausts, green chartreuse paint-job, dark-tint windshield, a little poof on top. Let me just turn him on. (*Snap.* JOHNNY *walks to stage center with a* PACHUCO *bounce.*)

SECRETARY: What was that?

SANCHO: That, señorita, was the Chicano shuffle.

SECRETARY: Okay, what does he do?

SANCHO: Anything and everything necessary for city life. For instance, survival: he knife fights. (*Snaps.* JOHNNY *pulls out a switchblade and swings at* SECRETARY. SECRETARY *screams.*) He dances. (*Snap.*)

JOHNNY: (*Singing.*) "Angel Baby, my Angel Baby . . ." (*Snap.*)

SANCHO: And here's a feature no city model can be without. He gets arrested, but not without resisting, of course. (*Snap.*)

JOHNNY: En la madre, la placa. I didn't do it! I didn't do it! (JOHNNY *turns and stands up against an imaginary wall, legs spread out, arms behind his back.*)

SECRETARY: Oh no, we can't have arrests! We must maintain law and order.

SANCHO: But he's bilingual.

SECRETARY: Bilingual?

SANCHO: Simón que yes. He speaks English! Johnny, give us some English. (*Snap.*)

JOHNNY: (*Comes downstage.*) Fuck-you!

SECRETARY: (*Gasps.*) Oh! I've never been so insulted in my whole life!

SANCHO: Well, he learned it in your school.

SECRETARY: I don't care where he learned it.

SANCHO: But he's economical.

SECRETARY: Economical?

SANCHO: Nickels and dimes. You can keep Johnny running on hamburgers, Taco Bell tacos, Lucky Lager beer, Thunderbird wine, yesca . . .

SECRETARY: Yesca?

SANCHO: Mota.

SECRETARY: Mota?

SANCHO: Leños . . . marijuana. (*Snap.* JOHNNY *inhales on an imaginary joint.*)

SECRETARY: That's against the law!

JOHNNY: (*Big smile, holding his breath.*) Yeah.

SANCHO: He also sniffs glue. (*Snap.* JOHNNY *inhales glue, big smile.*)

JOHNNY: Tha's too much man, ese.

SECRETARY: No, Mr. Sancho, I don't think this . . .

SANCHO: Wait a minute, he has other qualities I know you'll love. For example, an inferiority complex. (*Snap.*)

JOHNNY: (*To* SANCHO.) You think you're better than me, huh, ese? (*Swings switchblade.*)

SANCHO: He can also be beaten and he bruises. Cut him and he bleeds, kick him and he... (*He beats, bruises and kicks* PACHUCO.) Would you like to try it?

SECRETARY: Oh, I couldn't.

SANCHO: Be my guest. He's a great escape goat.

SECRETARY: No really.

SANCHO: Please.

SECRETARY: Well, all right. Just once. (*She kicks* PACHUCO.) Oh, he's so soft.

SANCHO: Wasn't that good? Try again.

SECRETARY: (*Kicks* PACHUCO.) Oh, he's so wonderful! (*She kicks him again.*)

SANCHO: Okay, that's enough, lady. You'll ruin the merchandise. Yes, our Johnny Pachuco model can give you many hours of pleasure. Why, the LAPD just bought 20 of these to train their rookie cops on. And talk about maintenance. Señorita, you are looking at an entirely self-supporting machine. You're never going to find our Johnny Pachuco model on the relief rolls. No, sir, this model knows how to liberate.

SECRETARY: Liberate?

SANCHO: He steals. (*Snap.* JOHNNY *rushes to* SECRETARY *and steals her purse.*)

JOHNNY: ¡Dame esa bolsa, vieja! (*He grabs the purse and runs. Snap by* SANCHO, *he stops.* SECRETARY *runs after* JOHNNY *and grabs purse away from him, kicking him as she goes.*)

SECRETARY: No, no, no! We can't have any more thieves in the State Administration. Put him back.

SANCHO: Okay, we still got other models. Come on, Johnny, we'll sell you to some old lady. (SANCHO *takes* JOHNNY *back to his place.*)

SECRETARY: Mr. Sancho, I don' think you quite understand what we need. What we need is something that will attract the women voters. Something more traditional, more romantic.

SANCHO: Ah, a lover. (*He smiles meaningfully.*) Step right over here, señorita. Introducing our standard Revolucionario and/or Early California Bandit type. As you can see, he is well-built, sturdy, durable. This is the International Harvester of Mexicans.

SECRETARY: What does he do?

SANCHO: You name it, he does it. He rides horses, stays in the mountains, crosses deserts, plains, rivers, leads revolutions, follows revolutions, kills, can be killed, serves as a martyr, hero, movie star. Did I say movie star? Did you ever see *Viva Zapata? Viva Villa, Villa Rides, Pancho Villa Returns, Pancho Villa Goes Back, Pancho Villa Meets Abbott and Costello?*

SECRETARY: I've never seen any of those.

SANCHO: Well, he was in all of them. Listen to this. (*Snap.*)

REVOLUCIONARIO: (*Scream.*) ¡Viva Villaaaa!

SECRETARY: That's awfully loud.

SANCHO: He has volume control. (*He adjusts volume. Snap.*)

REVOLUCIONARIO: (*Mousey voice.*) Viva Villa.

SECRETARY: That's better.

SANCHO: And even if you didn't see him in the movies, perhaps you saw him on TV. He makes commercials. (*Snap.*)

REVOLUCIONARIO: Is there a Frito Bandito in your house?

SECRETARY: Oh yes, I've seen that one!

SANCHO: Another feature about this one is that he is economical. He runs on raw horse-meat and tequila!

SECRETARY: Isn't that rather savage?

SANCHO: Al contrario, it makes him a lover. (*Snap.*)

REVOLUCIONARIO: (*To* SECRETARY.) Ay, mamasota, cochota, ven pa 'ca! (*He grabs* SECRETARY *and folds her back, Latin-lover style.*)

SANCHO: (*Snap.* REVOLUCIONARIO *goes back upright.*) Now wasn't that nice?

SECRETARY: Well, that was rather nice.

SANCHO: And finally, there is one outstanding feature about this model I know the ladies are going to love: he's a genuine antique! He was made in Mexico in 1910!

SECRETARY: Made in Mexico?

SANCHO: That's right. Once in Tijuana, twice in Guadalajara, three times in Cuernavaca.

SECRETARY: Mr. Sancho, I thought he was an American product.

SANCHO: No, but...

SECRETARY: No, I'm sorry. We can't buy anything but American made products. He just won't do.

SANCHO: But he's an antique!

SECRETARY: I don't care. You still don't understand what we need. It's true we need Mexican models, such as these, but it's more important that he be American.

SANCHO: American?

SECRETARY: That's right, and judging from what you've shown me, I don't think you have what we want. Well, my lunch hour's almost over, I better...

SANCHO: Wait a minute! Mexican but American?

SECRETARY: That's correct.

SANCHO: Mexican but... (*A sudden flash.*) American! Yeah, I think we've got exactly what you want. He just came in today! Give me a minute. (*He exits. Talks from backstage.*) Here he is in the shop. Let me just get some papers off. There. Introducing our new 1970 Mexican-American! Ta-ra-ra-raaaa! (SANCHO *brings out the* MEXICAN-AMERICAN *model, a clean-shaven middle class type in a business suit, with glasses.*)

SECRETARY: (*Impressed.*) Where have you been hiding this one?

SANCHO: He just came in this morning. Ain't he a beauty? Feast your eyes on him! Sturdy U.S. Steel Frame, streamlined, modern. As a matter of fact, he is built exactly like our Anglo models, except that he comes in a variety of darker shades: naugahide, leather or leatherette.

SECRETARY: Naugahide.

SANCHO: Well, we'll just write that down. Yes, señorita, this model represents the apex of American engineering! He is bilingual, college educated, amibitious! Say the word "acculturate" and he accelerates. He is intelligent, well-mannered, clean. Did I say clean? (*Snap.* MEXICAN-AMERICAN *raises his arm.*) Smell.

SECRETARY: (*Smells.*) Old Sobaco, my favorite.

SANCHO: (*Snap.* MEXICAN-AMERICAN *turns toward* SANCHO.) Eric? (*To* SECRETARY.) We call him Eric García. (*To* ERIC.) I want you to meet Miss JIM-enez, Eric.

MEXICAN-AMERICAN: Miss Jim-enez, I am delighted to make your acquaintance. (*He kisses her hand.*)

SECRETARY: Oh, my, how charming!

SANCHO: Did you feel the suction? He has seven especially engineered suction cups right behind his lips. He's a charmer all right!

SECRETARY: How about boards, does he function on boards?

SANCHO: You name them, he is on them. Parole boards, draft boards, school boards, taco quality control boards, surf boards, two by fours.

SECRETARY: Does he function in politics?

SANCHO: Señorita, you are looking at a political machine. Have you ever heard of the OEO, EOC, COD, WAR ON POVERTY? That's our model! Not only that, he makes political speeches.

SECRETARY: May I hear one?

SANCHO: With pleasure. (*Snap.*) Eric, give us a speech.

MEXICAN-AMERICAN: Mr. Congressman, Mr. Chairman, members of the board, honored guests, ladies and gentlemen. (SANCHO *and* SECRETARY *applaud.*) Please, please. I come before you as a Mexican-American to tell you about the problems of the Mexican. The problems of the Mexican stem from one thing and one thing only; he's stupid. He's uneducated. He needs to stay in school. He needs to be ambitious, forward-looking, harder-working. He needs to think American, American, American, American, American! God bless America! God bless America! God bless America! (*He goes out of control.* SANCHO *snaps frantically and the* MEXICAN-AMERICAN *finally slumps forward, bending at the waist.*)

SECRETARY: Oh my, he's patriotic too!

SANCHO: Sí, señorita, he loves his country. Let me just make a little adjustment here. (*Stands* MEXICAN-AMERICAN *up.*)

SECRETARY: What about upkeep? Is he economical?

SANCHO: Well, no, I won't lie to you. The Mexican-American costs a little bit more, but you get what you pay for. He's worth every extra cent. You can keep him running on dry Martinis, Langerdorf bread . . .

SECRETARY: Apple pie?

SANCHO: Only Mom's. Of course, he's also programmed to eat Mexican food at ceremonial functions, but I must warn you, an overdose of beans will plug his exhaust.

SECRETARY: Fine! There's just one more question. How much do you want for him?

SANCHO: Well, I tell you what I'm gonna do. Today and today only, because you've been so sweet, I'm gonna let you steal this model from me! I'm gonna let you drive him off the lot for the simple price of, let's see, taxes and license included, $15,000.

SECRETARY: Fifteen thousand dollars? For a Mexican!!!!

SANCHO: Mexican? What are you talking about? This is a Mexican-American! We had to melt down two pachuchos, a farmworker and three gabachos to make this model! You want quality, but you gotta pay for it! This is no cheap run-about. He's got class!

SECRETARY: Okay, I'll take him.

SANCHO: You will?

SECRETARY: Here's your money.

SANCHO: You mind if I count it?

SECRETARY: Go right ahead.

SANCHO: Well, you'll get your pink slip in the mail. Oh, do you want me to wrap him up for you? We have a box in the back.

SECRETARY: No, thank you. The Governor is having a luncheon this afternoon, and we need a brown face in the crowd. How do I drive him?

SANCHO: Just snap your fingers. He'll do anything you want. (SECRETARY *snaps.* MEXICAN-AMERICAN *steps forward.*)

MEXICAN-AMERICAN: ¡Raza querida, vamos levantando armas para liberarnos de estos desgraciados gabachos que nos explotan! Vamos . . .

SECRETARY: What did he say?

SANCHO: Something about taking up arms, killing white people, etc.

SECRETARY: But he's not supposed to say that!

SANCHO: Look, lady, don't blame me for bugs from the factory. He's your Mexican-American, you bought him, now drive him off the lot!

SECRETARY: But he's broken!

SANCHO: Try snapping another finger. (SECRETARY *snaps.* MEXICAN-AMERICAN *comes to life again.*)

MEXICAN-AMERICAN: ¡Esta gran humanidad ha dicho basta! ¡Y se ha puesto en marcha! ¡Basta! ¡Basta! ¡Viva la raza! ¡Viva la causa! ¡Viva la huelga! ¡Vivan los brown berets! ¡Vivan los estudiantes! ¡Chicano power! (*The* MEXICAN-AMERICAN *turns toward the* SECRETARY, *who gasps and backs up. He keeps turning toward the* PACHUCO, FARMWORKER, *and* REVOLUCIONARIO, *snapping his fingers and turning each of them on, one by one.*)

PACHUCO: (*Snap. To* SECRETARY.) I'm going to get you, baby! ¡Viva la raza!

FARMWORKER: (*Snap. To* SECRETARY.) ¡Viva la huelga! ¡Viva la huelga! ¡Viva la huelga!

REVOLUCIONARIO: (*Snap. To* SECRETARY.) ¡Viva la revolución! (*The three models join together and advance toward the* SECRETARY, *who backs up and runs out of the shop screaming.* SANCHO *is at the other end of the shop holding his money in his hand. All freeze. After a few seconds of silence, the* PACHUCO *moves and stretches, shaking his arms and loosening up. The* FARMWORKER *and* REVOLUCIONARIO *do the same.* SANCHO *stays where he is, frozen to his spot.*)

JOHNNY: Man, that was a long one, ese. (*Others agree with him.*)

FARMWORKER: How did we do?

JOHNNY: Pretty good, look at all that lana, man! (*He goes over to* SANCHO *and removes the money from his hand.* SANCHO *stays where he is.*)

REVOLUCIONARIO: En la madre, look at all the money.

JOHNNY: We keep this up, we're going to be rich.

FARMWORKER: They think we're machines.

REVOLUCIONARIO: Burros.

JOHNNY: Puppets.

MEXICAN-AMERICAN: The only thing I don't like is how come I always get to play the goddamn Mexican-American?

JOHNNY: Here it comes right now. $3,000 for you, $3,000 for you, $3,000 for you and $3,000 for me. The rest we put back into the business.

MEXICAN-AMERICAN: Too much, man. Heh, where you vatos going tonight?

FARMWORKER: I'm going over to Concha's. There's a party.

JOHNNY: Wait a minute, vatos. What about our salesman? I think he needs an oil job.

REVOLUCIONARIO: Leave him to me. (*The* PACHUCO, FARMWORKER, *and* MEXICAN-AMERICAN *exit, talking loudly about their plans for the night. The* REVOLUCIONARIO *goes over to* SANCHO, *removes his derby hat and cigar, lifts him up and throws him over his shoulder.* SANCHO *hangs loose, lifeless. To audience.*) He's the best model we got! ¡Ajúa! (*Exit.*)

CHAPTER 7

Contemporary Reflections on Identity

José Yglesias (1919–1995)

The Truth about Them (excerpt)

Born in Tampa, Florida, to immigrant cigarmakers from Spain and Cuba, much of José Yglesias's writing explores his bicultural, working-class roots and the politics of his hometown Latin enclave, Ybor City. Yglesias was a young man when he left Tampa for New York in 1937. However, the first twenty years of Yglesias's life were marked by events that shaped his career as a writer and a journalist, such as the early loss of his father, the wildness of "Cigar City" in the 1920s, the Depression, and the Spanish Civil War. Much of his nonfiction work, about places of social and political interest, such as revolutionary Cuba, fascist and post-Franco Spain, and Brazil, provides a personal, insider viewpoint on these societies that was uncommon in the United States at that time. His fiction, which draws heavily on his own life in Tampa and New York, explores the struggles and triumphs of immigrant Hispanics in the United States, particularly working-class, Cuban émigré families. The following excerpt from *The Truth About Them* (1971) portrays a young Latino in Tampa experiencing his first funeral, a humble yet dignified ritual. He subsequently explores cultural differences between American and Hispanic attitudes toward mourning and burial practices. (KDM)

Further reading: José Yglesias, *Break In* (Houston: Arte Público Press, 1996), *The Guns in the Closet* (Houston: Arte Público Press, 1996), *A Wake in Ybor City* (1963; rpt., Houston: Arte Público Press, 1996), *The Truth About Them* (Houston: Arte Público Press, 1999).

How undignified for a grocery delivery truck, liable at any moment to an attack of the shimmy, to form part of the cortege following the funeral car to the cemetery. With me at the wheel. Only Mama Chucha and Papa Leandro could have thought it appropriate. I said so to Cousin Pancho, who accompanied me to the cooperative to ask for the use of it in the family's name, and he didn't laugh, as I expected, but simply said, "It is for the children to ride in." There were compensations. Celia sat next to me and kept the small children on the benches in the back quiet. At first she didn't have to, for they were still awed by the sight of their dead grandmother. Papa Leandro had stood them in line before the coffin when the funeral car drove up to the house, and he told them to kiss her good-bye. I did not see it, I heard my aunts tell it, and they thought Papa Leandro had acted correctly.

This was my first funeral. I didn't own a jacket but wore a long-sleeved shirt and a tie that belonged to a cousin. Celia looked at me out of the corner of her eyes. She wore a borrowed dress; probably an older woman's, for she looked more grown up and subdued, her breasts lost in its fullness. "I am glad you're driving and not my brother Cuco," she said. "He's crazy."

Given the old truck, my trouble with the clutch, Celia's presence, my strangled Adam's apple, the children behind me, the line of cars—all these things should have turned the ride to the cemetery into a disaster, a funny-sad disaster of the poor. Heart-warming too. Darling enough to make you cry. Even right by Ybor City predictions: Oh, the things that happen at a Cuban's funeral, especially one arranged by Papa Leandro. And Mama Chucha with her broken arm. Neo-realism, to be sure. I could tell it that way—the path has been smoothed—and what, after all, was so extraordinary about the funeral but my perception of it?

Papa Leandro went straight to the open grave, and Mama Chucha found her own way there. She didn't take his arm—Latin women never did that; it would have been too intimate a gesture to make in public—but looked back to see how big a crowd had come. Some seventy people. Not bad. Then she saw Celia with the children and she raised her good arm and waved for them to come to her. The two youngest pulled back because they were afraid of the grave, and Mother and Aunt Titi each took one and kept them with them there in the second rank where the fresh hole was too far to be seen. They themselves could not bear to look at an open grave; it gave them vertigo, they said. A seven-year-old immediately closed her fist on one leg of Papa Leandro's pants; twice he had to unstick it, pulling the fingers away from the cloth one at a time.

There was no ceremonial lowering of the coffin; it was simply placed at the bottom of the pit, and from where I stood I saw Papa Leandro lean forward curiously. A man called El Maestro stepped up on the pile of earth nearby, so that he was a head taller than the group, and slowly looked around to signify that he was about to speak. Papa Leandro straightened and stared ahead, at attention.

El Maestro was a reader at one of the cigar factories. From his vantage on the platform built in the middle of the factory floor, he was used to speaking over the heads of cigar-makers. Early in his career in Ybor City and West Tampa he had adopted so didactic a tone and maintained so upright a posture of his short body that he was immediately nicknamed El Maestro. He was not unapproachable, however; he played dominoes at the Cuban Club, poker at the Centro Español, never missed a drawing of the numbers at Serafin's Café; and for thirty years had been singing in the zarzuelas, Spanish light operas, staged by the amateur group at the Centro Asturiano, going from romantic tenor roles in his youth to grandfatherly baritones now without anyone's having complained that his vocal range hadn't shifted; in fact, it was comforting that it had not. Just as it was comforting to those at the cemetery—you could feel it in a certain relaxation that came over the group when he got up on the mound—to know he was going to *despedir el duelo*, a phrase I heard then as one word. It means Farewell to the Mourning.

"*Compañeros*," he began, "one of our own has died."

The words that followed were like a song, and how El Maestro connected one to another was a mystery and a wonder to me. I cannot remember them and I will not invent them. I know now that they were flowery and sentimental and the Farewell to the Mourning was as rule-ridden as the letters for all occasions that I had been taught in junior high school. I daresay that no child of my generation in Ybor City ever had the opportunity to write or receive a bread-and-butter letter, but even for me, who had been surprised to hear two days earlier that Papa Leandro had a mother, El Maestro's speech had a function. Solace.

That was the effect of the speech's inviolable rules: praising the enduring qualities of the dead; naming the mourners so that all eyes turned to them for one beneficent moment; suggesting to each resignation not in the name of religion—that was not popular—but of their own good conduct in life toward the dead; and recalling to those who stood beyond the first rows of the stricken the now bearable old griefs. The women wept. The men made short, abrupt movements of their heads as if suddenly distracted. I thought of the death of my father some years earlier while he was in Spain. I believed I was mourning him, but it was the power of the Spanish language that moved me, those swells and pauses that El Maestro conducted, an eloquence so unlike the prosaic commands of Aunt Titi and my mother, the gossip of the women on the porch at night, the teasing, hectoring exchanges of the men over coffee, that it resolved our separate beings in the unity of art.

El Maestro swooped and picked up some sand and dropped it into the grave. Papa Leandro moved forward, picked up some too, and threw it with an effort, and Mama Chucha, as if afraid to find herself standing alone, gave a small, thin shriek. The seven-year-old howled. My aunts stepped toward Mama Chucha, but they did not get to her in time to prevent Papa Leandro throwing himself on her. "Mamita, Mamita, you are all I have left now," he cried, and the two wobbled, threatening to fall to the ground. "You and the children!" Next to me Uncle Candido shook his head: You could not trust Papa Leandro to maintain the tone of stoicism proper to a funeral.

Those great secular funerals—they were the first to go. Or, rather, when their form began to change, when the dead were no longer laid out at home but at funeral parlors and it was there you went, for a few brief hours, to mourn and pay your respects; when that happened, it was already too late to reclaim Ybor City and West Tampa. They were mortally wounded and we didn't know it. Such a sensible change, particularly under the special circumstances of Aunt Titi's death three years later, why should it lead to a freeway cutting a swath through the community and to urban renewal bulldozers leveling block after block of wooden houses? You stand on the steps of the Cuban Club today and see all the way to Twenty-second Street, and the fuss that Mama Chucha raised about laying out Aunt Titi at a funeral parlor seems now full of prophecy. No one walks, not even on Seventh Avenue (only the Americans ever got to call it East Broadway), although the Chamber of Commerce has given it a center island with palms, and the sidewalks, once so crowded, have been decorated with iron grillwork that looks like plastic. Bad Negroes from Mississippi and Tennessee have moved into the old, termite-ridden houses, and the old men who still go to the clubs to play dominoes start home early so they will not be assaulted by one of them. I walked down Seventh Avenue the other day and a car slowed down alongside me and a voice called out,

"What you doing here, man?" It belonged to a boy with whom I played marbles, and his face appeared streaked, puffed, and drained of color. I almost asked what had happened to him.

Aunt Titi was not, indeed, laid out at a funeral parlor. My aunts and mother had planned it that way when they left New York with her body on a train called the Silver Meteor, having been urged to do so by their husbands and children, all adults and working in perfume factories and caféteria kitchens in Manhattan. But Mama Chucha had never left Tampa. She, Papa Leandro, and the younger children survived the Depression on relief and the money orders that Cuco and the other boys in New York sent each week. Unlike the rest of us who had gravitated to New York, Mama Chucha had never seen a Jewish newspaper, a Chinese restaurant, the morning twenty-five-cent show at the Paramount; she had never sat in a subway underground and been hurtled—suddenly, astoundingly—into the open air to ride alongside the tops of buildings and see beyond them the Hudson River and, out the opposite windows, the dark valley of Harlem. Mama Chucha had not felt that little click inside her—like the uncoupling of noiseless trains—that separates one from the ways of West Tampa and Ybor City. She screamed when she learned at the railroad station in Tampa that Aunt Titi's body was not going directly home.

"I shall take my sister to my home," she announced.

"What a thing to say!" Aunt Angela said. "Anyway, Titi has been dead three days."

"The more reason, the more reason," Mama Chucha said. "My home is not too fine for Titi's smell."

"Oh, oh!" Aunt Lulu turned to my mother. "Did you hear her! If Mama heard—"

"What do you think she would say?" Mama Chucha asked. "And Titi—what would she say? My sister who helped me with all my children and my broken arm, they want to treat her like a parcel now!"

Mother was unimpressed. "Titi was our sister too, and it was we who gave her a home."

"Americans, that is what you are," Mama Chucha yelled. "Florida crackers. Without feelings. I am the oldest now and she is going to my home."

Piri Thomas (1928–)

Down These Mean Streets (excerpt)

Piri Thomas is one of the most widely known writers of ethnic autobiography. His *Down These Mean Streets* was so successful as a powerful chronicle of growing up in the barrio that it spawned a host of Puerto Rican imitators. Born in New York City to a Puerto Rican mother and a Cuban father, Thomas grew up during the Depression, facing both poverty and double racism, for his black skin and Hispanic background. As a teenager on the mean streets, he began a career as a small-time criminal and eventually served prison time, a period which allowed him to discover the Black Pride movement and his own ethnic roots and his genius for writing. After release from prison, Thomas became one of the most renowned members of the Nuyorican generation of writers, following up his best-selling first book with a continuing series of memoirs and autobiographical stories, poems, and plays. In addition to his writing, Thomas also developed a career as a public speaker and performer of his verse and prose. In the excerpt below, the young Piri grapples with differences in skin color and racial and ethnic identity within his own family. (NK)

Further reading: Piri Thomas, *Down These Mean Streets* (New York: Knopf, 1967), *Stories from El Barrio* (New York: Knopf, 1992), *Seven Long Times* (Houston: Arte Público Press, 1995).

Chapter Fifteen: Brothers Under the Skin

My daydreaming was splintered by my brother José kicking at the door in sheer panic. "Hey, who's in there?" he yelled.

"Me, man, me," I yelled back. "Whatta ya want?"

"Let me in. I gotta take a piss so bad I can taste it."

"Taste good?" I asked softly.

"Dammit, open up!"

I laughed, and reached out a dripping hand and flipped the latch. José rushed in like his behind was on fire. His face had a pained look on it. "Chri-sus sake," he said, "you made me piss all over my pants."

"It'll dry, man, it'll dry."

"Aggh," he said as he relieved himself. "That feels good." I looked at my brother. *Even his peter's white,* I thought, *just like James's. Only ones got black peters is Poppa and me, and Poppa acts like his is white, too.*

"Poppa's home."

"Yeah. Hand me the towel, simple."

"Damn, Piri, you made me piss all over my pants," José said again. He pulled back the towel he was offering me and began to wipe his pants with it.

"Man, turkey, what you doin'?" I said. "You drying that piss and I gotta wipe my face with that towel."

"It'll dry, man, it'll dry."

I yanked the towel outta his hand and carefully wiped with what seemed to be the part he hadn't used. "You know somethin', José?" I said.

"What? Jesus, I hope this piss don't stink when it dries."

"I'm goin' down South."

"Where?"

"Down South."

"What for?"

"Don't know all the way," I said, "except I'm tryin' to find somethin' out."

"*Down South!*" He said it like I was nuts.

"*Sí.* I want to see what a *moyeto*'s worth and the paddy's weight on him," I said.

"Whatta ya talking about? You sound like a *moto* who's high on that *yerba* shit. And anyway, what's the spade gotta do with you?"

"I'm a Negro."

"You ain't no nigger," José said.

"I ain't?"

"No. You're a Puerto Rican."

"I am, huh?" I looked at José and said, "Course, you gotta say that. 'Cause if I'm a Negro, then you and James is one too. And that ain't leavin' out Sis and Poppa. Only Momma's an exception. She don't care what she is."

José didn't look at me. He decided that looking at the toilet bowl was better. "So whatta you got to find out, eh?" he said. "You're crazy, stone loco. We're Puerto Ricans, and that's different from being *moyetos.*" His voice came back very softly and his hand absent-mindedly kept brushing the drying wet patch on his pants.

"That's what I've been wanting to believe all along, José," I said. "I've been hanging on to that idea even when I knew it wasn't so. But only pure white Puerto Ricans are white, and you wouldn't even believe that if you ever dug what the paddy said."

"I don't give a good shit what you say, Piri. We're Puerto Ricans, and that makes us different from black people."

I kept drying myself even though there was nothin' to dry. I was trying not to get mad. I said, "José, that's what the white man's been telling the Negro all along, that 'cause he's white he's different from the Negro; that he's better'n the Negro or anyone that's not white. That's what I've been telling myself and what I tried to tell Brew."

"Brew's that colored guy, ain't he?" José said.

"Yeah—an' like I'm saying, sure there's stone-white Puerto Ricans, like from pure Spanish way back—but it ain't us. Poppa's a Negro and, even if Momma's *blanca,* Poppa's blood carries more weight with Mr. Charlie," I said.

"Mr. Charlie, Mr. Charlie. Who the fuck is he?"

"That's the name Brew calls the paddies. Ask any true *corazón* white motherfucker what the score is," I said.

"I'm not black, no matter what you say, Piri."

I got out of the shower and sat on the edge of the tub. "Maybe not outside, José," I said. "But you're sure that way inside."

"I ain't black, damn you! Look at my hair. It's almost blond. My eyes are blue, my nose is straight. My motherfuckin' lips are not like a baboon's ass. My skin is white. White, goddamit! White! Maybe Poppa's a little dark, but that's the Indian blood in him. He's got white blood in him and—"

"So what the fuck am I? Something Poppa an' Momma picked out the garbage dump?" I was jumping stink inside and I answered him like I felt it. "Look, man, better believe it, I'm one of 'you-all.' Am I your brother or ain't I?"

"Yeah, you're my brother, and James an' Sis, and we all come out of Momma an' Poppa—but we ain't Negroes. We're Puerto Ricans, an' we're white."

"Boy, you, Poppa and James sure are sold on that white kick. Poppa thinks that marrying a white woman made him white. He's wrong. It's just another nigger marrying a white woman and making her as black as him. That's the way the paddy looks at it. The Negro just stays black. Period. Dig it?"

José's face got whiter and his voice angrier at my attempt to take away his white status. He screamed out strong, "I ain't no nigger! You can be if you want to be. You can go down South and grow cotton, or pick it, or whatever the fuck they do. You can eat that cornbread or whatever shit they eat. You can bow and kiss ass and clean shit bowls. But—I—am—*white!* And you can go to hell!"

"And James is *blanco*, too?" I asked quietly.

"You're damn right."

"And Poppa?"

José flushed the toilet chain so hard it sounded as if somebody's neck had broken. "Poppa's the same as you," he said, avoiding my eyes, "Indian."

"What kinda Indian?" I said bitterly. "Caribe? Or maybe Borinquén? Say, José, didn't you know the Negro made the scene in Puerto Rico way back? And when the Spanish spics ran outta Indian coolies, they brought them big blacks from you know where. Poppa's got *moyeto* blood. I got it. Sis got it. James got it. And, mah deah brudder, you-all got it! Dig it! It's with us till game time. Like I said, man, that shit-ass poison I've been living with is on its way out. It's a played-out lie about me—us—being white. There ain't nobody in this fucking house can lay any claim to bein' paddy exceptin' Momma, and she's never made it a mountain of fever like we have. You and James are like houses—painted white outside, and blacker'n a mother inside. An' I'm close to being like Poppa—trying to be white on both sides."

José eased by me and put his hand on the doorknob.

"Where you going?" I said. "I ain't finished talking yet."

José looked at me like there was no way out. "Like I said, man, you can be a nigger if you want to," he said, as though he were talking with a ten-ton rock on his chest. "I don't know how you come to be my brother, but I love you like one. I've busted my ass, both me and James, trying to explain to people how come you so dark and how come your hair is so curly an'—"

I couldn't help thinking, *Oh, Crutch, you were so right. We shouldn't have moved to Long Island.* I said, "You and James hadda make excuses for me? Like for me being *un Negrito?*" I looked at the paddy in front of me. "Who to?" I said. "Paddies?"

Lights began to jump into my head and tears blurred out that this was my brother before me. The burning came up out of me and I felt the shock run up my arm as my fists went up the side of his head. I felt one fist hit his mouth. I wondered if I had broken any of his nice white teeth.

José fell away and bounced back with his white hands curled into fists. I felt the hate in them as his fists became a red light of exploding pain on my tender, flat nose. *Oh, God!* I tried to make the lights go away. I made myself creep up a long sinking shit-hole agony and threw myself at José. The bathroom door flew open and me, naked and wet with angry sweat, and José, his mouth bleedin', crashed out of the bathroom and rolled into the living room. I heard all kinds of screaming and chairs turning over and falling lamps. I found myself on top of José. In the blurred confusion I saw his white, blood-smeared face and I heard myself screaming, "You bastard! Dig it, you bastard. You're bleeding, and the blood is like anybody else's—red!" I saw an unknown face spitting blood at me. I hated it. I wanted to stay on top of this unknown what-was-it and beat him and beat him and beat him and beat him and *beat beat beat beat beat*—and feel skin smash under me and—and—and—

I felt an arm grab me. It wasn't fair; it wasn't a *chevere* thing to do. In a fair rumble, nobody is supposed to jump in. "Goddammit, are you crazy?" a voice screamed. "God-damn you for beating your brother like that. My God!—"

I twisted my head and saw Poppa. And somewhere, far off, I heard a voice that sounded like Momma crying, "What's it all about? What's it all about? Why do brothers do this to each other?"

I wanted to scream it out, but that man's arm was cutting my air from sound. I twisted and forced out, "Lemme go, Poppa. *Coño*, let me go!" And the arm was gone. I stayed on bended knees. My fists were tired and my knuckles hurt at this Cain and Abel scene. As the hurting began to leave me, I slowly became a part of my naked body. I felt weak with inside pain. I wondered why.

"José, José," Momma screamed, and I wondered why she didn't scream for me, too. Didn't she know I had gotten hurt the worst?

"Why in God's name?" Poppa was saying.

Fuck God! I thought.

"Why in God's name?"

I looked at Poppa. "'Cause, Poppa," I said, "him, you and James think you're white, and I'm the only one that's found out I'm not. I tried hard not to find out. But I did, and I'm almost out from under that kick you all are still copping out to." I got up from my knees. "Poppa," I added, "what's wrong with not being white? What's so wrong with being *tregeño*? Momma must think it's great, she got married to you, eh? We gotta have pride and dignity, Poppa; we gotta walk big and bad. I'm me and I dig myself in the mirror and it's me. I shower and dig my peter and it's me. I'm black, and it don't make no difference whether I say good-bye or *adiós*—it means the same."

Nobody said anything; everyone just stood there. I said, "I'm proud to be a Puerto Rican, but being Puerto Rican don't make the color." Still there was silence. "I'm going," I said.

"Where?" Poppa asked.

"I don't know . . ."

"He's going down South," said José, sitting on the floor with his head in his hands and the almost-blond hair, the good, straight hair that could fall down over his forehead.

"*Where?*" Poppa asked.

I looked at José and felt sorry for me. I looked at the wall and said, "Down South. I joined the merchant marine and me and Brew's going, and—"

"Who? Brew? That's that colored boy, ain't it?" Poppa said.

"—and I wanna find out what's happening, and . . ." I wondered why everything I was saying didn't sound like it was so important to anybody, including me. I wondered why James wasn't there. I wondered why Sis wasn't there . . .

I walked away. Momma put her hand on me and she asked, "Why does it hurt you so to be *un Negrito?*"

I shook my head and kept walking. I wished she could see inside me. I wished she could see it didn't hurt—so much.

Miguel Piñero (1946–1988)

A Lower East Side Poem

Miguel Piñero, as a playwright, poet, and anthologizer, was one of the leading figures in the Nuyorican literary movement. Born in Gurabo, Puerto Rico, Piñero was raised on the Lower

East Side of New York, which he memorialized as a rich cultural space for the development of Nuyorican identity. Piñero literally lived on the streets of "Loisaida" the life of a member of the "underclass," the phrase *Time* magazine coined to describe the lowest, most disadvantaged sector of U.S. society. Piñero was raised in a fatherless home, became a gang leader, was involved in petty crime and drugs, was a junior high school dropout, and by the time he was twenty-four had been sent to Sing Sing for armed robbery. While in Sing Sing, Piñero began acting and writing in a theater workshop. There he began his first hit play, *Short Eyes*, which won the New York Drama Critics Circle Award for Best American Play, an Obie, and the Drama Desk Award, all in 1974. Soon after his release from prison, Piñero saw his play move successfully to Broadway, and he became a sought-after screenwriter for television crime shows and a playwright in demand. While his fame as a writer helped him to spread the Nuyorican literary movement, principally in his roles as an oral, bilingual poet, his work for Hollywood all but stymied his play production, which could not provide the payoffs in cash that he needed to sustain the drug addiction, which he had since late childhood. Despite his continuous run-ins with the law and his perennial homelessness and his poverty—and despite his consistent, highly paid Hollywood script work—Piñero managed to publish a slim collection of poems, *La Bodega Sold Dreams*. He also published *Short Eyes* and two collections of plays—some of them unfinished and unpolished, but all staged or workshopped. Miguel Piñero died of cirrhosis of the liver in 1988. (NK)

Further reading: Miguel Piñero, *Short Eyes* (New York: Hill and Wang, 1975), *La Bodega Sold Dreams* (Houston: Arte Público Press, 1980), *The Sun Always Shines for the Cool, Midnight Moon at the Greasy Spoon, Eulogy for a Small Time Thief* (Houston: Arte Público Press, 1984), *Outrageous One Act Plays* (Houston: Arte Público Press, 1986).

Just once before I die
I want to climb up on a
tenement sky
to dream my lungs out till
I cry
then scatter my ashes thru
the Lower East Side.

So let me sing my song tonight
let me feel out of sight
and let all eyes be dry
when they scatter my ashes thru
the Lower East Side.

From Houston to 14th Street
from Second Avenue to the mighty D
here the hustlers & suckers meet
the faggots & freaks will all get
high
on the ashes that have been scattered
thru the Lower East Side.

There's no other place for me to be
there's no other place that I can see
there's no other town around that
brings you up or keeps you down
no food little heat sweeps by
fancy cars & pimps' bars & juke saloons
& greasy spoons make my spirits fly
with my ashes scattered thru the
Lower East Side . . .

A thief, a junkie I've been
committed every known sin
Jews and Gentiles . . . Bums and Men
of style . . . run away child
police shooting wild . . .
mother's futile wails . . . pushers
making sales . . . dope wheelers
& cocaine dealers . . . smoking pot
streets are hot & feed off those who bleed to death . . .

all that's true
all that's true
all that is true
but this ain't no lie
when I ask that my ashes be scattered thru
the Lower East Side.

So here I am, look at me
I stand proud as you can see
pleased to be from the Lower East
a street fighting man
a problem of this land
I am the Philosopher of the Criminal Mind
a dweller of prison time
a cancer of Rockefeller's ghettocide
this concrete tomb is my home
to belong to survive you gotta be strong
you can't be shy less without request
someone will scatter your ashes thru
the Lower East Side.

I don't wanna be buried in Puerto Rico
I don't wanna rest in long island cemetery
I wanna be near the stabbing shooting
gambling fighting & unnatural dying

& new birth crying
so please when I die . . .
don't take me far away
keep me near by
take my ashes and scatter them thru out
the Lower East Side . . .

Nicholasa Mohr (1935–)

Uncle Claudio

Nicholasa Mohr is the Hispanic woman with the longest career as a creative writer. Since 1973, her books, in both adult and children's literature categories, have won numerous awards and outstanding reviews. Part and parcel of her work is the experience of growing up a female, a Hispanic, and a minority in New York City. Born in New York City and raised in Spanish Harlem, Mohr finally escaped poverty after graduating from the Pratt Center for Contemporary Printmaking in 1969. From that date until the publication of her first novel, *Nilda* (1973), Mohr developed a successful career as a graphic artist. *Nilda*, a novel that traces the life of a young Puerto Rican girl confronting prejudice and coming of age during World War II, won the Jane Addams Children's Book Award and was selected as Best Book of the Year by *School Library Journal*. After *Nilda*'s success, Mohr was able to produce numerous stories, scripts, and novels, many of which have been reprinted and/or excerpted in anthologies and textbooks. Mohr has contributed some of the most honest and memorable depictions of Puerto Ricans in New York with warmth and empathy. In *Uncle Claudio*, from her collection of stories *El Bronx Remembered* (1975), Mohr explores the difference between Puerto Ricans native to the city and recent migrants, who have great difficulty in adjusting to the new environment, where different race and class distinctions operate. (NK)

Further reading: Nicholasa Mohr, *Nilda* (New York: Harper, 1973), *El Bronx Remembered* (New York: Harper, 1975), *Rituals of Survival: A Woman's Portfolio* (Houston: Arte Público Press, 1985).

Jaime and Charlie sat on the stoop waiting for the rest of their family to come down. They were all going to the airport to see Uncle Claudio and Aunt Chela take the plane back to Puerto Rico.

Charlie had arrived in the Bronx very early this morning with his parents and older sisters. They had driven in from Manhattan. The two boys were first cousins. They saw each other only on special holidays and at family meetings, and today they were glad to be together again.

It was a warm spring Saturday morning. People were still in their apartments and the streets were empty. The boys sat silently, watching the traffic roll by and listening to the faraway sounds coming from inside the tenements. People were beginning to open their windows and turn on their radios. After a while, Jaime stood up and stretched.

"How about a game of stoop ball, Charlie?" he asked, smiling and holding up a Spalding ball.

"Better not," warned Charlie. "I got my good clothes on. You too, Jaime. We'll get it if we get dirty."

Bouncing the ball quickly against the stoop steps a few times, Jaime stopped and sighed. "You're right," he said.

"They sure are taking their sweet time coming down, ain't they?"

"True," answered Jaime, "but they gotta be at the airport at a certain time, so they can't be too late."

"Jaime, do you know why Uncle Claudio is going back to Puerto Rico so fast?" asked Charlie. "He only been here a few months. My mother and father were just talking this morning about how foolish he is to leave. Giving up a good job and good pay and all."

"My mother and father say the same thing like yours. But I know why he's going back to Puerto Rico."

"You do?"

"Yeah," answered Jaime, "I do."

"Tell me."

"Well, I came home from playing ball one day, I guess about a couple of weeks ago. As I came up the stairs I heard a noise, like someone crying. When I came to my floor, there was Uncle Claudio, standing in front of our door. He had his face buried in his hands and was crying out loud."

"Crying?" interrupted Charlie.

"Yes, he was. Because I tapped him and he turned around. His face was full of tears, and when he saw me he just took out his handkerchief, blew his nose, and went into our apartment real quick."

"Why was he crying?"

"I didn't know why, then. He went right into his room, and I forgot about it. But later that evening, I was doing my homework in my room and I heard a lotta noise coming from the kitchen. It sounded like a big argument so I went to see what was happening. Papi was standing and shouting at Uncle Claudio, and Aunt Chela was crying and wiping her eyes. My mother was trying to calm down my father."

"What were they saying?"

"Well, Papi was telling Uncle Claudio that he was an ungrateful brother to be going back to Humacao, after all he and Mami had done for him and Aunt Chela. You know, get them jobs and all. Well, all of a sudden Uncle Claudio jumped up, clenching his fists at Papi. You know what a bad temper my father has, so I thought, Uh-oh, here it comes; they are gonna stomp each other. But when Papi put up his hands to fight back, Uncle Claudio sat down and began to cry. Burst right out into tears just like in the hallway!" Jaime paused and nodded.

"Wow," said Charlie. "Did he tell why he was crying?"

"Wait, I'm coming to that. At first, everybody started asking him a whole lotta questions. He kept saying in Spanish, 'No puede ser,' something like that, you know, like 'It can't never be.' Like that. Then he started to tell why he can't stay here in this country. First, he says there are too many people all living together with no place to go. In his own home, in Humacao, people take it easy and know how to live. They got respect for each other, and know their place. At home, when he walks down the street, he is Don Claudio. But here, in New York City, he is Don Nobody, that's what he said. He doesn't get no respect here. Then he tells something that happened to him that day, in the subway, that he says made him make up his mind to go back home."

"What was that?"

"Well, he got on at his regular station downtown and there was no seats. So he stands, like always, and he notices two young men whispering to each other and pointing at him. At first he don't recognize them. But then one of them looks familiar. They are both well dressed, with suits and ties. One guy waves to him and smiles, so he waves back. Then the guy starts to call out to him by his first name. He says he is Carlito, the son of a lady called Piedad. She used to work for my father and Uncle Claudio's family back in Puerto Rico. The lady used to do the cleaning and cooking, and she was fired. Uncle Claudio says that this young guy is talking real loud and thanks him for firing his mother, because they came to this country and now are doing real well. He even told Uncle Claudio he has no bad feelings and offered him his seat. Then he asked Uncle Claudio where he worked and offered him a better job in his place. Well, Uncle Claudio said he was so embarrassed he got off before his stop, just to get away from that young guy."

"He did?" asked Charlie. "Why?"

"That's exactly what my Papi asked him. Why? Well, Uncle Claudio got real red in the face and started hollering at Papi. He said that in Humacao the maid's son would never talk to him like that. Here, that punk can wear a suit and tie while he has to wear dirty clothes all day. Back home in Humacao, Uncle Claudio says he could get that guy fired and make him apologize for the way he spoke to him, calling him by his first name like that. His mother was caught stealing food and was fired . . . and that she was lucky they did not put her in jail! Anyway, Papi tries to explain to him that things are different here. That people don't think like that, and that these things are not important. That there are better opportunities here in the future for Uncle Claudio's sons. And that Uncle Claudio has to be patient and learn the new ways here in this country." Jaime stopped talking for a moment.

"What did Uncle Claudio say?"

"He got really mad at Papi," said Jaime. "He says that Papi is losing all his values here in New York, and that he don't want his boys to come here, ever. That he is glad he left them in Humacao. There, they know that their father is somebody. He says he is ashamed of his younger brother—you know, my father. Anyway, everybody tried to calm him down and talk him out of going. Even Aunt Chela. I think she likes it here. But he got so excited he jumped up and made the sign of the cross and swore by Jesucristo and la Virgen María that he will never come back to El Bronx again! That was it, he made up his mind to go back, right there!"

"That was it?"

"Yes," Jaime nodded. "That's what happened."

"I don't know," said Charlie, shaking his head. "But I don't care who I meet on the subway, because I may never meet them again. I never see the same people on the subway twice even. Do you? Maybe Uncle Claudio didn't know that."

"You are right, but it wouldn't make no difference because he just made up his mind to leave."

"Anyway," Charlie said, "what's so bad about what that guy said? In fact I thought he seemed nice—giving him his seat and all. Maybe it was something else, and he's not saying the truth."

"No," Jaime said, "that was it. I know; I was there."

"Well, that's no big deal if you ask me. I thought it was something bad," Charlie said.

"I know," said Jaime, "and when I asked Papi why Uncle Claudio got so excited and has to leave, he said that Uncle Claudio lives in another time and that he is dreaming instead of facing life."

"What does that mean?" asked Charlie.

"I asked him the same thing. I don't know what that means neither. And Papi told me that when I grow up I'll understand. Then he started to laugh a whole lot and said that maybe I'll never understand."

"That's what your father said?"

"That's what he said. Nothing else," answered Jaime.

"Well . . ." Charlie shrugged his shoulders and looked at Jaime.

They sat silently for a while, enjoying the bright sun as it warmed their bodies and the stone steps of the stoop.

Very young children played, some on the sidewalk, others in the street. They chalked areas for different games, forming groups. The men were lining up in front of their parked cars with buckets of water, detergent, car wax, and tool boxes. They called out to one another as they began the long and tedious ritual of washing, polishing and fixing their secondhand automobiles.

Windows opened; some of the women shook out the bedclothes, others leaned against the mattresses placed on the sills for an airing and looked out along the avenue. The streets were no longer empty. People hustled and bustled back and forth, and the avenue vibrated with activity.

Jaime and Charlie grew restless.

"Too bad we can't go over to the schoolyard and play ball," said Jaime.

"Here they come at last!" said Charlie.

Uncle Claudio walked by with his wife, Chela. The boys noticed that he wore the same outfit he had arrived with last year: a white suit, white shirt with a pale-blue tie, white shoes, and a very pale beige, wide-brimmed, panama hat. Aunt Chela had a brand-new dress and hat.

The adults talked among themselves as they decided how to group the families into the two cars.

"We wanna ride together, Papi. Please, me and Charlie!" Jaime pulled his father's arm.

"O.K.," said his father, "you two jump in." He pointed to one of the cars.

Jaime and Charlie sat together, enjoying the ride.

"What do you think? If we get back in time, how about going to the schoolyard and have a game of stickball? You can meet all my friends," said Jaime.

"Right!" answered Charlie.

Tato Laviera (1950–)

my graduation speech; the africa in pedro morejón

Jesús Abraham "Tato" Laviera is the best-selling Hispanic poet of the United States, and he bears the distinction of still having all of his books in print. Born in Santurce, Puerto Rico, he migrated to New York City at age ten with his family, who settled in a poor area of the Lower

East Side. After graduating high school with honors and taking courses at various colleges, Laviera worked as a social services administrator until he published his first book, *La Carreta Made a U-Turn* (1979), the success of which led him to pursue full-time his work as a writer. In 1980, Laviera was received by President Jimmy Carter at the White House gathering of American poets, and in 1981, he published his second book, *Enclave*, which achieved the American Book Award of the Before Columbus Foundation. Laviera has continued to publish poetry collections, tour, and produce cultural events around the nation. He is celebrated by critics within the context of Afro-Caribbean poetry and Hispanic bilingualism and performance art. *La Carreta Made a U-Turn* is bilingual jazz-salsa poetry that presents the reader with a slice of life drawn from the Puerto Rican community of the Lower East Side. As such, it examines both the oppression of the migrant community and its alienation; it probes crime and drug addiction while affirming the spiritual and social values of the community and the place of art in what many may consider the most unlikely of social environments. Laviera affirms and supports the existence of authentic Latino culture. He also explores African heritage and prejudice against it both in the United States and in Puerto Rico. (NK)

Further reading: Tato Laviera, *La Carreta Made a U-Turn* (Houston: Arte Público Press, 1979), *Enclave* (Houston: Arte Público Press, 1981), *AmeRícan* (Houston: Arte Público Press, 1985).

my graduation speech

i think in spanish
i write in english

i want to go back to puerto rico,
but i wonder if my kink could live
in ponce, mayagüez and carolina

tengo las venas aculturadas
escribo en spanglish
abraham in español

abraham in english
tato in spanish
"taro" in english
tonto in both languages

how are you?
¿cómo estás?
i don't know if i'm coming
or si me fui ya

si me dicen barranquitas, yo reply,
"¿con qué se come eso?"
si me dicen caviar, i digo,
"a new pair of converse sneakers."

ahí supe que estoy jodío
ahí supe que estamos jodíos

english or spanish
spanish or english
spanenglish
now, dig this:

hablo lo inglés matao
hablo lo español matao
no sé leer ninguno bien

so it is, spanglish to matao
what i digo
¡ay, virgen, yo no sé hablar!

the africa in pedro morejón

slowly descending, as if from the clouds above,
thinking of africa, i find myself enthralled!
rhythmic africanism swell and dwell inside
the fingers of my cuban mambo eyes.

the african rhythms i hear are native, native
from my cuban land, it is as if my guaguancó
was shipped to africa, when it was the other
way around, but nevertheless all my colors are the same.

i hear the merengue in french haiti
and in dominican blood,
and the guaracha in yoruba,
and the mambo sounds inside the plena
so close to what i really understand,
sometimes i think
that cuba is africa,
or that i am in cuba and africa at the
same time, sometimes i think africa
is all of us in music,
musically rooted way way back
before any other language.

yes, we preserved what was originally african,
or have we expanded it? i wonder if we have
committed the sin of blending? but i also hear
that AFRICANS love electric guitars clearly misunderstanding they are the root,

or is it me who is primitive?
damn it, it is complicated.

i had a dream that i was in africa,
it took me a long time
to find the gods inside
so many moslems and christians,
but when i did, they were the origin of everything!
then i discovered bigger things,
the american dollar symbol,
that's african;
the british sense of loyalty, that's african;
the colors in catholic celebrations,
that's african; and . . .
ultimate . . . listen here . . . closer . . .
come on . . . closer . . . sshhhhhh . . .
two whites can never make a black . . .
two whites can never make a black . . .
two whites can never make a black . . .
but two blacks, give them
time . . . can make mulatto . . .
can make brown . . . can make blends . . .
and ultimately . . . can make white.

óyeme consorte, pero no repita esto,
porque si me coge el klu klux klan
me caen encima con un alemán
me esparrachan con una swastika
y me cortan la cabeza. pero, es verdad:
dos blancos no pueden hacer un prieto.

i went to africa and all of it seemed cuban,
i met a cuban and all of him was african,

this high-priest, pedro, telling me all of this
in front of an abandoned building.

Cherríe Moraga (1952–)

La Güera [The fair-skinned one]

When *This Bridge Called My Back* was published, Gloria Anzaldúa and Cherríe Moraga created a space for exploring issues affecting the lives of women of color in the United States, positioned as they were between the racism and classism of the mainstream feminist movement and the sexism of male-led ethnic movements. From this moment on, Moraga proved herself relentless in her commitment to giving voice to discourses excluded from the Chicano literary canon, among them the expression of female sexuality and a critique of homophobia. Her own multiracial, working-class, and lesbian background provided the foundation for a corpus of work including poetry, essays, drama, and fiction. In the essay included here, Moraga begins the difficult work of teasing out the various strands that make up the knot of internalized racism, homophobia, and class oppression. Crucial to her understanding of these issues is the exploration of her mother's experiences as a dark-skinned woman of the working class in juxtaposition with her own experience as a fair-skinned woman who is able to avoid discrimination by "passing." This exercise reveals to Moraga the source of her lesbian desire and opens the door to an encounter with her Chicana cultural identity. Moraga received a master's degree from San Francisco State College and has taught high school and university writing classes. She is a recipient of the American Book Award from the Before Columbus Foundation, the Fund for New American Plays Award from the Kennedy Center for the Performing Arts, and a National Endowment for the Arts Theater Playwriting Fellowship. (EGB)

Further reading: Cherríe Moraga, *Loving in the War Years: O que nunca pasó por sus labios* (Boston: South End Press, 1983), *Heroes and Other Plays* (Albuquerque: West End Press, 1994).

> It requires something more than personal experience to gain a philosophy or point of view from any specific event. It is the quality of our response to the event and our capacity to enter into the lives of others that help us to make their lives and experiences our own.
>
> —Emma Goldman

I am the very well-educated daughter of a woman who, by the standards in this country, would be considered largely illiterate. My mother was born in Santa Paula, Southern California, at a time when much of the central valley there was still farm land. Nearly thirty-five years later, in 1948, she was the only daughter of six to marry an anglo, my father.

I remember all of my mother's stories, probably much better than she realizes. She is a fine story-teller, recalling every event of her life with the vividness of the present, noting each detail right down to the cut and color of her dress. I remember stories of her being pulled out of school at the ages of five, seven, nine, and eleven to work in the fields, along with her brothers and sisters; stories of her father drinking away whatever small profit she was able to make for the family; of her going the long way home to avoid meeting him on the street, staggering toward the same destination. I remember stories of my mother lying about her age in order to get a job as a hat-check girl at Agua Caliente Racetrack in Tijuana. At fourteen, she was the main support of the family. I can still see her walking home alone at 3 A.M., only to turn all of her salary and tips over to her mother, who was pregnant again.

The stories continue through the war years and on: walnut-cracking factories, the Voit Rubber factory, and then the computer boom. I remember my mother doing piecework for the electronics plant in our neighborhood. In the late evening, she would sit in front of the T.V. set, wrapping copper wires into the backs of circuit boards, talking about "keeping up with the younger girls." By that time, she was already in her mid-fifties.

Meanwhile, I was college-prep in school. After classes, I would go with my mother to fill out job applications for her, or write checks for her at the supermarket. We would have the scenario all worked out ahead of time. My mother would sign the check before we'd get to the store. Then, as we'd approach the checkstand, she would say—within earshot of the cashier— "oh honey, you go 'head and make out the check," as if she couldn't be bothered with such an insignificant detail. No one asked any questions.

I was educated, and wore it with a keen sense of pride and satisfaction, my head propped up with the knowledge, from my mother, that my life would be easier than hers. I was educated; but more than this, I was "la güera": fair-skinned. Born with the features of my Chicana mother, but the skin of my Anglo father, I had it made.

No one ever quite told me this (that light was right), but I knew that being light was something valued in my family (who were all Chicano, with the exception of my father). In fact, everything about my upbringing (at least what occurred on a conscious level) attempted to bleach me of what color I did have. Although my mother was fluent in it, I was never taught much Spanish at home. I picked up what I did learn from school and from over-heard snatches of conversation among my relatives and mother. She often called other lower-income Mexicans "braceros," or "wet-backs," referring to herself and her family as "a different class of people." And yet, the real story was that my family, too, had been poor (some still are) and farmworkers. My mother can remember this in her blood as if it were yesterday. But this is something she would like to forget (and rightfully), for to her, on a basic economic level, being Chicana meant being "less." It was through my mother's desire to protect her children from poverty and illiteracy that we became "anglocized"; the more effectively we could pass in the white world, the better guaranteed our future.

From all of this, I experience, daily, a huge disparity between what I was born into and what I was to grow up to become. Because, (as Goldman suggests) these stories my mother told me crept under my "güera" skin. I had no choice but to enter into the life of my mother. *I had no choice.* I took her life into my heart, but managed to keep a lid on it as long as I feigned being the happy, upwardly mobile heterosexual.

When I finally lifted the lid to my lesbianism, a profound connection with my mother reawakened in me. It wasn't until I acknowledged and confronted my own lesbianism in the flesh, that my heartfelt identification with and empathy for my mother's oppression—due to being poor, uneducated, and Chicana—was realized. My lesbianism is the avenue through which I have learned the most about silence and oppression, and it continues to be the most tactile reminder to me that we are not free human beings.

You see, one follows the other. I had known for years that I was a lesbian, had felt it in my bones, had ached with the knowledge, gone crazed with the knowledge, wallowed in the silence of it. Silence is like starvation. Don't be fooled. It's nothing short of that, and felt most sharply when one has had a full belly most of her life. When we are not physically starving, we have the luxury to realize psychic and emotional starvation. It is from this starvation that other starvations can be recognized—if one is willing to take the risk of making the connection—if one is willing to be responsible to the result of the connection. For me, the connection is an inevitable one.

What I am saying is that the joys of looking like a white girl ain't so great since I realized I could be beaten on the street for being a dyke. If my sister's being beaten because she's Black, it's pretty much the same principle. We're both getting beaten any way you look at it. The connection is blatant; and in the case of my own family, the difference in the privileges attached to looking white instead of brown are merely a generation apart.

In this country, lesbianism is a poverty—as is being brown, as is being a woman, as is being just plain poor. The danger lies in ranking the oppressions. *The danger lies in failing to acknowledge the specificity of the oppression.* The danger lies in attempting to deal with oppression purely from a theoretical base. Without an emotional, heartfelt grappling with the source of our own oppression, without naming the enemy within ourselves and outside of us, no authentic, non-hierarchical connection among oppressed groups can take place.

When the going gets rough, will we abandon our so-called comrades in a flurry of racist/heterosexist/what-have-you panic? To whose camp, then, should the lesbian of color retreat? Her very presence violates the ranking and abstraction of oppression. Do we merely live hand to mouth? Do we merely struggle with the "ism" that's sitting on top of our own heads?

The answer is: yes, I think first we do; and we must do so thoroughly and deeply. But to fail to move out from there will only isolate us in our own oppression—will only insulate, rather than radicalize us.

To illustrate: a gay male friend of mine once confided to me that he continued to feel that, on some level, I didn't trust him because he was male; that he felt, really, if it ever came down to a "battle of the sexes," I might kill him. I admitted that I might very well. He wanted to understand the source of my distrust. I responded, "You're not a woman. Be a woman for a day. Imagine being a woman." He confessed that the thought terrified him because, to him, being a woman meant being raped by men. He *had* felt raped by men; he wanted to forget what that meant. What grew from that discussion was the realization that in order for him to create an authentic alliance with me, he must deal with the primary source of his own sense of oppression. He must, first, emotionally come to terms with what it feels like to be a victim. If he—or anyone—were to truly do this, it would be impossible to discount the oppression of others, except by again forgetting how we have been hurt.

And yet, oppressed groups are forgetting all the time. There are instances of this in the rising Black middle class, and certainly an obvious trend of such "unconsciousness" among white gay men. Because to remember may mean giving up whatever privileges we have managed to squeeze out of this society by virtue of our gender, race, class, or sexuality.

Within the women's movement, the connections among women of different backgrounds and sexual orientations have been fragile, at best. I think this phenomenon is indicative of our failure to seriously address ourselves to some very frightening questions: How have I internalized my own oppression? How have I oppressed? Instead, we have let rhetoric do the job of poetry. Even the word "oppression" has lost its power. We need a new language, better words that can more closely describe women's fear of and resistance to one another; words that will not always come out sounding like dogma.

What prompted me in the first place to work on an anthology by radical women of color was a deep sense that I had a valuable insight to contribute, by virtue of my birthright and background. And yet, I don't really understand first-hand what it feels like being shitted on for being brown. I understand much more about the joys of it—being Chicana and having family are synonymous for me. What I know about loving, singing, crying, telling stories, speaking with my heart and hands, even having a sense of my own soul comes from the love of my mother, aunts, cousins . . .

But at the age of twenty-seven, it is frightening to acknowledge that I have internalized a racism and classism, where the object of oppression is not only someone outside of my skin, but the someone inside my skin. In fact, to a large degree, the real battle with such oppression, for all of us, begins under the skin. I have had to confront the fact that much of what I value about being Chicana, about my family, has been subverted by anglo culture and my own cooperation with it. This realization did not occur to me overnight. For example, it wasn't until long after my graduation from the private college I'd attended in Los Angeles, that I realized the major reason for my total alienation from and fear of my classmates was rooted in class and culture. CLICK.

Three years after graduation, in an apple-orchard in Sonoma, a friend of mine (who comes from an Italian Irish working-class family) says to me, "Cherríe, no wonder you felt like such a nut in school. Most of the people there were white and rich." It was true. All along I had felt the difference, but not until I had put the words "class" and "color" to the experience, did my feelings make any sense. For years, I had berated myself for not being as "free" as my classmates. I completely bought that they simply had more guts than I did—to rebel against their parents and run around the country hitch-hiking, reading books and studying "art." They had enough privilege to be atheists, for chrissake. There was no one around filling in the disparity for me between their parents, who were Hollywood filmmakers, and my parents, who wouldn't know the name of a filmmaker if their lives depended on it (and precisely because their lives didn't depend on it, they couldn't be bothered). But I knew nothing about "privilege" then. White was right. Period. I could pass. If I got educated enough, there would never be any telling.

Three years after that, another CLICK. In a letter to Barbara Smith, I wrote:

> I went to a concert where Ntosake Shange was reading. There, everything exploded for me. She was speaking a language that I knew—in the deepest parts of me—existed, and that I had ignored in my own feminist studies and even in my own writing. What Ntosake caught in me is the realization that in my development as a poet, I have, in many ways, denied the voice of my brown mother—the brown in me. I have acclimated to the sound of a white language which, as my father represents it, does not speak to the emotions in my poems—emotions which stem from the love of my mother.
>
> The reading was agitating. Made me uncomfortable. Threw me into a week-long terror of how deeply I was affected. I felt that I had to start all over again. That I turned only to the perceptions of white middle-class women to speak for me and all women. I am shocked by my own ignorance.

Sitting in that auditorium chair was the first time I had realized to the core of me that for years I had disowned the language I knew best—ignored the words and rhythms that were the closest to me. The sounds of my mother and aunts gossiping—half in English, half in Spanish—while drinking cerveza in the kitchen. And the hands—I had cut off the hands in my poems. But not in conversation; still the hands could not be kept down. Still they insisted on moving.

The reading had forced me to remember that I knew things from my roots. But to remember puts me up against what I don't know. Shange's reading agitated me because she spoke with power about a world that is both alien and common to me: "the capacity to enter into the lives of others." But you can't just take the goods and run. I knew that then, sitting in the Oakland auditorium (as I know in my poetry), that the only thing worth writing about is what seems to be unknown and, therefore, fearful.

The "unknown" is often depicted in racist literature as the "darkness" within a person. Similarly, sexist writers will refer to fear in the form of the vagina, calling it "the orifice of death." In contrast, it is a pleasure to read works such as Maxine Hong Kingston's *Woman Warrior*, where fear and alienation are described as "the white ghosts." And yet, the bulk of literature in this country reinforces the myth that what is dark and female is evil. Consequently, each of us—whether dark, female, or both—has in some way *internalized* this oppressive imagery. What the oppressor often succeeds in doing is simply *externalizing* his fears, projecting them into the bodies of women, Asians, gays, disabled folks, whoever seems most "other."

call me
roach and presumptuous
nightmare on your white pillow
your itch to destroy
the indestructible
part of yourself
—Audre Lorde

But it is not really difference the oppressor fears so much as similarity. He fears he will discover in himself the same aches, the same longings as those of the people he has shitted on. He fears the immobilization threatened by his own incipient guilt. He fears he will have to change his life once he has seen himself in the bodies of the people he has called different. He fears the hatred, anger, and vengeance of those he has hurt.

This is the oppressor's nightmare, but it is not exclusive to him. We women have a similar nightmare, for each of us in some way has been both oppressed and the oppressor. We are afraid to look at how we have failed each other. We are afraid to see how we have taken the values of our oppressor into our hearts and turned them against ourselves and one another. We are afraid to admit how deeply "the man's" words have been ingrained in us.

To assess the damage is a dangerous act. I think of how, even as a feminist lesbian, I have so wanted to ignore my own homophobia, my own hatred of myself for being queer. I have not wanted to admit that my deepest personal sense of myself has not quite "caught up" with my "woman-identified" politics. I have been afraid to criticize lesbian writers who choose to "skip over" these issues in the name of feminism. In 1979, we talk of "old gay" and "butch and femme" roles as if they were ancient history. We toss them aside as merely patriarchal notions. And yet, the truth of the matter is that I have sometimes taken society's fear and hatred of lesbians to bed with me. I have sometimes hated my lover for loving me. I have sometimes felt "not woman enough" for her. I have sometimes felt "not man enough." For a lesbian trying to survive in a heterosexist society, there is no easy way around these emotions. Similarly, in a white-dominated world, there is little getting around racism and our own internalization of it. It's always there, embodied in someone we least expect to rub up against.

When we do rub up against this person, *there* then is the challenge. *There* then is the opportunity to look at the nightmare within us. But we usually shrink from such a challenge.

Time and time again, I have observed that the usual response among white women's groups when the "racism issue" comes up is to deny the difference. I have heard comments like, "Well, we're open to *all* women; why don't they (women of color) come? You can only do so much . . . " But there is seldom any analysis of how the very nature and structure of the group itself may be founded on racist or classist assumptions. More importantly, so often the women seem to feel no loss, no lack, no absence when women of color are not involved; therefore, there is little desire to change the situation. This has hurt me deeply. I have come to believe that the only reason women of a privileged class will dare to look at *how* it is that *they* oppress, is when they've come to know the meaning of their own oppression. And understand that the oppression of others hurts them personally.

The other side of the story is that women of color and working-class women often shrink from challenging white middle-class women. It is much easier to rank oppressions and set up a hierarchy, rather than take responsibility for changing our own lives. We have failed to demand that white women, particularly those who claim to be speaking for all women, be accountable for their racism.

The dialogue has simply not gone deep enough.

I have many times questioned my right to even work on an anthology which is to be written "exclusively by Third World women." I have had to look critically at my claim to color, at a time when, among white feminist ranks, it is a "politically correct" (and sometimes peripherally advantageous) assertion to make. I must acknowledge the fact that, physically, I have had a *choice* about making that claim, in contrast to women who have not had such a choice, and have been abused for their color. I must reckon with the fact that for most of my life, by virtue of the very fact that I am white-looking, I identified with and aspired toward white values, and that I rode the wave of that Southern Californian privilege as far as conscience would let me.

Well, now I feel both bleached and beached. I feel angry about this—the years when I refused to recognize privilege, both when it worked against me, and when I worked it, ignorantly, at the expense of others. These are not settled issues. That is why this work feels so risky to me. It continues to be discovery. It has brought me into contact with women who invariably know a hell of a lot more than I do about racism, as experienced in the flesh, as revealed in the flesh of their writing.

I think: what is my responsibility to my roots—both white and brown, Spanish-speaking and English? I am a woman with a foot in both worlds; and I refuse the split. I feel the necessity for dialogue. Sometimes I feel it urgently.

But one voice is not enough, nor two, although this is where dialogue begins. It is essential that radical feminists confront their fear of and resistance to each other, because without this, there *will* be no bread on the table. Simply, we will not survive. If we could make this connection in our heart of hearts, that if we are serious about a revolution—better—if we seriously believe there should be joy in our lives (real joy, not just "good times"), then we need one another. We women need each other. Because my/your solitary, self-asserting "go-for-the-throat-of-fear" power is not enough. The real power, as you and I well know, is collective. I can't afford to be afraid of you, nor you of me. If it takes head-on collisions, let's do it: this polite timidity is killing us.

As Lorde suggests in the passage I cited earlier, it is in looking to the nightmare that the dream is found. There, the survivor emerges to insist on a future, a vision, yes, born out of what is dark and female. The feminist movement must be a movement of such survivors, a movement with a future.

Gloria Anzaldúa (1942–)

How to Tame a Wild Tongue

Published in 1987, Gloria Anzaldúa's *Borderlands/La Frontera: The New Mestiza* quickly became a must-read in cultural, postcolonial, feminist, queer, border, and Latino studies. The blending of history, myth, personal testimony, poetry, and oral genres in both Spanish and English and of writing styles ranging from academic to stream-of-consciousness make this work a quintessential hybrid text. By blurring genre and linguistic boundaries, Anzaldúa drives home her point that borders invite transgression and that it is in the process of crossing them that mestiza identity is given shape. The excerpt below focuses on the hybrid nature of Chicano Spanish and suggests that it is precisely its illegitimate status that contains its potential for breaking the silence of Chicanas imposed by centuries of colonization. Anzaldúa was raised in the Rio Grande Valley of Texas where, as a young girl, she followed the crops with her family. She received a master's degree in English from the University of Texas and has held teaching positions at Vermont College, the University of California at Santa Cruz, and San Francisco State College. Anzaldúa received the Before Columbus Foundation American Book Award and the Sappho Award of Distinction. (EGB)

Further reading: Gloria Anzaldúa, *Borderlands/La Frontera: The New Mestiza* (San Francisco: Aunt Lute Press, 1987).

"We're going to have to control your tongue," the dentist says, pulling out all the metal from my mouth. Silver bits plop and tinkle into the basin. My mouth is a motherlode.

The dentist is cleaning out my roots. I get a whiff of the stench when I gasp. "I can't cap that tooth yet, you're still draining," he says.

"We're going to have to do something about your tongue," I hear the anger rising in his voice. My tongue keeps pushing out the wads of cotton, pushing back the drills, the long thin needles. "I've never seen anything as strong or as stubborn," he says. And I think, how do you tame a wild tongue, train it to be quiet, how do you bridle and saddle it? How do you make it lie down?

> Who is to say that robbing a people of
> its language is less violent than war?
> —Ray Gwyn Smith

I remember being caught speaking Spanish at recess—that was good for three licks on the knuckles with a sharp ruler. I remember being sent to the corner of the classroom for "talking back" to the Anglo teacher when all I was trying to do was tell her how to pronounce my name. "If you want to be American, speak 'American.' If you don't like it, go back to Mexico where you belong."

"I want you to speak English. *Pa' hallar buen trabajo tienes que saber hablar el inglés bien. Qué vale toda tu educación si todavía hablas inglés con un 'accent,'"* my mother would say, mortified that I spoke English like a Mexican. At Pan American University, I, and all Chicano students were required to take two speech classes. Their purpose: to get rid of our accents.

Attacks on one's form of expression with the intent to censor are a violation of the First Amendment. *El Anglo con cara de inocente nos arrancó la lengua.* Wild tongues can't be tamed, they can only be cut out.

Overcoming the Tradition of Silence

> *Ahogadas, escupimos el oscuro.*
> *Peleando con nuestra propia sombra*
> *el silencio nos sepulta.*

En boca cerrada no entran moscas. "Flies don't enter a closed mouth" is a saying I kept hearing when I was a child. *Ser habladora* was to be a gossip and a liar, to talk too much. *Muchachitas bien criadas,* well-bred girls don't answer back. *Es una falta de respeto* to talk back to one's mother or father. I remember one of the sins I'd recite to the priest in the confession box the few times I went to confession: talking back to my mother, *hablar pa' 'trás, repelar.* Hocicona, repelona, chismosa, having a big mouth, questioning, carrying tales are all signs of being *mal criada.* In my culture they are all words that are derogatory if applied to women—I've never heard them applied to men.

The first time I heard two women, a Puerto Rican and a Cuban, say the word "*nosotros,*" I was shocked. I had not known the word existed. Chicanas use *nosotros* whether we're male or female. We are robbed of our female being by the masculine plural. Language is a male discourse.

> And our tongues have become
> dry   the wilderness has
> dried out our tongues   and
> we have forgotten speech.
> —Irena Klepfisz

Even our own people, other Spanish speakers *nos quieren poner candados en la boca.* They would hold us back with their bag of *reglas de academia.*

Oye como ladra: El lenguaje de la frontera

Quien tiene boca se equivoca.
—Mexican saying

"*Pocho*, cultural traitor, you're speaking the oppressor's language by speaking English, you're ruining the Spanish language," I have been accused by various Latinos and Latinas. Chicano Spanish is considered by the purist and by most Latinos deficient, a mutilation of Spanish.

But Chicano Spanish is a border tongue which developed naturally. Change, *evolución, enriquecimiento de palabras nuevas por invención o adopción* have created variants of Chicano Spanish, *un nuevo lenguaje. Un lenguaje que corresponde a un modo de vivir.* Chicano Spanish is not incorrect, it is a living language.

For a people who are neither Spanish nor live in a country in which Spanish is the first language; for a people who live in a country in which English is the reigning tongue but who are not Anglo; for a people who cannot entirely identify with either standard (formal, Castilian) Spanish nor standard English, what recourse is left to them but to create their own language? A language which they can connect their identity to, one capable of communicating the realities and values true to themselves—a language with terms that are neither *español ni inglés*, but both. We speak a patois, a forked tongue, a variation of two languages.

Chicano Spanish sprang out of the Chicanos' need to identify ourselves as a distinct people. We needed a language with which we could communicate with ourselves, a secret language. For some of us, language is a homeland closer than the Southwest—for many Chicanos today live in the Midwest and the East. And because we are a complex, heterogeneous people, we speak many languages. Some of the languages we speak are:

1. Standard English
2. Working class and slang English
3. Standard Spanish
4. Standard Mexican Spanish
5. North Mexican Spanish dialect
6. Chicano Spanish (Texas, New Mexico, Arizona and California have regional variations)
7. Tex-Mex
8. *Pachuco* (called *caló*)

My "home" tongues are the languages I speak with my sister and brothers, with my friends. They are the last five listed, with 6 and 7 being closest to my heart. From school, the media and job situations, I've picked up standard and working class English. From Mamagrande Locha and from reading Spanish and Mexican literature, I've picked up Standard Spanish and Standard Mexican Spanish. From *los recién llegados*, Mexican immigrants, and *braceros*, I learned the North Mexican dialect. With Mexicans I'll try to speak either Standard Mexican Spanish or the North Mexican dialect. From my parents and Chicanos living in the valley, I picked up Chicano Texas Spanish, and I speak it with my mom, younger brother (who married a Mexican and who rarely mixes Spanish with English), aunts and older relatives.

With Chicanas from *Nuevo México* or *Arizona* I will speak Chicano Spanish a little, but often they don't understand what I'm saying. With most California Chicanas I speak entirely in English (unless I forget). When I first moved to San Francisco, I'd rattle off something in Spanish, unintentionally embarrassing them. Often it is only with another Chicana *tejana* that I can talk freely.

Words distorted by English are known as anglicisms or *pochismos.* The *pocho* is an anglicized Mexican or American of Mexican origin who speaks Spanish with an accent characteristic of North Americans and who distorts and reconstructs the language according to the influence of English. Tex-Mex, or Spanglish, comes most naturally to me. I may switch back and forth from English to Spanish in the same sentence or in the same word. With my sister and my brother Nune and with Chicano *tejano* contemporaries I speak in Tex-Mex.

From kids and people my own age I picked up *Pachuco. Pachuco* (the language of the zoot suiters) is a language of rebellion, both against Standard Spanish and Standard English. It is a secret language. Adults of the culture and outsiders cannot understand it. It is made up of slang words from both English and Spanish. *Ruca* means girl or woman, *vato* means guy or dude, *chale* means no, *simón* means yes, *churo* is sure, talk is *periquiar, pigionear* means petting, *que gacho* means how nerdy, *ponte águila* means watch out, death is called *la pelona.* Through lack of practice and not having others who can speak it, I've lost most of the *Pachuco* tongue.

Chicano Spanish

Chicanos, after 250 years of Spanish/Anglo colonization have developed significant differences in the Spanish we speak. We collapse two adjacent vowels into a single syllable and sometimes shift the stress in certain words such as *maíz/maiz, cohete/cuete.* We leave out certain consonants when they appear between vowels: *lado/lao, mojado/mojao.* Chicanos from South Texas pronounced *f* as *j* as in *jue (fue).* Chicanos use "archaisms," words that are no longer in the Spanish language, words that have been evolved out. We say *semos, truje, haiga, ansina,* and *naiden.* We retain the "archaic" *j,* as in *jalar,* that derives from an earlier *h* (the French *halar* or the Germanic *halon* which was lost to standard Spanish in the 16th century), but which is still found in several regional dialects such as the one spoken in South Texas. (Due to geography, Chicanos from the Valley of South Texas were cut off linguistically from other Spanish speakers. We tend to use words that the Spaniards brought over from Medieval Spain. The majority of the Spanish colonizers in Mexico and the Southwest came from Extremadura—Hernán Cortés was one of them—and Andalucía. Andalucians pronounce *ll* like a *y,* and their *d*'s tend to be absorbed by adjacent vowels: *tirado* becomes *tirao.* They brought *el lenguaje popular, dialectos y regionalismos.*)

Chicanos and other Spanish speakers also shift *ll* to *y* and *z* to *s.* We leave out initial syllables, saying *tar* for *estar, toy* for *estoy, hora* for *ahora* (*cubanos* and *puertorriqueños* also leave out initial letters of some words). We also leave out the final syllable such as *pa* for *para*. The intervocalic *y*, the *ll* as in *tortilla, ella, botella*, gets replaced by *tortía* or *tortiya, ea, botea*. We add an additional syllable at the beginning of certain words: *atocar* for *tocar, agastar* for *gastar*. Sometimes we'll say *lavaste las vacijas*, other times *lavates* (substituting the *ates* verb endings for the *aste*).

We use anglicisms, words borrowed from English: *bola* from ball, *carpeta* from carpet, *máchina de lavar* (instead of *lavadora*) from washing machine. Tex-Mex argot, created by adding a Spanish sound at the beginning or end of an English word such as *cookiar* for cook, *watchar* for watch, *parkiar* for park, and *rapiar* for rape, is the result of the pressures on Spanish speakers to adapt to English.

We don't use the word *vosotros/as* or its accompanying verb form. We don't say *claro* (to mean yes), *imagínate*, or *me emociona*, unless we picked up Spanish from Latinas, out of a book, or in a classroom. Other Spanish-speaking groups are going through the same, or similar, development in their Spanish.

Linguistic Terrorism

> *Deslenguadas. Somos los del español deficiente.* We are your linguistic nightmare, your linguistic aberration, your linguistic *mestizaje*, the subject of your *burla*. Because we speak with tongues of fire we are culturally crucified. Racially, culturally and linguistically *somos huérfanos*—we speak an orphan tongue.

Chicanas who grew up speaking Chicano Spanish have internalized the belief that we speak poor Spanish. It is illegitimate, a bastard language. And because we internalize how our language has been used against us by the dominant culture, we use our language differences against each other.

Chicana feminists often skirt around each other with suspicion and hesitation. For the longest time I couldn't figure it out. Then it dawned on me. To be close to another Chicana is like looking into the mirror. We are afraid of what we'll see there. *Pena*. Shame. Low estimation of self. In childhood we are told that our language is wrong. Repeated attacks on our native tongue diminish our sense of self. The attacks continue throughout our lives.

Chicanas feel uncomfortable talking in Spanish to Latinas, afraid of their censure. Their language was not outlawed in their countries. They had a whole lifetime of being immersed in their native tongue; generations, centuries in which Spanish was a first language, taught in school, heard on radio and TV, and read in the newspaper.

If a person, Chicana or Latina, has a low estimation of my native tongue, she also has a low estimation of me. Often with *mexicanas y latinas* we'll speak English as a neutral language. Even among Chicanas we tend to speak English at parties or conferences. Yet, at the same time, we're afraid the other will think we're *agringadas* because we don't speak Chicano Spanish. We oppress each other trying to out-Chicano each other, vying to be the "real" Chicanas, to speak like Chicanos. There is no one Chicano language just as there is no one Chicano experience. A monolingual Chicana whose first language is English or Spanish is just as much a Chicana as one who speaks several variants of Spanish. A Chicana from Michigan or Chicago or Detroit is just as much a

Chicana as one from the Southwest. Chicano Spanish is as diverse linguistically as it is regionally.

By the end of this century, Spanish speakers will comprise the biggest minority group in the U.S., a country where students in high schools and colleges are encouraged to take French classes because French is considered more "cultured." But for a language to remain alive it must be used. By the end of this century English, and not Spanish, will be the mother tongue of most Chicanos and Latinos.

So, if you want to really hurt me, talk badly about my language. Ethnic identity is twin skin to linguistic identity—I am my language. Until I can take pride in my language, I cannot take pride in myself. Until I can accept as legitimate Chicano Texas Spanish, Tex-Mex and all the other languages I speak, I cannot accept the legitimacy of myself. Until I am free to write bilingually and to switch codes without having always to translate, while I still have to speak English or Spanish when I would rather speak Spanglish, and as long as I have to accommodate the English speakers rather than having them accommodate me, my tongue will be illegitimate.

I will no longer be made to feel ashamed of existing. I will have my voice: Indian, Spanish, white. I will have my serpent's tongue—my woman's voice, my sexual voice, my poet's voice. I will overcome the tradition of silence.

> My fingers
> move sly against your palm
> Like women everywhere, we speak in code . . . .
> —Melanie Kaye/Kantrowitz

"Vistas," corridos, y comida: My Native Tongue

In the 1960s, I read my first Chicano novel. It was *City of Night* by John Rechy, a gay Texan, son of a Scottish father and a Mexican mother. For days I walked around in stunned amazement that a Chicano could write and could get published. When I read *I Am Joaquín* I was surprised to see a bilingual book by a Chicano in print. When I saw poetry written in Tex-Mex for the first time, a feeling of pure joy flashed through me. I felt like we really existed as a people. In 1971, when I started teaching High School English to Chicano students, I tried to supplement the required texts with works by Chicanos, only to be reprimanded and forbidden to do so by the principal. He claimed that I was supposed to teach "American" and English literature. At the risk of being fired, I swore my students to secrecy and slipped in Chicano short stories, poems, a play. In graduate school, while working toward a Ph.D., I had to "argue" with one advisor after the other, semester after semester, before I was allowed to make Chicano literature an area of focus.

Even before I read books by Chicanos or Mexicans, it was the Mexican movies I saw at the drive-in—the Thursday night special of $1.00 a carload—that gave me a sense of belonging. "*Vámonos a las vistas*," my mother would call out and we'd all—grandmother, brothers, sister and cousins—squeeze into the car. We'd wolf down cheese and bologna white bread sandwiches while watching Pedro Infante in melodramatic tear-jerkers like *Nosotros los pobres*, the first "real" Mexican movie (that was not an imitation of European movies). I remember seeing *Cuando los hijos se van* and surmising that all Mexican movies played up the love a mother has for her children and what ungrateful sons and daughters suffer when they are not devoted to their mothers. I remember the singing-type "westerns" of Jorge Negrete and Miguel Aceves Mejía. When watching Mexican movies, I felt a sense of homecoming as well as alienation. People who were to amount to something didn't go to Mexican movies, or *bailes* or tune their radios to *bolero, rancherita*, and *corrido* music.

The whole time I was growing up, there was *norteño* music sometimes called North Mexican border music, or Tex-Mex music, or Chicano music, or *cantina* (bar) music. I grew up listening to *conjuntos*, three- or four-piece bands made up of folk musicians playing guitar, *bajo sexto*, drums and button accordion, which Chicanos had borrowed from the German immigrants who had come to Central Texas and Mexico to farm and build breweries. In the Rio Grande Valley, Steve Jordan and Little Joe Hernández were popular, and Flaco Jiménez was the accordion king. The rhythms of Tex-Mex music are those of the polka, also adapted from the Germans, who in turn had borrowed the polka from the Czechs and Bohemians.

I remember the hot, sultry evenings when *corridos*—songs of love and death on the Texas-Mexican borderlands—reverberated out of cheap amplifiers from the local *cantinas* and wafted in through my bedroom window.

Corridos first became widely used along the South Texas/Mexican border during the early conflict between Chicanos and Anglos. The *corridos* are usually about Mexican heroes who do valiant deeds against the Anglo oppressors. Pancho Villa's song, "*La cucaracha*," is the most famous one. *Corridos* of John F. Kennedy and his death are still very popular in the Valley. Older Chicanos remember Lydia Mendoza, one of the great border *corrido* singers who was called *la Gloria de Tejas*. Her "*El tango negro*," sung during the Great Depression, made her a singer of the people. The everpresent *corridos* narrated one hundred years of border history, bringing news of events as well as entertaining. These folk musicians and folk songs are our chief cultural mythmakers, and they made our hard lives seem bearable.

I grew up feeling ambivalent about our music. Country-western and rock-and-roll had more status. In the 50s and 60s, for the slightly educated and *agringado* Chicanos, there existed a sense of shame at being caught listening to our music. Yet I couldn't stop my feet from thumping to the music, could not stop humming the words, nor hide from myself the exhilaration I felt when I heard it.

There are more subtle ways that we internalize identification, especially in the forms of images and emotions. For me food and certain smells are tied to my identity, to my homeland. Woodsmoke curling up to an immense blue sky; woodsmoke perfuming my grandmother's clothes, her skin. The stench of cow manure and the yellow patches on the ground; the crack of a .22 rifle and the reek of cordite. Homemade white cheese sizzling in a pan, melting inside a folded *tortilla*. My sister Hilda's hot, spicy *menudo, chile colorado* making it deep red, pieces of *panza* and hominy floating on top. My brother Carito barbecuing *fajitas* in the backyard. Even now and 3,000 miles away, I can see my mother spicing the ground beef, pork and venison with *chile*. My mouth salivates at the thought of the hot steaming *tamales* I would be eating if I were home.

Si le preguntas a mi mamá, "¿Qué eres?"

> Identity is the essential core of who
> we are as individuals, the conscious
> experience of the self inside.
> —Gershen Kaufman

Nosotros los Chicanos straddle the borderlands. On one side of us, we are constantly exposed to the Spanish of the Mexicans, on the other side we hear the Anglos' incessant clamoring so that we forget our language. Among ourselves we don't say *nosotros los americanos, o nosotros los españoles, o nosotros los hispanos.* We say *nosotros los mexicanos* (by *mexicanos* we do not mean citizens of Mexico; we do not mean a national identity, but a racial one). We distinguish between *mexicanos del otro lado* and *mexicanos de este lado.* Deep in our hearts we believe that being Mexican has nothing to do with which country one lives in. Being Mexican is a state of soul—not one of mind, not one of citizenship. Neither eagle nor serpent, but both. And like the ocean, neither animal respects borders.

> *Dime con quién andas y te diré quién eres.*
> (Tell me who your friends are and I'll tell you who you are.)
> —Mexican saying

Si le preguntas a mi mamá, "¿Qué eres?" te dirá, "Soy mexicana." My brothers and sister say the same. I sometimes will answer *"soy mexicana"* and at others will say *"soy Chicana" o "soy tejana."* But I identified as *"Raza"* before I ever identified as *"mexicana"* or "Chicana."

As a culture, we call ourselves Spanish when referring to ourselves as a linguistic group and when copping out. It is then that we forget our predominant Indian genes. We are 70 to 80% Indian. We call ourselves Hispanic or Spanish-American or Latin American or Latin when linking ourselves to other Spanish-speaking peoples of the Western hemisphere and when copping out. We call ourselves Mexican-American to signify we are neither Mexican nor American, but more the noun "American" than the adjective "Mexican" (and when copping out).

Chicanos and other people of color suffer economically for not acculturating. This voluntary (yet forced) alienation makes for psychological conflict, a kind of dual identity—we don't identify with the Anglo-American cultural values and we don't totally identify with the Mexican cultural values. We are a synergy of two cultures with various degrees of Mexicanness or Angloness. I have so internalized the borderland conflict that sometimes I feel like one cancels out the other and we are zero, nothing, no one. *A veces no soy nada ni nadie. Pero hasta cuando no lo soy, lo soy.*

When not copping out, when we know we are more than nothing, we call ourselves Mexican, referring to race and ancestry; *mestizo* when affirming both our Indian and

Spanish (but we hardly ever own our Black ancestry); Chicano when referring to a politically aware people born and/or raised in the U.S.; *Raza* when referring to Chicanos; *tejanos* when we are Chicanos from Texas.

Chicanos did not know we were a people until 1965 when Cesar Chavez and the farmworkers united and *I Am Joaquín* was published and *la Raza Unida* party was formed in Texas. With that recognition, we became a distinct people. Something momentous happened to the Chicano soul—we became aware of our reality and acquired a name and a language (Chicano Spanish) that reflected that reality. Now that we had a name, some of the fragmented pieces began to fall together—who we were, what we were, how we had evolved. We began to get glimpses of what we might eventually become.

Yet the struggle of identities continues, the struggle of borders is our reality still. One day the inner struggle will cease and a true integration take place. In the meantime, *tenemos que hacer la lucha. ¿Quién está protegiendo los ranchos de mi gente? ¿Quién está tratando de cerrar la fisura entre la india y el blanco en nuestra sangre? El Chicano, sí, el Chicano que anda como un ladrón en su propia casa.*

Los Chicanos, how patient we seem, how very patient. There is the quiet of the Indian about us. We know how to survive. When other races have given up their tongue, we've kept ours. We know what it is to live under the hammer blow of the dominant *norteamericano* culture. But more than we count the blows, we count the days the weeks the years the centuries the eons until the white laws and commerce and customs will rot in the deserts they've created, lie bleached. *Humildes* yet proud, *quietos* yet wild, *nosotros los mexicanos*-Chicanos will walk by the crumbling ashes as we go about our business. Stubborn, persevering, impenetrable as stone, yet possessing a malleability that renders us unbreakable, we, the *mestizas* and *mestizos*, will remain.

Alicia Achy Obejas (1956–)

Above All, a Family Man

Achy Obejas was born in Havana, Cuba, on June 28, 1956, under the name of Alicia Obejas. Her family arrived in Florida in 1963, when Achy was six years old. The family lived in Miami for approximately a year and a half; then they were sent to Indiana through the "Mainstream Refugee" government program. Achy Obejas is well known as a fiction writer, poet, and freelance writer for the *Chicago Tribune, Latina, Poz, The Advocate, The Catalyst, Hispanic Link*, and *Insider Watch*, among others. *We Came All the Way from Cuba So You Could Dress like This?* is a collection of short stories published in 1994 which captured the attention of a cross-cultural audience. The suffering and preoccupation she endured through her exile are central topics in her writing. Obejas describes her own life of diversity as an exiled, immigrant, lesbian, Jewish woman through the voices of her characters, and focuses on the problems faced by exiles and immigrants telling stories about men and women who struggle to find their identity and love. In *Above All, a Family Man*, from *We Came All the Way*, Obejas captures the cultural conflicts through two of her characters, Tommy Drake, a white gay man with AIDS, and Rogelio, a married Mexican immigrant. (CV)

Further reading: Achy Obejas, *We Came All the Way from Cuba So You Could Dress like This?* (Pittsburgh: Cleis Press, 1994), *Memory Mambo* (Pittsburgh: Cleis Press, 1996).

There's a whole subterranean world under the Arch: a museum, a video show, a couple of souvenir stores. There's also a snake of a line to the elevators. I'm surprised there are so many people, especially because it's a weekday, but then I realize most of the ticket holders are tourists, primarily Asians. Even though the line moves relatively well, I have to squat and lean against the wall. It's getting harder to swallow, too, and I keep seeing little bursts of orange and blue light in front of my eyes.

During all this, Rogelio is a phantom. He stands pale and quiet next to me, but he wants to run. His fingers are folded into tentative fists, and he keeps shifting his eyes from side to side. I know the crowd scares him; there are too many people in uniform. I tell him these are only Arch security people, not covert INS agents. But although he has never gotten so much as a traffic ticket, authority types frighten him, and he won't be reassured.

Me, I resent everything. I hate that with a mouthful of thrush I'm the one having to tell him everything's okay. For once, I want him to do the talking, I want him to be brave, to take my hand, push his way to the front of the line and demand our own elevator. At the top of the Arch, I want us to grope and run our tongues along each other's stubbly chins, right there in front of all the tourist groups and grade-school field trips.

"Tommy?" There's a hand on my cheek. "Tommy?" I lift my eyes and see Rogelio's face emerging from a gray haze. "We should go," he says. "You don't look good." He glances nervously next to me, where a woman with two small children is staring at us.

"Fuck what I look like," I say, my lips sticking to each other. I reach up to undo my mouth, but I can barely feel my fingers.

"Tommy, let's go," Rogelio insists, and he starts to take my elbow.

"No, damn it," I say, standing up and jerking away. "I don't want to go to Santa Fe yet." I think of those ghostly buffalo skulls hung so artfully in Ron and Paul's gallery. "I have a fashionable disease, you know." Rogelio blanches, and I laugh. "Hey, don't worry, you're not going to get it," I add, winking at him. I start to laugh again, but something gets caught in my throat, and I cough instead, my head rocking back and forth. After a minute, I see him through the watery channel in my eyes. He has stepped away a bit, almost as if he's scared of me.

"You look like shit," he says in a whisper.

Soon we're in front of the elevators, and I understand why the wheelchair women were disenfranchised: You have to step up and hunch down to get in the elevators, which aren't elevators at all but tiny little holding pens in which no one can stand. The doors open and shut like a vault. As I watch the tourists get in, I can't help but think of Nazi ovens. A few people refuse to ride these little torture chambers, and I think they look suspiciously Jewish.

"Get in, Tommy," Rogelio orders, and I lift my legs one at a time, but I fall anyway, finally crawling up to a chair. I want to tell Rogelio I don't think we'll survive, but the only thing out of my mouth is air. I finally settle in, wiping my face on my sleeve, which is so wet I could wring it. I feel bruised and weary.

Rogelio says nothing, he just sits quietly across from the two Asians assigned with us to this elevator. They are blank-faced and embarrassed. I supply the soundtrack for the trip, breathing like an iron lung. When the elevator starts moving—not a modern vacuum up some gigantic shaft but a jerky Ferris wheel ride—they're relieved to hear the creaking and groaning of the gears.

I look out the little window and realize we have no view at all. Instead, we're traversing the very bowels of the St. Louis Arch—ancient stairwells, a landing filled with janitorial supplies, a caged room with lockers for maintenance workers. I start to laugh, quietly at first, but then I can't help it, and I slap my thigh hysterically.

Rogelio ignores me at first, then finally reaches over and reluctantly pats my shoulder. "Don't cry, Tommy," he says. But I'm not crying at all. I wipe my nose and brush my hair out of my face. I pull my pants up and dry my eyes. Then I tuck in my shirt, feeling the vast distance between my bones and the waistband.

"I don't ever want to get to Santa Fe," I say after much effort, and Rogelio shakes his head. He can't hear me above the mechanical noises. The Asians across from us shift in their seats, and Rogelio sits as far away from me as space allows. "I don't want to go to Santa Fe," I repeat, but I can't feel my lips move.

When the elevator doors part, we tumble out to a steep, narrow stairway. We're all crushed together, the Asians, Rogelio, and me, and traffic keeps going around us. I feel Rogelio's hands on my hips, secretly guiding me up toward the fresh-faced student at the top of the stairs, a red-haired girl with a walkie-talkie strapped to her belt. She's on the lookout for trouble, or troublemakers, and it feels like Rogelio's turning me in. I jerk him loose, pushing my way through the crowd. It's cold up here, and the air feels thin.

At the top, the observation deck is a small room that resembles a space capsule. There are no windows to speak of, just horizontal slits maybe a yard wide and ten inches deep. To get a peek you lean over, resting your body against the incline of the walls. On the east side, there's no lake, just the Mississippi River looking muddy and small. On the west, there's no city, just generic St. Louis. Straight down, I can see the kidney-shaped pond next to the Arch and the walkway to the parking lot. I'm nauseous.

"Rogelio?" I whisper. I don't see him anywhere. A couple of kids are running between adult legs, but none belong to Rogelio. I try to find him by stretching up above the crowd, but I can't seem to muster the strength. I lean my back against the wall and feel my throat with my hand. My fingers seem to be working again, and my glands aren't as tender. I lick my lips, but there's something salty on them. I turn away from the crowd, which keeps brushing against me, and flap my sleeve up to my mouth. My lips feel sore.

It's then I hear unmistakable laughter behind me: high-pitched, kind of girlish. I turn to find it, but whole family groups keep coming and going by me as quickly and enthusiastically as if we were at a political rally. Everybody's got souvenir tee-shirts. There's a grandmother with a Confederate flag sewn on the back of her jacket. Teenage girls cackle with disappointment over the Arch's antiquated futurism. They smack their gum and sigh, barely noticing me. They're so close, I can smell their shampoo and cigarettes.

"St. Louis used to have another baseball team, before the Cardinals," someone is saying; it's a voice I could recognize in the dark. "But the St. Louis Browns left the city and became the Baltimore Orioles in 1954." There's a man with a cowboy hat in front of me, and as the hat dances away, I see Rogelio, cocky, giving away no secrets. He's talking to another man, propped casually against the wall on the other side.

"Well, it's karma then," the man says. He's big and white and wearing a cap with the logo from Rogelio's union local. "You know, Baltimore had a team sneak out on 'em a couple of years ago—the Colts."

"Yes, the football team," Rogelio says. "They're in Indianapolis now."

The man, who's about fifty and graying, hunches forward to look out one of the little windows. I can't keep them in my line of vision because the tourist flow is constant. But I hear them both laugh. Then I see the man slap Rogelio's shoulder in a friendly, manly sort of way. They're obviously friends, and when a small woman in a pair of yellow cotton pants comes up to them, the man goes through a series of introductory motions. Rogelio shakes her hand.

I'm watching from across the way, but he has no idea I'm here. So many people have bumped into me, I feel raw and beaten. I want to leave now; I want to collect my lover and go. "Rogelio," I say, but he doesn't hear me. A girl walking inches in front of me focuses my way. She's not sure if I'm talking to her. "I'm just trying to get my boyfriend's attention," I tell her, nodding in Rogelio's direction. The girl looks frightened, and I feel something wet on my shirt. Someone says something to her over her shoulder, but her eyes are wary and still on me.

I try to get away, but my knees wobble, and I quickly lean back against the wall. I touch my uneasy stomach, rubbing it with my hand. When I reach up to my pounding heart, I find a puddle and follow the trail of saliva up to my chin. I shove my wrist up to my mouth, rubbing my sleeve against it. I turn around slowly, facing the wall, and swallow hard. My forehead throbs. I tell myself it's not a good idea to panic. I remind myself the St. Louis Arch is not accessible, and I'm going to have to walk back to one of those little Nazi elevators. But I don't want to move, I don't want anything to happen now. I want to close my eyes and open them up to the aftermath of a simple dizzy spell in a normal world, where Rogelio comes up from behind me while I'm doing the dishes and wraps me up, nuzzling against my neck.

"Mister, are you all right?"

The red-haired girl with the walkie-talkie is standing next to me. She is all business, and her look is firm. I'd tell her I'm fine, but I'm not. And besides, I could never fool her.

"Do you need help?" she asks, and it's obvious I do. "Here," she says, offering her shoulder as a crutch. She uses a free hand to unhook the walkie-talkie from her belt and gives emergency instructions across the air waves. Then she efficiently snaps it back on her belt and turns to me, holding me with strong, muscular arms. I push slowly off the wall and turn.

The entire observation deck is quiet now, and the crowd has created a space for me. The only sounds are the elevators in the distance and the shuffling of feet. The red-haired girl walks with me, and I hear whispers behind me. As we head toward the stairway, the noise level returns to normal. I hear Rogelio's voice again, and my head jerks toward it. The red-haired girl turns with me.

"Rogelio—"

His back is to us, and he stabs the air with his finger to make a point in an argument. The gray-haired man with whom he's talking sees us and juts his chin our way. Rogelio turns quickly, registering everything with a shiver. Suddenly, he looks just like any other South Side greaser—the too-tight blue jeans and black tee-shirt, his hands rough and calloused. His chest moves up and down with heavy breathing.

My eyelids drop against my will, and the red-haired girl shifts under me. I hear her say something, and Rogelio responds, but when I finally look up all I see is his shoulder turning back to the gray-haired man and the woman in the yellow pants, their voices unnaturally bright. I hear him say something about his son, about football, about his wife. I don't know, I don't know.

I want to throw up. Both Rogelio and I have keys to the car, but I know neither one of us would leave the other. The thing is, I've seen him turn now, and I've heard his voice bob and sink away from me. That means something.

When the red-haired girl leads me away, I look over her shoulder, wanting by sheer force, by the volume of both my love and hatred, to make Rogelio look at me. When he finally does, just this side of the heterosexual couple pretending not to notice our intensity, he's terrified. He sticks his hands in his jeans pockets and balls them up, causing the jeans themselves to hike up an inch or so. He looks at me, then looks away. Then he looks back again, his eyes pleading for understanding. But my heart is pounding its thin walls, and I don't understand. I want to ask him how much he expects me to take.

Sandra María Esteves (1948–)

My Name Is Maria Christina; Anonymous Apartheid

The most important female poet to come out of the Nuyorican literary movement, Sandra María Esteves is a performance poet whose works have deep roots in community life and popular culture. Born in New York City, the daughter of a Dominican factory worker and a Puerto Rican shell-shocked veteran of the Korean War, Esteves received her early education in a Catholic boarding school, where on weekdays her Spanish language and Hispanic culture were targeted by the nuns; on weekends she lived with her mother in the heart of the Puerto Rican community in New York. Thus, at an early age she recognized and grappled with the language and culture conflicts that Hispanics experience in the United States. In the early 1970s, Esteves began writing during the heat of the civil rights movement and the movement to gain independence for Puerto Rico. In connection with the latter, she sang and recited her poetry with the socialist music ensemble El Grupo, whose recordings became anthems for the independence movement. One of her most famous works that was recorded with El Grupo, *My Name Is Maria Cristina*, attempts to bring a traditional conception of womanhood together with an Afro-Caribbean consciousness and the militant struggle for rights and independence. In *Anonymous Apartheid*, Esteves explores the psychological and spiritual effects of constant oppression and resistance, worldwide, not just in the urban barrios. (NK)

Further reading: Sandra María Esteves, *Yerba buena* (New York: Greenfield Review Press, 1980), *Bluestown Mockingbird Mambo* (Houston: Arte Público Press, 1990).

Trans.: CLM

My Name Is Maria Christina

My name is Maria Christina
I am a Puerto Rican woman born in el barrio

Our men . . . they call me negra because they love me
and in turn I teach them to be strong

I respect their ways
inherited from our proud ancestors
I do not tease them with eye catching clothes
I do not sleep with their brothers and cousins
although I've been told that this is a liberal society
I do not poison their bellies with instant chemical food:
our table holds food from earth and sun

My name is Maria Christina
I speak two languages broken into each other
but my heart speaks the language of people
born in oppression

I do not complain about cooking for my family
because abuela taught me that woman is the master of fire
I do not complain about nursing my children
because I determine the direction of their values

I am the mother of a new age of warriors
I am the child of a race of slaves
I teach my children how to respect their bodies
so they will not o.d. under the stairway's shadow of shame
I teach my children to read and develop their minds
so they will understand the reality of oppression
I teach them with discipline . . . and love
so they will become strong and full of life

My eyes reflect the pain
of that which has shamelessly raped me
but my soul reflects the strength of my culture

My name is Maria Christina
I am a Puerto Rican woman born in el barrio
Our men . . . they call me negra because they love me
and in turn I teach them to be strong.

Anonymous Apartheid

There is a stranger in our house
who looks half blind at us,
does not know our name,
assumes our earth is flat,
wraps a ball and chain around our tired legs,
barricades our windows with formless visions,
illusions of no consequence.

This stranger thinks we are alley cats, purring
in heat for violent attentions,
feeds us day-old fish and dead meat,
leaves our fruit basket empty,
does not speak our language, wear our colors,
nor understand the soul of these tender thoughts.

The stranger upsets our garden,
turning over seeds of potential into desert soil,
laying waste the promise of life's harvest,
denied, for no better reason than greed,
chopping down innocent buds to feed
their wealth of scavengers, and thieves,
growing fat from the treasures we are.

This stranger steals us from our mother,
separates us from our brothers and sisters,
does not listen to our million crying petitions,
cuts off our rebellious tongues,
laughs when our tears fall on stone,
orders us to kneel, though we refuse.

Each day the stranger drinks a nectar of blood at high noon,
wears clothing spun from blood,
worships a heathen blood god made of gold,
destroys the covenant of humanity
for the sake of a synthetic blood mirror, cracked,
tarnished quicksilver, ungrounded and formless,
traveling a broken spiral of blood.

This stranger lives here uninvited,
an unwelcomed alien ravaging us in gluttonous consummation,
throwing a soiled shroud over our altar,

expecting us to accept a life of disgrace.
Yet, we refuse.

There is a ruthless stranger in our house
who has no voice of its own,
mimics our words in crude scorn,
suggests we are low, worthless, incompetent,
grinning at itself
while we are held hostage in a doomed drama
where act one lasts more than five hundred years,
in plots of bigoted abuse,
dialogues of racial condescension, poverty,
transitions of rapes, muggings, lynchings,
scenes of jailhouse tortures and hangings,
life sentences to minimum security housing projects.

There is a stranger in our house
plundering our womb,
stealing our newborn with a dry knife,
drug-thirsty for their blood,
bargains in exchange for their lives,
tells us to throw away our weapons, love one another,
rejecting our religion,
forcing us to sell our worth,
poisoning the rich center of our spiritual essence,
speaking the lecherous tongue of split truth.

Yet we refuse, and will continue to refuse,
along with our planetary relatives who also refuse
this stranger in our house
who has no face.

Aurora Levins Morales (1954–) and Rosario Morales (1930–)

Ending Poem

Born to an American Jewish father and a Puerto Rican mother, Levins Morales lived on the island for the first thirteen years of her life before moving permanently to the United States. A committed feminist, in the late 1970s she participated in the effort to build cultural and political alliances between different communities of radical women of color. Among the fruits of this project was her participation in the pioneering collection *This Bridge Called My Back* (1981), edited by Cherríe Moraga and Gloria Anzaldúa (see entries in this anthology). But nothing is more symbolic of Levins Morales's feminist stand than her exceptional literary relationship with her mother Rosario Morales, with whom she coauthored her first major book,

Getting Home Alive (1986), and the *Ending Poem*. These works are examples of an intergenerational dialogue rooted in love as well as an ethical drive for female solidarity. Also central to her work is the question of the individual self, both through historical memory and through multiple social positions in the present. (ALO)

Further reading: Aurora Levins Morales and Rosario Morales, *Getting Home Alive* (Ithaca, N.Y.: Firebrand Books, 1986); Aurora Levins Morales, *Medicine Stories: History, Culture, and the Politics of Integrity* (Boston: South End Press, 1998); Cherríe Moraga and Gloria Anzaldúa, eds., *This Bridge Called My Back: Writings by Radical Women of Color*, foreword by Toni Cade Bambara (Watertown, Mass.: Persephone Press, 1981).

I am what I am.
A child of the Americas.
A light-skinned mestiza of the Caribbean.
A child of many diaspora, born into this continent at a crossroads.
I am Puerto Rican. I am U.S. American.
I am New York Manhattan and the Bronx.
A mountain-born, country-bred, homegrown jíbara child,
up from the shtetl, a California Puerto Rican Jew
A product of the New York ghettos I have never known.
I am an immigrant
and the daughter and granddaughter of immigrants.
We didn't know our forbears' names with a certainty.
They aren't written anywhere.
First names only or mija, negra, ne, honey, sugar, dear

I come from the dirt where the cane was grown.
My people didn't go to dinner parties. They weren't invited.
I am caribeña, island grown.
Spanish is in my flesh, ripples from my tongue, lodges in my hips,
the language of garlic and mangoes.
Boricua. As *Bóricuas* come from the isle of Manhattan.
I am of latinoamerica, rooted in the history of my continent.
I speak from that body. Just brown and pink and full of drums inside.

I am not African.
Africa waters the roots of my tree, but I cannot return.

I am not Taína.
I am a late leaf of that ancient tree,
and my roots reach into the soil of two Americas.
Taíno is in me, but there is no way back.

I am not European, though I have dreamt of those cities.

Each plate is different.
wood, clay, papier mâché, metals, basketry, a leaf, a coconut shell.
Europe lives in me but I have no home there.

The table has a cloth woven by one, dyed by another,
embroidered by another still.
I am a child of many mothers.
They have kept it all going

All the civilizations erected on their backs.
All the dinner parties given with their labor.

We are new.
They gave us life, kept us going,
brought us to where we are.
Born at a crossroads.
Come, lay that dishcloth down. Eat, dear, eat.
History made us.
We will not eat ourselves up inside anymore.

And we are whole.

Oscar Hijuelos (1951–)

Our House in the Last World (excerpt)

The work of Oscar Hijuelos can be characterized as an ongoing search for identity, particularly Cuban identity. Throughout his first four novels, Hijuelos explores how immigration, isolation, or orphanhood can bring about language loss and cultural displacement. The characters in these works are challenged, each time more abstractly, by the extreme difficulty or impossibility of recovering their lost Hispanic identities. It is only in his latest novel, *The Empress of the Splendid Season*, that Hijuelos once again takes on the experiences of a New York Cuban immigrant family as seen through the eyes of a disillusioned wife and mother who must work as a domestic to help her family survive. In 1990, Hijuelos received the Pulitzer Prize for his second novel, *The Mambo Kings Play Songs of Love.* The following excerpt, taken from Hijuelos's first novel, captures the pain endured by a Cuban American child when he is forced to believe that Cuba, his homeland, is the cause of his serious illness and hospitalization. The child must also sacrifice his Spanish and speak only English in order to receive water and comfort from a sadistic, English-speaking nurse. (KDM)

Further reading: Oscar Hijuelos, *Our House in the Last World* (New York: Persea, 1983), *The Mambo Kings Play Songs of Love* (New York: Farrar, Straus and Giroux, 1989), *Mr. Ives' Christmas* (New York: Harper Collins, 1995), *The Fourteen Sisters of Emilio Montez O'Brien*

(New York: Harper Collins, 1996), *Empress of the Splendid Season* (New York: Harper Collins, 1999).

The Cuban Illness: 1954–1955

1

They were in New York for a few months when the pains returned to Hector's lower back. At night he called out to Alejo and Mercedes, and they came down the hall to see what was wrong. Alejo figured that Hector was just afraid of the dark, a phase kids go through. After all, Hector was at the age when devils and shadowy animals roam wild in the mind. Horacio had screamed from nightmares at that age. Alejo used to come down the hall and, sitting on the edge of the bed, hold down Hector's hands, say, "Estoy aquí, estoy aquí," "I am here, I am here." He would sit there with a confused expression on his face until Hector went to sleep. But sometimes Hector woke from his sleep with a violent wretching inside, jumping up and screaming as if fighting someone or something in that room. This always made Alejo a little angry, that the kid could get this way, after having such a nice time in Cuba . . . a little kid, "my son." "But don't worry, su papá está aquí."

Other times Mercedes took care of him. She was not always as patient or as sympathetic as Alejo. Sometimes her answer to everything was an aspirin or Alka Seltzer. She'd come into the dark room, ask what was wrong, and, hearing the usual, come back with either a glass of plain or fizzling water. Horacio, who was in the very next room at the end of the hall, used to stay up listening to Hector moan. He tried to understand why no one would take Hector to a doctor, but that was the way things were done in that house.

On a bad night, when Hector called out three or four times, Mercedes came down the hall, sat on the bed, and started pounding on his chest, one, two, three times.

"Now we're going to get the little devils out," she said, pounding his chest again. "You'll cry until it all comes out." Then she twisted his ears until he cried out, but the devils did not leave. Instead he heard a buzz, as if an angel was standing in the doorway with hand on chin, checking them out and saying, "Hmmmmmmm . . . . "

This continued for a few weeks. Then Mercedes finally decided to call a doctor uptown who knew about illnesses and fakery. He was from the Dominican Republic and was practicing medicine in the United States without a license. He came to the house with his wife. She dressed like a widow in black and was the witch part of the team. She performed everything from exorcisms to rituals that cured impotence and changed a man's luck with women. The doctor brought her along to gain credibility with the more superstitious clients who did not trust modern medicine or doctors. He examined Hector and told Mercedes that a specialist's help was in order, but she didn't want to believe him. Too much trouble, too much money. The doctor left some pills and went away.

That evening, when the screams continued, Alejo came and sat with Hector, and then Mercedes came. She was convinced that he was calling out only for attention. So she pounded his chest again and told him a story: "You know, child, if you keep complaining you'll never be able to get along in this world. like the little girl we used to hear about in Cuba. She was afraid of everything: shadows, flies, dogs, the wind, and even people in her own family. She was always standing at the window of her house looking out at the people walking by, but she wouldn't go out herself. She was so afraid, the slightest noise made her cry out for help, and someone would come along and tell her, 'You have to get along by yourself,' the way I'm telling you, child. And she said yes, but as the years went by and all her friends went to school and grew up, she never left her house. Soon she was a young woman, unmarried and without a novio. Then more years passed and she became an old woman, still unmarried. But she was lonely and called for people to help her, but no one came because she had been calling out all her life. So she finally got her nerve back, and having nothing to lose, she went outside. You know what happened? When she left the house by herself, she was run over by a truck and died."

Laughing, she took hold of Hector's hands and squeezed his wrists. Pounding his chest, she said, "In the morning you're going to wake up and everything bad inside of you will have gone away." Then she left him and went back to bed.

Afraid of getting into trouble or being pounded, Hector didn't call out to her again. He tried to fall asleep. Finally, after a long time, he began to dream about the ocean and Spanish galleons with foamy decks, and he could feel the mattress under him soaked and cakey as if crystal wafers had been broken. He dreamed about the whoosh of the Cuban current, Manny's laughter, Mercedes's voice, and he touched his hands to the bed, which was all wet, and in the middle of the dream he woke up again, calling out, "Mama, Mama," but it was Horacio who came instead. And he really yelled, because Hector had been urinating blood.

In the morning Mercedes was in a panic to take Hector to the hospital. "I should've known how my luck would go," she kept saying. The kid looked sort of healthy. He was fat; his limbs and belly had bloated out, and he slept like a turtle on his back. It hurt him to move. Things were dark . . . His muscles really hurt, he was boneless, and he felt like soaked rags inside. Horacio tried to carry him out, but Hector was too heavy. Mercedes went to the window. There were kids playing stickball outside on the street, and she called to them, "Please get me a taxi," and they got him out into a cab.

At the hospital Mercedes and Horacio waited in the hall outside the examination room where all the complicated tests were being performed. Nurses pushed many geared machines with screens and tubes in and out of rooms. Mercedes looked down into her cupped hands, trying to have faith in science, about which she knew almost nothing. When the machines passed she looked at them in awe, as if they were saintly coffins. And she nodded to the doctors, who knew all the baffling secrets of the human body. All these machines were so new, not like what she had seen in Holguín. Medicine in Holguín was nineteenth-century medicine. People died easily. But here in America? The machines would help Hector. Miraculously, they would stop the blood, heal the broken vessels, purify the internal organs. Poor Mercedes knew practically nothing about the body, only that the heart could burst and blood was very important. And that the soul resided in the backbone and that real prayer could turn God's head so that he would squeeze out cures. She knew all kinds of old wives' tales about the curative properties of rosaries, holy water, and dreams. The power of eucalyptus, garlic, and lilies—hit-and-miss stuff that sometimes worked. Mercedes saw the body as a mystery, like a huge house with winding halls and endless rooms where food was eaten and blood pumped and where little monsters like microbios swarmed in thick streams through the halls, a house where the walls were on the verge of collapse. She had the kind of faith in science that the ignorant have: It will do everything. She had a faith like the faith hoods with knife wounds that spill their guts have, who come to the hospitals thinking they won't die. They come walking in nonchalantly and then fall to the floor, dead.

Horacio drew pictures, and Mercedes prayed into the streams of thought that passed through her mind. She was thinking that Alejo was going to hit her, call her no good, send her away, or prove her crazy. She thought about what Buita would say, that she was not fit to be a mother. She remembered the time when Buita accused her of poisoning Horacio, and Buita's threats of sending her to the asylum. Would these things happen? No, he'll get better, don't you worry. She kept telling Horacio, "He'll get better." But after a while a doctor came out and told her bluntly, "Señora Santinio, your child is most gravely ill." For hours she remained motionless, thinking about the children she knew in Cuba who died. Tuberculosis and yellow fever were the big killers. Overnight a bad fever would bring on pneumonia, and by the morning the child would be dead. Names came to mind: poor Theodocia, poor Alphonso, poor Pedro, poor Mariaelena. For a moment, Cuba became a place of disease and death. She saw tiny coffins, cemetery stones, flowers, stoic-faced families walking through cemetery gates and down winding paths, heads bowed; she saw children crying and her mother crying. She saw her father's funeral winding through the cobblestone streets of Holguín.

Occasionally a nurse who knew Spanish came by to speak to her, but this did nothing to allay her fears. A terrible infection had spread through Hector's body. A doctor elaborated, and this was translated by the nurse: "He may have a bad inflammation of the kidneys. This condition has gone on for months. His kidneys do not work, nothing works. He cannot get the poison out of his system. He's bloated with dirty water, and it's everywhere inside him. Already the infection has spread to his liver and heart."

The doctor was holding a folder that would grow thick over the years with the bird script of specialists. Three hundred pages of blood pressure and pulse readings, diagnosis, appraisal of blood samples and urinalysis . . . *All from the dirty water of Cuba?*

"Just tell the Señora," the doctor said, "that we don't know what will happen."

The room was cheerless with no windows. There were two doors with wire windows. Around eight o'clock, Alejo came in. He had been at the hotel when a family friend went to get him. He looked very confused; he would not say a word to Mercedes. She called out his name, but he did not answer. He was at the desk signing papers and presenting union insurance forms and the like. There were many questions. Citizen? Yes. Occupation? Cook. Age? Forty-two. Birthplace? San Pedro, Cuba. Date? January 17, 1912. Faith? Catholic. *(Worried? Yes, yes, yes, I'll kill that witch!)*

He stood patiently by the desk, smoking one cigarette after another. He signed forms, shook his head, blew smoke from his mouth. When the nurse left, Mercedes went over to him and rested her head on his shoulders. She was waiting to be lifted away from the situation, but he told her, "This is your fault, no one else's."

Horacio was falling asleep in a chair. His eyes kept closing and opening. In his striped shirt, he looked like a tomcat having dreams. Hector was going to die. He was sure it was going to happen. Then he would sing at the funeral. In the next few days he would go to the funeral parlors with Alejo, pricing coffins. Just a few weeks before, Horacio had punched Hector around in anger. He came home, and boom! he hit Hector in the face and turned the lights off and twisted his arm. It was really nothing, but when he thought Hector might die, then every thought swirled into the fear that the dead would come back to get revenge. He did not like to think about it. He remained curled up in his seat, trying to sleep, but kept flinching each time he saw his pop's face and felt the sadness, thick in that room. He knew, too, things would explode once they got home.

Alejo sat beside Horacio, his brown felt, black-banded hat in his hands. Mercedes was beside him, but did not say a word. She kept looking off into the dark hallway, thinking about the illness. It had come almost supernaturally from the Cuban water, making her look bad before Alejo. Microbios malos, little malicious spirits had penetrated Hector's flesh. She shook her head in confusion. The doctor said he got sick from drinking something bad. Water from the puddle? Water dripping from branches in the yard? All she could do was sit there terrified, whispering, "No me diga, no me diga"—"Don't tell me, don't tell me." She was watching the hall and Alejo's exhausted face, wishing he would move his hand a few inches closer to hers.

They remained overnight. Around two the next afternoon, a nurse led them to the room where Hector was sleeping. He was propped up, and there were needles and tubes of blood and more tubes sticking out from his nose. There was some kind of catheter shoved up his penis, and a thick tube coming out of his ass. Alejo looked him over for a moment and then left the room. Mercedes made the sign of the cross. Horacio stood, just watching. Hector seemed to him to be asleep, but he could also be near the land of the dead. A nurse called them out and said they might as well go home, and so they left the hospital.

They spent the evening with company. A Cuban family from next door brought them dinner in pots and casserole dishes, and everyone sat in the living room, eating and making small talk. Alejo disappeared. He would be gone for three days. Later, Mercedes's friend, Mary, invited Horacio upstairs to watch their television set, which he did. And Mercedes passed her time in bed, nervous and shaking, trying to sleep.

2

After a month they sent Hector to a hospital in Connecticut that was a terminal home for children. It was near Hartford, and there was a convenient cemetery along the way, shaded by drooping willow trees and dotted with white- and blue-streaked tombstones. The road curved into an estate of hilly greens, duck ponds, stone walks, and benches. It was very beautiful. Hector stayed in a ward at the end of a long corridor. There were two rows of simple metal beds and windows high up on the bare walls. Not one of the kids could leave the building. To get into the ward, you had to get past a guard and three double doors. Even the sunlight seemed to sneak in clandestinely, illuminating the faces of the other children like little El Dorados. The patients were innocent children. Most were filled with water and bad air and with microbios. They came to this place from all over the East Coast, and there was even a little girl with pigtails who came from California. The children were very sick and had to take pills five times a day and were required to piss in bedpans, whose contents were examined under microscopes. Blood samples, ugly in thick hypos, were taken every week. Gas was always being administered through tubes into the noses of the children, and metallic rods were shoved up into the privates, rods so cold and violating that the children's bones would leave their bodies and walk around in the outer hall waiting for the flesh's temperature to rise again. Little adorable girls, who would have certainly grown up to be real beauties, went to sleep without a mark on their faces and woke in the morning black and blue, as if they had received the worst beatings. Then they became pale like fish and started to cry. Some crawled along the floor like lizards, while others ran wildly, banging into the walls and shaking. And when the nurses came by with their medicines, the children crawled into shelves and, wracked with pain, spoke to themselves, asking to be helped. If a beam of sunshine shot through the window, spotlighting the floor, they would crawl in it, letting it warm their insides. They would sail around the floors in their boats of light, until they could not move. The pretty girls sang until their bellies cramped and they keeled over and the crying began again. Sometimes at night two men in white hats, dressed like garbage collectors, came into the ward and would lift one of the sleeping children quietly out of bed, put him in a bag, and carry him off. In the morning one of the nurses would calmly make the bed of the missing child, without so much as a word to the kids. But they knew. Another one gone to the skeletons, vanished like so many other things: like the shaky sunlight, sucked into the mirrors and never returned, like toys and tiny shoes and dolls and mirrors, one second there and then poof! gone. Like the Superman funny books! Like Mama and Papa! Like their homes and the whole world and the sun, poof! gone so fast, pulled out from under them.

But they had their fun. They had a television set that was the greatest wonder on Earth. Howdy Doody was a mannequin and he looked just like one of them, except Howdy could still walk around. And now and then the nurse took everyone down the corridor and let them stand on a bench to look out the window, through which they sometimes could see snow falling over the meadow and the countryside.

The parents came into the hospital on visiting days. The kids who were well enough were brought down the long hallway, into a visiting room. The parents sat facing the children and did not always like what they could see. The parents had faces like rubber masks stretched out on nails. They spoke quietly and gave presents but could not kiss the kids because their kisses carried too many microbios.

Hector was lucky. After the third or fourth month he was allowed to see Mercedes. She started to come up every couple of weeks on Sundays, with a friend from down the street who was married to a gangster, or with Mary, who had a black Oldsmobile. The nurse would come down the long hallway with Hector and put him into the room with the screen wall. Then, after a time, he was improved enough to sit face to face with her. They would sit on a bench by the window. Hector had no idea what was going on. She would hold him while he squirmed in her arms. He knew her face, recognized the jittery voice. Sometimes she didn't look him in the eyes and just started speaking her Spanish so fast, fast, while Hector wondered where the rest of his family and their friends had gone. He kept seeing Alejo in the shadows, but Alejo was never there. And when he asked Mercedes for Pop, she always grew uncomfortable, spoke about the weather, gossip, or the neighbors. Sometimes, at these moments, he noticed she had bruises under her eyes.

"Your papa," she would say in Spanish, "they won't let him in here. They say he has a cold and can't come in. He's standing outside."

Once she went so far as to show him the window facing the field and in the distance, a stark denuded tree about which she said, "See him over there, he's smoking a cigarette. They won't let him in until he's finished."

But he never finished the cigarettes and never came inside to visit Hector, who wanted to see him very much.

Hector looked everywhere for Alejo, squirming in Mercedes's arms and trying to break free from her grasp. No matter how hard Mercedes tried to take care of Hector she would always lose. Even though she often visited him, in the future Hector would swear that it was Alejo who made the trip every weekend, showering him with toys he got from a neighbor in the building. He would recall Alejo removing his hat by one of the large arched, yellow windows in the hallway. Alejo with packages of gifts. Alejo kissing him. Alejo with the most concerned expression on his face. He swore he heard Alejo's soft voice saying, "Estoy aquí"—"I am here"—and "I nearly died when you got sick," over the hissing radiator noises. He would remember Alejo walking through the ward of the terminal home, tipping his hat to the nurses and the staff, remember looking forward to the next week, an interminable length of time, and seeing Alejo again.

"Sure, Pop came every week," he would say, years later, to Horacio.

"He never came to see you."

"Sure he did. I saw him myself."

"Listen brother, I have no reason to lie to you. He never showed up to see you even once, not even once, because he was always out on those Sundays having a good time."

"Yeah, well you're just jealous."

"Well, you take it for the truth, brother."

Hector wanted to see Alejo because he remembered the good days before the illness, how Alejo emptied rooms of their sadness and used to let him sleep beside him and brought him presents and took him walking in the park on spring days and did not once fall down. Alejo wasn't like Mercedes, who filled the house with nervousness and worry. She had the high cackling laugh, the crazy eyes, she started the arguing, and she made Alejo turn red in the face and pant.

So maybe Hector did see Alejo in the shadows or in the light that fell onto the bed-sheets or onto the walls of the hospital. He believed that Alejo had shown up even though everybody in the world swore differently. (And where was Alejo? He passed his days holed up with friends, getting stewed and worrying about bills, and crying about human mortality and about his sick kid, made sick by that woman, a thorn in his side, who couldn't even take care of the boy for a few lousy months, crying about his son named after his dead brother and now ready to go into the next world, "no, that kid isn't going to go . . . no, give me a drink . . . ah, qué bueno, nothing to fill up the empty like a drink . . . qué bueno.")

Alejo's presence made Hector feel calm, but Mercedes's presence was a punishment. The ordeal made her overly strict and protective. The few hours she saw him, she spent reminding him about how he almost died. And then she would go away, and he would be left alone, murmuring, "Cuba, Cuba . . . "

And that was the other thing. The origin of the disease. Cuba, as Mercedes always said. "The water made you sick." Cuba gave the bad disease. Cuba gave the drunk father. Cuba gave the crazy mother. Years later all these would entwine to make Hector think that Cuba had something against him. That it made him sick and pale . . . and excluded from that life that happy Cubans were supposed to have.

"Cuba, Cuba . . . "

Even the nurses made something of this. Hector, being a little Cuban, didn't speak much English. The nurses figured they would help him by teaching him English. After all, he was blond and fair and didn't look Spanish. There was one nurse who took special care of him: meals, bedpans, injections, tubes.

"Do you know something," she said to him, "you're very stupid for not speaking in English. This is your country. You live here and should know the language."

To teach him English she would lock him up in a closet. He would be quiet for a while then get scared and start banging on the door. She'd say, "Not until you say, 'Please let me out!'" But he wouldn't even try. He'd pull on the door of the closet and cry out in Spanish. He was afraid: All the clothes on the shelves were haunted. They had belonged at one time or another to children now dead, and they seemed to be puffed up and to move around, as if hundreds of invisible kids had crawled into them. Dead children were like normal children except their eyes were closed. He would bang on the door and scream out in Spanish, "¡Abra la puerta! ¡Abra la puerta!"—"Open the door! Open the door!" wishing in his deep dreams to open the door to Aunt Luisa's kitchen in Cuba and find a glass of the magic concoction, or to see Alejo as he went down the hall to work. He kept on saying it, in a panic, crazy, as if on fire inside. Then the voice on the other side would return, "Say it in English. *Let me out!*" Then she would shout it. "Now don't be stupid," she would tell him, "say it!"

The hours would drag and the door would not open.

Day after day, she badgered him with the same punishments and repeated phrases. In time she made him suspicious of Spanish. Spanish words drifted inside him, he dreamed in Spanish, but English began whooshing inside. English forced its way through him, splitting his skin. Sometimes he called out for Horacio and Mercedes and Alejo, Luisa and Rina, and the others, but they did not come. A few times he yelled out, "Cuba, Cuba." But no one and nothing came to save him.

Hector began to feel as if he deserved to be locked up. Each day was like the next. Vague, recent memories invaded him. He would be lifted from paradise in Cuba and dropped into a dark room. Each time he spoke Spanish and the nurse was nearby, she slapped his hands. The same nurse mocked his mother's ignorance of English. He was slowly improving, but his sentences were sprinkled with Spanish. Holding a glass of water before him, she would ask, "And how do you ask for this?"

"May I have some *agua?*"

"No! Water!"

"May I have some water?"

"Oh yes," she answered. "That's it!" And she kissed him.

In time he believed Spanish was an enemy, and when Mercedes came to visit and told him stories about home, he remained silent, as if the nurse were watching him. Even his dreams were broken up by the static of English, like a number of wasps overcoming the corner of a garden. Suddenly he could understand what his friends were saying, "Hector, I hurt. I'm so thirsty . . . "

This stay in the Connecticut hospital lasted for nearly a year. Tubes went into his penis, and he listened to the kids' crying and saw them shaking in the dark and watched some of the kids who had been watching Ding Dong School and Howdy Doody with him get carried off in garbage bags. He would one day remember a little girl who was carried off. She told him a story about a dog she used to have, named Fluffy, the kind of dog you throw sticks to on a fine spring day, who goes running around and pants so happily. She told him how much she missed her dog, and she kept speaking of Fluffy running in a field, his tongue feeling so nice when he came up to lick her face. And this little girl told him she would be leaving the home to play with Fluffy, but then she disappeared in the middle of the night. He never saw her again.

One day the doctors took Hector into the examination room, and instead of pushing a tube into his body, they stuck a needle into his arm, withdrawing blood. The doctor looked at the blood through a microscope, sent it off for the tests, and that afternoon announced ecstatically, "This one will be fine."

In a week Mercedes went to see the doctor, who told her she could take Hector home. The doctor behaved like a schoolteacher that day, pointing to a chart of the human body and finding the diseased kidneys, which were shaped like the island of Cuba on maps.

"You must be careful with him, Mrs. Santinio. The kidney is a vital organ, subject to rapid and easy deterioration, and it must be treated properly. You must be attentive when administering all antibiotics and medications. He must be careful about what he eats. His diet must contain little or no salts, fats, sweets. Everything must be boiled. No fried foods, no sweets, no rich food of any kind. Recovery is rare and there is a high incidence of recurrence, but as long as you are careful and give him all the prescribed medicines, he may live for many years . . . "

With such happy tidings, Mercedes went into the ward to gather his things. She was nervous about taking him back into the world. As he passed down the hall with its wobbly rectangles of sunlight cast by the corridor windows, the prospect of true sunshine excited him. It was the spring, and when the door from the hospital opened, in the sky was the astonishing sun. A beautiful spring day with smell of grass and buzz of insects in the air, and with hospital attendants lounging in short-sleeved shirts on benches by a small river that passed through the grounds. But Hector was wearing a heavy coat! Mercedes did not want to risk his catching a cold. They followed a path through the high grass, past little gardens with busy dragonflies and bees, past a gazebo, a willow tree, a lily pond. Mercedes noticed that Hector was starting to perspire, melting like a snowman. So she hurried with him to the car. Behind the wheel was the gangster from down the street, chainsmoking, and beside him, his wife, and Horacio, waiting as usual, silent because strange things were going on at home. Mercedes and Hector got into the back seat. Each time Hector tried to undo the coat's buttons, Mercedes redid them. Each time he tried to roll down the window to get some fresh air, she rolled it back up. Whenever Hector tried to get close to Horacio, she pulled him back, or else Horacio moved away. Hector possessed microbios contracted in Cuba. He would be unable to touch anyone but Alejo for years.

At home Alejo was sitting in the kitchen, pretty much as if nothing had happened. When he saw Hector, he looked at him with pity and then opened his arms, and Hector ran to him. Then he started to speak to Hector in Spanish, and Hector nodded and listened but he did not speak back. When Hector finally spoke, he used English, which surprised Alejo. Alejo asked him all kinds of questions, "Why don't you speak in Spanish?" and Hector, feeling ashamed and afraid, became silent. Alejo looked at Hector, wondering if this was his son. There he was, a little blondie, a sickly, fair-skinned Cuban who was not speaking Spanish. He patted the kid on the head, turned around, and took a swig of beer.

Later that night Alejo rushed down the hallway to save Hector from a bad dream. He put his big meat-smelling hands on Hector's face until the kid fell back to sleep. Then he went back into the kitchen to have a drink. He slammed doors and began swearing. He told Mercedes, "You made the boy that way. You'd better take care of him, or out you go!" In this simple way, he wanted the best for Hector, for all the family. But from now on, whenever Alejo's friends came to the house, they would look Hector over and make jokes in Spanish. They laughed, rolled their eyes, patted his head. Now he looked American and spoke mostly American. Cuba had become the mysterious and cruel phantasm standing behind the door.

Graciela Limón (1938–)

The Day of the Moon (excerpt)

Graciela Limón became a novelist only after many years of teaching literature and history as a university professor. Born and raised in East Los Angeles the daughter of Mexican immigrants, writing seemed always beyond her means. Finally, in 1993, she published her first book, *In Search of Bernabé*, which won an American Book Award and was named "Critic's Choice" by the New York Times Book Review. Limón has gone on to write three more highly acclaimed novels and in 2001 retired from teaching at Marymount College in Los Angeles. In *Day of the Moon*, Limón weaves a spellbinding tale that spans the twentieth century, moving from Mexico to Los Angeles and through four generations of the Betancourt family. The selection below reveals how nine-year-old Alondra is made to feel inferior because of her dark skin color and her indigenous heritage. After hearing again and again these tales of racial superiority, Alondra covers herself in flour in an attempt to change her skin color. Limón captures the dynamics of living in a world filled with racism, where children are taught to measure self-worth by the color of their skin. The author successfully challenges this observation by introducing Ursula, Alondra's Indian grandmother, who advises the young girl to treasure her differences. (GBV)

Further reading: Graciela Limón, *In Search of Bernabé* (Houston: Arte Público Press, 1993), *The Memories of Ana Calderón* (Houston: Arte Público Press, 1994), *Song of the Hummingbird* (Houston: Arte Público Press, 1996), *En busca de Bernabé* (Houston: Arte Público Press, 1997), *They Day of the Moon* (Houston: Arte Público Press, 1999), *Erased Faces* (Houston: Arte Público Press, 2001).

Chapter Fifteen: Los Angeles, 1947

"My brother Flavio had two daughters: a good one, and a bad one."

Nine-year-old Alondra dusted the table as she listened to Doña Brígida. She glanced over at Samuel. She smiled when she saw that he was making eyes at her as he snickered at his great aunt's story. The old woman had her thin, beaked face turned toward the window and was unaware of the boy's mocking.

The elderly Doña Brígida held herself erect as she sat stiffly in a high-backed chair. The porcelain-white skin of her face contrasted with the black dress she wore, its high collar wrapped snugly around her stringy neck. When she turned to look at Samuel, she held her long, bony arms against her stomach, accentuating spotted hands.

"The good daughter was your mother, Samuel. She was lovely, and she was as white and pure as a lily. No one but your father ever put a finger on her so she was like the finest crystal. She was flawless and chaste. But she died, and the bad one drifted away. Just like a—"

"She-goat!" Samuel blurted out. He could not help it; laughter spilled out of his mouth. His face was red from suppressed giggling, but he hardly had time to enjoy himself before Doña Brígida lashed out, whacking him on the top of his head.

"Have respect for your great aunt! I was speaking to you so that you'll never forget that it's possible to have bad blood, even if a child is the offspring of good people."

"Sí, Tía Grande."

The boy responded timidly as he wriggled under Doña Brígida's glare. He did not know which great aunt he liked best: the one who lingered in moody silence, or this one, who invented names and dates. He did know that he acted differently according to her swings in disposition. When he and his grandfather Flavio sat at the dinner table with her, she was almost mute, speaking only to ask for the salt or a glass of water. At those times, Samuel felt grown up, and he liked helping her. When Brígida was in one of her moments, he acted like a little boy despite his fourteen years, sometimes feeling even younger than Alondra.

"And you, Alondra, you have no right to smirk at the history of people far better than those who hatched you."

Alondra felt shaken, as she always did whenever Doña Brígida reminded her that she was an orphan. But then the girl thought of what Abuela Ursula told her: This was not the real Doña Brígida. She had only fallen into one of her moments.

"As I was saying, the bad one drifted away. Just like the cabra that is pulled by evil desires up to the craggy mountain, where she can do the vile things that her condition demands of her."

Alondra wondered what horrible things a she-goat could do. She had the feeling that Doña Brígida meant that she, Alondra, was like that perverted cabra. The girl looked up from the polished surface of the table to take a look at Samuel. His skin was as milky white as that of his great aunt. The only difference was that the boy's skin was smooth. Alondra glanced down at her own hands and arms, dark brown just like the hot chocolate they drank every morning at breakfast.

Samuel listened as intently as he could because he knew that if his great aunt even suspected that he was not paying attention, she would punish him. When Brígida was caught up in her imaginary world, the ritual of reciting the family history took place every afternoon, when she would repeat each episode with details and dates. The boy hated the long, tedious story. Nothing ever changed and he now knew it by memory.

The voice droned on, lulling the boy; he was getting sleepy. Suddenly, he began thinking of Alondra and how he wished he could be like her. Except—this thought jerked him out of his drowsiness—she, too, was forced by his great aunt to listen to the dreary story, as if part of the family.

Samuel was intrigued by this new realization. He looked up at his great aunt and saw that her eyes were riveted on the girl as she spoke. It was clear to Samuel that Doña Brígida was using her words to hurt Alondra.

"Why are your making faces, Samuel? You are hearing about your dead, saintly mother and I see you making the face of a bad, ungrateful boy."

"Tía Grande, I don't want to hear this part any more."

Samuel looked over at Alondra, hoping that she would be relieved because of what he had just blurted out, but she went on polishing the table surface. She did not look up or even show that she had heard his words. Doña Brígida's shoulders creaked forward; and she stretched to take hold of her walking stick, from against the wall.

"What did you say?"

For the first time, Samuel did not cringe at the thin, imposing figure. When he answered his voice was soft but steady. "Tía, I don't want to hear about the she-goat anymore."

"Samuel, I have no forgiveness for such disrespect. You will be punished, I assure you. And part of that punishment will be that you will not be allowed to play with that girl anymore."

Doña Brígida pointed at Alondra, who was by now staring back at the old woman. Doña Brígida had never been so grumpy; this was one of her worst days.

"But . . . what does Alondra have to do with—"

"Silence! You are never again to question your elders. If you do it one more time, Samuel, you will surely bring down a curse on yourself. One's ancestors are everything in this life and you have been blessed with a good family. You must never again refuse to hear the important things about those who came before you."

"I don't understand. Why can't I be with Alondra? All we do is—"

"It is not for you to ask for reasons! You must obey and that is all!"

The old woman had risen to her feet. She pointed the silver-handled cane in her hand at Samuel. Her voice was not loud, but it was steady, powerful. As she stood, she seemed to grow taller, longer, leaner; she almost reached the ceiling, he thought. He was stunned into silence.

"Because you have been so disrespectful to the story of your ancestors, you will have to hear it once again, from the beginning. And when I am finished, you will have to repeat it to me, word for word."

The old woman banged her cane on the hardwood floor. After a few seconds, she returned to the high-backed chair and seated herself. She placed her elbows on the armrests as she motioned to Alondra to go on dusting the table. Doña Brígida slowly passed her tongue over her withered upper lip and began again her demented version of the Betancourt family history.

. . .

Later that afternoon, Ursula went to the kitchen to prepare dinner and found Alondra standing by the pantry. Her back was to Ursula, and she saw that the girl was patting flour over her face and arms. Rushing to her, Ursula took her by the shoulders and turned her around.

"What are you doing?"

"I want to have white skin like Samuel."

Ursula took the sack of flour from Alondra's hands and pulled her to her, embracing the girl. She fought a knot of tears trapped in her throat. Not knowing what to say, Ursula tried to wipe off the flour with a wet cloth, but it was little use because Alondra was nearly covered with the powdery dust.

"You look like a cookie. You need a bath."

In the bathroom, Ursula undressed Alondra and helped her into the tub, which was filling with warm water. Slowly, she rubbed soap into the girl's skin, then poured water over her head and shoulders. She did this several times before speaking.

"Alondra, the color of your skin is beautiful. Look at how it glistens. It is brown like so many beautiful things that we love. It is the color of wood and of the beans that give us chocolate. It has the tones of herbs and plants that heal us."

That night, Ursula had already turned out the lights and was sitting up in bed trying to pray, but she was distracted thinking about what had happened that afternoon. Alondra was on a cot near her grandmother's; she, too, was thinking of Doña Brígida.

Alondra and Ursula shared the service porch of the house as a bedroom. One side of the room was used as a laundry. Large wicker baskets filled with the day's ironing took up one of the corners. Next to an ironing board stood a washing machine; its ringer was used as a hook for dust rags and aprons. Behind this was a storage closet for brooms, buckets and mops. Alondra's and Ursula's cots took up the other part of the porch, which was screened in on all four sides. A door led out to the back yard. There was a full moon that night and its light filtered through the screens, flooding the room, casting silvery tones on Ursula's hair.

"Abuela, Doña Brígida was acting loca today."

"Niña, you know that's the way she is sometimes."

"I know, but today she said a lot about good and bad blood."

"Alondra, that's nothing new. You know Doña Brígida."

"It was different today. She said that Samuel's mother was the good hija, and when she talked about the bad one, the she-goat, Doña Brígida looked straight at me."

"¡Ah! La cabra tira hacia el monte."

"What did you say, Abuela?"

"It's an old saying, Alondra. The she-goat yearns for the mountain."

Alondra sat up and leaned against the wall. She liked the times she could speak with her grandmother, especially at night when the light was turned off. The girl liked Ursula's way of speaking; it was full of words and sayings that captivated her.

"But, Abuela, what does that mean?"

Ursula looked over at the girl; she, too, enjoyed these moments. She liked Alondra's questions and curiosity and, most of all, she was fond of her manner of speaking: a tangle of English learned in school and Spanish spoken at home.

"It means that no matter what we look like, or what we tell others we are, we will always be pulled by what we really are. It means that what is inside of us is more powerful than what is outside."

"The cabra?"

"Sí."

"Is the cabra inside of me?"

Ursula cocked her head as she peered at Alondra through the darkness. She was beginning to feel uneasy with the direction their conversation was taking. It bothered her that Doña Brígida was lately concentrating on the example of the two daughters. She thought again of Alondra with flour smeared on her face and arms. She reclined on the pillow, thinking, trying to understand the meaning of the two daughters in the old woman's mind. It was clear that it was Isadora, but why the two sides? Why had the memory of Isadora split into two persons somewhere inside of Doña Brígida? Did she think that Isadora had become bad when she loved Jerónimo and gave birth to Alondra? That could not be, because the old woman had loved her niece. Everyone knew that. Ursula shook her head, trying to unravel the tangled threads spiraling in her mind.

"Hija, what is inside of me and you is special and different. We have our own spirit."

"But the cabra sounds wicked."

"Only if you want to think of it that way. Remember, it's better if a person doesn't pretend to be what she isn't. It's better to be yourself, hija, because sooner or later the truth will come out."

"And the she-goat?"

"If that's what is in me, that's what is in me!"

Ursula's words were charged with finality. They announced the end of the conversation and she returned to her prayers. Alondra slid back under the covers, but her eyes were open. She was watching Ursula, right arm lifted in mid-air tracing the sign of the cross in different directions. She closed her eyes, expecting the sound of her grandmother's whispered prayers to lull her to sleep.

"¡Abuela!"

"Niña, go to sleep! Can't you see that I'm praying?"

"What are ancestors?"

Ursula sighed deeply, letting her breath filter slowly through her teeth. She turned toward Alondra, squinting as she peered at the girl. "Ancestors are family, people who live before our time. They are the abuelas and abuelos who gave life to our mothers and fathers."

"Are there bad ancestors?"

Ursula's back snapped forward and she sat erect, ears straining as she listened to what Alondra was saying. She felt a pang of worry at what Doña Brígida might have told the girl about her Rarámuri side. The old woman's mind strayed more and more each day. Recently, her spells had brought out a different side, a meanness that had not been there in the past.

"Why do you ask?"

"Doña Brígida said that Samuel was blessed with good ancestors. Better than the ones who hatched me."

Ursula pressed her back against the pillow as she shook her head. Then she scratched her head and rubbed her eyes, thinking of what to say to the girl.

"Doña Brígida's spirit has lost its way and her words are messages that it is sending. It is searching for help because she no longer remembers the truth. You were not hatched. You were conceived in moonlight and born in the light of the rising sun. You do have good ancestors. Don't forget what I've told you about the Rarámuri. Our history is long and so is our memory. We have known the secrets of dreams and healing from the beginning of time. We know the arts of carving stone and of dancing. We speak the language of Tata Hakuli and Tata Peyote. Know also that your ancestors are the people who run with the wind. They are the distance runners."

"Tell me more, Abuela."

Ursula smiled because she heard sleepiness overcoming Alondra's voice. She went on speaking, transported to the sierra and to the kitchens of Casa Miraflores where Rarámuri, Hicholes, Mexicas, Zapotecas and Chichimecas worked together, exchanging beliefs and legends.

"Your ancestors, Alondra, walked the floors of deserts and jungles, climbed the heights of the barranca, prayed to the gods of the north countless cycles before Samuel's ancestors came to these parts of the world."

"Tell me about my father."

"Your father was El Rarámuri, the distance runner who was swifter than the wind. His speed was so great that even the fastest deer could not match him."

"Tell me about my mother."

"Your mother was Xipe Totec, the one who did not die but was reborn instead."

"Tell me . . ."

Alondra's voice trailed and Ursula knew that she had fallen asleep. Rising, Ursula went to the child, fluffed her pillow, and tucked the blanket around her feet.

Gustavo Pérez Firmat (1949–)

Anything but Love (excerpt)

Born in Havana, in 1949, Gustavo Pérez Firmat left Cuba with his family in 1960, at the age of eleven. Much of his writing, poetry, prose, and even literary criticism uses bilingualism and biculturalism, particularly in the Cuban American context, as its main themes. A master of linguistic play, in both English and Spanish equally, Pérez Firmat reveals the cultural and linguistic battleground immigrants and exiles must negotiate on a daily basis in their efforts to survive "life on the hyphen," the "hyphen" in Cuban-American. In *Next Year in Cuba*, an autobiographical book, he recreates the eternal longing he feels for the place he has seemingly lost forever, Cuba, and his misgivings about ever truly fitting into American society. Pérez Firmat establishes clearly that the hyphen is a place of eternal exile, a place that is neither easy to inhabit nor easy to leave, one end of it linked to a desired place, the other to an uncomfortable reality. In the following excerpt, from his first novel, *Anything but Love*, a Cuban macho's desire to control his American wife leads to his obsessing over his wife smoking behind his back—among other behaviors. His zealousness or jealousy, which drives him to search in garbage bags and read grocery receipts, causes him to experience serious misgivings about his wife's trustworthiness and their bicultural, Cuban-American marriage. (KM)

Further reading: Gustavo Pérez Firmat, *Life on the Hyphen: The Cuban-American Way* (Austin: University of Texas Press, 1994), *Next Year in Cuba: A Cubano's Coming of Age in America* (New York: Doubleday, 1995), *Anything but Love: A Novel* (Houston: Arte Público, 2000).

Chapter Ten

Like this, two years passed.

Then, late one Friday evening, Frank went into the bathroom to brush his teeth before going to bed, a habit that he had recently acquired. As he reached over for the red-white-and-blue tube of toothpaste, he noticed a cigarette butt stirring ever so slightly on the clear water of the toilet bowl. The white filter showed a lipstick smudge, and the stem had been smoked a little more than halfway.

To say that Frank was distressed would be misleading. He was stunned. But he had his reasons.

When Frank met Catherine, she had been smoking continuously since she was fourteen, even though her parents had both died of cancer, her mother of lung cancer, within a few weeks of each other. Puffing away to the end, Catherine's mother endured a slow and atrocious death, which her eldest daughter witnessed first hand, since Mrs. Thomas spent her last months wasting away in Catherine and Richard's own bed. Early in their acquaintance, Frank asked Catherine why she smoked. "Because I have no incentive not to," she replied, staring off into space the way she sometimes did.

Frank didn't say another word about it until after they became engaged. At that point he felt he had a right to intervene. His motives were both selfish—he was afraid to turn his life upside down for someone who didn't take care of herself—and selfless—he loved Catherine, and he didn't want her to continue to damage her health. They were under the mobile of the solar system, looking out to the woods where their romance had germinated and bloomed. Reaching into her purse, she pulled out a pack of Salem Lights and held it up to her eyes, the plastic wrapping glistening in the afternoon light. Then she threw it into the wastebasket next to the bookcase.

That was the last time Frank and Catherine talked about smoking, and the last time he saw her with any cigarettes. When they got married, several months later, Frank had put the whole issue out of his mind. If he thought about her smoking at all, he emphasized to himself her ability to quit, proof of Catherine's inner strength. Unlike Marta, Catherine wasn't given to showy gestures. Just as she didn't flaunt her looks, she didn't advertise her willpower. What she did, she did quietly. It was one of the many things about her that he loved.

Frank emerged from the bathroom without brushing his teeth or flushing the toilet. Catherine was dozing, half-covered by the pastel comforter, which he still called by its Polish name, *chejol.* When she cuddled up against him, he didn't respond. She asked what was the matter.

"Nothing," he replied.

"Are you sure?"

"Yes."

Catherine nestled against him again, and again he drew away. She sat up on the bed.

Then he said, "Can I ask you a question?"

"Of course."

"Do you smoke?"

"No, of course not."

"I want to show you something."

He grabbed her by the wrist—it was so slender that he could almost make a fist around it—and led her to the bathroom.

He pointed to the cigarette butt.

"Oh," she said, "is that what you're upset about?"

"I thought you didn't smoke."

"I don't. It isn't mine."

She explained that one of her teacher friends—the frumpy redhead at the wedding, remember?—had been having a cigarette in her portable that afternoon. Since she couldn't throw the butt in the wastebasket—no smoking on school grounds—Catherine wrapped it in a tissue and put it in her purse. That evening she dumped it into the toilet. That was all.

Frank's heart stopped thumping. He apologized for having doubted her. He cuddled up to her, and this time it was she who didn't respond.

"What's the matter?" he asked.

"You didn't brush your teeth."

"I'd rather sleep with your taste in my mouth."

"Is it good?"

"I've had better."

"Let me see." She kissed him tenderly, and they fell back on the bed. After making love again, this time slow and tender, they went to sleep with Frank's knee wedged between Catherine's thighs, the way they always did.

Three weeks later, at the convention of the Association of Teachers of Spanish and Portuguese in San Diego, Frank woke up in the middle of the night with stomach cramps, an old affliction. Rooting around in the cosmetics bag for paregoric, he came across a blue vinyl pouch where, instead of the little amber bottle that he got without a prescription in Miami, he found two crumpled packs of Salem Lights and a Bic lighter.

When is a cigarette just a cigarette? He might as well have discovered his wife in bed with the Marlboro Man.

He ran back into the room and shook Catherine awake. In spite of his last name, Guerra, Frank wasn't especially belligerent, but he knew he was irascible. He told himself that he needed to keep his cool, to deal with the situation the way Catherine's family would: not by ranting and raving, but by talking it out, working it through, coming to a consensus. Even if Catherine was smoking, it wasn't the end of the world. So his wife smoked. There were a lot worse things in life.

Catherine looked at him wide-eyed, as if she didn't recognize him—the same expression she had on her driver's license. Instantly forgetting his best intentions, Frank flung the pouch at her chest. She winced. Between screams in English and curses in Spanish, he demanded an explanation. Catherine had one: Yes, she admitted that those cigarettes were hers, but she had begun to smoke only because Frank had doubted her.

"I don't understand what you're saying." He was kneeling on the bed, towering over her.

Catherine rubbed her eyes. The eyeliner left a black streak on her cheek. "I know it sounds crazy."

"Why did you lie to me?"

"I didn't."

"But those cigarettes are yours."

"I was resentful that you assumed that I would lie to you when I wasn't."

"But you are now."

She was finally awake. "I'm sorry." The green pouch had come to rest between the headboard and the mattress. She pulled it out. "I really don't know why I did it. I smoked one and then another and then I couldn't stop. I told myself that if you didn't believe that I didn't smoke, then I might as well smoke. It doesn't make sense."

"So you were doing it just to spite me?" The word in his mind was *despecho.*

"The thing is I didn't really enjoy it. It made me sick. I don't want to get hooked again." She paused. "I'm glad you found them."

Frank Guerra wasn't ready to smoke a peace pipe just yet. "Why didn't you tell me? I could have helped you. We could have worked on it together."

"I knew you'd be disappointed in me," she said.

Beyond the floor-to-ceiling window of their hotel room, dawn was breaking. It promised to be another overcast day.

"How much did you smoke?"

"Not very much."

"What do you call not very much?"

"One or two a day, that's all. I'm pretty sure these are the only packs I bought."

"Pretty sure?"

"Let me think." She took the crumpled packs out of the pouch and a cigarette fell out. "I'm sure these are it." Frank picked up the loose cigarette from the floor. He had not held one in his hands in twenty years. As a teenager he had smoked a few, the same as everybody else, but when his mother had a heart attack in 1972, he convinced himself that her Camels were to blame. From then on he looked upon her silver cigarette case, one of the prized possessions she had snuck out of Cuba, as a Pandora's box of evils. Aware of the risks of smoking, Frank's mother switched to Carltons, but she couldn't quit. Frank had always found it reassuring that Marta was too sensible to smoke.

Pinching the Salem Light as if it were a wet worm, Frank was struck by its smallness. He was used to holding cigars, which were made to be held in your hand, your index finger curling around the brightly-colored band. Cigarettes were much too slight for fondling, he thought; the only way to make them graspable was to use a holder—the Spanish word was *boquilla,* little mouth—but no one had those anymore.

He glanced out through the window at the Pacific, an unfamiliar ocean, and then again at Catherine, an unfamiliar wife. The morning light had brightened the room. Sitting on the bed with her legs crossed, she looked like a Girl Scout, demure and pretty.

A forty-two-year-old Girl Scout who had just been caught smoking by her husband, who didn't understand why his wife should lie to him.

The next day, when they got back to Seagroves after a long and tense plane ride, Frank resisted the temptation of accompanying Catherine to the supermarket. He didn't want her to think that he didn't trust her. But the moment she got back home, he began wondering whether she had bought cigarettes. As he put away the groceries, he located the receipt at the bottom of one of the bags, under a package of ground meat. The condensation had blurred the faint blue markings, which he couldn't examine closely because Catherine was standing next to him. Although it occurred to him that she could have paid separately for the cigarettes, he didn't believe she would go to such lengths to avoid detection. After all, she had kept the other packs where he could easily find them.

Ten minutes later, nervous that his wife would see him through the kitchen window, Frank Guerra was digging his soft writer's hands into egg shells, coffee grounds, frozen fricassee, jellied gravy, pasta salad, black beans, Dr. Pepper cans, baby jars of Beechnut Tropicales (his favorite snack), and a couple of glossy catalogs mottled with grease stains. Scouring his garbage for the receipt, he had the distinct impression that he was being absurd, that his life had become a comedy of terrors. He was not a raccoon and this was not Cuba. And yet, although perhaps he wouldn't admit it, some part of him would be disappointed if he found nothing.

But nothing was what he found.

Then it occurred to him that the moist receipt could have gotten stuck to the bottom of the paper bag. (Confronted by the contemporary American conundrum—"Plastic or paper?"—Catherine always opted for the latter.) Frank retied the plastic handles, lifted the bag into the trash can, and secured the lid with a bungee cord. Back inside, he told Catherine that he was going to take the stash of folded bags to the recycling center. Using the hatch back of the Integra as a shield, he rummaged through the brown bags.

There it was! With his hand quivering slightly—whether from fear or excitement, he could not tell—Frank began to read:

CAPTAIN CRUNCH	2.59 G
BORDON AMER SWS	1.89 R
TROP PREM ORA	4.19 G
CANS COKE CLASSIC	1.99 G
OM FAT FREE HONEY	1.99 M
LO FAT GR BEEF	3.11 M
HAMBURGER RLS	1.69 D
STRAWBS/PINT	1.29 P
CK FOR TWO	3.59 D

No Salem Lights. No Winstons. No Newports. Nothing that Frank recognized as a cigarette brand. Except for the last item on the list:

LT WHITE	1.79 G

How much were cigarettes? (He remembered that he and Angel used to buy them for thirty cents at the Seven Eleven near his house.) Wasn't a pack now a couple of dollars? But the "G" was for "groceries," right? Or was it "generic"? He wasn't sure. Frank went to the supermarket as often as his wife, perhaps more often, but this was the first time he had stopped to read a receipt. It was a more interesting text than he would have anticipated, almost like something written in a foreign language. As he threw the bags into the blue bin, his mind was traveling on more than one track. While the fast track fretted that Catherine might still be smoking, the slow track pondered grocery receipts, which could provide an entertaining way to teach the names of foods, numbers and currency terms. Perhaps he could include a receipt from a Mexican *mercado* or Cuban *bodega* in a textbook, which would then allow him to develop activities blending language with culture, as he liked to do. But he didn't recall ever reading a *recibo* either.

For the rest of the afternoon Frank Guerra puzzled over the instructional uses of receipts and brooded about smoking. He and Catherine spent the evening peacefully—she had grown used to his occasional moodiness—but the next morning, after she left for school, Frank resumed his search. Detergent? On the top shelf of the laundry closet he found Wisk and Clorox. Butter? Nothing but Land O'Lakes in the refrigerator. Toilet Paper? *Charmin Ultra: Ultra Strong, Ultra Soft.* Can a man be like Charmin? Before giving up, he decided to give the kitchen a last once-over.

If LT WHITE had really stood for a pack of cigarettes, they would have burned twenty holes in his face. Looking up from the kitchen counter, he spotted the answer to the mystery: an unopened package of Light White Wonder Bread, sitting placidly on top of the refrigerator. The only wonder was that he hadn't seen it before.

Frank was ecstatic. He repeated to himself, "Catherine doesn't smoke! Catherine doesn't smoke!" How could he have doubted her? How could he be so clueless about white bread? Overflowing with love and confidence, feeling ultra-soft and ultra-strong, he waited for her planning period to tell her how much she meant to him. "Cat, my darling, my baby, my princess. *Mi vida, mi corazón, mi cielo.*" Surrounded by report cards that needed to be completed by the end of the day, Catherine didn't have time to ask herself what has gotten into her changeable husband. "I love you too," she said. "*Te quiero mucho.*"

CHAPTER 8

Rites of Passage

Evelio Grillo (1920–)

Going Up North

Born in Tampa, Florida, to black Cuban cigarworkers, Evelio Grillo grew up on the border between Ybor City's white Latin community and African American community. This reality, particularly in a Jim Crow, highly segregated town like Tampa, taught Grillo a valuable lesson: his marginalization was two-fold because of blackness among white Latino immigrants, most of them Cubans with whom he shared a great deal of culture, and his foreignness among Southern blacks with whom he shared the legacy of racial discrimination. The young boy soon learned that in his world, the color of his skin would supercede any other consideration of him, which prompted him to establish his alliances, make his connections to the world of African Americans, and get caught up in the struggle for racial and ethnic equity. In *Going Up North,* a chapter from *Black Cuban, Black American*, an autobiographical memoir, the octogenarian Grillo shares the pain and pride he experienced when he took up an opportunity to abandon the stifling and downtrodden South and finish his studies in Washington, D.C. Given the paucity of written material on the life of black Cubans in the United States, Grillo's contribution to our understanding of the true complexity of the Hispanic/Latino experience in this country is invaluable. (KDM)

Further reading: Evelio Grillo, *Black Cuban, Black American* (Houston: Arte Público Press, 2000).

"Boy, when are you going up north to get an education?" Mr. Martin had been after me all spring with the oft-repeated question. I didn't have the vaguest notion of how one went "up north." Ultimately, during one of our Saturday morning trips to do his grocery shopping in the big markets downtown, where mostly white and mostly rich people shopped, he turned to me and said, "Boy, tell your momma to pack your clothes and give you five dollars. I'm taking you up north so you can get an education. Tell your momma to bring you to the insurance company at nine o'clock Wednesday morning ready to travel. You are going to Washington where you belong!"

Mr. Martin was the controller of the Central Life Insurance Company, a successful black-owned firm that served blacks in Florida. Very fair of skin, tall, thin, and lanky, he towered over black Tampa, determined to point every black adolescent possible towards college. He did not cajole, exhort, or give too much advice. He simply made friends of us, so that we would have a first-hand experience of someone for whom college was a given, and who thought it was a given for us. He was especially helpful to us children of black Cuban immigrants, whose life experience did not include college as a vision of the possible.

The early generation of black Cubans, including my mother, had come in waves of migration to the United States. Most were, on the whole, literate. Some were very well read. But I do not know of any that attended college.

Had it not been for Mr. Martin and our black American teachers, it would have been very difficult for us to land places in black American life and, however limited, in the American society. They shoe-horned us in, the very few lucky ones among us.

We gathered in front of the insurance company at nine o'clock, as Mr. Martin had told me. My mother, my uncle Rojelio, my sister Sylvia, and I all joined Mr. Martin, Mr. G. D. Rogers, the president of the insurance company, and his son, G. D. Rogers, Jr. We transferred the paper shopping bag that held my clothes to Mr. Roger's car.

"Hi, Evelio, we're ready," greeted the ebullient Mr. Martin. He moved easily among his small crew of employees, which had gathered to wish us goodbye. He exchanged greetings with my mother.

"Now don't you worry, Mrs. Grillo, this is the best thing for Evelio. He'll be all right," Mr. Martin consoled my sad-faced mother. Letting me go took all of her emotional strength. She had pawned her engagement ring for five dollars. She would redeem it for seven dollars and fifty cents two weeks later.

I thought I caught a certain wistfulness in my sister's face and voice. Four years older than I, Sylvia had watched each of the older boys leave Tampa seeking opportunity. Now I, younger than she, had my opportunity. Why did she always have to stay behind?

"We'll have to hurry along," remarked Mr. Martin, eager to begin the trip. It was a long way to Jacksonville, the first stop. So the leave takings were brief, almost abrupt, while yet noisily happy.

The scene became a blur as we pulled away, Mr. Rogers and Junior in the front seat, and Mr. Martin and I in the rear. My mother's face, its severity softened by sadness, was but background to the chatter of leave taking. I had neither the time nor the inclination to give her the attention she sought from me. I was going up north!

Jacksonville lay two hundred miles away, a long trip by 1934 standards. After we left Tampa and were well on the road, things began to unfold for me. Mr. Martin and Mr. Rogers were going to Richmond, Virginia, to attend an insurance convention. Mr. Rogers had brought his son along for a vacation. At seventeen, Junior was two years older than I, so he could help with the driving. Mr. Martin, I surmised, had been planning for some time to take me along.

Mr. Martin and Mr. Rogers were in their late forties or early fifties. Mr. Rogers, a civil and gentle man, engaged me in brief conversation about my hopes and plans. G. D. Junior felt that he was much older than I was, and rightfully so. More experienced than I was by quantums, he clearly took charge when he and I were alone together.

I was subdued and quiet during the drive to Jacksonville. At one point, I gave Mr. Martin the five dollars my mother had procured. Mr. Martin took it quietly and, without drawing the attention of Mr. Rogers and Junior, placed it in an envelope and then placed the envelope in his inside jacket pocket.

The last time I remember thinking of my mother throughout the trip and in the months ahead in Washington, the years of fearing her had ended. Without being even vaguely aware of what was transpiring, I was pushing her deep into the recesses of my spirit. While relatively quiet, within I boiled with self-centered excitement. I had not even said goodbye to my sister or to my uncle.

We arrived in Jacksonville while yet enough light remained for us to make the complicated arrangements for lodging, which the times imposed. We went to a local funeral parlor where blacks could be guided to a local home that rented rooms to black travelers. The motels and hotels were off limits, restricted to whites only. Mr. Martin and Mr. Rogers went into the funeral parlor, leaving G. D. Junior and me in the car.

When they returned, they had connected to the home. We drove there. When Mr. Martin and Mr. Rogers had arranged for their lodging, G. D. Junior drove the two of us back to the funeral parlor.

We parked under a street light in front of the mortuary and settled in for the night, stopped in what seemed to be the commercial section within the black ghetto. Junior and I slept in the car the entire night without the slightest interruption. We were sojourners escaping to the north, and we were not to be bothered. The police and kindly adults saw to that.

We awakened with the first streak of light. G. D. Junior, pleased with the responsibility given him, drove us back to the house where his father and Mr. Martin had spent the night.

I don't remember where—or if—G. D. Junior and I washed our hands and faces. Mr. Rogers and Mr. Martin were waiting for us; bags packed and ready to be placed again in the car. We drove back to the commercial district.

Dawn had yielded to bright, sparkling day. We went to a good-sized restaurant for breakfast. Mr. Martin led the way in. He did not rush, but he smoothed his imposing frame past the door and called out to the waiter in a folksy, raspy, drawl: "Hi there! I hear you cook up some fine grits here, and I hear that your biscuits aren't bad at all."

His presence filled the room. His simple, open, manner quickly caught the attention of the waiter, who bustled towards him, all smiles. While the waiter was showing us to our table, Mr. Martin kept up a continuous banter about the proper way to cook grits, and the proper way to make biscuits. He waited for us to be seated, but he did not sit down. Instead, he walked to the kitchen, the waiter at his side, chattering that he wanted to talk it over with the cook and that, after all, he hailed from Tampa, where grits and biscuits were cooked to perfection. He disappeared into the kitchen. Shortly, we could hear voices in mock dispute over the relative merits of Jacksonville and Tampa grits and biscuits. He emerged a few minutes later with the entire kitchen staff in tow, smiling and talking animatedly. His voice carried throughout the restaurant.

"Come with me. I have someone I want you to meet." This was vintage Mr. Martin, and I was enjoying him thoroughly. He led the procession of four staff members, dressed in kitchen whites, until they formed a semi-circle around the table where Mr. Rogers, G. D. Junior, and I were seated. Then he said, his eyes ablaze with delight, "Meet my friend Evelio. He's going up north to get an education."

A happy buzz of chatter followed as they each shook my hand warmly, gleefully commenting about my going to college, asking me what I intended to be, and, generally, making a happy fuss over an absolutely splendid young man, a future leader, no less!

The center of a warm circle of love and encouragement, I felt special and very important to those surrounding me. It was not until this ceremony of indoctrination had played its full course that we ordered our grits and biscuits.

Mr. Martin and Mr. Rogers kept up a steady stream of commentary about the countryside as we made our way through the cotton and tobacco fields of Georgia, South Carolina, and North Carolina. They loved the land, yet hated it, too, for they were under constant assault because they were black.

We had an accident between Fayetteville and Raeford. G. D. Junior drove this long stretch of lonely, narrow concrete, recently built. Red dirt, through which the dozers had but recently gashed, lay on either side of the highway. A heavy rain-washed mud lay across the road.

G. D. Junior, all seventeen years of him, drove downhill into this invitation to disaster. He drove without having the knowledge of how to gear the car down from free-wheeling. The car spun all the way around, rolled over and then landed, almost gently, on its side in the soft mud.

We survived the crash. The only injury was to Mr. Roger's arm, and that was not very serious. Every second of the experience as the car was spinning and rolling over is recorded in my memory, like a sequence from a slow-motion film. As we were speeding down the hill, Mr. Martin started giving Junior warnings about road conditions and the speed of the car. But Junior did not know how to control the car or even how to reduce its speed. As the car went into a spin near the bottom of the hill, Mr. Martin cried out, "See there! See there! Oh! Oh! We're going to Hell!"

Mr. Rogers softer voice pleaded with Junior to exercise caution, and, as we went into the spin, he cried out softly, "Oh! My goodness!" He was a gentleman even in this moment of fear and great crisis.

During the infinite seconds between the beginning of the spin and the landing of the car in the mud, we were rigid and steeled for the calamity. Frozen in time and space, not a sound came from any of us.

As soon as the car finished its hurtle, pandemonium descended. Mr. Rogers called out frantically for Junior, and Mr. Martin called out, "Evelio! Evelio! Are you all right?" I answered quickly, "I'm all right, Mr. Martin, I'm all right!"

Junior was simultaneously giving Mr. Rogers the same assurances. A moment of quiet settled over the disordered scene, as we realized that our worst fears had not come to pass. We extricated ourselves from the morass, slowly. Mr. Rogers and Mr. Martin were all over Junior and me, assuring themselves that we were not hurt. Mr. Martin's affection and concern showed demonstrably in his face and in his eyes as he checked to see that I was, indeed, unharmed. This interlude with Mr. Martin I savored as a fathering moment, though I could not have expressed it that way at the time. I basked in the radiance of his love, his care, and his concern. I had not been that close to a man since my father's death, eleven years previously. This was a very rare and special moment. My father had died when I was three. I do not remember his face. But I remember his presence and his love, as when he was talking gently to me as he handed me some new trinket. Mr. Martin's tenderness stirred in me a surge of great affection for him, similar to the feelings I remember having for my father.

A white farmer came running in a few moments and helped us to gather our disheveled selves together. A police auto shortly followed and, some time thereafter, a tow truck. They towed us into Fayettesville, where arrangements to make the car operable were made.

The awkward arrangements to find lodging for the night were completed also, but I do not remember them. My memory kicks in the next morning, when we were having breakfast, before we took off for Richmond, the last leg of our journey together.

Mr. Martin again brought out the kitchen staff to meet me and to offer words of congratulations and encouragement. By this time the cultural indoctrination was taking. I began to feel the purpose of going to college forming within me. For the first time in my life I began to see myself in a college setting.

We arrived in Richmond in the very late afternoon. Mr. Rogers and Junior left Mr. Martin and me at the house of Mr. Martin's uncle, where Mr. Martin was staying during the convention, and where I was to spend the night.

The uncle, Mr. Brown, was a gray-headed delight. He was a retired post-office clerk (a very prestigious position for a black American at that time), and his house was the most luxurious I had ever slept in. In the perspective of time, though, I now believe it to have been simply a solid, well-kept home in what was then a middle-class black neighborhood.

Mr. Martin and Mr. Brown turned their attention to my continued acculturation. In the early evening, Mr. Martin took me into the black commercial district, which excited me almost unbearably.

We walked past the main theater, where the marquee screamed in foot-high letters against a dazzling white lighted background that BUTTERBEANS AND SUSIE were playing in person. Mr. Martin, aware of my excitement and of the absolute strangeness of the experience for me, explained that Butterbeans and Susie were a very popular comedy act. We walked down the street taking in all that there was to see. It was all new, very bright, and very beautiful. I had never been close to a big extravagantly lighted marquee before. This was my first experience with the bright lights of a big city. Not even New York City generated the excitement of my evening in Richmond.

We stopped at a restaurant. Mr. Martin, impelled by the desire to provide new experiences for me, suggested that I have a club sandwich. He must have known that I had never had one before. In fact, I never had eaten in a restaurant before this trip. Nor had I ever eaten turkey. The club sandwich was a transforming experience. I gazed with fascination at the layers of turkey, ham, and strips of bacon, the slices of tomato, and the garnish of lettuce. Even the mayonnaise was a new taste for me. In my home, a sandwich had been, invariably, a slice of bologna between two slices of white bread lightly splashed with mustard, nothing else. Three slices of bread contained this sandwich. More than one sandwich, as I knew sandwiches. I took my time eating this new, huge, delicious concoction, savoring every mouthful.

Mr. Martin watched me with obvious great pleasure at my enjoyment of what was clearly a totally new cultural experience for me. He urged me to have a slice of pie and a glass of milk to finish the meal.

We walked home slowly. I was happy, excited, tired, and a little sobered by the realization that this was my last evening with Mr. Martin. I did not understand what he had done for me, but I felt it viscerally. He had given me himself. My excitement was not so much about the trip, the places we had seen, the people we had met. I was moved by very deep feelings. I had been very close to an older, loving, man for three whole days, an experience unique in my childhood after my father's death.

The next morning at six o'clock, Mr. Martin's uncle came to the room in which I slept. I was awaiting him eagerly. He had asked me to take a walk along the St. Charles River with him. The river could not have been far from the house, for I do not remember walking a long distance. We started along its grassy shore, all the while Mr. Martin's uncle pointing out one interesting sight or the other. Then, as though he had known me all my life, he began to talk gently and seriously to me.

"You have made me very happy man," he began. "Ever since Mr. Martin told me that you were going up north to go to school, I have been feeling good. I know you are a good student, because you have a fine mind and a very pleasant disposition. I just had to say that to you because what you are about to do is important for all of us."

I did not quite understand everything he said to me but I did grasp the tenor and the emotion of it. Without planning it, he had participated in the process whereby college came for the first time to loom as a possibility for me.

That's what Mr. Martin's goal had been during the journey from Tampa to Richmond. That had been his goal when he first hired me to chase balls on the tennis court where he and Dr. Ervin, Mr. Broughton, and others of the black middle class played.

Mr. Martin provided the final episode in what I now understand clearly as an acculturation process. They led me deliberately and lovingly into the assumption that college was a matter-of-fact choice for me. By the end of the trip, attending college became a given. The only thing remaining to be worked out was how I would pull it off.

Mr. Martin was his most engaging self as he drove me to the bus station, where I was to take a bus to Washington, D.C. He kept up a steady chatter, letting me know that he was going to miss me and talking about the wonders of Washington.

We arrived at the bus station. Mr. Martin purchased a ticket and handed it to me. Then he walked with me to the bus. Then, just before I boarded, he reached into his inside jacket pocket, brought out an envelope, took out the very same five-dollar bill my mother had given me, and that I had in turn given to him, and gave it back to me. His last words, imprinted indelibly in my memory, were: "Son, now you go up there and show them what a southern colored boy can do."

Sabine Ulibarrí (1919-)

My Wonder Horse

Poet, essayist, and short story writer, Sabine Ulibarrí holds an important place in the development of contemporary Chicano literature. He was born in Tierra Amarilla, a small town in northern New Mexico. His parents were descended from old New Mexico families. Both college graduates, they instilled in their children the importance of education. Ulibarrí interrupted his college education to serve with distinction in the U.S. Army Air Corps from 1942 to 1945. Through the G.I. bill, he was able to return to the University of New Mexico, where he graduated in 1947 with degrees in English and American literature. He went on to graduate school at UCLA, where he received his Ph.D. in 1958. His entire career was spent at the University of New Mexico, where he distinguished himself as a gifted teacher, scholar, creative writer, and popular lecturer. He is best known for his bilingual collection of short stories, *Tierra Amarilla: Cuentos de Nuevo México,* originally published in Spanish in 1964 and in translation in 1971. This and his later collections of short stories can best be characterized as a kind of intrahistory, that is, the chronicling and recording of the values, sentiments, and relationships of the daily lives of the Nuevo Mexicano inhabitants of his beloved childhood home. The writer himself has commented that his intent was to document the aspects of the history of his people, often ignored by scholars, before the onslaught of Anglo culture destroyed the Hispanic heritage of the region where he was raised. *The Wonder Horse*, a selection from *Tierra Amarilla: Cuentos de Nuevo México*, is an excellent example of how Ulibarrí brings to bear his poetic sense upon his childhood memories. (ChT)

Further reading: Sabine Ulibarrí, *Tierra Amarilla: Stories of New Mexico/Cuentos de Nuevo México* (Albuquerque: University of New Mexico Press, 1971), *Mi abuela fumaba puros y otros cuentos de Tierra Amarilla/My Grandma Smoked Cigars and Other Stories of Tierra Amarilla* (Berkeley: Quinto Sol Publications, 1977), *El Cóndor and Other Stories* (Houston: Arte Público Press, 1989).

Trans.: TCN

He was white. White as memories lost. He was free. Free as happiness is. He was fantasy, liberty, and excitement. He filled and dominated the mountain valleys and surrounding plains. He was a white horse that flooded my youth with dreams and poetry.

Around the campfires of the country and in the sunny patios of the town, the ranch hands talked about him with enthusiasm and admiration. But gradually their eyes would become hazy and blurred with dreaming. The lively talk would die down. All thoughts fixed on the vision evoked by the horse. Myth of the animal kingdom: Poem of the world of men.

White and mysterious, he paraded his harem through the summer forests with lordly rejoicing. Winter sent him to the plains and sheltered hillsides for the protection of his females. He spent the summer like an Oriental potentate in his woodland gardens. The winter he passed like an illustrious warrior celebrating a well-earned victory.

He was a legend. The stories told of the Wonder Horse were endless. Some true, others fabricated. So many traps, so many snares, so many searching parties, and all in vain. The horse always escaped, always mocked his pursuers, always rose above the control of man. Many a valiant cowboy swore to put his halter and his brand on the animal. But always he had to confess later that the mystic horse was more of a man than he.

I was fifteen years old. Although I had never seen the Wonder Horse, he filled my imagination and fired my ambition. I used to listen open-mouthed as my father and the ranch hands talked about the phantom horse who turned into mist and air and nothingness when he was trapped. I joined in the universal obsession—like the hope of winning the lottery—of putting my lasso on him some day, of capturing him and showing him off on Sunday afternoons when the girls of the town strolled through the streets.

It was high summer. The forests were fresh, green, and gay. The cattle moved slowly, fat and sleek in the August sun and shadow. Listless and drowsy in the lethargy of late afternoon, I was dozing on my horse. It was time to round up the herd and go back to the good bread of the cowboy camp. Already my comrades would be sitting around the campfire, playing the guitar, telling stories of past or present, or surrendering to the languor of the late afternoon. The sun was setting behind me in a riot of streaks and colors. Deep, harmonious silence.

I sit drowsily still, forgetting the cattle in the glade. Suddenly the forest falls silent, a deafening quiet. The afternoon comes to a standstill. The breeze stops blowing, but it vibrates. The sun flares hotly. The planet, life, and time itself have stopped in an inexplicable way. For a moment, I don't understand what is happening.

Then my eyes focus. There he is! The Wonder Horse! At the end of the glade, on high ground surrounded by summer green. He is a statue. He is an engraving. Line and form and white stain on a green background. Pride, prestige, and art incarnate in animal flesh. A picture of burning beauty and virile freedom. An ideal, pure and invincible, rising from the eternal dreams of humanity. Even today my being thrills when I remember him.

A sharp neigh. A far-reaching challenge that soars on high, ripping the virginal fabric of the rosy clouds. Ears at the point. Eyes flashing. Tail waving active defiance. Hoofs glossy and destructive. Arrogant ruler of the countryside.

The moment is never ending, a momentary eternity. It no longer exists, but it will always live . . . . There must have been mares. I did not see them. The cattle went on their indifferent way. My horse followed them, and I came slowly back from the land of dreams to the world of toil. But life could no longer be what it was before.

That night under the stars I didn't sleep. I dreamed. How much I dreamed awake and how much I dreamed asleep, I do not know. I only know that a white horse occupied my dreams and filled them with vibrant sound, and light, and turmoil.

Summer passed and winter came. Green grass gave place to white snow. The herds descended from the mountains to the valleys and the hollows. And in the town they kept saying that the Wonder Horse was roaming through this or that secluded area. I inquired everywhere for his whereabouts. Every day he became for me more of an ideal, more of an idol, more of a mystery.

It was Sunday. The sun had barely risen above the snowy mountains. My breath was a white cloud. My horse was trembling with cold and fear like me. I left without going to mass. Without any breakfast. Without the usual bread and sardines in my saddle bags. I had slept badly, but had kept the vigil well. I was going in search of the white light that galloped through my dreams.

On leaving the town for the open country, the roads disappear. There are no tracks, human or animal. Only a silence, deep, white, and sparkling. My horse breaks trail with his chest and leaves an unending wake, an open rift, in the white sea. My trained, concentrated gaze covers the landscape from horizon to horizon, searching for the noble silhouette of the talismanic horse.

It must have been midday. I don't know. Time had lost its meaning. I found him! On a slope stained with sunlight. We saw one another at the same time. Together, we turned to stone. Motionless, absorbed, and panting, I gazed at his beauty, his pride, his nobility. As still as sculptured marble, he allowed himself to be admired.

A sudden, violent scream breaks the silence. A glove hurled into my face. A challenge and a mandate. Then something surprising happens. The horse that in summer takes his stand between any threat and his herd, swinging back and forth from left to right, now plunges into the snow. Stronger than they, he is breaking trail for his mares. They follow him. His flight is slow in order to conserve his strength.

I follow. Slowly. Quivering. Thinking about his intelligence. Admiring his courage. Understanding his courtesy. The afternoon advances. My horse is taking it easy.

One by one the mares become weary. One by one, they drop out of the trail. Alone! He and I. My inner ferment bubbles to my lips. I speak to him. He listens and is quiet.

He still opens the way, and I follow in the path he leaves me. Behind us a long, deep trench crosses the white plain. My horse, which has eaten grain and good hay, is still strong. Undernourished as the Wonder Horse is, his strength is waning. But he keeps on because that is the way he is. He does not know how to surrender.

I now see black stains over his body. Sweat and the wet snow have revealed the black skin beneath the white hair. Snorting breath, turned to steam, tears the air. White spume above white snow. Sweat, spume, and steam. Uneasiness.

I felt like an executioner. But there was no turning back. The distance between us was growing relentlessly shorter. God and Nature watched indifferently.

I feel sure of myself at last. I untie the rope. I open the lasso and pull the reins tight. Every nerve, every muscle is tense. My heart is in my mouth. Spurs pressed against trembling flanks. The horse leaps. I whirl the rope and throw the obedient lasso.

A frenzy of fury and rage. Whirlpools of light and fans of transparent snow. A rope that whistles and burns the saddle tree. Smoking, fighting gloves. Eyes burning in their sockets. Mouth parched. Fevered forehead. The whole earth shakes and shudders. The long, white trench ends in a wide, white pool.

Deep, grasping quiet. The Wonder Horse is mine! Both still trembling, we look at one another squarely for a long time. Intelligent and realistic, he stops struggling and even takes a hesitant step toward me. I speak to him. As I talk, I approach him. At first, he flinches and recoils. Then he waits for me. The two horses greet one another in their own way. Finally, I succeed in stroking his mane. I tell him many things, and he seems to understand.

Ahead of me, along the trail already made, I drove him toward the town. Triumphant. Exultant. Childish laughter gathered in my throat. With my newfound manliness, I controlled it. I wanted to sing, but I fought down the desire. I wanted to shout, but I kept quiet. It was the ultimate in happiness. It was the pride of the male adolescent. I felt myself a conqueror.

Occasionally the Wonder Horse made a try for his liberty, snatching me abruptly from my thoughts. For a few moments, the struggle was renewed. Then we went on.

It was necessary to go through the town. There was no other way. The sun was setting. Icy streets and people on the porches. The Wonder Horse full of terror and panic for the first time. He ran and my well-shod horse stopped him. He slipped and fell on his side. I suffered for him. The indignity. The humiliation. Majesty degraded. I begged him not to struggle, to let himself be led. How it hurt me that other people should see him like that!

Finally we reached home.

"What shall I do with you, Mago? If I put you into the stable or the corral, you are sure to hurt yourself. Besides, it would be an insult. You aren't a slave. You aren't a servant. You aren't even an animal."

I decided to turn him loose in the fenced pasture. There, little by little, Mago would become accustomed to my friendship and my company. No animal had ever escaped from that pasture.

My father saw me coming and waited for me without a word. A smile played over his face, and a spark danced in his eyes. He watched me take the rope from Mago, and the two of us thoughtfully observed him move away. My father clasped my hand a little more firmly than usual and said, "That was a man's job." That was all. Nothing more was needed. We understood one another very well. I was playing the role of a real man, but the childish laughter and shouting that bubbled up inside me almost destroyed the impression I wanted to create.

That night I slept little, and when I slept, I did not know that I was asleep. For dreaming is the same when one really dreams, asleep or awake. I was up at dawn. I had to go to see my Wonder Horse. As soon as it was light, I went out into the cold to look for him.

The pasture was large. It contained a grove of trees and a small gully. The Wonder Horse was not visible anywhere, but I was not worried. I walked slowly, my head full of the events of yesterday and my plans for the future. Suddenly I realized that I had walked a long way. I quicken my steps. I look apprehensively around me. I begin to be afraid. Without knowing it, I begin to run. Faster and faster.

He is not there. The Wonder Horse has escaped. I search every corner where he could be hidden. I follow his tracks. I see that during the night he walked incessantly, sniffing, searching for a way out. He did not find one. He made one for himself.

I followed the track that led straight to the fence. And I saw that the trail did not stop but continued on the other side. It was a barbed-wire fence. There was white hair on the wire. There was blood on the barbs. There was red stains on the snow and little red drops in the hoofprints on the other side of the fence.

I stopped there. I did not go any further. The rays of the morning sun on my face. Eyes clouded and yet filled with light. Childish tears on the cheeks of a man. A cry stifled in my throat. Slow, silent sobs.

Standing there, I forgot myself and the world and time. I cannot explain it, but my sorrow was mixed with pleasure. I was weeping with happiness. No matter how much it hurt me, I was rejoicing over the flight and the freedom of the Wonder Horse, the dimensions of his indomitable spirit. Now he would always be fantasy, freedom, and excitement. The Wonder Horse was transcendent. He had enriched my life forever.

My father found me there. He came close without a word and laid his arm across my shoulders. We stood looking at the white trench with its flecks of red that led into the rising sun.

Tomás Rivera (1935–1984)

First Communion

Tomás Rivera was one of the early leaders of the Chicano literary movement, winning the Quinto Sol literary prize with *. . . y no se lo tragó la tierra/ . . . And the earth did not devour him* (1971). Presented through a series of stories and vignettes, this fragmented form depicts the attempt by an adolescent, who serves as the central consciousness of the novel, to piece together his personal past, discovering in the process that his past is inseparable from that of the experiences of his community of migrant workers. The novel thus functions on two levels: As a *Bildungsroman*, coming-of-age novel, the work depicts an adolescent protagonist proceeding through the universal rites of passage and overcoming his alienation; and as social protest, the novel documents the brutal cycle of dehumanizing labor endured by the community of Mexican-American migrant workers. On this level, the protagonist represents the entire community. Himself a migrant laborer, Tomás Rivera overcame the social and economic barriers of migrant labor to earn a Ph.D. in romance literatures (University of Oklahoma, 1969). Only ten years later, he became Chancellor at the University of California, Riverside, a position which he held when he died in 1984. The story *First Communion* deals with two rites of passage, the initiation into a religious body and into adulthood through sexual knowledge. (JO)

Further reading: Tomás Rivera, *The Complete Works,* ed. Julián Olivares, 2nd ed. (Houston: Arte Público Press, 1995), *. . . y no se lo tragó la tierra/ . . . And the earth did not devour him* (Houston: Arte Público Press, 1996).

Trans.: EVP

The priest always held First Communion during mid-spring. I'll always remember that day in my life. I remember what I was wearing and I remember my godfather and the pastries and chocolate that we had after mass, but I also remember what I saw at the cleaners that was next to the church. I think it all happened because I left so early for church. It's that I hadn't been able to sleep the night before, trying to remember all of my sins, and worse yet, trying to arrive at an exact number. Furthermore, since Mother had placed a picture of hell at the head of the bed and since the walls of the room were papered with images of the devil and since I wanted salvation from all evil, that was all that I could think of.

"Remember, children, very quiet, very very quiet. You have learned your prayers well, and now you know which are the mortal sins and which are the venial sins, now you know what sacrilege is, now you know that you are God's children, but you can also be children of the devil. When you go to confession you must tell all your sins, you must try to remember all of the sins you have committed. Because if you forget one and receive Holy Communion, then that would be a sacrilege and if you commit sacrilege, you will go to hell. God knows all. You cannot lie to God. You can lie to me and to the priest, but God knows everything; so if your soul is not pure of sin, then you should not receive Holy Communion. That would be a sacrilege. So everyone confess all your sins.

Recall all of your sins. Wouldn't you be ashamed if you received Holy Communion and then later remembered a sin that you had forgotten to confess? Now, let's see, let us practice confessing our sins. Who would like to start off? Let us begin with the sins that we commit with our hands when we touch our bodies. Who would like to start?"

The nun liked for us to talk about the sins of the flesh. The real truth was that we practiced a lot telling our sins, but the real truth was that I didn't understand a lot of things. What did scare me was the idea of going to hell because some months earlier I had fallen against a small basin filled with hot coals which we used as a heater in the little room where we slept. I had burned my calf. I could well imagine how it might be to burn in hell forever. That was all I understood. So I spent that night, the eve of my First Communion, going over all the sins I had committed. But what was real hard was coming up with the exact number like the nun wanted us to. It must have been dawn by the time I finally satisfied my conscience. I had committed one hundred and fifty sins, but I was going to admit to two hundred.

"If I say one hundred and fifty and I've forgotten some, that would be bad. I'll just say two hundred and that way even if I get lots of them I won't commit any kind of sacrilege. Yes, I have committed two hundred sins . . . Father, I have come to confess my sins . . . How many? . . . Two hundred . . . of all kinds . . . The Commandments? Against all of the Ten Commandments . . . This way there will be no sacrilege. It's better this way. By confessing more sins you'll be purer."

I remember I got up much earlier that morning than Mother had expected. My godfather would be waiting for me at the church and I didn't want to be even one second late.

"Hurry, Mother, get my pants ready. I though you already ironed them last night."

"It's just that I couldn't see anymore last night. My eyesight is failing me now and that's why I had to leave them for this morning. But tell me, what's your hurry now? It's still very early. Confession isn't until eight o'clock and it's only six. Your godfather won't be there until eight."

"I know, but I couldn't sleep. Hurry, Mother, I want to leave now."

"And what are you going to do there so early?"

"Well, I want to leave because I'm afraid I'll forget the sins I have to confess to the priest. I can think better at the church."

"All right, I'll be through in just a minute. Believe me, as long as I can see I'm able to do a lot."

I headed for church repeating my sins and reciting the Holy Sacraments. The morning was already bright and clear but there weren't many people out in the street yet. The morning was cool. When I got to the church I found that it was closed. I think the priest might have overslept or was very busy. That was why I walked around the church and passed by the cleaners that was next to the church. The sound of loud laughter and moans surprised me because I didn't expect anybody to be in there. I thought it might be a dog but then it sounded like people again and that's why I peeked in through the little window in the door. They didn't see me but I saw them. They were naked and embracing each other, lying on some shirts and dresses on the floor. I don't know why but I couldn't move away from the window. Then they saw me and tried to cover themselves, and they yelled at me to get out of there. The woman's hair looked all messed up and she looked like she was sick. And me, to tell the truth, I got scared and ran to the church but I couldn't get my mind off of what I had seen. I realized then that maybe those were the sins that we committed with our hands. But I couldn't forget the sigh of that woman and that man lying on the floor. When my friends started arriving I was going to tell them but then I thought it would be better to tell them after communion. More and more I was feeling like I was the one who had committed a sin of the flesh.

"There's nothing I can do now. But I can't tell the others 'cause they'll sin like me. I better not go to communion. Better that I don't go to confession. I can't, now that I know, I can't. But what will Mom and Dad say if I don't go to communion? And my godfather, I can't leave him there waiting. I have to confess what I saw. I feel like going back. Maybe they're still there on the floor. No choice, I'm gonna have to lie. What if I forget it between now and confession? Maybe I didn't see anything? And if I hadn't seen anything?"

I remember that when I went in to confession and the priest asked for my sins, all I told him was two hundred and of all kinds. I did not confess the sin of the flesh. On returning to the house with my godfather, everything seemed changed, like I was and yet wasn't in the same place. Everything seemed smaller and less important. When I saw Dad and my Mother, I imagined them on the floor. I started seeing all of the grown-ups naked and their faces even looked distorted, and I could even hear them laughing and moaning, even though they weren't even laughing. Then I started imagining the priest and the nun on the floor. I couldn't hardly eat any of the sweet bread or drink the chocolate. As soon as I finished, I recall running out of the house. It felt like I couldn't breathe.

"So, what's the matter with him? Such manners!"

"Ah, *compadre*, let him be. You don't have to be concerned on my account. I have my own. These young ones, all they can think about is playing. Let him have a good time, it's the day of his First Communion."

"Sure, *compadre*, I'm not saying they shouldn't play. But they have to learn to be more courteous. They have to show more respect toward adults, their elders, and all the more for their godfather."

"No, well, that's true."

I remember I headed toward the thicket. I picked up some rocks and threw them at the cactus. Then I broke some bottles. I climbed a tree and stayed there for a long time until I got tired of thinking. I kept remembering the scene at the cleaners, and there, alone, I even liked recalling it. I even forgot that I had lied to the priest. And then I felt the same as I once had when I had heard a missionary speak about the grace of God. I felt like knowing more about everything. And then it occurred to me that maybe everything was the same.

Helena María Viramontes (1954–)

The Moths

Helena María Viramontes, one of nine children of a working-class family, was born and raised in East Los Angeles, a setting that shows up frequently in her work. Her first collection of stories, *The Moths*, brought her swift recognition for her compassionate rendering of marginal voices. Women, old and young, strong in their abilities to survive loneliness, abandonment, and abuse, fill her urban landscapes. In the story below, a young girl engages in a hauntingly beautiful ceremony of departure and coming of age as she seeks escape from an oppressive father and restrictive cultural mores. Viramontes received a B.A. in English from Immaculate Heart College and an M.A. in creative writing from the University of California, Irvine. She is an NEA Fellow and currently an Assistant Professor of Creative Writing at Cornell University in Ithaca. (EGB)

Further reading: Helena María Viramontes, *The Moths and Other Stories* (Houston: Arte Público Press, 1985), *Under the Feet of Jesus* (New York: E. P. Dutton Press, 1996), *Their Dogs Came with Them* (New York: E. P. Dutton, 2000).

I was fourteen years old when Abuelita requested my help. And it seemed only fair. Abuelita had pulled me through the rages of scarlet fever by placing, removing and replacing potato slices on the temples of my forehead; she had seen me through several whippings, an arm broken by a dare-jump off Tío Enrique's toolshed, puberty, and my first lie. Really, I told Amá, it was only fair.

Not that I was her favorite granddaughter or anything special. I wasn't even pretty or nice like my older sisters and I just couldn't do the girl things they could do. My hands were too big to handle the fineries of crocheting or embroidery and I always pricked my fingers or knotted my colored threads time and time again while my sisters laughed and called me bull hands in their cute waterlike voices. So I began keeping a piece of jagged brick in my sock to bash my sisters or anyone who called me bull hands. Once, while we all sat in the bedroom, I hit Teresa on the forehead, right above her eyebrow, and she ran to Amá with her mouth open, her hand over her eye while blood seeped between her fingers. I was used to the whippings by then.

I wasn't respectful either. I even went so far as to doubt the power of Abuelita's slices, the slices she said absorbed my fever. "You're still alive aren't you?" Abuelita snapped back, her pasty gray eye beaming at me and burning holes in my suspicions. Regretful that I had let secret questions drop out of my mouth, I couldn't look into her eyes. My hands began to fan out, grow like a liar's nose until they hung by my side like low weights. Abuelita made a balm out of dried moth wings and Vicks and rubbed my hands, shaping them back to size. It was the strangest feeling. Like bones melting. Like sun shining through the darkness of your eyelids. I didn't mind helping Abuelita after that, so Amá would always send me over to her.

In the early afternoon Amá would push her hair back, hand me my sweater and shoes, and tell me to go to Mama Luna's. This was to avoid another fight and another whipping, I knew. I would deliver one last direct shot on Marisela's arm and jump out of our house, the slam of the screen door burying her cries of anger, and I'd gladly go help Abuelita plant her wild lilies or jasmine or heliotrope or cilantro or hierbabuena in Red Hills Brothers coffee cans. Abuelita would wait for me at the top step of her porch holding a hammer and nail and empty coffee cans. And although we hardly spoke, hardly looked at each other as we worked over root transplants, I always felt her gray eye on me. It made me feel, in a strange sort of way, safe and guarded and not alone. Like God was supposed to make you feel.

On Abuelita's porch, I would puncture holes in the bottom of the coffee cans with a nail and a precise hit of a hammer. This completed, my job was to fill them with red clay mud from beneath her rose bushes, packing it softly, then making a perfect hole, four fingers round, to nest a sprouting avocado pit, or the spidery sweet potatoes that Abuelita rooted in mayonnaise jars with toothpicks and daily water, or prickly chayotes that produced vines that twisted and wound all over her porch pillars, crawling to the roof, up and over the roof, and down the other side, making her small brick house look like it was cradled within the vines that grew pear-shaped squashes ready for the pick, ready to be steamed with onions and cheese and butter. The roots would burst out of the rusted coffee cans and search for a place to connect. I would then feed the seedlings with water.

But this was a different kind of help, Amá said, because Abuelita was dying. Looking into her gray eye, then into her brown one, the doctor said it was just a matter of days. And so it seemed only fair that these hands she had melted and formed found use in rubbing her caving body with alcohol and marihuana, rubbing her arms and legs, turning her face to the window so that she could watch the Bird of Paradise blooming or smell the scent of clove in the air. I toweled her face frequently and held her hand for hours. Her gray wiry hair hung over the mattress. Since I could remember, she'd kept her long hair in braids. Her mouth was vacant and when she slept, her eyelids never closed all the way. Up close, you could see her gray eye beaming out the window, staring hard as if to remember everything. I never kissed her. I left the window open when I went to the market.

Across the street from Jay's Market there was a chapel. I never knew its denomination, but I went in just the same to search for candles. I sat down on one of the pews because there were none. After I cleaned my fingernails, I looked up at the high ceiling. I had forgotten the vastness of these places, the coolness of the marble pillars and the frozen statues with blank eyes. I was alone. I knew why I had never returned.

That was Apá's biggest complaint. He would pound his hands on the table, knocking the sugar dish or spilling a cup of coffee and scream that if I didn't go to Mass every Sunday to save my goddamn sinning soul, then I had no reason to go out of the house, period. Punto final. He would grab my arm and dig his nails into me and make sure I understood the importance of catechism. Did he make himself clear? Then he strategically directed his anger at Amá for her lousy ways of bringing up daughters, being disrespectful and unbelieving, and my older sisters would pull me aside and tell me if I didn't get to Mass right this minute, they were all going to kick the holy shit out of me. Why am I so selfish? Can't you see what it's doing to Amá, you idiot? So I would wash my feet and stuff them in my black Easter shoes that shone with Vaseline, grab a missal and veil, and wave goodbye to Amá.

I would walk slowly down Lorena to First and Evergreen, counting the cracks on the cement. On Evergreen I would turn left and walk to Abuelita's. I liked her porch because it was shielded by the vines of the chayotes and I could get a good look at the people and car traffic on Evergreen without them knowing. I would jump up the porch steps, knock on the screen door as I wiped my feet and call Abuelita, mi Abuelita? As I opened the door and stuck my head in, I would catch the gagging scent of toasting chile on the placa. When I entered the sala, she would greet me from the kitchen, wringing her hands in her apron. I'd sit at the corner of the table to keep from being in her way. The chiles made my eyes water. Am I crying? No, Mama Luna, I'm sure not crying. I don't like going to mass, but my eyes watered anyway, the tears dropping on the tablecloth like candle wax. Abuelita lifted the burnt chiles from the fire and sprinkled water on them until the skins began to separate. Placing them in front of me, she turned to check the menudo. I peeled the skins off and put the flimsy, limp-looking green and yellow chiles in the molcajete and began to crush and crush and twist and crush the heart out of the tomato, the clove of garlic, the stupid chiles that made me cry, crushed them until they turned into liquid under my bull hand. With a wooden spoon, I scraped hard to destroy the guilt, and my tears were gone. I put the bowl of chile next to a vase filled with freshly cut roses. Abuelita touched my hand and pointed to the bowl of menudo that steamed in front of me. I spooned some chile into the menudo and rolled a corn tortilla thin with the palms of my hands. As I ate, a fine Sunday breeze entered the kitchen and a rose petal calmly feathered down to the table.

I left the chapel without blessing myself and walked to Jay's. Most of the time Jay didn't have much of anything. The tomatoes were always soft and the cans of Campbell soups had rusted spots on them. There was dust on the tops of cereal boxes. I picked up what I needed: rubbing alcohol, five cans of chicken broth, a big bottle of Pine Sol. At first Jay got mad because I thought I had forgotten the money. But it was there all the time, in my back pocket.

When I returned from the market, I heard Amá crying in Abuelita's kitchen. She looked up at me with puffy eyes. I placed the bags of groceries on the table and began putting the cans of soup away. Amá sobbed quietly. I never kissed her. After a while, I patted her on the back for comfort. Finally: "¿Y mi Amá?" she asked in a whisper, then choked again and cried into her apron.

Abuelita fell off the bed twice yesterday, I said, knowing that I shouldn't have said it and wondering why I wanted to say it because it made Amá cry harder. I guess I became angry and just so tired of the quarrels and beatings and unanswered prayers and my hands just hanging helplessly by my side. Amá looked at me again, confused, angry, and her eyes were filled with sorrow. I went outside and sat on the porch swing and watched the people pass. I sat there until she left. I dozed off repeating the words to myself like rosary prayers: when do you stop giving when do you start giving when do you . . . and when my hands fell from my lap, I awoke to catch them. The sun was setting, an orange glow, and I knew Abuelita was hungry.

There comes a time when the sun is defiant. Just about the time when moods change, inevitable seasons of a day, transitions from one color to another, that hour or minute or second when the sun is finally defeated, finally sinks into the realization that it cannot with all its power to heal or burn, exist forever, there comes an illumination where the sun and earth meet, a final burst of burning red orange fury reminding us that although endings are inevitable, they are necessary for rebirths, and that time came, just when I switched on the light in the kitchen to open Abuelita's can of soup, it was probably then that she died.

The room smelled of Pine Sol and vomit, and Abuelita had defecated the remains of her cancerous stomach. She had turned to the window and tried to speak, but her mouth remained open and speechless. I heard you, Abuelita, I said, stroking her check, I heard you. I opened the windows of the house and let the soup simmer and overboil on the stove. I turned the stove off and turned the soup down the sink. From the cabinet I got a tin basin, filled it with lukewarm water and carried it carefully to the room. I went to the linen closet and took out some modest bleached white towels. With the sacredness of a priest preparing his vestments, I unfolded the towels one by one on my shoulders. I removed the sheets and the blankets from the bed and peeled off her thick flannel nightgown. I toweled her puzzled face, stretching out the wrinkles, removing the coils of her neck, toweled her shoulders and breasts. Then I changed the water. I returned to towel the creases of her stretch-marked stomach, her sporadic vaginal hairs, and her sagging thighs. I removed the lint from between her toes and noticed a mapped birthmark on the fold of her buttock. The scars on her back, which were as thin as the lifelines on the palms of her hands, made me realize how little I really knew of Abuelita. I covered her with a thin blanket and went into the bathroom. I washed my hands, turned on the tub faucets and watched the water pour into the tub with vitality and steam. When it was full, I turned off the water and undressed. Then I went to get Abuelita.

She was not as heavy as I thought and when I carried her in my arms, her body fell into a V. And yet my legs were tired, shaky, and felt as if the distance between the bedroom and bathroom was nine miles and years away. Amá, where are you?

I stepped into the bathtub one leg first, then the other. I bent my knees slowly to descend into the water slowly so I wouldn't scald her skin. There, there, Abuelita, I said, cradling her, smoothing her as we descended, I heard you. Her hair fell back and spread across the water like eagles' wings. The water in the tub overflowed and poured onto the tile of the floor. Then the moths came. Small gray ones that came from her soul and out through her mouth fluttering to light, circling the single dull light bulb of the bathroom. Dying is lonely and I wanted to go to where the moths were, stay with her and plant chayotes whose vines would crawl up her fingers and into the clouds; I wanted to rest my head on her with her stroking my hair, telling me about the moths that lay within the soul and slowly eat the spirit up; I wanted to return to the waters of the womb with her so that we would never be alone again. I wanted. I wanted my Amá. I removed a few strands of hair from Abuelita's face and held her small light head within the hollow of my neck. The bathroom was filled with moths, and for the first time in a long time I cried, rocking us, crying for her, for me, for Amá, the sobs emerging from the depths of anguish, the misery of feeling half-born sobbing until finally the sobs rippled into circles and circles of sadness and relief. There, there, I said Abuelita, rocking us gently, there, there.

Roberta Fernández (1940–)

Amanda

Born in Laredo, Texas, the bilingual writer Roberta Fernández has explored border culture in most of her creative work. After receiving her primary education in her native state, Fernández received a Ph.D. in Spanish from the University of California, Berkeley in 1990 and went on to pursue a career in higher education. She currently teaches at the University of Georgia. In her scholarship and in her creative writing, Fernández has searched for a Hispanic third-world feminist aesthetic. Her beautifully crafted short stories have been the product of this diligent artistic inquiry and ideological commitment. After publishing her stories in various magazines throughout the country in English and Spanish, Fernández published *Intaglio: A Novel in Six Stories*, in which she constructs a literary style and approach to writing that derive from handicrafts and trades that have been traditionally considered "women's work" in Hispanic culture: dress-making, braiding hair, orally recording the family history. The stories of *Intaglio* are framed by the devise of a young writer–narrator coming of age, piecing together her own identity by remembering the strong, creative women who most influenced her development. *Intaglio*'s chapter "Amanda" is one of the most haunting coming-of-age stories in all of Hispanic literature. Here, the young writer-to-be is initiated into the world of magic and art as a spiritual apprentice to a dressmaker—or is she really, as the townspeople gossip, that most free and powerful woman of all times: a witch? (NK)

Further reading: Roberta Fernández, *Intaglio: A Novel in Six Stories*, (Houston: Arte Público Press, 1990).

I

Transformation was definitely her specialty, and out of georgettes, piques, peaux de soie, organzas, shantungs and laces she made exquisite gowns adorned with delicate opaline beadwork which she carefully touched up with the thinnest slivers of iridescent cording that one could find. At that time I was so captivated by Amanda's creations that often before I fell asleep, I would conjure up visions of her workroom where luminous whirls of *lentejuelas de conchanacar* would be dancing about, softly brushing against the swaying fabrics in various shapes and stages of completion. Then, amidst the colorful threads and iridescent fabrics shimmering in a reassuring rhythm, she would get smaller and smaller until she was only the tiniest of gray dots among the colors and lights, and slowly, slowly, the uninterrupted gentle droning of the magical Singer sewing machine and her mocking, whispering voice would both vanish into a silent, solid darkness.

By day, whenever I had the opportunity I loved to sit next to her machine, observing her hands guiding the movement of the fabrics. I was so moved by what I saw that she soon grew to intimidate me and I almost never originated conversation. Therefore, our only communication for long stretches of time was my obvious fascination with the changes that transpired before my watchful eyes. Finally she would look up at me through her gold-rimmed glasses and ask "¿*Te gusta, muchacha*?"

In response to my nod she would proceed to tell me familiar details about the women who would be showing off her finished costumes at the Black and White Ball or at some other such event.

Rambling on with the reassurance of someone who has given considerable thought to everything she says, Amanda would then mesmerize me even further with her provocative gossip about the men and women who had come to our area many years before. Then, as she tied a thread here and added a touch there, I would feel compelled to ask her a question or two as my flimsy contribution to our lengthy conversation.

With most people I chatted freely but with Amanda I seldom talked since I had the distinct feeling by the time I was five or six that in addition to other apprehensions I had about her, she felt total indifference towards me. "How can she be so inquisitive?" I was positive she would be saying to herself even as I persisted with another question.

When she stopped talking to concentrate fully on what she was doing, I would gaze directly at her, admiring how beautiful she looked. Waves of defeat would overtake me, for the self containment that she projected behind her austere appearance made me think she would never take notice of me, while I loved everything about her. I would follow the shape of her head from the central part of her dark auburn hair pulled down over her ears to the curves of the bun she wore at the nape of her long neck. Day in and day out she wore a gray shirtwaist with a narrow skirt and elbow-length sleeves which made her seem even taller than she was. The front had tiny stitched-down vertical pleats and a narrow deep pocket in which she sometimes tucked her eyeglasses. A row of straight pins with big plastic heads ran down the front of her neckline and a yellow measuring tape hung around her neck. Like the rest of the relatives, she seemed reassuringly permanent in the uniform she had created for herself.

Her day lasted from seven in the morning until nine in the evening. During this time she could dash off in a matter of two or three days an elaborate wedding dress or a classically simple evening gown for someone's fifteen-year-old party, which Verónica would then embroider. Her disposition did not require her to concentrate on any one outfit from start to finish, and this allowed her to work on many at once. It also meant she had dresses everywhere, hanging from the edge of the doors, on a wall-to-wall bar suspended near the ceiling and on three or four tables where they would be carefully laid out.

Once or twice, she managed to make a hysterical bride late to her own wedding. In those hectic instances, Amanda would have the sobbing bride step inside her dress, then hold her breath while she sewed in the back zipper by hand. Somehow people did not seem to mind these occasional slip-ups, for they kept coming back, again and again, from Saltillo and Monterrey, from San Antonio and Corpus Christi, and a few even from far-off Dallas and Houston. Those mid-Texas socialites seemed to enjoy practicing their very singular Spanish with Amanda, who never once let on that she really did speak perfect English, and, only after they were gone, would she chuckle over her little joke with us.

As far as her other designs went, her initial basic dress pattern might be a direct copy from *Vogue* magazine or it could stem from someone's wildest fantasy. From then on, the creation was Amanda's and every one of her clients trusted the final look to her own discretion. The svelte Club Campestre set from Monterrey and Nuevo Laredo would take her to Audrey Hepburn and Grace Kelly movies to point out the outfits they wanted, just as their mothers had done with Joan Crawford and Katherine Hepburn movies. Judging from their expressions as they pirouetted before their image in their commissioned artwork, she never failed their expectations except perhaps for that occasional zipperless bride. She certainly never disappointed me as I sat in solemn and curious attention, peering into her face as I searched for some trace of how she had acquired her special powers.

For there was another aspect to Amanda which only we seemed to whisper about, in very low tones, and that was that Amanda was dabbling in herbs. Although none of us considered her a real *hechicera* or enchantress, we always had reservations about drinking or eating anything she gave us, and whereas no one ever saw the proverbial little figurines, we fully suspected she had them hidden somewhere, undoubtedly decked out as exact replicas of those who had ever crossed her in any way.

Among her few real friends were two old women who came to visit her by night, much to everyone's consternation, for those two only needed one quick stolen look to convince you they were more than amateurs. Librada and Soledad were toothless old women swathed in black or brown from head-to-toe and they carried their back sack filled with herbs and potions slung over their shoulder, just as *brujas* did in my books. They had a stare that seemed to go right through you, and you knew that no thought was secret from them if you let them look even once into your eyes.

One day, in the year when it rained without stopping for many days in a row and the puddles swelled up with more bubbles than usual, I found myself sitting alone in the screened-in porch admiring the sound of the fat rain-drops on the roof; suddenly I looked up to find Librada standing there in her dark brown shawl, softly knocking on the door.

"The lady has sent a message to your mother," she said while my heart thumped so loudly its noise scared me even further. I managed to tell her to wait there, by the door, while I went to call my mother. By the time mother came to check on the visitor, Librada was already inside, sitting on the couch, and since the message was that Amanda wanted mother to call one of her customers to relay some information, I was left alone with the old woman. I sat on the observed Librada's every move. Suddenly she broke the silence asking me how old I was and when my next birthday would be. Before I could phrase any words, mother was back with a note for Amanda, and Librada was on her way. Sensing my tension, mother suggested we go into the kitchen to make some good hot chocolate and to talk about what had just happened.

After I drank my cup, I came back to the porch, picked up one of my *Jack and Jill's* and lay on the couch. Then, as I rearranged a cushion, my left arm slid on a slimy greenish-gray substance and I let out such a screech that mother was at my side in two seconds. Angry at her for having taken so long to come to my aid, I kept wiping my arm on the dress and screaming, "Look at what the *bruja* has done." She very, very slowly took off my dress and told me to go into the shower and to soap myself well. In the meantime she cleaned up the mess with newspapers and burned them outside by the old brick pond. As soon as I came out of the shower, she puffed me up all over with her lavender-fragranced bath powder and for the rest of the afternoon we tried to figure out what the strange episode had meant. Nothing much happened to anyone in the family during the following wet days and mother insisted we forget the incident.

Only, I didn't forget it for a long time. On my next visit to Amanda's I described in detail what had happened. She dismissed the entire episode as though it weren't important, shrugging, "Poor Librada. Why are you blaming her for what happened to you?"

With that I went back to my silent observation, now suspecting she too was part of a complex plot I couldn't figure out. Yet, instead of making me run, incidents like these drew me more to her, for I distinctly sensed she was my only link to other exciting possibilities which were not part of the everyday world of the others. What they could be I wasn't sure of but I was so convinced of the hidden powers in that house that I always wore my scapular and made the sign of the cross before I stepped inside.

After the rains stopped and the moon began to change colors, I began to imagine a dramatic and eerie outfit which I hoped Amanda would create for me. Without discussing it with my sisters, I made it more and more sinister and finally, when the frogs stopped croaking, I built up enough nerve to ask her about it. "Listen, Amanda, could you make me the most beautiful outfit in the world? One that a witch would give her favorite daughter? So horrible that it would enchant everyone ... maybe black with wings on it like a bat's."

She looked at me with surprise. "Why would you want such a thing?"

"Cross my heart and hope to die, I really won't try to scare anyone."

"*Pues, chulita,* I'm so busy right now, there's no way I can agree to make you anything. One of these days, when God decides to give me some time, I might consider it, but until then, I'm not promising anyone anything."

And then I waited. Dog days came and went, and finally when the white owl flew elsewhere I gave up on my request, brooding over my having asked for something I should have known would not be coming. Therefore the afternoon that Verónica dropped off a note saying that *la señora* wanted to see me that night because she had a surprise for me, I coolly said I'd be there only if my mother said I could go.

II

All the time I waited to be let in, I was very aware that I had left my scapular at home. I knew this time that something very special was about to happen to me, since I could see even from out there that Amanda had finally made me my very special outfit. Mounted on a little-girl dress-dummy, a swaying black satin cape was awaiting my touch. It was ankle-length with braided frogs cradling tiny buttons down to the knee. On the inside of the neckline was a black fur trim. "Cat fur," she confessed, and it tickled my neck as she buttoned the cape on me. The puffy sleeves fitted very tightly around the wrist, and on the upper side of each wristband was attached a cat's paw which hung down to my knuckles. Below the collar, on the left side of the cape, was a small stuffed heart in burgundy-colored velveteen and, beneath the heart, she had sewn-in red translucent beads.

As she pulled the rounded ballooning hood on me, rows of stitched-down pleats made it fit close to the head. Black chicken feathers framed my face, almost down to my eyes. Between the appliques of feathers, tiny bones were strung which gently touched my cheeks. The bones came from the sparrows which the cats had killed out in the garden, she reassured me. She then suggested I walk around the room so she could take a good look at me.

As I moved, the cat's paws rubbed against my hands and the bones of the sparrows bounced like what I imagined snowflakes would feel like on my face. Then she slipped a necklace over my head that was so long it reached down to my waist. It too was made of bones of sparrows strung on the finest glittering black thread, with little bells inserted here and there. I raised my arms and danced around the room, and the bells sounded sweet and clear in the silence. I glided about the room, then noticed in the mirror that Librada was sitting in the next room, laughing under her breath. Without thinking, I walked up to her and asked what she thought of my cape.

"Nenita, you look like something out of this world. Did you notice I just blessed myself? It scares me to think of the effect you are going to have on so many. *¡Que Dios nos libre!*"

I looked at Librada eye-to-eye for the first time, then felt that the room was not big enough to hold all the emotion inside of me. So I put my arms around Amanda and kissed her two, three, four times, then dramatically announced that I was going to show this most beautiful of all creations to my mother. I rushed outside hoping not to see anyone on the street and since luck was to be my companion for a brief while, I made it home without encountering a soul. Pausing outside the door of the kitchen where I could hear voices I took a deep breath, knocked as loudly as I could and in one simultaneous swoop, opened the door and stepped inside, arms outstretched as feathers, bones and *cascabeles* fluttered in unison with my heart.

After the initial silence, my sisters started to cry almost hysterically, and while my father turned to comfort them, my mother came towards me with a face I had never seen on her before. She breathed deeply, then quietly said I must never wear that outfit again. Since her expression frightened me somewhat, I took off the cape, mumbling under my breath over and over how certain people couldn't see special powers no matter how much they might be staring them in the face.

I held the *bruja* cape in my hands, looking at the tiny holes pierced through the bones of sparrows, then felt the points of the nails on the cat's paws. As I fingered the beads under the heart I knew on that very special night when the green lights of the fire flies were flickering more brightly than usual, on that calm transparent night of nights I would soon be sleeping in my own witch's daughter's cape.

III

Sometime after the Judases were all aflame and spirals of light were flying everywhere, I slowly opened my eyes to a full moon shining on my face. Instinctively my hand reached to my neck and I rubbed the back of my fingers gently against the cat's fur. I should go outside I thought. Then I slipped off the bed and tip-toed to the back door in search of that which was not inside.

For a long time I sat on a lawn chair, rocking myself against its back, all the while gazing at the moon and the familiar surroundings which glowed so luminously within the vast universe while out there in the darkness, the constant chirping of the crickets and the cicadas reiterated the reassuring permanence of everything around me. None of us is allowed to relish in powers like that for long enough, and the vision of transcendence exploded in a scream as two hands grabbed me at the shoulders, then shook me back and forth. "What are you doing out here? Didn't I tell you to take off that awful thing?"

Once again I looked at my mother in defiance, but immediately sensed that she was apprehensive rather than angry, and I knew it was hopeless to argue with her. Carefully I undid the tiny rounded black buttons from the soft, braided loops and took off the cape for what I felt would be the last time.

IV

Years passed, much faster than before, and I had little time left for dark brown-lavender puddles and fanciful white owls in the night. Nor did I see my cape after that lovely-but-so-sad, once-in-a-lifetime experience of perfection in the universe. In fact, I often wondered if I had not invented that episode as I invented many others in those endless days of exciting and unrestrained possibilities.

Actually, the memory of the cape was something I tried to flick away on those occasions when the past assumed the unpleasantness of an uninvited but persistent guest; yet, no matter how much I tried, the intrusions continued. They were especially bothersome one rainy Sunday afternoon when all the clocks had stopped working one after another as though they too had wanted to participate in the tedium of the moment. So as not to remain still, I mustered all the energy I could and decided to pass the hours by poking around in the boxes and old trunks in the store-room.

Nothing of interest seemed to be the order of the afternoon, when suddenly I came upon something wrapped in yellowed tissue paper. As I unwrapped the package, I uttered a sigh of surprise on discovering that inside was the source of the disturbances I had been trying to avoid. I cried as I fingered all the details on the little cape, for it was as precious as it had been on the one day I had worn it many years before. Only the fur had stiffened somewhat from the dryness in the trunk.

Once again I marvelled at Amanda's gifts. The little black cape was so obviously an expression of genuine love that it seemed a shame it had been hidden for all those years. I carefully lifted the cape out of the trunk, wondering why my mother had not burned it as she had threatened, yet knowing full well why she had not.

V

From then on I placed the little cape among my collection of few but very special possessions which accompanied me everywhere I went. I even had a stuffed dummy made, upon which I would arrange the cape in a central spot in every home I made. Over the years, the still-crisp little cape ripened in meaning, for I could not imagine anyone ever again taking the time to create anything as personal for me as Amanda had done when our worlds had coincided for a brief and joyous period in those splendid days of luscious white gardenias.

When the end came I could hardly bear it. It happened many years ago when the suitcase containing the little cape got lost en route on my first trip west. No one could understand why the loss of something as quaint as a black cape with chicken feathers, bones of sparrows and cat's paws could cause anyone to carry on in such a manner. Their lack of sympathy only increased my own awareness of what was gone, and for months after I first came to these foggy coastal shores I would wake up to *lentejuelas de conchanacar* whirling about in the darkness, just as they had done so long ago in that magical room in Amanda's house.

VI

Back home, Amanda is aging well, and although I haven't seen her in years, lately I have been dreaming once again about the enchantment which her hands gave to everything they touched, especially when I was very tiny and to celebrate our birthdays, my father, she and I had a joint birthday party lasting three days. During this time, he would then use bamboo sticks to make a skeletal frame for a kite, and then Amanda would take the frame and attach thin layers of marquisette to it with angel cords. In the late afternoon, my father would hold on to the cords, while I floated about on the kite above the shrubs and bushes; and it was all such fun. I cannot recall the exact year when those celebrations stopped, nor what we did with all those talismanic presents but I must remember to sort through all the trunks and boxes in my mother's storeroom the next time that I am home.

Judith Ortiz Cofer (1952–)

Volar; María Elena; Exile

Judith Ortiz Cofer was born in Hormigueros, Puerto Rico, into a family that was destined to move back and forth between Puerto Rico and Paterson, New Jersey. She became the first Puerto Rican writer to express from a middle-class point of view this disjuncture of migrating from the island to the mainland. When she was sixteen, Ortiz Cofer's father retired from the Navy and moved the family to Augusta, Georgia. After graduating from high school in Augusta, Ortiz Cofer studied literature and writing, eventually attaining a Master's degree in English from Florida Atlantic University. Ortiz Cofer is known for both her poetry and her prose. In her poems, she struggles to create a history for herself out of the cultural ambiguity that characterized her childhood. Many of her stories, on the other hand, are coming-of-age narratives that explore in very poetic language the subtleties of learning about one's self and about choosing roles to play in life. In all of her works, Ortiz Cofer explores through a feminist perspective her own and her characters' relationships with father, mother, and grandmother, while considering the different expectations for the males and the females in Anglo-American and Hispanic cultures. Ortiz Cofer is a Professor of Creative Writing at the University of Georgia. (NK)

Further reading: Judith Oriz Cofer, *Terms of Survival* (Houston: Arte Público Press, 1987), *The Line of the Sun* (Athens: University of Georgia Press, 1989), *Silent Dancing: A Remembrance of a Puerto Rican Childhood* (Houston: Arte Público Press, 1990), *The Year of Our Revolution* (Houston: Arte Público Press, 1999).

Volar

At twelve I was an avid consumer of comic books—*Supergirl* being my favorite. I spent my allowance of a quarter a day on two twelve-cent comic books or a double issue for twenty-five. I had a stack of *Legion of Super Heroes* and *Supergirl* comic books in my bedroom closet that was as tall as I. I had a recurring dream in those days: that I had long blonde hair and could fly. In my dream I climbed the stairs to the top of our apartment building as myself, but as I went up each flight, changes would be taking place. Step by step I would fill out: my legs would grow long, my arms harden into steel, and my hair would magically go straight and turn a golden color. Of course, I would add the bonus of breasts, but not too large; Supergirl had to be aerodynamic, and sleek and hard as a supersonic missile. Once on the roof, my parents safely asleep in their beds, I would get on tip-toe, arms outstretched in the position for flight, and jump out of my fifty-story-high window into the black lake of the sky. From up there, over the rooftops, I could see everything, even beyond the few blocks of our barrio; with my x-ray vision I could look inside the homes of people who interested me.

Once I saw our landlord, whom I knew my parents feared, sitting in a treasure-room dressed in an ermine coat and a large gold crown. He sat on the floor counting his dollar bills. I played a trick on him. Going up to his building's chimney, I blew a little puff of my super-breath into his fireplace, scattering his stacks of money so that he had to start counting all over again.

I could more or less program my Supergirl dreams in those days by focusing on the object of my current obsession. This way I saw into the private lives of my neighbors, my teachers, and in the last days of my childish fantasy and the beginning of adolescence, into the secret rooms of the boys I liked. In the mornings I'd wake up in the tiny bedroom with its incongruous—at least in our tiny apartment—white "princess" furniture my mother had chosen for me, and find myself back in my body; my tight curls still clinging to my head, my skinny arms and legs and flat chest unchanged.

In the kitchen my mother and father would be talking softly over a *café con leche.* She would come and "wake me" exactly forty-five minutes after they had gotten up. It was their time together at the beginning of each day, and even at an early age I could feel their disappointment if I interrupted them by getting up too early. So I would stay in my bed recalling my dreams of flight, perhaps planning my next flight. In the kitchen they would be discussing events in the barrio. Actually, my father would be carrying that part of the conversation; when it was her turn to speak she would, more often than not, try shifting the topic toward her desire to see her *familia* on the Island: How about a vacation to Puerto Rico together this year, *querido*? We could rent a car, go to the beach. We could . . . And he would answer patiently, gently: *Mi amor,* do you know how much it would cost for all of us to fly there? It is not possible for me to take the time off . . . *Mi vida,* please understand . . . And I knew that soon she would rise from the table. Not abruptly. She would light a cigarette and look out the kitchen window. The view was of a dismal alley that was littered with refuse thrown from windows. The space was too narrow for anyone larger than a skinny child to enter safely, so it was never cleaned. My mother would check the time on the clock over the sink, the one with a prayer for patience and grace written in Spanish. A birthday gift. She would see that it was time to wake me. She'd sigh deeply and say the same thing the view from her kitchen window always inspired her to say: *"Ay, si yo pudiera volar."*

María Elena

My hair started turning gray that year, seeing the turmoil on the streets of America and waiting for my daughter to come home from her rallies, demonstrations and sit-ins. Late into the night, I sat in my rocker by the window, waiting to see the pretty girl with the wild black mane of hair hiding herself inside a huge poncho. I watched her coming down the block, clutching her books and papers, head bowed as if she were burdened with the worries of the whole world. Such a serious child. So intent on righting wrongs that she missed all of the good things that I thought a young girl would want: pretty clothes, fiestas, fun with other teen-agers. I knew that she liked boys, although those years I had to look very closely to tell the difference between the sexes. Both wore ragged blue jeans, painted t-shirts and ridiculous jewelry. They let their hair grow and wore it wildly and tangled as moss on a tree. From my window I could not always tell if her occasional companions were girlfriends or *novios.*

There was no doubt, however, the night I saw the obscene kiss in front of our building. By the light of the street lamp, I could clearly see the entire spectacle. Although I did not want her to know that I watched her in such a clandestine manner, I was alarmed one night to see the groping and abandoned caresses. It was *el poeta*, Gerald, she wrapped herself around one night. The boy looked like he needed a good night's sleep, a hot meal and a hair-brush. I did not understand what she saw in him. Perhaps her enchantment with words and poetry was embodied in the unkempt boy. I knew I had to say something to her about the display on the street. She walked in preceded by the wave of that patchouli oil that permeated her person and everything she touched in those days. It was a pagan smell, calling up for me images of naked people dancing around a fire. I was sitting in the dark living room, so I startled her when I spoke her name.

"Elenita. Please come here for a minute, *niña*," I said, trying to calm myself before speaking.

"What are you doing up so late, Mother? Hey, have you been spying on me?"

"*I* will ask the questions, Elenita." I reached over and turned on the light. Her hands shot up to cover her face as if she had something to hide. But she regained her rebel pose quickly.

"Have you thought about what people in this barrio will say if they see you being intimate with a man right on the sidewalk?"

"You *were* spying on me!"

She was furious, as I knew she would be, but I was determined to speak my thoughts.

"You are forgetting something, *hija*." I spoke calmly so that she would know that I did not intend to be intimidated by her anger. "You live in my house. And as long as you call this home, you will answer to me and your father for your moral behavior."

"Then maybe it's time that I leave your *home*," she answered sharply. And the way she says *su casa* hurt me. "Perhaps you haven't noticed, stuck as you are behind these four walls, that there's been a sexual revolution going on out in the real world." She continued speaking in the same sarcastic tone. "People don't have to ask their parents or anyone for permission before they make love. It's a personal matter, Mother!"

"I call what you are suggesting immoral behavior, *hija*. If you are saying that for girls to pass their bodies around to many men is not a sin, then you are wrong. The body is a temple—"

"My body is *my* temple, and I will conduct services any way I want!"

I saw that I could never hope to win a battle of words with my daughter: They were her domain. Even then she could use language to her advantage like no one else I knew. So I brought out my most dangerous and final weapon. Trembling in fear, I said, "I cannot *live* with you if you have given yourself over to a life of sin. I do not want you to go, but you have become a stranger to me."

She looked at me in horror. I knew I had shocked her because she thought that my devotion to her was greater than my objections to anything she could do. And it was. I was playing this game of chance, risking my whole life and my soul—for I could no more give up my child than I could stop breathing—hoping she would understand the gravity of our moral dilemma.

"You're throwing me out?"

She had to sunk to the floor in front of my rocker. Her heap of bright rags spread around her, she seemed to shrink into a little girl again. I held back my need to comfort my child, keeping my hands locked together so as not to reach out to her.

"No, Elenita," I spoke firmly although my throat felt constricted by fear. "I am telling you that if the morals we taught you mean nothing, then we are no longer a family. You must make a choice. If you want to live without rules, then you must make a life away from us. On your own."

She sank back on her knees staring at me in disbelief, as if I had suddenly turned into a monster right there in front of her. She had never known that I too could rebel against injustice.

"You don't understand, Mother. Things have changed in the world. A modern woman makes her own choices . . . She has the freedom to choose."

Now she was going to give me a lecture on free love, but I interrupted her.

"Nothing of value to your life is free, Elenita. *Nada. ¿Entiendes?* Not even love. Especially not love. Look around you. Women have always paid a high price for love. The highest price. I am telling you that if you want to be an adult, you have to learn the first lesson: Love will cost you. It is not free."

She sat there taking in my pronouncements. Not in the usual way that people process things. Not *my* Elenita. She was translating and transforming what I had said inside that unknowable mind of hers. And when I would hear my own words again, coming out of her mouth, they would sound foreign to me.

My plan was to walk out on *her* for once, leaving her there to think about the choices I had given her. But I could not help myself. As I walked past my *niña* sitting stiffly in her pagan costume, I stroked her hair. She lay her wild head inside the circle of my arms for one brief moment, then rushed to her room to drown out the world with her long-playing albums. I will remember that night as the beginning of the end of the worst year in the history of parents and children: 1968, the year of our revolution.

Exile

I left my home behind me
but my past clings to my fingers
so that every word I write bears
the mark like a cancelled postage stamp
of my birthplace

There was no angel to warn me
of the dangers of looking back.
Like Lot's wife, I would trade
my living blood for one last look
at the house where each window held
a face framed as in a family album.
And the place lined with palms
where my friends and I strolled in our pink
and yellow and white Sunday dresses, dreaming
of husbands, houses, and orchards where
our children would play in the leisurely summer
of our future. Gladly would I spill
my remaining years like salt upon the ground,
to gaze again on the fishermen of the bay
dragging their catch in nets glittering
like pirate gold, to the shore.
Nothing remains of that world, I hear,
but the skeletons of houses, all colors
bled from the fabric of those
who stayed behind
inhabiting the dead cities
like the shadows of Hiroshima.

CHAPTER 9

New Directions in Poetry

Mercedes de Acosta (1893–1968)

Day Laborer; Strange City

Mercedes de Acosta, born in New York City to Spanish parents of noble lineage, spent most of her life there. Although she wrote in many different genres, including poetry, novels, and theater and screen plays, she enjoyed little success with the critics or the public during her lifetime, and her work is mostly forgotten today. De Acosta struggled to make her place in society as a woman, keeping her maiden name after she had married and fighting for women's right to vote. Today, as she is rediscovered, her writing is rapidly gaining importance for the simple elegance of her literary style and for her perspective on the gay and lesbian arts world of the 20s and 30s. Sadly, de Acosta is most often not remembered as a writer, but as the lover of some of Hollywood's most prominent women, including Greta Garbo, Isadora Duncan, and Marlene Dietrich. The poems below are impressionistic observations of life in New York City. In simple and direct language, de Acosta records rhythms and sites in the urban environment, thus adding substantially to the extensive portraits of the metropolis by Hispanic authors. (JM)

Further reading: Mercedes de Acosta, *Here Lies the Heart* (New York: Reynal and Company, 1960), *Streets and Shadows* (New York: Moffat, Yard and Company, 1922).

Day Laborer

Massive shoulders
Convulsed with muscle—
A bright red blouse
Standing out like a scarlet wound,
Across the breast of the snow.
Easy swing and handling of the shovel;
Brown face and hands
Proclaiming warmer skies.
Brown face and hands,
Sad—alien—amidst Northern whiteness,
And a voice and song that sing of Southern lands.

Strange City

O Strange city.
City wherein I am a stranger.
I look down at you from this high window
And watch the contour of your face
Pressed against the night sky.
I see a tower rising in the distance,
Pale, thin, with a faint light flickering from its eyes—
Like a tired woman
Wearied with incessant clamoring of voices she does not understand
I see a clock whose face stands out silvery and ghost-like,
Passing its slender hands across its face,
And feeling the breath of time as it slips between its fingers.
I see black roofs
Like crouching beetles,
And endless streets
Fading into the night.
Then far away and deep within the distance—
Looms a corner of the sea.
Strange city with your harbor, streets and houses,
I am lonely. Befriend me!

Víctor Hernández Cruz (1949–)

The Latest Latin Dance Craze; today is a day of great joy; Loisaida; energy

Víctor Hernández Cruz is the Nuyorican poet most recognized and acclaimed by mainstream literary critics. Born in Aguas Buenas, Puerto Rico, he moved with his family to New York's Spanish Harlem at the age of five. Cruz attended Benjamin Franklin High School, where he began writing poetry. In the years following graduation, his poetry began to appear in the *Evergreen Review*, the *New York Review of Books, Ramparts,* and other small magazines. Hernández Cruz from the outset was treated as a prodigy, and he published his first chapbook at age sixteen and, at age twenty, his first highly lauded collection, *Snaps* (1969). Classifying his poetry as Afro-Latin, Hernández Cruz has developed as a consummate bilingual poet and experimenter who consistently explores the relationship of music to poetry in a multiracial, multicultural context. Because of this, and because he quite often reproduces salsa percussion rhythms in his work, Cruz has often been considered a jazz poet, but the April 1981 *Life* magazine survey of poetry in the United States concluded that Víctor Hernández Cruz was among a mere handful of outstanding American poets all around. In the poems that follow can be appreciated the musicality of Hernández Cruz's verse, its homage to salsa as well as to Puerto Rican identity. In *Loisaida*, Hernández Cruz expresses his belief that the Lower East Side, and New York City in general, is home turf, the result of a Latinization that will eventually spread across the entire United States. (NK)

Further reading: Víctor Hernández Cruz, *Snaps* (New York: Random House, 1969), *Tropicalization* (San Francisco: Reed and Canon, 1976), *Rhythm, Content and Flavor* (Houston: Arte Público Press, 1989), *Red Beans* (Minneapolis: Coffee House Press, 1991).

The Latest Latin Dance Craze

First
You throw your head back twice
Jump out onto the floor like a
Kangaroo
Circle the floor once
Doing fast scissor works with your
Legs
Next
Dash towards the door
Walking in a double cha cha cha
Open the door and glide down
The stairs like a swan
Hit the street
Run at least ten blocks
Come back in through the same
Door
Doing a mambo-minuet
Being careful that you don't fall
And break your head on that one
You have just completed your first
Step.

today is a day of great joy

when they stop poems
in the mail & slap
their hands & dance to
them

when the women become pregnant
by the side of poems
the strongest sounds making
the river go along

it is a great day

as poems fall down to
movie crowds in restaurants
in bars

when poems start to
knock down walls to

knock down walls to
choke politicians
when poems scream &
begin to break the air

that is the time of
true poets that is
the time of greatness

a true poet aiming
poems & watching things
fall to the ground

it is a great day

Loisaida

By the East River
of Manhattan island
Where once the Iroquois
Canoed in style
Now the jumping
Stretch of Avenue D
housing projects
Where
Rican / Blacks
Johnny Pacheco / Wilson Pickett
Transistor
the radio night
Across the Domino sugar
sign
Red Neon on stage
It's the edge of Brooklyn

From heaven windows
megalopolis light
That's the picture
Into a lizard mind
Below the working
class jumps like frogs
Parrots with new raincoats
Swinging canes of bamboo
Like third legs
Strollers of cool flow
A didy-bop keeping step

time with the finest
Marching through
Red bricks aglow

Hebrew prayers
inside metals
Rolled into walls
Tenement relic
living in Museum
Home driven carts
arrive with the morning
slicing through the
curtains
Along with a Polish
English
Barking peaches and melons
The ice man sells
his hard water
Cut into blocks
Buildings swallowing
coals through their
Basement mouth

Where did the mountains
go
The immigrants ask
The place where houses
and objects went back
In history and entered
The roots of plants
And become eternal again
Now the plaster of Paris
The ears of the walls
The first utterances
in Spanish
Recalled what was left
behind

People kept arriving
as the cane fields dried
They came like flying bushes
from another planet
which had pineapples for moons
Fruits popping out of luggage
The singers of lament

into the soul of Jacob Riis
The Bible tongues
Santa María
Into the Torah
La liturgical lai le lo le
A Spanish never seen
before
Inside the gypsies
Parading through
Warsaw ghetto
Lower East Side
Rabbinicals
Begin to vanish
into the economy
Left Loisaida
a skeleton
The works quarter

Orchard Street
garments
Falling off the torso
in motion down the avenue
It seems it could not hold
the cold back

The red Avenue B bus
disappearing down
The drain of Man
Hat on
Dissolving into the
pipes of lower Broadway
The Canals of streets
direct to factories

After Foresite Park
Is the begining of Italy
Florence inside Mott
Street windows
Palmero eyes of Angie

Criss crossing these
mazes I would arrive
At Lourdes home
With knishes she threw
next to red beans

Broome Street Hasidics
with Martian fur hats
Gone with their brims
Puerto Ricans with Pra
Pras
Atop faces with features
thrown out of some bag
Of universal racial
stew
Mississippi sharecroppers
through Avenue D black
Stories
All in exile from broken
Souths
The amapolas the daffodils
were cement tar and steel
Within architectural
gardens remembering
the agriculture of mountain
and field

From the guayava bushels
outside a town with a
Taíno name
I hear a whistle
In the aboriginal ear
With the ancient I
that saw Andalucía
Arrive on a boat
To distribute Moorish
eyes on the coast
Loisaida was faster
than the speed of light
A whirlpool within which
you had to grab on to something
It took off like a spauldine
hit by a blue broom stick
on 12th street
Winter time summer time
seasons of hallways
And roofs
Between pachanga and duwap
Thousands of Eddies and Carmens
Stars and tyrants
Now gone

From the temporary station of
desire and disaster
The windows sucked them up
The pavement turned out to
be a mouth
Urban vanishment
Illusion
Henry Roth
Call it Sleep.

energy

is
red beans
ray barretto
banging away
steam out the
radio
the five-stair
steps
is mofongo
cuchifrito stand
outside down
the avenue
that long hill
of a block
before the train
is pacheco
playing with
bleeding
blue lips

Lorna Dee Cervantes (1954–)

Beneath the Shadow of the Freeway

Beneath the Shadow of the Freeway is perhaps the best-known poem of Cervantes's collection *Emplumada* (1981). In this poem, Cervantes explores the intergenerational lives of three women—grandmother, mother, and narrative speaker—with regard to their relationship with the men in their lives, and how they deal with their own sense of identity and independence. While the grandmother has endured twenty-five years of marriage to a man who tried to kill her, she has become independent and trusts "only what she builds with her own hands." The mother advises the lyric speaker to not "count on nobody." But the speaker has learned to trust her own instincts both with what she builds with her own hands and about men. The many bird images in the poem and throughout the book symbolize freedom as well as the ability to sing. Other poems in *Emplumada* deal with social issues, identity, and the difficulties of writing. Born in California, Cervantes has been the publisher of Mango Press and teaches creative writing at the University of Colorado. (TDR)

Further reading: Lorna Dee Cervantes, *Emplumada* (Pittsburgh: University of Pittsburgh Press, 1981), *From the Cables of Genocide: Poems on Love and Hunger* (Houston, Arte Público Press, 1991).

1
Across the street—the freeway,
blind worm, wrapping the valley up
from Los Altos to Sal Si Puedes.
I watched it from my porch
unwinding. Every day at dusk
as Grandma watered geraniums
the shadow of the freeway lengthened.

2
We were a woman family:
Grandma, our innocent Queen;
Mama, the Swift Knight, Fearless Warrior.
Mama wanted to be Princess instead.
I know that. Even now she dreams of taffeta
and foot-high tiaras.

Myself: I could never decide.
So I turned to books, those staunch, upright men.
I became Scribe: Translator of Foreign Mail,
interpreting letters from the government, notices
of dissolved marriages and Welfare stipulations.
I paid the bills, did light man-work, fixed faucets,
insured everything
against all leaks.

3
Before rain I notice seagulls.
They walk in flocks,
cautious across lawns: splayed toes,
indecisive beaks. Grandma says
seagulls mean storm.
In California in the summer,
mockingbirds sing all night.
Grandma says they are singing for their nesting wives.
"They don't leave their families
borrachando."

She likes the ways of birds,
respects how they show themselves
for toast and a whistle.

She believes in myths and birds.
She trusts only what she builds
with her own hands.

4
She built her house,
cocky, disheveled carpentry,
after living twenty-five years
with a man who tried to kill her.

Grandma, from the hills of Santa Barbara,
I would open my eyes to see her stir mush
in the morning, her hair in loose braids,
tucked close around her head
with a yellow scarf.

Mama said, "It's her own fault,
getting screwed by a man for that long.
Sure as shit wasn't hard."
soft she was soft

5
in the night I would hear it
glass bottles shattering the street
words cracked into shrill screams
inside my throat   a cold fear
as it entered the house in hard
unsteady steps   stopping at my door
my name   bathrobe   slippers
outside a 3 A.M. mist heavy
as a breath full of whiskey
stop   it go home   come inside
mama if he comes here again
I'll call the police

inside
a gray kitten   a touchstone
purring beneath the quilts
grandma stitched
from his suits

the patchwork singing
of mockingbirds

6
"You're too soft . . . always were.
You'll get nothing but shit.
Baby, don't count on nobody."
—a mother's wisdom.
Soft. I haven't changed,
maybe grown more silent, cynical
on the outside.

"O Mama, with what's inside of me
I could wash that all away. I could."

"But, Mama, if you're good to them
they'll be good to you back."

Back. The freeway is across the street.
It's summer now. Every night I sleep with a gentle man
to the hymn of mockingbirds,

and in time, I plant geraniums.
I tie up my hair into loose braids,
and trust only what I have built
with my own hands.

Pat Mora (1942–)

Legal Alien; Curandera

Pat Mora, perhaps the most productive of the contemporary Chicana writers, is the author of several collections of poetry, a novel, a collection of essays, a contemporary hagiography, and numerous children's books. A keen observer of details and surroundings, Mora draws on her fervent sense of place for her creative inspiration. The desert landscape of her native El Paso, its flora and fauna, climate, sounds, smells, and colors weave in and out of her writing. Blending nature with her intimate knowledge and respect for Mexican cultural customs, Mora's writing fills the page with rich imagery and enduring cultural traditions. The celebratory tone of her work is punctuated with critical social observations, compassionate renderings of the humble people, and portrayals of indomitable women. Mora is a Fellow of the National Endowment for the Arts and the Kellogg Foundation. She received the Pellicer Frost Binational Poetry Award, four Southwest Book Awards, and the Premio Aztlán. (EGB)

Further reading: Pat Mora, *Chants* (Houston: Arte Público Press, 1984), *Borders* (Houston: Arte Público Press, 1986), *Communion* (Houston: Arte Público Press, 1991), *Nepantla: Essays from the Land in the Middle* (Albuquerque: University of New Mexico Press, 1993), *Agua Santa/Holy Water* (Boston, 1995).

Legal Alien

Bi-lingual, Bi-cultural,
able to slip from "How's life?"
to *"Me'stan volviendo loca,"*
able to sit in a paneled office
drafting memos in smooth English,
able to order in fluent Spanish
at a Mexican restaurant,
American but hyphenated,
viewed by Anglos as perhaps exotic,
perhaps inferior, definitely different,
viewed by Mexicans as alien,
(their eyes say, "You may speak
Spanish but you're not like me")
an American to Mexicans
a Mexican to Americans
a handy token
sliding back and forth
between the fringes of both worlds
by smiling
by masking the discomfort
of being pre-judged
Bi-laterally.

Curandera

They think she lives alone
on the edge of town in a two-room house
where she moved when her husband died
at thirty-five of a gunshot wound
in the bed of another woman. The *curandera*
and house have aged together to the rhythm
of the desert.

She wakes early, lights candles before
her sacred statues, brews tea of *yerbabuena.*
She moves down her porch steps, rubs
cool morning sand into her hands, into her arms.
Like a large black bird, she feeds on
the desert, gathering herbs for her basket.

Her days are slow, days of grinding
dried snake into powder, of crushing

wild bees to mix with white wine.
And the townspeople come, hoping
to be touched by her ointments,
her hands, her prayers, her eyes.
She listens to their stories, and she listens
to the desert, always to the desert.

By sunset she is tired. The wind
strokes the strands of long gray hair,
the smell of drying plants drifts
into her blood, the sun seeps
into her bones. She dozes
on her back porch. Rocking, rocking.

At night she cooks chopped cactus
and brews more tea. She brushes a layer
of sand from her bed, sand which covers
the table, stove, floor. She blows
the statues clean, the candles out.
Before sleeping, she listens to the message
of the owl and the *coyote.* She closes her eyes
and breathes with the mice and snakes
and wind.

Alberto Alvaro Ríos (1952–)

Mi abuelo; Wet Camp; Nani

Ríos was born in Nogales, Arizona, close to the U.S.–Mexico border where, in his words, he could put "one foot in Mexico and one foot in the United States, at the same time." Born to a Mexican father and an English mother, he stood between cultures in a larger sense as well and this dimension of his early experience has had an influence on his writing. He received an MFA in creative writing from the University of Arizona and has taught in the Creative Writing Program (a program he was instrumental in founding) at Arizona State University since 1980. He has published several collections of poetry, two collections of short stories, and, most recently, a memoir. He is a recipient of a Guggenheim Fellowship and a fellowship from the National Endowment for the Arts. His first book of poems, *Whispering to Fool the Wind*, won the prestigious Academy of American Poets Walt Whitman Award in 1981. The following selections, which are taken from this book, illustrate his ability to transform seemingly the most casual language into images that deepen our understanding of personal and family relationships. Ríos draws from an oral culture that his father's family passed on to him. (ChT)

Further reading: Alberto Ríos, *Whispering to Fool the Wind* (New York: Sheep Meadow Press, 1982), *Capirotada: A Nogales Memoir* (Albuquerque: University of New Mexico Press, 1999).

Mi abuelo

Where my grandfather is is in the ground
where you can hear the future
like an Indian with his ear at the tracks.
A pipe leads down to him so that sometimes
he whispers what will happen to a man
in town or how he will meet the best
dressed woman tomorrow and how the best
man at her wedding will chew the ground
next to her. Mi abuelo is the man
who speaks through all the mouths in my house.
An echo of me hitting the pipe sometimes
to stop him from saying *my hair is a*
sieve is the only other sound. It is a phrase
that among all others is the best,
he says, and *my hair is a sieve* is sometimes
repeated for hours out of the ground
when I let him, which is not often.
An abuelo should be much more than a man
like you! He stops then, and speaks: *I am a man*
who has served ants with the attitude
of a waiter, who has made each smile as only
an ant who is fat can, and they liked me best,
but there is nothing left. Yet I know he ground
green coffee beans as a child, and sometimes
he will talk about his wife, and sometimes
about when he was deaf and a man
cured him by mail and he heard groundhogs
talking, or about how he walked with a cane
he chewed on when he got hungry.
At best, mi abuelo is a liar.
I see an old picture of him at nani's with an
off-white yellow center mustache and sometimes
that's all I know for sure. He talks best
about these hills, *slowest waves*, and where this man
is going, and I'm convinced his hair is a sieve,
that his fever is cooled now underground.
Mi abuelo is an ordinary man.
I look down the pipe, sometimes, and see a
ripple-topped stream in its best suit, in the ground.

Wet Camp

We have been here before, but we are lost.
The earth is black and the trees are bent

and broken and piled as if the game
of pick-up-sticks were ready and the children
hiding, waiting their useless turns.
The west bank of the river is burned
and the Santa Cruz has poured onto it.
The grit brown ponds
sit like dirty lilies in the black.
The afternoon is gone grazing
over the thin mountains.
The night is colder here without leaves.
Nothing holds up the sky.

Nani

Sitting at her table, she serves
the sopa de arroz to me
instinctively, and I watch her,
the absolute *mamá*, and eat words
I might have had to say more
out of embarrassment. To speak,
now-foreign words I used to speak,
too, dribble down her mouth as she serves
me albondigas. No more
than a third are easy to me.
By the stove she does something with words
and looks at me only with her
back. I am full. I tell her
I taste the mint, and watch her speak
smiles at the stove. All my words
make her smile. Nani never serves
herself, she only watches me
with her skin, her hair. I ask for more.

I watch the *mamá* warming more
tortillas for me. I watch her
fingers in the flame for me.
Near her mouth, I see a wrinkle speak
of a man whose body serves
the ants like she serves me, then more words
from more wrinkles about children, words
about this and that, flowing more
easily from these other mouths. Each serves
as a tremendous string around her,
holding her together. They speak
nani was this and that to me
and I wonder just how much of me

will die with her, what were the words
I could have been, was. Her insides speak
through a hundred wrinkles, now, more
than she can bear, steel around her,
shouting, then, What is this thing she serves?

She asks me if I want more.
I own no words to stop her.
Even before I speak, she serves.

PART III

The Literature of Immigration

CHAPTER 10

Encounters with the Modern City

José Martí (1853–1895)

Two Views of Coney Island (excerpt)

José Martí was not only a political revolutionary who devoted his life to the cause of Cuban independence (see second entry on Martí in this anthology). He was also a poet and a highly innovative prose writer. His first published book of poems, *Ismaelillo* (1882), is considered a landmark in the development of modern Hispanic literature and is seen as the first sign of the late nineteenth-century Spanish-American revolution in poetic language known as "Modernismo." Likewise, Martí's prose, ranging from his political discourses to art and literary criticism to journalistic chronicles, is characterized by its formal audacity. Restlessness, tension, speed, and syntactical unruliness are all terms that describe the structure and rhythm of his prose that in many ways echoes the electric pace of the hectic modern city. Martí's exile in the United States (1882–95), and particularly in New York, was crucial to his literary evolution. An avid reader of American literature and a fervent admirer of Emerson and Whitman, Martí's unique writing crystallizes in the creative encounter of two distinct literary traditions: the Spanish that nourished his early literary vocation, and the North American that comforted him in his exilic homelessness. *Two Views of Coney Island* (1881) is an early example of this symbiosis, as well as of the terror and fascination with which Martí approached the experience of modern urban culture. The transformation of traditional moral values, the sense of anonymity amidst the mesmerizing presence of the crowds, the draining of one's vital energies by the sensual dynamics of the city, and the emergence of the concept of leisure and incipient mass culture—represented below by the recently opened Coney Island amusement park—are all themes that appear in these insightful pieces. (ALO)

Further reading: José Martí, *Major Poems: A Bilingual Edition,* ed. Philip S. Foner, trans. Elinor Randall (New York: Holmes and Meier, 1982); *On Art and Literature: Critical Writings*, ed. Philip S. Foner, trans. Elinor Randall, Luis A. Baralt, Juan de Onís, and Roslyn Held Foner (New York: Monthly Review Press, 1982).

Trans.: ER

1

Nothing in the history of mankind has ever equaled the marvelous prosperity of the United States. Time will tell whether deep roots are lacking here; whether the ties of sacrifice and common sorrow that bind some people together are stronger than those of common interests; whether this colossal nation carries in its entrails ferocious, tremendous elements; whether a lack of that femininity which is the origin of the artistic sense and the complement of nationality, hardens and corrupts the heart of this wonderful country.

For the present, the fact is that never has a happier, a jollier, a better equipped, more compact, more jovial, and more frenzied multitude living anywhere on earth, while engaged in useful labors, created and enjoyed greater wealth, nor covered rivers and seas with more gaily dressed ships, nor overflown lovely shores, gigantic wharves, and brilliant, fantastic promenades with more bustling order, more childlike glee.

United States newspapers are full of hyperbolic descriptions of the unusual beauty and singular attraction of one of these summer resorts, with crowds of people, numerous luxurious hotels, crossed by an elevated railroad, studded with gardens, kiosks, small theaters, saloons, circuses, tents, a multitude of carriages, picturesque assemblies, vending wagons, stands, and fountains.

French newspapers echo its fame. From all over the Union come legions of fearless ladies and country beaux to admire the splendid scenery, lavish wealth, blinding variety, Herculean push, and surprising aspect of famous Coney Island, an island which four years ago was nothing but an abandoned heap of earth and is now an ample place for rest, seclusion, or entertainment for the one hundred thousand New Yorkers who visit its shores daily.

It is composed of four hamlets joined by carriage, tram, and steam railroads. One is Manhattan Beach, where, in the dining room of one hotel, four thousand people can comfortably sit at the same time; another, Rockaway, has arisen, as Minerva arose with lance and helmet, armed with steamers, squares, piers, murmuring orchestras, hotels as big as cities, nay, as nations; still another, less important, takes its name from its hotel, the vast, heavy Brighton. But the most attractive place on the island is neither far-off Rockaway, nor monotonous Brighton, nor aristocratic, stuffy Manhattan Beach, but Cable, smiling Cable with its elevator, higher than Trinity Church steeple in New York, twice as high as the steeples of our Cathedral, to the top of which people are carried in a tiny, fragile cage to a dizzying height; Cable, with its two iron piers projecting on elegant piles three blocks into the sea, its Sea Beach Palace, now only a hotel, but which in the Philadelphia Fair was the famous Agricultural Building, transported to New York and reassembled as if by magic, without a piece missing, on the shores of Coney Island; Cable, with its fifty-cent museums where human monsters, freakish fish, bearded ladies, melancholy dwarfs, and rickety elephants, ballyhooed as the biggest elephants in the world, are shown; Cable with its one hundred orchestras, its lively dances, its battalions of baby carriages, its gigantic cow being perpetually milked, its fresh cider at twenty-five cents a glass, its countless couples of loving pilgrims which bring back to our lips García Gutiérrez's tender cries:

In pairs they go
Over the hillocks
The crested larks,
The turtle-doves

Cable, where families resort in search of wholesome, invigorating sea breezes instead of New York's foul and nauseating air; where poor mothers, as they open great lunch baskets with provisions for the whole family press against their breasts their unfortunate babes who seem consumed, emaciated, gnawed by that terrible summer sickness which mows down children as a sickle does wheat, *cholera infantum.*

Steamers come and go, trains whistle and smoke, leave and arrive emptying their serpent belly full of people on the shore. Women wear rented blue flannel suits and coarse straw hats which they tie under their chins; men in still simpler suits lead them to the sea, while barefooted children at the water's edge await the roaring breakers and run back when the waves are about to wet them, disguising their fear with laughter. Then, relieved of the smoldering heat of an hour ago, they charge, tirelessly, against the enemy, or, like marine butterflies, they brave the fresh waves, play at filling each other's pails with shovelfuls of burning sand, or, after bathing—imitating in this the behavior of grown-up people of both sexes who do not heed the censure and surprise of those who feel as we do in our countries—they lie on the sand and allow themselves to be buried, patted down, kneaded into the burning sand. This practice, considered a wholesome exercise, lends itself to a certain superficial, vulgar, and boisterous intimacy to which these prosperous people seem so inclined.

But the most surprising thing there is not the way they go bathing, nor the children's cadaverous faces, nor the odd headdresses and incomprehensible attire of those girls noted for their extravagance, their eccentricity, and their inordinate inclinations to merrymaking, nor the spooners, nor the bathing booths, nor the operas that are sung at café tables in the guise of *Edgar* and *Romeo*, and *Lucia* and *Juliet*, nor the grimaces and screams of Negro minstrels, surely not like the Scottish minstrels, alas!, nor the majestic beach, nor the soft, serene sun. The surprising thing there is the size, the quantity, the sudden outburst of human activity, that immense valve of pleasure open to an immense people, those dining rooms which, seen from afar, look like bivouacked armies, those roads which, from two miles away, do not seem like roads but like carpets of heads, that daily outpouring of a portentous people upon a portentous beach, that mobility, that change of form, that fighting spirit, that push, that feverish rivalry of wealth, that monumental appearance of the whole place which makes a bathing establishment worthy of competing with the majesty of the country that supports it, the sea that caresses it and the sky that crowns it, that swelling tide, that dumbfounding, overwhelming, steady, frenzied expansiveness, and that simplicity in the marvelous; *that* is the surprising thing.

Other peoples—we among them—live devoured by a sublime inner demon who pushes us tirelessly on in search of an ideal of love or glory. When we hold the measure of the ideal we were after, delighted as though we were holding an eagle, a new quest makes us restless, a new ambition spurs us, a new aspiration heads us toward a new vehement desire, and out of the captive eagle emerges a rebel, free butterfly, daring us to follow it, chaining us to her circuitous flight.

Not so these tranquil souls, only disturbed by the craving of owning a fortune. Our eyes scan the reverberating beaches, we go in and out of those halls as vast as pampas, we climb to the peak of those colossal structures as tall as mountains. Promenaders in comfortable chairs by the seaside fill their lungs with that bracing, benign air. But a melancholy sadness, as it were, takes hold of the men of our Latin American countries who live here, for they seek each other in vain and no matter how much first impressions may have lured their senses, charmed their eyes, dazzled and puzzled their reason, they are finally possessed by the anguish of solitude, while the homesickness for a superior spiritual world invades them and grieves them. They feel like stray sheep without their mothers or their shepherd. Tears may or may not flow to their eyes, but their astounded souls break in bitter weeping, because this great land is devoid of spirit.

What a bustle! What flow of money! What facilities for pleasure! What absolute absence of all sadness or visible poverty! Everything is in the open air; the noisy groups, the vast dining halls, that peculiar courtship of North Americans into which enter almost none of the elements which make up the modest, tender, exalted love found in our lands. The theater, the photographic studio, the bathing booths; everything in the open. Some get weighed, for to North Americans to weigh a pound more or less is a matter of positive joy or real grief; for fifty cents, others receive from a stout German woman an envelope containing their fortune; still others, with incomprehensible delight, drink certain unsavory mineral waters out of tall, narrow glasses like mortar shells.

Some ride in roomy carriages from Manhattan to Brighton at the soft twilight time. One fellow shores his boat, in which he had been rowing with his smiling girlfriend, who holds on to his shoulder as she jumps, frolicking like a child, onto the bustling beach. A group of people admire an artist who cuts silhouettes out of black paper of whoever wishes to have this kind of portrait of himself and glues them on white cards. Another group watch a woman in a tiny shop less than a yard wide and praise her skill at fashioning strange flowers out of fish skins. Others laugh uproariously when one fellow succeeds in hitting a Negro on the nose with a ball, a poor Negro who, for a miserable wage, sticks his head out of a hole in a cloth and is busied day and night eluding with grotesque movements the balls pitched at him. Bearded, venerable citizens ride gravely on wooden tigers, hippogriffs, sphinxes, and boa constrictors that turn like horses around a central pole where a band of would-be musicians play unharmonious sonatas. The less well-to-do eat crabs and oysters on the beach or pies and meats on tables that some large hotels offer free for such purpose. The wealthier people lavish large sums on fuchsin infusions passed off as wine and on strange, massive dishes which our palates, fond of the artistic and light, would certainly reject. To these people eating is a matter of quantity; to ours, of quality.

And this lavishing, this bustle, these crowds, this astounding anthill lasts from June to October, from morning till midnight, without respite, without interruption, without change.

What a beautiful spectacle at night! True enough, a thinking man is surprised at seeing so many married women without their husbands and so many mothers strolling by the humid seaside, concerned with their pleasure, and heedless of the piercing wind that might harm the squalid constitution of the babies they hold against their shoulder.

But no city offers a more splendid view than Cable Beach by night. More lights shine at night than heads could be seen by day. When descried from a distance offshore the four towns shine in the darkness as though the stars of heaven had suddenly gathered and fallen to the sea.

The electric lights that bathe with magic brightness the approaches to the hotels, the lawns, the concert pavilions, even the beach whose every grain of sand can be counted, seem from afar like restless sprites, like blithe, diabolic spirits romping about the sickly gas jets, the garlands of red lanterns, the Chinese globes, the Venetian chandeliers. One can read everywhere, as though it were day: newspapers, billboards, announcements, letters. All is heavenly: the orchestras, the dances, the clamor, the rumble of the waves, the noise of men, the ringing of laughter, the air's caresses, the loud calls, the rapid trains, the stately carriages, until the time comes to return home. Then, as a monster emptying its entrails into the hungry gullet of another monster, the colossal, crushed, compact crowds rush to catch the trains, which, bursting under their weight, seem to pant in their ride through solitude, until they deliver their motley load onto gigantic ships. These latter, livened by harps and violins, take the exhausted tourists to the piers of New York and distribute them in the thousand cars and along the thousand tracks that like veins of steel traverse the sleeping city.

Francisco Gonzalo "Pachín" Marín (1863–1897)

New York from Within: One Aspect of Its Bohemian Life

Pachín Marín was the pressman for the Puerto Rican and Cuban revolutionary groups who resided in New York at the end of the nineteenth century. As a political activist, journalist, and poet, Pachín Marín was forced into exile from his native Puerto Rico, and penned some of the most famous poems of exile, works that became foundational to Puerto Rican letters. However, his residence in New York also led him to contemplate the life of Hispanic immigrants. *New York from the Within* is part of a group of *crónicas* he published in New York's *La Gaceta del Pueblo*, and is considered one of Pachín Marín's most important works. Filled with irony with regard to the suffering in the metropolis by all humans, he describes a city overflowing with difficulty for the newcomer, but also one that beckons to men of little or no ambition, picaresque characters who prey on the immigrants—themes that are all too frequent in immigrant literature. As in much of the literature of immigration written in Spanish, Pachín Marín's *crónica* satirizes social customs and highlights linguistic conflicts. In his *crónicas*, as in his poems, his patriotism and political ideals, shared with his collaborators in the press and in politics, José Martí and Sotero Figueroa, are quite visible. (CV)

Further reading: Francisco Gonzalo Marín, *Romances* (New York, 1892), *En la arena* (New York, 1898).

Trans.: LPG

If you present yourself in this metropolis in the enviable guise of a tourist, and bring, as it is customary, suitcases stuffed with Mexican *soles* or shimmering gold doubloons, things will naturally go very well for you, my amiable reader. But you will not have known New York from within, as it really is, with its grand institutions and prodigious marvels.

To attain an intimate knowledge of this elephant of modern civilization, you will need to set foot to the ground without a quarter to your name, though you may bring a world of hope in your heart.

Indeed! To arrive in New York, check into a comfortable hotel, go out in an elegant carriage pulled by monumental horses every time an occasion presents itself, visit the theaters, museums, *cafés*, chantants, cruise the fast-flowing East River, lulled by the ebb and flow and murmur of the waves, visit Brooklyn Bridge—that frenzy of North American initiative—, and the Statue of Liberty—that tour de force of French pride—, pay twenty dollars or more to hear La Pattissi sing, as she is doing now, at the Metropolitan Opera House, frequent, in short, the places where elegant people of good taste gather, people who can afford to spend three or four hundred dollars in one evening for the sole pleasure of looking at a dancer's legs, oh!, all that is very agreeable, very delicious, and very . . . singular; but it doesn't give you the exact measure of this city which is, at one and the same time, an emporium of sweeping riches and rendezvous-point for all the penniless souls of America.

The convenient—if you prefer, the reasonable—thing to do, is for you to present yourself at one of the vast New York docks without even a semblance of resources; ready and agile as a student and as hungry as a schoolteacher. You have already realized your most cherished dream; you are overjoyed because since childhood your happiness has centered on great voyages . . . What! You don't speak any English? Are you overwhelmed by the incessant howling of the locomotives, the vertiginous agitation of the factories, and the vista of a million people hurrying past, trampling each other, yet going on their way as if nothing had happened? Well, don't you stop. Let's walk, walk! Here in New York time is sacred, since it is the most genuine representation of money. Don't stand there in perplexed contemplation of an eleven- or twelve-story building whose highest windows seem to look down on you as if mocking your smallness. Time is urgent. Walk hurriedly, as if you had most-important business at hand. One must find a friend, a friend or countryman, at all cost. Where? How? Don't you know how? Well, by asking everyone. Come on; try it out on that gigantic policeman looking at you so tenaciously. Throw care to the wind and plunge in. Gentleman, would you be so kind as to point out where I can find a friend . . . How stupid of me! Now I get it, this man can't speak any Spanish . . . You're beginning to grow sad. You see no familiar faces. My God!, you exclaim. I'm a wretch! Some identical incidents read in novels dart past your imagination with the speed of lightning. Jean Valjean, Jean Valjean . . . If the same thing that happened to Jean Valjean were to happen to you . . .

If there is a civilized country capable of astonishing the most indifferent and stoic, the United States, or better yet, New York, is the place.

Its buildings, its portentous architectural works, its elevated railways fantastically crisscrossing through the air, its streets—broad arteries roamed by inexhaustible hordes from all countries of the world—, its parks—austerely and aristocratically designed—, its steam engines, its powerful journalistic institutions, its treacherously beautiful women, its wonders, all instill, at first sight, a deep malaise on the foreigner, because it occurs to one that these large cities, deafening in their progress, are like the mouth of a horrible monster constantly busy simultaneously swallowing and vomiting human beings; and it is amidst these great noises and grand centers that our soul finds itself increasingly besieged by that horrendous malady called sadness, and assumes the somber character of isolation and silence . . .

For the poor in money but rich in ambition, arriving here in the circumstances outlined above, however, New York is a great house of asylum where all who believe, more or less vigorously, in the virtue and sanctity of work, ultimately find their niche.

Are you very poor? Have you not succeeded yet in finding something on which to invest your talents and energies? Are you feeling the sting of hunger? Are you cold?

Don't distress yourself. Don't despair in any way. Do you see that establishment on the corner whose door continuously opens and closes? Well, it is commonly known here by the name of Lager Beer Hall. Have you been inside? Such cleanliness and tidiness everywhere! Isn't it true that places like these are better decorated than the presidential palaces of our republics? But we shouldn't waste time in useless ramblings, not even in here. Take that table nearby; throw five cents on it; it's a tip in advance; don't go believing anything else. Pay attention now. In the first place, they bring you a big mug of beer, fresh, foamy, poured on smooth glass. Drink it. In this country, beer is a necessity; it fortifies and warms limbs numbed by the cold. But . . . don't be a fool! Take care. Let us, before draining the contents of the glass, eat ham, beef, sausage, cheese, etc. That stuff you gobble down for starters. At least that's what gastronomy calls it. Well! Good heavens! But principles be gone! You must eat it all. Here comes the waiter; this time he's bringing you a succulent soup preceded by its wafting aromas. Eat until you've had your fill: I am your host, you honorable Maecenas . . .

Are you pleased? Yes? Let's not waste time, then, take a toothpick, light this cigarette I'm offering you and . . . onto the street.

"But, sir, didn't you offer to pay the check? We can't leave without paying . . . I am an honest man . . ."

"Come now, blockhead. The sum of what you have gobbled down amounts to five cents. You have already paid . . ."

And after leaving the place, satiated and proud of our find, forgetting the novelistic tortures that made Jean Valjean suffer from such acute hunger, then we recall the real New York, the wise and good New York, hospitable and gay; and we laugh our heads off at the admirers of the Brooklyn Bridge and the Statue of Liberty, of the elevated railway and gigantic buildings, of all the great institutions of this surprising republic, since, never fear, I doubt that there is in this country of inventions and colossal enterprises anything as grand, as portentous, as human as those establishments where for five coppers they feed the hungry and give drink to the thirsty.

Ample reason has my philosopher friend, who, every day, upon returning from heaven-knows-where with an enormous toothpick in his hand, says to me:

"Oh! A Lager Beer Hall is indeed an institution."

Nicanor Bolet Peraza (1838–1906)

Fourth Missive

Published in New York in 1900, *Cartas gredalenses* adopts the epistolary genre to compare life in the United States and Latin America. Silvestre Montañés, the main character, writes to Don Frutos del Campo, who has stayed in El Gredal (a fictive country that could be anywhere in Latin America). In their correspondence, Silvestre Montañés criticizes, with humor, the way Americans run their country, describing details such as their meticulous lives ruled by the weather and issues of great transcendence, such as women's right to vote. In this sense, the six letters that compose this text, especially the *Cuarta Misiva*, portray the reality of the immigrant who gravitates between two worlds, making poignant observations on the different political cultures of the United States and Latin America. It is the immigrant who laughs, knowing that in the United States "todo marcha al pelo, y por allá todo marcha al palo" (everything functions perfectly, but over there [in Latin America] everything is always screwed up). Nicanor Bolet Peraza was a writer, journalist, soldier, and politician who lived his last fifteen years in New York, directing the Hispanic periodicals *La Revista Ilustrada* and *Las Tres Américas*. Bolet Peraza's columns were widely circulated through Hispanic newspapers in the United States. (KW)

Further reading: Nicanor Bolet Peraza, *Cartas gredalenses* (New York: Las Novedades, 1900), *Impresiones de viaje* (New York: Las Novedades, 1906).

Trans.: KDM

New York: May 1894

Mr. Fruits of the Field, Esquire

Dearest Friend of Fondest Memory:
Although it will not be long before I can greet you with a hearty embrace, the good Lord and salty sea permitting, I write these few lines to tell you that of late I have done nothing more than think of you, my good Mr. Fruits, upon seeing our flora here so suddenly bursting with life, with the arrival of Spring, after the poor trees had spent the whole winter like brushwood, without even a leaf to protect them. And I say that seeing them has reminded me of you, my compatriot, because they bring me a memory of that green suit that you wear as though you had just been dressed by little cloistered nuns.

One can really hear the grass grow here, my friend. Here one can go to bed one night surrounded by trees as naked as prison brooms, and spend the night hearing the popping of the buds that bloom, so that when one wakes up one finds the trees all properly dressed and uniformed in green, some even crowned by flowers. Anyone would say that we even have steam engines here to move the seasons.

What is truly a fact, my dear Mr. Fruits, is that these folks have everything arranged and figured out as if this were a matter for stage machinery. This is an immense machine, nothing more, despite the fact they tell you it is a great Republic. What Republic are they talking about?! I have studied this what-d'ye-call-it and can assure you that it is nothing more than legally draped despotism, where not even a fly takes flight without there being an article of law or an ordinance that says the fly can fly. What more do you want? Even the temperature is regulated by these Yankee gentlemen in whatever way they like. You know very well, my compatriot, that back home we say: "In summer carry your blanket, in winter you'll know what to do." Because there is true liberty amongst us; no government would do what Washington does: have some idlers employed who do nothing more than prepare weather reports, which they declare are authoritative, and then publish them in daily newspapers, forecasting cold or wind for a certain time, or heat, or a storm.

And, that's all; it is carried out to the letter, like when in Gredal the Prefect receives a little order from the President in this tone: "Comrade Ovejón; slap the reins on so-and-so, and send him to me. It's not convenient for me to have him living in that town." And he does it like there's no tomorrow.

That's just the way it is here. The difference is that everything goes ahead by the book, and everything back home is by the blow.

Notwithstanding, it might be the reason why I am what they call a stick in the mud, but I much prefer our way of killing fleas as regards liberty. You have no more than to see that there the Almanac is an authority to which one turns a blind eye, and its rules are like our constitutions, that is, like a religious primer, just for children. I keep going on about the Almanac. Back home some man tells us that there ought to be four different seasons a year. Naturally. The principle of change, yes sir. But, what do we get from change, what good comes to us because of this wonder? And there you have it, my compatriot. We long for an eternal Spring, and once that idea is stuck in our brains, no one can get it out. That is why you will see that all of us back home want to perpetuate ourselves, when we have a budding, new government in our hands.

Here, in this land of lambs, the opposite happens; here, when one says law, even if it is a lynching-type law, everybody respects it and submits to it. My compatriot, it is just that these people have no blood. They just have cold water in their veins. Let's get to the point. The Almanac says that Winter ends on March 20th; and there is nothing more to it. People fold up Winter so that Spring may come. There is no: "Let me have just one more drink." No: "The first one doesn't count, but this next one will." No: "Yesterday was pretend but today it's for real." It is all useless, my compatriot, because that very same day, the thermometers, which are also somewhat fearful of the law, begin to rise, which is the way they have of saying that they are not in favor of a perpetual Winter or anybody.

So that you might be able to form a more complete idea of just how stubborn these people are, when it comes to laws and constitutions, it would suffice for you to see how they topple governments. You would split your sides laughing. Here, voting is taken very seriously; and he who gets the most ballots is the one who will sit in the president's chair. I was just asking around a few days ago why they didn't carry out their elections with cannons blazing, like us, and everybody answered quite horrified: "Oh! What about the Constitution? And this canon and that canon?" Man, get rid of that which in English you call canons; in Spanish we call them cannons.

Nevertheless, I figure that this doll's house wants to go bad. And if not, you should see what the women here are up to: they want to vote in elections, just like men.

May God who is everywhere, even among all women, forgive me. Last night, my cousin took me to a meeting that almost turned into a riot, because some women were in favor of using pants while others were in favor of bloomers.

A very finicky and refined woman spoke a few words that my cousin translated for me: "I believe we should not vote. This business of voting is just a new burden that is going to be placed on women, who already have enough to do with taking care of the house, of the children, and of the master of the house, who gets furious every time the soup is short on salt or the roast is overcooked. What do we need more people to vote for? We do not need great numbers at the voting booths; we just need for the few who vote to be of quality. Too many cooks spoil the broth."

So you see, my compatriot Mr. Fruits, that diminutive blonde was explaining herself. And I agree with her. That whole idea that every living being should participate in government is repulsive to me. But the little Yankee did not stop there. She continued by saying: "When the master of the house votes, it should be understood that he votes for the whole family, even for the cat. We women, from the kitchen, say amen, and that's all. Why go to the assemblies and repeat the same litanies? What if while we're out playing men one of the children breaks his head or the stew burns?

"Man and woman," the little Yankee fighter continued, "were made by God. He knew what He was doing."

All of these reasons seemed like gems to me, and I almost stuck my two cents' worth in as well, to talk about that business of "a woman wed, a broken leg, and home," or the other one about "a woman and her labors, no farther than the neighbors." But a very corpulent, good looking brunette, with a shortly cropped, mannish haircut, began to unleash her fury, and didn't let me: "Don't come to me with that story that we're trying to impose a new burden in asking you to vote. And if suffrage is a burden, why did the Negroes ask for it and why was it given to them?" Do you see, my compatriot, how this one began her spurring? "That would mean," she continued, "that those who support Negro rights are not of goodwill, and that what they were asking for were not rights but something more like a job. Come on, ladies, this business about a burden seems ridiculous to me. I also think that the idea that we only need a select few to vote is rather funny. That solution smacks of monarchy to me. In republics, the many should vote, no matter whom it bothers. It makes me feel like saying that the vote should go only to those who understand and not to the ignorant. Come on, that would be something. And now I say that my cook should stay home in the kitchen while I go take his place at the voting booth. No sir: even the dishwasher can elect a government. The lady of the house can't vote. How will she know how to exercise her right, if that knowledge belongs only to trousers, even if they are mended?!"

What do you say, my compatriot, Mr. Fruits? The little dickens could kick one in the shins. I, who had bet ten to one on the feisty female, regretted I had done so.

Here is another voice out of the riffraff: "It has been said that the Divine gave different destinies to man and woman. As for myself, I have never spoken to God on this particular, and very much doubt that the lady who just spoke has done so either, to confirm this."

Boy, do these women come up with stuff, my compatriot. I assure you that they are akin to the devil, and I don't know what hand to play with them. I hear one of them and think that she makes all the sense in the world; I hear another, and then I think that that one makes all the sense.

And now I ask: Why all this nonsense about voting, my compatriot and friend Mr. Fruits? To split hairs, to further ruin this Republic? I have told them once and again; I have told them at public auction, like our friend and teacher in Gredal has said. I have told these Yankees that they should learn from us, that back home no citizen is yanked from his job so that he might stick a little piece of paper in a box, and that from that box should spring our elected president, as if he were the grand prize in a lottery raffle. "Look here," I say to them, "in my country, all of that is done by the government, and good or bad, we live on, the people working and the government governing, and that is a true republic. Like that of Anton Perulero, in which everybody looks out for himself.

And you should see, my compatriot, the looks these guys give me when I suggest some simple and good things to them, that they find far out, as if they'd heard them by telephone from the moon. "Doesn't everybody vote over there?" they ask, with great naturalness, as if they were asking me: "Don't turtles fly there?" And I answer: "When it comes to voting, we all vote. I, for example, without going any further, and you can attest to this, my compatriot, vote for my stubble field, I vote for my four cows, I vote for my roadhouse at the entrance to the town. And even the dead vote, even though they don't receive any votes themselves." Watch out, my compatriot; I have become a master of words. These gentlemen keep asking me in astonishment: "Don't citizens sign up to vote?" To which I reply: "Of course they sign their names on lists. The government requests that the funeral home provide them with the names of people they invite to funerals, and all they have to do is copy them. Each one of those is a vote for the government's candidate; and if the funeral home lists are not enough, they take the calendar and start taking Christian names from it, to which they add names taken from objects for last names. For example (and here I thought it would be appropriate to mention you), they write the name Fruits, which is the name of a saint, and they add it to del Campo, which is the name of a silvan thing. And that's how they go about baptizing voters, with names taken from fruits, woods, animals; in that way the president is elected by the populace without the people having had to worry about said election, because those who have truly voted are the Pines, Oaks, Pineapples, Apples, Rocks, Lions and the rest of the inanimate people or quadrupeds."

How wide those good Yankees open their mouths when I explain to them the republican system with which we have achieved our happiness until now and that will take us into a future of good fortune!

I have a great idea, Field, my friend, and it is to apply myself seriously to learning English. Once I can overcome my linguistic limitations, that don't allow me to explain myself, I will be become a speaker, like the ones here, who make a lot of money giving so-called speeches. I would make a fortune speaking about the true republic, the Gredal Republic. I just need to be able to speak. That way these pale faces could see what a real republic with blood in its eye is. And they'd better not come to me saying that what we learned about republics we read in books; because the truth be told, with no bragging intended: Our things, my compatriot, are not written down.

I will soon have the pleasure of embracing you, my compatriot and friend,
Silvestre Montañés

Alirio Díaz Guerra (1862–1925)

Lucas Guevara (excerpt)

Born in Sagamosa, Colombia, into a wealthy and privileged family, Alirio Díaz Guerra was initiated into politics early in life, perhaps because his father was a government official. From his early days, as well, he published poetry and, in 1884, began publishing a newspaper in opposition to the government. By 1885, he had become part of a liberal revolution, which ultimately resulted in his exile in Venezuela, where once again he became part of the established government. In Venezuela, he became involved in revolutionary activities, and was forced into exile in 1895. This time, he took up permanent residence in New York, where he spent the last thirty years of his life. Initiated as a romantic poet in Colombia and Venezuela, Díaz Guerra began writing prose fiction as an immigrant to the United States and authored the earliest novel of immigration that researchers have been able to recover to date: *Lucas Guevara* (1914). In this early novel, Díaz Guerra constructed most of the literary formulas that would come to typify this genre: the coming to the United States full of high expectations for success in the opportunities offered by the great society only to be disillusioned in the end; the insistence on return to the homeland; the description of the iniquitous and oppressive metropolis; the positing of U.S. culture in opposition to Hispanic culture; the slice-of-life portrayal of the underclass populated by picaresque characters; and so on. In the selection below, the narrator moralistically depicts, with lurid detail, the evils of New York's Bowery, the infamous port of entry for many immigrants. Díaz Guerra continued to write and publish poetry throughout his life, in book form as well as in periodicals in New York, Panama, Colombia, and Venezuela. He authored a second novel, *May*, also set in New York and dealing with social issues; unfortunately, it has been lost to posterity. (NK)

Further reading: Alirio Díaz Guerra, *Lucas Guevara* (Houston: Arte Público Press, 2001).

Trans.: ECB

IV

If not the first, then one of the first terms heard by the uninitiated when arriving to New York City is the Bowery.

The Bowery is the name of one of the precincts in the great metropolis, understood to be on the East side, between the Brooklyn Bridge up to Eighth Street, that is to say constituting a span of nearly two miles.

The Bowery is really a commercial district; but, at the same time, it is a neighborhood in which hundreds of families seek refuge or asylum, some directly or indirectly related to the merchants who have established their places of business on the ground floors of their buildings, while others agglomerate in those one-of-a-kind constructions known as tenement houses, which have achieved one of the century's greatest exploits: the enslavement of freedom or vice-versa.

The Bowery is a cosmopolitan region to the nth degree. To provide it with its own characteristic vitality and flavor, they draw from the large Chinese community which populates Mott Street and from even the most eccentric models of the Hebrew race; in addition, among the former and the latter, there are subjects of every monarchy and citizens of every democracy in the world.

If some Machiavellian or ridiculous fop were to appear in the city streets, one could trace his origins to the Bowery's vicinities; if a heinous crime were to be committed, it is more than likely that one of the accomplices pertains to the hierarchy of the Bowery's denizens; if one wishes to obtain cheap merchandise—almost always of the most wretched quality—the Ciceros suggest that one searches the Bowery; if an unlucky soul has only a few bits to attend to life's basic necessities, the Bowery offers him room and board at the level of his financial standing: living quarters with all of the distinctive features that befit a buffoon, and sustenance which is the by-product of chemical concoctions and residuum from gastronomic institutions of only the highest caliber; if one speaks of Eves condemned to the four walls of a jail cell by the police's divine providence, one would not be mistaken imagining that they are the Bowery's own tempting sirens; if one solicits a tight-fisted Pharisee or savvy loan-shark, they can be found by the hundreds in the Bowery; if one is in search of the comic, the dramatic, or even the tragic, between the Bowery's cross streets and cross-hairs one can light upon the merry-Andrew who pesters with all of his drunken pleas, down to the pauper who drives people insane with all of his pan-handling; charlatans live there having purchased at the lowest price possible the right to place a plaque in their office window advertising the practice of their medical profession; there are the worst sorts of pettifoggers to be found there, from those who entrust themselves with looking for young brides then availing themselves to a thousand stratagems in order to break up happy homes, up to those who, without any scruples whatsoever, would send their own family members to prison for the right price; there are apothecaries who, without batting an eyelash, would sell all kinds of drugs and would not hesitate to perform illegal obstetric operations in the back rooms of their pharmacies; there are hotels which hire out beds to those corrupt of body and soul, upon whose straw mattresses, rarely ventilated or ever tidied, have sprawled out consummate drunks, consumptive fools, scrofulous syphilitics and herpetics; and, during the day, they practice their right to make themselves at home in a hotel lobby, chatting or snoring away, smoking a pipe or reading lascivious magazines; treachery, deception, gambling, greed, and the premeditation of crime have all found their place in the Bowery.

It's a two-faced coin: which shows certain features during the day, but a totally different side at night.

It's a neighborhood that never rests; everyone works while the sun is still out; but no one sleeps under the cover of night. One can feel the heat of the feverish marketplace from dawn till the last bloody tinge of dusk; all of the devices of progress and ambition come into play; the buyer must match wits with the vendor; like two adversaries that show mutual respect upon encountering one another, they inspect each other from head to toe; they evaluate and analyze each other, then prepare to strike and defend. The consumer is almost always bound to lose, for it is impossible to compete with such an entrenched opponent capable of such a powerful attack. Foreigners who stroll the streets of the Bowery seem to have their nationality painted across their faces, and for as forewarned and intelligent as they may be, they are doomed to submission; they may be able to prevent the countless tugs at their shirts and clever tricks to overcome them, but they will never be able to make it out of the Bowery with their wallets unscathed.

And if they do not fall at the hands of the daring con artists who bewitch and beguile, it is difficult to escape from the despicable women of ill repute or the pickpockets which inundate the sidewalks and occupy the bars.

The merchants begin to cloud one's vision and test one's mettle and innocence by promising the best prices on countless goods which they exhibit in their shop windows. The unwary becomes enraptured with the display model; he inspects it; he compares it to similar items he has seen in the Broadway and Sixth Avenue boutiques; and he discovers that they are exactly the same, but with the added bonus that in the Bowery it can be purchased for a quarter of the original price. He enters the store; he inquires about the merchandise; five or six salesmen surround the client; they inform him that, regrettably, they sold the last remaining model just a moment ago and that they couldn't possibly hand over the one on display; however, they compel him to peruse a thousand other items, until he becomes so flabbergasted, that, in a fit of exasperation, he escapes further torture by purchasing his surrendered freedom for its weight in gold.

And that's how they live in the Bowery: at the expense of the impotence of the hapless souls who frequent the vicinity and who, when they least expect it, are humiliated and defeated after an intense battle with the swarm of swindlers who, for some incomprehensible reason, enjoy the benefits which the Mercantile Code bestows upon these so-called businessmen of the most impeccable moral character. However, the comedy of errors which makes up the Bowery in broad daylight cannot be compared in any way to the scenes which, in constant procession, cloak themselves under the black canopy of night. The little playhouses, which cost between ten to fifteen cents to enter, become saturated with spectators. Situated about vile tables, with foul smelling pipes stuffed full of Virginia tobacco and enormous pitchers of beer in front of them, half dazed workers mingle with thrill seekers, petty larcenists, audacious gents, and in the end, an army of suspicious individuals: magnificent models for artistic study, with flared nostrils, disheveled hair and beards, eyes that inspire fear, and mouths invigorated by contemptuous grins. And like nocturnal butterflies that flutter one by one around the light, those fiendish ladies of the night, the dregs of a social vice driven from the large civic centers onto the sordid alleyways, teem in these smoke filled saloons, satisfying themselves by catching a malicious glance over here, a sip of beer or a shot of whiskey over there, or even an unkept promise way over there. And while on stage, the dancers make all manner of pirouettes; the songbirds sing more and more off key; and the comedians lower themselves to performing the most obnoxious and vulgar routines. Cultural centers of this singular sort display gigantic posters smeared by shady artists in the doorway, hoping to pique the tourists' curiosity about what surprises he might find inside: but it so happens that these surprises do not exist; and if the curious sightseer, hurt or angered due to the money he has lost and the ridicule he has suffered, ventures to register any form of complaint, the owner will invite him to take a walk down to the end of a dark alley where he's sure to find what he's looking for; this is a situation which sound judgement will naturally avoid; so, the visitor is left with no other recourse than to retreat and to be content to return to contemplate the cartoon-like pictures which don the theater's entrance.

Assuming meditative postures or engaging in loquacious prattle with their elbows on the tavern bar, many of the infallible patrons of those establishments, if they are not all unable to take a step without the support of another blind-drunk friend, contrary to the standards of proper modicum, do not give the waitresses a moment's rest; those fine ladies make use of the special entrances for courtesans into these little public houses, and, while separated from one another by thin partitions, they answer to the ding-a-ling-a-ling of the glasses which they refill with expressions of carnal knowledge and prolonged, sonorous kisses. And out in the streets, the human harum-scarum ebbs and flows with nervous anticipation; squadrons of irreverent Romeos and alluring Juliets can be seen; the ambulatory and servile businesswomen of smoke filled halls exhort dinner companions; stalwart Dionysiacs make their way through the multitude, which spreads itself across both sides of the sidewalk, and they direct discourteous gallantries towards the women they encounter; professional beggars with mellifluent voices and pitiful miens fall upon the passers-by once they discover that they are foreigners, and they begin to ask for spare change and end up making pennies; the police redouble their vigilance as the burglars take incivility to new extremes; and then there's the young, the old, and the children: the elderly remembering the good ole days when so much debauchery did not exist, the youth walking down the path to the penitentiary or to the hospital, and the children learning what they should have never known.

And at every moment, on every street corner, side-stepping the light of the street lamps, a man verifies a meeting settled upon by way of a glance that he came across a few moments before; the pair of love birds then goes forth from their cache and is lost in the crowd directing their steps to the first hostel they see, in whose main lobby, the hotel manager asks the transitory guests to sign their names as if they were husband and wife into a registry which is required by law to perform acts which the same law prohibits. And down the poorly lit hallways of these establishments, the couples who enter rub elbows with those who are leaving; the porters who are responding to the guests' requests crisscross with those who have just furnished beverages to the other inhabitants of those god forsaken alcoves; the proprietor runs up and down the stairs pacifying excitable tempers and playing the role of referee during the bouts; there is no shortage of clients who leave swearing for having seen their hopes shattered and worrying at the thought of being compelled to later solicit therapeutic instructions from some druggist; and if by chance a moment of peace and quiet were to prevail, one could hear the indecipherable whispers and suspicious noises coming from inside the bedrooms.

As a compliment to everything else, like a carnival explosion, one must suffer the endless departures of the railcars overhead that extend to each of the city's extremities; the vibrant echo of the warning bells and whistles of the trolley cars which storm off in opposite directions crammed full of passengers, many of whom have their arms wrapped affectionately around the figures of their neighboring sweethearts with their heads languishing on their shoulders while they snore sweetly to the side with burned out cigarettes imprisoned between their lips and crumpled up newspapers drooping over their legs; laborers who return from work or from the bar and are not bothered by witnessing these saucy groups of lovers in adjacent seats, so close that their whispered words cannot be heard but can easy be guessed at; and as an accompaniment to all the commotion, there are teamsters who curse and scream, cars that pile up, fire engines that hasten to put out the blazes ignited by some criminal hand or originated in some moment of carelessness; and, finally, there are the organ barrels of traveling musicians who, with the greatest indiscretion, brutalize and rip works of operas like *Trovador, Traviata, Rigoletto,* and *La Fille de Madame Angot* to shreds.

The night hours move forward, but the Bowery does not sleep. Tumultuous, shameless, maddening, it waits for the first lights of morning to dissipate the last shadows of night, so that the unbridled orgy may give way to unbridled gambling and usury.

Salomón de la Selva (1893–1959)

A Song for Wall Street; The Secret

Born the son of a physician in Leon, Nicaragua, Salomón de la Selva left his home and family at the age of eleven with a scholarship to study in the United States. In 1916, he began teaching Spanish and French at Williams College in Massachusetts and became a member of the Northeastern literati, most notably as a friend of poet Edna St. Vincent Millay, who exerted a great influence over his creative development. De la Selva loved the United States dearly, despite his being torn by the U.S. interventions in his homeland, and had hoped to enlist in the U.S. Army during World War I; but he was refused admittance because he was not a U.S. citizen and he would not renounce his Nicaraguan citizenship. It was at this psychological and cultural juncture in his life that he published *Tropical Town and Other Poems* (1918), the first of a number of books that he would write, but most of the later works would appear in Spanish. Shortly thereafter, de la Selva left the United States to join the British army. After the war he returned to Nicaragua, where he became an important literary figure, whose works in Spanish form part of the national literary canon. In the following poems from *Tropical Town*, his description of the Metropolis follows in the long tradition of immigrant verse, as do his mixed emotions about his relationship with the United States. (NK)

Further reading: Salomón de la Selva, *Tropical Town and Other Poems*, ed. Silvio Sirias (Houston: Arte Público Press, 1999).

A Song for Wall Street

In Nicaragua, my Nicaragua,
What can you buy for a penny there?—
A basketful of apricots,
A water jug of earthenware,
A rosary of coral beads
And a priest's prayer.

And for two pennies? For two new pennies?—
The strangest music ever heard
All from the brittle little throat
Of a clay bird,
And, for good measure, we will give you
A patriot's word.

And for a nickel? A bright white nickel?—
It's lots of land a man can buy,
A golden mine that's long and deep,
A forest growing high,
And a little house with a red roof
And a river passing by.

But for your dollar, your dirty dollar,
Your greenish leprosy,
It's only hatred you shall get
From all my folks and me;
So keep your dollar where it belongs
And let us be!

The Secret

This, in the lower Berkshires,
Was most like witchery,
At evening, in the Springtime,
The bark of a white birch tree
Turned flesh, for my sake only,
So soft to touch, so rose to see.

When the cool sun was setting
The sky spread out her hair
Over the pillowy mountains
Heaped for her comfort there,
And I saw, like bathing women,
White birches tossing in the air.

But the good folk grew sulky
Because I would not pay
A compliment to the Springtime
In that New England day;
And they murmured because I wanted
To pack my things and run away.

A. Ortiz-Vargas

The Hispanic Barrio (El barrio hispanoparlante)

Virtually nothing is known of A. Ortiz-Vargas, a Hispanic immigrant who in 1939 was able to have his book-length epic poem in praise of Manhattan and the American Empire published in Spanish. What is certain is that, following a long tradition of visions of the metropolis by immigrants, he compared Manhattan to the monumental sites of Babylon and Egypt in the ancient world and to the grandeurs of the Inca and Maya civilizations of the New World.

While eloquently celebrating the technological and economic success of this new Nineva, Ortiz-Vargas was not blind to the excesses of the empire nor to the exploitation of the peoples of the world drawn to New York's urban ghettoes, which is evident in his vision of the disillusioned immigrants in the "Spanish Harlem" section of his epic. Despite his bemoaning the plight of Latinos, blacks, and Jews, Ortiz-Vargas goes on to predict a glorious future for this New World empire, precisely because of its incorporating within itself the peoples and cultures of the world. (NK)

Further reading: A. Ortiz-Vargas, *Las torres de Manhattan* (Boston: Chapman and Grimes, 1939).

Trans.: PP

You find Harlem
and identify it
in more than one way:
jovial inconstancy,
dangerous life,
quiet defeats.

Life without rhythm
or horizon or purpose;
poor obscure lives
at the mercy of chance.
In dream of triumph,
they left their homes
for the Land of Success.
but only failure triumphs.

They are adventurous souls,
crazy butterflies
without goal or course,
leaving no footprint.
blinded by the flashy
luminous advertisements,
they search Manhattan
for the light of their star.

Incautious Argonauts,
they deserted their beaches
for the false lure
of the triumphant fleece . . .
They deserted their beaches,
and a serpent of anguish
braided their destiny.

Se encuentra con Harlem
y se identifican
en más de un sentido:
jovial inconstancia,
vivir azaroso,
derrotas sin ruido.

Existencias sin rumbo
ni horizonte ni objeto;
pobres vidas obscuras
a merced del acaso.
De los triunfos soñados
al dejar sus comarcas
por la Tierra del Exito,
triunfó sólo el fracaso.

Almas de aventura,
locas mariposas
sin meta y sin ruta
y sin huella
que, ofuscadas por el llamativo
anuncio luminoso,
buscan por Manhattan
la luz de su estrella.

Argonautas incautos,
desertaron sus playas
por el falso señuelo
del triunfal vellocino . . .
Desertaron sus playas
y una sierpe de angustia
se trenzó a su destino.

Marijuana and boredom
on the weekdays,
and cheap whiskey
on Saturdays,
Aafter collecting their pay . . . .

Boredom without remedy
inside a small room
where the air is as heavy
as the existence
of its dwellers:

The women sew blouses
for the Semites;
the men wash plates
in the eateries of Broadway,
run elevators
and paint screens
in gloomy factories,
and on the docks, carry with the
stevedores.

From so much struggle,
day after day,
with never a tomorrow,
the only thing left them
is the smile that cries
in the red smile of marijuana.

A sad Nepenthes
detains the rushing hours . . . .

How it interweaves
through the labrinthean columns
of steely smoke—
a macabre nightmarish vision!

How slowly time passes!
How that minute lasts a thousand years!
How they go passing
—without passing at all—
the grim looks and grays and long years.

After? . . . ah, the sonorous light
of the triumphant streets.

Marihuana y tedio
los días ordinarios,
y whisky barato,
los sábados,
después de los pagos . . . . .

Tedio sin remedio
dentro de un cuartucho
donde pesa el aire
como la existencia
de sus moradores.

Ellas cosen blusas
para los semitas;
ellos lavan platos
en fondas de Broadway,
suben ascensores
y pintan pantallas
en lóbregas fábricas,
y en el muelle cargan
con los cargadores.

De tanta porfía,
un día y otro día
y nunca un mañana,
quedóles tan sólo,
la risa que llora
en la risa roja de la marihuana.

Nepentes del triste
que la fuga de la hora detiene . . . . .

¡Cómo va tejiéndose
entre el laberinto de sus columnillas
de humo acerado,
la visión macabra de las pesadillas!

¡Cómo tarda el tiempo!
¡Cómo ese minuto perdura mil años!
¡Cómo van pasando
—sin que pasen nunca—
los torvos y grises y luengos años!

¿Después? . . . . .ah, la luz sonorosa
de las rúas triunfantes.

The gold that shines, the skins that grope, the car that honks calling to the date, the clear diamonds	El oro que fulge, las pieles que tientan, el auto que grita llamando a la cita, los claros diamantes . . . . .
And what of the sad ones?	¿Y ellos los tristes?
The women sew blouses for the Semites; the men wash dishes in the eateries of Broadway, run elevators and paint screens in gloomy factories, and on the docks, carry with the stevedores.	Ellas cosen blusas para los semitas; ellos lavan platos en fondas de Broadway, suben ascensores y pintan pantallas en lóbregas fábricas, y en el muelle cargan con los cargadores.
They corrupted their language with the bizarre mix of a foreign tongue they never learned. And in the indulgent shade of the foreign flag, in their sorrowful failure, they were forever drowned.	Corrompieron su lengua con la mezcla bizarra de la lengua extranjera que jamás aprendieron. Y a la sombra indulgente de la extraña bandera, en sus pobres derrotas para siempre se hundieron.

Guillermo Cotto-Thorner (1916–1983)

Tropics in Manhattan (excerpt)

Born in Juncos, Puerto Rico, Guillermo Cotto-Thorner came to New York City in the 1930s, where he was a student at Columbia University. After finishing his studies at Columbia and at the University of Texas, he was ordained a Baptist minister in 1942. Cotto-Thorner became widely known in Hispanic communities in Milwaukee and New York because of his social work among Hispanics, but his religious writings in Protestant periodicals were reprinted throughout Spanish-speaking communities in the United States and Latin America. Cotto-Thorner also wrote columns for New York newspapers, such as *Liberación* and *Pueblos Hispanos*, in which he supported Puerto Rican independence and other liberal causes. It was his firm belief that Christianity promoted democracy, and this he argued repeatedly in books and articles. In the course of his ministry, Cotto-Thorner published a number of books on religious themes. However, he is most widely known for his first-hand narrative on life in Spanish Harlem, which was one of the first book-length endeavors not only to coin the oft-repeated phrase of *trópico en Manhattan*, the "tropics in Manhattan," but to actually describe the Hispanic transformation of the metropolitan environment, something that many

Nuyorican writers, such as Victor Hernández Cruz, would later repeat in their cultural claims on the city. In the selection below, Cotto-Thorner describes the Puerto Rican presence in Spanish Harlem. (NK)

Further reading: Guillermo Cotto-Thorner, *Trópico en Manhattan* (San Juan: Editorial Occidente, 1951), *Gambeta* (San Juan: Editorial Cordillera, 1986).

Trans.: PP

When summer arrives, New York turns into an overhelming steambath. The whole world searches in vain for a slight breath of fresh air. The rich in the southern part of Manhattan sun themselves high above on flat roofs, contemplating the two rivers that belt the crowded little island, and drink their Tom Collins stretched-out on comfortable chairs, placidly smoking while the penetrating rays of the sun tan their seminude bodies. But in the northern part of the city, up Madison and above, and in the rest of the Barrio, and even further uptown, in the Bronx, the poor, the thousand of Hispanos who live like sardines in dark, narrow apartments, search for a little air by going out into the streets.

Summer in the Barrio. Tables come out in front of restaurants and fry stands; men without shirts; women without stockings, girdles, or brassieres; children stark naked bathing themselves in the cold jet spewing from the mouths of fire hydrants; men in hitched-up shirts looking like doves on a rusty bar of the ladder of salvation; students on vacation, towel in hand, heading for the beach; crazy mothers gathering together and pushing their strollers to the park while their babies sleep calmly in the shade; coconut water, tamarind and *guanábana* drinks, slices of pineapple on blocks of manufactured ice . . . hot tar, tiresome vapor, smoke from the chimneys, humidity in the air sticking and thickening; shouts from little children playing in some revolting yard among hills of garbage; regal and lanky dogs smelling the putrefaction at the foot of the stairwells; banana peels in the middle of the street; bark juice, Pepsi, beer and lemonade . . . the bored in the movie houses; those who work pouring sweat in their labors; juke boxes playing *sones* and *rumbas* with such a racket as if they wanted to lift the heavy buildings into the air, with their noise; gatherings of vagrants on stoops and in hallways; billiard halls and taverns crammed full and noisy; the smell of fish in vinaigrette, sausages and salamis; excess and frenzy in the green plants and trees of Central Park; snow cones on every corner: strawberry, peach, lime, and coconut . . . . The Barrio in full summer.

And by night the tumult is much worse, because those who do not work continue in the streets, with the mob of those who, after a day of anxious and suffocating struggle, also want to take a little walk to refresh themselves. And the parade of people has no end. There goes a young man with his shirt open to his navel; over there one can see two men half-drunk, with stupid looks, reddened eyes, and leaden feet; and there goes a little girl about six years old with her dirty face and her worn clothes, radiating a singular independence. On the corner is Domitilo, surrounded by two or three admirers.

Domitilo once enjoyed a era of popularity. An olive-skinned young man, muscular, tough, he was a great boxer in his time—so much so that he had two or three victories in the ring at the Garden. But he was ruined by the bad environment. Even the press had eulogized him as being "championship material"; but rum and women took away his toughness, and now, after working days as a mechanic in a garage, at night he consoles himself by evoking his days of glory to a familiar crowd at the street corner. Despite being a fallen hero, Domitilo contents himself among an army of admirers.

And who is that dressed as though he was going to a funeral? You don't know him? It's Raphael Larra, the representative of the Latinos. Representative? Yes, he has given himself the title, and it's true, it's no joke. He comes dressed in black, purple tie, and his shoes . . . white. Marvelous! He walks alone because he has no friends, but he walks as if he owned the entire Barrio. And what's straight about this ambitious one is that he's become a real estate salesman and has bought various old buildings; after giving them a whitewash, without even killing one cockroach, he sells them to his own friends at fantastic and exorbitant prices. He's a swindler—the whole world knows it—but he still has his dental work intact, despite everyone talking about getting him one day (or night) in a dead-end alley and teach him a lesson. But it seems that to this day no one has discovered a dead-end alley in the Barrio. Most people foresee Raphael ending up in jail with all he owns: his black suit and the shoes . . . white.

Marching down the other side of the street comes Teodora. From the rapid click of her heels you can tell she's in a hurry and doesn't deign to ever glimpse out of the corner of her eye at the suitor with the trim mustache. "Hello, beautiful, what a dish?" She is mourning because her mother died only fifteen days ago. The poor old lady. Teodora in pain and feeling remorse, because she thinks she's the cause of her mother's death. Doña Tuna was doing very well in Puerto Rico, her days passing very calmly tending her chickens in the corral and frightening off the boys who'd throw stones on her zinc roof every time the mango tree outside the kitchen window bore delicious fruit. But Teodora pledged to bring her mother to New York. What abuse! She did not want to come, but there comes an age in life when the parents are obligated to obey their children. So poor little Doña Tuna arrived in New York, and New York killed her. She arrived in Winter, and the cold slipped into her bones and that wearisome rheumatism made a disaster of her. She passed her days shivering and gnashing her gums in an apartment that looked to her like a long coffin with divisions and little doors. There was no one there to heat a little bit of coffee on the gas stove, for fear of an explosion. Somebody back on the island had told her that those machines exploded and blew-up houses completely. That little blue flame was, for her, the symbol of death, or hell. Wrapped-up in a chair, near the window, surrounded by a draft, she spent the whole day until Teodora would come from work. When Summer arrived, the poor old lady was so drained that she declined overall her until she died. The Italian doctor who attended her scratched his head and admitted defeat because he didn't know the exact cause of her death. Some one should have whispered in the ear of this quack that what killed her was the move . . .

And a few steps behind Teodora, Lolín, comes rolling her hips down the block . . . with no good in mind. A very light skinned girl, shapely and with black hair. Apparently very serious, but spirited. Lolín's husband is a grocer, who weighs about two hundred and fifty pounds and always swings his weight around . . . including on his own wife. That's why the lady makes an effort to look very modest as she walks in the street. But follow her to the theater, and you'll see what happens. There in the half-dark (not as dark as in the theaters on the island), she can flirt as she wants. After entering, she sits alone, in a place separate from the rest of the people. Magnificent! Then, since it is hot, she coquettishly raises her skirt, crosses her legs . . . and waits. In a few moments a young man about twenty-five years old arrives. Despite the darkness, he discovers those legs so white and beautiful, outlined in the shadows, voluptuously, and he reacts; he makes a show of not seeing the seats in front of him, and he sits very close to her. She doesn't move, feigning indifference in her solitude; he has already lost all interest in the picture. For an instant their gazes meet. He offers her chewing gum, which she accepts gladly, thanking him and letting the young man's hand slowly brush against hers. Then comes an exchange of smiles, and after a few minutes they're both seated there snuggled together, whispering to each other and holding hands.

"The picture will end soon. Tell me, beautiful, when will I see you again so that we can be really alone?"

"Ah! That I cannot do. Tell me, tell me, what time is it now?"

"It's almost ten thirty, but at least wait until the picture is ends."

"No, I have to go. My husband must be waiting for me by now."

"But . . ."

"Go on, let me out . . . Goodbye, good looking, and good luck . . ."

And the play goes on. There goes Martita, that beautiful girl from Cabo Rojo who came to New York in search of excitement and ended up in the gutter. And over there is Juanchín, the popular photographer, married and with four children, who never misses a dance and no one's ever seen his wife. Ahead is a little sickly man, beautifully dressed, with a large book; he's coal black and has a golden voice. That's Andrés, the religious fanatic, who never tires of pounding his chest and barking at his wife.

Crossing at the corner against the stoplight is a young man who through some miracle has just escaped being run over by a heavy truck. His name is José Berteaga, and for days now he's been looking for a certain individual named Juan Marcos Villalobos.

CHAPTER 11

Negotiating New Realities

Wen Gálvez (1867–?)

My Valise

Upon retiring from the practice of law and the bench, Cuban-born Wenceslao (Wen) Gálvez turned to writing poetry, literature of manners, and chronicles during a tumultous period in his country's history. He lived through much of Cuba's late nineteenth-century revolutionary activity, which sent him to U.S. shores, where thousands of Cubans and Spaniards sought better working conditions in places like Key West and Tampa. Gálvez had first-hand experience with Cuban independence fever and its manifestation among immigrant cigar-making communities, where factory workers raised money to help finance Cuba's war for independence from Spain in 1895. A keen observer, he is ever sensitive to the plight of the immigrant working class. In the following selection, Gálvez offers us a painful glimpse of the life of a recently arrived door-to-door salesman trying to eke out a livelihood selling trinkets to customers who themselves can barely afford basic necessities and do not understand him because of his almost nonexistent English skills. (KDM)

Further reading: Wen Gálvez, *Tampa: Impresiones de un emigrado* (Tampa: Establecimiento Tipográfico Cuba, 1897).

Trans.: PP

I came to know Ybor City inch by inch and, I would dare say, house by house, except for one house or another recently constructed. I have entered all the others hawking trinkets because I was a trinket seller, although it pains me to say it. I didn't go into the streets loaded with a monstrosity strapped to my back, but I carried a valise in my hand with cheap perfumery and trinkets for women. How many times have I heard "Nothing today," "I don't want anything today," which sound like "Please forgive me, brother!" How many times, at the end of a long journey over the red-hot sand, have I earned a miniscule profit! Oh! Those who use that metaphor, "the red-hot sand of politics" don't know what they're saying. Hot sand is a truly disagreeable thing. The heat subtly penetrates through the soles of your shoes and produces an unpleasant sensation on the bottom of your feet. And so, with your feet hot and your head cold, you have to enter the houses happily, offering cheap perfume. And so, street by street, house by house, I have journeyed through Ybor City, this neighborhood that extends without order or harmony like a misguided climbing plant. And so I also saw, day by day, that poverty was the queen and mistress of almost all the households. Many times I stopped selling my trinkets because of my customers' absolute lack of money. To spend five cents on a little tin jar (which cost me four cents) some would ask me to come back in eight days. Others would delay the order of a packet of fifteen hairpins. The poor black women of the most segregated neighborhoods remained open-mouthed, scratching the lining of their pockets to pay full price for a colorful ribbon. My valise full of trinkets! Sometimes it felt so heavy.

"Are you going on a trip, sir?" an acquaintance once asked me on the street.

"No, sir, I'm selling trinkets."

"You're always such a hard worker!" he answered. And he smiled, twirling his cane and breathing the smoke from a fake Cuban cigar.

Some American families taught me some English phrases, and I was led not so much by the hand, but by the valise, in an effort to enlarge my business to the houses of Americans.

Those who have seen the anguish of the mute trying to make themselves understood would comprehend the effort in mimicry that I squandered, offering my merchandise to these good-natured families who understood not even the names of currency in Spanish.

I once offered an indisputably useful ceramic jar. I said "ten cents" because "cents" is the first thing understood in all countries. The family, for its part, wanted to understand me. "Milk?" they asked. "Eggs? water?" . . . . I finally left, vanquished, and with the ceramic jar in my hand. My effort to sell was for naught. I should have demonstrated a liveliness superior even to my wishes, so that not even the little respect due to a passer-by would hold me back. Once again I approached with another jar in my hand, a tin jar that wouldn't fit in my valise. In the opposite direction came a peasant on his small cart. And once again history repeated itself. "Five cents," I said to him. And this man answered in English, "five cents worth of beans?"

Oh, my valise of trinkets! Preserve our memories, preserve them, so that no one profanes them. . . .

Gustavo Alemán Bolaños (1884–?)

The Factory (excerpt)

The Nicaraguan journalist, poet, and novelist Alemán Bolaños dedicated much of his journalistic work to political reportage and commentary, advocating throughout his life the creation of a Central American federation and opposing dictatorships. Alemán Bolaños worked for many of the most important Spanish American newspapers of his time: *El Diario de Nicaragua, Diario de El Salvador, Diario de Panamá, El Excélsior* (México), *El Mercurio*

(Chile), *La Nación* (Argentina). In the United States, he worked for New York's *La Prensa* and the *Herald Tribune*, in the latter as a translator. *The Factory* is his novel of immigration, published in Guatemala in 1925. It relates the experiences of an immigrant from an undisclosed Spanish American republic and presents a realistic portrayal of the life of a worker in manufacturing and on the streets of the big city. Bolaños's personal struggles are reflected in the beginning of the first-person narrative when the protagonist is unsuccessful in finding intellectual work appropriate to his own education and profession because he does not speak English. At work in the handbag factory, the reader never learns the name of the protagonist, only his employee number. Throughout the novel there is a subtle protest against this dehumanization and exploitation and a call for the defense of workers' rights. As a novel of immigration, return to the homeland is promoted after destroying the myth of the "streets of gold" in the metropolis, and at the end of the novel the protagonist does return home. (EO)

Further reading: Gustavo Alemán Bolaños, *La factoría* (Guatemala City: Tipografía Sánchez and de Guise, 1925).

Trans.: PP

Chapter One

Today I have become a man-machine. I am a thinker, in so far as I have the use of reason, but I had never had the fortune of being a factory worker in front of a machine that I must operate. The instrument and I become one: I am, then, a man-machine.

Necessity, which I have felt and experienced at other times, had never taken me to that extreme, which, while indeed difficult, in truth is beautiful, for work, as someone once said, ennobles man, and I am proud to be a worker in this great country where the worker is as noble as the boss, even if he is the most unhappy laborer under the patronage of the most distinguished magnate of the dollar. This is a cause for satisfaction, to be as equals, at least in the eyes of the law and society in general: a manufacturer, a factory man, a miner at a level with the owners of those emporiums of wealth. For here, in the immense country of the United States, he who engages in the lowliest and most modest of tasks enjoys this equality.

My education, my intellectual culture, my physical build, strong as they make me feel, are not what have made me, day after day, one of them, a factory worker. But rather, my words have carried me, and I have gone with pleasure because I know that man, cursed or blessed by God—nobody knows—must earn his bread with the sweat of his brow. Such are the circumstances that have forced me to earn my bread. Unable to find any occupation in my field—which is intellectual in essence and I can practice only in my natural language—or any other similar vein, and not wanting to sacrifice my self-esteem by becoming an office employee of the lowest class, or a peddler of trinkets, I have chosen to work in a factory.

What kind of factory? *Any kind.* There are circumstances in which one cannot choose, and in order to meet one's needs one thing is as good as another. I was told that there was work at such and such a place, and I went there. As luck would have it, this same morning and in said place, I found a position in the manufacture of paper purses and handbags. In a vast hall there are many people working. The machines are noisy. There is much activity. A friend also looking for work, who accompanied me and served as my guide, signed us in; we began to work at that very moment. To work! We were sent to the machine section, medium-sized pedal driven machines.

All the machines are working at this hour, eight o'clock on a cold morning, when inside it is eternally warm and the vast room is illuminated *a giorno*. I'm mistaken: not all are working, because two are missing their operators; they are alone, inactive, nostalgic for those who would give them life, movement, for machines do not like the ugly rust that cramps, that paralyzes, that hurts, that kills iron.

We were each assigned our own machine. My friend, who has had experience in this department, explains the operation, simple indeed, and, stripped of my jacket—we are under the rigor of winter—of my hat, and of my fine leather gloves, I begin to test my skills. I have understood the operation, and am now, before the machine, a man-machine.

Chapter Seven

After a Sunday of rest when one can rise at whatever hour he pleases, and when one can do whatever he pleases, a disagreeable Monday dawns, and one must go to the factory, obligated by the hard law of necessity. But I confess that I have returned happy and animated to my work.

The task is becoming easier. I feel like an expert, and without noticing the time, I had filled the first hundred purses. This morning's corrections were few, and consequently I conclude that I am perfecting—refining, as they say—my labor.

I have noted today a curious phenomenon of acoustics; the noise of the factory's machines is musical, let us say. It occurs not unlike the sound of the ironwork on a moving train, perceived by the traveler riding drowsily in his coach seat: from such infernal clatter there escapes a soft, cadenced music, a waltz is heard, or something like it, continuous, with a whimsical *leit motif*. It is not exactly what I have observed but rather what my ear has registered this morning: the cadence in the beating of the drill presses much the ticking of a metronome. One could call it an orchestra of dry sounds, an extraordinary iron symphony.

This morning, another discovery: I have started observing my companions at work nearby, and I have discovered, almost in front of me, a beautiful blond girl. Young, robust, she has a pleasant appearance. Her face is interesting, and some locks of gold, semi-unruly, lend it charm. She dresses poorly—as to be expected—and she works incessantly, almost without lifting her head. When she goes to carry her purses, or when she brings materials, I observe her walk, which is graceful, and her body, which under her working clothes, seems languid and youthful. Under some pretext, I speak to the woman on the first chance I get. The conversation is brief. She is Romanian and arrived in this country a few years ago with a brother, in search of the golden fleece, the fleece that—alas!—not everyone can win. Her brother had to return to Europe to take-up arms in the war, and as of today she hasn't heard a word from him. Did he die? Those blue eyes—those of the girl, my companion—cloud at my question; her mouth tells me nothing, but her heart surely speaks, under the coarse sweater of gray wool. . . . We remain friends, acquaintances. She, lacking curiosity, ordinarily not interested in knowing anything about the workers who march through the factories—they are so many!—asks not one word about my life, but returns once again to her work, to the incessant hammering, after giving to me a soft smile, a sorrowful smile of resignation, of gratitude for my cordial words, my words of affection. . . . Just like this, in the whirlwinds of the world, friendships are born, are constantly being born. Work—one of the forms, undoubtedly, of social life—bring together individuals who, if they are in tune, make contact, exchange thoughts, ideas, and intentions. And from such occasions sprout the good, sometimes fraternal, friendships, and numerous cases have been cited in which there, in these places, the spark of love has ignited. Love! The attraction of souls and bodies, which, when it reaches beyond the pale, elevates instinct from the human, the savage, to the divine.

I have returned to my machine to continue working. From my post, I watch the blond girl who works almost in front of me. She, in her turn, for a moment has raised her enormous eyes—which are blue as I said—and has rested them upon me. . . .

Conrado Espinosa (1897–1977)

The Texas Sun (excerpt)

Conrado Espinosa was an educator, a revolutionary and a newspaper man who fled during the height of the Mexican Revolution to the United States, where he continued to write political articles in Mexican and American newspapers. He was also involved in the struggle for human rights, and became an activist in both countries. *The Sun of Texas*, a novel of immigration published in 1926, tells the story of a Mexican couple who, along with their children, arrive in the United States with high hopes for a better life than the one they left behind in Mexico. What the family encounters is hard, unforgiving labor without rest under the hot, scorching sun of the Texas fields. The husband clings to the one hope that keeps him going: to earn enough money to return to his own land, where he can work for himself. Unfortunately, this hope also brings back memories of the unproductive labor as a sharecropper in the Mexican fields. He decides that being abused by foreigners is preferable to being abused by those of his own blood in Mexico. So he continues to toil and dream in a foreign land at the hands of the bosses that ridicule him and strip him of his dignity. This novel of immigration, like many others of its kind, reveals the plight of the immigrant who discovers that the American Dream has turned into the American Nightmare, and with it comes the ultimate dilemma—whether to remain or return. (MMG)

Further reading: Conrado Espinosa, *El sol de Texas* (San Antonio: Viola Novelty, 1926), *Fray Sebastián de Aparicio, primer caminero mexicano* (Mexico City: Editorial Jus, 1959).

Trans.: TEW

Panting and dripping sticky, filthy sweat, he follows the harvest, pulling himself along, on the verge of collapsing in the furrow. Still strong, he carries his forty years like a light and joyful load. But this, the harvest, is a bad hand dealt him by fate, a foolish misstep. He'll come out of it. He can recuperate. He'll get some money together; better days and more prudent endeavors will come. No more craziness. But the foreman arrives and the man must continue. They are waiting to weigh the crop. Lugging a huge sack that gets heavier with each step, he follows the furrow, pulling himself along, panting and dripping sticky, filthy sweat. It is overwhelming. He is like a kangaroo, unable to skip gracefully and barely able to walk, carrying the cursed load of a deformed body behind him. The mother of his offspring—some of them youngsters, some toddlers—walks behind him. Also burnt by the sun and by hope, the children, who together number four, walk along harvesting those snow-like tufts of cotton that are ignited under the fiery sun. It is the same sun that beats down on their moist backs, burns their skulls until they go mad, and turns the earth into a black, dull and eternal persecuting ember for their blistered feet . . .

Under the foreman's gaze they walk along—father, mother and children—like six miserable, condemned criminals. Spurred on by crude jokes and the enticing, ever-present next payday, they go on. They have to continue. They have to collect loads of cotton . . . more . . . always more. It's the only way you can escape from that hell!

The field fans out. It is immense, like a sea. The small bushes swell and the bundles of cotton, exalted in their whiteness, are the foam. The tufts multiply, glistening like an omen of prosperity, a guarantee of riches for the proprietor, a taunting storehouse . . . a storehouse whose worst leftovers will fall into the hands of these unhappy workers in order to sustain them a little longer, to prolong their existence, so that they can continue to harvest.

The intensely blue sky is clear of all clouds and its curves seem to be resting upon the wretched hills at the border. The sun marches along deliberately. It hardly progresses and is distracted in its sluggishness by spitting fire, shooting at the earth and at men with darts that singe. There is no shade, no brisk breeze. Everything is suffocating and still. Over there, the only movement is that of the strained walking of the farm workers and the routine trotting of the mules that pull carts and carts loaded with cotton. At times, a car races by wildly, passing along the nearby highway. It carries contented folks on their way from a happy seaside resort, a wealthy city, or a small town that is all spruced-up and lively in celebration of its yearly festival.

The time comes when she cannot take it any longer. The woman has stopped suddenly, overcome with a sharp pain that drives needles into her back and her waist. With a dull expression, the children watch their mother's contorted face. They remain standing there, dripping sweat, with their mouths wide open. A little bit ahead, he continues. The ploughed earth is asking him to work more; the cotton offers itself up out of the bud. Drunk from work and sun, he continues, gaining strength with his imagination crazed over this illusion that he perceives in the glare between earth and sky . . .

Every day he'll harvest one hundred pounds . . . three hundred . . . a thousand . . . or whatever it takes to get together at least one hundred dollars. He'll have all of them harvest. He'll return to San Antonio to buy himself rags. He'll dress his woman and children in the best clothes; there will be extra money for that. With the money, he'll go to Mexico, to his land, to his farm that they never should have left, in order to work for himself. Now he'll be able to do it without relying on loans . . .

This reminds him of when he was exploited by his town's leaders, when he was planting as a sharecropper and was the victim of their theft, and the hardship that he suffered cultivating the land whose products were blatantly stolen from him. Now, he is almost happy to suffer on foreign soil, to feel exploited by foreigners! They are not of his blood, but of their own . . . !

He would continue day-dreaming, but a scream—a death-cry—brings him back to reality. He regains his senses and sees how his woman falls, flat-out on the furrow, like an abused bag of meat without a soul. He sees how the children surround her and hears sobs. He sees how the foreman smiles from the awning that shades him and, furious and enraged, leaves the sack and runs toward his family. He lifts his wife so that someone can give her water; it is a lukewarm, nauseating water. He calms his children. The foreman laughs.

Irate and feeling his blood boil with all the rage of his ancestors, the man runs toward the joker, takes out a knife, opens it and is about to plunge it into the foreman's mocking flesh, when two pistols are pointed at him.

The foreman laughs and his friends laugh. They are strong, blonde, well-armed young men who are weighing the harvest and affirming their authority. They are powerful, in-charge and untouchable.

He understands that if he touches one of them, he can die like a dog. His family would be abandoned under this fiery sun, on the land that burns, among these men that only know how to ridicule and exploit life. He stops himself, lowers his head, swallows his pride and returns to the furrow!

He cannot even say a thing to them! Oh, how he wants to! They wouldn't understand him, like he doesn't understand the gibberish they emit between laughter and gestures of comradery!

The woman has recuperated and continues harvesting on her knees. The children have emptied their bags and, tuft by tuft, go to fill them again. He does that much more.

Days, weeks and months pass in this way. The cotton runs out in one tract of land and they go to another. Many times they travel for miles and miles, resting from the furrow in the hardship of the trip, heaped on a dilapidated truck. Other times, the sky opens up unexpectedly, water floods the furrows, mud confines their feet and they have to wait. . . . The owner gets impatient because of his losses, wages are lowered and their savings disappear. Barely able to sustain the family, they endure by purchasing the worst food with rotten left-overs. Their clothes have been wearing out and their backs are naked. When the sun comes out again and the family returns to the furrow there is more oppression and more pain . . . but there is new hope.

Yes, there is new hope. It can be weaved in the night under the moon . . . weaved under these bright August moons, whose rays are made of silver, whose rays are like dollars as they filter through the holes in their battered, canvas tent, or the branches of their lean-to.

He dreams again. The woman also dreams. The children trustingly surrender themselves to the paternal delirium!

A few days later, there is already some money knotted in his filthy bandanna. He has cleared some debts and has already found a kinder boss. There is hope . . .

But the sun returns and he comes to his senses. To the harvest!

With flesh lacerated by pebbles and thorns, they pull themselves along the furrows, lugging those huge bags. Perhaps they find themselves again under an inclement sun or a cursed downpour. Then, it's off to the city that is hungry for all of their money and, living like beggars, they stay there. They are unable to return to their land and wait for another year, dreaming of making a lot of money and resigned to suffering new abuses for the chance to get a crust of bread . . .

Daniel Venegas (dates unknown)

The Adventures of Don Chipote or, When Parrots Breast Feed (excerpt)

The Adventures of Don Chipote; or, When Parrots Breast Feed is a picaresque novel of Mexican immigration, published in Los Angeles in 1928. Written by a self-described Chicano (Mexican immigrant laborer), the novel oscillates between humorous satire and outright protest of the inhumane working and living conditions Mexican immigrants suffered. In this bittersweet road story, Don Chipote and his partner Policarpo leave their families and sharecropping back in Mexico to find their fortune in the United States, only to discover that Mexicans are treated by industry like beasts of burden and by city slickers as easy marks. As literature that emerges directly from working-class life, the novel incorporates the rural folk and laborers' dialects of the times, rendered in the translation below in similar English-language dialects. Like many other novels of immigration, the message counters the American Dream while leading Chicanos to analyze their plight, albeit through laughing at themselves and their ingenuousness in this hostile environment. Venegas was a self-taught journalist, a playwright, and creative prose writer who, during the 1920s, was an activist as the president of the Mexican Journalists Association of California. (NK)

Further reading: Daniel Venegas, *The Adventures of Don Chipote; or, When Parrots Breast Feed*, trans. Ehtriam Cash Brammer, introduction by Nicolás Kanellos (Houston: Arte Público Press, 2000); Nicolás Kanellos, with Helvetia Martell, *Hispanic Periodicals in the United States: A Brief History and Comprehensive Bibliography* (Houston: Arte Público Press, 2000).

Trans.: ECB

It was Don Chipote, then, who bumped into another fellow, who was one of those who, even though he had all the mannerisms of one who has lived in the United States for a long time, has only learned a mongrel form of English.

"Hey, boss," Don Chipote said, "look, we ain't got a single cent 'tween the two of us. Ya wouldn't happen ta know of anywheres that we might be able ta swing a job, now, would ya?"

"Ha! Get a load o' these fellas!" replied the man. "Looks like you two are green from head to toe and fresh off the turnip truck. Well, sure—over there are the recruiters who send out everyone who stops by for a job. Heck, it's workin' on the *traque.* But there ain't nothin' else here that they'll let a Chicano do. Look, o'er there's the agency askin' for folks to go to California. Jus' go up there. Only folks that don't want a job don't git one."

Policarpo, upon hearing that bit of information, removed the scowl from his face. He said to the guy, "Hey, buddy, would ya be so kind as ta do us the favor of takin' us to see if they'd find us a spot? You know this place awready. So we'd be much obliged if'n you could lend us a hand."

The fellow understood Don Chipote and Company's predicament, and, remembering the jams that he had gotten himself into when he had first arrived, he volunteered to take them to the office and arrange for their employment. And so, said and done, they crossed the street and went up to the office which recruited people to go to California.

As usual, a work contractor went straight to them, like a cat to a saucer of milk, purring at them the litany which they know in their sleep: "Come in, friend, we have assignments in all parts of the United States. Thirty-five cents an hour. It doesn't matter where you want to go: the Santa Fe or the Southern Pacific . . . They'll take you there and give you a return ticket after six months."

In the border cities, El Paso among them, there exists a certain class of people who are Mexican and who devote themselves to taking advantage of the innocence of our countrymen. Without any scruples whatsoever, they become instruments for the companies and landowners, who, knowing that Mexican braceros can be useful in all types of work, put Mexicans in those recruitment offices, drawing most of their employees from them, the majority of times, as frontmen or callers, who attend to shipping out greenhorns to the *traque* or to the cottonfields, where the workers are usually treated like animals. Those slavedrivers, who make their living from Mexican disgrace, appear to be our guardian angels when we come across them. Because the majority of us cross the border without a nickel and only dreams, and because those lobsters go out even to the middle of the street to offer us jobs, where they promise us not only a good salary and fair treatment, but even a trip back home to boot. Caramba, one can't help but believe that there are angels walking the Earth. And to receive their blessings, all the Chicanos dive in and tie themselves down, which is how they get all of us to carry a pickax and shovel.

This or something similar had to have happened to our chums after seeing that the work contractor, who without a doubt had a job order to fill, invited them with thousands of salutations to come in so that they could sign up. And with the dignified air of a skilled orator, he offered them some grub and a bunk.

It didn't take much spit to convince Don Chipote and Associates, because this was exactly what they were begging for. So, in less than two shakes of a dog's tail, they were jotted down for the first tour out of town, only they would have to wait until the entire order was filled.

"This's made it all worth while," said Don Chipote, giving thanks to the guy who had taken them. "At least, we hope so. The only thing that gits me is how're we gonna make it 'til we start workin', 'cause we don't have a thing ta eat."

"Don't worry," the other answered. "The Supply will give you food when taking you to the worksite and until you receive your first check. I don't wanna make it seem like they'll give it to you for free. No, siree, they'll give you the food on credit, then take it out of your wages."

"That's jus' fine with us, sir. 'Cause being how we are, we ain't got nothin' more than pitchers of water keepin' us filled," observed Policarpo. And, with that, the recruiter left, wishing them farewell.

Almost immediately afterward, the work contractor called for his contractees to go eat. Our chums, not knowing where their next meal would come from, had stuffed themselves with the leftovers they had been given at the restaurant and, now, did not have much of an appetite. Notwithstanding, since one shouldn't look a gift horse in the mouth, they went in to eat so as not to snub their tutelary angel.

The railroad companies and the Supply are in cahoots. And, like the recruitment offices, they are dependent upon the same system. Thus, once the braceros are assigned to a job, they are forced to buy from the Supply which, from that moment on, has a forced clientele, obligated to buy merchandise at their whimsical prices, with the one and only advantage of being able to charge the first payment. And this is why the work contractors give food to those they bring in, because they know that as soon as they begin to work, the Supply wrings every last penny from them to the point of leaving them with nothing but a bill when it's time to get paid.

Don Chipote and Policarpo had thought of only smelling the food, which consisted of soda crackers and cans of sardines and were already so old that they weren't any good except to stimulate the digestive juices and make their mouths water.

The only one who did not hold back but took advantage of his ration was Skinenbones. For, notwithstanding the tummy that he had put on in the restaurant, he stuffed himself on all that his masters threw away and that they would have to pay for later.

13

In the morning, after washing their mugs and completing their morning routines, they left to go gobble down something to quiet the hangovers they were experiencing. So they went to a Mexican restaurant and threw back a bowl of menudo, very much to the delight of Skinenbones, who attacked the bones to the point of leaving them bare, even more than what his owners had left them. Later, Policarpo decided to go look for work and asked his pal to loan him a little something for food in case he landed a job. Then he told Don Chipote to meet him in the hotel room in the afternoon, because he wasn't coming back until he found work. After Don Chipote gave him a dollar, Policarpo beat it, and Don Chipote found himself on Main Street, looking around to figure out which way to go.

It didn't take Don Chipote long to get his bearings. He went to the Placita, because he didn't know where else to go. Also, there he was sure to come across fellow countrymen who could speak to him in his own tongue. He had already spent the greater part of the morning there, sleeping and smoking, until it appeared as though he was getting drunk again. In the end, he was getting bored and extremely sunburned.

Not knowing how to kill time, he thought about taking a stroll along Main Street. So he hit the pavement, just to rid himself of the doldrums.

That's how, step by step, he happened across a movie house and went inside, drawn by the comic always posted at the front door to lure people inside. The announcer was shouting himself hoarse, yelling about the attractions, which according to him were the season's best, and that they had the best movies ever. He was practically shoving passers-by into the theater by force.

Don Chipote, who couldn't find anything to do and excited by the announcer's spiel, asked how much a ticket cost. After finding out that it only cost ten cents, he bought his ticket and went inside to be entertained.

Skinenbones, upon seeing his master go inside and realizing he didn't even buy him a ticket, chased after him so that he too could watch the "sho."

Never in his life had Don Chipote seen a cinematographic projection—that is to say, he didn't even know that the "sho" would be in the dark. So when the house lights grew dim and he couldn't see anything, he wanted to run out of the theater, for he thought that he had descended into Hell. And with the lights completely dark, he couldn't see where he was going and smacked into one of the pillars in the auditorium.

Skinenbones caught up to his owner. But Don Chipote didn't want to let go of the pillar that he had run into. Skinenbones whimpered as Don Chipote's knees knocked.

Little by little, his eyes finally adjusted to the darkness and he began to make out the seats and everything around him. Once he could get a good look at things and see well, he took to the aisle. And without looking at where he was sitting down, he plopped himself down before the silver screen. It wasn't until Don Chipote realized that the fellows who appeared on the big screen were moving on their own that he began to get nervous; or more clearly stated, he started to get scared. So he made the sign of the cross, entrusted his soul to Divine Providence, and prepared to make a dash for the exit. But he stopped, thinking that he might fall while running and, that after he fell, they would do him in.

In the end, he decided to just bow his head and not look around, praying that Our Lady of Perpetual Help would get him out of this fix.

He had already spent some time with his head down beseeching God's grace, when a cry of laughter grabbed his attention away from his predicament. Unable to withstand his curiosity, he lifted his head and watched the screen as a funny-looking actor threw a cake at an old man but hit his girlfriend instead. The rest of the audience continued to laugh at the lunacies which comprised the comic scenes. Don Chipote felt the blood rush back into his veins, and also felt like laughing at those wise guys' shenanigans. It didn't take long for him to let fly with his guffaws and for him to shake the room with his chortles, which called the attention of the others, who, now being entertained by watching him, stopped watching the screen to laugh at Don Chipote instead. He thought that those pictures were so hilarious that they made him want to laugh even harder than he had on his honeymoon, when his Doña Chipota had tickled him in the morning so that he would wake up laughing with her, which made him fall more deeply in love.

Don Chipote then confessed to himself that he had no reason to be scared and that his fears were the seeds of his ignorance, because he now realized that, if he were being dragged down into Hell, they wouldn't have made him pay first. Once pacified by this thought, he occupied himself with watching the entertainment on the screen. And so that Skinenbones could see too, he picked him up and placed him on his lap and showed him what he was looking at. Of course, the pooch didn't give a straw about what was making his master laugh so hard, but he felt swell sitting on his lap, because it had been a long time since Don Chipote had so much as pet him.

Don Chipote, all the while, kept rocking back and forth with laughter, giving the others in the crowd reason to laugh at him.

While he was still laughing at the screen, and the others at him, the movies ended and it was announced that the variety show was to follow shortly. Even though Don Chipote had no idea what this was, he remained seated, only because the rest had stayed put as well. He began to get annoyed by so much waiting around, when to his delight, he saw a musician with a drum make himself comfortable next to the piano. And he thought, without a doubt, that they were going to dance the matachines like back home.

The piano maestro arrived at last. After giving the keyboard a few general passes, he attacked the piano furiously, in harmony with his sonorous companion, playing the pasodoble, which even the local barn owls recognize as "Sangre Mexicana." After they thought they had played the tune, for in reality nothing could be heard except for the drumming and crashing, the curtain rose and a dame appeared wearing almost nothing at all, making Don Chipote cover his face, which turned red from the embarrassment of seeing a woman in such regalia. And don't go thinking that this was false modesty on the part of our compatriot, for as you well know, in his homeland, he had never seen the body of any woman—dare we say, not even his wife—higher up than the ankle. So you can just imagine what happened to him when seeing that doll-face showing off her legs to the crowd, looking more like streams of atole than legs.

Because temptation is the worst thing that mankind can face, enabling the devil to take us away, Don Chipote could not resist. And, little by little, he went opening his fingers to see what would startle him once more. And that's how, little by little, he continued until he peeled his hand from his face straight away and began to study the beautiful performer and even drool with delight.

When the dull monotonous singing had ended, Don Chipote's sweet temptress gave her thanks and took off. People in the audience stomped their feet, yelled out loud and applauded. And our pal, corrupted by the others, cheered until suddenly standing up and letting Skinenbones fall from his lap with a crash, for he could not resist joining the tremendous ovation without howling his approval, which redoubled the cheers, because the crowd thought that it was the performer who had started singing again from the middle of the song.

The poor song-and-dance gal was not the greatest, but for the Mexican masses before her, she was out of this world, especially for Don Chipote.

The singer let the crowd go wild for a few moments, then decided to repeat the number, only, this time—and you should understand that what really made the audience go bonkers was the exhibition of her scrawny chicken legs—she sang and danced while trying to reveal herself all the way up to where her bloomers were fastened. With such an artistic display, the reader can imagine how the crowd must have reacted, particularly Don Chipote, who was going blind with ecstasy. Fortunately, now that he had nearly lost his sight, the artist wrapped up her routine and exited the stage to the cheers and stomping feet of the audience which wanted her, at all cost, to do more of the same.

The pack of Mexicans went rabid. They shouted and did all they pleased and could do to compel an encore, but that piece of eye-candy didn't come back out. Instead, a guy dressed like his compatriots in the audience—who had taken their turns with distilled cactus juice—attempted to win their praise as well by telling them jokes and babbling baloney as dirty or more bawdy than his predecessor's songs and legs. In short, that buffoon gave them a kick, not so much from his jokes, but rather because the pantomime he did made them recall getting hooched up back home. And that's why they awarded his evil deeds with a salvo of applause, which he received while doing cartwheels off the stage, his heart full of gratitude for those who knew how to recognize his talents so warmly. Surely, he thought they would make him do an encore, but as soon as he was out of sight backstage, the clapping came to an end.

Another number followed; rather, it was basically the same, only, this time, both performers came out on stage. The woman was now dressed like a country girl and the comedian just as before, only this time he didn't have on his huaraches and instead carried a charro's sombrero, which in its day had been braided with gold, but now shone with a mountain of sequins embroidered onto it. In these get-ups, our artists engaged in a street dialogue which they presented as a novelty but even children know it by heart.

Following this lovely exchange, in which they exhausted their vast repertoire, the maestro started in on his piano with thumps on the keyboard, sending out the discordant chords of the "Jarabe Tapatío," while the artists par excellence started more or less into stomping their heels and kicking their legs to the music.

The row created defies description. The dust cloud cannot be described either, for, with each one of the dancers' steps, enough dirt came out of the slits between the stage's floorboards to build an adobe house.

Alberto O'Farrill (1899–?)

Easy Jobs

Pegas Suaves (Easy Jobs), published in New York's *Gráfico* in 1927, tells of the daily perils of a Caribbean man who lives in New York and wanders through the city every day in search of a job. "Pegas" in colloquial Caribbean Spanish means "jobs." Likewise, "suave" means "easy." The main character is a rascal who wakes up every morning determined to find an easy job that will provide him with enough money to survive in New York, but he fails. In this piece, O'Farrill employs satirical humor to portray the social and labor conditions of Hispanic immigrants in the city. *Pegas Suaves*, like other immigration texts, shows the contrast between people's lifestyles in New York and the homeland, from the perspective of a member of the underclass. His treatment of women is critical, seen through the portrayal of the "flapper," considered to be the embodiment of feminist liberation in the United States. Immigrant authors often view Hispanic women as the guardians of traditional morals. They fear that their wives and daughters might imitate American ways, thus endangering family integrity and, of course, Hispanic men's privileges. The following excerpt involves a young Anglo woman who mocks the demeanor and style of the main character while he works distributing advertising pamphlets. Alberto O'Farrill was born in Santa Clara, Cuba, and moved to the United States around 1922. He was a playwright, actor, dancer, and editor of periodicals in Cuba and New York. O'Farrill used different pseudonyms to signs his works: O'Fa, Domifá, Gavitofa. The following selection was signed by O'Fa. (AB)

Trans.: TEW

I find myself up.

Now I really am doing great, just great. I'm turned-around like a small-fishing boat caught in the sand on the beach, like a guppy in lye water or like a cat in a patch of catnip. And, for whoever might be the judge, however, I don't owe anyone anything for this "little job" that I found all by myself. . . .

As you know, I have to get up at the same time every day. I am never without my lucky charm, my five kilos, and much less without singing my little waltz. The fact that I like it so much contributes to its popularity and, it gets me up when it does because the words say that it's time to wake-up. But let's forget about this, which is of no interest to anyone but me, and move on to the matter of my little job.

I am an advertising agent at one of the most famous stores in this district. Or better said, I am a distributor of advertisements, as I am the one responsible for putting them in all of the mailboxes of the private houses. And, I am wonderful at it. The boss entrusts this to me because he knows that I am the best person to advertise the location of his business, and, actually, I take advantage of the cool morning air to do so. I begin really early with a satchel full of papers stuck to my ribs and walk to the beat of my whistling, to make the little job less boring.

I go along, darting into all of the houses on both sides of the street, and place five or six fliers in each mailbox. This is the most efficient way to do it. A person who would think to throw one into the trash doesn't throw away six because it takes more energy. Consequently, everybody reads the little flier and I finish my job faster.

As would be expected, while walking in the street I have to give 25 copies each to all of the "Valentinos." I like to get all dressed-up, as I consider myself an 11, and do it in such a way that there is not one Eve out there who can help but stare at me. They stare, I suppose, because of how elegant I look with my new straw hat. That proves that your appearance is what matters most: other men have caps that cost five or six dollars and don't get half as much attention as I do, wearing such a cheap one. It only cost me one semolian.

The only one who dared to speak to me was a little blonde who, it seems, couldn't control herself and said: "How elegant you are with that straw hat and monkey-colored coat!" She accompanied this with such a mocking laugh that, if I didn't know the truth (that I am gorgeous), I would have thought that she was laughing *at me*. Any other interpretation was impossible. If I'm wearing a straw hat, it's because it is in season. And, if I put on a coat it's because I was cold. It is not my fault that you have to be fashionable here and nobody bothers to control the weather. In Cuba, for example, when you feel like going around with a straw hat all year long, that's just fine with everybody. Here, they break you for it. If I'm cold, they can stomp on my soul, but I won't take off my coat! And from this, I come to understand who the Americans really are: a bunch of reverends. . . . They pretend to know more than everyone else, and often the proof of this is women in summer-coats and men in coats in the summer.

Only with this passing distraction did I finish my easy job today. I am inclined to continue tomorrow with more of the same, so that they can see that I am a man who likes to work . . .

Bernardo Vega (1885–1965)

Memoirs of Bernardo Vega (excerpt)

Bernardo Vega was a Puerto Rican community activist in New York City, from his arrival in 1916 and well into the years of World War II, during which time he began to write his memoirs. His activism, which extended from organizing unions of tobacco workers to leadership in the cultural life, also included his buying the newspaper *Gráfico* in 1927 and serving as its editor. Situated at the heart of the Hispanic community during the years of heavy immigration and political ferment, Vega was later able to produce what has come to be considered the most detailed and politically coherent account of Puerto Rican life in New York. Born in 1885 in Cayey, Puerto Rico (the same hometown as Jesús and Joaquín Colón), Vega began his labor activism as a tobacco worker in Puerto Rico, not only in organizing labor but also in working for the Socialist party. He carried these perspectives with him to New York, where he intensified his commitment after witnessing first-hand the exploitation of Hispanic immigrants in the city he called the "Iron Tower of Babel." Vega spent the years after World War II until his death in Puerto Rico, where he continued his militancy and came under surveillance for his protest against the House Un-American Activities Committee. The self-taught author turned his manuscript over to his friend and comrade César Andreu Iglesias to edit and it was published in Spanish in 1977, from which time it has been considered a foundational text of Puerto Rican culture. (NK)

Further reading: Bernardo Vega, *Memoirs of Bernardo Vega,* ed. César Andreu Iglesias, trans. Juan Flores (New York: Monthly Review Press, 1984).

Trans.: JF

Day-to-Day Life in New York and Other Details

In about 1918 entertainment for Puerto Ricans in New York was confined to the apartments they lived in. They celebrated birthdays and weddings and, of course, Christmas Eve, New Year's Day, and the Feast of the Epiphany. But always at home, with friends and neighbors.

There would be dancing, and between numbers somebody would recite poetry or hold forth about our distant homeland. At some of the parties there were *charangas,* lively groups of Puerto Rican musicians. But most of the time we played records. By that time Columbia Records was recording *danzas, aguinaldos,* and other kinds of music from back home.

Almost every family owned a vicrrola, and many even had a pianola. The fact is that once this music gained in popularity, Puerto Ricans were exploited mercilessly. Pianolas cost about $500.00, on credit. Many was the worker who wound up losing what little he earned by falling behind on his payments. Not to mention the times a family would move and have to leave their pianola behind . . . Just getting it from one place to another cost more than moving the rest of their belongings!

Those boisterous Puerto Rican parties would often disturb neighbors of other nationalities, which led to some serious conflicts and unpleasant quarrels.

And there were some less innocent events as well. In the more spacious apartments in Harlem some people threw parties on Saturdays and Sundays that weren't just family parties, but full-scale dances with a cover charge and all. And once you were in they'd take you for whatever else you had, for drinks and tidbits. Which is not the least of the shameful things that went on.

There was none of that in the homes of the *tabaqueros.*

By then there were over ten thousand Puerto Ricans living in El Barrio. The first stores and restaurants that were like those back home were opening up. Every week a new shipload of emigrants would arrive in the city. The landlords up in Harlem were making good money by charging the Puerto Ricans high rents—relative, that is, to what they were getting for their money. I remember a building on 113th Street off Fifth Avenue where, back when the Jews were still living there, apartments were renting for only $17.00 . . . When the Puerto Ricans moved in, the rents went up to $35.00.

In the winter of 1918, Manuel Noriega's theater company made its debut at the Amsterdam Opera House. Thanks to Noriega the Puerto Rican community in New York was able to see Spanish theater for the first time. One night more than two hundred Puerto Ricans attended, many of them theater-loving *tabaqueros.*

Another happy memory is of a reading by Mexican poet Amado Nervo, held in Havermeyer Hall over at Columbia University.

All this time the Brooklyn Círculo de Trabajadores, which I mentioned earlier, remained active. To give you an idea of how the Círculo got started; it was founded in the previous century and was largely made up of *tabaqueros.* They were all progressive in their thinking—anarchists, socialists, or at the very least left-wing republicans. Back then most of them were getting on in years, but their minds were young and alert, their hearts filled with optimism.

I went to the Círculo often. On any given night, in wintertime, they would get together at tables to play dominoes, checkers, or chess, or just to talk. I went from one group to another. The venerable old man Castañeda would be sitting in a corner. I can still hear him saying, "It was a shame that Martí took that rumormongering by Trujillo and Collazo so much to heart, and that his own pride brought him to his end in Dos Ríos. If he had only stayed on to direct and guide the revolution, Cuba today would be the freest and most democratic republic in the world . . ."

I then went to another group, where Miguel Rivera, a native of Cayey, was enthusiastically reporting the resolutions submitted by the Mexican delegation to the Congress of Laredo. "Even though the A.F. of L. accepted them," he commented, "the Yankees are sure to go on holding the Mexicans down, the same as before . . ."

From another group I heard cheerful laughter. I went over and found them enjoying the latest story by "El Malojero"—the "Corn Seller," as he was called—an anecdote passed on to him by Luis Bonafoux.

Making the rounds, I met up with Pepín and Anastasio Fueyo over by the Círculo's little office. They were discussing the events scheduled for that winter. I found out about a production of Guimera's *Tierra Baja* and Gorky's *The Vagabonds.* They were also thinking of staging Chekhov's *Uncle Vanya,* the Spanish version by the Puerto Rican worker Alfonso Dieppa.

Going over to the canteen for a cup of coffee, I overheard a discussion between the Spaniard José López, an *escogedor*, and the anarchist Rojas. "The Bolsheviks," Rojas was saying, "have betrayed the Russian workers. They should have set up free communities and not those iron-clad Soviets." To which López responded: "All of you anarchists have a screw loose. Only yesterday man left his wild, untamed state and already you're talking about showing them a new world, free of all restraint, and all in one fell swoop? If we are ever to arrive at a just society, you have to force men to be good and not animals."

That's what it was like in those days.

Years later I got to know a Puerto Rican cigarworker named Pedro Juan Bonit, who had been living in New York since 1913. Here is a conversation I had with him, which fills out my picture of the emigrants' life in those times.

"When did you arrive here?"

"On December 22, 1913."

"What town do you come from?"

"I was born and raised in San Juan."

"Why did you leave Puerto Rico?"

"To get to know the world. And, of course, because I thought I would be better off economically."

"Where did you live when you arrived here?"

"In a roominghouse run by Ramón Galíndez. The address was 2049 Second Avenue, between 105th and 106th."

"Was it easy to find work?"

"Immediately. There were a lot of jobs for cigarmakers back then. Besides, the cigar manufacturers had agents who would find them workers, and for every cigarworker they delivered they'd get $5.00. I still remember one of those agents; his name was Damián Ferrer, alias 'Batata,' or 'Sweet Potato.'"

"Where was that first job?"

"In a little factory. Later I worked at Samuel I. Davis's factory on 81st Street and First Avenue. Over a hundred Puerto Rican *tabaqueros* were working there."

"Were there any other places that hired so many Puerto Ricans?"

"Many."

"And did those factories have readers like the ones in Puerto Rico?"

"Practically all of them did. In the Davis factory there were two—Fernando García, who would read us the newspapers in the morning, and Benito Ochart, who read novels in the afternoon."

"Was there any difference between the works they read here and the ones they read back in Puerto Rico?"

"Well, I think the quality of the readings here was somewhat higher. They would read books of greater educational value."

"Do you remember any of them?"

"There was *Le Feu* by Barbusse and *La Hyène enragée* by Pierre Loti . . ."

"Who paid the readers?"

"We did. Each of us donated 25 cents a week."

"Were any other collections taken?"

"Yes. Every week we also contributed to the working-class press. And then they were always raising money to support some strike movement or another."

"Were there already Puerto Rican businesses in El Barrio?"

"No. No *bodegas* or restaurants had been established yet. There were only boarding houses and a few barber shops."

"Then where did people buy plantains and other vegetables?"

"There was a Latin grocery on 136th Street near Lenox Avenue, in the middle of the black community. And as for Spanish products, you could get them at Victoria's down on the corner of Pearl and John."

"Did you know of any authentic Puerto Rican businesses?"

"None that I am aware of. But yes, come to think of it, there was a drugstore owned by a certain Loubriel on 22nd Street and Seventh Avenue."

"Do you remember any Puerto Ricans who lived near you?"

"Sure. There was Andrés Araujo, Juan Nieto, Antonio Díaz, Agustín García, Felipe Montalbán, and many more. I think that by then there were already a good hundred and fifty Puerto Rican families living on 105th and 106th off of Second Avenue."

"How about in what we now know as El Barrio?"

"No. For the most part that was where the Jewish people lived. There were only a handful of Hispanic families. In those times the Puerto Ricans were scattered in other areas—in Chelsea, and over in Brooklyn around the Armory and Boro Hall. There were also Puerto Rican neighborhoods on the East Side, in the 20's and along Second and Third avenues from 64th Street up to 85th. And the professionals and better-off families were over on the West Side, on the other side of Central Park. That's where people like Dr. Henna and Dr. Marxuach lived . . ."

"How did people get along in the community?"

"Well, each class had its own way of associating. The *tabaqueros* were the only ones who were organized collectively. There were no exclusively Puerto Rican organizations. But we *tabaqueros* did have mutual aid societies like La Aurora (Dawn), La Razón (Reason), and El Ejemplo (The Example) . . . The educational circles were almost all anarchist except for the Brooklyn Círculo de Trabajadores, which admitted workers of different ideological leanings. The trade unions were the International Cigarmakers' Union and La Resistencia . . . Where I lived there was a club called El Tropical, which had dances and where meetings were held from time to time. It was presided over by Gonzalo Torres. Over on the West Side I remember that Dr. Henna was president of the Ibero-American Club."

"What were the Spanish-language papers published here in those days?"

"*Las Novedades*, a Spanish publication put out by a man by the name of García, whom we nicknamed 'Little Priest.' And there was the anarchist weekly *Cultura Proletaria*, and *La Prensa*, which also came out weekly back then."

"Where did you buy clothes for the first time when you got to New York?"

"I got them from Markowsky, a Jew who had a store downstairs in the building where I lived. A lot of *tabaqueros* bought things there on credit."

"Were there any notable racial differences among the Puerto Ricans?"

"Not among the *tabaqueros*; for us there were no problems of race or religion. But when it came to the so-called better-off people, some of them were even more prejudiced than the Americans."

"How much were your earnings back then?"

"At Davis's I was averaging about $30.00 a week."

"And what were your expenses like?"

"For a room, food, and clean clothes I paid about $10.00 a week."

"Did anyone play *bolita*, or lottery?"

"Yes. I've been told that game started back in 1870."

"What about problems between Puerto Ricans?"

"There would be a fight now and then, but never anything serious."

"What kind of parties did you have?"

"We celebrated Christmas, New Year's, and the Feast of the Epiphany in people's homes."

"Was there much concern over the situation in Puerto Rico?"

"Of course."

"Would you like to go back?"

"Don't make me sad. I've been back twice and if I could I'd be off again tomorrow."

News from Puerto Rico at the end of 1918 and the beginning of 1919 told of widespread misery and of strikes that crippled the country. Thousands of agricultural workers went out on strike, and many were persecuted and beaten. The *tabaqueros* also had frequent work stoppages. And on top of that there were the victims of the earthquakes . . . *La Prensa* called for donations from the public to help those struck by the catastrophe. Angered at the lukewarm response of its readers, it published an editorial complaining of the lack of charity in the Hispanic community. A lively debate ensued, involving Luisa Capetillo, Gabriel Blanco, and other writers of note.

The most widely discussed position was the one Luisa held. She openly blamed the people in power for the miserable living conditions in Puerto Rico. She called for making progressive people in the United States aware of this situation, and ended by saying that "Tyranny, like freedom, has no country, any more than do exploiters or workers."

I should say something about that great Puerto Rican woman. At that time Luisa Capetillo was employed as a reader in a cigar factory. She belonged to the leadership of the Federación Libre de Trabajadores and took part in meetings and strikes all over Puerto Rico. She could rightly be called the first woman suffragist in the Antilles. Aggressive and dynamic by temperament, she was devoted body and soul to defending the rights of workers and the cause of woman's liberation. She came to New York from Havana, where she had created a scandal by showing up in the streets dressed in culottes, which only the most advanced women at that time dared to wear.

The last time I spoke with Luisa was at a boarding house she ran on 22nd Street and Eighth Avenue. She worked interminable hours and always looked tired. But that didn't stop her from using every chance she had to propound her revolutionary and strongly anarchistic ideas to her boarders. Nor did that prevent anyone from eating very well at her place, because aside from her enthusiasm for the revolution, Luisa had a great love for cooking. And as that noble woman from Puerto Rico never cared very much about money, everyone who came there hungry got something to eat, whether he could pay for it or not. Needless to say, her "business" was in a constant crisis, and she was often hard put even to pay her rent.

Younger generations, especially women in our own day, should know of Luisa Capetillo and her exemplary life as a tireless militant. It is a story of great human interest. I do not know what became of her after that meeting.

Meanwhile, thousands of Puerto Rican workers continued to land in New York. The apartments of those already here filled up with family, friends; and just anyone who was down and out. The number of Puerto Ricans climbed to 35,000. According to statistics kept by the International Cigarmakers' Union, there were over 4,500 Puerto Ricans enrolled in its various locals around the city. But the majority of the workers lacked a skilled trade, and made a large labor supply willing to take on the lowest paying jobs in New York.

No serious effort was made to organize the community and fight for its civil rights. The groups that did exist, as I have pointed out, had no other purpose than to organize dances. The only exception was the Club La Luz, located on the corner of Lenox and 120th Street, which in addition to dances would hold occasional cultural evenings.

In early 1919 the first issue of *El Norteamericano* circulated among us. Published by the South American Publishing Co. at 310 Fifth Avenue, that weekly became very popular in Hispanic homes. But it did not last long.

Around the same time the great Spanish novelist Vicente Blasco Ibáñez visited New York. He gave three lectures at Columbia, the first and most controversial on the subject of "How Europeans View America."

But the only event really worth remembering, the one that had a lasting impact on the Puerto Rican community, was the Floral Games sponsored by *La Prensa.* This was, in fact, the most outstanding event in the Spanish-speaking community in New York since the turn of the century. The nominating judges were Federico de Onís, Orestes Ferrara, Pedro Henríquez Ureña, and the North American Hispanist Thomas Walsh.

Prizes were awarded on May 5 at an event held in Carnegie Hall. All of the Spanish-American peoples were represented. At no other event did I ever see so many beautiful women—Mexican, Spanish, Dominican, Cuban, and Puerto Rican. First prize went to José Méndez Rivera, a Colombian poet who received the Flor Natural prize. The Dominican writer M. F. Cesteros won another prize. And as for the Puerto Ricans in the audience, all of us left happy. A young Puerto Rican poet had been given Honorable Mention for his poem, "Yo soy tu flauta." His name: Luis Muñoz Marín.

Anonymous

The Dishwasher (El Lavaplatos); The Deportee (El Deportado)

El Deportado and *El Lavaplatos* were composed in the late 1920s or early 1930s and belong to a corrido subgenre known as "immigration" corridos, that is, the travails and tragedies of Mexican nationals as they trekked northward to the U.S.–Mexico border, crossed legally or illegally, avoided U.S. authorities, and tried to survive as farm laborers, dishwashers, construction workers, and so on. *El Deportado* captures a young man's regret at having to leave his beloved Mexico for the United States during the revolution, the humiliating treatment to which he is subjected in the United States, his eventual disillusionment, deportation, and his happy return to Mexico once the revolution has ended. *El Lavaplatos* deals with the vast difference between what a young Mexican male dreams the United States will offer him and the reality he finds once he has crossed the border. As in the previous selection, he, too, returns to Mexico, poorer but happier. (ChT)

Further reading: Américo Paredes, *A Texas-Mexican Cancionero* (Urbana: University of Illinois Press, 1975).

Trans.: MAT

The Dishwasher	*El lavaplatos*
I dreamed in my youth	Soñaba en mi juventud
Of being a movie star,	ser una estrella de cine
And one of those days I came	Y un día de tantos me vine
To visit Hollywood	A visitar Hollywood.
One day very desperate	Un día muy desesperado
Because of so much revolution	por tanta revolución
I came over to this side of the border	Me pasé para este lado
Without paying the immigration.	Sin pagar la imigracion.
What a fast one I pulled,	Qué vacilada,
What a fast one,	qué vacilada,
I crossed without paying anything.	me pasé sin pagar nada.
On arriving at the station,	Al llegar a la estación,
I ran into a friend,	Me tropecé con un cuate
Who gave me an invitation	Que me hizo la invitación
To work on the track.	De trabajar en "el traque."
I supposed the track	Yo "el traque" me suponía,
Would be some kind of a store.	Que sería algun almacén.
And it was to repair the road	Y era componer la vía
Where the train ran.	Por donde camina el tren.
Oh, my buddy,	Ay, qué mi cuate,
Oh, my buddy,	Ay, qué mi cuate.
How he took me to the track.	Cómo me llevo pa'l traque.
When I had enough of the track,	Cuando me enfadé del traque
He invited me again,	Me volvió a invitar aquél
To the picking of tomatoes	A la pizca del tomate
And the gathering of beets.	Y a desahijar betabel.

And there I earned indulgences
Walking on my knees,
About four or five miles
They gave me as penance.

Oh, what work,
And so poorly paid,
For going on one's knees.

My friend, who was no fool,
Continued struggling.
And when he saved enough for his fare,
He returned to his land.

And I earned but a trifle
And I left for Sacramento.
When I had nothing left to do,
I had to work with cement.

Oh, what torment,
Oh, what torment,
Is that famous cement.

Toss some gravel and sand
In the cement mixer,
Fifty cents an hour
Until the whistle blows.

Four or more of us
Strained at that famous pulley
And I, how could I stand it,
I was better off washing dishes.

How repentant,
How repentant,
I am for having come.

It is the decent work
Done by many Chicanos,
Although with the hot water,
The hands swell a little.

To make it short,
I got tired of so many dishes,

Y allí me gané indulgencias
Caminando de rodillas.
Como cuatro o cinco millas
Me dieron de penitencia.

Ay qué trabajo.
Tan mal pagado.
Por andar arrodillado.

Mi cuate, que no era mage,
El siguió dándole guerra
Y al completar su pasaje,
Se devolvió pa' su tierra.

Y yo hice cualquier bicoca,
Y me fui pa' Sacramento.
Cuando no tenía ni zoca,
Tuve que entrarle al cemento.

Ay, qué tormento,
Ay, qué tormento,
Es el mentado cemento.

Echale piedra y arena
A la máquina batidora,
Cincuenta centavos hora
Hasta que el pito no suena.

En la carrucha mentada
Se rajaron más de cuatro.
Y yo pos cómo aguantaba,
Mejor me fuí a lavar platos.

Qué arrepentido,
Qué arrepentido
Estoy de haberme venido.

Es el trabajo decente
Que lo hacen muchos chicanos,
Aunque con l'agua caliente,
Se hinchan un poco las manos.

Pa' no hacérselas cansadas,
Me enfadé de tanto plato,

And the thought came to me
Of working in the theater

Y me alcancé la puntada
De trabajar en el teatro.

Oh, how pretty,
Oh, how pretty,
Circus, somersaults and little shows.

Ay qué bonito,
Ay qué bonito,
Circo, maroma y teatrito.

I ask your leave
To give this advice
To the young and old,
Who are inexperienced.

Yo les pido su licencia
Pa' darles estos consejos
A los jóvenes y viejos,
Que no tengan experiencia.

Whoever doesn't want to believe
That what I say is true,
If he wants to be convinced
Let him come over here.

Aquél que no quiera creer
Que lo que digo es verdad,
Si se quiere convencer
Que se venga para acá.

Let him remember
This ballad,
Is all that I ask.

Y que se acuerde
De este corrido,
Es único que le pido.

The coach is about to leave,
Soon we will get going.
Eyes that saw you leave
When will they see you return?

Ya el estage va salir,
Ya empezamos a correr,
Ojos que te vieron ir,
¿cuándo te verán volver?

Goodbye dreams of my life.
Goodbye movie stars.
I am going back to my beloved homeland,
Much poorer than when I came.

Adiós sueños de mi vida.
Adiós estrellas del cine.
Vuelvo a mi patria querida.
Más pobre de lo que vine

We take our leave.
Goodbye my countrymen.
Because now we are leaving for good.

Nos despedimos.
Adiós paisanos.
Porque ahora sí ya nos vamos.

The Deportee

I'm going to sing to you, gentlemen,
I'm going to sing to you, gentlemen,
All about my sufferings,
Since I left my country,
Since I left my country
To come to this nation.

It must have been about ten at night,

El deportado

Voy a cantarles, señores,
Voy a cantarles, señores,
Todo lo que yo sufrí,
Desde que dejé mi patria,
Desde que dejé mi patria
Por venir a este país.

Serían las diez de la noche,

It must have been about ten at night,
The train began to whistle.
I heard my mother say,
"There comes that ungrateful train
That is going to take my son away."

"Goodbye my beloved mother,
Goodbye my beloved mother,
Give me your blessings.
I am going abroad,
I am going abroad,
Where there is no revolution."

Run, run little train,
Run, run little train,
Let's leave the station.
I don't want to see my mother
Cry for her beloved son,
For the son of her heart.

Finally the bell rang,
Finally the bell rang,
The train whistled twice.
"Don't cry, my buddies,
Don't cry, my buddies,
For you'll make me cry as well."

Right away we passed Jalisco,
Right away we passed Jalisco,
My, how fast the train ran.
La Piedad, then Irapuato,
Silado, then La Chona,
And Aguas Calientes as well.

When I remember these hours,
When I remember these hours,
My heart beats fast.
When I saw from afar
When I saw from afar
That infamous city of Torreón.

When we passed Chihuahua,
When we passed Chihuahua,
We noticed great confusion.
The employees from the customhouse,

Serían las diez de la noche,
Comenzó un tren a silbar.
Oí que dijo mi madre,
"Ahí viene ese tren ingrato
Que a mi hijo se va a llevar."

"Adiós mi madre querida,
Adiós mi madre querida,
Echame su benedición.
Yo me voy al extranjero,
Yo me voy al extranjero,
Donde no hay revolución."

Corre, corre maquinita,
Corre, corre maquinita,
Vámonos de la estación.
No quiero ver a mi madre
Llorar por su hijo querido,
Por su hijo del corazón.

Al fin sonó la campana,
Al fin sonó la campana,
Dos silbidos pegó el tren.
"No lloren, mis compañeros,
No lloren, mis compañeros,
Que me hacen llorar también."

Pasamos pronto Jalisco,
Pasamos pronto Jalisco,
Ay qué fuerte corría el tren.
La Piedad, luego Irapuato,
Silado luego La Chona,
Y Aguas Calientes también.

Al recordar estas horas,
Al recordar estas horas,
me palpita el corazón.
Cuando divisé a lo lejos,
Cuando divisé a lo lejos
A ese mentado Torreón.

Cuando Chihuahua pasamos,
Cuando Chihuahua pasamos
Se notó gran confusión.
Los empleados de la aduana,

<table>
<tr><td>The employees from the customhouse,
Who were conducting inspections.</td><td>Los empleados de la aduana,
Que pasaban revisión.</td></tr>
<tr><td>We arrived at Juarez at last,
We arrived at Juarez at last,
There I ran into trouble.
"Where are you going, where do
You come from?
How much money do you have
To enter this nation?"</td><td>Llegamos por fin a Juárez,
Llegamos por fin a Juárez,
Y allí fué mi apuración.
"¿Que 'onde vas que de 'onde vienes?

¿Que cuánto dinero tienes
Para entrar a esta nación?"</td></tr>
<tr><td>"Gentlemen, I have money,
Gentlemen, I have money
So that I can emigrate."
"Your money isn't worth anything,
Your money isn't worth anything,
We have to bathe you."</td><td>"Señores, traigo dinero,
Señores, traigo dinero
Para poder emigrar."
"Tu dinero nada vale,
Tu dinero nada vale,
Te tenemos que bañar."</td></tr>
<tr><td>Oh, my beloved countrymen,
Oh, my beloved countrymen,
This is idle conversation.
They were making me feel,
They were making me feel,
Like going right back.</td><td>Ay, mis paisanos queridos,
Ay, mis paisanos queridos,
Yo les platico no más.
Que me estaban dando ganas,
Que me estaban dando ganas,
De volverme para atrás.</td></tr>
<tr><td>At last I crossed the border,
At last I crossed the border,
And left on a contract.
Oh my beloved countrymen,
Oh my beloved countrymen,
I suffered a lot.</td><td>Crucé por fin la frontera,
Crucé por fin la frontera,
Y en un renganche salí.
Ay, mis queridos paisanos,
Ay, mis queridos paisanos,
Fue mucho lo que sufrí.</td></tr>
<tr><td>The white skinned men are very wicked,
The white skinned men are very wicked,
They take advantage of the occasion.
And all the Mexicans,
And all the Mexicans,
Are treated without compassion.</td><td>Los güeros son muy maloras,
Los güeros son muy maloras,
Se valen de la ocasión.
Y a todos los mexicanos,
Y a todos los mexicanos,
Los tratan sin compasión.</td></tr>
<tr><td>There comes a large cloud of dust,
There comes a large cloud of dust,
With no consideration,
Women, children and old ones
Are being driven to the border.
We are being kicked out of this country.</td><td>Ahí traen la gran polvadera,
Ahí traen la gran polvadera,
Y sin consideración,
Mujeres, niños y ancianos
Los llevan a la frontera.
Nos hechan de esta nación.</td></tr>
</table>

Goodbye, beloved countrymen,
Goodbye, beloved countrymen,
We are being deported.
But we are not bandits,
But we are not bandits,
We came to work like beasts.

I will wait for you in my homeland,
I will wait for you in my homeland,
There is no more revolution.
Let's leave, my dear friends,
We will be welcomed
By our beautiful nation.

Adiós, paisanos queridos,
Adiós, paisanos queridos,
Ya nos van a deportar.
Pero no somos bandidos,
Pero no somos bandidos,
Venimos a camellar.

Los espero allá en mi tierra,
Los espero allá en mi tierra,
Ya no hay más revolución.
Vámonos, cuates queridos,
Seremos bien recibidos
De nuestra bella nación.

Miguel Angel Figueroa and Anonymous

A Jíbaro's Lament (Lamento de un jíbaro); A Jíbaro in New York (Un jíbaro en Nueva York)

The following are the lyrics of two songs composed in the traditional *décima* verse form. Made up of ten–line stanzas, *décima* have been composed orally by highland bards since the colonization of Puerto Rico. Recorded in the 1960s, like many others that can be harvested from popular culture in New York, they express the ethos of the Puerto Rican migrant to the city, the nostalgia for their pastoral homeland, and fears of loss of language and identity. Miguel Angel Figueroa's *A Jíbaro's Lament* was recorded by its composer with a traditional ensemble of guitar, cuatro (four double-string, higher pitched guitar), and güiro (scraping gourd), in true highlander style, but *A Jíbaro in New York* (anonymous) was orchestrated in big-city salsa dance music, and sung very much tongue-in-cheek. (NK)

Further reading: Pedro Carrasquillo, *Requinto, poemas jíbaros* (New York: Las Américas, 1958).

Trans.: NK

A Jíbaro's Lament

I've come from the mountains
from the famed Guilarte slopes
and the proud song that I sing
is the plaintive chant of Adjuntas.
That's where I left behind
the yoke of oxen that was mine
in order to cross that ocean wide
to here, New York City,
and no one can ever imagine
how I am made of those mountains.

Lamento de un jíbaro

Yo vengo desde las montas
del gran cerro de Guiarte
y traigo como estandarte
el canto hondo de Adjuntas.
Allí yo dejé mi yunta
de bueyes que poseía
para hacer la travesía
a esta ciudad nuyorquina
y hoy ninguno se imagina
cuánto es yo mi serranía.

That's where I left my little farm
with all of my little animals
and the sweet unending love
of my poor old mother dear.
Today I pray God permits me
someday to be able to return
to contemplate my mountain view
where from childhood I grew
and to spend my aged years
in Borinquen, my homeland.

Oh how I have missed
everything there I left behind.
I can't begin to explain why
I came to someone else's land
when I lived back there in peace
and calm in my homestead
surrounded by mountain scenery
all its beauty and greenery
created only by Nature herself
for my sweet little land.

Here on New York soil
deep within me I feel
a hole deep in my heart
for my absent countryside.
Maybe it was my destiny
to come to foreign lands,
but someday I'll go return
to the mountains of Adjuntas
to deposit my mortal remains
in the care of her womb again.

Allí yo dejé mi finquita
y todos mis animalitos
y el amor más infinito
de mi pobre viejecita.
Y hoy ruego a Dios me permita
poder volver algún día
y contemplar la serranía
en donde tuve mi niñez
para pasar mi vejez
en Borinquen, tierra mía.

Estoy echando de menos
todo lo que allí dejé.
Yo no me explico por qué
vine a este país ajeno
y allí vivía más sereno
y más tranquilo en mi bohío
contemplando la serranía
su verdor y su belleza
que dio la Naturaleza
a ese terruñito mío.

Aquí en suelo nuyorquino
siento dentro de mi pecho
la falta que a mí me ha hecho
el ambiente campesino.
Tal vez sería mi destino
venir a tierras extrañas
Pero algún día a las montañas
de Adjuntas yo volveré
y mis despojos dejaré
guardados en sus entrañas.

A Jíbaro in New York

I'm talking about Hispanos
who on arriving in New York
on descending from the plane
forget their castellano.
That's where I met Mariano,
a jíbaro from Jagüey,
when I got on the subway
I asked him how he was,
listen how he answered me:

Un jíbaro en Nueva York

Me refiero a los hispanos
que llegando a Nueva York
que al tirarse del avión
se les olvida el castellano.
Allá encontré a Mariano
un jíbaro de Jagüey
que al montarse en el subway
Le pregunté cómo estaba
y lo que me contestaba

"I don't know what you say!"

But as I had known him for years
since our days back in Jayuya,
I kept asking to him questions
just to see what he would say,
only he would not confess
that indeed he was Hispano.
I asked him about the others.
He said, "Listen to me, brother,
I love my father and mother,
just like any americano."

And finally, at last, he says,
"Look, bud, I'm only joking,
but I always keep on talking
en español y en inglés."
He kept on saying "yes,"
between Spanish and inglés.
And on getting out of the train—
this is no lie, it's so—
instead of saying adiós, amigo,
he says, "Goodbye, my friend!"

Era, "I don't know what you say!"

Y como yo lo conocía
desde que estaba en Jayuya
seguí haciéndole preguntas
a ver lo que me decía.
Aún por eso no quería
declararse que era hispano.
Le pregunté por su hermano.
Y me dijo, "Oye esto, brother,
I love my father and mother
igual que un americano."

Y ya por última vez
me dijo, "Estoy vacilando
pero siempre sigo hablando
en español y en inglés."
Siguió diciéndome "yes"
siempre en el mismo vaivén
y al desmontarse del tren,
no es mentira lo que digo
por decirme, "Adiós, amigo,"
me dijo, "Goodbye, my friend!"

Américo Meana (dates unknown)

Prayer to Home Relief (Oración al Home Relief)

Like so many working-class poets who contributed their verse to the popular media, Américo Meana was an acute observer of the urban scene. His poems appeared during the Depression years in Spanish-language periodicals of New York, and little else is known of this Puerto Rican poet. (A corpus of Meana's work has also been found among the papers of Jesús Colón.) In his prose–poetry "prayer" below, which appeared in the June 1935 issue of Brooklyn's *El Curioso*, Meana satirizes the welfare program that helped so many poor people to survive during the Depression by maintaining the comparison throughout between a god and the "relief" program, as it was known at least until the 1960s. (NK)

Further reading: Bernardo Vega, *Memoirs of Bernardo Vega,* ed. César Andreu Iglesias, trans. Juan Flores (New York: Monthly Review Press, 1984).

Trans.: TEW

Oh, compassionate Home Relief, you who gives everything, who pays the rent, who pays the electric bill and the gas bill, make all the saints and virgins under you be punctual and that way, my father won't run up his tab at the bodega!

Oh, Home Relief, God of My Wallet, send me some clothes and a good bolt of cloth!

Oh, Wealthy Home Relief, order them to bring me a ticket to buy a suit for bathing and another for the theater!

Oh, Humanitarian Home Relief, don't let the all-powerful Mr. Hudson come by with that tired joke of giving me a job, and tell him to increase my father's pay, so that he can buy me the dress suit that I need!

¡Oh, Home Relief Piadoso, tú que todo lo das, que pagas la renta, que pagas la luz y pagas gas, haz que todos los santos y las vírgenes que están a tu mando sean puntuales y así mi papá no cogerá mucho en la bodega!

¡Oh, Home Relief, Dios del Bolsillo, mándame ropa y un buen pestillo!

¡Oh, Home Relief Adinerado, ordena que me traigan un ticket para comprar un traje de baño y atro para el teatro!

¡Oh, Home Relief Humanitario, no dejes que el Todopoderoso Mr. Hudson venga con la broma pesada de darme trabajo y dile que le aumente el cheque a mi papito, para que me compre un traje largo que necesito!

Oh, my beloved Home Relief: You've come to kill my hunger. I welcome you with frenzy, knowing how much you love me.	Adórote Home Relief, que a matar el hambre vienes. Te acojo con frenesí. pues sé el amor que me tienes.
You love me with such determination, you bring ham sandwiches, and to fight-off the cold of winter, you stock me up with coal.	Tú me amas con tal brío, que me das pan y jamón. Y para mitigar el frío, tú me regalas carbón.
You're so good you provide it all. You pay my light and you pay my gas; but not satisfied, I beg you for more.	Tú eres tan bueno que todo lo das, tú me pagas luz y me pagas gas; pero no conforme yo te pido más.
(A devotional is said to Saint Comehither.)	(Se le reza una salve a San Acércate.)
Come hither, Home Relief. Please let me see you when you bring the check for groceries; if you're slow to pay, you assure my death today, but pay me off, and you give me life. Amen	Acércate Home Relief, que quiero verte cuando traes el cheque de la comida; si me atrasas el cheque, me das la muerte, pero si me lo traes, me das la vida. Amén

Note: This prayer should be recited three days before the check comes, then a Saint Forgetmenot prayer should be said, and your front door be showered in sacred water powder.

Next week: The Prayer to the God Bacchus.

Nota: Esta oración debe hacerse tres días antes de venir el cheque, luego se debe rezar un San Noteolvides y hay que regar la puerta con agua bendita en polvo.
Próxima semana: La Oración al dios Baco.

Gonzalo O'Neill (?–1942)

Take the Dead Man Away (excerpt)

Born and educated in Puerto Rico, upon graduating from the island's Civil Institute, Gonzalo O'Neill immigrated to the United States before the Spanish-American War and became a wealthy businessman. Despite his financial success, O'Neill never severed his ties from the Hispanic community nor did he ever abandon his lifelong pursuit of Puerto Rican independence. In fact, O'Neill became something of a godfather to the Puerto Rican community of East Harlem, offering shelter to recent arrivals and investing in and helping to administer cultural institutions, such as the Teatro Hispano and the newspaper *Gráfico*. O'Neill was also a well known poet and playwright in the community, and he possessed the financial resources to publish a number of his own books. The 1920s was a particularly fruitful period for O'Neill. In New York he was able to publish three books, including *Sonoras bagatelas o sicilianas* (1924), which includes poetry and a dialog in verse meant to be dramatized on stage; *La indiana borinqueña* (*The Puerto Rican Indians*); and two full-length patriotic dramas: *Moncho Reyes* (1923), named after the nickname for the military governor of Puerto Rico, and *Bajo una Sola Bandera* (*Under Just One Flag*, written and produced in 1928), with a romantic plot symbolizing the choices of government and culture Puerto Ricans had to make. O'Neill penned other plays, such as *Take the Dead Man Away* (1937), a short, comic one-act following the style and structure of Cuban farce, so popular in the 1920s. The play was recovered from the archive of actor–playwright Erasmo Vando (see the Vando entry in this anthology). In this excerpt, three characters debate Puerto Rico's relationship to the United States. (NK)

Further reading: Gonzalo O'Neill, *Sonoras bagatelas o sicilianas* (New York: America, 1922), *Moncho Reyes* (New York: Spanish American Printing, 1923), *Bajo una Sola Bandera* (New York: Spanish American Printing, 1934).

Trans.: KDM

Scene II

QUINTÍN: (*He enters through the foyer door wildly shaking a newspaper in his hand. He speaks loudly, affected by his intense reaction. It seems that Don Quintín has lost his mind. On entering in that state, all the people in the scene stand and slowly and conclude that he is mad.*) No sir, no sir, no sir. Irrevocably no, no, and no. This is terrible. Just what we needed. No sir, no sir, no sir. No, no, and no. It would be a disaster. A veritable hecatomb.

SÁNCHEZ: (*Like the rest, he does not know what is wrong with Quintín.*) But tell us, Don Quintín, what is the matter? What has happened?

GRACIANO: (*With expressive affect.*) That's it. Tell us why you're so upset?
ANDRÉS: Yes, yes. Explain it to us.
ANICETO: (*Expressing pity.*) Be frank with us. Tell us everything.
QUINTÍN: (*Trying to control himself but still short of breath.*) Listen, gentlemen, to what the newspaper says. (*Everyone gathers around Quintín, who reads the newspaper with great difficulty.*) A law has just been presented in Congress to give Puerto Rico its independence. (*Newly upset and speaking directly to those who surround him.*) Have you ever heard such an atrocity? No sir, no sir, no way. (*Not giving the others a chance to speak.*) Can you imagine it? If that evil law is passed and sovereignty is proclaimed, I will be stripped of my citizenship and goodbye to my free lunch because I'll never see another home relief check.

(*Music. It starts a little before Quintín starts to sing.*)

Take the food out of my mouth
And leave me to my indigence
'Cause Marcantonio has a mind for them
To give us our independence.

CHORUS: No sir, no sir, no sir.

If we stir up that old Congress
That citizenship to us gave
Annoyed it will become
And take it back some day.

CHORUS: No sir, no sir, no sir.

If that ever were to happen
Depressed, I would become
I wouldn't ever receive
Any more relief income.

CHORUS: No sir, no sir, no sir.

Don Antonio has always said
To be careful and quite mindful
If not, the fox will find a way
To send us all to the devil.

CHORUS: No sir, no sir, no sir.

It doesn't matter if we spell "pies"
Like a dummy or a squire

Our stomachs will be telling us
It's English we must acquire.

CHORUS: No sir, no sir, no sir.

That is what that pelican
From Fajardo does proclaim
Yglesias repeats it likewise
And Gallardo does the same.

CHORUS: No sir, no sir, no sir.

Take the food out of my mouth
And leave me to my indigence
Because those foolish jokers want
The Congress to grant us our independence.

CHORUS: No sir, no sir, no sir.

GRACIANO: (*Putting his hand on Quintín's shoulder.*) Don't get so upset, Don Quintín, because Congress or no Congress, there is no danger of that disaster you so fear coming about.

ANDRÉS: (*Trying to console Don Quintín.*) Don Graciano is right. Our island is the lock and key to the Panama Canal, and they are not going to give it up so easily. Besides, don't forget that once those Saxons take control of something, they're not going to release it. There's no way.

GRACIANO: (*With emphasis.*) There's no way.

SÁNCHEZ: (*Interrupting Graciano.*) Another thing. Our Funerary Agency has been formally inaugurated and it is going to be a gold mine under my directorship. You'll see, Don Quintín. We are going to receive cadavers by the ton.

QUINTÍN: I hope to heaven it is so.

Luis Pérez (1904–1962)

El Coyote/The Rebel (excerpt)

Luis Pérez was one of the first Mexican immigrant writers to author an autobiography in English and have it issued by a major American publisher. Pérez was born in San Luis Potosí, Mexico, and immigrated as a teenager to Los Angeles, after having served in combat during the Mexican Revolution. He received a B.A. from Los Angeles State College in 1956. For many years he worked as a translator and later as a Spanish teacher, while also writing novels, plays, and children's stories. *El Coyote* is both a novel of the revolution and a novel of immigration, two genres that were dominant in Mexican immigrant communities. The novel spans twenty-five years in the life of protagonist Luis, the son of an Aztec-Spanish mother and a

French nobleman, who gets drawn into the chaos and violence of the Revolution and eventually makes his way to Los Angeles, California. The novel ends with Luis achieving U.S. citizenship. *El Coyote* accurately portrays the factors accounting for Mexican working-class emigration—the push from the Revolution and the pull of the expanding U.S. economy—as well as the psychology of, first, a boy confused by the wartime chaos and, then, an immigrant looking for work and a better life through education in the United States. In the excerpt below, the process of entering the United States at the border is related in detail. (NK)

Further reading: Luis Pérez, *El Coyote/The Rebel,* ed. Lauro Flores (Houston: Arte Público Press, 2000).

31

The twenty-fifth morning of November, 1918, the families and I were in the United States immigration office at Nogales, patiently waiting to be examined by the officials. When my turn came, the person who examined me said, "Young man, let it be known that you are entering the United States of America to pick cotton and to work as a farm hand for the term of one year. At the end of a year you shall return to Mexico. This is in accordance with the laws adopted by Congress and enforced by the Department of Labor of the United States." Then he took a form from his desk and the regular routine of questioning began. When he had finished asking questions and filling the blank spaces, he said, "Raise your right hand."

By mistake I raised my left hand.

"Your right hand," he commanded.

When I had my arm up in the air, he said, "Repeat with me: 'I, the undersigned, do solemnly swear that the statements made by me in answer to the foregoing questions are full and true to the best of my knowledge and belief. So help me God.'" Then he asked me to sign the documents, which I did by making a cross as a signature.

By three in the afternoon of the same day, our fast train was speeding its way through the Arizona desert to Phoenix. We arrived at the capital of the state late that night, and our coach was uncoupled and switched onto a side track. In the morning, when we got out of the coach, the "big shots" were nervously walking about with other well-dressed men. Don Pánfilo followed them like a faithful dog after his master. At about ten in the morning a lot of farmers came to the station driving old carts, buggies, and "flivvers." The farmers would talk with the "big shots," and after a short conversation they would sign some papers, and would come to where we were, pointing, "I want these these—and these." Then they would take with them three or four of the families.

Somewhere about three in the afternoon I noticed a tall, red-faced man driving a beautiful team of black horses hitched to a four-wheeled rack. When he had pulled the restless animals to an abrupt stop, the three bosses greeted him, and one of them said, pointing to us, "Benson, this is all we have left. You came too late."

Mr. Benson jumped off the cart and asked, "Do all these children belong to one family?"

"No," said one of the men who greeted him. "Those six over there belong to this man and this woman. This boy here is alone," he said, touching my shoulder. Then he pointed to a young man, who was seated on his suitcase, and said, "He is single."

"Benson, I think you should take all of them to your ranch," suggested one of the partners.

"I guess so," mumbled Mr. Benson. After he had signed the papers to own us, he came to each one of the workers, and asked, "Do you speak English?" When the person who was questioned said, "No, *señor,* me no espeaka dee Eengleesh," then Mr. Benson would say, "*Mucho malo, mucho malo*—too bad." When he asked me the question, I answered, "*No, señor, yo no hablo inglés.*" Immediately Don Pánfilo, who was standing near by, said to Mr. Benson, "Deesa *muchacho*—boy hee says hee no espeaka da Eengleesh."

"*Mucho malo, mucho malo,*" repeated Mr. Benson. To that I said, "Oh, no, *señor,* me no *mucho malo—yo* estrong—me wanta worka."

"Fine, fine," he said, and laughed.

The reason why I was able to say "strong," "wanta," and other words, was because Don Pánfilo was teaching me English the way he had learned it. The first night we were on the train he had said to me, "Luis, I like you, and I am going to tell you something that is going to be for your own good. You might just as well know that the only way you can get a good job in the United States is by knowing how to speak English." Then, holding the upper part of the lapels of his blue jumper, he continued, "Look at me, I have a good job—I espeaka da Eengleesh. There is no Mexican in the United States to espeaka da Eengleesh the way I do. I can read it, write it, and teach it. Yes, I can teach it, and because you have been such a good fellow, I am going to teach it to you in ten lessons so you can get a good job in the United States like the one I have. I got a good job."

While he was parading up and down the aisle like a proud peacock, telling me what a good job he had, and bragging about his good fortune, a fellow countryman, who was reading a newspaper, asked, "Say, Don Pánfilo, if hot air and gas makes balloons go up, what in the name of *Jesucristo* holds you down?"

"His big belly keeps him anchored to the ground," shouted an old man, who was eating a piece of dry bread.

At this last remark the crowd laughed, and Don Pánfilo said to me, "Don't pay any attention to them fellows. All they like to do is to eat and to make foul remarks. They will never amount to anything." Then he proceeded, "The only way you can learn English in ten lessons is by reading a book like this," and taking a small dictionary from his pocket, he pointed, "You see—you read the Spanish word and then the English. After you have learned both words you pronounce them like this: '*Beso*—kees,' '*Señorita*—meess,' and so on. Is it not simple? The English language is one of the easiest languages to master. I have tried all the languages—yes—all of them." Suddenly he asked, "Can you read?"

"No, I can't."

"Oh, well, you have to learn to read before you can speak any language. However, you are young, and you can learn. I can teach you a few words—I am a good teacher." In this manner he proceeded to instruct me in the art of learning to speak English in ten lessons; thus I was able to talk to Mr. Benson.

The first afternoon at the ranch, Mr. Benson gave the family a large tent, and a small one to the single man and me. Then he issued us a ration of groceries and let us use some old cooking utensils which were stored in the barn.

The next morning our employer took us to the cotton field and taught us the proper method of removing the wool-like material from the pod. He said, "You should be able to pick from a hundred to a hundred and fifty pounds a day. The more cotton you pick, the more money you'll get. Go to it and make a fortune."

The first day I picked only seventy pounds and the boss said, "Mucho malo."

The following day I picked a little more, and by the end of the cotton season I was able to pick ninety-five pounds per day.

After the cotton season was over, we stayed on the ranch to cultivate the fields for the following year.

By the middle of March of 1920, I told Mr. Benson that since I had been with him over a year I wanted to go back to Mexico. He said, "Luis, you may do as you please. Come to my office and I will go over your account." In the office he continued, "Luis, you came to my ranch the twenty-sixth of November 1918, I paid the recruiting men thirty dollars for your train fare and the food you ate on the way. I gave them eight dollars for the immigration fees. Now you owe me seventy-five dollars for food and shelter, twenty-three dollars for clothes, and twenty dollars that I have given you in cash. Let me see." Mumbling between his teeth, he added, "Thirty, plus eight, plus seventy-five—twenty-three and twenty is forty-three. Well, well, well—you owe me exactly one hundred and fifty-six dollars. Now we take this amount from the money you have earned, which is—let me see six from eight—two, seven and one eight, and two is—well, well, well—you have ten dollars coming to you."

"The whole amount of ten dollars!" I exclaimed.

"Yes, ten dollars."

"For a moment I thought I was going to owe you ten dollars."

"Oh, no! I am very honest—I don't steal money from anybody."

"Thank you, Mr. Benson. And may I have my ten dollars."

"Yes, of course. Here they are and if you ever want to come back to work for me, you are welcome to do so."

I thanked Mr. Benson again and left his ranch with my ten dollars, my blanket, my suitcase, and my black suit. Later I found that Mr. Benson, the honest man, had cheated me out of the greater part of my wages.

From the ranch I went to Phoenix, and after a few days in the capital of the state, I went to Glendale, Arizona.

René Marqués (1919–1979)

The Oxcart (excerpt)

Written in 1951, *The Oxcart* is the play of Puerto Rican emigration par excellence. In each of its three acts, the text dramatizes the tragic experiences of a family of *jíbaros* (peasants) in their migrant movement from the mountains of Puerto Rico to the urban ghettos of San Juan, and from there to metropolitan New York. Driven by an almost religious zeal regarding the potential of machines—the symbols of a modern industrial economy—to improve human life, the older son (Luis) convinces his family of the need to abandon their land and its demands for agricultural work. A series of calamitous events ensues, throwing the family into a downward spiral of moral degradation and unhappiness. The play is written in a poetic realist style, and the Spanish original fictionalizes the dialect of the *jíbaros*. René Marqués was not an emigrant himself and spent most of his life in Puerto Rico. Nevertheless, his works have been considered foundational for the representation of Puerto Rican migrant experience and crucial to the formation of a Puerto Rican migrant literature. His polemical image of migration as a sort of "voyage to hell" has been one with which younger generations of migrant Puerto Rican writers have had to contend during the last three decades. Although professionally trained as an agronomist, Marqués abandoned this career to become one of the country's foremost writers. In 1949 he accepted a grant from the Rockefeller Foundation to study dramaturgy at Columbia University and Piscator's Dramatic Workshop; and in 1957 he spent another brief interval in the city on a Guggenheim Fellowship. Shortly after his return to Puerto Rico in 1950, he began to write *The Oxcart,* which debuted in New York City in 1953. The following excerpt corresponds to the last scenes of the play, after Doña Gabriela (the mother) has revealed to her daughter Juanita a secret unknown to Luis: that he is not a legitimate child of the family. (ALO)

Further reading: René Marqués *The Oxcart* (New York: Charles Scribner's Sons, 1969), *The Look* (New York: Senda Nueva de Ediciones, 1983).

Trans.: ChP

DA. GABRIELA: There's somebody there.
JUANITA: You go in the bedroom. I'll open the door.
DA. GABRIELA: No, no. You go get the lunch. I'll see who it is.
(DA. GABRIELA *goes to the entrance hall.* JUANITA *hesitates a moment, then exits rear;* DA. GABRIELA *opens the door and* MR. PARKINGTON *enters. He is a tall, thin American about forty years old. He is dressed in black and carries a fall overcoat on his arm. He has a leather briefcase in his hand and an extremely friendly smile on his face.*)
PARKINGTON: Good day!
DA. GABRIELA: Good . . .
PARKINGTON: The lady of the house, no doubt?
DA. GABRIELA: Can I help you?
PARKINGTON: If it's no trouble, I'd like very much to talk to you about the Lord.
PARKINGTON: What lord . . . ? The landlord?
PARKINGTON: The Lord Creator of Heaven and Earth. I have named Jehovah, my dear sister! May I come in?
(*Enters without waiting for an answer.*)
Thank you. You're very kind.
(DA. GABRIELA *looks at him in amazement, shuts the door, and follows him to the living room.)*
(With a friendly smile.)
May I sit down, madam?
(*Sits down before* DA. GABRIELA can indicate for him to do so.)
Thank you.

JUANITA: (*Out of sight in the kitchen.*) Who is it, mamá?

DA. GABRIELA: I dunno. Some American . . .

PARKINGTON: My name is Parkington, sister.

JUANITA: (*Appearing in the rear doorway with a can of chopped ham in one hand and the opener in the other.*) What does he want?

DA. GABRIELA: I'm still waitin' for him to tell me.

PARKINGTON: (*Rising politely on seeing* JUANITA.) Pleased to meet you, miss.

JUANITA: (*Giving him the once over as she speaks to* DA. GABRIELA.) Mamá, I've told you not to open the door here to people you don't know.

DA. GABRIELA: The door o' my house has always been open. If I shut it here it's on account o' the cold. Well, mister, say what you have to say.

(JUANITA *exits rear.*)

PARKINGTON: Thank you, madam. The hospitality of you Latins is marvellous. I've always said so. Well then, here's my card.

(*Hands it to her and sits down again.*)

As you can see, I represent the Church of God, Incorporated.

DA. GABRIELA: (*Surprised.*) God incorporated? Incorporated to what?

PARKINGTON: No, no. God is not incorporated. What's incorporated is the Church.

DA. GABRIELA: And what does that mean?

PARKINGTON: (*In a tight spot.*) It means . . . Let's see . . . Incorporated is . . . a corporation.

JUANITA: (*Out of sight in the kitchen.*) Like the sugar mills, mamá! Like the sugar mills in Puerto Rico!

DA. GABRIELA: I don't understand. But go on . . .

PARKINGTON: Well, you must've read about it in the papers . . . it's had magnificent publicity, front page publicity . . . the creation of the Municipal Committee for the Betterment of the Puerto Ricans. The mayor of this great democratic city of New York is terribly interested in you people.

(JUANITA *appears in the doorway and listens skeptically.*)

The mayor, following the doctrine of Jehovah, makes no discriminations between Negroes or whites, rich, or poor, Puerto Ricans or Americans.

JUANITA: Since when?

PARKINGTON: (*Interrupted*). What did you say, miss?

JUANITA: The miss says since when don't the mayor make distinctions.

PARKINGTON: (*In another tight spot.*) Well . . . Since always. Of course, errors have been made in the past . . . Errors that we all lament . . . It won't happen again! It'll be different from now on.

JUANITA: How different?

PARKINGTON: What?

JUANITA: I said, how will it be different from now on?

PARKINGTON: Well . . . the betterment of the Puerto Rican colony, miss. So it can be on the same level . . .

(*Realizes he is putting his foot in it.*)

I mean, so it can be equal . . .

(*Bites his tongue in time.*)

Well . . . so it won't be an object of discrimination.

JUANITA: (*Leaning in the kitchen doorway.*) So they're gonna make us better. They're gonna make us as good as the Americans. That means that we're not any good now, that we're not equal to the rest o' you.

PARKINGTON: Please, miss! You misunderstand me.

JUANITA: (*Taking a step forward.*) Look, mister, what you're sayin' I'd understand even in Chinese. It's as clear as daylight.
(*Looks toward the window and corrects herself.*) Like the daylight in my country, of course.
(*Exits rear.*)

PARKINGTON: Oh, what a shame! The girl doesn't understand. But the thing is that the Church of God, Incorporated, is going to cooperate fully with the Municipal Committee for the Betterment of the Puerto Ricans. It's a titanic job, my sister. But we'll do it! You can be sure we'll do it.
(*Takes out some leaflets and keeps handing them to* DA. GABRIELA.)
Our mission is not only religious. It's also social . . .

DA. GABRIELA: (*Wanting to be pleasant and show an interest in something the visitor proposes.*) Oh, you're gonna hold dances!

PARKINGTON: (*Jumping back.*) Dances?

DA. GABRIELA: But didn't you say . . . ?

PARKINGTON: We are part of the Committee for the Betterment of the Puerto Ricans. And we don't solve social problems with dances. What we hold are meetings. And problems are discussed. And orientation work is performed.
(*Takes out another series of folders.*)
The Puerto Ricans must become orientated to this mechanized civilization. They must give up superstitions and idolatry. They must become familiar with the world of machines. Look, here are some very useful folders. They're in Spanish, very well translated.
(*Keeps handing folders to* DA. GABRIELA.)
The Puerto Rican workers must recognize their responsibilities and yield the maximum labor. We orient them. In that way difficulties are avoided. And accidents are prevented. Like the one that just happened there in the boiler factory.

DA. GABRIELA: In the boiler factory?

PARKINGTON: Yes, madam, yes. I ran into all the commotion just minutes before coming here.
(JUANITA *appears in the doorway.*)
And all because of carelessness and clumsiness on the part of a Puerto Rican worker. That's why I say . . .

JUANITA: (*Coming forward.*) A Puerto Rican worker?

PARKINGTON: Yes, miss. That's why I say the orientation of the workers is essential in a highly mechanized society.

DA. GABRIELA: What happened in the boiler factory?

PARKINGTON: The accident I mentioned. Because New York, as our democratic mayor strongly affirms, opens its arms to the Puerto Ricans. But . . .

JUANITA: What accident? What accident?

PARKINGTON: (*Annoyed by the interruptions.*) But haven't I told you already?

DA. GABRIELA: (*Terribly upset.*) No, you haven't said a thing! For the love o' God, tell us what happened!

PARKINGTON: Well, one of those frequent accidents when you're dealing with people not accustomed . . .

JUANITA: (*Going to him, violently.*) Cut out the stupid talk and tell us once and for all what happened! What happened in the boiler factory?

PARKINGTON: But, miss, you won't let me get a word in. It seems that a worker was examining the inside of one of the machines. The machine began to work and the man was trapped among the many steel parts that kept going full speed. The unfortunate fellow's body . . .

(*Violent knocking is heard on the door, and at the same time* LIDIA's voice is heard calling urgently: "Juanita! Juanita! Juanita, open the door! Juanita!" JUANITA *runs to the door at the right and opens it.* LIDIA *enters, her expression changed. She tries to speak softly to* JUANITA. DA. GABRIELA *takes a step toward the hall but stops in the living room, her eyes wide open, the fingers of both hands pressed against her lips as if she wanted to prevent something vital from escaping from her body.*)

LIDIA: (*Out of breath, in a low voice.*) Juanita! Telephone. In the janitor's office! It's urgent! Come right away. It's urgent!

(JUANITA *and* LIDIA *exit rapidly through the right.* DA. GABRIELA *goes slowly to the sofa. She stops in front of it, before the image of the Sacred Heart. She falls to her knees and sinks her face in the sofa cushion. We see only her bent back, which moves in rhythm to her difficult breathing.* MR. PARKINGTON, *disconcerted, doesn't know what to do. He finally collects his things quietly. Then he takes a step toward* DA. GABRIELA. *He stops, turns, slowly, and exits through the right. Interval, Immobility. Silence.* JUANITA *enters through the right. Then* LIDIA. JUANITA *is very pale, and her movements give the impression of a momentary somnambulism. She slowly enters the living room.* LIDIA, *crying, quietly, follows a short distance behind her. When she gets to the end of the hall and sees* DA. GABRIELA *kneeling,* LIDIA *stops and puts both hands to her mouth to drown her sobs. Leaning against the wall, her face between her hands, she cries silently.* JUANITA *keeps going forward. She stops beside* DA. GABRIELA, *and with a look lost in space, speaks.*)

JUANITA: The orphan found what he was looking for, mother. Luis finally discovered the mystery of the machines that give life.

(DA. GABRIELA *remains still.* JUANITA *slowly lowers her eyes toward the kneeling figure.*)

Did you hear what I said, mamá?

(DA. GABRIELA *slowly raises her head and looks at the Sacred Heart.*)

DA. GABRIELA: Take him to your bosom, Lord. Be a good father to my son!

JUANITA: They'll take him from the hospital to the nearest funeral parlor. Within an hour we can go see him.

(DA. GABRIELA *gets up.*)

DA. GABRIELA: I don't want them to bury him in this land of no sunshine. Will it cost much to take him to Puerto Rico?

JUANITA: It doesn't matter what it costs. We'll do whatever you say.

DA. GABRIELA: (*Noting* LIDIA's *presence.*) How's your little, girl, Lidia?

(LIDIA *runs and throws herself in* DA. GABRIELA's *arms and sobs convulsively on her shoulder.* DA. GABRIELA *caresses her in a motherly fashion.*)

There. There. Don't cry. My son is happy now. The land where he was born will always be the mother who lets him sleep without toil or sorrow.

(LIDIA *leaves* DA. GABRIELA'S *arms, goes more calmly to the hall, drying her tears, and exits right.* DA. GABRIELA *speaks in an illumined tone.*)

Because now I know what was happening to us all. The curse of the land! The land is sacred. The land cannot be abandoned. We must go back to what we left behind so that the curse of the land won't pursue us any more. And I'll return with my son to the land from where we came. And I'll sink my hands in the red earth of my village just as my father sunk his to plant the seeds. And my hands will be strong again. And my house will smell once more of patchouli and peppermint. And there'll be land outside. Four acres to share. Even though that's all! It's good land. It's land. It's land that gives life. Only four acres. Even if they're not ours!

JUANITA: They will be ours. They'll be yours, mamá! 'Cause I'm goin' back with you to my village.

DA. GABRIELA: (*Gently, as if waking from a dream.*) You? You too? But you always said that from now on you were gonna drive the oxcart of your life wherever you wanted.

JUANITA: For that very reason, mamá, for that very reason! 'Cause I do drive it wherever I want. And we'll get back before Miguel sells those acres. And if it's true that he wants me, I'll be his wife and the land will be ours. And we'll save Miguel from comin' here in search o' the mystery that killed my brother. And we'll save Chaguito. 'Cause it's not a question o' goin' back to the land to live like we were dead. Now we know the world don't change by itself. We're the ones who change the world. And we're gonna help change it. We're gonna help change it. We're gonna go like people with dignity, like grandpa used to say. With our heads high. Knowin' there are things to fight for. Knowin' that all God's children are equal. And my children will learn things I didn't learn, things they don't teach in school. That's how we'll go back home! You and I, mamá, as firm as ausubo trees above our land, and Luis resting beneath it!

DA. GABRIELA: Yes, just like you say. Like ausubos. As firm as ausubos.

(*Her voice begins to break.*)

Like ausubos that machines can never cut down! (*Sobs. Her crying, so long held back, breaks forth noisily until her entire body shakes and begins to bend. Little by little* DA. GABRIELA *slips to the floor, beside* JUANITA, *and remains kneeling, then seated on her heels, then bent over herself like a small, insignificant ball, shaken by sobs and pierced by sorrow, at the feet of her daughter who stands firm and decided.*)

CURTAIN

Pedro Juan Soto (1928–)

Scribbles

Scribbles is part of Pedro Juan Soto's first collection of short stories, *Spiks*, originally published in Spanish in 1957. Like other Puerto Rican writers of his generation (such as René Marqués and José Luis González), the stories in *Spiks* present a sordid image of the life of Puerto Rican immigrants in New York City through a violently realist and often poetic style. Poverty and discrimination, filth and moral degradation, hopelessness and insensitivity are some of the attributes of the fictional world inhabited by the characters. *Scribbles* also thematizes the view—shared by many of Soto's fellow writers at the time—that migrant life was not only antagonistic to the artistic creativity of the Puerto Rican male writer but culturally emasculating as well. At the age of eighteen Soto emigrated with his parents to New York, where he attended college while performing menial jobs. He was later drafted to fight in the Korean War. In 1954 he returned to Puerto Rico, working first in a state-sponsored educational project (the Publishing Unit of the Division for Community Education) and eventually becoming professor of Spanish-American literature at the University of Puerto Rico. In 1979, Soto suffered an immense tragedy when his son, Francisco Soto Arriví—a militant in the Puerto Rican independence movement—was ambushed and killed by the police in a politically motivated operation known as the Massacre of Cerro Maravilla. (ALO)

Further reading: Pedro Juan Soto, *Ardiente suelo, Fría estación* (Xalapa, Mexico: Universidad Veracruzana, 1961), *Spiks: Stories by Pedro Juan Soto* (New York: Monthly Review Press, 1973), *Usmaíl*, 5th ed. (Río Piedras, Puerto Rica: Editorial Cultural, 1981).

Trans.: VO

The clock said seven and he woke up for a moment. His wife wasn't in bed and the children weren't on their cot. He buried his head under the pillow to close out the racket coming from the kitchen. He didn't open his eyes again until ten, forced to by Graciela's shaking.

He rubbed his small eyes and wiped away the bleariness, only to see his wife's broad body standing firmly in front of the bed in that defiant attitude. He heard her loud voice and it seemed to be coming directly from her navel.

"So? You figured you'd spend your whole life in bed? Looks like you're the one with a bad belly, but I'm carryin the kid."

He still didn't look at her face. He fixed his eyes on the swollen stomach, on the ball of flesh that daily grew and threatened to burst the robe's belt.

"Hurry and get up, you damned good-for-nothin! Or do you want me to throw water on you?"

He shouted at the open legs and the arms akimbo, the menacing stomach, the angry face: "I get up when I want to and not when you tell me. Hell! Who do you think you are?"

He turned his face back into the sheets and smelled the Brilliantine stains on the pillow and the stale sweat on the bedspread.

She felt overpowered by the man's inert mass: the silent threat of those still arms, the enormous lizard his body was.

Biting her lips, she drowned her reproaches and went back to the kitchen, leaving the room with the sputtering candle for Saint Lazarus on the dresser, the Holy Palm from last Palm Sunday and the religious prints hanging on the wall.

They lived in the basement. But even though they lived miserably, it was a roof over them. Even though overhead the other tenants stamped and swept, even though garbage rained through the cracks, she thanked her saints for having someplace to live. But Rosendo still didn't have a job. Not even the the saints could find him one. Always in the clouds, more concerned with his own madness than with his family.

She felt she was going to cry. Nowadays she cried so easily. Thinking: *Holy God all I do is have kid after kid like a bitch and that man doesn't bother to look for work because he likes the government to support us by mail while he spends his time out there watching the four winds like Crazy John and saying he wants to be an artist.*

She stopped her sobs by gritting her teeth, closing off the complaints which struggled to become cries, returning sobs and complaints to the well of her nerves, where they would remain until hysteria opened them a path and transformed them into insults for her husband, or a spanking for the children, or a supplication to the Virgin of Succour.

She sat down at the table, watching her children run through the kitchen. Thinking of the Christmas tree they wouldn't have and the other children's toys that tomorrow hers would envy. Because tonight is Christmas Eve and tomorrow is Christmas.

"Now I shoot you and you fall down dead!"

The children were playing under the table.

"Children, don't make so much noise, *bendito!*"

"I'm Gene Autry!" said the oldest one.

"An I'm Palong Cassidy!"

"Children, I gotta headache, for God's sake . . ."

"You ain Palong Nobody! You the bad guy and I kill you!"

"No! Maaaaaaaa!"

Graciela twisted her body and put her head under the table to see them fighting.

"Boys, geddup from under there! *Maldita sea mi vida.* What a life. ROSENDO, HURRY AND GET UP!"

The kids were running through the room again, one of them shouting and laughing, the other crying.

"ROSENDO!"

Rosendo drank his coffee and ignored his wife's insults.

"Waddaya figure on doin today, lookin for work or goin from store to store and from bar to bar drawin all those bums?"

He drank his breakfast coffee, biting his lips distractedly, smoking his last cigarette between sips. She circled the table, rubbing her hand over her belly to calm the movement of the fetus.

"I guess you'll go with those good-for-nothin friends of yours and gamble with some borrowed money, thinkin that manna's gonna fall from the sky today."

"Lemme alone, woman . . ."

"Yeah, its always the same: lemme alone. Tomorrow's Christmas and those kids ain gonna have no presents."

"Kings Day's in January . . ."

"Kings don' come to New York. Santa Claus comes to New York!"

"Well, anyhow, whoever comes, we'll see . . ."

"Holy Mother of God! What a father, my God! You only care about your scribbles. The artist! A grown man like you."

He left the table and went to the bedroom, tired of hearing the woman. He looked out the only window. All the snow that had fallen day after day was filthy. The cars had flattened and blackened it on the pavement. On the sidewalks it had been trampled and pissed on by men and dogs. The days were colder now that the snow was there, hostile, ugly, at home with misery. Denuded of all the innocence it had had the first day.

It was a murky street, under heavy air, on a grandiosely opaque day.

Rosendo went to the bureau and took a bundle of papers from the drawer. Sitting on the window sill, he began to examine them. There were all the paper bags he had collected to tear up and draw on. He drew at night, while the woman and children slept. From memory he drew the drunken faces, the anguished faces of the people of Harlem: everything seen and shared during his daytime wanderings.

Graciela said he was in his second childhood. If he spent time away from the grumbling woman and the crying children, exploring absentmindedly in his penciled sketches, the woman muttered and sneered.

Tomorrow was Christmas and she was worried because the children wouldn't have presents. She didn't know that this afternoon he would collect ten dollars for the sign he painted yesterday at the corner bar. He was saving that surprise for Graciela. Like he was saving the surprise about her present.

For Graciela he would paint a picture. A picture that would summarize their life together, in the midst of deprivation and frustration. A painting with a melancholy similarity to those photographs taken at saints' day parties in Bayamón. The photographs from the days of their engagement, part of the family's album of memories: they were both leaning against a high stool, on the front of which were the words "Our Love" or "Forever Together." Behind was the backdrop with palm trees and the sea and a golden paper moon.

Graciela would certainly be pleased to know that in his memory nothing had died. Maybe afterward she wouldn't sneer at his efforts anymore.

Lacking materials, he would have to do the picture on a wall, and with charcoal. But it would be his, from his hands, made for her.

Into the building's boiler went all the old and useless wood the super collected. From there Rosendo took the charcoal he needed. Then he went through the basement looking for a wall. It couldn't be in the bedroom. Graciela wouldn't let him take down her prints and palms.

The kitchen wall was too cracked and grimy.

He had no choice but to use the bathroom. It was the only room left.

"If you need to go to the bathroom," he said to his wife, "wait or use the pot. I have to fix some pipes."

He closed the door and cleaned the wall of nails and spiders' webs. He sketched out his idea: a man on horseback, naked and muscled, leaning down to embrace a woman, also naked, wrapped in a mane of black hair from which the night bloomed.

Meticulously, patiently, he repeatedly retouched the parts that didn't satisfy him. After a few hours he decided to go out and get the ten dollars he was owed and buy a tree and toys for his children. On the way he'd get colored chalks at the candy store. This picture would have the sea, and palm trees, and the moon. Tomorrow was Christmas.

Graciela was coming and going in the basement, scolding the children, putting away the laundry, watching the lighted burners on the stove.

He put on his patched coat.

"I'm gonna get a tree for the kids. Don Pedro owes me ten bucks."

She smiled, thanking the saints for the miracle of the ten dollars.

That night he returned to the basement smelling of whiskey and beer. The children had already gone to sleep. He put up the tree in a corner of the kitchen and surrounded the trunk with presents.

He ate rice and fritters, without hunger, absorbed in what he would do later. From time to time he glanced at Graciela, looking for a smile that did not appear.

He moved the chipped coffee cup, put the chalk on the table, and looked in his pocket for the cigarette he didn't have.

"I erased all those drawins."

He forgot all about the cigarette.

"So now you're paintin filth?"

He dropped his smile into the abyss of reality.

"You don' have no more shame . . ."

His blood became cold water.

". . . makin yer children look at that filth, that indecency . . . I erased them and that's that and I don't want it to happen again."

He wanted to strike her but the desire was paralyzed in some part of his being, without reaching his arms, without becoming uncontrolled fury in his fists.

When he rose from the chair he felt all of him emptying out through his feet. All of him had been wiped out by a wet rag and her hands had squeezed him out of the world.

He went to the bathroom. Nothing of his remained. Only the nails, bent and rusted, returned to their holes. Only the spiders, returned to their spinning.

The wall was no more than the wide and clear gravestone of his dreams.

José Luis González (1926–1996)

The Night We Became People Again

José Luis González is considered the pioneer of what is known in Puerto Rican literary historiography as "the generation of 1940," a group of writers who strove to modernize Puerto Rican national literature by renewing their repertoire of narrative techniques and by shifting their themes from the dramas of rural life to the complexities of urban culture, colonial domination, and migration. Born in Santo Domingo to a Dominican mother and a Puerto Rican father, González moved to Puerto Rico with his family at age four. He lived on the island until 1957, when he left for New York City to conduct graduate studies in political science at the New School for Social Research. Shortly after, in 1963, he established permanent residence in Mexico City and soon became a Mexican citizen. Once he had renounced his U.S. citizenship, U.S. immigration authorities forbade his return to Puerto Rico for a period of twenty years as a punishment for González's Marxist ideology and for his vocal position in favor of Puerto Rican independence. *The Night We Became People Again* (1970) introduces a shift in the representation of migrant life dominant among many of the writers of his generation. Humorous in tone, the narration does not dwell on the sense of impossibility and despair we find in a Pedro Juan Soto, for example, but reveals to the reader how joy and light are found within darkness. (ALO)

Further reading: José Luis González, *En Nueva York y otras desgracias* (México: Siglo Veintiuno Editores, 1973), *El país de cuatro pisos,* 3rd ed. (Río Piedras, Puerto Rico: Huracán, 1982).

Trans: KW

Do I remember? The whole Barrio remembers, if you want to know the truth; even Crazytop won't forget, and he couldn't even tell you where they buried his mother fifteen days later. I can tell you about it better than anybody because of a coincidence you don't know about. But first let's have a couple of nice cold beers, because this damn heat is even affecting my memory.

Ah, now, *salud y pesetas* . . . and plenty of strength you know where. Well, it's been four years already; I can even tell you how many months and days, because to remember all I've got to do is take a look at the chubby little fellow you saw at home when you came to get me this morning. Yeah, the oldest one, who's named after me, but if he'd been born a girl we would have had to call her Estrella, or Luz María, or something like that. Or even Milagros, because that was really . . . but if I keep on like this I'll tell you the whole thing backwards.

Well, I won't mention the date, because you already know that. Turns out, that day I had told the foreman, a Jewish fellow, nice guy, knows a bit of Spanish, that I wanted some overtime, because I would need the dough for my wife's pregnancy, she was in her final months, and there were plenty of things to get. The crib, the midwife . . . ah, because she wanted to give birth at home, not in the clinic, because the doctors and the *norsas* don't speak Spanish, and anyways it's more expensive.

So at four o'clock I finished my first shift and went down to the Italian's snack bar in front of the factory. Wanted to put something into my belly, until I got home and my wife reheated the supper, you see. Well, I gulped down a couple of hot dogs with a beer while I flipped through the Spanish paper I'd bought that morning, and while I'm reading about this Latino who had cut up his girlfriend because she'd been running around with a Chinaman, I don't know if you believe in those things, but like I had a funny feeling. I felt that something big was going to happen that night. I think a person has to believe, because you might ask what's the thing about the Latino and his girlfriend and the Chinaman got to do with what I began to feel. Feel, you see, because I wasn't thinking it, which is different. Well, I stopped reading the paper and hurried back to the factory to start my overtime.

Then the other foreman, the first one had already left, he says to me, "Say, do you plan to become a millionaire and open a casino in Puerto Rico?" He's just fooling around, and then I tell him, still fooling, "No, I've already got a casino. Now I wanna open a factory." And he says, "What kinda factory?" And I tell him, "A smoke factory." So he says, "Ah, really? And what are you gonna do with the smoke?" And me, real serious, deadpan, I say, "Do with it? I'm gonna can it!" Just fooling around, y'know, because that foreman was an even nicer guy than the first. That's because it's to his benefit. He puts us in a good mood and gets us to work that much harder. He thinks I don't know, but any day now I'm going to tell him that I'm not as dumb as he might think. These people think that you come from the sticks and don't know the difference between sandpaper and toilet paper, especially if you're a bit dark-skinned, and your hair is kind of kinky.

Well, anyway, that's old news, and I've got something else to tell you. That damn heat . . . and our glasses are empty. Same brand, right? Okay. Well, as I was saying, after the foreman started joking around, we got down to some serious work. Because around here goofing and work don't mix. Time is money, you know. Radios started coming at me along the assembly line and I started sticking tubes into them, bam, bam. Yeah, that was my job then, putting tubes in. Two for every radio, one in each hand, bam, bam, bam. At first, when I was new at it, a radio would pass me right by and—oh, boy!—I had to run after it and also keep an eye on the next radio coming up; thought I would go crazy. When I left work, I felt like my whole body had St. Vitus dance. That's why I think there's so much drinking and vice in this country. Yeah, because after all that, you feel like having a shot of rum, or something, and you start getting into the habit. I think that's why women get along better in factory work, because they entertain themselves with gossip and tongue-wagging, you see, and they don't need to drink. Well, I was working along, sticking tubes into radios, and thinking silly thoughts, when the foreman comes up and says, "Say, someone's looking for you." "Who, me?" I say. "Yeah," he tells me, "you're the only one here with that name." So they got someone to take my place, because they can't stop the line, and I go to see who was looking for me. It was Crazytop. Doesn't even say hello. He spits it right out. "Hey, go home, your wife's having a baby." Just like that. You see, poor Crazytop fell out of his crib in Puerto Rico when he was little, and according to his mother, may she rest in peace, he fell on his head, and it seems that the blow softened up his brains. There was a time, when I met him here in the Barrio, that he would suddenly start spinning around, like a nut, and wouldn't stop until he was dizzy, and fell to the floor. That's where his nickname comes from. Now, nobody makes fun of him, because his mother was a good person, a spiritualist medium, you know, and she helped lots of people without charge. You gave her whatever you could, you see. And if you were broke, you didn't give her anything. So there are lots of people who kind of look after Crazytop. Because he was always an orphan on his father's side, and he had no brothers or sisters, so as they say, he's all alone in the world.

Well, Crazytop comes along and says that to me, and I say, "*Ay, mi madre*, what'll I do now?" The foreman, who was keeping an eye on us, because those people never take their eyes off you at work, comes over and asks, "What's the trouble?" And I tell him, "They came to get me because my wife is giving birth." And the foreman says, "Well, what are you waiting for?" Let me tell you, that foreman was Jewish, too, and for the Jews the family is always number one. In that sense they're not like the rest of the Americans, who between fathers and brothers and sons insult each other, even hit each other, for the slightest reason. I don't know if it's because of the kind of life people lead in this country. Always running after the dollar, like dogs at the track, after a rag rabbit. Have you seen that? They wear their lungs out and never catch the rabbit. Oh yeah, they feed them and care for them, so they'll run again another day, which is the same thing they do with people, if you really look at the way things are. In this country we're all like racing dogs.

Well, when the foreman asked me what was I waiting for, I told him, "Nothing, just to put on my coat and grab a subway before my son arrives and doesn't find me in the house." I was really happy, you see, because this was going to be my first child, and you know what that's like. And the foreman says, "Don't forget to punch out, so that you get credit for the half-hour you worked; from now on, you're going to really need money." And I tell him, "That's right," and grabbed my coat, punched my card, and I tell Crazytop, who was standing there, looking open-mouthed at all the machines, "Let's go, Crazytop, we'll be late!" And we ran down the stairs rather than wait for the elevator, and we got to the sidewalk, which was plenty crowded, because everyone was going home from work. "Damn it," I said, "I would have to get mixed up in the rush hour!" But Crazytop didn't want to run. "Wait a minute, man, wait a minute, I wanna buy candy." Crazytop is like that, you see, just like a baby. He's good for running errands, if it's something simple, or for washing floors in a building, or anything that doesn't need thinking. But if it's a question of using the old calculator, look for someone else. So I tell him, "No, no," he says, "they don't have the kind I want in the Barrio. You can only get them in Brooklyn." And I say to him, "*Ay*, you're crazy," and right away I'm sorry, because that's the one thing you can't say to Crazytop. He stops right there on the sidwalk, looking sadder than a penny's worth of cheese, and says to me, "No, no, not crazy." I tell him, "No, man, I didn't say crazy. I said silly. You didn't hear me right. C'mon! I'll get you the candy tomorrow!" And he says, "You sure you didn't call me crazy?" "Sure I am, man!" "And you'll get me the candy tomorrow?" He may be crazy, but he's pretty shrewd, too. I'm almost laughing and I say, "Sure, I'll even get you three candies if you want." So he smiles and says, "All right, let's go, but three candies, all right?" And I'm walking towards the subway entrance with Crazytop behind me. "Sure, man, three. You tell me later which kind."

We practically ran down the stairs and found the station packed with people, you know how it gets. And I was worried about Crazytop falling behind, because with all the pushing and shoving he might get scared. When the express train pulls in, I grab him by the arm and say: "Get ready to push, or we'll be left behind." And he tells me not to worry, and when the door opened and a few people got out, we pushed in and wound up so squeezed that we couldn't even move our arms. Just as well, that way we didn't have to hold on. Crazytop looked a bit scared, because I think it was the first time he'd been on the subway at rush hour, but since I was next to him there was no problem. So we got to Columbus Circle and changed trains, because we had to go to 110th and Fifth to get home, you see, and again we were just like sardines in a can.

I was counting the minutes, wondering if my son had already been born, and how my wife was. Suddenly it occurs to me: here I am so sure it'll be a boy, and what if it winds up being a girl? You know how a fellow wants a son at first. Truth is, it's selfishness on our part, because it's better for the mother if the eldest is a girl, so she can help with the housework and raising the little ones. Well, I'm thinking about all those things, and feeling very much like a father, you see, when . . . , wham! The lights go out and the train starts to lose power, and stops right in the middle of the tunnel, between stations. Nobody got frightened right away. Lights going out in the subway isn't such a rare thing, you know: they usually come right back on, and people don't even blink. And the train stopping for a bit isn't so strange, either. They put on the emergency lights, and everyone seemed fine. But time went by, and the train didn't move. And I'm thinking, "Shit, what luck, just when I'm in a hurry." But I'm still believing it was just a question of a few minutes, you see, and about three minutes go by, and this lady next to me starts to cough. An American lady, a bit on the old side. I looked at her and saw that she was coughing, but not very hard. I thought to myself: that's no cold, she's scared. Another minute went by and the train wasn't moving and the lady says to a young fellow next to her—tall, blond, tough-looking, with like an Irish face—she says, "Young man, doesn't this seem a bit odd?" And he says, "No, don't worry, it's nothing." But the lady didn't seem satisfied with that, and she kept on with her little cough, and other passengers tried to look out the windows, but they could barely move, and anyway it was so dark you couldn't see anything. I tried to look, too, but all I got out of it was a stiff neck, which lasted quite a while.

Well, time went by and I started getting a cramp in my leg, and that's when I started feeling nervous. Not because of the cramp, but I thought I'd never get home on time. I said to myself, "Something must've happened; we've been stuck here too long." Since I had nothing else to do I started my head working, and that's when I thought about suicide. It seemed logical, right? You know that there are lot of people here who don't give a damn about themselves and they climb up the Empire State Building and jump, and by the time they reach the street they're already dead from the fall. I don't know, but that's what I've heard. And there are others who jump in front of subway cars, and you have to pick up what's left with a shovel. The ones who jump from the Empire State, I guess you'd need tissue paper to pick them up. No, but seriously, because a person shouldn't joke about such things, I figured someone had thrown himself in front of a train, and I thought: "Well, may he rest in peace, but he really screwed me up, because now I'll be late." By now, my wife must be thinking that Crazytop got lost, or that I'm drunk and don't care about what's happening at home. It's not that I'm a lush, but once in a while, you understand . . . Well, now that we're on that subject, if you want to change brands, but make sure they're plenty cold.

Ah! Where was I? Oh yeah, thinking about the suicide, when suddenly—bang!—they opened the doors. Right there in the tunnel. I'd never seen anything like that, and I thought to myself, there's gotta be trouble. Down below, in front of the door, I see a few inspectors, they're wearing uniforms, and carrying lanterns. One of them says, "Take it easy, there's no danger. Come down slowly, without pushing." Right away people start asking the mister: What's happened? What's happened? And he says, "When you're all down here, I'll tell you." I grabbed Crazytop by the arm and told him, "Did you hear? There's no danger, but don't get separated from me." He nodded. I think the fright had robbed him of his voice. He didn't say a thing, but it seemed that his eyeballs would pop right out of his head; they were shining in the dark, just like a cat's.

Well, we all got out of the train, and when we're all lined up the inspectors started walking along the line and explaining what happened. There had been a blackout in the entire city, and nobody knew when the lights would come back on. Then the lady with the little cough, who was still close to me, asked the inspector, "Say, when will we get out of here?" And he says, "We have to wait a bit, because there are other trains ahead of us, and we can't all get out at the same time." So we began to wait. And I'm thinking,

"Dammit, this having to happen today," when I feel Crazytop pulling at my coat sleeve. He says to me real low, like in secret, "Say, buddy, I'm practically peeing in my pants." Imagine! That's all we needed. "*Ay*, Top," I say to him, "hold on. Can't you see it's impossible here?" And he says, "But I've had to go for a long time now, and I can't hold it in." So I start thinking fast, because this is an emergency, right? All I could think of was asking the inspector. "Wait right here," I say to Crazytop, "and don't move." I get out of line and walk up to the inspector. "Listen, mister, my friend wanna take a leak." And he says to me, "Goddamit to hell, can't he hold it in awhile?" I let him know that's just what I told my friend, to hold it in, but he says he can't. So he says, "Well, go ahead, but don't wander off too far." So I go back to Crazytop and tell him, "Come with me; let's see if we can find someplace there in back." We start walking, but the line of people never ended. We had already gone quite a distance when he pulls my sleeve again and says, "I really can't hold it anymore, brother." So I tell him, "Well, look, get behind me, right next to the wall, but be careful not to wet my shoes. And do it slow, so nobody hears." I hadn't even finished talking when I hear, you know how a horse sounds? Well, it was like two horses, not one. It's a wonder he hadn't ruptured his bladder. Oh, it was terrible. "*Ave María*," I think to myself, "he's gonna splash my coat." And I was wearing just a short coat, didn't even reach my knees, because I like to be in style, right? Well, of course, the people nearby had to notice, and I hear them whispering. I think to myself, "Just as well it's dark, and they can't see our faces. If they notice that we're Puerto Ricans . . ." You know how things are here. I'm thinking, and Crazytop still isn't finished. *Cristiano!* The things that happen to a fellow in this country! And people don't believe you. Well, Crazytop finally finished, or at least I thought he did, because I didn't hear any more noise, but he still stood there. So I say, "Hey, did you finish?" He says, "Yes." "Well," I say, "let's go." Then he says, "Wait a minute. I'm shaking it." That's when I blew my top. I ask him, "What've you got there, a garden hose? Get going, or these people are going to shake even your bones after making such a flood here." I think he finally understood the situation, and he says, "Okay, all right, let's go."

So we go back to where we were, and we're waiting for about half an hour more. I hear people around me talking English, complaining, and griping about the mayor, and everything. And suddenly I hear someone over there, in Spanish, say, "Well, it's just as well to die here as up there. At least down here the government has to pay for the funeral." Yeah, some *boricua* trying to be funny. I tried to spot him, and tell him that his funeral was going to be paid for by the animal shelter, but it was too dark. His little joke affected me, believe it or not. Standing there, with all my worries, you know what I thought? Imagine, I thought, if the inspector was lying, and the Third World War had really started. No, don't laugh. I'll bet I wasn't the only one thinking it. With all the things you read in the papers, about Russians, and Chinese, and Martians in flying saucers. Why do you think there are so many nuts in this country? They don't even fit in Bellevue anymore, and I think they're going to have to build another insane asylum.

Well, just then, the inspectors come and tell us it's our turn to get out, but to stay in line and be calm. We start walking and finally reach the station, which was at 96th. We weren't too far from home, but not too close either. Imagine if we'd stopped at 28th, or something. Up shit creek, right? Well, we get to the station and I tell Crazytop, "Let's hurry." We climb the stairs with that crowd of people, it looked like when you throw hot water on an anthill, and when we reach the street, *ay bendito!* The cars had their lights on, but there wasn't a single light on in the street, or in the buildings. A guy comes by with one of those portable radios. Since I was walking in the same direction I got close to him and started listening. Just what the inspector had told us down in the tunnel, so I stopped worrying about the war. But then I got to thinking again about my wife, and I tell Crazytop, "Well, my friend, now we use a special kind of transportation: a little on foot, and another while walking, to see who gets there first." And he says, "Let's race, let's race," laughing, as though he'd gotten over his fright.

We started walking real fast, because it was cold. When we reached 103rd, I wonder, "If there's no lights at home, how did they do the delivery? Maybe they had to call an ambulance to take her to some clinic, and I won't even know where she is." With that idea in my head, I looked like a champ in the stretch. I don't think it took us even five minutes from 103rd to home. I start running up the stairs, and they were in pitch darkness, couldn't even see the steps. Ah, but now the good part starts, because you weren't in New York that day, right? Okay. Well, let's get a couple more beers, because my throat is drier than the sand dunes of Salinas, where I grew up.

Well, as I was saying, that night I broke the world record for climbing three flights of stairs in the dark. I didn't even notice if Crazytop was behind me. When I reached the apartment door I grabbed my key and shoved it right into the lock on the first try, just as though I could see it. When I open the door the first thing I see are four candles lit in the parlor, and quite a few lady neighbors sitting there, looking plenty relaxed, and gossiping away. It looked like the Olympics for tongue-wagging. *Ave María*, that must be the ladies' favorite sport. I think that when the day comes that they abolish gossiping, there'll be a revolution bigger than Fidel Castro's. But as soon as they spotted me, they all turned quiet. I didn't even say good evening; right away I asked, "What's happened to my wife? Where is she? Did they take her away?" One of the ladies comes over and says, "No, she's in there, and she's fine. We were just saying that for a first pregnancy . . ." And just then I hear those squeals from my son there in the room. Well, I still didn't know if it was a boy or a girl, but I'll tell you, he was shouting more than Daniel Santos [a Puerto Rican singer] in his good times. So I tell the lady, "Excuse me, *doña*," and I rush into the room and the first thing I see is so many candles I thought it was a church altar. And the midwife there fussing with the pans, and rags, and things, and my woman in bed, nice and still, but with her eyes wide open. When she sees me, she says, her voice very slight, "*Ay*, my boy, how good that you got here. I was worried about you." Imagine, she's worried about me, and she's been going through labor pains, and all that. Yeah, women are like that sometimes. I think that's why we put up with their foolishness and love them so much, right? Well, I was just going to tell her about the problem with the subway when the midwife says, "That little boy has got your identical face. Come see him, look." He was in the bed, right next to my woman, but since he was so tiny you could hardly see him. I go over and look at his little face, which is all you could see, since he was wrapped up more than a *pastel* [meat pie], and when I'm looking at him, my woman says, "Doesn't he resemble you?" I say, "Yes, quite a bit." But I'm thinking to myself, "No, he doesn't look like me or anybody else. Looks like a newborn mouse." But we're all like that when we come into the world, right? And my woman says to me, "He's a little boy, just what you wanted." And I, just to say something, answered,

"Well, let's see if next time we can make a nice match." I didn't want her to notice how proud I felt and how happy, you see? And the midwife asks, "Well, what are you going to name him?" My woman says, "The same as his papa, so he won't forget it's his." Just joking, you see, but with her little dig. And I say, "Well, baby, if it pleases you." My son had stopped crying by then, and I start to hear like the sound of music coming from the upper part of the building. But it wasn't from a radio or phonograph, you see. It was like a combo, right there, because I heard laughing and talking. Lots of people. And I ask my woman, "Is there a party?" And she says, "I don't know, but it seems so, because we've been hearing it for quite a while. Maybe it's a birthday party." And I say, "But without any light?" And then the midwife says, "Maybe they did the same as we did, went out and bought candles." Then I hear Crazytop calling to me from the parlor, "Hey, hey, c'mere." Crazytop had gone to check. "What's happening?" I asked him. "*Muchacho*," he says, "thing's are really swell up there on the *rufo*." And I say, "Well, let's go see what's happening."

So we go up the stairs and onto the roof and I find almost the whole building there. *Doña* Lula, the widow from the first floor; Cheo, the guy from Aguadilla, who had closed down his coffee shop when the lights went out; the girls from the second floor, who neither worked nor collected welfare, according to the tongue-waggers; *don* Leo, the Pentecostal minister who has four children here and seven in Puerto Rico; Pipo and *doña* Lula's boys, and one of *don* Leo's had formed a combo with a guitar, a *güiro*, some maracas, and even some drums, I don't know where they got them because I'd never seen them before. Yeah, a quartet. Say, and they were really making quite a racket! When I got there, they were playing "*Preciosa*," and the singer was Pipo, you know he's an *independentista*, and when he got to the part where it says, "*Preciosa, preciosa*, you're called by the sons of liberty," he raised his voice so much I think they heard him in Morovis. And I'm standing there looking at all those people, and listening to the song, when one of the girls from the second floor comes over, a little heavyset, I think her name is Mirta, and she says to me, "Say, how good it is that you're here. Come over and have a little shot." Ah, they had bottles and paper cups atop a chair, and I don't know if it was Bacardi or Don Q, because it was dark, but right away I tell her, "Well, if you're offering, I accept with great pleasure." She serves me the rum and I ask, "Say, can you tell me what the party's all about?" And *doña* Lula, the widow, comes over and says, "Haven't you noticed?" I look all around, but *doña* Lula says, "No, no, not there. Look *up*." And when I raise my eyes she says, "What do you see?" "Well, the moon." "And what else?" "Well, the stars."

Ave María, muchacho! That's when I realized! I think *doña* Lula saw it in my face, because she didn't say a thing more. She put her two hands on my shoulders and stood there looking, too, nice and still, as though I were asleep, and she didn't want to wake me. Because I don't know if you're going to believe me, but it was like a dream. The moon was this big, and yellow, yellow, as though it were made of gold, and the whole sky was full of stars, as though all the fireflies in the world had gone up there to rest in that immensity. Just like in Puerto Rico, 'most any night of the year. But it had been so long since I'd seen the sky, because of the glow of millions of electric bulbs that are turned on here every night, and we had already forgotten that the stars existed. When we stood there contemplating that miracle for I don't know how long, I hear *doña* Lula say, "It seems we're not the only ones celebrating." It was true. I can't tell you on how many rooftops in the Barrio there were parties that night, but there were quite a few, because when our combo stopped playing, we could hear music from other places, nice and clear. Then I thought of so many things. I thought of my newborn son, and what his life would be like here; I thought of Puerto Rico and my folks, and everything that we left behind, just out of need; I thought of so many things that I've already forgotten some of them, because you know that your mind is like a blackboard, and time is like an eraser that sweeps across it when it's full. But what I'll always remember is what I said then to *doña* Lula, which is what I want to tell you now, to finish my story. And that is, according to my poor way of understanding things, that was the night we became people again.

Iván Acosta (1943–)

El Súper (excerpt)

Born in Santiago de Cuba, Iván Acosta arrived in the United States in 1961. A graduate of the NYU Film Institute, Acosta has been active in the New York theater scene since 1969. He has directed the Spanish-language drama department at the Henry Street Playhouse and the New Federal Theater, and received the Thalia, O.C.L.A, and ARIEL awards for his musical hit *Grito 71* in 1971. Acosta founded the Centro Cultural Cubano de New York and produced numerous plays there. *El Súper*, which was debuted at the CCC, went from stage to silver screen, winning four prestigious film awards. The following scene finds several members of the Amador family in a discussion with a door-to-door missionary, who is trying to convert this Cuban Catholic family. The discrepancies between their beliefs and those of their interlocutor, exasperated by Roberto Amador's anticommunist paranoia and his family's nostalgia for pre-Castro Cuba, cause them to confuse religious propaganda with political propaganda, providing us with a humorous yet poignant look at the U.S. experiences of many post-1959 Cuban exiles. What began as a potential conversion experience ends up being a raucous remembrance of Cuban food, music, and daily life on the island. (KDM)

Further reading: Iván Acosta, *El Súper* (Miami: Ediciones Universal, 1982), *Un cubiche en la luna: Tres obras teatrales* (Houston: Arte Público Press, 1989).

Trans.: TEW

AURELIA: Lower your voices, someone's at the door. It must be Philip.
ROBERTO: At this hour?
PREACHER: Good evening. (*He enters without permission.*)
AURELIA: What can we do for you?
PREACHER: The eternal purpose of God now triumphs for the good of man . . .
AURELIA: Young man, please forgive me, but . . .
PREACHER: In the Bible it is written that Jesus resurrected Lazarus from the dead after four days.
AURELIA: That's fine son, but . . . I believe in Santa Bárbara . . .

PREACHER: Does it make sense to you that some people live on earth in perpetual hunger, as is the case with millions today?

PANCHO: Yeah, we'll take care of that right away, bro' . . .

AURELIA: What? . . . Okay, I don't think that . . .

PREACHER: So, what you mean is that the Bible story about Jesus providing food for thousands of people isn't—perhaps—important to you?

AURELIA: Well, yes, but look, couldn't you come another day? Right now we're. . . .

PREACHER: Christ is the only Savior. You have to save yourselves. It's better late than never. We all have to be born again . . . (*He hands Ophelia a religious pamphlet.*)

OPHELIA: Okay, but I'm Catholic, son.

PREACHER: (*He goes to the living room and hands pamphlets to Roberto and Pancho.*) The super-powers spend more than 40 billion dollars on weapons, and to keep one soldier armed, uniformed and equipped. . . . I'm telling you, just one soldier . . . (*He sits down.*)

ROBERTO: (*Roberto stands up quickly.*) Okay, okay. Young man, I understand what you're sayin', but you've got to understand that we have visitors. We're busy.

PREACHER: You should never be too busy to receive the word of God. For that reason I urge you, in the name of Christ, for everyone to speak with one voice, end the divisiveness, everyone come together in one mind, with a unified point of view . . .

PANCHO: Bro', that's what they call Communism. Get'm outta here already!

PREACHER: That is the Bible, the word of God . . .

OPHELIA: But he won't leave!

PREACHER: Does it make any sense that a simple turtle lives more than 150 years while the superior creation, man, despite modern medical science has to resign himself to a life expectancy half as long, or less?

ROBERTO: All right. Young man, we're busy. I've already told you. (*He escorts him to the door.*) Do me the favor of hittin' the road. If you like, come another day, but for now, that's enough.

PREACHER: Jehovah has declared his plans for the future in symbolic language. (*He continues talking as he is leaving.*) Read Genesis 3:15, read Galatians 3:18, read Ezekiel 38:23, and Joseph 9:11. The creator, God, Jehovah . . . (*From outside.*) Save yourselves now. Your names will be praised on earth and in heaven when you settle your score with Satan, the demons and the wicked people on earth.

(*The words of the preacher continue to be heard backstage. Roberto begins to talk to Aurelia and an improvisation starts among the four people.*)

AURELIA: What was that all about?

ROBERTO: Remember, I've told you not to open the door without lookin' out the window first.

OPHELIA: That's why I don't open the door for anyone without lookin' first to see who it is.

PANCHO: They line up right here and grab whatever they can.

ROBERTO: It's just not right, and especially with the bunch of nuts runnin' around this city. What about that serial killer? That son of Sam? Right? That woman never learns. If I've told her once, I've told her a thousand times, but she just doesn't learn.

AURELIA: I thought it was Philip.

ROBERTO: The bottom line is that you have to be careful. (*They all talk at the same time about the same topic.*)

PANCHO: Hey Roberto, you know what? This reminds me of when we were down there durin' the invasion and there's this guy, like the one who just left. Well . . . (*Roberto interrupts him.*)

ROBERTO: That's enough, Pancho. Why don't we talk with the women some, okay? Ophelia, come 'ere. Aurelia, give it a rest in the kitchen. Come 'ere. (*Aurelia and Ophelia go to the living room.*)

PANCHO: Ophelia, bring me another beer, would ya'?

AURELIA: You wanna 'nother too, Roberto?

ROBERTO: (*He rubs his stomach.*) No, no more. I don't wanna mess up my diet.

OPHELIA: Speakin' of diets, look at you Aurelia. You're lookin' thinner, right? Or is it that dress?

AURELIA: Oh, come on, girl, trapped in that kitchen, who can resist stuffin' their face?

ROBERTO: Now Aurelita, she's the one who's careful about what she eats. She doesn't touch bread, or rice, or beans, and she won't eat meat fried in oil.

OPHELIA: Think about it. She's in her prime. Here, it's fashionable to be skinny. Even so, back home, the fatter you were, the healthier they thought you were. I remember when I was in high school and they'd call me "skinny cat." Here they'd h've said I had a great figure.

PANCHO: A figure like Mahatma Ghandi's! As far as I'm concerned, I'm not interested in any skinny cat, 'cause the way I like it is to have some meat before I get to the bones! (*He laughs loudly.*)

AURELIA: There're so many ads about diets that ya' just get sucked in. I mean, they use those young models, who are perfect: perfect teeth, perfect hair, those legs, those eyes. They're genuine little dolls. People see that on TV, and then everybody wants to look like 'em.

ROBERTO: That reminds me of when I was young . . . you know, those American movies, about cowboys and the war. Everybody was blond with blue eyes, there wasn't one Black.

PANCHO: Yeah, right. And they were six and seven feet tall. Not one of 'em was short. Think about what happened to Alan Ladd. That guy was 5'4", and when his movie was comin' out, they made him taller by havin' him stand on an empty milk crate.

ROBERTO: Don't forget, they never lost a battle either.

PANCHO: Lose a battle? Are you crazy? To the Japanese, to the Germans, to the Koreans? Forget it. They were always the heroes and the enemy was always sent packin'. And the heroes never even got shot either. You better believe it. I mean come on, these are the same folks who invented Superman.

OPHELIA: That's right, and those Americans just eat it all up.

ROBERTO: (*Yawning.*) Right. And by eatin' so much, they get indigestion. (*The conversation shifts to a slower pace.*) How much longer do we have to shovel snow for these people, my friends?

PANCHO: Until you decide to move to the Exile capital.

AURELIA: Fine. I'll tell you Pancho that I prefer the snow and the boiler and all the rest compared to going to Miami. Geez! The whole Cuban thing and all that gossip! Here, at least nobody sticks their nose into other people's lives.

PANCHO: Yeah, well, what about when you have a little heart attack in the morning and there isn't one neighbor who even prepares ya' a cup of coffee or tea. Forget it. There's nothing can replace Cuba. (*Aurelia yawns, and without speaking, gestures to Roberto asking for the time, and he answers her in the same way. Ophelia also yawns.*) The rooster's cock-a-doodle-doo in the morning, a little cup of hot coffee, greetings from the neighbor passin' by, that sun that burns like the devil, the juice of the sugar cane. Oh, my dear Cuba, dear little Cuba! (*Singing badly.*) When I left Cuba, I left my life. La, la, la, la, la. Guantanamera, guajira, guantanameeera . . . (*The lights have been dimming.*)

OPHELIA: Pancho, whadda ya' say we go?

PANCHO: Okay, you're the boss. Right? (*He laughs.*)

Ramón "Tianguis" Pérez (dates unknown)

Diary of an Undocumented Immigrant (excerpt)

Ramón "Tianguis" Pérez is nicknamed for his birthplace, San Pablo Macuiltianguis, a Zapotec village in the Sierra Juárez region of Oaxaca, where his family ran a cabinet-making shop. While still in his teens, he became involved with the revolutionary movement of Florencio Medrano (known as "El Güero" or "Tío") in southern and central Mexico. After the collapse of Medrano's movement, Pérez survived by working variously as a carpenter, busman, laborer, printer, and furniture maker in both the United States and Mexico. His experiences as a "mojado," or undocumented worker, were chronicled in his first book, *Diary of an Undocumented Immigrant*, which is an honest and direct testimonial of the process of immigration and labor contracting that Mexican workers experience in the world of labor smuggling and pursuit by the U.S. Immigration and Naturalization Service. Despite skepticism that an uneducated worker from the indigenous highlands of Mexico could be an accomplished writer, "Tianguis" proved his abilities once again with his second book, *Diary of a Guerrilla*, detailing his experiences in Medrano's movement. In the excerpt below from the *Diary of an Undocumented Immigrant*, "Tianguis" recalls following the migrant farm work trail in the Northwest. (NK)

Further reading: Ramón "Tianguis" Pérez, *Diary of an Undocumented Immigrant,* trans. Dick J. Reavis (Houston: Arte Público Press, 1991) *Diary of a Guerrilla;* (Houston: Arte Público Press, 1999).

Trans.: DJR

In My Father's Footsteps

The bus advances into extensive plains, so extensive that you can't see where they end. All of the land is cultivated, perfectly clean of plants and perfectly plowed in straight lines that seem to open out before the bus, like a fan extending itself. Soon, we are passing by big vineyards and fields of onion, beets, avocado, tomatoes and other types of fruits and vegetables, so many that I assume that the harvests will be in tons.

Back at home, villagers also plant these types of crops, but only for family consumption, and from time to time, to sell to neighbors. My mother has for years kept and supervised such a garden on a plot by our house. She knows what to plant, depending upon the climate, whether in times of hot or cold, rain or snowfall. My brothers and I prepare the seed beds in our off-hours after school. In addition to vegetables, our garden has apple, plum, peach, cherry, avocado and pecan trees.

My father also traveled the immense plains of California, "bending his back," as he put it, during his time as a *bracero.* Once when we were weeding our cornfield, he told my younger brother and I the story of a tomato harvest here. At the time that dad told the story, my younger brother wasn't big enough to use the *coa* to weed. Instead, he pulled weeds with his hands, and, as I recall, spent most of his effort chasing after the crickets he found in his path.

My father said that in California, the rows of fields were long and perfectly flat, like those I see through the window of the bus. But when he described the plains for us, because there are no such lands near our village, we weren't sure we believed him. I remember looking on a map, to see if his description could be true, but all I could tell from looking at it was that California was a long way from home.

My father said that among the foremen who were hired by the contractor was a type of trainer. His job was teaching the newly arrived *braceros* how to work at the speed the company wanted. All the *braceros* feared him. He was a tall man, as thin as a rail. He wore cowboy boots, had a big moustache, wore a wide-brimmed hat and had a stare of steel. His name was Pierre, but the *braceros* nicknamed him "*El Perro,*" "The Dog." He was so demanding that nobody could for long keep the pace he wanted. Whenever he came near, somebody would say, "Here comes the Dog," and as word passed, everybody would start working at full speed. But there was no way to satisfy him. At first, he only insulted them: "Bend over, lazy, you've come here to work, so get to work!" When he was watching, nothing distracted him. If a *bracero* stood up to stretch and rub his back, the Dog immediately blew a whistle, and made a signal—by raising his hand and doubling his index finger—to show the bracero that he should bend back to his work. Of course there were a few rebels who refused to obey, but they ran the risk of being laid off for a couple of days while they "recuperated"—the company said—from their strains, or worse, of having their contracts cancelled and being returned to Mexico, as a few men were.

Only the contractor admired the foreman, since the foreman squeezed maximum productivity out of his *braceros.* Among the *braceros,* no one liked the foreman, though they obeyed him. One day a man from Querétaro, whom the others called the Queretano, a short, thin and quick-witted fellow, stopped in the middle of a row to rub his back. Then he and another *bracero* started pushing against one another, each one trying to topple the other, all in an effort to rest and distract themselves a minute. The Dog blew his whistle immediately, but only one of the men bent over the row again. The Queretano stayed on his feet, stretching. The Dog whistled a second time; a second whistle, he had taught the men, meant that the offending worker had to take off the rest of the day. The Queretano, without showing any fear, but also without trying to be offensive, shouted, "Why do you dog us so much? We're not machines. You should come out here with us, for just one row, so that you can feel like we do."

The Dog ordered him to take the day off, and that meant, without pay. The Queretano had to obey, but everybody admired him for having spoken up in the way he did.

Everyone warned him to be on guard, because the next time the Queretano said anything to the Dog, he risked being sent back to Mexico.

Instead of being frightened, the Queretano proposed to his friends an idea for getting even with the Dog. Several days passed before his friends agreed, because even the closest of them warned against any action that might get them returned, since getting the contracts had not been easy, in the first place. But finally, they all consented. One day at lunch, to the surprise of the field crew, they heard the Dog yelling curses inside his pickup, where he was accustomed to eat at a distance from the *braceros.* "Those sons of whores!" they heard him exclaim. Then they saw him walking towards them, still cursing and, my father said, with saliva dripping from his mouth. His fists were doubled and his eyes shot sparks. He went group-to-group among the *braceros*, asking who had played the trick on him, but no one said anything.

The Queretano's idea had been to simply go to the foreman's pickup, throw out his lunch, and put in its place in his lunch pail a note saying, "Dog, go fuck your mother."

"All of us were glad to see that the trick had infuriated the Dog, but we were also afraid he'd discover its origins," Dad had told us. "But thanks be to God," he added, "nobody said anything." The Queretano had broken the immaculate authority of the Dog. The trick had gained the respect of all the *braceros*, even though most of them weren't sure whether the Queretano or one of his friends had played it.

But, to take his own vengeance, the Dog became even more demanding and punitive. His ferocity grew bolder by the day. After a week or two of this harsher treatment, the Queretano proposed that everybody throw tomatoes at the Dog. "And after that, we'll have to pack our bags," one of the *braceros* told him. "The contractor won't forgive us if we treat his best foreman like that," another one said. But little by little, the idea grew popular.

The plan was for the Queretano to stand in the middle of the field, scratching himself, to attract the foreman's attention, while everyone else continued working at a fast pace. When the foreman saw the Queretano standing, he shouted, "What has happened to you today, you son of a whore? Are you sick? Or do you want at least a week of layoff? Doesn't it make you ashamed to see everybody else working?" The Queretano withstood several insults, until the appropriate moment, when the Dog came out into the middle of the field, where the Queretano was standing. Then one of the workers behind the Dog rose up and threw an overripe tomato, hitting the Dog in the back. The Dog turned and looked and, seeing no one, fell upon the Queretano. But when he did, he was hit again, and again from the backside. Before long, tomatoes were raining upon the Dog, who could do nothing but run. As he ran back towards the edge of the field, several times he tripped and fell on tomato plants. Everything had gone according to plan.

By the time he reached his pickup, his clothing was badly spotted from the tomato attack. He got in his pickup and went roaring off. The *braceros* lost sight of him in the dust he left behind. Then, rapidly, the others helped the Queretano catch up on the row he'd been working when he had stopped. They did that in order to show the contractor that they knew how to work, without the foreman's insults. When the contractor came a little later in the afternoon, he saw that the work had advanced at a normal rate, and when he couldn't find the Dog, he asked a *bracero* what had become of the foreman.

The *bracero* pointed in the direction in which the foreman had gone. The contractor drove off to find him. He came back about an hour later. Everybody expected an exemplary punishment and some were sure that they'd all be sent home. But the contractor merely watched, until quitting time came. Then he spoke to the crowd of them. "So that's what you did to Pierre, eh? Nobody liked him, I already knew that. You guys were within your rights." Then he told them that he had found the Dog down the road a mile or two, bent over the steering wheel of his pickup, crying with rage. The contractor said that he'd told the foreman not to come back to work.

Junot Díaz (1969–)

No Face

Born in Santo Domingo in 1969, Junot Díaz came to the United States at the age of seven. His family settled in New Jersey, where, surviving poverty and a father's abandonment, he managed to attend Kean College and Rutgers University. He later earned an MFA degree in creative writing from Cornell University. After publishing his first piece of short fiction in *Story*, he launched a career that *Newsweek* described as an "overnight success." His debut collection *Drown* was hailed for the calm command of his craft. Texts of his have appeared in *The Best American Short Stories* three times (1996, 1997, and 1999). *The New Yorker* included him in the June 1999 summer fiction issue entitled "20 Writers for the 21st Century: The Future of American Fiction." Upon completing a year as a Guggenheim Fellow, he received the Lila Wallace Readers Digest Grant for three years. Díaz teaches in the English Department at Syracuse University. *No Face*, the ninth of the ten pieces collected in *Drown*, is set in Santo Domingo, and features Ysrael, a boy who has to wear a mask because a pig disfigured him when he was a baby. The idea of traveling abroad looms large in the boy's mind where medical science might rescue him from his daily horrors. (STS)

Further reading: Junot Díaz, *Drown* (New York: Riverhead Books, 1996).

In the morning he pulls on his mask and grinds his fist into his palm. He goes to the guanábana tree and does his pull-ups, nearly fifty now, and then he picks up the café dehuller and holds it to his chest for a forty count. His arms, chest and neck bulge and the skin around his temple draws tight, about to split. But no! He's unbeatable and drops the dehuller with a fat Yes. He knows that he should go but the morning fog covers everything and he listens to the roosters for a while. Then he hears his family stirring. Hurry up, he says to himself. He runs past his tío's land and with a glance he knows how many beans of café his tío has growing red, black and green on his conucos. He runs past the water hose and the pasture, and then he says FLIGHT and jumps up and his shadow knifes over the tops of the trees and he can see his family's fence and his mother washing his little brother, scrubbing his face and his feet. The storekeepers toss water on the road to keep the dust down; he sweeps past them. No Face! a few yell out but he has no time for them. First he goes to the bars, searches the nearby ground for dropped change. Drunks sometimes sleep in the alleys so he moves quietly. He steps over the piss-holes and the vomit, wrinkles his nose at the stink. Today he finds enough coins in the tall crackling weeds to buy a bottle of soda or a johnnycake. He holds the coins tightly in his hands and under his mask he smiles.

At the hottest part of the day Lou lets him into the church with its bad roof and poor wiring and gives him café con leche and two hours of reading and writing. The books, the pen, the paper all come from the nearby school, donated by the teacher. Father Lou has small hands and bad eyes and twice he's gone to Canada for operations. Lou teaches him the English he'll need up north. I'm hungry. Where's the bathroom? I come from the Dominican Republic. Don't be scared.

After his lessons he buys Chiclets and goes to the house across from the church. The house has a gate and orange trees and a cobblestone path. A TV trills somewhere inside. He waits for the girl but she doesn't come out. Normally she'd peek out and see him. She'd make a TV with her hands. They both speak with their hands.

Do you want to watch?

He'd shake his head, put his hands out in front of him. He never went into casas ajenas. *No, I like being outside.*

I'd rather be inside where it's cool.

He'd stay until the cleaning woman, who also lived in the mountains, yelled from the kitchen, Stay away from here. Don't you have any shame? Then he'd grip the bars of the gate and pull them a bit apart, grunting, to show her who she was messing with.

Each week Padre Lou lets him buy a comic book. The priest takes him to the bookseller and stands in the street, guarding him, while he peruses the shelves.

Today he buys Kaliman, who takes no shit and wears a turban. If his face were covered he'd be perfect.

He watches for opportunities from corners, away from people. He has his power of INVISIBILITY and no one can touch him. Even his tío, the one who guards the dams, strolls past and says nothing. Dogs can smell him though and a couple nuzzle his feet. He pushes them away since they can betray his location to his enemies. So many wish him to fall. So many wish him gone.

A viejo needs help pushing his cart. A cat needs to be brought across the street.

Hey No Face! a motor driver yells. What the hell are you doing? You haven't started eating cats, have you?

He'll be eating kids next, another joins in.

Leave that cat alone, it's not yours.

He runs. It's late in the day and the shops are closing and even the motorbikes at each corner have dispersed, leaving oil stains and ruts in the dirt.

The ambush comes when he's trying to figure out if he can buy another johnnycake. Four boys tackle him and the coins jump out of his hand like grasshoppers. The fat boy with the single eyebrow sits on his chest and his breath flies out of him. The others stand over him and he's scared.

We're going to make you a girl, the fat one says and he can hear the words echoing through the meat of the fat boy's body. He wants to breathe but his lungs are as tight as pockets.

You ever been a girl before?

I betcha he hasn't. It ain't a lot of fun.

He says STRENGTH and the fat boy flies off him and he's running down the street and the others are following. You better leave him alone, the owner of the beauty shop says but no one ever listens to her, not since her husband left her for a Haitian. He makes it back to the church and slips inside and hides. The boys throw rocks against the door of the church but then Eliseo, the groundskeeper says, Boys, prepare for hell, and runs his machete on the sidewalk. Everything outside goes quiet. He sits down under a pew and waits for nighttime, when he can go back home to the smokehouse to sleep. He rubs the blood on his shorts, spits on the cut to get the dirt out.

Are you okay? Padre Lou asks.

I've been running out of energy.

Padre Lou sits down. He looks like one of those Cuban shopkeepers in his shorts and guayabera. He pats his hands together. I've been thinking about you up north. I'm trying to imagine you in the snow.

Snow won't bother me.

Snow bothers everybody.

Do they like wrestling?

Padre Lou laughs. Almost as much as we do. Except nobody gets cut up, not anymore.

He comes out from under the pew then and shows the priest his elbow. The priest sighs. Let's go take care of that, OK?

Just don't use the red stuff.

We don't use the red stuff anymore. We have the white stuff now and it doesn't hurt.

I'll believe that when I see it.

No one has ever hidden it from him. They tell him the story over and over again, as though afraid that he might forget.

On some nights he opens his eyes and the pig has come back. Always huge and pale. Its hooves peg his chest down and he can smell the curdled bananas on its breath. Blunt teeth rip a strip from under his eye and the muscle revealed is delicious, like lechosa. He turns his head to save one side of his face; in some dreams he saves his right side and in some his left but in the worst ones he cannot turn his head, its mouth is like a pothole and nothing can escape it. When he awakens he's screaming and blood braids down his neck; he's bitten his tongue and it swells and he cannot sleep again until he tells himself to be a man.

Padre Lou borrows a Honda motorcycle and the two set out early in the morning. He leans into the turns and Lou says, Don't do that too much. You'll tip us.

Nothing will happen to us! he yells.

The road to Ocoa is empty and the fincas are dry and many of the farmsteads have been abandoned. On a bluff he sees a single black horse. It's eating a shrub and a garza is perched on its back.

The clinic is crowded with bleeding people but a nurse with bleached hair brings them through to the front.

How are we today? the doctor says.

I'm fine, he says. When are you sending me away?

The doctor smiles and makes him remove his mask and then massages his face with his thumbs. The doctor has colorless food in his teeth. Have you had trouble swallowing?

No.

Breathing?

No.

Have you had any headaches? Does your throat ever hurt? Are you ever dizzy?

Never.

The doctor checks his eyes, his ears, and then listens to his breathing. Everything looks good, Lou.

I'm glad to hear that. Do you have a ballpark figure?

Well, the doctor says. We'll get him there eventually.

Padre Lou smiles and puts a hand on his shoulder. What do you think about that?

He nods but doesn't know what he should think. He's scared of the operations and scared that nothing will change, that the Canadian doctors will fail like the santeras his mother hired, who called every spirit in the celestial directory for help. The room he's in is hot and dim and dusty and he's sweating and wishes he could lie under a table where no one can see. In the next room he met a boy whose skull plates had not closed all the way and a girl who didn't have arms and a baby whose face was huge and swollen and whose eyes were dripping pus.

You can see my brain, the boy said. All I have is this membrane thing and you can see right into it.

In the morning he wakes up hurting. From the doctor, from a fight he had outside the church. He goes outside, dizzy, and leans against the guanabana tree. His little brother Pesao is awake, flicking beans at the chickens, his little body bowed and perfect and when he rubs the four-year-old's head he feels the sores that have healed into yellow crusts. He aches to pick at them but the last time the blood had gushed and Pesao had screamed.

Where have you been? Pesao asks.

I've been fighting evil.

I want to do that.

You won't like it, he says.

Pesao looks at his face, giggles and flings another pebble at the hens, who scatter indignantly.

He watches the sun burn the mists from the fields and despite the heat the beans are thick and green and flexible in the breeze. His mother sees him on the way back from the outhouse. She goes to fetch his mask.

He's tired and aching but he looks out over the valley, and the way the land curves away to hide itself reminds him of the way Lou hides his dominos when they play. Go, she says. Before your father comes out.

He knows what happens when his father comes out. He pulls on his mask and feels the fleas stirring in the cloth. When she turns her back, he hides, blending into the weeds. He watches his mother hold Pesao's head gently under the faucet and when the water finally urges out from the pipe Pesao yells as if he's been given a present or a wish come true.

He runs, down towards town, never slipping or stumbling. Nobody's faster.

Mario Bencastro (1949–)

Odyssey to the North (excerpt)

Mario Bencastro was born in El Salvador, where he began his artistic career as a painter, but eventually concluded that the political and social conditions in his country required that he express himself through written language. After emigrating to the United States during the civil wars that disrupted life in his native land, Bencastro began writing and publishing poetry and short stories; in 1989, his first novel, *A Shot in the Cathedral,* was published in Mexico, where it won the prestigious Diana y Novedades International Literary Prize. Bencastro's subsequent books have also won awards in Spain and in El Salvador. While these first literary efforts must be considered as exile literature, Bencastro's latest work, *Odyssey to the North,* is the first to explore the life of immigrants in the modern city. The selection below explores the precarious, hand-to-mouth existence of the immigrants, culture conflict, and alienation in the big city. Bencastro's novel is loosely based on his own experiences and his direct observations in social service work in Hispanic immigrant communities in Washington, D.C. (NK)

Further reading: Mario Bencastro, *A Shot in the Cathedral* (Houston: Arte Público Press, 1997), *The Tree of Life: Stories of Civil War* (Houston: Arte Público Press, 1997), *Odyssey to the North* (Houston: Arte Público Press, 1999).

Trans.: SGR

1

"It's going to be a beautiful day here in Washington!" exclaimed the voice on the radio. "Clear blue skies, seventy degrees, sunny with no threat of rain. A perfect spring day!"

Two policemen were making their rounds in the Adams Morgan district, the windows of their patrol car open to receive the cool breeze which caressed the groves of trees in Rock Creek Park, carrying the perfume of the multicolored flowers, outlined against the delicate blue sky.

The metallic voice coming over the transmitter from headquarters shook them out of their deep thoughts, ordering them to proceed immediately to a building on Harvard Street, across from the zoo, just a few minutes away.

When they arrived on the scene, they had to fight their way through the crowd of residents who had come running in response to the desperate shouts of a woman.

They ordered the people to move aside and then they saw the cause of the commotion: a smashed body stuck to the hot cement. The cranium was demolished. The facial features were disfigured by a grimace of pain. The eyes were still open, with an enigmatic gaze. The arms and legs were arranged incoherently, not at all in the normal symmetry of the human body. One leg was bent with the foot up by the neck. One shoulder was completely separated from the body; as if it had been chopped off.

"Spiderman!" someone exclaimed.

One of the policemen approached the man who had shouted and said to him, "Hey, show some respect; this is no joke!"

The man turned around and walked away, hanging his head. But as soon as he was out of the officer's reach, he turned around and screamed, "Spiderman! Spiderman!" and took off running toward the zoo, where he hid among some bushes.

The policeman started to chase him, but settled for insulting the man silently, biting his lip to keep the words from escaping.

"Is there anyone here who knows the victim?" asked the other officer, scrutinizing the group of curious onlookers with an indecisive expression.

No one dared to say a word.

"You?" he asked a brown-skinned man. "Do you know him?"

"I don't speak English," the man answered fearfully.

"*¿Tú, conocer, muerto?*" insisted the officer, stammering in thickly accented Spanish.

"I don't speak Spanish either," said the man in broken English. "I'm from Afghanistan."

The policeman appeared utterly disconcerted at the people's silence. The loud sound of a lion's roar came from the zoo.

Finally, a woman approached the men in uniform and, in an anxious voice, stated, "I was coming home from the store and when I was climbing the stairs to go into the building I heard a scream . . . Then I saw the shape of a man in the sky . . . With his arms stretched out like he was flying . . . But he came crashing down headfirst on the cement . . . He was just a ball of flesh and blood . . . He didn't move anymore . . ."

The people listened openmouthed as the terrified woman described what had happened. One of the officers took down all the details in a small notebook. A reporter took countless photographs per second, as if unable to satisfy his camera.

The shouts of "Spiderman! Spiderman!" were heard again, but this time they were completely ignored.

Calixto was among the spectators, stunned, terrified, and livid, unable to say a word about the tragedy, incapable of testifying that as they were washing the windows outside the eighth floor, the rope tied around his companion's waist broke. Calixto feared they would blame him for the death and he would end up in jail, if not deported for being undocumented. "And then," he thought, "who would support my family?"

The superintendent of the building was observing the scene from the lobby. He was not willing to talk either. He feared he would lose his job for permitting windows at that height to be washed without proper equipment for such a dangerous task. It would come out that he employed undocumented workers and paid them only a third of what cleaning companies usually charged.

The ambulance siren sounded in the neighborhood with such shrillness that it frightened the animals in the zoo. The lion roared as if protesting all the commotion.

The paramedics made their way through the crowd and laid a stretcher on the ground near the body. After a brief examination, one of them said dryly. "He's dead," confirming what everyone already knew.

"Who is he?" one of the paramedics asked the police. "What's his name?"

"No one knows," responded the officer. "Nobody seems to recognize him."

"He looks Hispanic," stated the other paramedic, observing the body closely.

"Maybe he's from Central America," said a woman, clutching her purse to her chest. "A lot of them live in this neighborhood . . . You know, they come here fleeing the wars in their countries . . ."

"If he's not from El Salvador, he must be from Guatemala," agreed one of the paramedics. "Although now they're coming from all over: Bolivia, Peru, Colombia. We used to be the ones who invaded their countries; now they invade ours. Soon Washington will look like Latin America."

"Poor devils," said the other paramedic. "They die far from home, like strangers."

Meanwhile, in the zoo, the lion's loud roar was answered by that of the lioness. The pair of felines, oblivious to the conflicts going on around them, were consummating the reproduction of their species, part of the ancient rites of spring.

The paramedics put the body into the ambulance. The policemen left. The crowd dispersed. A strange red stain remained on the cement.

Calixto entered the zoo and began to walk absent-mindedly among the cages, thinking about his co-worker who just half an hour ago had been telling him that he had already bought his ticket to return to his country, where he planned to open a grocery store with the money had saved from five years of hard work in the United States.

Suddenly Calixto realized that in a matter of minutes he had become unemployed. Despair seized him as he remembered that it had taken him a month and a half of constant searching to get the window washing job.

He spent the entire day at the zoo and, as he agonized over whether to return to his country or stay in Washington, he walked from one end of the zoo to the other several times. When they closed the park, he began to walk down long streets with strange names, until finally night fell and he had no choice but to return to the place where he lived, a tiny one-bedroom apartment occupied by twenty people.

"At least I'm alive," he said to himself. "That's good enough for me."

2

Calixte got up early and, without eating breakfast, left the apartment to look for work. He stopped at several businesses along Columbia Road where, according to the comments he had heard at the apartment, Spanish was spoken. But they gave him no hope of a job because he did not have a Social Security card or a green card. Nevertheless, he did not give up; he knew he would find something. "Even if it's cleaning bathrooms, it doesn't matter; in this country people aren't ashamed to do anything."

To alleviate his desperation a little, he paused in front of the window of a clothing store. His gaze fell on the tiny alligator that adorned one of the shirts, and the price of the shirt startled him. He remembered that in his country they made clothing like that. In his neighborhood, in fact, everyone went around with that little figure on their chests. It made no difference that the crocodile faded with the first washing, came loose with the second, and that after the third washing nothing was left of the reptile but a hole in the shirt. Calixto realized it was pointless to dream about new things when he did not even have a job, and he continued walking along Columbia Road. When he reached the corner of 18th Street, he decided to go into McDonald's. A fellow countryman from Intipucá whom Calixto had met at the apartment had heard that there were job opportunities there. He noticed a dark-skinned man who looked Latin American picking up papers from the floor and wiping off tables. He approached him, and asked in Spanish, "Do you know if they're hiring here?"

The man responded with a smile and strange gestures.

"Work," repeated Calixto. "Washing dishes or anything."

But the man did not understand him because he was Indian and did not speak Spanish.

CHAPTER 12

Early Perspectives on Class and Gender

Leonor Villegas de Magnón (1877–1955)

The Rebel Is a Girl

Leonor Villegas de Magnón is one of the very few women memoirists of the Mexican American as well as Mexican traditions. Born in northern Mexico, Villegas was educated at elite Catholic schools in San Antonio and Austin, Texas, and received her bachelor's degree and teaching credentials from the Academy of Mount St. Ursula in New York in 1895. By 1913, Villegas was married, teaching school, and living in Laredo. She was also one of the local representatives of Ricardo Flores Magón's (see entry in this anthology) revolutionary movement against dictator Porfirio Díaz. That same year, she organized and commanded a corps of military nurses, La Cruz Blanca (The White Cross), made up mostly of Texas Mexican and Anglo women, that crossed the border and entered the hostilities of the Mexican Revolution in support of Venustiano Carranza's army. During the extent of the Carranza army participation in the war, Villegas served at his side, practically as a general of the women, and took charge of the hospital in Nuevo Laredo. After the war, Villegas noted that the extensive contribution of women to the revolution had been ignored, so she decided to write a memoir to document the work of La Cruz Blanca and women in battle. Her memoir was rejected by publishers in Mexico; her English-language version of the tale was similarly rejected in the United States. Her manuscripts, as well as her humanitarian and cultural leadership in Texas and Mexico, became the legacy of her family, which over the years continued to pursue recognition and publication. Success was finally achieved when her granddaughter, Leonor Smith, was able to place the memoir with the Recovering the U.S. Hispanic Literary Heritage project for publication. What follows below is chapter 1, which recalls the birth of the Rebel herself. (NK)

Further reading: Leonor Villegas de Magnón, *The Rebel,* ed. Clara Lomas (Houston: Arte Público Press, 1994).

Chapter One: The Rebel Is a Girl

The Río Bravo or Río Grande defines the dividing line between the two nations, Mexico and the United States. As the years pass the river appears to be in a state of inactivity. Its waters seek a lower level, until it eventually leaves its banks exposed. In some places it becomes a thin stream that can be easily crossed on foot. The least cautious, or perhaps the most daring and hard-pressed people, take advantage of the fertile soil and, at their own risk, build huts, plant vegetables, raise chickens, cows, and a pig or two. The river maintains this happy mood for years, and the poor are hopeful that it will thus continue.

By some whim of nature, or it may be that Neptune, God of the Seas, wishes to amuse himself, the water awakens from its tranquil slumber and transforms itself into a gigantic serpent that crawls slowly, but gains a momentum of such menacing form that carries with it everything that it contacts. Soon on its surface floating with the torrent cows, sheep, chickens, snakes, and huts struggle to keep above the waters until they are finally engulfed by the churning undercurrent. Nothing escapes the furious waters that rush on as if in answer to a challenge presenting a grotesque contrast to the many years of defiant lethargy.

On a night like this, the twelfth of June, 1876, the shrill whistle of the night guards gave the alarm. Civil guards on horses rode from town to town along the river, warning the inhabitants of the approaching peril. Shrill cries and terrifying screams filled the air and the Laredos, two border towns across the river from each other, rose to the emergency. The darkness of the night became more terrifying as thunderclap after thunderclap intermingled with the cries of those in danger. The lightning illuminated their path momentarily only to leave it again and again in intense darkness.

The trees whipped by a gale of wind blew back and forth, beating against the walls of the big homes, while rampant waters gaining ground curled around the foundations, menacing homes and huts till they yielded to the mighty pressure of the water and fell like sugar toys.

The poor who lived on the edge of the river were making powerful efforts to save the little they possessed. They moved forward like beasts of burden, carrying as much as their strength allowed them. Women with children tied to their back in *rebozos* had their hands free to drag their animals. Men burdened with chattel also dragged their beasts, going ahead to find a safe foot path to scale the river banks. If they dared to halt, those behind gave a cry of warning.

"Go up higher! Higher! Higher!"

Again they redoubled their steps in an effort to gain safe ground; the waters were already flooding Nuevo Laredo on the Mexican side. The town was in darkness; only the lanterns carried by helpers provided the means to light the way of the refugees. The *mozos*, caretakers of the rich ones, were kept busy guarding the homes, and running back and forth with news of the rising water, its level, its perils, providing an excuse for wild excitement.

Emperor Maximilian had been dethroned, tried, and executed. Benito Juárez and Porfirio Díaz had dickered for power between themselves. After overthrowing the government of Lerdo de Tejada, General Profirio Díaz had taken the Capital of Mexico proclaiming his Plan de Tuxtepec. Slow means of communication and the rapid changes in governments left many guerrilla bands of either side scattered over the country. These groups, unaware of peace, continued to roam about attacking towns.

A band of these scattered rebels, taking advantage of the storm-frightened people of the little town of Nuevo Laredo, found it opportune to attack and loot the homes which had been temporarily abandoned or neglected either from fear of the rising river or out of curiosity to view the damage. The terror of the night meant nothing to the rebel looters. They rode unchallenged to the heart of town, determined to break down the gates of a rich Spanish merchant to whom it was rumored a large consignment of fine wines had recently arrived by barge from the Gulf of Mexico.

Quickly they made their way through the darkness to the front of a strong gate, or *portón*, with the master's name, Don Joaquín, on the stone arch overhead.

"This is the place," they yelled, banging on the gate with the butts of their guns. "Open the gate! Open!"

Don Joaquín, a prudent man, ordered the gate opened. Pancho, the *mozo*, was accustomed to obeying orders, but he hesitated.

"Go, Pancho. Open the gate."

Slowly Pancho proceeded to accomplish the task which was always so easy, but tonight his trembling fingers refused to pull the heavy lock that held the door tight.

"Señor," he said, "they are bandits."

"You cannot do it, Pancho? I will do it myself." Don Joaquín, carrying a lantern in one hand, approached and opened the door that yielded softly.

Pancho hid behind the door. The Indian guessed the reason for this visit. Holding his lantern high, Don Joaquín got a quick view of the intruders. He saw the group of armed bandits and at once guessed their motive.

"Follow me," he said in a low voice, escorting them down the tile-paved courtyard.

Don Joaquín's establishment covered a long city block on the main plaza, a quarter of a mile from the river. Surrounded by a thick wall well over a man's height were the house, the *bodega* (warehouse), and the store. In the house lived the young master and his family. In rooms built along the side of the warehouse lived the young boys who had come from Spain to learn the merchandising business. Along the back wall was an open space behind the house and the *bodega*, where garlic was stored.

Entering the warehouse, Don Joaqíun led the way down into the cellar where the big assortment of Spanish wines had been stowed away. The intruders at once became his guests, sitting around on the benches, but still holding their guns in a prominent position. Wine casks stacked on top of each other lined the sides of the room. The light from Don Joaquín's lantern on the rough wooden table was reflected in the tin wine cups. Where the wine had dripped from the spigots there were stains on the stone floor. The sweet smell of wine was heavy in the air.

Serving the wine Don Joaquín drew, Pancho faltered among the rough men. Grabbing a cup from Pancho, the leader held it up close to his eyes to see if it was full. Then flinging back his head he poured it down his throat. Putting his cup back on the table with a heavy thump he looked meaningly at Pancho.

"His cup, Pancho. We do not want our friends to leave thirsty." Don Joaquín held out his hand for the empty cup.

"Ah, we are not leaving yet, Señor. Not until we have searched the house." The leader nodded to his men who forgot their wine and jümped up.

Don Joaquín pushed through the men and started toward the door near the gate, but the men were already attracted by a closed door across the patio, where voices were heard coming from within.

"Open this door, señor," commanded the boldest one making a sign to his companions to present arms. "Open this door."

Without hesitating, the master raised his lantern to throw a better light in the dimly lit room. At that moment cries of a newborn baby broke the silence.

Outside, the increasing fury of the stormy night threatened at any moment to demolish the house. The waters were slapping against the walls, slipping in through the low windows. Inside the bandit-held mansion, beaten by the wind, threatened by the water, a woman in majestic dignity had given birth to a child.

The rebels were touched by the familiar sacredness of the scene. Putting away their guns, some among them made the sign of the cross on their foreheads and on their hearts. They returned to the patio to resume their drinking.

"Pardon, señor," the leader murmured.

But before the band could descend to the wine cellar, loud knocks and threats of breaking in the gate were heard. A Federal commander in command of his own troops demanded entrance to search for bandits. Frightened by the Federals, the rebels scattered wildly over the courtyard, climbing the wall in back of the warehouse and escaping in the opposite direction.

Gripping his lantern, the master walked to the gate. He again held his light high. Opening the door, he signaled to the Federals to walk in and be quiet.

"Follow me," said Don Joaquín, starting toward the wine cellar.

The Federals in their anxiety to find some victim on whom to discharge their fury, pushed one another into the hall, some bouncing clear across the patio.

"The rebels are here," the commander said, seeing that Don Joaquín was leading them away from the direction of the house.

"Sí, señor," answered Don Joaquín quickly. "I am hiding one rebel." He walked toward the door, hesitated, then flung it open. The crying of the baby silenced the men.

"A man child, señor?" asked the commander.

Pancho shook his head at Don Joaquín.

"No, señor," the master answered. He drew himself up in pride. "My rebel is a girl."

"A girl!" one of the men said, and making excuses for their intrusion, turned away from the door.

"Pardon us, señor. We already knew that you were an honest man. But in these awful times, what about it? Anything may happen. All the people are alarmed with so many rumors of bandits."

Don Joaquín ushered the Federals to the same cellar where the bandits had just been. With their cups filled, the men held them high and offered a toast of welcome to the new arrival, the Rebel. They drank a second toast to the mother of the baby.

"This toast we offer," the commander said, "to the mother of this border town on the banks of the Río Bravo." He wished to appear in a good light before the eyes of the owner of such good wines.

"¡Viva! ¡Viva!" the men called out in high spirits because their bandit hunt had turned into a party.

Finally, Don Joaquín, who was impatiently awaiting their departure, began to show signs of restlessness. Pancho appeared with his lantern to lead the way out. As the Federals filed out of the gate, passersby reported that the river was now at a standstill and the storm had abated.

Pancho, lantern in hand, did not think it time to go to bed, but preferred walking the streets, telling the double good news of the baby and the dying storm. As he started out the gate, Don Joaquín called, "Pancho, go put on dry clothes while Julia makes coffee for us all."

Julia was considered part of the family. She was a young Indian girl whom Doña Valerianna, Don Joaquín's wife, had taken as a child and raised.

Meanwhile, Don Joaquín personally examined all the doors and windows; though the storm had ceased, the strong wind might blow them open. While he was walking about the place, his thoughts were filled with scenes from the year. He remembered that just one year before, his first son had been born in Corpus Christi.

"Strange coincidence," he recalled. On the night Leopoldo was born there had been a tempest and the waves had lashed his home on the bay.

"My son born on American soil. My daughter in Mexican territory, and I, a Spanish subject. Who will be more powerful, he or she?"

In bed, Doña Valerianna held her child in a warm embrace, whispering a benediction.

"A Mexican flag shall be yours. I will wrap it together with your brother's. His shall be an American flag, but they shall be like one to me."

Her eyes searched into the darkness for her husband's flag, murmuring in her semiconsciousness, "His country I shall never see; it is beyond the great ocean."

María Cristina Mena (1893–1965)

The Emotions of María Concepción

With Mexico on the verge of a revolution, María Cristina Mena's family sent her to live with family friends in New York City. She was fourteen at the time, and she was to spend the rest of her life in the United States. Mena, who moved in literary circles, which included the likes of D. H. Lawrence and Aldous Huxley, published her first short story when she was twenty-one. Soon she became known as an apt translator of Mexican culture for readers of *Century, Cosmopolitan, Household,* and *American Magazine*. While some critics have taken her to task for propagating stereotypes, others have come to her defense by pointing out that on many occasions her own perspective and voice were sacrificed to the demands of editors interested in presenting an exotic and romantic Mexico to their journals' readership. Indeed, Mena draws on her rarified class background and employs a rose-colored-lens perspective in her portrayal of Mexican culture; but she also allows the reader to glimpse the fissures that were beginning to appear in an entrenched colonial hierarchy, prompted not only by the revolutionary masses but by rebellious sons of privilege as well as by daughters and wives restrained by rigid gender codes. In *The Emotions of María Concepción*, Mena depicts the predicament of a young woman caught between loyalty to a possessive father and sexual desire for a dashing matador. The reader might be disappointed to discover that despite having engaged in a daring flaunting of tradition, in the end, María Concepción opts for the traditional pattern of honor gained through fulfilling duty. Literary critic Amy Doherty has suggested a more interesting reading: as a comment on the colonial relation between Mexico and Spain, with a final affirmation of the Mexican side. (EGB)

Further reading: María Cristina Mena, *The Collected Stories of María Cristina Mena*, ed. Amy Doherty (Houston: Arte Público Press, 1997); María Cristina Chambers, *The Boys and Heroes of Chapultepec: A Story of the Mexican War* (Philadelphia: Winston, 1953).

María Concepción, having a favor to ask of her *papá* that morning, listened at the door of his dressing-room, which adjoined her own, and tried to augur an auspicious mood from the accent of the abstruse little cough with which he punctuated every delicate task. She heard his measured pacing to and fro, his opening and shutting of drawers, and the clash of dainty cup and saucer as he sipped his black coffee. Her delicate nose identified the aroma generated by *papá*'s hair under the cordial embraces of a curling-iron, and the lilac perfume of the cosmetic with which those rampant waves and the heavy mustache and imperial were licked into lustrous immobility. At last—welcome sound!—a cough of finality, and Senator Montes de Oca marched forth, serene in spotless, frock-coated, patent-leathered perfection.

Not yet, however, would his daughter present herself before him. First he must make his morning *reflexiones*, a solemnity which involved his pacing for five minutes the circuit of the gallery, with head bent, and hands clasped behind his back, sometimes pausing to glance over the flower-decked railing into the patio, or to order his *mozo* to remove some linnet or canary whose pipings interfered with his cerebral operations. According to domestic tradition, the senator, during that daily perambulation, exercised his intellect to a degree beyond the capacity of less formidable mortals to comprehend. Watching him furtively from the shelter of her room, María Concepción applied an extra coat of powder to her already well-whitened features, and dexterously encircled her large eyes with artificial shadows, those *ojeras* which promote luster and spirituality. She found time, too, to rehearse a languid comportment, and she gave some consideration to the project of sinking at her *papá's* feet in a graceful swoon, a maneuver sometimes effective as a stimulant to the granting of special indulgences.

Intense in all things, she had an intense desire to attend a brilliant affair at the Plaza de Toros on the following Sunday. All society would be there, and El Mañoso was to kill—El Mañoso, the youngest and greatest swordsman of Spain, who was now to make his first bow to the cream of Mexican fashion. María Concepción had never been present at a bull-fight. Before her arrival at an age for such fiestas her mother had died, and for five years the house of Montes de Oca had dragged through the successive stages of ceremonious mourning prescribed by Mexican etiquette. The senator had testified his grief *á lo gran señor*, causing the finest chamber in his house to be converted into an exquisite private chapel, duly consecrated, where masses were celebrated daily in memory of the beloved. Upon his daughter, during those springtime years of hers, he had imposed the most rigid austerities. If ever a young gallant found opportunity to make "eyes of deer" at her, though he might possess all the virtues of St. Thomas, the indignant senator would suddenly discover in him all the hypocrisies of Judas. Maria Concepción often declared with tears to her adored twin-brother, Enrique, that it if were not for her expansions of soul with him, and with the heroines of innumerable surreptitious novels, she would have perished in the bud. Soon she would be eighteen. That very morning she had discovered a wrinkle, a very little one, it was true, and possibly no deeper than the powder; but it had made her weep. *¡Qué fatalidad!*

Decisive as a signal-gun was the cough with which *El Senador* Don Enrique Montes de Oca y Quintana Ruiz announced to all the world that he had concluded his *reflexiones.* The household sprang into audible activity. The great doors of the coach-house rolled open, and the senator's coupé swung into the patio. Now was the ordained moment for the bestowal of his benediction upon his daughter.

Even as the thought came to him, she approached—pale as a gardenia, her humid, dark eyes fixed upon him in a faint smile of reverence, submission, and affection. At what cost of vigilance and self-discipline she had studied to obliterate herself until the instant of need, and then to sparkle from oblivion with a smile, her *papá* never reflected, not deeming it any concern of his to discover the technique by which women compass the proprieties of their sex. But it did occur to him that she was growing every day more like her lamented mother, and that observation brought him an access of paternal tenderness as she kissed his hand.

She had brought a flower for his coat, a single violet selected from the mass which Refugio, the coachman's daughter, had placed on her dressing-table.

"But thy *papá* is too old for these fiestas," he protested indulgently as she sought to put it in his buttonhole. "Have more formality, Conchita!"

"It is so little and so pale," she pleaded—"so pale, dear *Papá,* that I think it must have grown in the moonlight."

Touched on his poetic side, he unbent so far as to permit himself to be decorated. But then—then, before she could frame the tactful phrases which were to lead up to the theme of the bull-fight, he made an announcement which swept that festival from her thoughts, and canceled every check that her imagination had ever drawn upon the bank of destiny. With an air of conferring an honor far beyond her aspirations, he said:

"Daughter of my soul, thou hast been this morning the subject of my reflections, with the consequence that God has illumined me to guide thee to happiness by making thee the companion and consolation of my remaining years on earth."

Her eyes and breathless mouth rounded in a trinity of O's. Pleased that his words had produced a palpable impression, and proud of the discretion with which he had attacked that delicate task, the making of an old maid, he coughed rhetorically and continued:

"Thou wilt rejoice that I have made thy future secure by liberating thee from the anxieties of youth and, above all, from the banalities of coquetry. Study to make thyself worthy of the consecration to which thou art elected. Invoke the sanctified spirit of thy mama, who doubtless is in heaven commending us to God. Preserve thy health, taking with diligence thine emulsion of oil of liver of codfish, that thou mayest be a comfort and not a care to thy desolate *papá,* who in a short time will have fulfilled half a century of this life, and who requires thy gentle ministrations to alleviate the dolorous path which he must follow to the tomb."

These words, pronounced in a deep and vibrating tone, affected María Concepción so piteously that, without one thought of artifice, she sank sobbing to the floor and embraced the paternal knees, entreating the senator to abandon such gloomy thoughts and to believe that she, his child, thanked Heaven for the privilege of dedicating her life to her beloved *papacito.* Touched at this proof of a becoming feminine spirit, he raised her to her feet, and rewarded her with an affectionate embrace. His heart expanded, and it occurred to him that he was feeling uncommonly young and lively; nevertheless he thought it proper to utter a few pensive reflections on mortality.

When he had given her his benediction and departed for the palace María Concepción ran to change her dress. She had a habit of changing her dress under the stimulus of every new emotion, whether derived from life or from a novel. *Papá*'s ministering angel! Never had she experienced an emotion so difficult to fit with the psychological frock. She must design a costume, something very spiritual, with a Sarah Bernhardt collar. In the meantime she would put on her habit of the Daughters of Mary, which she had worn at the College of the Sacred Heart—black silk, with a silk cord about the waist, the only touch of color being the broad ribbon of blue sackcloth by which the blessed medal of the order was suspended from the devotee's neck.

Feeling particularly angelic in that demure but bewitching costume, María Concepción sought the chapel of her mama, and earnestly invoked the Virgin to purify her heart and to make her as worthy as possible of her tender and distinguished mission. And she felt herself uplifted as on wings. Returning to her own apartments and consulting the mirrors, she was impressed by the unearthly, soft splendor of her eyes, turned upward under their sweeping lashes in this new rapture of devotion. The contemplation of her own delicate beauty moved her to tears of appreciation. *Papá* should see that he had not been mistaken in her, that she did indeed rejoice at his having set her free from—what were his words? The "anxieties of youth," yes, yes, and the "banalities of coquetry." Coquetry, with those eyes of hers! What sacrilege!

Luisa Capetillo (1879–1922)

How Poor Women Prostitute Themselves

Known as the first feminist militant in Puerto Rico, Luisa Capetillo is also a legendary figure in the history of the Puerto Rican working-class movement. In many ways, she was a working-class intellectual, dedicated not only to political journalism and to the defense of workers' rights, but also to the ideological and practical integration of the principles of anarchism, women's liberation, and Allan Kardec's "spiritism." For Capetillo, revolution entailed both structural changes in the oppressive relationships of production under capitalism, as well as the transformation of personal life and values. Thus, she became a vocal critic of bourgeois notions of marriage and family and of dominant definitions of women's cultural roles. The fact that she was the first Puerto Rican woman to publicly wear pants is emblematic of her politically and culturally defiant behavior. While engaged in these activities, Capetillo continued to work as a *lectora* (reader) in cigar factories. The *lectores* were literate workers who read newspapers, novels, and political essays to their peers while they worked at their tasks. Capetillo emigrated to the United States early in the twentieth century. There she continued her activism, becoming a member of the Free Workers Union. The text below, "How Poor Women Prostitute Themselves," is a sample of the kind of dramatic productions generated within the working-class movement at the time. Later, this sketch was printed in *Influencia de las ideas modernas* (*Influence of Modern Ideas*), a collection of Capetillo's writings published in 1916. (ALO)

Further reading: Luisa Capetillo, *Ensayos libertarios* (Arecibo: Imprenta Unión Obrera, 1907), *La humanidad en el futur* (San Juan: Tipografía Real Hermanos, 1910), *Influencia de las ideas modernas: Notas y apuntes* (San Juan: Tipografía Negrón Flores, 1916).

Trans.: PP

A One Act Play

Scene: A simple living room

WOMAN: (*Enters scene in a house dress, followed by a well-dressed man who gives her money.*)

YOUNG MAN: Are you happy with this life?

WOMAN: No, but what choice do I have?

YOUNG MAN: Work at a factory.

WOMAN: I don't know a trade, and besides, how much would I make?

YOUNG MAN: Enough to feed yourself.

WOMAN: You're telling me to go earn a miserable wage, to breath bad air, and to listen to the impertinences of some vulgar foreman. That won't fix the harm done: we women will always be sacrificed in this infinite holocaust to a hypocritical social lie. It's all the same, for me or for someone else: it's human flesh that is humiliated or despised, that is sold and that atrophies, that is outraged, that is used and trampled on in the name of Christian morality. (*with energy*) What could you say to me that any other woman doesn't deserve to hear? It's all the same: treat me the same. We can only vindicate ourselves as a whole, or not at all—I'm no better than any other woman.

YOUNG MAN: That's true, one person alone is powerless. All women have the right to be happy, to be respected.

WOMAN: Along with stupid courtesies, social respect is a farce. If it can't prevent a poor tubercular girl from getting sick, why should she give a damn? Would respect give her the means to live comfortably? Because of the rich people's virtue and decorum they'll give her an apology when her soul has been left twisted and her body in the factory; why doesn't respect guarantee health and get rid of deprivation? Useless words!

YOUNG MAN: You're selfishness incarnate in an ignorant lady.

WOMAN: Why isn't that virtue inaccessible to the poor people in the grave? Why doesn't it take the stench out of the fermentation in the ditch? If you buried two girls of equal size and age, one an immaculate virgin, the other surrounded by vice and misery, would the dirt respect one more than the other? Would the dirt free the virgin from the worms?

YOUNG MAN: No, Mother Nature doesn't make those choices. For her, the virgin is the same as the prostitute. She is the equalizer, the lever par excellence.

WOMAN: Then, friend, what's the sense of living one way or the other? It's all the same: social hypocrasies don't bother my soul or disturb my mind.

YOUNG MAN: I understand. But if those things don't matter to you, I should remind you that you're exposed to thousands of diseases, and you practice vices that pleasure the mob of degenerates that use you and then treat you with scorn.

WOMAN: All that is very splendid to say, but if you were in my circumstances you would surely accept it one way or the other. One day a drunk came, and my opinions meant nothing to him. I was disgusted to go near him. He usually comes every Friday; he'll surely come this evening. What can I do about it?

YOUNG MAN: Well, I need to go. Please excuse my questions. Until another day. (He salutes her courteously with his hat.)

WOMAN: (*Alone*) An excellent young man. But it is already very late—what can I do?—and besides, it's the same to do it with only one as to do it with many. Aren't they all brothers, like in the Bible and all other religions? All that mess of uselessness seems ridiculous and stupid to me. If everything is for sale, why worry so much because we charge a fee? If she who joins herself with a man—through civil marriage or through some religion—also sells herself, doesn't the husband have to cover all the costs? Very few of them go to the factories, but isn't that a kind of sale? They don't want to call it that, but it's a sale just like ours.

DRUNK MAN: Good evening!

WOMAN: Come in.

THE MAN: May I? Very good then, let's hurry, I have to go. (*Shaking*)

WOMAN: Then enter, so you can go . . .

MAN: No, you go first. You want to do it, right? Look—you thieves—not even paying you makes you listen. Let's go, or I'll whip you! (*Pushing her*)

WOMAN: I'm going, pig, what do you think! . . . I'd be better off killing myself. . . .

MAN: For what you're worth, you may as well have already done it. (*They enter the house, he pushing her forward.*)

María Luisa Garza (1887–1990)

The Intelligent Woman

The Intelligent Woman is a *crónica* that depicts the ideology of "México de afuera" as manifested among twentieth-century immigrant writers. Through her regular column entitled "Crónicas Femeninas" in *El Imparcial de Texas* (San Antonio), under the pseudonym of Loreley, Garza criticized the Americanization of Mexican women in the United States. This specific chronicle analyzes the manner in which women are censured and scrutinized because they do not dedicate themselves to matters of the home or society. Loreley's intention was to motivate women to study and partake in reading and the intellectual life. Nevertheless, she concludes her chronicle by stating that an intelligent woman is one who despises filth, maintains a clean home, tends to her garden, and surrounds herself with birds. Loreley does create a place for women in her writing, making them active participants. But she cannot do away with bonds that tie her to tradition and, in the end, places women back at home, tending to their duties as intelligent homemakers. Loreley was a journalist and writer who also worked as editor in chief for *La Epoca* and wrote for *El Demócrata, El Universal,* and *Gráfico.* (GBV)

Further reading: María Luisa Garza, *La Novia de Nervo* (San Antonio: Librería Quiroga, 1922), *Los amores de Gaona, apuntes por Loreley [pseud.]* (San Antonio: Art Advertising, 1922), *Escucha* (México: Editorial Cultura, 1928).

Trans.: TEW

Much has been said about intelligent women, and intelligent women have been criticized for many things also. In my opinion, this is one of the principal reasons that there are few women writers. From a young age, females hear the interminable little phrase: "Hey . . . that one over there, she's a bluestocking."

Under these circumstances, beginning in childhood girls are afraid of intelligent women. Instead of reading books, they find it better to dedicate themselves to coquettishness, or they surrender completely to the talons of the fashion world.

There is nothing more misguided than this, because an educated woman is attractive, charming and seductive, from the very minute you meet her.

Napoleon once said that a pretty woman is a charm and a good woman a treasure. I cannot imagine how goodness can illuminate a dull soul. Goodness is attractive, but only if it is a characteristic of knowledge.

The woman who reads and educates herself, not in the shallow works of Luis de Val, but in vital and informative books—the seeds of fruitful illumination—is the woman who can dare to venture out alone into the raging sea of life.

It is common to observe how many young girls are perverted and fall into prostitution, enticed by nothing more than the lure of silks and the sparkle of jewels. I am sure that these gullible creatures never opened any book other than a fashion magazine.

I met a girl who was born into luxury and wealth but, through some misfortune, came to be enveloped by poverty. She was young and attractive and could have married, but her suitors turned away when they found out that she was poor.

One or another suitor who would continue the courtship was able to recognize the young lady's intelligence, but was not interested in her for such a respectable reason. Like so many naive women, she could have continued to live her lavish life at the cost of her honor, but this woman was smart. She was educated and looked to her erudition for the shield that would protect her from vice.

Once banished, her exceptional intelligence opened the redemptive doors of work to her. When she was thought to have been completely defeated, she was able to ascend the luminous path to success, something that is attained through knowledge.

It is often said: "She is an intellectual . . . and doesn't know anything about managing her home." Do those women who go dancing, walking or out visiting friends not waste time that should be invested in house work? It is not true that they actually waste more time than the bookworms, who everyone ridicules? If only these critics would really think about it. If only they would reflect on who wastes more time. Would they conclude that it is the woman who is always at home with her books, or the one constantly out in the streets?

An intelligent woman hates filth and ensures that her house is clean, the garden well-tended, and birds are close by.

Everyone would agree that not even a man could be happy having as his companion a frivolous wife who does not know how to brighten the home with her intelligence. Not even honor can be entrusted to such a woman, for she is capable of selling it in order to buy a suit *à la derniere* or a string of pearls from the Far East.

Julio G. Arce (1870–1926)

The Stenographer

Among the cultural elites who disseminated the ideology of "México de afuera" was one political refugee who, through writing as well as publishing a newspaper, became immensely influential. Julio G. Arce was a newspaper publisher from Guadalajara who took up exile in San Francisco, vowing never to return to Mexico, as he was so disillusioned with the revolution. Arce's series, entitled "Crónicas Diabólicas" (Diabolical Chronicles), published under the pseudonym of "Jorge Ulica," became the most widely syndicated *crónica* in the Southwest because of its ability to comment humorously on life in the Mexican immigrant community. By and large, Ulica assumed the stance of satirist, observing the human comedy as a self-appointed conscience for the community. Ulica's particular talents lay in caricature, in emulating the colloquialisms and popular culture of the working-class immigrant and in satirizing the culture conflict and misunderstandings encountered by greenhorn immigrants from the provinces in Mexico. In *The Stenographer*, he is not only scandalized but titillated by the Mexican American flapper whom he employs as a stenographer. The flapper was seen by *cronistas* as the most representative figure of American female liberation and loose morality. Hispanic women who adopted their dress and customs were subjected to the harshest censure as men sought to preserve their male prerogatives and power. (NK)

Further reading: Julio G. Arce, *Crónicas diabólicas de "Jorge Ulica"/Julio G. Arce,* ed. Juan Rodríguez (San Diego: Maize Press, 1982).

Trans.: TEW

The following are pages taken from my diary.

MONDAY.—I now have a stenographer. The promise of a boom in business, uttered by the prophetic lips of big U.S. financiers, has resulted in the presence in my humble office of a girl who takes dictation, types my letters, signs them by imitating my bad handwriting and mails them. What a wonder of a woman.

She is not a beauty, but does have some fine and delicate features. She was sent to me by an employment agency, and upon introducing herself, embarked on the following speech:

"At your request, The Horses, Mules and Stenographers Agency has sent me. I am 'efficient,' 'fine' and 'educated.' I am 25 years old and was born to 'Spanish' parents in Stockton. I graduated from grammar school, high school and Spanish class. Here are my certificates."

Next, she placed in my hands the documents that accredited her as a three-time graduate or, as a graduate in the three ways she had indicated. Then, instead of me being the one who asked her questions, she subjected me to an interrogation.

"Are you married or single?"

"Married."

"By the state or the church?"

"By everybody."

"How long ago did you get married?"

"A long time. One loses track of dates as time passes."

"Do you hit your wife?"

"So far, no."

"Fine. I'll agree to work at this office for 100 dollars a month."

"That is a lot of money. . . ."

She lowered her price and we agreed on sixty dollars, not a large sum of money if you keep in mind that the girl does all of the work of a private secretary, she smiles provocatively, looks sideways with a subdued sweetness and, the smell of black Narcissus, her favorite scent, fills the entire office.

She took off her coat, revealing her huge, fat and beautifully shaped arms, discreetly passed them in front of my face, and went about taking dictation. I don't know what I could have dictated to her because I felt queasy from the scent of Narcissus and the fluttering of her arms. When we finished, my stenographer—with an unequaled grace and posture—took out several articles of clothing from a giant suitcase she had brought with her. She took off her shoes and stockings in front of me, saying that at work they get worn down a lot and that she always changes her street things for those for work. She put her shoes and stockings behind my file cabinet and went to her office to work.

TUESDAY.—I had two quarrels with my employee. The first was because I did not call her by her name, which is Rosie, and instead I said to her Miss Pink, because that word "Pink" is her last name. The second conflict occurred because I begged her to bring me the letters she had typed in order to review them.

"Nobody reviews what I write. Either you trust me or you don't."

She wept and sobbed, and I had to give her a few pats on her arms in order to console her. She got very close to my face, as if for me to kiss her, but I didn't dare.

WEDNESDAY.—New trouble, but of a different kind. The ladies who direct the High Morality Society, an institution that monitors proper conduct between office managers and their female employees, were here to visit me. They were thrilled with the signs of my uprightness and with my unblemished integrity, but then they discovered the stenographer's shoes and stockings behind the file cabinet.

I tried to explain the situation to them, but they would not accept excuses and offered to publish the findings in their newspaper and contact my family about the sultry discovery, and they reprimanded Rosie. She was a sea of tears and sought solace in my words, but I didn't say a thing to her, afraid that I might complicate matters.

THURSDAY.—As usual, my stenographer changed her shoes and stockings and put them behind the file cabinet. I took them from there, fearing a new conflict, and put them in my desk drawer.

I went out at lunchtime, having forgotten about Miss Pink's things, and when I returned to the office I found my secretary in a state of rage.

"Where have you put my shoes and stockings?" she asked me angrily.

I realized inmediately what was going on and tried numerous apologies, but Rose refused to accept them.

"Are you the same as all the rest?" she yelled. "They begin by taking your stockings and shoes in order to kiss them and to smell them, I don't know what for, and then come the little 'jokes' and flirtations . . ."

I have sworn to my employee that it had never crossed my mind to kiss or smell her footware and in order to placate her, I gave her three dollars for a late lunch and the rest of the afternoon off.

FRIDAY.—My secretary took the following short note during dictation: "Sr. Pascual Torumes.—Hacienda del Big Huizache.—Dear friend Pascual: I feel a bit gray and I'm going to spend the weekend with you. See you soon.—Ulica."

My employee's slanderous accusation—that I am the same as the rest and that I have kissed or sniffed the things she wears on her feet—does not stop churning over in my mind.

I was struck by a tremendous, overwhelming and uncontrollable obsession.

When Rosie left for her apartment, I grabbed her slippers and stockings and sniffed them. The girl had emptied at least an ounce of Narcissus on them. I put everything back in its place but, as luck would have it, I spilled a bottle of ink and stained one of her shoes.

I explained the occurrence to Rosie as an accident and gave her ten dollars for some new shoes. She left saying, "You are worse than the others!"

SATURDAY.—My friend Pascual, who doesn't have a stenographer, responded to my letter saying that he would not tolerate what I had written to him, not even as a joke. The letter stated: "I feel a bit GAY and I'm going to spend the weekend with you . . ." It was as if I had suggested that this old friend of mine was effeminate. I was impatient, called Rosie and showed her the letter . . .

"You have made a serious mistake . . . Gray is written with an R."

"Listen," she said, "I write with whichever letter inspires me, and I don't follow 'spelling foolishness.' I'm leaving. You are the worst of the many bosses that I have had. You have not even once asked me to dinner or to a show. Blockhead . . . blockhead, don't you know what you are missing?"

She collected her salary and has left, leaving behind the scent of black Narcissus.

Jesús and Netty Rodríguez (dates unknown)

I'm Going to Mexico

Jesús and Netty Rodríguez were a husband-and-wife song, dance, and stand-up comedy act that was popular on Hispanic vaudeville circuits throughout the Southwest during the 1920s and in New York during the Depression and into the early 1950s. The star attraction of the act was Netty, who often received solo billing on fliers and marquees as La Bella Netty, for her beauty, her lovely voice, and her quick-witted comic repartee. Through their humorous dialogs, Jesús and Netty dramatized the culture conflict felt by both native Mexican Americans and Mexican immigrants. They often chose the Anglified *agringado* or *pocho* as the butt for their jokes and often reflected the tensions felt by men and women because of conflicting social and gender roles among Mexicans in the United States. As in the comic sketch below, which ends quite conventionally so as not to scandalize working-class audiences, the character Netty pushes, stretches, and attempts to broaden her woman's rights as she challenges male prerogatives. Throughout the skit the complete set of double references to Mexican and Anglo cultures is glossed on and explored, as in much of immigrant literature; but it was precisely through these types of cultural explorations—and in the Spanish original, language explorations—that a Mexican American cultural sensibility arose (as opposed to a Mexican immigrant stance). (NK)

Further reading: Chris Strachwitz and James Nicolopulos, eds., *Lydia Mendoza: A Family Autobiography* (Houston: Arte Público Press, 1993).

Trans.: PP

NETTY: When are we leaving, Panchito?
JESUS: Well, who knows, honey?
NETTY: What we did was real bad, and the thing is, I won't be leaving.
JESUS: Be a little patient.
NETTY: Patience! I've had enough.
JESUS: You're so impatient! It's worth it to keep on. We shouldn't back down about seeing our homeland.
NETTY: I'm not hesitating anymore. I'm staying here and looking for work. You can go if you want, 'cause no matter what, honey, I'm out of it.
JESUS: What's the matter, sweety? What's wrong? Shut your smart little mouth! You can't stay, your husband's leaving!
NETTY: Well, go ahead, if you want, leave. Because I'm fine right here. And you don't give me orders, got it? I'm not going!
JESUS: Look at you getting all worked up! The man gives the orders, you hear?
NETTY: I'm not your errand girl. Here, the man orders, and . . . doesn't.
JESUS: And doesn't give the orders? That's what you think.
NETTY: I don't just think it, I know it.
JESUS: You learned that pretty fast! And what I taught you, how soon you forgot it. A man is a man anywhere, and he should always be respected by his woman. When you snared me back in Celaya with your romantic illusions, I wore the pants and you wore the skirt. And because you've heard talk that here the law is a tyrant, you want me to turn everything upside down. Well, this ungrateful woman is mistaken! If she squawks because she's here, I'll break her leg, just to remind her of me.
NETTY: Ah, aren't you the tough guy! Get out of here with your threats! If you call a cop, you'll see if he pays attention to me!
JESUS: I'll show you!
NATTY: Go ahead! Hit me!

JESUS: Why should I hit you? Back home Mexico in there are plenty women who'll want me!

NETTY: Boy, aren't you exaggerating, Pancho! But I don't care, *compadre*, I've got the road wide open to go whereever I want.

JESUS: Well, I hope you're happy, baby. If you don't want to come, go ahead and stay. It won't kill me. Down there there's lots of women who'll love me. When I get to Manzanillo, I'll hook up with somebody else. And down there I won't be so stupid, I'll look for a real woman who doesn't give up, and who knows how to be grateful for her husband's hard work. A completely Mexican woman who doesn't change her mind and doesn't give up tortillas for hot cakes and ham.

NETTY: Now you've gone too far.

JESUS: Why did you give up, you sad woman?

NETTY: What are you talking about, loud mouth! Shut up!

JESUS: Why should I shut up? When did I not love you enough to make you want to stay here? Didn't I work nice and hard to buy you those tennis shoes?

NETTY: Sure.

JESUS: Didn't your good man take you for a good time at Venice Beach?

NETTY: Uh huh.

JESUS: Didn't I work like a dog for you for a whole year without a break? And you just havin' a good time learnin' to make yourself up? You are so ungrateful! You've given me such a hard time! My woman treats me so bad! She's even forgotten her homeland!

NETTY: That's it, don't you say that to me.

JESUS: Then why don't you come with me?

NETTY: How can you ask me to go with you if you don't have any more land down there?

JESUS: She's really laying it on heavy. She has no shame at all. Man, has she picked up the customs up here. I'm getting a divorce!

NETTY: All right, very well, all right!

JESUS: Lady, speak gibberish to me. I know how to speak that language, but talk to me like you know how, and don't get me all tangled up.

NETTY: Don't tell me I tangle you up, nothing could be clearer! If you leave, I'm staying. Goodbye, Panchito! Bye bye, toodeloo!

JESUS: Why does your love rule me like some kind of tyrant, even if I know that money makes you love me? And if your love is unhealthy and impure, it dishonors me. Because Mexico is in my heart, I'm going back, you'll see. Our love dies right here. Love down there will be even better. In my beloved Mexico to be in love is an honor. The only price for love there is love in return.

NETTY: Oh, Panchito baby, I can't stand it anymore. My homeland has won out. I want to go, too.

JESUS: At last, she's coming with me.

NETTY: I hope you'll forgive me, I'll follow you anywhere.

JESUS: To Mexico, baby, to Mexico.

Jesús Colón (1901–1974)

The Flapper (La Flapper)

In the period following the passage of the Jones Act of 1917, which made Puerto Ricans citizens of the United States, Jesús Colón became one of the most ardent social and political activists in the Hispanic immigrant community of New York. An autodidact whose roots lay in the tobacco culture of Cayey, Puerto Rico, Colón produced a steady stream of *crónicas*, editorials, and poetry that tended to promote his moral views among the Hispanic working classes. Colón gradually made the transition to writing in English, to greater political radicalism, and to staking out native entitlements for the Hispanic community in New York. However, in this early poem satirizing the adoption of American ways by Hispanic women, he echoed the common theme of immigrant literature: Hispanic cultural loyalty. Published as a sonnet in New York's *Gráfico* newspaper in 1927, *The Flapper* gives an intimate view of the culture clash that was occurring in the Hispanic communities at a time when women's roles were being liberalized in the United States. As in much immigrant literature, the past and present, the Hispanic and the Anglo cultures are contrasted in the last stanza of the poem. (EP)

Further reading: Jesús Colón, *A Puerto Rican in New York and Other Sketches* (New York: Masses and Mainstream, 1961); *The Way It Was and Other Writings,* eds. Edna Acosta-Belén and Virginia Sánchez Korrol (Houston, Arte Público Press, 1993).

Trans.: PP

Like a mestizo girl from New York,
The "flapper" rips the air with her wiggle,
her sway.
Her dress, a futurism of the latest style,
A thousand things suggest with its
divine silk.

Her greatest desire is to make men look
As she walks by. If a man speaks to her
of marriage
She answers with a burst of laughter
that kills
The most sublime illusion. An assassin's
laugh!

Expert queen of the final, mortal, dancing
leap;
Made-up, superficial, inconstant
Like the freed slave attempting a new life.

Como una niña Chole que fuera
neoyorquina,
rasga el aire la "flapper" contoneándose
toda.
Su traje, un futurismo de la última moda,
hace mil sugerencias con su seda divina.

Que la miren los hombres mientras ella
camina
es su supremo anhelo . . . Si hay quien le
hable de boda,
contesta con alguna carcajada que poda
la ilusión más sublime ¡Carcajada asesina!

Reina experta del último salto mortal
bailable,
niña pintarrajeada, superficial, variable,
como el liberto esclavo al probar nueva
vida.

In contrast, they remind me of my grandmother,	Por contraste me hacen recordar a mi abuela,
Who, while knitting, told me of a flying giant	que hilando me contaba del gigante que vuela,
With a thundering voice like a lost prayer.	con su voz temblcrosa cuál plegaria perdida.

Consuelo Lee Tapia (1909–?)

Women and Puerto Rican Identity

Patriot, poet, journalist, and pianist, Consuelo Lee Tapia is best known as the cofounder, with her husband, poet Juan Antonio Corretjer, of the weekly *Pueblos Hispanos*. This important, although short-lived (1943–44), New York–based anti-imperialist and antifascist publication not only advocated for Puerto Rico's independence from the United States but also stood against any form of U.S. military intervention in Latin America. The granddaughter of one of Puerto Rico's most important nineteenth-century writers, Alejandro Tapia y Rivera, Lee Tapia moved to New York City in the first decades of the twentieth century. A militant member of the Communist Party of America since 1937, her political convictions were to exert a tremendous influence on the ideological reorientation of her renowned husband (see entry on Juan Antonio Corretjer in this anthology). The two met in New York City around 1942, when Corretjer was freed from his five-year imprisonment in a federal jail due to nationalist militancy. From New York both went to Cuba in 1945, and the following year they were finally able to return to their country. Back in Puerto Rico, Lee Tapia founded the People's Union, a school for adult literacy, and continued her political activism. Later in life she published her only collection of poems, *Con un hombro menos (With One Shoulder Less)*. The article below was published in *Pueblos Hispanos* on September 23, 1944, to commemorate a nineteenth-century Puerto Rican revolutionary uprising against Spanish colonialism known as the "Grito de Lares" (1868). In her piece, Lee Tapia pays homage to one of the protagonists of this rebellion, the patriot Mariana Bracetti—known as "Brazo de oro" (Golden Arm) for having embroidered the flag that was to become the national symbol for an independent Puerto Rico. Written in the context of World War II, the article is a nationalist call to action to Puerto Rican women on the basis of an intensely politicized, although still traditional, conception of motherhood. (ALO)

Further reading: Consuelo Lee Tapia, *Con un hombro menos* (San Juan: Instituto de Cultura Puertorriqueña, 1977).

Trans.: TEW

When Mariana Bracetti dedicated her life to the emancipation of our country from Spanish tyranny, she also committed Puerto Rican mothers to fighting for their passions and to giving birth to free citizens.

Mariana Bracetti gave us her life so that no child of a Puerto Rican mother would be born into slavery. The Puerto Rican woman who does not fight for the freedom of her homeland is not fulfilling her maternal and sacred duty, as this valiant woman did through her sacrifice. Mariana Bracetti is more than a champion for the redemption of her country from the tyrants; she is also a champion of liberty for Puerto Rican mothers. Mariana Bracetti did not think it enough to just have a son; she found out that giving birth, by itself, is not maternity if one does not battle to ensure that the new life breathes the air of liberty.

Mariana paved the way for us. We, the women of Puerto Rico, have a promise to keep . . . a sacred promise . . . a maternal promise. It is now time for Puerto Rican mothers to take hold of the flag. With full rights, courage, sacrifice—and in the name of justice and obligation—we will confront the enemy face to face. We will submerge our enemy's resistance in a wave of protests, until we free our country.

In Lares, Mariana was a lone woman in a world that still considered the female sex unfit to vote. Today, we have a history of victories for women: suffrage, better conditions and the sense to raise our children as sound and brave citizens. The women of the world are doing it; we will do it. Now is the time. If only every town on our island would hear the battle cry of Mariana . . . and one daughter would be inspired to protest: against our country's enslavement, against our enslavement as women, and against the enslavement of our children. Now that the whole world is fighting for the same principle that caused our Mariana to give birth in a Spanish prison, we shall fight also. We shall fight so that none of the Puerto Ricans who gave their lives in the fight for freedom will have done so in vain. We also shall fight for the Puerto Ricans who sacrifice their lives today and die on foreign soil while fighting in order to guarantee Puerto Rico a place among the world's democracies. They shall not die without the assurance that all Puerto Rican mothers are equally responsible for them. It is our duty to ensure that our heroic children return to an independent and sovereign country. It is the duty of all Puerto Ricans.

Women of Puerto Rico, hear the battle-cry of Lares! Hear the voice of Mariana Bracetti! Fulfill the promise of Lares! Let us all join together for the immediate independence of Puerto Rico!

CHAPTER 13

Editorial Discontent

Sara Estela Ramírez (1881–1910)

Speech Read by the Author on the Evening that the "Society of Workers" Celebrated the Twenty-Fourth Anniversary of Its Founding

At the age of seventeen, Sara Estela Ramírez came to Laredo, Texas, in 1898. During this period, Mexican teachers were recruited by Mexicans in Texas who founded their own schools in order to preserve language and culture, as well as to protect their children from segregation and discrimination. During her short, very productive life in the border city, she not only taught in elementary schools but also founded and edited newspapers, assisted in organizing labor, and became an active member of Flores Magón's movement against the dictatorial regime of Porfirio Díaz in Mexico. A sought-after poet, whose verses were often published in Laredo Spanish-language newspapers, Ramírez was equally in demand for her passionate speeches on behalf of labor and liberal causes at organizing meetings for farm workers, miners, industrial workers, and women. In the speech below, Ramírez extols the benefits of workers organizing themselves into mutual aid societies and unions. (NK)

Further reading: Inés Hernández Tovar, "Sara Estela Ramírez: The Early Twentieth Century Texas-Mexican Poet," Ph.D. diss., University of Houston, 1984.

Trans.: Inés Hernandez Tovar

I beseech the honorable president, the respected Society of Workers, and this most distinguished audience to forgive my lack of ability. Invited to take part in this celebration, pleasant for more than one reason, and wishing to cooperate with this united effort, though my part may be insignificant, I come as a fervent admirer of the mutual benefit movements, to call on all workers, my brothers, and say: Combatants, forward!

For such a simple expression I need no elegance of language, rhetoric, nor any wisdom. To call a worker my brother, I need only my heart, and to tell him "Forward!" I need only, like him, a soul swollen with the desire to struggle.

We celebrate the twenty-fourth anniversary of the well known as it is respected Society of Workers.

The twenty-fourth anniversary! How much that date tells us!

Twenty-four years of noble struggle against so many morbid germs that would annihilate the collective effort, that terribly and vilely devote themselves to devouring mutualism; twenty-four years of having to kill egotisms and ambitions, of holding down rebelliousness and joining hands over those fallen rebellions; twenty-four years of joining souls through the principle of humanity, through the sentiment of innate altruism in the heart, an altruism that permits us to fulfill our obligation to our beloved comrade, to visit him in sickness, to console him in sorrows and to give him our hand in every bitter hour and in every test, even to bid him farewell when his turn comes to be called to eternity.

That is mutualism, a noble mission of truth, sublime and holy mission, mission of charity that nations ignore or have forgotten; nations, whose workers are dispersed, segregated, strangers to each other, and . . . how many times, sad to say, more than strangers, subject to ruinous enmities, that workers' element divides instead of seeking [union], becomes offended instead of giving aid and, no, rejects with hatred its own [members], rather than embracing [all workers] with love; [workers] reject each other without seeing that their blood and their anguish kneaded together become the bitter bread that they devour together; without seeing that their arms are what sustain the industry of nations, their richness and their greatness.

How many times also through apathy do the workers' guilds remain isolated, through the lack of that invigorating spirit that gives energy and patience to confront setbacks and survive difficulties?

Mutualism needs the vigor of struggle and the firmness of conviction to advance in its unionizing effort; it needs to shake away the apathy of the masses, and enchain with links of abnegation the passions that rip apart its innermost being; it needs hearts that say: I am for you, as I want you to be for me; mutualism has need of us workers, the humble, the small gladiators of the idea, it needs for us to salvage from our egotisms something immense, something divine, that can make us a society, that can make us nobly human. And the worker should not think of his humbleness, nor of his insignificance, he should not reason that he is unimportant and so remove himself discouraged from the social concert. What does it matter that he is but an atom, what does it matter?

The atoms invisible for their smallness are the only elements of the universe.

That is how he is. The worker is the arm, the heart of the world.

And it is to him, untiring and tenacious struggler, that the future of humanity belongs. May you, beloved workers, integral part of human progress, yet celebrate, uncounted anniversaries, and with your example may you show societies how to love each other so that they may be mutualists and to unite so that they may be strong.

Tomás Gares (1892–?)

The Castilian Language and Puerto Rico (El idioma castellano y Puerto Rico)

Little is known of the life of Tomás Gares, the Puerto Rican poet who seems to have been ubiquitous in community life in Hispanic New York from the 1920s through the 1940s. In 1923, Gares was a founding member and vice-president of one of the most important and extensive mutual aid societies in U.S. Hispanic communities: the Puerto Rican Brotherhood. Gares was also on the staff of the important community newspaper *Gráfico*, but he did not limit the publication of his work to that periodical alone; his poetry appeared in many others throughout the years. The poem below, which appeared in *Artes y letras* (*Arts and Letters*) in 1934, dedicated to fellow New York Puerto Rican poet and playwright Antonio González, was a response to the imposition of English by the United States military government in Puerto Rico as the official and only language of instruction in the public schools of Puerto Rico. Tomás Gares's double gaze as an economically displaced immigrant looking back to his native soil is made even more bitter by the displacement of his history and culture by that of Anglo America. (NK)

Further reading: Bernardo Vega, *Memoirs of Bernardo Vega*, ed. César Andreu Iglesias, trans. Juan Flores (New York: Monthly Review Press, 1984).

Trans.: PP

They say the beautiful Castilian language
Is mortally wounded in my land;
They say it's a question of time, Castilian's
abandonment
For another, non-secular language.

They say Cervantes' rich language
By Shakespeare's will be supplanted,
Now that my land studies Scott and Byron
To leave behind Espronceda and Castelar.

That we are a sick, subdued people,
Easy to conquer;
and that the slave kisses the chains
that still bind him.

That like slaves at the end, we say it all:
With our sacroscant liberty;
The tradition, the customs, the language,
And even to the appraisal
Of our own human dignity.

And still . . . everything is possible in this
life . . .
Even the drying of the ocean . . .
The rocks changing themselves into
mountains
And the sun abandoning its course.

Time could stop its movement
and the flowers stop smelling so sweet.

Dicen que el sonoro idioma castellano
Herido está de muerte en mi solar;
Dicen que es cuestión de tiempo su
abandono
Por otro idioma que no es el secular.

Dicen que el rico idioma de Cervantes
Por el de Shakespeare se habrá de suplantar,
Que ya mi tierra estudia a Scott y a Byron
Al dejar a Espronceda y Castelar.

Que somos un pueblo enfermo, sometido,
Fácil de conquistar;
Y que el esclavo besa las cadenas
Que le suelen atar.

Que como esclavos al fin, lo dimos todo:
Con nuestra sacrosanta liberta;
La tradición, las costumbres, el idioma,
Y hasta el aprecio,
A nuestra propia humana dignidad.

Más . . . todo es posible en esta
vida . . .
Hasta secarse el mar . . .
Convertirse las piedras en
montañas
Y el sol su derrotero abandonar.

Podrán los tiempos detener su marcha
Y las flores dejar de perfumar;

And still . . . this language of my
Grandparents,
Children have learned to recite . . .
That language will be eternal in my
homeland,
Never, never will we change it.

While the memory endures in the mind
And the mind continues to function . . .
While the knowledge endures in my land
Of its breeding and ancestral legacy . . .

While the blood of the Boricua woman
in her home
Circulates through my veins . . .
And in her body new children are
conceived
In my land of birth . . .

While in our minds De Diego
Is a symbol of the national language . . .
While my Homeland remembers its past,
It will speak the language of Castile . . .

Más . . . el idioma aquel de mis
abuelos
Aprendido de niños al rezar . . .
Ese idioma en mi Patria será eterno
Nunca, nunca, le habremos de cambiar.

Mientras dure el recuerdo en la memoria
Y la mente prosiga a funcionar . . .
Mientras dure en mi tierra la conciencia
De su estirpe y de su herencia ancestral . . .

Mientras circule sangre por las venas
De la mujer Boricua en el hogar . . .
Y en sus entrañas conciban nuevos hijos
En mi país natal . . .

Mientras De Diego en nuestras mentes
sea
Símbolo del idioma nacional . . .
Mientras recuerde mi Patria su pasado
La lengua de Castilla se hablará . . .

GRÁFICO

Editorial, August 7, 1927

With talented writers such as Jesús Colón, Alberto O'Farrill, Gustavo O'Neill, and Bernardo Vega serving on its editorial board and as columnists, it is difficult to discern who exactly the authors of the following editorial are, but what is clear is that its political stance marks a transition from purely immigrant consciousness to that of a citizen and permanent resident. In fighting for the rights of their community, the editorial indicts the racism and discrimination prevalent against the citizens of Spanish Harlem while promoting a multicultural United States, so prevalent today as a basis for entitlement and defense of the community. (NK)

Further reading: Nicolás Kanellos, *Hispanic Periodicals in the United States: A Brief History and Comprehensive Bibliography* (Houston: Arte Público Press, 2000).

The mayority of those who "knock" us from time to time seem to forget that those citizens who reside in Harlem enjoy to the full extent all privileges and the like that American citizenship most assuredly defines. The greater majority of us being natives of Porto Rico and naturally Americans, while others have become citizens through the medium of naturalization. Any one knowing the history of this country undoubtedly knows that in speaking of foreigners, in reality, we mean all of us, as the inhabitants of this young and progressive nation are in a sense foreigners. The United States is a young country and we believe the work of assimilation of the various races within its borders indicates very clearly indeed that its people belong to all races, creeds and nations. Therefore, it will be absurd and ridiculous for us to attempt to discriminate against anybody, because like ourselves, he be a foreigner or at any rate his ancestors.

Many of those who attempt to discriminate against our co-citizens in this vicinity were by no means any better before they themselves learned the customs and mannerism of the country. One indeed must be blind if he fails to note amongst those who call themselves complete citizens some trace or other of their old country, as well as old customs. To make a hue and cry because a certain few are of the opinion that one class is low and unworthy, when in all probability it is relative to citizens who respect the rights, liberties and pursuits of their fellow-men, indicates but a poor degree of intellect.

It is not our desire nor do we ever wish to take part in what is noted above, or revert to any means that will result in no good. Nevertheless we think both prudent and wise to bring this most important factor to the attention of those who are at present planting the seed, the fruit of which brings on a storm in this connection.

A grain of common sense and a little initiative will at once make us aware of the condition in which various foreign colonies live in this section; many are even far below our level.

We are not pigheaded enough to think that we are better than anybody else, but again, neither are we inferior. Last, but not least, because of a few differences that have taken place between the residents of the borough and some lesser authorities who by the way are ignorant on their surmise as regards our people, we are now more than ever ready to show the stuff we are made of and defend our good name.

Joaquín Colón (1889?–1964)

How to Unite the Puerto Rican Colony

Along with his brother Jesús Colón, Joaquín was part of the self-educated workers dedicated to organizing the Hispanic communities in New York during the early twentieth century. Joaquín Colón was a founder and president of the Puerto Rican and Hispanic League. This organization aimed to protect civil rights, especially those of the Puerto Rican community. As citizens of the United States, Puerto Ricans were entitled to certain privileges, but unlike immigrants from around the world, they had no consulates or embassies to assist and protect them. In addition to serving as a community leader, Colón was a frequent columnist and letter writer for Spanish-language periodicals in the city, including his organization's own *Boletin de la Liga Puertorriqueña e Hispana*. In the essay below, published in the bulletin in 1932, Colón was furthering his unifying mission by attacking those individuals, such as politicians, who were putting their own benefits above the needs of the community; he was proposing the development of a Puerto Rican conscience based on culture, tradition, and national character more than on political ideology. (EKP)

Further reading: Nicolás Kanellos, *Hispanic Periodicals in the United States: A Brief History and Comprehensive Bibliography* (Houston: Arte Público Press, 2000); Joaquín Colón, *Pioneros Puertorriqueños en Nueva York* (Houston: Arte Público Press, 2001).

Trans.: TEW

Before advancing my humble opinion about how to organize Puerto Ricans in this metropolis, let me touch briefly upon the causes of why, in my view, we are not organized.

Let us peer briefly over the edge of our crib. Let's contemplate, without rose-colored lenses, the workshop in which our character was formed. When has the spirit of dignifying solidarity—the true meaning of genuine fraternity—ever flourished there? And patriotism? Regional pride? What about a collective and perennial interest in the misery of the homeland? These qualities, indispensable to edifying and solidifying the spiritual unity of our people, have never been able to surpass pedantic and lowly individualism there. The Battle Cry of Lares has been the only vigorous feat of our people; but what else was it other than a game of treason, indifference, and lack of Puerto Rican solidarity? In Puerto Rico our leaders associate among themselves and form alliances, not to save the needy homeland or to resolve her many problems, but to save their political prestige and to protect their well-to-do and idle lives. Methodical organization, both political and economic, and HEROIC solidarity by and for Puerto Rico exclusively, have never germinated in our inconstant nation, which is frivolous and lacking in civic responsibility.

And after all, we came from there. Drowned in misery and a thousand times deceived by the "apostles" of our country, we arrived on these shores believing in nothing and nobody. If any trace of faith was left in us, those fake Puerto Rican redeemers who have followed us here have tried to kill it also, more than once. Those pseudo-emancipators here are simply a bad imitation of the ones there. Needless to say, they have fewer scruples, less compassion, less honor. Let us take a closer look at them. They hate work, live by cunning, fraud, and rhetoric. Some of them are talented, but lacking in character. And in men without character, ideals are merely part of the many items for sale to support them. As they do not have the fortitude to jeopardize themselves in any adventure that is risky, they dedicate themselves to selling Puerto Rican souls. They know that sentimentality is one of our biggest weaknesses, that we forgive and forget everything very quickly. They invent a reputation for themselves. Then they establish an association with an attractive name and altruistic principles. While everything is going according to their wishes, they jump up and raise their voices, boasting self-denial. After they have sucked all the blood out of the association and have mined its entire foundation, or have made a lucrative connection, then they retire. They always retire honorably . . . like the sacred colonial martyrs. Later, at another opportune moment, you hear outbursts, courageous voices boasting self-denial. You get closer and take a look. There they are again—those who apparently retired—the sacred colonial martyrs, selling their new patriotic prescriptions once more. And they triumph again. You can be sure of that. To triumph, they surround themselves with Puerto Rican mediocrity, people whose only fame lies in being friends with men with titles and seeing their names in print next to the names of men with titles. These are their pimps, who proclaim the new patriotic merchandise on the street corners and in the barber shops in exchange for a little familiarity with the prestigious men. Do you remember the poor people of the island who always gave John Doe and Mr. Smith money to baptize their children, even though they would come in through the back door? Remember those who always talked to you about a distant relative, doctor so-and-so, the degreed so-and-so, but never mentioned their brother the thief or their father the drunk? Well, they are also right here with us. And they are dressed like John Doe would dress back there during holy days. To look like Mr. Smith, that's all. These are the instruments of our imposters: the robots who work for them in exchange for an intelligently enthusiastic greeting.

We have among us another element that in good faith believes their ideas are the only sound and noble ones. Anyone who does not have their seal of approval is considered worthless. They do not recognize Puerto Rican loyalty in anyone who does not think and feel as they do.

There are some other Puerto Ricans among us whose obsession is the resolution of all of the problems of the United States and those of the rest of the world. For them, the sad picture of our colony in New York is secondary. First, the problems of the North and South Poles have to be resolved. We have many, a great many, who are waiting for everything to be done so that they will enter triumphantly and occupy the seats in the front row. And they do it. They have never known civic responsibility.

There are other things blocking Puerto Rican fellowship in this urban center. But I do not believe them to be of vital importance, nor does the limited space allow me to enumerate them properly.

Moreover, we have an idea about the site where we have to spread the seeds. Based on these observations, I think that we can only join together on the basis of Puerto Ricanism. We can join together by developing a kind of Boricua fascism in New York, where we will make room for all those people who feel Boricua, but will not tolerate any individual or group of individuals that thinks they are superior, in any way, to the idea of being Puerto Rican.

We have to, above all, recognize that we are all Puerto Ricans and that behind all socio-political ideology there is a culture . . . a tradition—a sovereign idiosyncracy—that links us together and characterizes us. Nobody has the right to ignore or de-emphasize this while still calling themselves Puerto Rican. We have to create a Puerto Rican consciousness without falling into a romantic, sentimental chauvinism that deprives us of thinking with judiciousness and balance. It is necessary to close the doors on the professional politician, no matter who it is. With him among us, solidarity is impossible. We should open the doors, in time, to the Puerto Rican historian, the academic, the educator, the man of sciences, the lecturer and the recognized artist. They demonstrate clearly to the United States and the world our true culture and character. Cooperatives absolutely must be organized and adopt all of those modern systems of mutual protection that tend to normalize our economic status. This is the task within reach of a great society for and by all Puerto Ricans.

Like an escape valve for our passions, our whims, our searching instinct, and our pedantic and lowly individualism, that is the direction in which we need to move, far away from this grand Puerto Rican society, our infinity of lodges, centers, dogmas, and social and political functions. There you will find me also, fighting . . . taking on one panther after another.

Let it be there that the wretched and heterogeneous battles continue their inevitable course. But in Puerto Rican unity par excellence we must present ourselves as a united front with fascist discipline in regards to the assimilation of all other ideas for saving our Puerto Rican personality. The factionist and disrupter must be boycotted if this Puerto Rican society is to survive.

We owe this to the distinguished exiles of our country, those who were pursued and jailed, those who sacrificed everything unselfishly for our cause. This, we owe to our children.

Let us prove that we are an entity . . . an entity that is more than four and a quarter centuries old . . . an entity that today knows how to live on the margins of the latest socioeconomic innovations of this civilization. And after? . . . After? . . . Anything is possible.

Rodolfo Uranga (dates unknown)

Those Who Return

In the piece below, editorialist Rodolfo Uranga demonstrates a deep commitment to advocating for the civil rights of the Mexican immigrant and Mexican American communities in the United States. The lack of jobs and the unbridled poverty that affected millions of Americans led Nativists to turn their wrath on the Mexican-origin population of the United States. This in turn led to massive deportations of immigrant workers as well as citizens. In their defense, Uranga extolled the virtues of his compatriots, offering an antidote to the virulent demonizing of Mexicans that fueled the media and the mainstream popular imagination. Uranga also called attention to an aspect of return migration that frequently tends to be ignored: the potential benefits to the home country resulting from the skills gained by living and working in "the belly of the beast." Research has failed to produce biographical data on Mr. Uranga. (EGB)

Trans.: PP

The largest migratory movement of modern times.

That is how we can describe the human river made of thousands of Mexicans that first ran from Mexico to the United States, and has now returned to the native country.

The return is much like the leaving. This human river has passed through scalding canals of dramatic pain: persecutions, expulsions, dispossessions, humiliations, assignments of slavery, miserable salaries; brutal treatment and injustice by the authorities and bosses; mass apprehensions; and other uncountable cruelties and penalties.

This has been the path run by hundreds of thousands or millions of Mexicans who first were expelled from their homeland by the militaries, the tyrannies and religious intolerances. Now they have returned, expelled again, because of the poverty in "the richest country in the world." Mexicans have been thrown out by Anglo intolerance, enemy of everything Spanish and Indian; in short, they have been cruelly cast aside by the "modern American inquisition," as the Wickersham Investigatory Commission has called the Immigration Service.

But behind so much darkness and so much pain, I have begun to see great benefits for our people.

In the first place, the emigration of millions of Mexicans came out of an audaciousness of spirit, enterprise and adventure—the type of cardinal virtues many thought dead. Those who left were the most sober and the most vigorous, as Master Vasconcelos said.

And their staying in the United States was a demonstration of our aptitude to struggle for life, our capacity for work, and our ability to mix in other lands with other races who believe themselves superior. In effect, our people have many times demonstrated equality and superiority (in multiple cases) over the Anglos in our work ethic, our constancy, our stamina, our ability, our application and intelligence for educational work, our unity and spirit of thrift, and even our skill and strength for athletics.

As a journalist specializing in the subject, I published and recorded a countless number of cases in which Mexicans—acting unknowingly, sometimes with hostility—became equal to or surpassed the other races in the United States of North America.

It has, thus, been demonstrated that the Ibero-American lineage is not fatally inferior, as the geography and history texts of North American schools and colleges poisonously affirm. I believe that, given half a chance, with favorable times and opportunities, our race is capable enough to lead a productive and civilized life.

By the hundreds, by the thousands, in trains replete with them, the "Mexico Outside Mexico" has returned to the homeland.

I have seen them arriving in automobiles, in trucks, in vehicles of every type and make. Many of them bring their furniture and other goods, and occasionally something of a "nest-egg," as they say. Others come in poverty from having been out of work, or because Immigration fell upon them unexpectedly, jailing and deporting them without giving them time to bring their things.

But all of them, or almost all of them, bring a rich baggage of experience, of practical and useful knowledge, of resources and purposes for work, and even good citizenship and honesty.

All of them have learned about Uncle Sam in depth. They lived in the monster and saw him from within his belly, like José Martí. When they arrived in the United States, they ingenuously believed they were in the promised land and that all virtues and all wonders dwelled there exclusively. The vices and defects—all things dark and bad—were Mexican, Hispano-American, originating in the criollos, Indians, and mestizos.

But in reality, experience opened the eyes of those who dwelled in "Mexico Outside Mexico," and now they return to tell the "Mexicans Inside Mexico" what they have really seen.

All or almost all of the Mexican expatriots who return to the country not only hate imperialism, because they have known its bad deeds, but they also strongly hate the servants of imperialism: bossism and puppet governments. They know that the three "isms" are terrible pustules that poison the Americas—a large part of the world—and that they should urgently eradicate this pustule with scalpel and cauterization, not with rose water and pomades.

Almost all of them also learned to think in broader terms, above patriotism and regionalism.

With the return of the "Mexicans Outside Mexico," many prodigal sons come back to the breast of our family. They are thousands of youths and children who, born and raised in the United States, have almost lost their way, lamentably becoming yankees, even forgetting their own language.

A great hope of economic and civic improvement—in no distant future—is what I foresee behind so much pain and injustice that has happened to these millions of our brothers who now participate in the largest migratory movement of modern times.

Erasmo Vando (1896–1988)

Open Letter to Don Luis Muñoz Marín, President of the Puerto Rican Senate; United States (Estados Unidos)

Poet, playwright, actor, *cronista,* and political activist, Erasmo Vando was born in Puerto Rico while it was still a colony of Spain. Vando emigrated to the Southern United States as a laborer and made his way to New York, where he became a community leader, most notably as the president of the Puerto Rican Nationalist Youth. Vando was considered by Bernardo Vega to be the best interpreter of the *jíbaro*, the Puerto Rican campesino, on the stages of New York, and like Vega and Jesus Colon, he often crafted his artistic and intellectual productions within that perspective. In the *Open Letter* below, Vando took up the cause of the uprooted and destitute Puerto Rican community in New York and elsewhere in the United States, challenging Puerto Rican politicians back on the island to tackle the problem of their emigrant brothers. In his poem, *United States*, Vando vented the resentment that many immigrants felt at their disillusionment in the "Land of the Free." (NK)

Further reading: Erasmo Vando, *Amores* (San Juan: Emelí Vélez de Vando e Hijos, 1996).

Trans.: TEW, PP

Open Letter to Don Luis Muñoz Marín, President of the Senate, Puerto Rico

Honorable Don Luis Muñoz Marín, President of the Puerto Rican Senate.
City of San Juan

My distinguished compatriot and friend:

Signs of the invading soldiers' footsteps had not yet disappeared from the beaches of Borinquen when the collective exodus of the native population began. The chorus "Don't die without going to Spain" was naturally succeeded by "Our salvation is in the North." Since then many of our countrymen, full of hope, have left the homeland in pursuit of a new El Dorado, full of abundance and bounty. They carried with them the traditional motto, Vini Vidi Vici, and arrived at these latitudes with determination, but were lacking in the most rudimentary preparation to find their way in an environment to which they were not accustomed. We do not know how many have come since then, but conservative estimates put the count of exiled Puerto Ricans at more than one million human beings, of which, it is estimated, three hundred thousand live in New York. There are also large concentrations of Boricuas in

California, Arizona, Alabama, Pennsylvania, Hawaii, Cuba, Santo Domingo, Venezuela, etc . . . , the common belief being that where there are human beings, there are Puerto Ricans. We know of two families living in the city of Nome, Alaska. And, in the city of Glen Cove, Long Island, there is the pathetic case of Mrs. Nemesia López with eleven children and thirty-some grandchildren. (We will discuss this case of surprising fertility on another occasion.) The reason they left their homeland, always warm and green, in search of a fortune in other exotic, bizarre and cold places is even more important than the numbers. The act of living and the right to life propelled this large human contingent in search of a chunk of bread, something their native land denied them. The farewell was always the same: spiritually devastated and teary-eyed, an expression of envy at not being the lucky ones who were leaving, and the tired words, "After you get the money for the ticket, send it to me. I prefer to die there of pneumonia to slowly dying here of starvation or tuberculosis." This is all terribly pathetic! Later, a little black dot on the horizon that disappeared like brown smoke and a pearly wake on the sea. And on land, a handkerchief agitating innocently, with tears in their eyes, much hope in their souls, and emptiness in their stomachs, much emptiness. . . . Already here: a marvelous, gigantic, solid, suffocating, bizarre city. Something that they say is ours, but that does not belong to us. It's like telling a child, "That doll is yours, but don't take it out of the display case." There is a mixture of many races whose colonies endeavor to destroy each other with cruel competition—except when it comes to the Puerto Rican colony, in which case everyone joins together to destroy, harass and disorient us. And here we are, floundering in our own simple-mindedness, disorganized, disoriented and beaten-down by intemperance, like a boat without a rudder in the middle of the sea. And, we are always dreaming of a new day in which we can return to our homeland with our pockets full and a smile on our faces. Everything is useless: as victims of politicking in Puerto Rico we are the easy prey of politicking here, except that in Puerto Rico our fellow countrymen exploited us, and here we are exploited by Puerto Ricans and foreigners alike. A lack of vocational training has been one of our greatest handicaps and divisiveness another. Our language and our customs are not important: other races have prospered without theirs and without citizenship, according to many, a ticket to happiness and freedom. That we have founded a thousand associations proves that we are divided and isolated. In spite of them all being patriotic, not a single one of them is vigilant for the care and guidance of the hopeful immigrant. We are forgotten by everyone else and forgotten by ourselves. All of the governments and all of the towns in the world take responsibility for the well-being of their subjects. The legislative bodies make laws and plan for their well-being, except for ours. Our past legislators, embroiled in cheap politics for personal benefit, remember little about those who have left. Face to face with the problem of extreme overpopulation, they closed their eyes to our misfortune. Their attitude resembles that gruff song by Rafael Hernández: "If you leave, well, goodbye. I am not throwing you out of my house, but if you want to go with another, goodbye. Goodbye!" Every few decades, a politician would come along and want to capitalize on our fortunate strategic position of being Yankee citizens with the right to vote in Yankee land. The reasons were varied, but this same divisive vice that I mentioned before was a life-saving drug. It was the bitter taste of the nut's shell: the politicians could not crack through it to the meat.

Our situation is terrible these days: there is misery, bad jobs, racial persecution, rhetoric, exploitation, and on top of all this, there is the nefarious moral problem that is slowly but surely ruining our youth. The young men are fertile ground for using marijuana, drinking rum and taking up other vices. Prostitution is lying in ambush for our young ladies. Our flesh is exploited and our spirit degraded. We are the steps that everyone else treads upon. That is what we are, a common staircase that is continually exploited. The Spaniard, the Cuban, the Mexican, the Jew and the black Yankee all exploit us and we calmly let them exploit us. We have a daily newspaper that every once in awhile makes a token gesture toward Puerto Ricans, but is really overwhelmingly Spanish. There are two theaters, one is the property of a Mexican and the other one is Cuban-Jewish. Naturally, the newspaper, like the theaters, makes use of the Boricua workers and labor, but that is not my point. If we are the majority, if the Puerto Rican colony in New York has more people than the three largest cities in Puerto Rico, then why aren't there dailies, theaters, markets, hotels and other businesses that are worth a damn and that belong to us? The answer calls for a close look and this is what I see: in regards to Island affairs, in reference to politics, the Popular Democratic Party, whose motto is "Bread, Land and Liberty," has done a commendable job until now. So why isn't the current island legislature interested in the problems of mismanagement of the Eighth Legislative District? We recommend that these gentlemen appropriate funds for a commission to study these problems and that they do not delay. The problem, yes, ours in all of its profundity, is also yours by reflex. No citizen should leave Puerto Rico without the assurance that he comes prepared for the life of an immigrant, that honorable laws protect him wherever he goes, and that a friendly institution will open its doors for him when he needs them opened.

United States (Estados Unidos)

> This republic, by its excessive cult of wealth, has fallen
> without any of the shackles of tradition, into the inequality,
> injustice and violence of the monarchistic nations.
>
> —Jose Martí

> Esta república, por el culto desmedido a ha riqueza, ha caído sin
> ninguna de las trabas de la tradición, en la desigualdad, injusticia y
> violencia de los países monárquicos.
>
> —José Martí

A lofty document that proclaims
the rights of man;
a starred flag;
a history that begins snorting rebellions
and ends smelling of imperialism;
a heterogenous people, the residues

Un documento excelso que proclama
los derechos del hombre;
una bandera constelada;
historia que comienza roncando rebeldías
y finaliza oliendo a imperialismo;
un pueblo heterogéneo, los residuos

of our old Europe made into a republic;
an alloy of passions and prejudices;
spoilage enthroned;
deceipt deified in America—
joke of the century,
satire of the age—
the United States!

In your port a statue,
which lies about liberty, insults the
cosmos.
within, injustice: Sacco and Vanzetti,
Mooney,
the blacks of Scottsboro;
the shout of the mothers whose sons
have died in imperial campaigns;
the shout of the sons whose mothers
are rolling in vice;
the Ku Klux Klan—grunting fanatics;
the Indian, a prisoner in the mountains;
the black, prostrate and persecuted;
the Bible feeding ignorance;
pain muffled
by the response of Puritans. . . .
Suffering! Suffering that chauvinism
silences!
Hatred! The rancor the religious incite!
The eternal smell of blood in the air;
mediocrity with a red tunic;
new life in the temple of Janus;
the altar of Minerva destroyed;
bits of rot in each soul;
the word of God on everyone's lips. . . .
the United States!

Ruling: Detroit,
Chicago, New York.
Great smoking beasts
that eat human flesh
with erect fangs
attempting to rip the sky!
Detroit wants to dirty the firmament
with the spit of its chimneys;
Chicago enters history through crime,

de nuestra vieja Europa hechos república;
aleación de pasiones y prejuicios;
engreimiento entronizado;
engaño hecho dios en América;
carcajada del siglo;
sarcasmo de la época:
¡los Estados Unidos!

En su puerto una estatua,
mintiendo libertad, insulta al cosmos.

Adentro, la injusticia: Sacco y Vanzetti,
Mooney,
los Negros de Scottsboro;
el grito de las madres cuyos hijos
han muerto en las campañas imperiales;
el grito de los hijos cuyas madres
rodaron en el vicio;
el Ku-Klux-Klan gruñendo fanatismos;
el Indio prisionero en la montaña;
el Negro postergado y perseguido;
la Biblia alimentando la ignoracia;
dolor amortiguado
con el responso de los puritanos. . . .
¡Dolor! ¡Dolor que el *chauvinismo* acalla!

¡Odios! ¡Rencor que el religioso enciende!
Eterno olor a sangre en el ambiente;
mediocridad con túnica encarnada;
nueva vida en el templo del dios Jano;
el altar de Minerva destruído;
ansias de poderío en cada alma;
la palabra de Dios en cada labio. . . .
¡los Estados Unidos!

Imperando: Detroit,
Chicago, Nueva York.
¡Grandes fieras ahumadas
que comen carne humana
con colmillos erectos
con que pretenden desgarrar el cielo!
Detroit quiere ensuciar el firmamento
con la saliva de sus chimeneas;
Chicago entra en la historia con el
crimen,

and assures its perpetual place in it
with the gunfire and abuses of its
gangsters.
New York makes itself unique, supreme
with its Tammany Hall (an airy cave
of twentieth century highwaymen)
and with the tentacles of Wall Street
—narrow, foul-smelling
lair of Ginart.

Never-ending activity:
large factories
that suck the blood of the worker;
politicos, bankers and bandits,
three distinct persons and one true
thief! . . . .

The United States!

se perpetúa en ella con el fuego
y los desmanes de sus pistoleros;

Nueva York se hace única y suprema
con su Tammany Hall—airosa cueva
de salteadores muy del siglo veinte—
y con su Wall Street tentacular
—estrecha y mal oliente
guarida de Ginart—

Movimiento continuo;
grandes fábricas,
que succionanan la sangre del obrero;
políticos, banqueros y bandidos,
tres personas distintas y un ladrón
verdadero! . . . . .

¡Los Estados Unidos!

CHAPTER 14

Cultural (Dis)Junctures

Eliseo Pérez Díaz (1871–1963)

The Key West Rose (excerpt)

Born in Guanajay, Cuba, Pérez Díaz emigrated to Key West at a young age and later moved to Tampa, Florida, where he became an active member of the Partido Revolucionario Cubano. He went to Cuba to fight for its independence and, after the war, returned to Tampa where he managed the newspaper *La Prensa*. A veteran of forty years of service with the Cuban Consulate in Tampa, Pérez Díaz died in 1963. His time in Tampa and Key West inspired him to write *La Rosa del Cayo (The Key West Rose)*, a historical novel that traces the footsteps of one young Cuban independence fighter's exploits in the revolution. The story centers on Rosa Valdés, who falls in love with Pablo González, a Cuban independence fighter who leaves Key West with the expeditionary forces of generals Sarafín Sánchez and Carlos Roloff. Hearing that Pablo has been killed in action, Rosa, upon the advice of her mother, marries Carlos Roberts, a successful merchant. Meanwhile, Pablo recovers from his wounds and is promoted to major in recognition of his bravery. When Rosa learns that Pablo is alive, she is torn between her loyalty to her husband and her love for Pablo. (CS)

Further reading: Eliseo Pérez Díaz, *La Rosa del Cayo* (La Habana: El Fígaro, 1947).

Trans.: PP

Consternation in Cayo Hueso

She looked at her husband, to read the impression on his face, and she asked him pointedly:

"Did you tell Rosa?"

"Yes, she knows it all now."

"And, what does she say?"

"Well, I won't deceive you. She took it calmly, telling me she was happy about the news."

"What did you say?" Doña Feliciana's calm words belied her expression, remaining as if petrified in front of Joseíto.

"Don't excite yourself woman, things that must come must be accepted. This I have told you many times and I repeat it to you, because you always want to fix everything with all guns blazing."

"Guns blazing, knives drawn, it's the same to me. You have the makings of a tired mule, you exasperate me so." Doña Feliciana chastised her husband a little with these jibes. She continued. "It's that I can't believe that our daughter can be happy with the news that will disgrace us all. And when Roberts finds out he will be very displeased."

"But why?" replied Joseíto Valdés, who knew how impassive Roberts was in solving his problems. "When he returns to the factory I will tell him. He won't think we're hiding anything maliciously."

Indeed, upon arriving at the factory he went to his son-in-law's desk and, placing his hand on his arm, he said:

"How goes it, Charlie, how are you today?"

"Very well. What news do you bring?"

"Nothing extraordinary, one of those things that happens in life, and that men analyze closely so they turn out well."

"I don't understand Joseíto. Speak a little more clearly."

"Well, it's nothing, not something out of this world," and the cigar-roller didn't stop talking.

"But José, please don't waste my time. Say what it is."

"According to Colonel Boza, who assured me that. . . . You know, that Cuban official who was here this morning to look for money to send supplies to Cuba . . ."

"Yes, I already know who you are talking about," interrupted the foreman, wishing he would finish with the message because he was getting tired of it.

"Well, he told me that Pablo González is alive."

"Oh, that's nothing, I already know that. I have confidence in Rosa. She's very good, I'm not afraid. If Pablo comes here and she wants to talk to him, why not? He won't take her."

Joseíto breathed a sigh. This was not passivity, this was a complete lethargy that affected the whole body. "Well, man," he thought, "thank God it wasn't what I expected. It's no doubt better that he take it philosophically. These Americans are very wise."

And he went calmly to his work table.

Rosa prayed at her house. When she married, she took with her the adored Saint, the Virgin of Charity, who always helped her escape difficult situations.

Prostrating herself before the image hung in her bedroom, and raising her supplicant hands to the heavens, she concentrated with great devotion on the face of the virgin, asking for help.

"My adored Virgin, once again, I am suffering. My heart is weakening. I can't help it, when they mention Pablo, who was my fiancé, so handsome, so sweet, so nice, so valiant in war. Remove me from this spell I'm under. I consulted with you—remember?—on whether to accept accept Robert's proposal and marry him and you winked one eye—yes, I'm sure I saw it, a sign for me to go through with it.

"Now I am worried, very worried, because he lives, Pablo lives, and I have no doubt that he will return to Cayo Hueso. Give me strength to pass this test. I don't want to be unfaithful to my husband, it wouldn't be fair. He is very good to me, and I am a decent woman. Virgin of Charity, help me!"

And the young woman remained in a trance, concentrating on her request, transported to the Almighty, her spirit inundated in the most sincere religious devotion.

She threw herself fully dressed on the bed and slept a little—a short nap—but one filled with hallucinations in which she saw Pablo angry, reproaching her for her actions while she tried to explain what happened. It was like a nightmare she struggled to expel from her mind, and the more she struggled, the more powerful it became. And she enjoyed the contact with her beloved, even while not allowing herself to accede to his desire to embrace her. And . . . she gave a shout, startled, finding herself alone in her house. She got up and drank a cup of tea to calm her nerves.

Feeling better, she went to her parent's house. Joseíto had gone to work, and she found her mother alone, knitting to pass the time.

"Hi mom, what's new around here?"

Doña Feliciana looked her in face and said: "Hum, there is something. That heart of yours isn't still. You'll see how the Devil will stick his hand in."

Rosa began to laugh. "Yes, I know what's on your mind. Don't be silly, I'm resigned to it. I just finished praying to the Virgin. Are you afraid of something?"

"That question better suits you. What are you thinking?"

"Me? Nothing. What am I going to think? I'm very happy that Pablo is alive. Why would I wish him dead when he has never shown me but kindness and goodness? No Mamá, you know that I don't have those feelings. He was my fiancé and never gave me any reason to leave him. It was the gossip in this town—may God punish it for the damage done to me, putting me in this mess without my consent, because I was very happy to marry Pablo, whom I still love. Yes, I love him and I can't do anything about it. I wouldn't say it in public or anywhere, only to you, Mamá, I'll confess it and unburden my heart." Upon saying this, two heavy tears ran down Rosa's face.

"But girl, you drive me crazy! What are you saying?" exclaimed Doña Feliciana, distressed with the declarations and weeping of her daughter.

"What if Charlie was informed of this attitude of yours—he'd immediately get a divorce."

"No, dear, you don't understand. I know that I'm married to a very good man who gives me everything I want. But I can't deny what I feel for Pablo, and that's all.

"Besides, Charlie won't ask for a separation from me, as you think. You don't know him like I do. He is crazy about me and would never leave me for anything in the world."

"Well, don't go around making this into a wake. Don't do anything silly that could cost too much, for you or us. Your father does very well in the factory, making money like never before, because Charlie's the foreman; and if we lose that, we'll return to the poverty that we had before you married him."

"But, dear, who told you I would do anything out of order? You're confused. That is not the question. It's that I once liked Pablo very much and still do. God and the Virgin forgive me. Look, I once saw a play in Spanish, here, in which the woman said to the man, 'Tear out my heart or love me because I adore you!' That is exactly what I feel. I declare it with no intention of committing a sin."

"Ah, yes, that's the drama of 'Don Juan Tenorio.' I too remember it. But our situation is more serious than enactments in a theater. I shudder to think . . . ! Praise God on high . . . !" Doña Feliciana crossed herself, making crosses on her face and on her chest and kissing her hands various times.

Rosa got up to leave, kissed her mother and said, "Now I am going to the shop of Luis, the jew, try on the silk dress that Roberts gave me for my birthday."

"You see, my daughter, you lack for nothing: good clothes, all kinds of comforts at home, on one of the best streets, Farola."

"Yes," replied Rosa, teasing her, "the cage is undoubtedly very beautiful, but instead of a mockingbird, it is occupied by a parrot. There is no comparison. Pablo recited poetry to me and sang for my ear sweet nothings that women like, while Charlie doesn't talk to me about anything but business. He's very dry. I love him because he is my husband, but he doesn't make the effort to awake in me the love that is so necessary in married life."

And she left.

On returning from the store, Roberts had arrived at his home. She greeted him as always: kind, but with no expression of happiness. The maid, a black Jamaican, prepared her bath and made the final touches to the supper, almost always the same, with nourishing dishes and few spices, to which Rosa had already become accustomed. Occasionally they had beer in the evening, never at lunch, excepting when they entertained a visitor.

The couple had no heirs, and they used the time that would otherwise be dedicated to their children in walking, almost always separately. They both had complete liberty to go through the streets alone, and to spend time in the refreshment salons. Once in a while—Charlie, for a change of pace, invited his wife to eat in a restaurant, or he would eat alone.

Sitting there at the table, Rosa did not say a word about Pablo. She had kept it back in order to see how her husband, who undoubtedly already knew, produced the news. But Roberts, without any hesitation, like a businessman who liked things clear to the end, mentioned the subject, repeating the rumor being spread about the soldier who was still alive.

The most powerful weapon that a woman has is her astuteness, and the young woman took great care to not demonstrate her emotions at finding out that her ex-fiancé had not died. She continued the conversation. "Yes, that is what they say. Now we only have to confirm it, because you know how this town is, inventing everything."

"No, my dear, it would not matter to me if it were true, because I have never lost confidence in you and I will not do so now." They always spoke to each other in English.

"Yes, I know, Charlie, but it's hard to find oneself in such a situation because of the gossips, people who do nothing more than look for reasons to whisper about others."

"Bah! Don't worry about that! The important thing is that you and I live in harmony. There are many envious people, and they can't see that you, who were a poor girl, now enjoys wealth. Let them say what they please. You did nothing wrong. González preferred going to war over marrying you. Because of that you were in your right to decide you didn't want to be alone. What's more, there is no comparison between what he could have offered you and what I have given you. A reasonable person, like you, had to resolve it in the way you did. A woman who does not take advantage of the opportunity offered to her commits an unpardonable error because, as I heard a cigar-roller sing in the factory one day, "There's an oversupply of women, but you can't put a price on a man."

Rosa looked at him smilingly. He spoke with such logic! But if he only knew what was in her heart.

Without doubt, her husband was so good that there was no human force that could make him change his character. Pablo González could come when he wanted; he would confront an impregnable wall. No, he would not do it, if by his growing passion he wanted to dominate her. She would resist to the death if it were necessary, before she gave in to whatever sexual desire her ex-fiancé intended.

They finished eating, and Charles Roberts, the famous foreman of the Mojasky & Company tobacco factory, sat down in a stuffed chair to read the *Key West Citizen* newspaper which was published in the evening.

Wilfredo Braschi (1918–?)

A Prayer in the Snow

Born in New York in 1918, Wilfredo Braschi is regarded by many as one of Puerto Rico's foremost journalists. After graduating from the University of Puerto Rico, Braschi received his doctorate from the University of Madrid, in 1953. He was an editorialist for the Puerto Rican newspapers *La Democracia* and *El Mundo*. In addition, he was Professor of Public Administration at the University of Puerto Rico. His book of literary criticism, *Cuatro Caminos* (1963), was the winner of the Instituto de Literatura Puertorriqueña Prize. His book *Metrópoli* (1968), a collection of thirty-one short stories, centers on revealing life in the big cities. Unlike other writers who concentrate on depicting the hopelessness and insensitive aspects of city life, Braschi's characters are guided by love, faith, and tenderness. In *A Prayer in the Snow*, Braschi narrates the relationship between a humble Puerto Rican orator and his employer, a Jewish funeral director. The message is clear: Human love transcends cultural boundaries. (JBF)

Further reading: Wilfredo Braschi, *Metrópoli* (San Juan: Ediciones Juan Ponce de León, 1968).

Trans.: TEW

In those days he was so poor that he would hardly go out into the street. When, as nervous as a rat, he would dare to set foot outside, a compelling reason would drive him: hunger.

There, in his small attic in Greenwich Village, he felt a pleasant warmth. Through the dirty window, which was covered with an almost historic grime, he was watching the paving-stones and the sidewalk as they played hide-and-seek under the snow.

Like a punished child, he would press himself against the little show-window of his lookout. The pedestrians down below were leaving tracks of mud that, seen from above, resembled blood. Then, the snowflakes would erase them, and the ground came to be a grand sheet of white crepe paper.

Suddenly, he heard footsteps on the stairs. A guttural voice yelled, "Mr. Gómez! Mr. Gómez! I wanna tell you one thing! You must pay working at the cellar! Hear me?"

He mentally reviewed his deal with Mrs. Bally. The agreement was simple. When he didn't pay, he had to go down to the basement and spend several hours shoveling coal in the building's boiler.

Poking his head out of his warm refuge, he answered, "Está bien, está bien! Ya mismo voy!"

Not understanding him, and displaying her gold-filled buck teeth, Mrs. Bally asked, "What the hell are you sayin'?"

Mr. Gómez apologized, "Pardon me, pardon me, Mrs. Bally. I was just speaking my language!"

The relentless Mrs. Bally descended into the stairwell. Antulio Gómez followed her with his eyes. The landlady's fake bun bobbed, while her sandals kept time with a monotonous beat.

Throwing shovels full of coal into the insatiable boiler, now that was hard work. After the intense task, his arms would ache. His hands would burn. A bitter taste of coal residue would seize his palate.

Whenever he would finish working as a coal man, he would peer out of the small window of his little room. Through the stained peephole he was contemplating his New York, his Greenwich Village. His image reflected in the passers-by surprised him, as if these transitory beings were small pieces of his own life.

He was unable to resist meditating. He recalled his days back on the island, then contemplated life in the Metropolis.

On the subject of his last job in the giant city, he wondered where his old boss, Jacob Baulman, had been hiding. The Semite would give him the chance, quite often, to earn a few dollars.

Baulman the Jew was a picturesque fellow. He was a funeral services entrepreneur who liked to surround himself with bohemians. Certainly, a sentimentalist was hiding under his black bowler hat.

Antulio struck up a friendship with him under the most dismal of circumstances. He had enjoyed his camaraderie since then, without being a close friend.

Baulman had made him into a public speaker . . . and at the same time, into a unusual agent of funeral pomp. . . .

How did he meet the Semite? Pressing his nose against the cold glass of the window, Antulio was reliving the scene of his first encounter with Jacob Baulman, his sporadic protector.

Gómez was attending one of those bizarre and sad New York-Latino wakes. In the undertaker's sitting room, pompously called the Chapel, a son of the deceased asked old man Baulman, "Do you have a preacher?"

The undertaker hit his wrinkled forehead. Oh, how these clients from Harlem would surprise him without proper notice!

"A burial with prayer, I didn't know you wanted . . ." he paused briefly and muttered, ". . . but a speaker I can find you . . . Don't worry mister."

The anonymous Hispanics who stream like ants along the Hudson do not want to go to the grave without a few words. And Jacob Baulman extracted, due to this spiritual inclination of his Catholic customers, the resultant economic benefit.

This afternoon, due to carelessness, he had not contracted a preacher. The family of the deceased felt degraded. Was their deceased to whirl around the afterlife without a Christian word? To hell with Jacob Baulman's chapel!

With his inner eye, the undertaker soon discovered a flowing mane, a bow tie and a little, bushy mustache. "Are you living in Greenwich Village?"

Antulio answered that, yes, he lived in the Village.

Baulman sputtered, "Would you be interested in eulogizing the deceased?"

And before he could answer yes or no, Jacob Baulman introduced him to the relatives. "This gentleman poet will eulogize the deceased."

"We'll be eternally indebted!"

Antulio pronounced the speech with an inspired accent. When the Jew Jacob Baulman placed ten dollars in his hand as an honorarium for his generous intervention in the burial, he became embarrassed. He felt the urge to press the money in his face! But he refrained, clutched his reward and put it in his coat pocket. Then, he went to eat at a fast-food restaurant.

He was almost a professional preacher, a burier with a gold pick-axe. His heart reproached him. Despite this, he was beginning to adapt to his peculiar job.

If only Baulman would come. If only he would call to assign him a funeral. Outside, the wind was blowing and the snow's white wing was beating on the surface of the tiny window.

He heard some very familiar footsteps. It was Mrs. Bally again. This time she brought a message that softened her voice, "I am sure it's business for you, Mr. Gómez."

She handed him a telegram from the funeral home. They were asking him to show up at the Green Memorial. The matter at hand: a presentation.

Soon he would get some cash! Next week he would not have to descend to that little hell of a basement to shovel coal.

He dressed for the occasion and threw himself into the inclement weather. Soon he was one more soul in the obscure mass of the subway.

What was the deceased's name? He did not know. In this instance, it did not matter if he knew or not. He would deliver a speech like so many others he had done.

Winter seemed to be centered at the Green Memorial. The snow stung his face. The cemetery was like a tiny ghost of a village.

The coffin arrived without mourners. Only Jacob Baulman's diligent workers, wrapped in their black suits, followed behind the casket.

Who could this solitary dead man be? Antulio Gómez could have satisfied his curiosity by asking the two stiff undertakers. For what? It was just one more Latino sinking into eternity!

He began the talk as a summary of the life of the deceased. The snow that accumulated on the coffin was turned to ice by the wind. He continued, constructing the eulogy for the man who was departing.

Yes, Baulman would come! It was certain that the Jew would take him to have a whisky. He eulogized the deceased with stereotypical words: a worthy man, an upstanding gentleman, exemplary citizen, noble exile. The Chapel workers remained standing, supporting the black box that was turning white under the snow. How could Baulman have left him at the Green Memorial with such frigid company?

This afternoon, the words flowed from his mouth. Despite the wasted phrases he was using, he bid farewell to the anonymous dead man with sincerity, and concluded emotionally, "Rest in peace, friend."

Everything had ended. The coffin of the unknown citizen remained in the tomb. The undertakers approached Antulio Gómez. They had his pay.

Almost with repulsion, he extended his hand just as one of the individuals said, "The boss left this for you."

"Where is he?" asked Antulio.

"Don't you know, pal? We put him down this minute. He's gone. You just talked for him."

Antulio opened the envelope that Jacob Baulman had sent him. Before dying, the old funeral services director had requested that Antulio Gómez speak at his wake. And he was paying him an extravagant sum: several thousand dollars.

That night, Antulio Gómez did not eat fast food or at Mrs. Bally's house. He went up to his little room, stuck his face against the window pane and cried for a while.

Ernesto Galarza (1905–1984)

Barrio Boy (excerpt)

Ernesto Galarza had a rich and varied career as a sociologist, labor expert, and organizer. Born in a small mountainous village in the western Mexican state of Nayarit, he came to the United States when, like thousands of Mexicans, his family fled the violence and tumult of the 1910 Mexican Revolution. The Galarza family settled in Sacramento, California, where the young Galarza began the process of acculturation. Galarza excelled academically, which eased the transition he was forced to make to English as a child. Galarza went on to earn a Ph.D. in sociology in 1946. Over the course of his career as a labor specialist, serving for twelve years as a field organizer for the newly formed National Agricultural Workers Union, he became a strong advocate for Mexican and other farm workers, often speaking out against the abuse by farm owners. Galarza was involved for the rest of his life in many Mexican American organizations that were fighting injustice. He also lectured and wrote extensively on social issues, particularly those involving labor rights and conditions. He is best known for *Barrio Boy* (1971), an autobiographical account of his own journey from Mexico to the United States and his process of acculturation. In the following excerpt, Galarza describes the Mexican barrio of Sacramento, evoking the strong sense of solidarity that existed among Mexican Americans and Mexicans as together they confronted the cultural differences and sometimes the hostility of Anglo Americans. (ChT)

Further reading: Ernesto Galarza, *Merchants of Labor: The Mexican Bracero Story* (Charlotte, N.C.: McNalley and Loftin, 1964), *Spiders in the House and Workers in the Field* (Notre

Dame, Ill.: University of Notre Dame Press, 1970), *Barrio Boy* (Notre Dame, Ill.: University of Notre Dame Press, 1971).

For the Mexicans the barrio was a colony of refugees. We came to know families from Chihuahua, Sonora, Jalisco, and Durango. Some had come to the United States even before the revolution, living in Texas before migrating to California. Like ourselves, our Mexican neighbors had come this far moving step by step, working and waiting, as if they were feeling their way up a ladder. They talked of relatives who had been left behind in Mexico, or in some far-off city like Los Angeles or San Diego. From whatever place they had come, and however short or long the time they had lived in the United States, together they formed the *colonia mexicana.* In the years between our arrival and the First World War, the *colonia* grew and spilled out from the lower part of town. Some families moved into the alley shacks east of the Southern Pacific tracks, close to the canneries and warehouses and across the river among the orchards and rice mills.

The *colonia* was like a sponge that was beginning to leak along the edges, squeezed between the levee, the railroad tracks, and the river front. But it wasn't squeezed dry, because it kept filling with newcomers who found families who took in boarders: basements, alleys, shanties, run-down rooming houses and flop joints where they could live.

Crowded as it was, the *colonia* found a place for these *chicanos,* the name by which we called an unskilled worker born in Mexico and just arrived in the United States. The *chicanos* were fond of identifying themselves by saying they had just arrived from *el macizo,* by which they meant the solid Mexican homeland, the good native earth. Although they spoke of *el macizo* like homesick persons, they didn't go back. They remained, as they said of themselves, *pura raza.* So it happened that Jose and Gustavo would bring home for a meal and for conversation workingmen who were *chicanos* fresh from *el macizo* and like ourselves, *pura raza.* Like us, they had come straight to the *barrio* where they could order a meal, buy a pair of overalls, and look for work in Spanish. They brought us vague news about the revolution, in which many of them had fought as *villistas, huertistas, maderistas,* or *zapatistas.* As an old *maderista,* I imagined our *chicano* guests as battle-tested revolutionaries, like myself.

As poor refugees, their first concern was to find a place to sleep, then to eat and find work. In the *barrio* they were most likely to find all three, for not knowing English, they needed something that was even more urgent than a room, a meal, or a job, and that was information in a language they could understand. This information had to be picked up in bits and pieces—from families like ours, from the conversation groups in the poolrooms and the saloons.

Beds and meals, if the newcomers had no money at all, were provided—in one way or another—on trust, until the new *chicano* found a job. On trust and not on credit, for trust was something between people who had plenty of nothing, and credit was between people who had something of plenty. It was not charity or social welfare but something my mother called *asistencia,* a helping given and received on trust, to be repaid because those who had given it were themselves in need of what they had given. *Chicanos* who had found work on farms or in railroad camps came back to pay us a few dollars for *asistencia* we had provided weeks or months before.

Because the *barrio* was a grapevine of job information, the transient *chicanos* were able to find work and repay their obligations. The password of the barrio was *trabajo* and the community was divided in two—the many who were looking for it and the few who had it to offer. Pickers, foremen, contractors, drivers, field hands, pick and shovel men on the railroad and in construction came back to the *barrio* when work was slack, to tell one another of the places they had been, the kind of *patrón* they had, the wages paid, the food, the living quarters, and other important details. Along Second Street, labor recruiters hung blackboards on their shop fronts, scrawling in chalk offers of work. The grapevine was a mesh of rumors and gossip, and men often walked long distances or paid bus fares or a contractor's fee only to find that the work was over or all the jobs were filled. Even the chalked signs could not always be relied on. Yet the search for *trabajo*, or the *chanza*, as we also called it, went on because it had to.

We in the *barrio* considered that there were two kinds of *trabajo*. There were the seasonal jobs, some of them a hundred miles or more from Sacramento. And there were the closer *chanzas* to which you could walk or ride on a bicycle. These were the best ones, in the railway shops, the canneries, the waterfront warehouses, the lumber yards, the produce markets, the brick kilns, and the rice mills. To be able to move from the seasonal jobs to the close-in work was a step up the ladder. Men who had made it passed the word along to their relatives or their friends when there was a *chanza* of this kind.

It was all done by word of mouth, this delicate wiring of the grapevine. The exchange points of the network were the places where men gathered in small groups, apparently to loaf and chat to no purpose. One of these points was our kitchen, where my uncles and their friends sat and talked of *el macizo* and of the revolution but above all of the *chanzas* they had heard of.

There was not only the everlasting talk about *trabajo*, but also the never-ending action of the *barrio* itself. If work was action the *barrio* was where the action was. Every morning a parade of men in oily work clothes and carrying lunch buckets went up Fourth Street toward the railroad shops, and every evening they walked back, grimy and silent. Horse drawn drays with low platforms rumbled up and down our street carrying the goods the city traded in, from kegs of beer to sacks of grain. Within a few blocks of our house there were smithies, hand laundries, a macaroni factory, and all manner of places where wagons and buggies were repaired, horses stabled, bicycles fixed, chickens dressed, clothes washed and ironed, furniture repaired, candy mixed, tents sewed, wine grapes pressed, bottles washed, lumber sawed, suits fitted and tailored, watches and clocks taken apart and put together again, vegetables sorted, railroad cars unloaded, boxcars iced, barges freighted, ice cream cones molded, soda pop bottled, fish scaled, salami stuffed, corn ground for masa, and bread ovened. To those who knew where these were located in the alleys, as I did, the whole *barrio* was an open workshop. The people who worked there came to know you, let you look in at the door, made jokes, and occasionally gave you an odd job.

This was the business district of the *barrio*. Around it and through it moved a constant traffic of drays, carts, bicycles, pushcarts, trucks, and high-wheeled automobiles with black canvas tops and honking horns. On the tailgates of drays and wagons, I nipped rides when I was going home with a gunnysack full of empty beer bottles or my gleanings around the packing sheds.

Once we had work, the next most important thing was to find a place to live we could afford. Ours was a neighborhood of leftover houses. The cheapest rents were in the back quarters of the rooming houses, the basements, and the run-down clapboard rentals in the alleys. Clammy and dank as they were, they were nevertheless one level up from the barns and tents where many of our *chicano* friends lived, or the shanties and lean-to's of the migrants who squatted in the "jungles" along the levees of the Sacramento and the American rivers.

Barrio people, when they first came to town, had no furniture of their own. They rented it with their quarters or bought a piece at a time from the secondhand stores, the *segundas*, where we traded. We cut out the ends of tin cans to make collars and plates for the pipes and floor moldings where the rats had gnawed holes. Stoops and porches that sagged we propped with bricks and fat stones. To plug the drafts around the windows in winter, we cut strips of corrugated cardboard and wedged them into the frames. With squares of cheesecloth neatly cut and sewed to screen doors holes were covered and rents in the wire mesh mended. Such repairs, which landlords never paid any attention to, were made *por mientras*, for the time being or temporarily. It would have been a word equally suitable for the house itself, or for the *barrio*. We lived in run-down places furnished with seconds in a hand-me-down neighborhood all of which were *por mientras*.

We found the Americans as strange in their customs as they probably found us. Immediately we discovered that there were no *mercados* and that when shopping you did not put the groceries in a *chiquihuite*. Instead everything was in cans or in cardboard boxes or each item was put in a brown paper bag. There were neighborhood grocery stores at the corners and some big ones uptown, but no *mercado*. The grocers did not give children a *pilón*, they did not stand at the door and coax you to come in and buy, as they did in Mazatlán. The fruits and vegetables were displayed on counters instead of being piled up on the floor. The stores smelled of fly spray and oiled floors, not of fresh pineapple and limes.

Neither was there a plaza, only parks which had no bandstands, no concerts every Thursday, no Judases exploding on Holy Week, and no promenades of boys going one way and girls the other. There were no parks in the *barrio*; and the ones uptown were cold and rainy in winter, and in summer there was no place to sit except on the grass. When there were celebrations nobody set off rockets in the parks, much less on the street in front of your house to announce to the neighborhood that a wedding or a baptism was taking place. Sacramento did not have a *mercado* and a plaza with the cathedral to one side and the Palacio de Gobierno on another to make it obvious that there and nowhere else was the center of the town.

It was just as puzzling that the Americans did not live in *vecindades*, like our block on Leandro Valle. Even in the alleys, where people knew one another better, the houses were fenced apart, without central courts to wash clothes, talk and play with the other children. Like the city, the Sacramento *barrio* did not have a place which was the middle of things for everyone.

In more personal ways we had to get used to the Americans. They did not listen if you did not speak loudly, as they always did. In the Mexican style, people would know that you were enjoying their jokes tremendously if you merely smiled and shook a little, as if you were trying to swallow your mirth. In the American style there was little difference between a laugh and a roar, and until you got used to them you could hardly tell whether the boisterous Americans were roaring mad or roaring happy.

It was Doña Henriqueta more than Gustavo or José who talked of these oddities and classified them as agreeable or deplorable. It was she also who pointed out the pleasant surprises of the American way. When a box of rolled oats with a picture of red carnations on the side was emptied, there was a plate or a bowl or a cup with blue designs. We ate the strange stuff regularly for breakfast and we soon had a set of the beautiful dishes. Rice and beans we bought in cotton bags of colored prints. The bags were unsewed, washed, ironed, and made into gaily designed towels, napkins, and handkerchiefs. The American stores also gave small green stamps which were pasted in a book to exchange for prizes. We didn't have to run to the corner with the garbage; a collector came for it.

With remarkable fairness and never-ending wonder we kept adding to our list the pleasant and the repulsive in the ways of the Americans. It was my second acculturation.

The older people of the *barrio*, except in those things which they had to do like the Americans because they had no choice, remained Mexican. Their language at home was Spanish. They were continuously taking up collections to pay somebody's funeral expenses or to help someone who had had a serious accident. Cards were sent to you to attend a burial where you would throw a handful of dirt on top of the coffin and listen to tearful speeches at the graveside. At every baptism a new *compadre* and a new *comadre* joined the family circle. New Year greeting cards were exchanged, showing angels and cherubs in bright colors sprinkled with grains of mica so that they glistened like gold dust. At the family parties the huge pot of steaming tamales was still the center of attention, the *atole* served on the side with chunks of brown sugar for sucking and crunching. If the party lasted long enough, someone produced a guitar, the men took over and the singing of *corridos* began.

In the *barrio* there were no individuals who had official titles or who were otherwise recognized by everybody as important people. The reason must have been that there was no place in the public business of the city of Sacramento for the Mexican immigrants. We only rented a corner of the city and as long as we paid the rent on time everything else was decided at City Hall or the County Court House, where Mexicans went only when they were in trouble. Nobody from the *barrio* ever ran for mayor or city councilman. For us the most important public officials were the policemen who walked their beats, stopped fights, and hauled drunks to jail in a paddy wagon we called *La Julia*.

The one institution we had that gave the *colonia* some kind of image was the Comisión Honorífica, a committee picked by the Mexican Consul in San Francisco to organize the celebration of the Cinco de Mayo and the Sixteenth of September, the anniversaries of the battle of Puebla and the beginning of our War of Independence. These were the two events which stirred everyone in the *barrio*, for what we were celebrating was not only the heroes of Mexico but also the feeling that we were still Mexicans ourselves. On these occasions there was a dance preceded by speeches and a concert. For both the *cinco* and the sixteenth queens were elected to preside over the ceremonies.

Between celebrations neither the politicians uptown nor the Comisión Honorífica attended to the daily needs of the *barrio*. This was done by volunteers—the ones who knew enough English to interpret in court, on a visit to the doctor, a call at the county hospital, and who could help make out a postal money order. By the time I had finished the third grade at the Lincoln School I was one of these volunteers. My services were not professional but they were free, except for the IOU's I accumulated from families who always thanked me with "God will pay you for it."

My clients were not *pochos*, Mexicans who had grown up in California, probably had even been born in the United States. They had learned to speak English of sorts and could still speak Spanish, also of sorts. They knew much more about the Americans than we did, and much less about us. The *chicanos* and the *pochos* had certain feelings about one another. Concerning the *pochos*, the *chicanos* suspected that they considered themselves too good for the *barrio* but were not, for some reason, good enough for the Americans. Toward the *chicanos*, the *pochos* acted superior, amused at our confusions but not especially interested in explaining them to us. In our family when I forgot my manners, my mother would ask me if I was turning *pochito*.

Turning *pocho* was a half-step toward turning American. And America was all around us, in and out of the *barrio*. Abruptly we had to forget the ways of shopping in a *mercado* and learn those of shopping in a corner grocery or in a department store. The Americans paid no attention to the Sixteenth of September, but they made a great commotion about the Fourth of July. In Mazatlán Don Salvador had told us, saluting and marching as he talked to our class, that the Cinco de Mayo was the most glorious date in human history. The Americans had not even heard about it.

In Tucson, when I had asked my mother again if the Americans were having a revolution, the answer was: "No, but they have good schools, and you are going to one of them." We were by now settled at 418 L Street and the time had come for me to exchange a revolution for an American education.

Jesús Colón (1901–1974)

Kipling and I

Colón is considered one of the major chroniclers of the Puerto Rican experience. Writing predominantly in the English language, his was the voice of the working class, the labor organizer, the militant socialist, the community activist, and the black man in racist America. Jesús Colón (see the other entry for his biography) experienced first-hand the discrimination and hostility that permeated life in the barrios. His writings exposed the injustice and promoted a political awareness intended to empower and unite his compatriots. Colón documented the infant migrant community of the interwar years to the massive movements of Puerto Ricans from the island to the city, known as the "great migration," to the struggles for civil rights in the 1960s. *Kipling and I* offers an excellent example of Jesús Colón's observations of the human condition and his literary conciseness. Initially published in the monthly magazine *Mainstream*, to which Colón was a contributing editor, the essay recounts a turning point in the author's life. Kipling's motivational poem *If* helped to soften the blows of countless hardships that Colón had suffered. (VSK)

Further reading: Jesús Colón, *A Puerto Rican in New York and Other Sketches* (New York: International Publishers, 1982); *The Way It Was and Other Writings*, ed. and introduced by Edna Acosta-Belén and Virginia Sánchez Korrol (Houston: Arte Público Press, 1993).

Sometimes I pass Debevoise Place at the corner of Willoughby Street . . . I look at the old wooden house, gray and ancient, the house where I used to live some forty years ago . . .

My room was on the second floor at the corner. On hot summer nights I would sit at the window reading by the electric light from the street lamp which was almost at a level with the window sill.

It was nice to come home late during the winter, look for some scrap of old newspaper, some bits of wood and a few chunks of coal and start a sparkling fire in the chunky fourlegged coal stove. I would be rewarded with an intimate warmth as little by little the pigmy stove became alive puffing out its sides, hot and red, like the crimson cheeks of a Santa Claus.

My few books were in a soap box nailed to the wall. But my most prized possession in those days was a poem I had bought in a five and ten cent store on Fulton Street. (I wonder what has become of those poems, maxims and sayings of wise men that they used to sell at the five and ten cent stores?) The poem was printed on gold paper and mounted in a gilded frame ready to be hung in a conspicuous place in the house. I bought one of those fancy silken picture cords finishing in a rosette to match the color of the frame.

I was seventeen. This poem to me then seemed to summarize the wisdom of all the sages that ever lived in one poetical nutshell. It was what I was looking for, something to guide myself by, a way of life, a compendium of the wise, the true and the beautiful. All I had to do was to live according to the counsel of the poem and follow its instructions and I would be a perfect man—the useful, the good, the true human being. I was very happy that day, forty years ago.

The poem had to have the most prominent place in the room. Where could I hang it? I decided that the best place for the poem was on the wall right by the entrance to the room. No one coming in and out would miss it. Perhaps someone would be interested enough to read it and drink the profound waters of its message . . .

Every morning as I prepared to leave, I stood in front of the poem and read it over and over again, sometimes half a dozen times. I let the sonorous music of the verse carry me away. I brought with me a handwritten copy as I stepped out every morning looking for work, repeating verses and stanzas from memory until the whole poem came to be part of me. Other days my lips kept repeating a single verse of the poem at intervals throughout the day.

In the subways I loved to compete with the shrill noises of the many wheels below by chanting the lines of the poem. People stared at me moving my lips as though I were in a trance. I looked back with pity. They were not so fortunate as I who had as a guide to direct my life a great poem to make me wise, useful and happy.

And I chanted:

If you can keep your head when all about you
Are losing theirs and blaming it on you . . .

If you can wait and not be tired by waiting
Or being hated don't give way to hating . . .

If you can make one heap of all your winnings
And risk it on a turn of pitch and toss . . .
And lose and start again at your beginnings . . .

"If," by Kipling, was the poem. At seventeen, my evening prayer and my first morning thought. I repeated it every day with the resolution to live up to the very last line of that poem.

I would visit the government employment office on Jay Street. The conversations among the Puerto Ricans on the large wooden benches in the employment office were always on the same subject. How to find a decent place to live. How they would not rent to Negroes or Puerto Ricans. How Negroes and Puerto Ricans were given the pink slips first at work.

From the employment office I would call door to door at the piers, factories and storage houses in the streets under the Brooklyn and Manhattan Bridges. "Sorry, nothing today." It seemed to me that that "today" was a continuation and combination of all the yesterdays, todays and tomorrows.

From the factories I would go to the restaurants looking for a job as a porter or dishwasher. At least I would eat and be warm in a kitchen.

"Sorry" . . . "Sorry" . . .

Sometimes I was hired at ten dollars a week, ten hours a day including Sundays and holidays. One day off during the week. My work was that of three men: dishwasher, porter, busboy. And to clear the sidewalk of snow and slush "when you have nothing else to do." I was to be appropriately humble and grateful not only to the owner but to everybody else in the place.

If I rebelled at insults or at a pointed innuendo or just the inhuman amount of work, I was unceremoniously thrown out and told to come "next week for your pay." "Next week" meant weeks of calling for the paltry dollars owed me. The owners relished this "next week."

I clung to my poem as to a faith. Like a potent amulet, my precious poem was clenched in the fist of my right hand inside my secondhand overcoat. Again and again I declaimed aloud a few precious lines when discouragement and disillusionment threatened to overwhelm me.

If you can force your heart and nerve and sinew
To serve your turn long after you are gone . . .

The weeks of unemployment and hard knocks turned into months. I continued to find two or three days of work here and there. And I continued to be thrown out when I rebelled at the ill treatment, overwork and insults. I kept pounding the streets looking for a place where they would treat me half decently, where my devotion to work and faith in Kipling's poem would be appreciated. I remember the worn out shoes I bought in a secondhand store on Myrtle Avenue at the corner of Adams Street. The round holes in the soles that I tried to cover with pieces of carton were no match for the frigid knives of the unrelenting snow.

One night I returned late after a long day of looking for work. I was hungry. My room was dark and cold. I wanted to warm my numb body. I lit a match and began looking for some scraps of wood and a piece of paper to start a fire. I searched all over the floor. No wood, no paper. As I stood up, the glimmering flicker of the dying match was reflected in the glass surface of the framed poem. I unhooked the poem from the wall. I reflected for a minute, a minute that felt like an eternity. I took the frame apart, placing the square glass upon the small table. I tore the gold paper on which the poem was printed, threw its pieces inside the stove and placing the small bits of wood from the frame on top of the paper, I lit it adding soft and hard coal as the fire began to gain strength and brightness.

I watched how the lines of the poem withered into ashes inside the small stove.

Roberto Fernández (1951–)

Miracle on Eighth and Twelfth

One of the most renowned Cuban-American prose fiction writers, Roberto G. Fernández, was born in Sagua la Grande, Cuba. Disaffected with the Cuban Revolution, his family migrated to the United States and settled in South Florida, in 1960. Fernández received his B.A. and M.A. degrees from Florida Atlantic University and his doctorate from Florida State University. Currently, he is Professor of Latin American literature at Florida State University. *Miracle on Eighth and Twelfth* is part of Fernández's first novel written in English, *Raining Backwards* (1988). Like all of his works, it parodies the cultural, linguistic, religious, political, and socioeconomic values of South Florida's Cuban community. The author often has declared his fatherland is still Cuba but his country is the United States; therefore, he turns to Miami and its Cuban population as a source of inspiration in his work. (HL)

Further reading: Roberto G. Fernández, *La montaña rusa* (Houston: Arte Público Press, 1985), *Raining Backwards*, 2nd ed. (Houston: Arte Público Press, 1997).

Me and Manolo were walking toward Eighth and Twelfth after we left Pepe's Grocery 'cause I needed a few things for Sunday when the grandchildren would be over. I know what you are thinking, but it's my very own shopping cart. I'm no thief. Well, I was guiding my Manny and thinking how hard life had got ever since he went blind after lighting that old kerosene kitchen. I warned him, but he's always been so hard-headed. You want some coffee? It's not American coffee. It's not watery. So the kitchen exploded right in his face, and my poor Manny pretended for weeks that he could still see, and he even tried to drive the car and ended up smashing it against Mr. Olsen's porch. Mr. Olsen never knew Manny did it 'cause he was vacationing in Georgia at the time. Let me tell you, life then was a lemon, and I didn't have no sugar to make it a lemonade.

So we were walking and it was Good Friday. Wait a second, I think something is burning in the kitchen. Manny, is that you, my little heart? I wonder what he is doing in the kitchen. Last week, he turned on all the burners and nearly burned the house down. Now that he can see again he still likes to pretend to be blind. I guess he enjoyed all that extra attention. I always took care of him, like the king of this house he is. So we were walking along Eighth and Twelfth and it was Good Friday. It must have been around a quarter to three since it was really getting dark and windy. I was saying a rosary, just to do something, and I was admiring this huge mango when I noticed next to the mango tree, near the fence, Mr. Olsen's sea grape crying. It wasn't really crying, but sap was oozing from its branches. Somehow I was inspired and I helped Manny jump the fence and then I jumped. Actually, it wasn't really that easy since Manny's privates got tangled in the fence and I had to help him. I remember he screamed: "Barbarita, they are useless. Let's leave them there."

I went straight to the tree, gathered some sap in my hands and rubbed it all over my poor Manny's sightless eyes. At first, he cursed me, but then he knelt, lifted his arms and shouted: "Coño, I can see. Barbarita, I can see!" I thought he was kidding, so I asked him what color my blouse was. "Red, white and blue," he said. I wasn't convinced yet, so I asked him again what color his shoes were. "Blue sneakers," he said with a grin. I quickly knelt and was beating my chest in gratitude when Mr. Olsen came out with his shotgun and threatened to kill us for trespassing. I tried to explain, but he wasn't interested.

Finally, I had to bribe him with some bubble gum. You know how Americans go crazy for stuff like that. He let us go, screaming that only Superman could save him from this foreign plague. While he was shouting, I was trying to scoop up some more holy sap in case Manny had a relapse, but he saw me and placed his gun right in my nose and said, "Lady, put that sap where it belongs . . . you . . . you tropical scum, or I'll blow your head off."

We were very scared of Mr. Olsen, but very thankful for Manny's sight, and now we go every day at a quarter to three to pray across the street from Mr. Olsen's house, facing the tree, while a watchful Mr. Olsen keeps his gun cocked. "Scuse me, just a minute. Manny is that you, my little heart?" It's Manny, all right. Every time he goes to the toilet he closes his eyes like he's blind and misses. I always have to go clean up after him. I want you to promise me by your mother's body lying in her funeral casket that you will tell everybody you know about this divine happening, so the faithless can become believers. But what I told about Manny's privates, keep it to yourself.

> ATTENTION PLEASE. MAY I HAVE YOUR ATTENTION PLEASE: WOULD YOU PLEASE DISPERSE AND GO HOME. GO CASA! THIS AREA IS BEING CORDONED OFF BY ORDER OF THE POLICE. POR FAVOR, GO AS QUICKLY AS POSSIBLE. ¡PRONTO!

That sure is a big helicopter up there! Please ma'am! Please, ma'am, don't push. Let me go by, please. Please don't push, don't you see I'm carrying a sick child! Who pinched my ass? Mima, where are youuuu? Hail Mary full of grace, the gentleman with the green shirt please get out of the way. Excuse me, please. Forget it, honey. I ain't moving, I saw this spot first. Out, out, out! This is private property, propiedad private! Hot dogs! Hot dogs! Get your hot dogs and cockfight tickets here. Oh, my tree! Oh Julia, if you could only see what they are doing to my tree. My beautiful sea grape! Who pinched my ass? The mother who pinched my ass! Hail Mary full of get your Bud, get your ice cold Bud here. This butt's for me. Ouch! If you touch my tree again, I'll kill you! Shut up, old man. Lois, Lois call the police! I am not. This is so much fun, olé! I swear by my little boy that I saw everything from my bathroom window. She was pushing the shopping cart with a man inside. The man had no legs. Then I saw her jump the fence and gather something from the sea grape tree and spreading it all over his stumps and the next thing I saw was the man sprouting a new pair of legs. I swear by my mother's grave that I saw everything from my bathroom window. That's why I'm here. You spic English? Yes, a little. What the police saying from the helicopter? They said that the Virgin is coming real soon. How they know she is coming? They are gringos, my friend, they know everything. If Superman could only hear me, but I can't get to my watch now. Holy cards, with the Pope blessing the holy tree, with your order of a small pizza and a Bud. Number, numbers, bolita. Coke, coke. Get your coke here. Snort, excuse meee, drink your Coke here. C'mon, Manny, rub a little bit of sap on your pipi, it might make it work again. Do it for me, Manny. Okay, Barbarita, but just a little bit! Let me go by, I have arthritis. Connie, just chip off a piece. It'll keep Bill at your side. And her royal highness for the Queen Calle Ocho Festival is, may I have the envelope: Lovee Martinez, a modeling student. Hey, don't take that whole branch. Shut up, viejo. My country tis of thee sweet land of liberty. And then he sprouted two legs and an arm. Caridad, our lady, is landing. She's landing upside down on top of the tree! Who pinched my ass? Oh, Manny, that's incredible. It's so big and hard!!!!

Isaac Goldemberg (1945–)

Chronicles; Self-Portrait

Isaac Goldemberg was born in Chepén, Perú, emigrated to the United States in 1964, and returned to his native country to write his first novel, *La vida a plazos de don Jacobo Lerner*. His prose and poetry reflects upon the uncomfortable reality of his Peruvian-Jewish experience. His highly personal works are characterized by a constant search for identity and meaning, an attempt to synthesize his cultural and experiential parts—the Peruvian, the Jew, the immigrant to the United States. The poems below, from his collection entitled *La vida al contado*, evoke the almost forbidden nature of Jewishness in a predominantly Hispano-Christian society and the difficulty of reconciling those distinctly different cultures. (KDM)

Further reading: Isaac Goldemberg, *The Fragmented Life of Don Jacobo Lerner* (translation: Robert S. Piciotto) (New York: Persea, 1976), *Hombre de paso/Just Passing Through* (Hannover, N.H.: Ediciones del Norte, 1981), *La vida al contado* (Lima: Lluvia Editores, 1989).

Trans.: KDM

Chronicles (Cronicas)

Saturday embedded in memory
The neighborhood kids have run off to
deliver the bread
and the prayers have been cut short
The house sinks, like a word, into silence

Hospitable grandmother reposes in the
dark like an idol
My father prays with his patriarchal and
watchful voice
My mother lights the oven
(there is still time)
She kneads our bread with her silences

Sábado aferrado a la memoria
Han corrido los muchachos del barrio a
repartirse el pan
y se ha cortado la oración
La casa se hunde como una palabra en el
silencio
La hospitalaria abuela reposa en la
penumbra como un ídolo
Mi padre reza con su voz de patriarca y
centinela
Mi madre enciende el horno
(aún queda tiempo)
Amasa nuestro pan con sus silencios

Self-Portrait (Autorretrato)

I and my Jew on my back
observing ourselves from behind
and yet
ear to ear
he, imperturbable
disdainful of death, one would say
tolling the bell against time
on his mission of roaming
through the abyss of history
he, his youthful countenance
lagging behind in mirrors
tattooed from sole to soul
I and my Jew on my back
indelibly marked up to my crooked nose
that we are wearing out
smelling the Kingdom of this Earth

Yo y mi judío a cuestas
observándonos de espaldas
y sin embargo
oreja a oreja:
él imperturbable
diríase desdeñoso de la muerte
dando campanazos contra el tiempo
en su misión de ir rodando
por el abismo de la historia
él su rostro adolescente
rezagado en los espejos
tatuado del pie al alma
Yo y mi judío a cuestas
calcamoniados hasta la corva nariz
que se nos gasta
en olfatear el Reino de la Tierra

Dolores Prida (1943–)

The Herb Shop

Born in the small town of Caibarién, Cuba, Dolores Prida was brought to the United States at the age of sixteen by her family, which was fleeing the triumph of the Cuban Revolution and Fidel Castro's rise to power. She began writing while still in Cuba and pursued her vocation throughout college and much of her professional life as an editor and correspondent. Prida's career is highlighted by successful runs of her award-winning plays in the United States, Venezuela, Puerto Rico, and the Dominican Republic. Her work entwines the universal with the specific, with carefully crafted, sometimes untranslatable bilingual codeswitching, elements of popular culture and religion, and a fine sense of irony and humor. She has received numerous international and national awards, and an honorary doctorate in Humane Letters from Mt. Holyoke College in Massachusetts. The following excerpt, which is from the first act of *The Herb Shop* ("Botánica" in Spanish), finds a homeless drunk, a Nuyorican college graduate, a septuagenarian herb shop owner, and two Yoruba deities discussing the trials and tribulations of keeping the faith and the business going while facing assimilation and tough times in the city. (KDM)

Further reading: Dolores Prida, *Beautiful Señoritas and Other Plays* (Houston: Arte Público Press, 1991).

Trans.: TEW

Characters

DOÑA GENO. Genoveva Domínguez, sixty-odd years old. She was born in Guayama, Puerto Rico and has lived in New York for more than 40 years. She is a widow. She owns and runs The Ceiba Herb Shop in the area of Manhattan (New York) known as The Barrio.

ANAMÚ. Forty-something. She is Doña Geno's daughter. She is divorced and is the mother of Milagros (Millie). She was born in Puerto Rico, but arrived in New York as a child. She is an indecisive women, somewhat loathsome of life.

MILLIE. Milagros Castillo, twenty-two years old. She was born in New York. She has just graduated from the university with a degree in Business Administration.

RUBÉN. Twenty-six years old. He is a friend of Millie's from childhood. He was born in New York. He works at a development organization for the Barrio community.

PEPE THE INDIAN. Of unknown age and nationality. He is a homeless drunk and philosopher who strolls around the neighborhood.

LUISA and CARMEN. Clients of the Herb Shop.

SAINT BÁRBARA and SAINT LÁZARO. Two saints.

The Scenery

All action takes place inside The Ceiba Herb Shop. While the scenery does not have to be realistic, it is necessary that a considerable amount of paraphernalia appear of the type sold in herb shops: candles, herbs, incense, small bottles of essential oils and potions, aerosols and saintly images. An enormous engraving or drawing of a Ceiba—a five-leafed, silk cotton tree—dominates the scene. Under it, Doña Geno's chair-throne is found. To one side there is a little counter. One door opens out into the street, and another to the interior of the house.

Act I

The lights go on. Doña Geno is attending to a customer in the herb shop.

LUISA: I don't think it's another woman, Doña Geno. With what time? The poor thing has two jobs. At first I though it was because of the hair . . . you know. . . .

GENO: What hair?

LUISA: My hair. A couple months ago, it began to fall out and lost its shine. I looked like a dead person . . . me . . . who had a tangle of beautiful hair. But I saw on TV, on "Five Minutes with Mirta Perales," that a woman, she wrote to her tellin' her how her husband didn't look at her no more 'cause she had her hair ugly. Mirta recommended to her her Mirta Lotion, and wham, her hair turned pretty and the husband fell in love with her again. I bought me the same lotion, and nothin'. Arturo doesn't even look at me. Whadda ya recommend, Doña Geno?

GENO: *Zabila.* The Americans call it Aloe Vera. I've got liquid, gelatine, capsules . . .

LUISA: For my hair?

GENO: (*Taking out bottles, boxes and envelopes of aloe and placing them on the counter.*) My child, it's proved aloe has medicinal properties for the treatment of arthritis, high blood pressure, asthma, vaginitis, dysentery, erysipelas, hemorrhoids, athletes foot, prickly heat, colitis, diarrhea, constipation, flu, apoplexy, dandruff, molar pain, and . . . (*Triumphantly*) hair loss! And that's not all, aloe's also a cleanser, refresher, humectant and nutrient for skin; it stimulates the pancreas, repels insects and eliminates foot odor . . . helps to lose weight, conditions hair . . . and, is a powerful aphrodisiac.

LUISA: Mother of Jesus! Give me six liquid, six of the gelatine and four of the capsules!

GENO: (*She takes out a manila folder.*) Just in case, I recommend you burn this incense "Everlasting Assistance," several times each day. And when you bathe, throw a couple a drops of this "Come Hither Bath Potion" in the tub. This, I prepared it myself. I'll also give you a spiritual cure to bring good luck to the house. Listen carefully: take an egg, tie a white ribbon and a blue ribbon 'round it, put a drop of your perfume on it . . .

LUISA: Mirta.

GENO: . . . put the egg on a plate and light a red candle, say three "Our Fathers" and blow out the candle. Put the egg at the foot of the bed all night. The next day, pick it up and throw it in the river.

LUISA: Which river?

GENO: Whichever.

LUISA: I think I'm gonna throw it in the Hudson. It's the biggest.

GENO: The Hudson's good, but throw it towards downtown. The Dominicans have overdone it uptown.

LUISA: Oh, you don't know how much I appreciate this, Doña Geno. How much do I owe you?

GENO: (*Geno tears off a piece of paper bag and writes with a dull pencil. She does the math moving her lips.*) It's $45.50.

LUISA: Oh, look, I didn't think it'd be so much. I didn't bring that much money with me.

GENO: Don't worry, dear. Give me what you can. I'll write the rest down and you bring it later.

LUISA: (*Gives her five dollars. Geno makes a note on the scrap paper and throws it in a paper shopping bag she has on the counter.*) For sure I'll bring it for you when I hit the numbers this week. Oh, another little thing . . . Doña Geno, I dreamed about Elsie last night. What number do you think I should play?

GENO: Who's Elsie?

LUISA: The cow on TV. Don't you remember?

GENO: Oh, yeah. Well, if you dreamed you saw a cow, this means relatives will visit. If you were milkin' a cow, this means you're gonna win money.

LUISA: I don't remember if I milked it or not.

GENO: Either way, play 744.

LUISA: 744 . . . hmmmmmm, it sounds nice . . . Listen, Doña Geno, how long do you think it'll take this other stuff to work?

GENO: Give it . . . might be . . . two weeks. And let me know as soon as you see a change.

LUISA: Thanks, Doña Geno. God bless you. Bye.

GENO: See ya' later, dear. Good bless you. (*She sits in her chair under the cotton tree. She fans herself with a straw fan.*)

ANAMÚ: Mamá, please, go and take a look at the dough. I think it came out too thin. And check the amount. It seems too little. I don't know if there's enough for fifty. Also, taste it for salt, maybe it's a bit salty.

GENO: Oh child, I just sat down . . .

ANAMÚ: Okay . . . When you can . . .

GENO: If I didn't know better, I'd say it was your first time makin' *pasteles.*

ANAMÚ: It's that I don't like the look of these. I don't know if it's such a good idea to show up there loaded down with frozen *pasteles.*

GENO: You don't think those Nu Hamprish gringos are gonna like 'em? There they don't eat nothing else but mitlof and boiled potatoes.

ANAMÚ: Mamá, they're not all from New Hampshire. There are folks from all over.

GENO: Fine, if the gringos doesn't like 'em, Milagritos can eat 'em herself. She's always liked *pasteles* a lot. Even though lately she's got somethin' against *tostones.* The last time she was here, she was so picky with food and going on with some vegetarianism. As if plantains wasn't vegetables!

ANAMÚ: Mamá, it's just that she has never liked *mofongo* for breakfast.

GENO: Anamú, you're exaggeratin'. When have I served *mofongo* for breakfast?

ANAMÚ: Well, almost . . .

GENO: What's wrong is you don't wanna accept Milagritos has changed a lot since she's been at that college for white people . . . (*There are voices coming from the street.*)

PEPE THE INDIAN: (*From outside.*) Rubén, Rubén, don't let them kill your buffalo!

RUBÉN: (*From outside.*) Don't worry, Chief, I'm taking good care of them.

ANAMÚ: Pepe the Indian is already out there with his babblin'. In a little bit he'll be in here askin' for change for lunch. You started a bad habit.

GENO: He's a good-natured beggar, Anamú. He doesn't have no place to sleep.

ANAMÚ: He's a drunk, Mamá. The money you give him to eat goes to drinkin' beer.

GENO: At least he don't spend it on drugs.

RUBÉN: (*Enters dressed in a baseball uniform, a bat in one hand. The uniform is of very outrageous colors. On his back it says "Neighborhood Lions."*) Greetings, ladies. What's new?

ANAMÚ: How's it goin', son?

GENO: (*Covering her eyes with the fan.*) Glory be, Rubén! That uniform's makin' me sick!

RUBÉN: (*He feels uncomfortable in the uniform.*) Well, you shouldn't look a gift horse in the mouth . . . . José, the owner of the "Beautiful Boricua" restaurant donated the uniforms. I told him that they were going to make fun of us, and he said it was to confuse the competition.

GENO: Maybe by makin' 'em nauseous.

RUBÉN: The worst part is there isn't anything disgusting enough to make "The Bronx Bulls" sick. But anyway, Doña Geno, just to be sure, put a little essence of "Tame the Bully" right here.

ANAMÚ: Hope it works, God willing. The last time you only scored five goose eggs.

RUBÉN: (*Geno gives him a little bottle.*) Thanks, Doña Geno. You'll make a note of it? (*Rubén opens the bottle and pours it on the bat.*)

GENO: Don't worry 'bout it, my boy. I'm gonna check the dough and (*pointing to the uniform*) rest my eyes from those crazy colors. (*Geno leaves.*)

RUBÉN: (*To Anamú.*) Did she say dough? By chance could it be dough to make those famous and unique *pasteles* a la Doña Geno Domínguez, the Empress of the Puerto Rican Pastel? (*He licks his lips.*)

ANAMÚ: Don't drool, Rubén. I'm makin' 'em. Mamá isn't feelin' well lately. And, they're for Milagros' graduation.

RUBÉN: Do you know the date?

ANAMÚ: Were waitin' for her to call. We left it at that. I think it's weekend after next. We're gonna freeze 'em to have 'em ready. You can't make fifty *pasteles* in a day.

RUBÉN: And Mila knows you're gonna take pastries to the graduation?

ANAMÚ: No, it's a surprise.

RUBÉN: A surprise, uh huh . . . Who would have thought, huh? Milagritos a graduate in Business Administration. I say it, hear it, and don't believe it.

GENO: (*She enters from behind, a caldron and ladle in hand.*) Anamú, not even a miracle could save this dough . . .

At that moment the front door opens and Millie enters carrying parcels and dragging a suitcase.

RUBÉN: Mila!

ANAMÚ: Milagros!

GENO: Milagritos!

ANAMÚ: Honey, but . . . (*Everyone tries to talk at the same time, surrounding her and hugging her.*)

RUBÉN: But, what are you doing here?

ANAMÚ: . . . And the graduation?

GENO: Is something wrong? Why didn't you call?

ANAMÚ: Why didn't you let us know you were coming?

RUBÉN: What happened?

GENO: You graduated, yes, right?

ANAMÚ: (*Confused and agitated.*) What about all those *pasteles*?!?

MILLIE: Calm down everyone, calm down.

ANAMÚ: You're not gonna tell me you didn't graduate. After so much work . . .

MILLIE: Mommy, I did graduate. It was yesterday. Look at my class ring . . . and here's the diploma.

GENO: Yesterday! How's it possible? And you couldn't tell us? Here, your mother and me were ready to drag ourselves on over there . . .

ANAMÚ: With fifty frozen *pasteles* . . . okay, they still need to be frozen . . .

RUBÉN: Milagritos . . .

MILLIE: (*Correcting him.*) Millie.

RUBÉN: Millie . . . I was going to take them up there in my car. I'd even bought an overcoat . . . and a real tie . . .

MILLIE: Mommy, grandma, Rubén . . . I'm really sorry . . . it's just that . . . there were some problems and they moved up the date . . . it was a private ceremony . . . there weren't many people . . . there was no time to tell anyone.

GENO: They don't have no phones in Nu Hamprish?

MILLIE: It's just that with being so nervous and in a rush, I thought I didn't want you to rush out of here from one minute to the next to get there. Anyway, you didn't miss anything special. Everything was so boring.

ANAMÚ: Nothing special! My daughter graduates from university and that's nothin' special. I was all ready to feel so proud.

Millie sits down. She is obviously uncomfortable and embarrassed. She doesn't know what to say. Doña Geno looks at her quizzically. Anamú looks away. Rubén realizes the general state of embarrassment and tries to make the best of the situation.

RUBÉN: Hey, people! We can feel proud right here. Isn't that true, Mila . . . , I mean, Millie? We'll celebrate the graduation right here. I'm not wearing my new overcoat, but hey, this uniform is new also! (*He takes out the cap that's sticking out of one of Millie's bags. He puts it on her head.*) Let's see . . . the diploma . . . where's it at? Here it is! Man, are we proud or what! (*He grabs the diploma and holds it up like a sword.*) Back to work! To boil *pasteles*! (*They leave.*)

Later that day. Rubén and Millie are alone in the store.

RUBÉN: Just between you and me, Mila . . . Millie, your mother's *pasteles* aren't as good as your grandmother's. But today, imagine, I thought they were great. Maybe because of the occasion. . . . You barely tasted them.

MILLIE: It's because I don't eat pork anymore. It poisons the body.

RUBÉN: Don't tell me that. If that was true, there wouldn't be one Puerto Rican alive today.

MILLIE: Can you imagine? Mommy and grandma arriving at my graduation with fifty frozen *pasteles* . . .

RUBÉN: You knew they were gonna bring 'em?

MILLIE: No, but I imagined it. I know them. When I was little, we'd go to Orchard Beach on the subway. All the other children were carrying their toys, life jackets, buckets, shovels, towels. Not me. I was there carrying a shopping bag full of *pasteles* and rice and beans. I think that's why I don't like the beach.

RUBÉN: Is that why you didn't want them to go to the graduation?

MILLIE: (*Evasive.*) Why would you say that? Of course not. It was because . . . there wasn't enough time . . . I didn't have the chance to . . . I thought I'd already explained all that.

RUBÉN: You've changed a lot, Milagros . . .

MILLIE: Millie. I don't like to be called Milagros.

RUBÉN: It's a really pretty name. What's wrong with it?

MILLIE: It's that at the university, every time I'd explain what it meant, they'd laugh. They'd say, "Miracles, what kind of a name is that?"

RUBÉN: You paid attention to that crap?

MILLIE: You don't understand, Rubén. It wasn't easy, you know? To arrive alone at a place where you don't know anyone. I'd never left the Barrio, as they say. And to end up there, in New Hampshire, at a university where almost everyone was so different from me. It wasn't easy, believe me. I had a lot of struggles. The thing about the name was one of the easiest. Milagros in the Barrio might be common and acceptable. But Miracles in New Hampshire . . . no way.

RUBÉN: Well, that's history. You're home now. Now you're here and your family is really happy—even though they couldn't go to the graduation.

MILLIE: Will you ever forget about that?

RUBÉN: You just don't know how excited they were . . . we were.

MILLIE: Okay, it's done. I don't want to talk about it anymore. What matters is the future.

RUBÉN: That's true. Doña Geno is older now, and lately she hasn't been feeling well . . .

MILLIE: How's that possible? With all these cures and miracles within reach? She looks really healthy to me. She's really strong. "There isn't a lighting bolt that could split this ceiba tree," that's what she always says.

RUBÉN: Yeah, but with your training, you'll be a great help to your grandma and mother in the store.

MILLIE: Rubén, if you think I got a degree in Business Administration to run an herb shop, you're out of your mind. I've got other plans.

RUBÉN: For example?

MILLIE: For example: Vice President of Chase Manhattan Bank, International Department.

RUBÉN: Get out, girl! If you're gonna start up there at the top, why not go for president?

MILLIE: In a couple of years. You'll see. The thing is that I already have a job. They went to recruit on campus and interviewed me.

RUBÉN: Does your family know this?

MILLIE: Mommy knows, but we haven't found the right time to tell grandma.

RUBÉN: Good luck! Doña Geno thinks you're staying here. I also thought the same thing.

MILLIE: Well no, as soon as I start work, I'm gonna move downtown. I want my own apartment.

RUBÉN: Now I am sure.

MILLIE: Of what?

RUBÉN: That you've got a screw loose upstairs. Even the *gringos* have a hard time finding apartments here, and you, who's got a free one upstairs here, are going to move downtown to pay at least $1,000 in rent.

MILLIE: What apartment?

RUBÉN: Doña Fela's. She's retiring and heading to Puerto Rico. Your grandmother isn't going to rent it out so she can give it to you. You didn't know?

MILLIE: Nobody's told me anything.

RUBÉN: The level of communication in this family is impressive.

MILLIE: It must be another surprise waiting for me . . . But I can't accept it. She needs the rent for the mortgage. This house isn't paid for yet.

RUBÉN: That's not a problem. You'll pay her the same rent as Doña Fela and that's it. Look, the apartment is really nice. I put in new wood floors, there's no carpet. I told Doña Geno, "Milagros doesn't like that five by ten linoleum. She likes the real thing: parquet floors . . ." It cost a mint, but turned out beautifully. Doña Fela almost changed her mind, girl!

MILLIE: Rubén, I don't want to live there. I'm not going to live there. I've got my own plans. I want something different. I want to get out of this. Forget the smell of fried plantains and *Agua de Florida.* I hate this business. I've always wanted to escape from here, from the incense, the camphor, the potions and the saints . . . the people looking for simple solutions to life's problems . . . my grandmother running everybody's lives, like a queen in a cholesterol and *pachuli* palace. I may have been born in the ghetto, but I don't have to live there.

RUBÉN: But look, there are many Hispanic professionals moving here again . . . helping to . . .

MILLIE: I don't care about that. I'm not a social worker. Out there, outside, there is a much bigger world, and I want to be part of it. For that, I've prepared myself. I don't want to be like you, dreaming about hitting home runs in Yankee Stadium and being happy with fly balls in Central Park. (*Rubén takes his hat off and lowers his head. He pauses.*) I'm sorry, Rubén. Forgive me, but since I arrived, I've felt pressured by everyone. The whole world has plans for me. You've got my life planned, without checking with me. It's MY LIFE, you know.

Isabel Allende (1942–)

The Argonauts

Isabel Allende was born in 1942 into a Chilean family in Perú, where her father was a diplomat. When she turned three, her parents divorced, and her mother went back to Chile, where Isabel and her brothers were raised. Allende began her career as a journalist for *Paula*, a Chilean magazine. She began writing novels in Venezuela during her exile following the military coup in 1973 in Chile. Her first novel, *The House of Spirits*, was born from a letter written to her grandfather in which she tells the story of her family. In this novel she creates a poetic biography in which magic and reality are intertwined, and the writer to find her place in the world as an exile. As an immigrant to the United States since 1988, Allende continued her biographical writing. In her memoir *Paula* she purges the pain and suffering caused by her daughter's illness and death. In the United States, she also wrote *The Infinite Plan*, one of the few novels attempted by an immigrant narrating a story from the perspective of an Anglo-American. *Daughter of Fortune*, her latest novel from which *The Argonauts* is taken, tells the story of a Chilean immigrant woman named Elisa, who travels from Valparaiso, Chile, to San Francisco during the Gold Rush in search of her lover, Joaquín Andieta, a character based on the legendary bandit Joaquín Murieta. As usual, Allende narrates from the perspective of a woman, who has to dress like a man in order to survive. The novelty in the *Daughter of Fortune* is that her perspective is also the immigrant's, her expectations, her difficulties adjusting to life here, her disillusionments, and, finally, her confident participation in the building of a new society. (CV)

Further reading: Isabel Allende, *The House of the Spirits,* trans. Magda Bogin (New York: Knopf, 1985); *The Infinite Plan,* trans. Margaret Sayers Peden (New York: Harper Collins, 1993); *Paula,* trans. Margaret Sayers Peden (New York: Harper Collins, 1995); *Daughter of Fortune* (New York: Harper Collins Publishers, 1999).

Trans.: MSP

Tao Chi'en's and Eliza Sommers' feet first touched the soil of San Francisco on a Tuesday in April of 1849, at two o'clock in the afternoon. By then thousands of adventurers had briefly passed through on their way to the placers. A persistent wind made walking difficult, but the day was clear and they could appreciate the panorama of the bay in all its splendid beauty. Tao Chi'en cut a bizarre figure with his doctor's case, which he was never without, his seabag, his straw hat, and a multicolored wool serape he had bought from one of the Mexican stevedores. It didn't matter, really; looks weren't what counted in that town. Eliza's legs were trembling; she hadn't used them in two months, and she felt as landsick as she had before at sea, but the man's clothing gave her an unfamiliar freedom; she had never felt so invisible. Once she got over the feeling that she was naked, she could enjoy the breeze blowing up her sleeves and pants legs. Accustomed to the prison of her petticoats, she could now breathe deeply. She was struggling to carry her small suitcase filled with the exquisite dresses Miss Rose had packed with the best intentions, and when he noticed her difficulty Tao Chi'en took it from her and slung it over his shoulder. The Castile wool blanket rolled up beneath her arm weighed as much as the suitcase, but she realized she couldn't leave it, it would be her most precious possession at night. Eyes to the ground, hidden beneath her straw hat, she stumbled along through the awesome anarchy of the port. The village of Yerba Buena, founded in 1769 by a Spanish expedition, had fewer than fifteen hundred inhabitants, but the adventurers had begun to flock in with the first news of gold. Within a few months, that innocent little village awakened with the name San Francisco and a fame that had reached the farthest points of the globe. More than a true city, it was an enormous camp for men on the move.

Gold fever left no one unaffected: smiths, carpenters, teachers, doctors, soldiers, fugitives from the law, preachers, bakers, revolutionaries, and harmless madmen of various stripes who had left family and possessions behind to traverse half the world in search of adventure. "They look for gold, and along the way lose their souls," Captain Katz had repeated tirelessly in the brief religious services he imposed every Sunday on the passengers and crew of the *Emilia,* but no one paid any attention, blinded by dreams of the sudden riches that would change their lives. For the first time in history, gold lay scattered on the ground, unclaimed, free, and plentiful, within the reach of anyone with the will to go after it. Argonauts came from distant shores; Europeans fleeing wars, plagues, and tyrannies; Americans, ambitious and short-tempered; blacks pursuing freedom; Oregonians and Russians dressed in deerskin, like Indians; Mexicans, Chileans, and Peruvians; Australian bandits; starving Chinese peasants who were risking their necks by violating the imperial order against leaving their country. All races flowed together in the muddy alleyways of San Francisco.

The main streets, laid out as broad semicircles touching the beach at both ends, were intersected by other, straight, streets descending from the steep hills to end at the dock, some so abrupt and deep in mud that not even mules could climb them. Suddenly a storm would blow in, raising whirlwinds of sand along the shore, but soon the air would be calm again and the sky blue. There were already several solid buildings and dozens under construction, including some announcing themselves as future luxury hotels, but everything else was a shambles of temporary dwellings, barracks, shacks of sheet metal, wood, or cardboard, canvas tents, and straw roofs. The recent rains of winter had turned the dock into a swamp; any vehicle that had ventured there sank hub-deep in mire, and planks were laid across ditches deep in garbage, thousands of broken bottles, and other refuse. There were no drains or sewers, and the wells were contaminated; cholera and dysentery reaped scores of lives—except among the Chinese, who by custom drank tea, and the Chileans, who had been raised on polluted water and were therefore immune to lesser bacteria. The heterogeneous throng pulsed with frenzied activity, pushing, bumping into building materials, barrels, boxes, burros, and carts. Chinese porters balanced their loads on each end of a long pole, indifferent to whom they struck as they went by; strong and patient Mexicans swung bundles equal to their own weight onto their backs and trotted off up the hills; Malaysians and Hawaiians seized any pretext to start a fight; Americans charged into temporary businesses on horseback, bowling over anyone in their way; native-born Californians strutted around in handsome embroidered jackets, silver spurs, and slit pants legs trimmed with a double row of gold buttons from belt to boot tops. Shouts from fights and accidents added to the din of hammers, saws, and picks. Shots rang out with terrifying frequency, but no one was affected by one more dead man; on the other hand, the theft of a box of nails immediately drew a crowd of indignant citizens ready to mete out justice with their own hands. Property was much more valuable than life; any robbery over a hundred dollars was paid for on the gallows. There were scores of gaming houses, bars, and saloons decorated with images of naked women in lieu of the real article. Everything imaginable—especially liquor and weapons—was sold at exorbitant prices because no one had time to bargain. Customers nearly always paid in gold, not even stopping to wipe up the dust clinging to the scales. Tao Chi'en decided that the famous Gum San, the Golden Mountain he had heard so much about, was a hell, and calculated that at these prices his savings would not go very far. Eliza's little bag of jewels would be worthless, because the only acceptable tender was pure gold.

Eliza made her way through the crowd as best she could, close behind Tao Chi'en and grateful to be wearing men's clothing because she saw no sign of a woman anywhere. The *Emilia*'s seven female passengers had been carried off to one of the many saloons, where undoubtedly they had already begun earning the two hundred seventy dollars they owed Captain Vincent Katz for their passage. Tao Chi'en had found out from the stevedores that the town was divided into sectors and that every nationality had its neighborhood. He was warned not to go near the Australian roughnecks, who might waylay a passerby for pure fun, and then was pointed the way to a cluster of tents and shacks where the Chinese lived. And that was the direction in which they started walking.

"How am I going to find Joaquín in all this uproar?" Eliza asked, feeling lost and helpless.

"If there is a Chinese barrio, there must be a Chilean one. Look for it."

"I'm not planning to leave you, Tao."

"Tonight," he warned, "I'm going back to the ship."

"Why? Aren't you interested in gold?"

Tao Chi'en walked faster, and she adjusted her pace to his in order not to lose sight of him. Soon they came to the Chinese sector—Little Canton, it was called—a couple of unwholesome streets where Tao immediately felt at home because not a single *fan wey* was to be seen; on the air floated delicious odors of the food of his country and he heard several Chinese dialects, mainly Cantonese. To Eliza, in contrast, it was like being transported to another planet; she did not understand a single word, and it seemed to her that everyone was furious because they were all yelling and waving their arms. Again she did not see any women, but Tao pointed to a couple of barred windows at which she saw despondent faces. Tao had been two months without a woman and those at the window called to him but he knew the ravages of venereal diseases too well to run that risk. These were peasant girls bought for a few coins and brought here from the most remote provinces of China. He thought of his sister, sold by his father, and was bent double by a wave of nausea.

"What's the matter, Tao?"

"Bad memories. Those girls are slaves."

"I thought there weren't any slaves in California."

They went into a restaurant, identified by the traditional yellow streamers. There was a large table crowded with men sitting elbow to elbow and wolfing down food. The sound of lively conversation and chopsticks clattering against tin plates was music to Tao Chi'en's ears. They stood in a double line until they could sit down. It wasn't a matter of choosing what to eat but of grabbing anything that came within arm's reach. It took skill to catch a plate on the fly before someone more enterprising intercepted it, but Tao Chi'en got one for Eliza and another for himself. She eyed with suspicion a dubious green liquid in which pale threads and gelatinous mollusks were floating. She prided herself on knowing any ingredient by its smell, but what sat before her did not look edible, it reminded her of swamp water swarming with polliwogs; it did, however, have the advantage of not requiring chopsticks, she could drink it directly from the bowl. Hunger overcame skepticism and she dared take a taste, while behind her a line of impatient customers yelled at her to hurry. The dish was delicious and she would happily have eaten more, but she was denied the opportunity by Tao Chi'en, who took her by one arm and led her outside. She followed him, first, from shop to shop to replace the medicinal supplies for his kit and to talk with the two Chinese herbalists in the town, and then to a gambling den, one of the many on every corner. This was a wooden building with a pretense of luxury and decorated with paintings of voluptuous, half-clad women. Gold dust was weighed to exchange for coins at the rate of sixteen dollars per ounce, or sometimes the whole pouch was laid on the table. Americans, French, and Mexicans made up the majority of the customers but there were also adventurers from Hawaii, Chile, Australia, and Russia. The most popular games were the monte that had originated in Mexico, *lasquenet*, and twenty-one. Since the Chinese preferred fan-tan, and wagered only a few cents, they were not welcome at the high-rolling tables. There were no blacks gambling, although some were providing music or waiting tables; Eliza and Tao later learned that if they went into a bar or gambling hall they would be given one free drink but would then have to leave or be thrown out. There were three women in the saloon, two young Mexican girls with large sparkling eyes, dressed in white and smoking cigarette after cigarette, and a pretty, rather mature Frenchwoman wearing a tight corset and heavy makeup. They made the rounds of the tables, urging the men to bet and drink, and often disappeared with some customer behind a heavy drapery of red brocade. Tao Chi'en was told that they charged an ounce of gold for an hour of their company in the bar and several hundred dollars to spend the night with a lonely man, although the Frenchwoman was more costly, and she had no truck with Chinese or blacks.

CHAPTER 15

Reflections on the Dislocated Self

Julia de Burgos (1914–1953)

I Was My Own Route (Yo misma fui mi ruta); Farewell in Welfare Island (Adios en Welfare Island)

Julia de Burgos is one of the most celebrated Puerto Rican poets of the twentieth century. Born into relative poverty in the then rural town of Carolina, Burgos was not an insider to the urban cultural circles of the Puerto Rican middle-class intelligentsia of her era. Nevertheless, she rapidly gained institutional recognition with her first collection of poetry, *Poema en veinte surcos* (1938), which was hailed as a major literary event and recited publicly for the first time in the Ateneo Puertorriqueño in 1939. Burgos began as a rural schoolteacher in 1933 and was later hired to write children's scripts for a public radio station. During these years she was also an active member of the Puerto Rican Nationalist Party. After spending a brief two-year interlude in Havana, Burgos emigrated to New York City in 1942. There she first worked as a journalist for the anti-imperialist publication *Pueblos Hispanos* and later performed menial jobs. Poor and suffering from an addiction to alcohol, Burgos died tragically in 1953, after being discovered unconscious and without identification on the streets of Spanish Harlem. Burgos's poetry ranges from metaphysical disquisitions to patriotic raptures, from lyrical love songs to emphatic social protests. Her work is also the poetry of exile, inhabited by images of flow and movement: rivers, infinite seas, skies, indefinite routes, and nothingness. It is poetry that celebrates the nomadic rather than the comfort of one's home or roots. (ALO)

Further reading: Julia de Burgos, *Song of the Simple Truth: Obra Poética Completa/The Complete Poems of Julia de Burgos,* bilingual edition compiled and translated by Jack Agüeros (Willimantic, Conn.: Curbstone Press, 1997).

Trans: MAT, MA

I Was My Own Route (Yo misma fui mi ruta)

I wanted to be like men wanted me to be:	Yo quise ser como los hombres quisieron que yo fuese:

an attempt at life;
a game of hide and seek with my being.
But I was made of here-and-nows,
and my feet level upon the promissory
earth
would not accept walking backwards,
and went forward, forward,
mocking the ashes to reach the kiss
of the new paths.

At each advancing step on my route to the
front
my back was ripped by the desperate
flapping wings
of the old guard.

But the branch was unpinned forever,

and at each new whiplash my look
separated more and more and more from
the distant
familiar horizons;
and my face took the expression that
came from within,
the defined expression that hinted at a
feeling
of intimate liberation;
a feeling that surged
from the balance between my life
and the truth of the kiss of the new paths.

Already my course now set in the present,
I felt myself a blossom of all the soils of
the earth,
of the soils without history,
of the soils without a future,
of the soil always soil without edges
of all the men and all the epochs.

And I was all in me as was life in me . . .

I wanted to be like men wanted me to be:

un intento de vida;
un juego al escondite con mi ser.
Pero yo estaba hecha de presentes,
y mis pies planos sobre la tierra
promisora
no resistían caminar hacia atrás,
y seguían adelante, adelante,
burlando las cenizas para alcanzar el beso
de los senderos nuevos.

A cada paso adelantado en mi ruta hacia
el frente
rasgaba mis espaldas el aleteo
desesperado
de los troncos viejos.

Pero la rama estaba desprendida para
siempre,
y a cada nuevo azote la mirada mía
se separaba más y más de los lejanos

horizontes aprendidos:
y mi rostro iba tomando la expresión que
le venía de adentro,
la expresión definida que asomaba un
sentimiento
de liberación íntima;
un sentimiento que surgía
del equilibrio sostenido entre mi vida
y la verdad del beso de los senderos
nuevos.

Ya definido mi rumbo en el presente,
me sentí brote de todos los suelos de
la tierra,
de los suelos sin historia,
de los suelos sin porvenir,
del suelo siempre suelo sin orillas
de todos los hombres y de todas las
épocas.

Y fui toda en mí como fue en mí la vida . . .

Yo quise ser como los hombres quisieron
que yo fuese:

an attempt at life;
a game of hide and seek with my being.
But I was made of here-and-nows;
when the heralds announced me
at the regal parade of the old guard,
the desire to follow men was warped in
me,
and the homage was left waiting for me.

un intento de vida;
un juego al escondite con mi ser.
Pero yo estaba hecha de presentes;
cuando ya los heraldos me anunciaban
en el regio desfile de los troncos viejos,
se me torció el deseo de seguir a los
hombres,
y el homenaje se quedó esperándome.

Farewell in Welfare Island (Adiós en Welfare Island)

It has to be from here,
right this instance,
my cry into the world.

Life was somewhere forgotten
and sought refuge in depths of tears

and sorrows
over this vast empire of solitude
and darkness.

Where is the voice of freedom,
freedom to laugh,
to move
without the heavy phantom of despair?

Where is the form of beauty
unshaken in its veil simple and pure?
Where is the warmth of heaven
pouring its dreams of love in broken
spirits?

It has to be from here,
right this instance,
my cry into the world.
My cry that is no more mine,
but hers and his forever,
the comrades of my silence,
the phantoms of my grave.

It has to be from here,
forgotten but unshaken,
among comrades of silence
deep into Welfare Island
my farewell to the world.

Tiene que partir de aquí,
en este mismo instante,
mi grito al mundo.

En algún lugar la vida fue olvidada
y buscó refugio en profundidades de
lágrimas
y pesares
sobre este gran imperio de soledad
y oscuridad.

¿Dónde está la voz de la libertad
libertad de reír,
de moverse
sin el pesado fantasma del desespero?

¿Dónde está la forma de la belleza
inquebrantable en su velo simple y puro?
¿Dónde está el calor del cielo
virtiendo sus sueños de amor en espíritus
quebrados?

Tiene que partir de aquí,
en este mismo instante,
mi grito al mundo.
Mi grito que no es más mío,
pero de él y de ella para siempre,
los camaradas de mi silencio,
los fantasmas de mi sepultura.

Tiene que partir de aquí
olvidado pero inquebrantable,
entre camaradas del silencio
muy adentro en Welfare Island
mi despedida al mundo.

Clemente Soto Vélez (1905–1993)

Horizons (Horizontes); Five-Pointed Stars (Estrellas de cinco puntas)

Clemente Soto Vélez was first brought to the United States as a political prisoner. An active member of the Puerto Rican Nationalist Party during the turbulent 1930s, he was sentenced (with fellow nationalist leaders Pedro Albizu Campos and Juan Antonio Corretjer) to seven years in federal penitentiaries, accused of attempting to overthrow U.S. colonial authority on the island. Once released in 1942, Soto Vélez moved permanently to New York City, where he became a member of the Communist Party of America and a contributor to the anti-imperialist and antifascist journals *Pueblos Hispanos* and *Liberación*. His first poetic works, however, date to the mid-1920s and are linked to one of the most daring Puerto Rican literary groups of the time: the Atalayistas. Stridently experimental and innovative, this group of poets aimed to alter conventions of poetic language by subverting established notions of logical coherence in favor of linguistic fragmentation. Likewise, for the Atalayistas, poetry was not just a verbal act but also a revolutionary lifestyle. It is not surprising, then, that in the early 1930s Soto Vélez and many of his peers became active in the nationalist movement. For them, poetry and politics were conceived as one and the same radical commitment to life. Yet Soto Vélez's most fruitful and creative literary period took place in New York during the 1950s. Throughout these years he further refined his early poetic principles, producing splendid collections such as *Caballo de palo* (*The Wooden Horse*, 1959), which established his reputation as a poet. He remained in New York until his death in 1993. (ALO)

Further reading: Clemente Soto Vélez, *Caballo de palo* (New York: Las Américas Publishing, 1959), *Obra poética* (San Juan: Instituto de Cultura Puertorriqueña, 1989), *The Blood That Keeps Singing/La sangre que sigue cantando,* trans. Martín Espada and Camilo Pérez-Bustillo (Willimantic, Conn.: Curbstone Press, 1991).

Trans.: ME and CPB

Horizons (Horizontes)

—Circumstances—speaking among ourselves—sometimes tend to thrust cruel practical jokes upon us. In truth, imperialism is a joke made out of ignorance.

Imperialism, at any point in the creative imagination, is the denial of freedom.

This book—a book does not consist of the number of its pages, but rather the degree to which it upholds the just and the truthful—, has traveled through all the whirlwinds of persecution. It has been in the intimate hands of honest revolutionaries; it has been on the shelves of printers; it has been in jail: always subject to being absorbed by imperialist ambition. Its author—better said, its compañero—, was arrested by imperialism, at the same moment he was at work writing "Revolution and the Revolutionary," with imprisonment, as well as exile, imposed upon him . . .

—Las circunstancias—hablando entre nosotros—suelen lanzar, a veces, bromas un tanto pesadas. En realidad, el imperialismo es una broma de la ignorancia.

El imperialismo, en cualquier punto de la imaginación creadora, es la negación de la libertad.

Este libro—un libro no consiste en el número de sus páginas, sino en su elevación de lo justo y lo verdadero—, ha viajado a través de todos los torbellinos de la persecución. Ha estado en las manos íntimas de veraces revolucionarios; ha estado en los anaqueles de las imprentas; ha estado en la cárcel: siempre expuesto a ser absorbido por la ambición imperialista. Su autor,—mejor dicho, su compañero—, fue arrestado por el imperialismo, en el momento mismo en que escribía "La Revolución y lo Revolúcionario," siéndole aplicado, además de la prisión, el destierro . . .

Five-Pointed Stars

Hands grasping hands that would hold
five-pointed stars:
five-pointed stars
with starless stars.
Hands that would awaken the ground
with the voices of roads
saturated in the sweat
of curves that swallow stones.
Hands that would tie the wind
which opens its legs to war
to drink the young blood
of all the earth.
Hands that would never know
that they killed knowingly
and that they killed killing
without killing all wars.
Hands that would cut the stalks
of ground sown
between wrought-iron fences,
with scissors of words
in alphabets of seed.
Hands that would hear the shout
which gathers the harvest
pregnant from the ploughs,
in the furrows of the tongue.
Hands that would ignite the sky
of the mouth closing
in fear of the iron
merging from miners' shadows.
Hands that together would conquer
the secrets of the grasses
that climb over the blond rooftiles
of spring.

Estrellas de cinco puntas

Manos con manos que tengan
estrellas de cinco puntas:
estrellas de cinco puntas
con estrellas sin estrella.
Manos que despierten suelos
con voces de carreteras
empapadas en sudor
de curvas que comen piedras.
Manos que amarren el aire
que abre a la guerra sus piernas
para beberse la sangre
joven de toda la tierra.
Manos que no sepan nunca
que mataron a sabiendas
y que mataron matando
sin matar todas las guerras.
Manos que corten los grillos
de sembrados entre rejas,

con tijeras de palabras
en alfabetos de siembras.
Manos que escuchen el grito
que se saca la cosecha
encinta de los arados,
en las zanjas de la lengua.
Manos que quemen el cielo
de la boca que se cierra,
por temor a que le pongan
hierro de sombras mineras.
Manos que conquisten juntas
los secretos de las yerbas
que suben por los tejados rubios
de la primavera.

Hands that would press the red fruit
of fences
which feed the red pathways

Manos que aprieten las frutas
coloradas de las cercas
que alimentan los caminos

Lucha Corpi (1945–)

Mexico (México); Dark Romance (Romance negro); Marina Mother (Marina madre)

Born in the small tropical village of Jáltipan, Mexico, Corpi moved to the United States and studied at the University of California, Berkeley, where she became involved in the free speech movement and the Chicano civil rights movement. She earned both a B.A. and an M.A. in Comparative Literature and has been a teacher in Oakland since 1977. Over the years, Corpi has published numerous poems in small magazines and anthologies, as well as two complete volumes of her poems, all written in her native Spanish. During the 1980s, Corpi began writing detective novels in English, which were met with much critical success as her poetry. Her poetry and prose works reveal a political involvement and strong feminist values. In addition, her poetry, while relying on standard international models of lyricism, also reveals her sensibility as an immigrant to the United States. The poems below make up a lyrical narrative of a woman's struggle against silence. Her work comes from an interior, enclosed space; the house, the domestic actions, and things that are found within the house are simultaneously symbols of oppression as well as of liberation. In Corpi's *Marina* poems, the problematic figure of Cortés's Indian interpreter is vindicated by Corpi, who sees her as a mystic, a sage steeped in tradition, and able to see into the future, the future of the Chicana writer and poet. (GBV)

Further reading: Lucha Corpi, *Delia's Song* (Houston: Arte Público Press, 1989), *Variaciones sobre una tempestad/Variations* on a Storm (1990), *Eulogy for a Brown Angel* (Houston: Arte Público Press, 1992), *Cactus Blood* (Houston: Arte Público Press, 1995), *Black Widow's Wardrobe* (Houston: Arte Público Press, 1999), and *Palabras de mediodía/Noon Words* (Houston: Arte Público Press, 2001).

Trans.: CRN

Mexico

I parted
like a note divided
in search of itself.

I looked
in the colors of night
for day's shadows.

I hunted
river lights
in old dreams.

México

Partí
como nota dividida
buscándose a sí misma.

Busqué
en colores de noche
sombras de día.

Perseguí
luces de ríos
en sueños viejos.

Double essence so closely bound
tightrope of my natural order.

Mexico.

Sometimes I think of you
on afternoons like this
An old distress comes over me.

Search for paths of earth
at the edge of the depth.

On warm banks
blue-feathered herons
cultivate red pearls.

There is no time for weeping
if you are to live in me.

Memories were never
the liquid measure of love.

Esencia doble tan cercana
Cuerda floja de mi orden natural.

México.

A veces pienso en ti
en tardes así
Me acaece viejo mal.

Buscar senderos de tierra
a vera de profundidades.

En bancales tibios
garzas de plumaje azul
perlas rojas cultivaron.

No hay tiempo de llorar
si has de vivir en mí.

Recuerdos nunca fueron
medida líquida de amar.

Dark Romance

A flavor of vanilla drifts
on the Sunday air.

Melancholy of an orange,
clinging still,
brilliant, seductive,
past the promise of its blooming.

Guadalupe was bathing in the river
that Sunday, late,

a promise of milk in her breasts,

vanilla scent in her hair,
cinnamon flavor in her eyes,

cocoa-flower between her legs,

and in her mouth a daze
of sugarcane.

Romance negro

Hay sabor de vainilla
en el aire dominical.

Melancolía de la naranja
que aún cuelga de la rama,
brillante y seductora,
sin esperanza de azahar.

Guadalupe se bañaba en el río
muy de tarde en un domingo.

Promesa de leche en los senos

Vainilla el olor de los cabellos
Canela molida el sabor de los ojos

Flor de cacao entre las piernas

Ah, la embriaguez de la caña
entre los labios.

He came upon her there
surrounded by water
in a flood of evening light.

And on the instant cut the flower
wrung blood from the milk

dashed vanilla on the silence
of the river bank

drained the burning liquid
of her lips

And then he was gone,
leaving behind him a trail of shadow
drooping at the water's edge.

Her mother found her, and at the sight
took a handful of salt from her pouch
to throw over her shoulder.

A few days later, her father
accepted the gift of a fine mare.

And Guadalupe . . . Guadalupe hung
her life
from the orange tree in the garden,
and stayed there quietly,
her eyes open to the river.

A scent of vanilla drifts
on the evening air.

Ancestral longing
seizes the mind.

An orange clings to the branch
the promise lost of its blooming.

Él se acercó y la miró así
rodeada del agua
inundada de tarde.

Y en un instante arrancó la flor
Estrujó la leche hasta cambiarla en sangre

Desparramó la vainilla por el
silencio de la orilla

Bebióse el candente líquido
de los labios

Y después . . . después desapareció
dejando sólo un rastro de sombra
lánguida al borde del agua.

Su madre la encontró y al verla
sacó de su morral un puño de sal
y se la echó por el hombro.

Y a los pocos días su padre
recibió una yegua fina de regalo.

Y Guadalupe . . . Guadalupe colgó
su vida del naranjo del huerto
y se quedó muy quieta ahí
con los ojos al río abiertos.

Hay sabor de vainilla
en el ambiente de la tarde.

Una nostalgia ancestral
se apodera de la mente.

De la rama cuelga una naranja
todavía sin promesa de azahar.

Marina Mother

They made her of the softest clay
and dried her under the rays of the
tropical sun.

Marina madre

Del barro más húmedo la hicieron,
al rayo del sol tropical la secaron,

With the blood of a tender lamb
her name was written by the elders
on the bark of that tree
as old as they.

Steeped in tradition, mystic
and mute she was sold—
from hand to hand, night to night,
denied and desecrated, waiting for the
dawn
and for the owl's song
that would never come;
her womb sacked of its fruit,
her soul thinned to a handful of dust.

You no longer loved her, the elders
denied her,
and the child who cried out to her
"mama!"
grew up and called her "whore."

con la sangre de un cordero tierno
su nombre escribieron los viejos
en la corteza de ese árbol
tan viejo como ellos.

Húmeda de tradición, mística
y muda fue vendida . . .
de mano en mano, noche a noche,
negada y desecrada, esperando el alba

y el canto de la lechuza
que nunca llegaban;
su vientre robado de su fruto,
hecha un puño de polvo seco su alma.

Tú no la querías ya y él la negaba

y aquél que cuando niño ¡mamá!
le gritaba
cuando creció le puso por nombre
"la chingada."

Virgil Suárez (1962–)

Spared Angola; Going Under (excerpts)

Born in Cuba and living in the United States since 1972, Virgil Suárez is the author of novels and poetry inspired by the Cuban immigrant and the Cuban American experience. In all, Suárez has covered the entire history of the recent Cuban diaspora, from the economic and political conditions in Cuba leading to emigration in his novel *The Cutter* (1991) to accommodation of immigrants in the new land in his novel *Latin Jazz* (1989) to the short stories in *Welcome to the Oasis* (1992) in which a generation of young Hispanics struggle to integrate themselves into an Americanized culture. In many of his works, Suárez has drawn heavily from his own displacement and migratory angst, as is evident in his autobiographical story *Spared Angola*; his struggle to survive in an Anglo world is not unlike that of Xavier, the antihero in his novel *Going Under* (1996), who in desperation dives into the ocean from Florida's southernmost point to swim back to Cuba. *Kirkus Review* described Suárez as "the leading spokesperson for his Cuban American generation." Suárez holds an MFA in creative writing and is a professor of creative writing at Florida State University. (NK)

Further reading: Virgil Suárez, *Latin Jazz* (New York: William Morrow, 1989), *The Cutter* (New York: Ballantine Books, 1991), *Welcome to the Oasis* (Houston: Arte Público Press, 1992), *Going Under* (Houston: Arte Público Press, 1996), *Spared Angola* (Houston: Arte Público Press, 1998).

Spared Angola

After a twenty-year absence, my grandmother, Donatila, flies from Havana to Miami for a visit. Waiting for her in the crowded and noisy lobby of Miami International Airport, I am struck by memories of my childhood in the arms of this woman who, except for vague moments, is a perfect stranger. To my mother she is Tina of the constant aches and headaches, of the bouts with rheumatism, of the skin disease that spotted her face and neck with pink blotches, of the hair the color of smoke and straw. *Abuela* Tina. Twenty years before this moment caught in the restless humdrum of waiting, this woman about to visit showed me many things: how to feed leftover rice to chickens, tie my shoelaces, brew the kind of watery coffee I like to drink with toasted bread. She kept my behind from feeling the wrath of my father's belt on numerous occasions; she stayed with me while I took a shower in the room by the side of the clapboard house because I was terrified of the bullfrogs that sought the humidity trapped there. She told me stories, most of which I've forgotten, except for the one about the old hag who would wait for a man to come by on horseback to cross the old bridge. The hag would jump on the horse and spook the animal and the rider. The horsemen knew never to look back or risk spooking themselves crazy. "Never look back," she said, "as you cross your bridges." The flight arrives and the waiting intensifies. My mother sinks her nails into my flesh as she holds my hand. My father every so often retrieves a handkerchief from his back pocket (he's never used one) and wipes his forehead and under his eyes. The first few passengers come out the glass doors of Customs and are greeted by relatives who have never forgotten these tired and worn faces, frail bodies. Parents, sisters, brothers, sons, daughters, all now looking thirty-six years older. "Time," my father says, "is a son of a bitch." Finally, I spot my aunt (I have not seen her for as long as I have not seen my grandmother), my father's sister who'd gotten cancer. She is holding on to my grandmother, and I realize my memory has served me better than I am willing to admit. Grandmother Tina looks the same except for the patches of the skin disease which have completely taken over her face. My mother screams and lets go of my hand and runs to the arms of her mother. My father to his sister. I stand back and brace myself. After the hugs and the kisses, my mother says, "There he is! Your grandson, Mamá!" She walks toward me and I find I cannot move, for I cannot believe in movement; I am still stuck in time. She comes toward me. "*¿No te acuerdas de mí?*" she says, her Spanish the necessary tug. I lean into her arms, for she is small and frail, and we stand there in the middle of the lobby. I tell her that I do remember. I remember everything. Slowly now we make our way out of the terminal to the parking lot, into the car, onto the freeway, home to my parents', up the stairs and into the living room of an apartment in which I've spent so very little time. All this time everybody has been talking except me; I've been driving and listening, bewildered by all the catching up. In the living room now, waiting for refreshments, my grandmother comes over to where I sit and she holds my face between her hands. She looks into my eyes. Can I? Can I remember this woman? My grandmother Donatila. She's an apparition, I think, but don't say it. She says, "You must tell me about you, all that the distance has taken from us." I tell her I am happy to see her, after so much time. "*¿Sabes?*" she says. "You are a lucky young man. Your parents did the right thing. When they took you out of Cuba, your parents spared you. Yes, you were spared. Spared Angola."

Going Under

Xavier glanced at the woman, but she was lost in the action on the screen. From where Xavier sat, the screen looked fuzzy, riddled with static.

"Do you know who I am?" the old man asked.

"I have no idea," Xavier said.

"Lázaro, *mi hermano*."

Xavier turned and gazed at the old man. His hair was white, cropped short.

"And I am Cuban. Nothing but Cuban."

Crazy bastard, Xavier mused, *been out in the sun and heat too long. Panhandler. How will I shake this guy?*

"Actually," he said, "I don't exist."

"But you said you were Cuban."

"I am a Parable," he said.

"Right."

"I'm lost here, though."

"I'll give you money," Xavier said, and smiled, "to get you where you want to go."

"Very kind of you," the old man said.

Xavier finished the last of his beer and left the man the change on the bar. He got up and walked toward the front. The woman ignored him. At the entrance, Xavier opened the door and walked out into the sunshine. The dog and shopping cart were gone. Then he turned and looked back in. The bar was empty except for the woman and the life-size San Lázaro keeping the vigil in the back.

I don't know what to believe.

Once in the car, Xavier took off southbound.

Without a map or a compass, Xavier headed south to the southernmost point of the United States, born out of sand and water and palm trees and mangroves. The mangroves merged in a flickering blur of green as he sped. He drove with a great sense of urgency. The easterly salty winds blew inland from an opaque sea and swept and rocked the car as if it had, like a Spanish galleon, great billowing sails. He drove on.

Behind him lay a city of spirits long turned to rubble, dust, grass, and soft earth. He sped down this river of ruin and tar and encrusted possum and armadillo carcasses, and rain. A car became a beige speck on the horizon where the blue of the sky met the ground in the shimmering distance, caught in splendor among the tall weeds and grass.

Motor oil veined the divided asphalt. Cars and trucks hummed and buzzed past. *So many lives destroyed and more on the brink. This is the end of the road that connects North and South with a single thread of loneliness and disillusionment.*

This road leads to the southernmost point . . .

No time left to forget from where the wind blew him like a tumbleweed.

It was hot, even in the air-conditioned car which seemed to be running out of freon. On the way, Xavier kept track of the names of the keys: Tavernier, Isla Morada, Upper and Lower Matacumbe, Long Key, Duck Key, Marathon, Bahia Honda, Big Pine, Ramrod Key . . . what alluring sounds.

The day was bright and sunny. Not a cloud on the magnificent sky. Xavier had never seen with such clarity. "Welcome to the Florida Keys," the signs read.

DON'T SPEED: IT IS BETTER TO ARRIVE LATE THAN NOT TO ARRIVE AT ALL!

In the Keys, life lingered like a slug, beat to a slow beat across nowhere but marshlands and a seven-mile bridge that reached further than the eye could see, past liquor stores, banks, fast-food restaurants, gift shops, tourist traps, sea-shell motels and dead-hour resorts.

Within city limits now, Xavier yearned for a way to be somewhere else.

He drove on.

This was the southernmost point of the mainland United States, and the hum inside the car whispered.

He arrived and parked by the side of the road. He got out of the car and walked over to the spot with the red- and white-painted buoy. The sign told him he had arrived, indeed. This was the end of the road.

The island of his birth lay 90 miles away. Xavier remembered some of his clients saying that they drove down here because on clear, windless nights, one could see the lights from Havana.

At the edge, where the asphalt ran out and turned into rocks and sand and the water started, Xavier stood and gazed at the open sea.

In the water, he swam, taking wide, long strokes. He moved away from the land, leaving all his troubles behind . . .

A voice speaking in a foreign tongue startled him Xavier turned to the voice. It was a man with a camera. The man, fat and dressed in shorts and a T-shirt, nose anointed with sunscreen, sunglasses on, a hat, was telling him something in what sounded like German.

The man *was* a German tourist, down here with his family, trying to take a group portrait, but he couldn't because Xavier was in the way of the background view.

"*Bitte, gehen Sie aus dem Weg!*" the man said.

In the awkward foreignness of the situation, Xavier couldn't understand.

"*Vielen dank.*"

Then, Xavier Cuevas turned to the sea and, clothes and all, dove off and plunged into the water. He went under, opened his eyes to the sting of the salt, held his breath, and swam.

In the pursuit of the unattainable, Xavier Cuevas was swimming home.

Elías Miguel Muñoz (1954–)

The Greatest Performance

At the age of fourteen, Elías Miguel Muñoz was sent from Cuba into exile by his parents. After extensive schooling in the United States, including obtaining a Ph.D. in Hispanic literature, and after pursuing a career as a university professor, Muñoz left academia to dedicate himself to writing. A prolific novelist, poet, essayist, and scriptwriter, Muñoz writes equally well in English as in Spanish. In many of his works, his narrators assume the posture of immigrants adjusting to a new society; in others, he observes the human comedy of acculturation and assimilation by Cuban Americans, as in his novel *Crazy Love*. Muñoz has stated that he has been preoccupied in his writing with the disjunctures—geographical, cultural, linguistic—and the search for identity, homeland, and love. In many of his books, as in *The Greatest Performance*, his characters are caught in ambiguous and undefined social and moral zones. (NK)

Further reading: Elías Miguel Muñoz, *Crazy Love* (Houston: Arte Público Press, 1988), *The Greatest Performance* (Houston: Arte Público Press, 1991), *Brand New Memory* (Houston: Arte Público Press, 1998).

The first couple of months in California I did nothing but bitch and ask that I be sent back to Spain. There was life there, good life. There were good-looking people who spoke pure Spanish and there was gorgeous music and crowded plazas. Here, in Garden Shore (a name that didn't fit the place at all), there were only cars, freeways and solitary houses. Nobody walked. The streets were always empty. How I detested that world. How I still detest it today, whenever I take a good look around me.

California was one enormous cemetery. Its inhabitants seemed ugly and haggard. Its music, *Baby baby baby I love you baby baby baby*, they called that unimaginative crap music. The weather was supposed to be the best on the entire globe. It was hot like Cuba's. Some rain, very little cold in the winter. And it would be easy for Papi to find employment there. Unfortunately not in an office, the way he would've liked to. But in a factory, where he could make lots of money right away. Yes, California was the promised land. Home away from home. Arcadia. But to me it became the vivid representation of hell.

Guess what I'm holding. What do you mean you can't tell? Records, you dope! Can't you see the faces on the covers? Look closely, *chico*. I know it's a super-old photo but try, look at it.

I found out through a Channel 35 commercial that there was a record store in Los Angeles, on Broadway, that sold Spanish music. The place, Discoteca Latina, was owned by a Cuban man, Señor Enrique, and most of his employees were Cuban. Reluctantly, Papi took me to Discoteca Latina one Saturday afternoon. He hated Los Angeles; he still does. He claimed that it was full of Mexican Indians and he hadn't come to the United States to mingle with an inferior race. That's why he tried to get our family located in Orange County, where there were more white people. We couldn't afford the ritzy places like Anaheim and Newport Beach, but Garden Shore—we were told by the Immigration authorities—was clean and moderately affluent, a predominantly middle-class city with a booming aircraft industry. It was far from the Mexican community of Santa Ana, and even further from downtown Los Angeles.

My record albums, yes. Papi complained the whole way to the music store. Why did I have to buy Spanish records, anyway? Weren't we in the United States? I should be studying English and listening to the American hits on the radio, not making him drive his '65 Rambler through those Indian-infested streets of the Angeleno metropolis. If anything happened to us, I'd be held responsible, he warned me. We'd risk our lives just to please me, the little lady, Baby Rosita. Why did I always have to have my way, he asked. Why did I consider myself so special?

I told him that I didn't consider myself special at all, that I was not a spoiled baby. My argument was simple: I hated American music and if I didn't find some way of entertaining myself, of alleviating my Cuban depressions, I'd surely commit suicide, as cut and dried as that. Suicide.

I bought, against his will, two Raphael's, one Massiel, one Karina, and one Marisol. "A fortune!" cried Papi. "Money I sweated for, money I bled for, wasted despicably on records!" Three of the albums turned out to be damaged; they were scratched and you could tell they were used or poorly manufactured. All of them, actually, were of the poorest quality. I was so broken-hearted. Papi drove me back to Discoteca Latina the next weekend, so we could return the damaged merchandise and get our money back. That's what you were supposed to do in America, he said; it was your right. But we were in for a not-so-American surprise.

"Impossible!" screamed one of the Cuban salesladies. "We don't take records back!" Papi was hyperventilating. "Well, you're gonna have to!" he wailed. But the lady was firm, "Don't blame us, blame your daughter! She was the one who ruined the records!" By now three other Cuban cows had shown up. You know the type: huge hips and butt, talcum-white skin, beady eyes heavily made-up, fake pearls and bracelets hanging from every limb, thinly disguised fuzz on the upper lip, the cow type. They were all telling Papi that if he didn't leave, he would have to deal with Mister Enrique himself, the owner, *El Dueño*. "Bring out that gangster! Tell him I wanna see him! Tell him I think he's a thief!"

Señor Enrique answered the call of duty, as was to be expected. He was predictably heavy-set, like his employees, had a black-bean belly and hairy arms, was balding and wore a *guayabera*. They just didn't make them more typical than that, I thought. (Oh, I guess he was missing the Havana cigar.) "How dare you speak that way to these ladies? Have you no manners?" he asked like a true Cuban gentleman. "Gangsters!" responded Papi. Mister Henry turned to one of his employees, the one who had been dealing with my father. "What seems to be the reason for the complaint?" he inquired. "This man!" she spat out her words, "this man came in here claiming that our records are bad! The nerve!" "My money back!" Papi restated his case. "Or I'll burn down your filthy pigsty!"

And just as Papi grabbed Señor Enrique's neck, and just as Señor Enrique's face turned red like a tomato, and just as Papi moved his fist into Señor Enrique's nose, the choking man shouted, "Give him back every penny!" Papi let go of his neck, leaving the clearly visible marks of his fingers on it. "That's more like it," said my father. And Mister Henry, trembling, handed him the money, twenty-five bucks more or less. "Don't you ever come here again!" the owner admonished. "Don't worry," Papi told him as we headed for the door, "I don't do business with pigs!"

On our way home Papi and I reveled in a wonderful fantasy. We'd buy a can of gasoline, we'd go to Discoteca Latina at night, when the store was closed and there was no one inside, and we'd set the whole place on fire. But maybe that would be dangerous, we could get burned ourselves. Better yet: we'd go into the store during the day, wearing disguises so they wouldn't recognize us, and we'd hide a bomb under a stack of albums. We would time the mechanism so it would explode later that night, so that it wouldn't hurt anybody. Just as long as it left the entire rats' nest in ruins.

"*Coño*! They make me feel ashamed to be a Cuban!" Papi kept saying. "*Coño*! Ashamed!"

That picture was taken when I was a Freshman in high school. Can't you tell? The name of the school is right behind me, see it on the wall? GARDEN SHORE HIGH. And here's a picture of my friends; I took this one. That's Leticia and that's Marco and that's Ramón and that's Luisita. The cute guy on the left, that's Francisco. He sort of had the hots for me. No, he wasn't my boyfriend. And I didn't have a girlfriend either! Are you kidding? I was totally and pathetically repressed in those days.

God, I was bored to tears with life in the great North! The world seemed flat and predictable, nothing moved me. No, not even gorgeous blonde Gringas or the prospect of speaking the American language fluently. I was convinced that I had left my heart buried behind, on the island, just like the song said. *Cuando salí de Cuba . . .*

I hated English and refused to speak it unless it was absolutely necessary. Papi used to get so pissed at me. Because, you see, I didn't always feel like translating his gross remarks when he was arguing with some clerk (which happened a lot). He'd tell me that I was stupid and lazy and that what the hell had he brought me to the North for and how did I expect to get ahead in life and get rich or catch a Gringo millionaire if I didn't "espeekee de eengleesh"?

My only source of happiness was the trips Mami and I took to downtown Los Angeles on Sundays to see old movies from Mexico at the Million Dollar Theatre. In that theatre that reeked of urine, I rediscovered, in ecstasy, handfuls of Mexican melodramas that took me right back to Cuba. Incredible, huh, that those dime-store stories and slapsticks featuring María Félix, Arturo de Córdoba, Sara García, Cantinflas, would make me long for Cuba. But they did. And I cried like a baby. Until one day when I got sick and tired of crying and decided not to go to the Million Dollar anymore. I need to stop living off memories the way my parents do, I said to myself. I began to see nostalgia as my enemy. And the images of my homeland that I carried inside as an obstacle for my success.

I stashed my Spanish albums away, my photos, my letters, my Cuban mementos in the closet. And I started to go to American movies with Pedro, because now I thought I was ready to understand them. The first American film I remember enjoying was *Valley of the Dolls*. The first American song I sang was "Aquarius." The first one I detested was "It's Your Thing." And the first American meal I remember savoring with gusto was a Sir Burger Supreme, with cheese. The rest I guess you could say is history.

Do you recognize me? Hard to believe that's me. Excellent polaroid shot, though, don't you think? That picture was taken right after I started high school. I was confused to the marrow. But fashionable. My hair dyed blonde, or rather what I thought was blonde (in reality a strange shade somewhere between red and brown, a barf-inducing color); wearing those dreadful bell-bottoms with the waist line below the hip, and that wide, scaly, worn-out leather belt, I was hot to trot.

The American students, compared to the ones in Madrid, seemed to me like people from another planet: tall, dead-white, distant, incomprehensible. Skinny girls with false eyelashes made of broom straw. Straight hair teased on top in the form of a nest, loose below, long and hanging as if all of a sudden there were a million greasy baby boas coming out of the high nest. Eyeshadow in blue, green, purple or all three colors smeared on their eyelids. Miniskirts that displayed long, feeble legs dressed in grey stockings. Platform shoes that forced them to drag themselves like war tanks.

Among the boys, needless to say, the blonde-boy type with T-shirts and pestilent tennis shoes predominated. The Koreans were gaining a reputation for being smart. Through a dirty trick of fate they had ended up first in Argentina and then in "America," so they spoke fluent Spanish with a Tango accent. There was also a species called Low-riders, drivers of Impalas, Chevrolets and Cadillacs at the level of asphalt. Mean-looking dudes who smoked marijuana and lived in Santa Ana. And the Blacks! How they had warned me at home to stay away from those Negroes! (Which I did, Heaven forbid.)

My GSH gang: The Colombian Leticia, who would one day become a flight attendant for Avianca and vanish into sidereal space. The Korean boy, Ramón (the name the Gauchos gave him), who would become a wealthy and stressed-out restaurateur. Marco the Ecuadorian, who would marry a Cheerleader and work in a factory all his life. Luisita the Cuban, whom I lusted after, today a mother of three and the resigned wife of a Marielito. Of all of them, I miss Francisco the most. Francisco El Mexicano.

Since I couldn't speak English, the school authorities "assigned" me to this Mexican guy, Francisco Valdés, from day one of my freshman year. He was an exemplary student, considering his "language handicap." I was told that he would help me with my classes and serve as my guide, until I felt ready to fend for myself. Whatever grades Francisco got (all of them Bs), I'd get, they informed me.

"Why are they doing this?" I asked Francisco. "Because," he said, amiably, smiling, "they don't know what to do with the recent arrivals."

Cristina García (1958–)

A Matrix Light

Born in Havana, Cuba, in 1958, Cristina García moved with her family to the United States in 1960, a year after the triumph of the Cuban Revolution. Her two novels and short stories are populated by exile characters, haunted by feelings of abandonment, dislocation, and uncertainly toward the future. They are forever in search of a new place to live or simply seeking to return to the one left behind, both difficult to achieve in the midst of semi-dysfunctional, displaced families. *Dreaming in Cuban*, García's much acclaimed first novel, chronicles the lives of three generations of Cuban women on the island and in the United States. Through a combination of first- and third-person narrative, the novel carefully weaves together the contents of twenty-five years' worth of love letters between a Cuban matriarch and the eternal object of her affection. García weaves a sometimes humorous but always poignant tale of abandonment, mediated triumph, and eternal longing. The following excerpt, *A Matrix Light*, portrays Lourdes, daughter of the island matriarch and mother of Pilar, who is struggling to achieve the American Dream by owning and operating a bakery, the Yankee Doodle Bakery. (KDM)

Further reading: Cristina García, *Dreaming in Cuban* (New York: Knopf, 1992), *The Agüero Sisters* (New York: Knopf, 1997), *The Golden Mage: The Prophecies of Seni's World* (Bryn Mawr, Penn.: Books on Web.com, 1998).

Lourdes Puente welcomes the purity, the hollowness of her stomach. It's been a month since she stopped eating, and already she's lost thirty-four pounds. She envisions the muscled walls of her stomach shrinking, contracting, slickly clean from the absence of food and the gallons of springwater she drinks. She feels transparent, as if the hard lines of her hulking form were disintegrating.

It is dawn, an autumn dawn, and Lourdes is walking. She is walking mile after mile, pumping her arms furiously, her eyes fixed determinedly before her. She is walking down Fulton Street in her mauve velour jogging suit, past the shabby May's department store with mannequins from another era, past shuttered shops and bus-stop benches draped with sleeping bums. Lourdes turns and strides past Brooklyn's sooty town hall, past the state supreme court, where the Son of Sam trial will take place. Lourdes can't understand what happened with Son of Sam, only that he exists and that he had a dog that commanded him to kill. His victims were girls with dark flowing hair, young girls like Pilar. But, no matter what Lourdes said, Pilar refused to pin up her hair or hide it under a knitted cap as other girls did. No, Pilar let her hair swing long and loose, courting danger.

Pilar is away at art school in Rhode Island. She won scholarships to Vassar and Barnard, but instead she chose a school of hippies with no future, delicate men with women's lips and a dissembling in their eyes. The thought of her daughter in bed with these men drives Lourdes to despair, to utter repugnance.

Lourdes was a virgin when she married, and very proud of it. The hip-splitting pain, the blood on the conjugal bed were proof of her virtue. She would gladly have hung out her sheets for everyone to see.

Pilar is like her grandmother, disdainful of rules, of religion, of everything meaningful. Neither of them shows respect for anyone, least of all themselves. Pilar is irresponsible, self-centered, a bad seed. How could this have happened?

Lourdes marches down Montague Street, her elbows jutting behind her like pistons. The Greek diner is open and there's a stoop-shouldered man in the back booth eyeing his bacon and eggs. The yolks are too orange, Lourdes thinks. She imagines their sticky thickness coating the old man's throat. It sickens her.

"One coffee, black," she tells the uniformed waiter, then heads for the public telephone. Lourdes dials her daughter's number in Rhode Island. The phone rings four, five, six times before Pilar answers sleepily.

"I know someone is there with you," Lourdes rasps. "Don't lie to me."

"Mom, not again. Please."

"Tell me his name!" Lourdes squeezes the words our between her teeth. "Whore! Tell me his name!"

"What are you talking about? Mom, it's five in the morning. Just leave me alone, okay?"

"I called you last night and you weren't in."

"I was out."

"Out where? To your lover's bed?"

"Out for a pastrami sandwich."

"Liar! You never eat pastrami!"

"I'm hanging up now, Mom. Nice talking to you, too."

Lourdes slaps two quarters on the counter and leaves the coffee steaming in its thick white mug. She hasn't had relations with Rufino since her father died. It's as if another woman had possessed her in those days, a whore, a life-craving whore who fed on her husband's nauseating clots of yellowish milk.

Lourdes lifts one arm, then the other to her face, sniffing them suspiciously for the scent of grease and toast.

The smell of food repels her. She can't even look at it without her mouth filling with the acrid saliva that precedes vomiting. These days, it's nearly impossible to endure even her own bakeries—the wormy curves of the buttery croissants, the gluey honey buns with fat pecans trapped like roaches in the cinnamon crevices.

Lourdes did not plan to stop eating. It just happened, like the time she gained 118 pounds in the days her father was dying. This time, though, Lourdes longs for a profound emptiness, to be clean and hollow as a flute.

She advances toward the Brooklyn Promenade. The abandoned shipyards display their corrugated roofs like infected scars. The East River, meeting the Hudson near its mouth, is quiet and motionless as the mist. On the other side of the river, the towers of Wall Street reach arrogantly toward the sky. Lourdes paces the quarter-mile-long esplanade eight times. A jogger runs by with a tawny Great Dane at his side. Cars hum on the highway below her, headed for Queens.

There is a moment of each dawn that appears disguised as dusk, Lourdes decides, and for that brief moment the day neither begins nor ends.

Lourdes has lost eighty-two pounds. She is drinking liquid protein now, a bluish fluid that comes in tubes like astronaut food. It tastes of chemicals. Lourdes rides her new Sears exercise bicycle until sparks fly from the wheels. She tacks up a full-color road map of the United States in her bedroom and charts her mileage daily with a green felt marker. Her goal is to ride to San Francisco by Thanksgiving, when her daughter will return home from school. Lourdes pedals and sweats, pedals and sweats until she pictures rivulets of fat, like the yellow liquid that pours from roasting chickens and turkeys, oozing from her pores as she rides through Nebraska.

Jorge del Pino is concerned about his daughter, but Lourdes insists that nothing is wrong. Her father visits her regularly at twilight, on her evening walks home from the bakery, and whispers to her through the oak and maple trees. His words flutter at her neck like a baby's lacy breath.

They discuss many topics: the worsening crime on New York City's streets; the demise of the Mets since their glory seasons in '69 and '73; day-to-day matters of the bakery. It was her father who had advised Lourdes to open a second pastry shop.

"Put your name on the sign, too, *hija*, so they know what we Cubans are up to, that we're not all Puerto Ricans," Jorge del Pino had insisted.

Lourdes ordered custom-made signs for her bakeries in red, white, and blue with her name printed at the bottom right-hand corner: LOURDES PUENTE, PROPRIETOR. She particularly liked the sound of the last word, the way the "r"'s rolled in her mouth, the explosion of "p"'s. Lourdes felt a spiritual link to American moguls, to the immortality of men like Irénée du Pont, whose Varadero Beach mansion on the north coast of Cuba she had once visited. She envisioned a chain of Yankee Doodle bakeries stretching across America to St. Louis, Dallas, Los Angeles, her apple pies and cupcakes on main streets and in suburban shopping malls everywhere.

Each store would bear her name, her legacy: LOURDES PUENTE, PROPRIETOR.

Above all, Lourdes and her father continue to denounce the Communist threat to America. Every day they grow more convinced that the dearth of bad news about Cuba is a conspiracy by the leftist media to keep international support for El Líder strong. Why can't the Americans see the Communists in their own backyards, in their universities, bending the malleable minds of the young? The Democrats are to blame, the Democrats and those lying, two-timing Kennedys. What America needs, Lourdes and her father agree, is another Joe McCarthy to set things right again. *He* would never have abandoned them at the Bay of Pigs.

"Why don't you go down and report on Cuba's prisons?" Lourdes taunted the journalists who questioned her last year about the opening-day fracas at the second Yankee Doodle Bakery. "Why are you wasting your time with me?"

Lourdes hadn't approved of Pilar's painting, not at all, but she wouldn't tolerate people telling her what to do on her own property.

"That's how it began in Cuba," Lourdes's father whispered hoarsely through the trees, counseling her. "You must stop the cancer at your front door."

After Pilar left for college, Lourdes stared at her daughter's painting every night before she walked home. If Pilar hadn't put in the safety pin and the bugs in the air, the painting would be almost pretty. Those bugs ruined the background. Without the bugs, the background was a nice blue, a respectable shimmering blue.

Why did Pilar always have to go too far? Lourdes is convinced it is something pathological, something her daughter inherited from her Abuela Celia.

It is Thanksgiving Day. Lourdes has lost 118 pounds. Her metamorphosis is complete. She will eat today for the first time in months. The aroma of food is appealing again, but Lourdes is afraid of its temptations, of straying too far from the blue liquid, from the pitchers of cleansing ice water. There is a purity within her, a careful enzymatic balance she does not wish to disturb.

The day before yesterday, Lourdes bought a red-and-black size-six Chanel suit with gold coin buttons. "You're so lucky you can wear anything!" the salesgirl at Lord & Taylor's had complimented her as she swiveled this way and that before the dressing-room mirror. Lourdes spent a week's profits on the suit. It was worth it, though, to see Pilar's astonishment at her weight loss.

"My God!" Pilar exclaims as she walks through the front door of the warehouse and stares at the fraction of her mother before her. "How did you do it?"

Lourdes beams.

"She starved herself," Rufino interjects irritably. He's wearing a toque like a fat white carnation on his head. Lourdes hushes him with a wave of her newly slender hand.

"I just made up my mind to do it. Willpower. Willpower goes a long way toward getting what you want, Pilar."

Her daughter's face registers suspicion, as if Lourdes is going to launch into a lecture. But Lourdes has nothing of the sort in mind. She ushers her daughter to the table, which is set with hand-painted china and an autumn-leaves centerpiece.

"Your father has been learning to cook since I stopped eating," Lourdes says. "He's been in the kitchen since Sunday, preparing everything."

"Are you going to eat today, Mom?"

"Just a few bites. The doctor says I have to start weaning myself back on food. But if it were up to me, I'd never eat again. I feel pure, absolutely clean. And I have more energy than ever before."

Lourdes begins reminiscing about the instant foods she made when she first came to New York. The mashed potatoes she whipped up from water and ashen powder, the chicken legs she shook in bags of spicy bread crumbs then baked at 350 degrees, the frozen carrots she boiled and served with imitation butter. But soon the potatoes and the chicken and the carrots had all tasted the same to her, blanched and waxen and gray.

"I think migration scrambles the appetite," Pilar says, helping herself to a candied yam. "I may move back to Cuba someday and decide to eat nothing but codfish and chocolate."

Lourdes stares hard at her daughter. She wants to say that nobody but a degenerate would want to move back to that island-prison. But she doesn't. It's a holiday and everyone is supposed to be happy. Instead, Lourdes turns her attention to a sliver of turkey on her plate. She tastes a small chunk. It's juicy and salty and goes straight to her veins. She decides to have another piece.

In a moment her mouth is moving feverishly, like a terrible furnace. She stokes it with more hunks of turkey and whole candied yams. Lourdes helps herself to a mound of creamed spinach, dabbing it with a quickly diminishing loaf of sourdough. The leek-and-mustard pie, with its hint of chives, is next.

"*Mi cielo*, you really outdid yourself!" Lourdes praises her husband between mouthfuls.

For dessert, there's a rhubarb-apple betty topped with cinnamon crème anglaise. Lourdes devours every last morsel.

The next morning, Lourdes scours the newspapers for calamities as she dunks sticky buns into her *café con leche*. A twin-engine plane crashed in the umber folds of the Adirondacks. An earthquake in rural China buried thousands in their homes. In the Bronx, a fire consumed a straight-A student and her baby brother, asleep in his crib. There's a photograph of their mother on the front page, ravaged by loss. She'd only gone to the corner store for a pack of cigarettes.

Lourdes grieves for these victims as if they were beloved relatives. Each calamity makes Lourdes feel her own sorrow, keeps her own pain fresh.

Pilar suggests they go to an exhibit at the Frick Museum, so Lourdes wriggles into her Chanel suit, the gold-coin buttons already straining across her middle, and they take the subway to Manhattan. On Fifth Avenue, Lourdes stops to buy hot dogs (with mustard, relish, sauerkraut, fried onions, and ketchup), two chocolate cream sodas, a potato knish, lamb shish kebabs with more onions, a soft pretzel, and a cup of San Marino cherry ice. Lourdes eats, eats, eats, like a Hindu goddess with eight arms, eats, eats, eats, as if famine were imminent.

Inside the museum, the paintings all look alike to Lourdes, smeared and dull. Her daughter guides her to an indoor courtyard, suffused with winter light. They settle on a concrete bench by the reflecting pool. Lourdes is mesmerized by the greenish water, by the sad, sputtering fountain, and a wound inside her reopens. She remembers what the doctors in Cuba had told her. That the baby inside her had died. That they'd have to inject her with a saline solution to expel her baby's remains. That she would have no more children.

Lourdes sees the face of her unborn child, pale and blank as an egg, buoyed by the fountain waters. Her child calls to her, waves a bare little branch in greeting. Lourdes fills her heart to bursting with the sight of him. She reaches out and calls his name, but he disappears before she can rescue him.

PART IV

The Literature of Exile

CHAPTER 16

Struggle for Spanish-American Independence

"The Friend of Men"

On Behalf of Mankind: To All the Inhabitants of the Islands and the Vast Continent of Spanish America

The following is an excerpt from a book, *On Behalf of Mankind . . .*, published under the pseudonym of El Amigo de los Hombres (The Friend of Men) in Philadelphia in 1812, two years after the Mexican declaration of independence by Father Miguel Hidalgo y Costilla. Its argument and tone are typical of the polemics conducted through Hispanic newspapers and other publications in the United States which discussed the need for the colonies of Spain to liberate themselves and adapt the U.S. Constitution and the structure of the American Republic to the as yet to be independent nations of Spanish America. The author's appeal to America in the text was the common usage of the time in Spanish to signify all the countries of the New World, as well as, more specifically, the colonies of Spanish America. The pseudonym was necessary because, at this date, the author was most certainly a Spanish citizen and subject to reprisals for his revolutionary ideas. Like much of the literature of exile, *On Behalf of Mankind* was meant to be smuggled into the Spanish colonies, in addition to challenging the editorial published in *The Spaniard* newspaper. The treatise was printed by early American printer Joseph Blockhurst, who was most likely paid by the author to issue the book. (NK)

Further reading: El Amigo de los Hombres, *A todos los que habitan las islas y el vasto continente de la América Española* (Philadelphia: Imprenta de José Blocquerst, 1812).

Trans.: TEW

People of the Americas: I have read number 16 of the newspaper, *The Spaniard*, and the work written by Mr. Alvaro Flórez de Estrada about the affairs of America and the means of reconciling her with the Spanish Peninsular Government. I am scandalized to see these two men, endowed with sufficient culture and steadfast character, prostitute themselves to the selfish and torturous designs of ministerial politics, declare themselves supporters of the Spanish government on the cliffs of the very powerful and proud Albion (England), and insult the rights and the high dignity of all the nations of the New World. *The Spaniard* has not had the shame to confess that its pen wavers in the same way political interests and concurrences do. And Flórez Estrada, who has proclaimed with such enthusiasm the inviolable and primary freedom of nations, contradicts and degrades himself now by contributing to the dreadful plans of tyranny. I am going to extract the principle propositions of their writings. Prepare yourselves to hear the most daring and absurd paradoxes.

Proposition I. The new American Governments have usurped the authority and made reforms and constitutions without relying on the people. There is no legitimate representation in the governments, nor is there any work undertaken that is willed by the general public.

Proposition II. Spanish America cannot be organized into independent states, imitating the Anglo American nation, because conditions there are absolutely different and will necessarily encourage her ruin.

Proposition III. Spanish America has recognized sovereignty in Ferdinand VII of the House of Bourbon, and in his absence before the Spanish governments that have successively represented him. Therefore, Spanish America cannot separate itself from this submission without violating the sanctity of an oath and feeling the loss of the government's most solemn favor.

Proposition IV. Spanish America obligated herself to support the Mother Country in the war against the French, and it would be an abomination to desist from this glorious obligation and abandon her brothers, the European Spaniards, to the claws of the tyrant.

Proposition V. Spanish America should assist Spain, even if only out of gratitude.

Proposition VI. Lastly, Spanish America should entrust herself to the generous embrace of the English Government, and trust that the English government will ensure an amicable and reasonable arrangement with the Spanish Peninsular Government.

An Impartial Reply to These Propositions

To the first proposition. The new Governments of America have reassumed sovereign authority under the same law as the governments of the Peninsula. The new American governments have called together the people of their provinces to make known the state of affairs and remitted to their examination and deliberation the party and the measures deemed necessary in the present crisis. The people of America elected their representatives in all freedom, and authorized all their actions and rights so the representatives would be reminded of that which would be most precipitous to the people's happiness and enact it. The people of the Americas announced all around their desire to be independent by way of a unanimous vote, decided by the general will. Note the authorization of the Congresses of Caracas, Buenos Aires, Santa Fe, etc. I doubt there has been or could ever be any authorization more solemn or more legitimate. To deny the people, in any part of the universe, the ability to attend to their preservation and improve their fate by adopting the means they consider most opportune is to blaspheme the sacred dogmas of nature, to offend the reason and dignity of man, to confound all principles, and to proclaim with horrid impudence the damned systems of tyranny. To charge as rebels and usurpers the first men who conceived the project of valiantly breaking their brother's chains and overthrowing and banishing insolent despotism is to condemn the most beautiful act of virtue and heroism. Anyone in these cases has the authority to protest and to depose tyrants and also to impede anarchy by taking the government reigns for a time and defending the liberty and rights of the entire union, until the people can be united and freely decide their destiny. May there be immortal glory for those who have the courage for such arduous and sublime purposes! In this same manner, in Greece, Rome, Switzerland, Holland, and English America, those who established liberty and brilliant prosperity in each of these nations were successful in their respective epochs.

The reaction to fight and overthrow tyranny can never be undertaken on the advice of the masses: it is indispensable that it always be the result of the calculations and generous efforts of certain individuals who sacrifice themselves for the good of their brothers and the glory of their country. There is no place in politics, or even in nature, for any other means of doing away with tyrants and reestablishing the freedom of the people. So then, everything that the Spanish publicists and writers say against these American regenerators comes to be nonsensical and absurd. The charges mounted against these celebrated men also indict, from the beginning of time until the present epoch, all the heroes who have been immortalized for recovering the independence and precious rights of their countries.

To the second proposition. The impossibility declared by the salaried declaimers from the ministerial party, or from abroad, confounds reason. To labor for, and support her independence, Spanish America has in her lap more fortunate means and resources that are much more powerful than those which the Anglo Americans had in a poor, ungrateful, deserted, and pillaged country. In order to know this, it is sufficient to have common sense and to know the physical and political geography of the American hemisphere. And because of this, I can do nothing less than laugh at the paradoxes and exaggerated false reasoning on the part of the writers to whom I am responding.

There is not one European power, except the government of Cadiz, that could have its interests in opposition to the liberty and independence of America. And if by misfortune, misguided politics, or the overly blind ambition of one savage government, they were to try to impede political regeneration in this part of the world, I would predict failure; because love of liberty is prolific in prodigies, and everything yields to their indefatigable and generous efforts. The history of all the ages and all nations is full of such admirable and immutable examples that should forever discourage the schemers of tyrannies.

The blacks and mulattos will always be a terrible obstacle to American Independence. (The superficial publicists say they are only judgmental of the party's petty ideas and the example of the French side of the island of Santo Domingo.) I do not agree with the basis for this prophecy. Firstly, there are only large numbers of slaves and people of color on the islands of Cuba and Puerto Rico, in Santo Domingo, the Spanish part of Hispaniola, in Caracas, and in the capital of Peru. But there are less than what has been exaggerated; and even on the island of Cuba, where they are most abundant, their numbers are lower than the number of whites. By the calculations of the Baron Von Humboldt, for each 100 inhabitants there are 54 whites and 46 colored; subtracting from this last figure the number who were born to free parents, who identify with the purposes and interests of whites, the superiority of the whites is evident.

Secondly, the bad politics of freeing the blacks all at once was, among things, what produced the frightening disasters on the island of Santo Domingo; secure measures to avoid such trouble are not unavailable or absent in the foresight of human understanding. It would be ridiculous to maintain that only the agents of a government, who reside 1,600 leagues away, can preserve the peace and good order among America's whites and blacks, and that this ability cannot be entrusted to any of America's natives. Lastly, with the dangers known, it is easy to forestall them and combine measures that will render them impossible. This is one of the points that should occupy the more serious and profound attention of the regenerators of America, and it can be expected that the pace of events will confound all the designs of their enemies.

To the example of the catastrophes that came about in the French part of Santo Domingo, one can compare the case of Roman slaves, who were known to be honest and, with the precious gift of civil liberty, conveniently were, for a long time, the most robust force in the eminent Republic that ruled the universe. Try to make men of all classes and conditions happy. Learn how to dole out goodness, distributing it impartially and with generous vigilance. Do not fear that the fruit of your noble and benevolent efforts will spoil.

It is said that antipathy and conflict among the races will be the ruin of Spanish America if she abandons the government of Cadiz and becomes independent.

It seems that this government, confined to a corner of the Spanish Peninsula, preserves for itself exclusively a miraculous talisman, giving it knowledge of everything and power over everything from this obscure corner, while the inhabitants of the vast and rich lands of the New World are capable of nothing. I know, indeed, that opposition actually exists between the dark-skinned and the blacks in the countries where they are populous, but I understand also that it is easier to neutralize the effect of these jealousies, or anti-patriotism, and take very useful advantage of what seems to be a dismal evil. The blacks aspire to the esteem of the whites, they want to be mistaken for them and in the second or third generation they are already tied together by blood and interests in such a way that they form one caste with the whites. For this reason the influence of the dark-skinned is null, and if the appropriate measures are taken with foresight, their physical and moral power will not be a threat.

The opposition between the European Spaniards and the Spanish Americans is born from other causes that politics and justice should quickly dissipate and suppress. The European Spaniards had a decided pre-eminence over the Spanish Americans and displayed unbearable vanity and pride, believing themselves to be a superior species to that of the Americans. The Spaniards possessed all the positions of honor and profitable businesses in America. The spectators and businessmen were the most insatiable and unpatriotic monopolists who drank the Americans' blood and, with a fierce look colored with satisfaction, watched them perish. The Viceroys and agents of the Spanish government authorized and defended these horrors, because it suited them to have the children of the Americas humbled and insignificant. So, then, the above mentioned opposition is not unusual: more so, it will end the minute the causes that produced it end. It will end when the Europeans see themselves at the same level as the

Americans, and when they feel obliged to brother their interests, existence, rights and respect with the Americans. Passions lose their individual animosity when legislation is judicious and the Government impartial, efficient and austere. Guided by love for the homeland and love for humanity—and with sweet and steady harmony—they will contribute to the well-being of the entire union, because in it the well-being of each individual is affirmed.

To the third proposition. The Viceroys and Spanish Authorities in America, and not their people, have recognized the sovereignty of Ferdinand the VII and the precarious and monstrous governments that have represented him since his absence from the Peninsula. Yes, violence had the Americans enslaved and unable, at the time, to manifest their feelings and votes. Who can deny this truth, which is as incontestable as it is notorious for everyone? Moreover, when the Americans pledge their obedience freely and with full knowledge, who can deny that these commitments are not irrevocable? Who can deny that they should be rescinded and canceled when it becomes known that they are in opposition to the rights and happiness of the people, and when the opportunity and means to do so arises? Is this not the same course of action that the Spaniards on the peninsula have taken, and that which has been confirmed by all the nations of the world that have had enough courage and virtue to overthrow obscene and dismal despotism and erect on its ruins the majestic work of freedom? In all cases, the welfare of the people is the supreme law and the only sacred one; all pacts or contracts that offend it are null by nature. No one can renounce the rights that are afforded him by the social contract and imprescriptible for his species, nor permit that these rights be taken away, as it is not possible to want that which is contrary to one's well being. The general will is necessarily decided by the greatest conformity of common interests, and by that which enables all the members of the union to be closest to the possession of their freedom and primary rights. Therefore, the people could not approve a fate of slavery, its degradation, unhappiness and opprobrium. Therefore, the people should have spoken out against the violence, broken the chains, and prepared themselves for the most fortunate destiny possible.

To the fourth proposition. The Viceroys, Governors, and Spanish authorities in America are the ones who seem to have committed to this obligation and not the Americans, because the general will could not be expressed freely under the tyrannical yoke, as I have demonstrated in the previous response. Despite this, if the Government of Cadiz does not harass the Americans with the most horrid ferociousness and vilest methods, and if it does not squander (as it has done thus far) America's vast treasures without compensating her, the Americans will be generous and continue helping their brothers in Spain.

To the fifth proposition. America owes Spain the same gratitude that the innocent slaves owe those who, armed with destructive weapons, stripped them of their freedom and burdened them with heavy and humiliating chains; the same debt that those who enjoyed a wealthy estate in peace owe those from which it was stolen, and who were not satisfied with this and have oppressed them more and more, considering them to be nothing more than animals. Nevertheless, the Americans would have forgotten three centuries of despotism, violence, theft, and other evils, only implicating the Spanish government, if the new despots, who have usurped Peninsular authority since the revolution, had not proceeded contrary to the interests of the Americans, and in offense to reason and humanity, erecting hateful and bloody barriers between the Spaniards of Europe and those of America. The Americans would be generous, I repeat, and would help those on the Peninsula with their terrible and unjust struggle, but everything is rendered impossible by the blind and atrocious conduct of the Government of Cadiz. This government is the one that should answer to the Spanish nation and the entire universe about this and other dreadful evils, which have been and continue to be voluntary. America needs everything now to strengthen and defend her independence against this same government and against all of those that intend to harass her.

To the sixth proposition. The English government's intervention is useless, as America is firmly resolved to support and defend the freedom and independence that she has recovered, and as her noble inhabitants have all sworn to perish, swathed in glory, in defense of their just rights before submitting to Spain again, or to any other world Power. The Spanish Americans now do not have to wait or to fear the European Spaniards. The Spanish Americans do not recognize or intend to recognize the Spanish Government, nor will they accept its offers under any circumstances or for any reason. When the Spanish nation finds itself free of its domestic and foreign tyrants, and when it forms a consolidated power worthy of figuring in the same political class as other civilized nations, then the independent states of America will recognize her and allow her diplomatic and trade relations according to natural law and under the same rights extended to all the other powers. Before then, there is nothing to be discussed or settled with the Spanish Government.

This simple and definite exposition, that is in agreement with the general will of Spanish Americans, serves ultimately as a response to that which one can read in the Philadelphia gazette, *La Aurora*, on the fifth of this month, relative to the appointment of English commissioners for the reconciliation of America. This news is said to be copied from the *Morning Chronicle*, and we cannot believe that it is true. Above all, the sacred interest of the freedom and happiness of the Americans demands that not one of these commissioners be allowed entry to her ports, because it would be a way to introduce the incendiary spirit of the Civil War and to mine the most beautiful and glorious foundations of the political regeneration of America. Have constancy and foresight, Americans! This is about imposing upon you the infamous yoke of slavery. Consider as your enemy all those who speak to you about reconciliation with, or consideration towards the proud and weak tyrants who claim to subjugate Columbus' entire hemisphere from Cadiz. Be wary of their offers—even the most liberal and generous ones—that inspire you to favor the Spanish government, or the foreign power; the means used in this case of ministerial, political Machiavellianism cannot be unknown to you. Noble magistrates and leaders who hold in your hands the fate of 16 million inhabitants—the fate of all the people of Spanish America—you should remember the maxim, *Timeo danaos y dona ferentes.* Protect the American people from the tricks and hateful plans that are designed to snatch the glory and treasured well-being that you have begun to enjoy. This well-being is the purest and most valuable of which the human species is capable; but great sacrifices and steady vigilance are needed to assure it. Do not lessen the esteem you have begun to receive and that should make eternal your names in the most brilliant splendors of history. I hope that you will execute it in this way, and soon I can laugh about the fiction and miserable stories that the ministerial intrigue will cultivate to discredit you and to put in doubt the firm resolution and grandiose efforts of the regenerated Americas. Coro and Maracaibo, the only points on the soil of the Venezuelan confederation that obey the tyrant in Puerto Rico, soon will open their doors to the Valencian re-conquerors and will join together, with great pleasure, with their brothers. On the walls of Montevideo they should fly the victory flags of the liberators of the Argentine people. And shortly, from one sea to another, crowned in triumph and delicious and pure peace, the glory of American independence for the entire Continent that was subjected to the European Spanish tyranny will be heard. I do not doubt that the news will spread to the islands, and that once and for all the prestige that still dazzles mean-spirited people and the agents of the Government of Cadiz or foreigners, will dissipate. I conclude, then, exhorting you to carry forward with insurmountable firmness so glorious an undertaking, because this is the most energetic and convincing means to respond to and confuse the Spanish newspapers and the foreigners who dedicate their pens to the detestable purposes of violence and despotism.

José Alvarez de Toledo y Dubois (1779–1858)

Mexicans: Signaled by Providence

Born in Havana, Cuba, on May 14, 1779, José Alvarez de Toledo y Dubois received a naval education in Cádiz and served briefly in the Spanish navy before being elected a representative from Santo Domingo to the Cortes (parliament) at Cádiz in 1810. During Alvarez de Toledo's formative years, Europe and the Americas underwent tumultuous and dramatic change. The independence of the United States, the French revolution, the rise of Napoleon, the Haitian revolution, and the French invasion of Spain helped spark independence movements throughout Latin America, starting with Mexico in 1810. As a member of the Spanish Cortes, Alvarez de Toledo expressed sympathy for Latin American independence and fled to the United States where he gained support from Secretary of State James Monroe to support independence activities in Cuba and Mexico. Alvarez de Toledo was a prolific writer, publishing numerous works in the United States aimed at inciting revolution in Mexico and the Americas. He was also one of the parties responsible for publishing the first newspapers in Texas. His most ambitious endeavor was participating with Mexican insurgent José Bernardo Gutiérrez de Lara in a U.S.-supported filibustering invasion of Texas in 1813. After the invading force took San Antonio, Alvarez de Toledo took command of the army, but was defeated by Spanish forces shortly thereafter. In 1816 he abandoned his insurgent activities, sought reconciliation with Spain, and worked with the Spanish government against the insurgents. He returned to Spain, where he served as an advisor to King Ferdinand VII and held several diplomatic posts. He died in Paris on April 16, 1858. The following political tract authored by Alvarez de Toledo and his insurgent colleague, José Bernardo Gutiérrez, in Philadelphia in 1811 reflects the Republican ideas and pro-U.S. attitudes popular among many Latin American insurgents of the period. (GP)

Further reading: José Alvarez de Toledo y Dubois, *Manifiesto ó satisfacción pundonorosa: Á todos los buenos españoles europeos, y á todos los pueblos de la América, por un diputado de las Cortes reunidas en Cádiz* ([Philadelphia], [1811]), *Contestación á la carta del Indio Patriota, con algunas reflexiones sobre el diálogo—entre el Entusiasta Liberal, y el Filósofo Rancio—y sobre las notas anonymas con que ha salido reimpreso el Manifiesto de dn. José Alvarez de Toledo* (Philadelphia: A. J. Blocquerst, 1812).

Trans.: TEW

Mexicans: signaled by Providence, the time has arrived for you to throw off the barbaric and shameful yoke with which the most insolent despotism has ignominiously oppressed you for 300 years. Now, the government of Cadiz wants to obligate you to continue to carry the same chains with which you were imprisoned by the Kings of Spain, who did not have more authority over you than that which you afforded them in exchange for being governed. Consequently, from the exact moment in which this repository of your power disappeared; or since you, for lack of justice, have been governed for said time by the most heedless tyranny; or since, by common agreement you wished to change the entire system and freely establish a new government and new workers to improve your miserable destiny, you can do so without there being any authority on earth that can legally impede it.

Mexicans: those of you who still live in fear that royal authority flows from Heaven, reflect upon how before kings were known, men existed and they existed under a more legitimate government. Who would doubt for one second that the Almighty, because of his infinite charity, authorized each man in particular, and all in general, with the necessary freedom and with enough reason to make use of that liberty; and in the same way allowed each society to select and form the type of government that seems most appropriate to its interests, preservation and customs; and located sovereignty in one or more persons—however it best suits them—with the purpose of limiting authority from which the people could never separate themselves, and that which no one could usurp from them lawfully. The desire to prove that God has prescribed a norm of government to which he subjected all men, as the superstitious claim and more so the tyrants and monopolists of Cadiz, is the most absurd, most blasphemous thing that has been said in politics. It is a ridiculous and crude pretense, and he who commits it does not know history nor does he know how to make use of reason. Until now, no type of government has been found whose establishment comes to us from God. To the contrary, we are sure by way of documentation that all forms of government known to us until now are entirely the work of men, without the All Powerful Divinity having any part other than to let them function freely. And from this we should infer that all forms of government are compatible with the ends intended by the Heavenly Father.

The Monarchic government is so praised, and is so recommended to as by the Sultans of Cadiz as an admirable work, because in it they include the religion that we profess. We know from the books of the Sacred Scripture that the ancient patriarchs never had nor aspired to royal authority: not by law and not by force; on the contrary, the beginnings and the continuation of royal power were incompatible with that of the patriarchs, and nobody denies the opposition that exists between these two powers. The first men left their children in complete freedom among themselves and with equal rights to procure for themselves their own particular sustenance and that of their entire families in a way that was easier for them, less dangerous and more convenient. It was these same men who were enjoying this liberty and happiness, while only a small number could agree on ideas and interests, that later multiplied; they began to split up, passions began to rise, and they were fearful one of the other. In this state, they understood the need to find means to avoid the disorder that reigned among them and to prevent that which henceforth would occur. They decided to join together—all the families that found it fitting to agree on ideas—to form one solitary body, or a small nation, with the goal of establishing a system that would proportion in the best way possible their happiness and comforts, and that at the same time would protect them from the attempts that could be made against them and their children in the future. And see here the way each individual began to contribute the real right he had to govern himself; and see at the same time the way sovereignty began to take shape, which can never be present except in the sum total of the individual or real rights that each one has received from the Almighty, so that nobody can usurp from another this sacred right—inclining them to contradict the ideas that directly protect their preservation and natural freedom—without committing a murder equal to that which a man armed with a dagger commits when he takes from another his life to steal his riches. All that is to force men to labor against their interests, that is what is called tyranny . . . despotism, etc. That is exactly what the Kings of Spain have done with you Mexicans, and it is what four miserable bandits want to continue exercising from Cadiz with even greater disregard for your rights and with more bias against your interests. More so, back to the point, I say that the first men who distinguished themselves most by their intelligence, moderation, knowledge, good habits, and bravery, were the first elected to rule, and the ones who worked more than ever for the benefit of the union, the establishment of the government, the improvements and reforms, and took advantage of human understanding. Those who were weak and cowardly, and unaware of the feelings and behaviors needed to contribute to the general well-being and to the most upstanding justice were subject to the first men by the unanimous will of the entire union.

From all of this followed that the first governments formed by mankind were founded on the most exact and distributive justice, on prudence and moderation; and see here the cause or origin from whence spring forth the terms "Government," "Republic," or "legitimate Kingdom." The first rules that these governments established through consensus and the general will of the entire alliance are what today we call Constitutional Laws of the Monarchy, of the Republic, etc. . . . Under this system of government, that is to say in which individuals reserve the sacred right to concur freely in the formation of the law that is to govern them, is where virtue, knowledge and love for the homeland have shined brighter, because it is where the sum of individual interests proportionally cultivates or augments the common interest and, consequently, the power of the entire union. Those governments that are not subject to the interests and whims of one solitary man are the ones that know how to maintain the precious and sweet goodness of peace for many more years, and are at the same time the ones more likely to go to war in defense of their rights in the way Rome, Holland, Switzerland and the United States of America have done. On the contrary, the governments like those most recently founded in Spain, including the one that currently exists in Cadiz—founded on the most extreme violence, on the most contradictory principles, and on the most corrupt injustice—are the ones that have always had the detestable and horrible name of tyrannies. In order to sustain themselves, these Mandarins, and agents of a similar government, have seen themselves in the cruel necessity of protecting the mob, favoring vices, and employing cunning meddlers in the prejudice and dishonor of men deserving of merit and justice; in this way, reducing those who had the bad luck to live under said governments to opprobrium, degradation and any number of calamities. These have been and are seen with horror and disgust by sensitive and judicious men, and more than anything, by the liberal, honest governments founded upon the majestic right of equality. I think I have proven sufficiently that God has not established with preference or exclusion any type of government, with the consequent result being that men can choose freely that which most agrees with their interests, security and preservation. With this surmised, and that the Almighty has nothing to do with anything, and that men can freely make use of the right that this same Author has conferred upon them, MEXICANS, I ask you: What is it that you expect from the government of Cadiz, dominated by foreigners and the monopolists of that center? Americans, in particular those who inhabit the Islands, believe that if you do not take care of yourselves, if you abandon your interests and security, if you do not in a timely fashion provide the means to shelter yourselves from the attempts of some ambitious European Power, that perhaps (and not doubting the government of Cadiz is working underhandedly to turn you over to said Power) you will pass without a doubt to another boss who will continue enslaving you with the same or worse tyranny than the Sultans of Spain. With this surmised, and also that it simply is the law of nature and not of the Divine as the Court in Cadiz pretends, why not make use of this same right to form an intelligent and liberal government that will assure your fate and that of your future generations? Are you not moved, Islanders and Mexicans, by the peaceful happiness that Venezuela, Santa Fe, Buenos Aires, Chile, and Peru enjoy, and that which Lima will soon enjoy? I advise you, noble children of the famous Montezuma, not to sheathe your swords until order has been re-established and your entire country been granted freedom. And you, Generals, keep in mind that you will not achieve the high responsibility that the people have entrusted to you unless you contribute by all means possible to the establishment of a provisional government, without which neither your efforts and sacrifices, nor the precious American blood spilled with such heroism and abundance on the battle fields will have the desired effect. What is it that can obstruct the establishment of such a government? I do not know anything more simple: issue from the Generals an order for the Municipalities of towns, villages and cities that are under their jurisdiction to elect a leader in whom the circumstances concur of being of American culture, liberal ideas, and a lover of his homeland's freedom. These representatives, that is how they should be called, should assemble at the safest place, and gathered together all, you should summarize the sovereignty of the people you represent, and in the interim, they cannot freely appoint representatives and establish legitimate government. The provisionally appointed government should continue consolidating itself a little at a time, as the armies advance; then, some other vocal folks and however many Church chapters can be gathered should join the governing assembly. This is the true path that should lead you to the temple of immortality and glory. In this way, that gang of tyrants will very soon disappear and your brothers immediately will join with the new government . . . with peace . . . with the sweet harmony that always reigns among true Republicans. In this way I repeat, my dear countrymen, those days of the horror, the desolation with which the new seat of government has been cloaked in mourning, and the fear that the opulent kingdom of Mexico will disappear. I await not long from now the glorious day in which each one of you, like another Cato, will address the grand palace and ask: What is the name of the monster who has sacrificed so many noble Republicans? Venegas, they will respond! Even though I surely hope that from now forward you will not have to say the likes of: Has Venegas sacrificed them? Does Venegas still exist? No, he will no longer exist if you follow my advice; moreover, if you abandon . . . if you prefer your individual happiness to the good and glory of your country . . . if you debase passions, then you will hinder moving forward with resolution and firmness the grand work that you have begun. I assure you that then you will be much more slaves than what you have been until now, because it is necessary that you know that the tyrants of Cadiz are trying (in accord with their fake alias) in going to that new capital to put new chains on you and to oppress you with greater ignominy than their predecessors have. So that Bravery, Unity and Firmness are recommended by an unfortunate American pursued by the European mob, who is certain that already in a free country, he will not miss an opportunity or any measure, even at the expense of the greatest sacrifices, to contribute to the successful regeneration of the New World. This, I offer you and I will accomplish.

Vicente Rocafuerte Bejarano (1783–1847)

Necessary Ideas for All Independent People of the Americas Who Want to Be Free

Necessary Ideas for the All Independent People of the Americas Who Want to Be Free is a political essay that Vincente Rocafuerte Bejarano published in Philadelphia in 1821 as a prologue to a translation of the works of Thomas Paine and John Quincy Adams and articles from the U.S. Constitution. Born in Guayaquil, Rocafuerte was a distinguished statesman of the Americas who militated for the independence of the Spanish colonies. During the early republican period, he served as president of Ecuador. In the essay below, he presents the model of United States independence and government organization for the countries that would soon gain their independence. He favorably compares the American Republic with the old monarchies of Europe, as well as with the Napoleonic Empire. In the highly rhetorical style common during this period, Rocafuerte details how easy it would be for his homeland to follow the model of the U.S. free-market economy and democracy. (EC)

Further reading: Vicente Rocafuerte Bejarano, *Ideas necesarias á todo pueblo americano independiente, que quiera ser libre* (Philadelphia: D. Huntington, 1821), *Bosquejo ligerisimo de la revolucion de Mégico: Desde el grito de Iguala hasta la proclamacion imperial de Iturbide* (Philadelphia: Imprenta de Teracrouef & Naroajeb, 1822).

Trans.: PP

Beloved friends: I cannot stop feeling in my chest the sharp joy I experienced upon knowing that the glorious standard of independence flutters over the joyful banks of the mighty Guayaquil. Permit me, to send you from this capital of Pennsylvania my most expressive good wishes, accompanying the ardent prayers that I direct to heaven for the happiness of my homeland. And where can I find more sublime memories, more heroic lessons, more examples of dignity, and examples more analogous to our present political situation, than in this famous Philadelphia? Yes, in this very city, asylum of the oppressed, center of knowledge, bastion of liberty, the genius of independence, defeater of deep-seated worry and the illusion of ignorance, arose on July 4th, 1776, an august voice with majestic accent as strong as thunder, and as pleasing as the harmony of heaven, that said to the union of all humanity:

"Tremble, tyranny, be buried in the abyss of the feudal monster, be banished false and dark dogmas of legitimacy by the brilliant light of the sublime truths that we proclaim:

"All men have been born equal. God has conceded inperscribable and inalienable rights, and they are: the right to life, the right to liberty, and the right to pursue happiness. All governments have been established to assure these rights; the governments do not have any power per se, nor do they enjoy more authority than the governors willingly want to concede. When there exists a form of government destroying of these principles, the people always have the right to alter it, change it, abolish it and organize their political powers in a way that will be more convenient to guarantee their security and achieve their prosperity.

"Prudence, in truth, counsels to not change governments established and secure for many years for light or transient causes; because men are more disposed to tolerate bad suffrage than to use their rights by taking away and abolishing laws which have grown old and molded by custom.

"But when a series of abuses and usurpations invariably following the same plan has as its object the enslavement of the people and their subjection to absolute despotism, then the people have the just right to insurrection; it is then their duty to destroy this government and substitute another that guarantees their present and future happiness.

"Such has been the patience and tolerance of Spanish America, and such is the need that today obliges it to change its government."

Félix Varela (1788–1853)

Essay on Slavery; Jicoténcal

Félix Varela came to the United States as a political exile in 1823, fleeing a death sentence by the Spanish absolutist government. After an active life of liberal political militancy, religious service, and pedagogical commitment in Cuba, he was never to return to his native country. Varela, the philosopher who first introduced the study of the experimental sciences into the

Cuban academic curriculum, was also a Catholic priest. Throughout his exile in the United States, he continued his vocational mission in Philadelphia and New York, polemizicing with Protestant theologians, championing the cause of poor Irish immigrants, and writing prolifically on religious matters. In 1837 he was appointed New York's General Vicar, but Varela also continued his militant political engagement. He wrote extensively on Cuban affairs, and from Philadelphia he started publishing a newspaper critical of Spanish colonial rule (*El Habanero*), which was circulated clandestinely on the island. The following selections convey a sense of the relentless commitment to critical thought that characterized Varela's intellectual life and that motivated his compatriots to call him "the first who taught us to think." Varela is one of the few Hispanic intellectuals commemorated on a U.S. postage stamp. (ALO)

Further reading: Félix Varela, *El Habanero* (Miami: Ediciones Universal, 1974), *Escritos políticos* (La Habana: Editorial de Ciencias Sociales, 1977), *Jicoténcal* (Houston: Arte Público Press, 1995).

Trans.: PP

Essay on Slavery

This essay demonstrates the need to extinguish the slavery of blacks on the island of Cuba, serving the interests of their owners.

The irresistible voice of nature clamors that the island of Cuba should be happy. Its advantageous location, its spacious and secure ports, its fertile lands serpentined by mountain ranges and frequent rivers all indicate its noble destiny to figure in an exceptional manner on this globe we inhabit. In ancient times it was covered by a simple and peaceful people who, without knowing the politics of men, enjoyed the just pleasures of frugality when the hand of the conqueror spreads death everywhere, creating a desert that their warriors could not fully occupy. The ancient race of Indians disappeared like smoke, preserved on the continent because of the immense regions where they interred themselves. Only the proximities of various ports were inhabited, where the horror of their own victory brought the victors, surrounded by a small number of their victims and the peaks of the distant mountains, where a few miserables hid in a spacious asylum and sadly contemplated their ruined homes and the beautiful plains on which they shortly before had their comforts.

I would not remember such disagreeable thoughts like these if their recollection were not absolutely necessary to understand the political situation of the island of Cuba. These offenses were the first links in a great chain that oppresses thousands of men and causes them to groan under the harshness of slavery on a land where others received death; an unhappy chain kept upon an island that seems destined by nature for pleasures: the sad image of degraded humanity.

It was impossible for the channel of communication between the two worlds not to receive torrents of enlightenments from the civilized world and the immense treasures that the uncultured world possessed, and it was even more impossible that, with such elements, one single century would not have been enough to form a new Atlantis. Despite this, the sinister politics of those times (if, in fact, Spain had a politics), after having left the island almost deserted, managed to block not only foreign immigration, but even the immigration of the Spanish nationals themselves, limiting the means of an immigration that would have consolidated the interests of the new owners.

Believing these countries were destined by Providence to enrich the new possessors, a tremendous war on their prosperity was declared by all. They ignored the real resources of enrichment for all. Sources that were, obstructed by the avarice of some to the harm of all.

This conduct of all government produced a backwardness in the population of this beautiful Island, and motivated a power who has always been inclined to varied and sure paths to find where its interests lie. It motivated, I say, England take on the business of supplying us with the black strength that cultivates our fields for us. England: the same England that now shows us a philanthropy so much a child to her vested interests as were her past cruelties—and I don't know how this speaks to her present but disguised oppressions—this same England, whose rigor with her slaves has no precedence, this same England who introduced on our soil the root of these evils. She was the first that, to the shock and abomination of all virtuous men, did not hesitate to sacrifice humanity in the name of avarice; and if she has ended these barbarous sacrifices, it is because these advantages have ceased. But what am I saying, "They have ceased?" . . . Brazil . . . I do not want to touch this theme . . . England, in accusing us of being inhuman, is similar to a warrior who, after immolating a thousand victims in his fury, climbs atop a pile of cadavers and pontificates leniency with his sword warm in his hand and his clothes bloodied. You English: on your lips the word philanthropy loses value; excise it; you are evil apostles of humanity.

Our government's deadly lack of foresight in those times was the cause of not only approving the traffic of blacks, but that, retaining it like a special benefit, assigned a premium of four good pesos for each slave that they introduced to the island of Cuba, besides permitting them to be sold at the price their owners wanted, as though the men were one of many articles of commerce. In this way they believed that they could supply the needed manpower. Without danger, with human slaves! What happened in Santo Domingo very early made clear to the government the error they had committed; nevertheless, the introduction of blacks continued . . .

Nevertheless, it gives me much pleasure to be able to manifest to the courts that the inhabitants of the island of Cuba looked-on in horror upon the slavery of Africans that they were forced to develop, not finding other recourse, given that besides the lack of workers for agriculture, the number of free servants is reduced to a few freemen. I say a few because it is known that even this class does not want to interact with slaves, and only when they find no other position do they dedicate themselves to domestic service. Much less are white maids found, because on the moment they arrive in Havana, even those who come from Europe, they do not want to be in the servant class. Because of this, the salaries are exorbitant, the current price ranging from fourteen to twenty *duros* a month, and a cook or maid of some merit costs never less than twenty-five *duros.*

I beg congress to forgive me for distracting it, narrating household details, since this news contributes much toward the understanding of the extraordinary phenomenon of why an illustrious and friendly people, like those in Havana, purchases more and more slaves. The government, I will repeat a thousand times, the government can end this, increasing proportionately the number of freemen who, by necessity, must be employed in domestic service, lowering the price of salaries that in time will become very moderate when slavery is abolished, and some whites no longer hesitate to work as servants. I dare to assure that it will resound to the general good fortune of the people of the island of Cuba when there are no slaves, and people find other ways to supply their needs. Although it is certain that the custom of dominating a part of the human race inspires in some certain insensibilities to the misfortune of these miserable people, many other people very much try to alleviate their misery, and more than owners are fathers to their slaves.

I am sure that in asking freedom for the Africans, reconciled with the interests of the owners and the security of public order through prudent measures, I only ask for what the public of Cuba wants. But I do not want to get ahead of myself, and I appeal to the Court to permit me to continue the narration of the deeds that serve as the basis for the propositions that I shall make about this matter.

The introduction of Africans on this island of Cuba gave origin to the class of mulattos, many of whom have received their freedom from their own fathers, while others suffer in slavery. This class, although less abused, experiences the effects caused by their birth. It is not so numerous, but it has not received the reinforcements that the blacks have in the repeated shipments of this human merchandise that has arrived from Africa; but because they are less abused, they multiply considerably. Both classes, reunited, form the natives from Africa, who, according to the most exact computations made early in 1821, exceed the white population three to one. The slaves are employed in agriculture and in domestic service, while the freemen are almost all dedicated to the arts, mechanical as well as liberal; it is estimated that for one white artist there are twenty of color. These have studied some, which should be no surprise, because most of them know how to read, write and count, and what's more effect their craft with a great deal of perfection, although they are not as capable as the foreign artists, because they have not had any more means to instruct themselves than their own genius. Many of them are initiated in other kinds of knowledge, and probably are not jealous of whites in general.

Necessity, teacher of men, made the natives of Africa derive benefits from their misfortune, since finding themselves without goods or social rank they have managed to overcome these drawbacks, as much as possible, through work, which not only has given them a comfortable subsistence, but also greater esteem from the whites; at the same time the whites have suffered a mortal blow from the civiling of the Africans. In fact, ever since the crafts have been practiced by blacks and mulattos, they have become too low an activity for the whites, who without degrading themselves could work with the blacks. Worry always has great power over men, and in spite of all the dictates of philosophy, men do not accept ignorance when a people, justly or unjustly, does not value one another's condition. From this it can be inferred how unfounded is the accusation that many have made of the natives of Havana, because of their lack of desire in dedicating themselves to crafts, and there are people who maintain that the climate inspires idleness. It is the government that has inspired idleness in them, and what's more, who has always demanded it. I only ask that you observe that those same artisans, the natives of Africa, are nothing less than citizens of Havana, since there is hardly a one that is not of Creole origin in the country.

Only the law can slowly cure such serious injustices, but they have unfortunately increased them, authorizing the principle from which they come. The African has, by nature, a sign of ignominy, and the African would not have been looked-down upon in our land if the laws had not made it so. Rusticity inspires compassion to just souls, not scorn; but the law, the tyrannical law, manages to perpetuate the misfortune of these miserable people, without noticing that time, calm spectator of the constant struggle against tyranny, has always seen the ruins of tyranny become, in glorious times, the trophies of that august universal mother of mortals.

As a result, because agriculture and the other arts on the island of Cuba depend absolutely on Africans, if this class wanted to ruin us, they would suspend their work and make a new rebellion. Their wealth in numbers could animate them to obtain by force that which they are denied by justice, which are liberty and the right to be happy. It has so far been the belief that their own rusticity makes such an undertaking impossible; but we now see that this is not so, and that, even if it were simplicity itself to free them, the best soldier is the most barbarous when he has someone to lead him. But do the blacks lack leaders? They had them on the island of Santo Domingo, and our officials surely have seen in the ranks of the blacks the uniforms of a potent enemy, whose engineers could perfectly direct a whole campaign of hostilities.

But why refer to the past? Why is it that independent nations cannot take this direction and supply other methods to complete this work? In the state of Haiti, they have an army that is numerous, veteran, well disciplined, and, what's more, has great captains; could they not engage in our ruin, which would be to their prosperity? They have already started; it is known that they sent two frigates loaded with troops to our coasts to form the basis of an army that very quickly would have been extraordinarily increased, but the wreck of these ships freed the island of Cuba from this great calamity. This belied a frequent communication between the islands, when before they hardly received two or three correspondences per year. In Santo Domingo's state of independence, even if the blacks overcome the whites and seize the whole island, even if they unite through peaceful treaties, neither the white nor the blacks should be so stupid as to not realize the damage that Cuba could inflict upon them, and the advantages they would experience by promoting a rebellion. It is, then, almost demonstrated that there is a war between the two islands, and that Santo Domingo will not throw away the advantage that our great number of slaves offer, who only wait a genius mentor to redeem them.

As for Bolivar, it was known in Havana that he said with two thousand men and the pennant of freedom he would take the island of Cuba, once this comes into his plans.

We should just as well wait for the Mexicans to help, and if, to our misfortune, have a war with the English, I think they would have no difficulty in ruining Cuba when they are masters of the sea, there is a surplus of talent and British sterling (no matter how poor they say they are), and they could introduce a thousands spies among us.

We must not lose sight of the fact that white population of the island of Cuba is almost all found in the cities and large towns, but the countryside could be said to belong to the blacks, since the number of overseers and other white persons who guard them is so low that they can be discounted. It should also be said that twenty leagues outside Havana are vast, entirely deserted lands, and deserted land like this comprises most of the island. All of this displays the facility with which they can disembark an organized army, and undertake their march without anyone knowing about it until it is almost on top of some of the most important targets, and that whichever enemy can take hold of our countryside, which will gladly be offered to them by its dwellers, and destroy in one blow our agriculture, which is to say our existence.

We only increase our fears with the knowing of the quick education that the free blacks daily acquire in the representative system, since the press unintentionally instructs them about their rights, which are none other than those of man, much repeated in all parts, and it makes them think of their desire to be happy like those to whom they only differ in color.

The image of their fellow men as slaves torments them very much, because it reminds them of the shame that reflects their origin, and it is very natural that these men attempt to remove, in any way possible, the obstacle of their happiness by freeing their equals. Moreover, their inferiority to the whites has never been so notable for them or so noticeable like on the day that they were constitutionally reprised of their political rights. This to them is only a door already almost shut, and even excludes them from forming a base of the representative population, which is Spanish, and not representative. They do not want it this way, because they feel the contempt of exclusion, because in the end an artist, a man useful to the society in which he was born, is much offended by being treated like a foreigner, and as such like a beast.

When freedom is discussed among slaves, it is natural that they make some terrible efforts to break their chains; if they do not, their envy will eventually devour them, and injustice will make them more sensitive. Whites on the island of Cuba do not stop congratulating themselves for having thrown down the ancient despotism, recuperating the sacred rights of free men. And who of the natives of Africa is calmly look upon these emotions? Their rabidity and their desperation obligate them to put themselves between the choice of freedom or death.

I should tell the courts that a remarkable disaffection with the constitution is noticed among the blacks, since they have never given the least sign of contentment, and it is known that at all the celebrations and public festivals they are the first to spread disorder everywhere. Sensible people observed that it seemed as if the earth had swallowed the blacks and mulattos in Havana at the news of the reestablishment of the system, because you could count the people in the streets on one hand. Despite the general happiness, they maintained a shaded and impotent air for some time. Do not think this was because of ignorance, or because of adhesion to the old system, since we already know that they have twice attempted to destroy it by declaring themselves free, and I am sure of that the first to give the shout of independence will have at his side almost all the blacks. Let's not delude our selves by terms: constitution, freedom, equality, are synonymous; and they are disgusted by terms such as slavery and unequal rights. We pretend to reconcile these contraries in vain.

But let us suppose that we have all the means for a glorious resistance to rebellion, and that we become the victors; of course at that point our trade relationships would have ended, entirely destroying agriculture and a large part of the population, white as well as black. For many years, our nation would not be in any condition to supply merchants with security, and this state of decay would motivate the same or another enemy to a new assault that would consume the rest. The island of Cuba, whose commerce is so well respected over on the entire globe, would remain reduced to an outpost of poor fishermen until another power seized the advantages that Spain had scorned. Let us not delude ourselves: the island of Cuba is a colossus, but it is built on sand; if it remains erect it is because of the constant calm of the atmosphere that surrounds it; but it is already possible that Cuba will be shaken by powerful hurricanes, and its fall would be so rapid and terrifying as if to seem inevitable, if we don't we strengthen its foundations.

No other recourse remains in such circumstances than to remove the cause of these evils while trying to not produce others that can compromise the tranquility of our island. Or should I say: give liberty to the slaves in such a way that their owners do not lose the capital they spent on their purchase, or the people of Havana do not suffer new burdens, or in a way that free black in their first unexpected do not, want to extend themselves beyond what has been granted to them, and finally by helping agriculture in whichever form possible so that it won't suffer, or that it would suffer less backwardness for the lack of slaves.

We lack means for such an arduous endeavor and the following project for a decree presents, some possibilities of whose usefulness the courts would judge with their accustomed prudence.

Jicoténcal

Jicoténcal is the first historical novel ever published in the Spanish language. It appeared anonymously in Philadelphia in 1826, but recent studies have revealed Father Félix Varela as the author (see previous entry). The subject of the novel *Jicoténcal* is the Conquest of Mexico by Hernán Cortés. Its hero, Jicoténcal, was a Tlaxcalan general who had sided with Cortés. However, shortly before the conquest of the Aztecs, Cortés accused Jicoténcal of treason and had him hanged, thus assuring Jicoténcal's place in Mexican history as a national hero. The author of *Jicoténcal* favored Aztecs and harshly criticized Cortés and the *conquistadores*. Although this is a historical novel (the first in the Spanish language), some of the characters, among them Teutila, Jicoténcal's betrothed, are fictitious. *La Malinche*, the Indian woman baptized by the Spaniards as Doña Marina, an evil woman, is the first prominent female historical character in Mexican literature and has endured until recently. Taking into consideration that Malinche was sold to the Spaniards by her own people, Mexicana and Chicana feminist critics have reevaluated her, recognizing her contribution to the creation of the mestizo people. (LL)

Before departing from Tlaxcala, Hernán Cortés had published various edicts stating that the death penalty was imposed for the slightest offenses, a cruel and rigorous discipline that was almost impossible to put into practice with a militia so little accustomed to the mechanical and servile obedience of European soldiers. The rigor of these edicts startled the various troops who, unaware of the reason behind them, would tremble, fearful of their being carried out. The lack of living examples had made everyone forget the announcement when the same edicts were once again published with great ostentation in Texcoco and other places occupied by the troops. These threatening devices drew the attention of the soldiers, who cast their eyes everywhere, looking with anxious solicitude for the victims at whom such an imposing demonstration of force was being directed.

Early one morning, two or three days later, a Spanish soldier was found hanged from one of the windows in his room. This spectacle, horrifying because of its novelty, the surprise it caused, and the circumstances that surrounded the executed man, produced a general commotion which manifested itself in different ways. Hernán Cortés informed the officers, and they in turn their respective ranks, of the horrible information that had been in the possession of Antonio de Villafaña (such was the name of the executed man) and the plot he had been hatching against him and many others, having beforehand passed along the word that Villafaña had swallowed a document, which had been torn to pieces, that, he thought, he had the names or signatures of the plotters.

In order to formulate an exact idea of the motive that occasioned the sacrifice of this individual, it is sufficient to see the result that it produced. Hernán Cortés placed around himself a powerful retinue of soldiers chosen from among those he trusted, a noteworthy, preventative action that laid bare his fears, badly concealed by the foolish invention of the paper with the signatures of the plotters. But the judgment and manner of Villafaña's execution is one of the traits that make known the character of the man who, in times of slavery, has been celebrated as a hero.

A panegyrist historian says that a soldier, one of those who had been in the army for a long time, betrayed himself as an accomplice in a plot against Cortés's life and those of all his friends. He states that the plotters had signed a paper which forced them to follow their leader, Villafaña. Their plan was to pretend that they had a number of letters from Veracruz and to turn them over to Cortés when he was at table with his companions. They would all enter under the pretext of having brought news, and while he opened the letters, they would kill him and his friends and then run through the streets clamoring in the name of freedom. This sacred word is heard coming from the mouths of our debased ancestors as a complement and recrimination of an assassination! How far has the degradation of the human race gone!

They promote as great heroic deeds the devastation of entire peoples, the unjust aggression against peaceful and remote countries, death and desolation inflicted by an ambitious man, accompanied by all the crimes and horrors of an uncontrolled soldiery; they venerate, as deeds of the most Christian piety, their having raised a cross atop the rubble of entire provinces and over the corpses of millions of men, and their having converted a few of the indigenous population, through coercion or out of fear, by despicable acts, or out of self-interest; they dare to desecrate something as venerable as Liberty in such a way!

On this basis, which does not go beyond being a secret denunciation that Hernán Cortés supposedly received, they set up Villafaña's trial and its verdict, which were as follows (these are the words of Antonio de Solís in his *History of the Conquest of Mexico*, book 5, chapter 19):

> This was the substance of the news given by the soldier, who asked for his life as a reward for his loyalty, since he was implicated in the sedition, and Hernán Cortés resolved to personally visit Villafaña's prison and attend to the first steps that had to be taken in order to convince him of his guilt, a procedure that can either clear up or muddle the truth. The importance of the affair required no less and time could not be taken to await the serious interrogation of the judicial authorities.

> He then departed in order to effect Villafaña's imprisonment, taking along minor officials with some of his captains, and he found him at his lodging place along with some of his supporters. He approached him so as to overcome his own confusion and, after ordering that he be imprisoned, indicated that all should leave, under the pretext of needing to carry out some secret interrogation and, making use of the news that he had received, he removed from Villafaña's vest, the paper with the pact signed by all the plotters.
>
> He read it and found on it the names of persons whose disloyalty made him very uneasy; but, being aware of the presence of the others, he ordered that those who were with the accused should be put in prison and he left, leaving word with the officials that the affair should be terminated in the briefest time possible, without turning to the accomplices for more information, and there was little need for it because Villafaña was convinced after the paper was seized and, believing that his friends had turned him in, quickly confessed the offense, and with this, the case against him quickly narrowed, as is customarily done in the military style, and sentence of death was pronounced against him, and it was carried out that very night, after his having been allowed to make his peace with his maker. And the next day he was there, hanged from a window in his very room.

What horror! Accusation, imprisonment, indictment, trial, sentence, execution, everything in the very same night! Undoubtedly an extremely powerful being watches over the human species, for we see it surviving against such monsters!

Such was the event that was to precede the horrifying attack that was to free Hernán Cortés from his powerful enemy, the brave and inflexible Xicoténcatl. Confined to a place where he was more a besieged man than a part of the army, and almost totally deprived of his forces, he finally came to recognize that his existence as a public man had been nullified and he decided to step down so as to thus be free as a person, serving the cause of justice as a private man.

The valiant American had planned to sacrifice his life for the country that had given birth to him, thus freeing it from the monster that was ravaging it. To carry out his plan, which was more generous than it was practicable, he wished to see himself freed from all public obligations and to run the risks as an individual, to discreetly avoid having Hernán Cortés use his plan as a way of again oppressing his homeland in case it failed. What a generous young man! Neither your resentments nor the justified indignation or disdainful acts that you were suffering, nothing was enough to have you understand the heart of your enemy. Tyrants do not need pretexts to work their evil: their oppression recognizes no boundaries other than those presented by the natural limits of their power. The most moderate one among them, if one can use that epithet with such monsters, sheds tears out of envy because he cannot surpass the Neros and Caligulas.

As the noble Tlaxcalan thought about these things, Hernán Cortés, having already decided to consummate his crime, reflected on the heroic patience with which Xicoténcatl had suffered an uninterrupted series of humiliations, and he trembled considering the danger that he would have been in as a result of removing him before taking all precautions. And in spite of them, his nights were disturbed by horrifying feelings of anxiety; his pleasures were embittered by a continuous and gnawing uneasiness; Xicoténcatl appeared as an exalted figure before his imagination and he wavered for a moment. But ambition and envy conquered him and he resolved to carry out the most infamous of all atrocities.

In order that his victim would provide some motivation to enable him to color his effrontery in any situation or, better, so that this type of evil act might always be accompanied by the despicable cowardice that spills an eternal dishonor over its originators, Hernán Cortés made sure that there would be a lack of provisions where Xicoténcatl was posted. The latter and his men suffered from shortages almost beyond endurance, thus prolonging the uneasiness of the leopard that lay in wait for him; but finally hunger forced him to come out in search of provisions for his troops in the surrounding area. The spies that surrounded him reported on his moves, and the weak Tlaxcalan regiment found itself surrounded by all the troops of the traitorous chief of Texcoco, the Chalco rebels, and several companies of Spaniards, the formidable force that Hernán Cortés sent so that his victim should not escape him.

Xicoténcatl and his men fought and defended themselves like lions, in spite of the depression in which hunger had placed them. But how much can an honest republican's bravery be humbled? He knows how to die before surrendering, and this was the resolution taken by the heroes of Tlaxcala, who made the enemy pay dearly for their victory, thus nobly avenging the honor of their republic. The unfortunate Xicoténcatl was wounded by a bullet shot from a harquebus which pierced his leg; still lying on the ground, he managed to knock down many of the enemy with his mace before being disarmed. Many men fell on top of him, finally, and through sheer force of numbers, the hero was tied up; he still made his guards tremble, nevertheless, as the lion does its own even when caged behind strong iron bars.

The prisoner was taken to Texcoco at night with the greatest of precautions and the most meticulous care. Hernán Cortés, trembling, could not make a decision; by then he had already scattered the Tlaxcalan troops among the members of his extensive army; nevertheless, he feared awakening the Tlaxcalan eagle. An ambitious man's anger must be very powerful, since he walks among so many horrible hurdles. Then he reminded himself with great ostentation of the authority that had been conferred upon him by the Senate of Tlaxcala, which allowed him to deal with Spanish military severity with any subjects of the republic who were insubordinate or lacked discipline, and, in spite of everything, even the farce of holding a war council was not followed.

The aim was, thus, to harshly extract from the brave general a confession of his guilt; but he, being above fear and dread, upset all the plans with his unbending steadfastness and his noble pride. The cruelest treatment and the vilest of insults had no better result. Xicoténcatl, his wounded legs covered in irons, tied by the waist with a thick chain that was affixed to a ring in the wall, and his hands secured behind by two strong manacles, Xicoténcatl in this horrendous condition was greater than his vile, lowly, cruel torturers. They showered him with blows and punches, as they insulted his honor with words unworthy of repetition, and the brave man looked upon the lowly subordinates of his tyrant as if they were poisonous vermin assaulting a corpse. Neither hunger, nor thirst, nor lack of sleep, no torment dreamed up by the frenetic delirium of oppressors could crush his pride. All was in vain.

Tired, finally, his tormentors left the brave man alone while they rested a bit before returning to the task once again. Xicoténcatl then gave in to his thoughts, and memories of Teutila drew a tear from his manly spirit. What an enviable tear, and more precious than all the laurels and triumphs of his oppressive tyrant! His homeland appeared in his mind's eye; his beloved homeland, torn apart, betrayed, dishonored, and weak. The bitter sighs that followed this pondering were the most unbearable of his torments.

"So!" he said to himself, "Tlaxcala will be the victim of a tyrant, and the fiery Tlaxcalans will prostrate themselves before a lord as much a coward as he is wicked and insolent! What stroke of fate has led you to this destiny, oh my homeland? But wait; your virtues lie drowned by the vapors of this drunkenness that has inebriated you. The horrendous death that awaits me, the torments that I am suffering, are going to awaken your former valor, and undoubtedly you, oh valiant Tlaxcalans, you will avenge an American, punishing the monsters that are tormenting me! A thousand times happy am I if my sacrifice makes you return to your former heroism! How could my life be any more useful to you than by its wrenching you away from your degradation and your lethargic drifting? And you, the most abominable of monsters ever aborted by the abyss! finish your work, for the more you multiply your horrors, the surer my sweet and consoling hopes will be."

The same wise providence that has put the world in order has made the souls of the just find in themselves effective consolation for even the greatest anguish. And thus Xicoténcatl appropriated this great and comforting idea that his unjust, tyrannical, and cruel death would reinstill courage in the hearts of the degenerated Tláxcalans, and he did not have to look outside of himself to assuage his horrendous situation. He was satisfied then with his destiny, and his love of country also mitigated the sorrows in his heart, all of which he laid before his wife, in the midst of her mourning and sobbing.

"No, beloved Tuetila," he exclaimed, "do not be downhearted by my misfortune. Your Xicoténcatl, vilely murdered, is going to engender the revenge of a great people and, as my blood flows, there is going to be an explosion of the volcano that must consume the assassins of liberty."

The time for the terrible execution was irrevocably set, and a gag was placed in the mouth of the Tlaxcalan general to guard against the potential effect of his valiant and manly eloquence. But faced with this unheard-of and unknown barbarity, a Texcocan, seeing the brave young man's mouth closed with iron, with only blood coming out of it rather than words, thus telling the world of the extremeness of the atrocious act about to be carried out, fainted and fell to the ground, horrified by such a spectacle. This occurrence made it necessary to have the gag's torment suppressed; but, at the same time, it became necessary to keep the heroic young man from addressing the public. Tyrants are fertile in resources and not very delicate in their selection of them; it matters not that they might be lowly and vile so long as they lead them to the achievement of their goals. It was determined, then, that the strong leader should be rendered unconscious with opium and then led, benumbed, to the altar of his glory and the monument to the dishonor of the oppressor.

Human imagination has no brush with which to depict the remainder of this catastrophe. One hundred and fifty thousand men at arms, each one looking at the others; everyone stirred up in a horrifying manner and visibly frightened; the European caliph, pale and trembling, wishing to conceal his anxiousness from those satellites that surrounded him no less anxiously; and all of this because an unconscious and weakened man, a corpse, was being dragged toward the scaffold. The criminal act was carried out! A lugubrious and frightening silence kept those present in an idiotic stillness, demonstrating their degradation and giving evidence of the fact that they had permanently succumbed to the yoke imposed on them by tyranny. Still, the Spanish leader kept the allied troops busy with maneuvers and repetitive and continuous movements with the intention of preventing them from reflecting too much on the serious events that they had witnessed.

Attributed to Enrique José Varona (1849–1933)

To the People of Cuba

The manifesto below, perhaps drafted by Enrique José Varona, was written on September 10, 1898, shortly after the U.S. victory over Spain in the War of 1898. An urgent call to peace and order, the text reveals the anxiety felt by many exiled Cuban revolutionaries about the fate of Cuban independence if the United States considered them incapable of stabilizing the political situation on the island. Many prestigious Cuban intellectuals and politicians living in exile signed the manifesto. Philosopher, poet, sociologist, journalist, university professor, and a prolific writer, Varona was one of the most respected Cuban figures of the time. A veteran of the first war for Cuban independence (The Ten Years War, 1868–1878) and an advocate for political autonomy during the interwar years (1878–1895), by 1895 Varona was convinced that Spain would not make any political concessions to Cuba. Once the war started, he sought refuge in New York City, and eventually became the director of the revolutionary newspaper *Patria* (after José Martí's death, see entry in this anthology). Varona returned to Cuba in 1898, and there he was named both Secretary of the Treasury and of Education and Culture by the U.S. military administration. Later a militant in the National Conservative Party, Varona was elected to the vice-presidency of the Republic in 1912. (ALO)

Further reading: Enrique José Varona, *Estudios literarios y filosóficos* (La Habana: Imprenta La Nueva Principal, 1883), *Artículos y discursos* (La Habana: Imprenta de A. Alvarez, 1891), *"Cuba contra España,"* Manifiesto del Partido Revolucionario Cubano a los pueblos hispano americanos (New York: Imprenta América, 1895).

Trans.: TEW

In moments decisive to the future of a nation, as are the present ones for the Cuban people, the supreme need for the unity of all vital elements in identity of goals and uniformity of conduct imposes itself.

The almost secular battle in which we have been involved to achieve a legal state that would permit us the free development of our material and moral activities is coming to an end. Our third War of Independence, supported by the indomitable spirit of an entire people, has produced a break in Spanish dominance. This has ended the loathing felt for the American invasion intended to bring down the sovereignty of Spain. Cuba has ceased to be a Spanish colony. Her people have come into possession of their freedom and independence with full rights.

The work begun by our heroic compatriots has been consummated by the people of the American Union, which has reinforced the arm of her children in order to finish breaking Cuba's chains. Obeying a Federal resolution from Congress, the United States Armed Forces today occupy part of the territory of our island, and soon, by virtue of an agreement with Spain, will occupy all of the rest.

This fact, no matter how important it may be, is only a casualty of the war that the United States has felt obligated to wage against Spain to force her to evacuate a country that she dominated against the express will of the majority of its inhabitants. The joint resolution of the Federal Congress on the nineteenth of April of this year determines the exact limits of the actions of the United States Armed Forces in the conflict between Cuba and Spain. They were to assist our island, as they did, in compelling Spain to abandon her so that the Cuban people, once again in possession of the benefits of peace, could organize in the way most adequate to their needs and aspirations.

It follows from the above exposition that the military occupation of Cuba by the American forces and accompanying regime are strictly transitory. It was a given in that situation, and for that reason accidental. That which is permanent is the freedom we have achieved and the right to independence that it has ascertained us.

By supposing this as a fundamental fact, we have no reason to disavow either the obligations of gratitude in which find ourselves with respect to the United States or the moral responsibility that they have procured before the world, appearing in some way as guarantors that the Cuban nation will know how to advance itself in peace and flourish in full light of justice and liberty. In no way are the obligations and emotions of the American people and ours incompatible, rather they are harmonious, as if they obey the same elevated ideal of civilization and progress.

We have battled for the principle the North Americans have affirmed as the foundation of public law in America: that the consent of those who are governed is that which makes lawful the power of governments. To obtain by entreaty our basic autonomy to organize and run ourselves according to the dictates of our conscience and the conditions of our collective existence, we affirm and put in practice the American principle, thus testing its potentiality and efficacy for the improvement of men and nations.

Working now for order and peace with the same vigor and steadiness with which we were engaged in the war, we will demonstrate that we are deserving of the sacrifices that the American nation has taken on in our favor, and we will undo all misgivings that the political freedom we have achieved is premature. In this way, we will reciprocate the favor we received, assuring that prejudice, or even serious vexation, is not caused for our helpers.

Because we know history and the spirit of our people—as laborious and skillful in times of peace as they are persistent and disposed to sacrifice when fighting for their rights—we have full confidence that they will rise to the occasion of this new situation and know how to forge a path among the obstacles that it presents, occasioned by that which we leave behind more than by that which we have ahead of us.

This conviction, and the responsibility of every citizen at critical times, has incited us to direct our voice to all our compatriots—to the inhabitants of Cuba who have identified their luck with that of our beloved country—to inform them of how we judge the situation, what we consider to be the purpose that should inspire us, and the conduct imposed upon us by foresight and patriotism. Nothing could be so lamentable now as the confusion of ideas and its consequence, the dispersion of forces. And no matter how natural uncertainty seems, upon embarking on an unbeaten path we should master it, setting our sights on the noble object we propose to reach.

We believe the fate of Cuba is basically in the hands of her children. Our well-directed effort will depend before all else upon it being shaped by our legitimate desires and inalienable rights. Firstly, let us affirm our political aspiration, which is the same one for which three generations of men have been sacrificed; and by affirming it, we declare our firm purpose of putting at its service all our activities, our intelligence, and our courage. We want for Cuba a government freely elected by her people. We want to guarantee the Republic of Cuba. Around this flag should gather all men of good will; no less, those who have defended the revolution, for they have waved it with inexpressible firmness, making the most bloody sacrifices for its triumph; and those who have wanted to approach this solution, looking for adjustments in the already frail laws of Spain; and still, those who accept it now as brought by the dominion of the events. Those who understand that the personality of Cuba should survive as a political entity and that in it the interests of all her inhabitants are supported will be with us.

More so, the first step to obtain this grand result in a definitive way that will also withstand the possible sudden attacks of old and new adversaries is to ensure peace in our country. Those of us who have served the revolution in any way, and those who have sympathized with it, should be the first to return to the new land, clot the old wounds as soon as possible, and work on the job of Cuba's economic and political reconstruction. The homeland demands it of us. The soldier and the agitator should be disposed to become citizens, defenders of their own ideals, surely, but in a new field and with new weapons. We are going to give Cuba the tranquility she demands, so that as soon as possible we can give her the definitive organization to permit her to assure prosperity, so easy for her to obtain, and the culture promised by the history of her great undertakings. We are going to carry to Cuba the unifying spirit of tolerance and concord. We are going to, all of us, gather together in the lap of peace that permits great efforts, as it allows the accumulation of riches and knowledge.

We feel obligated to invite the Cubans, and other inhabitants of Cuba who love her, to forget their past differences and join together in a large and well-organized configuration that has as its goal the restoration of the public wealth, advancement of culture, and the establishment of a stable government that represents our nation in a dignified manner and runs it with the reason of its own laws that are the reasoned expression of the intelligence and will of the Cuban community.

This is the imperious job of the present times. With this clear purpose we, the immigrants, should go to Cuba, and all who reside in the dear land and have consecrated or are disposed to consecrate their activity for her with perseverance and abnegation should await us.

We believe firmly there is no better way for us to serve the interests of our homeland or to more fittingly repay the favors bestowed upon us by the United States. Cuba—peaceful, orderly and progressive because of her grand commerce and tight relations with the Union—will be one more element of prosperity for the grand Republic, and a place where its political ideas will come to fruition without ceasing to be a factor in the general American concert and in the civilized world.

José Martí (1853–1895)

With All, and for the Good of All

The son of poor Spaniards who emigrated to Cuba around the mid-nineteenth century, in the 1890s José Martí was to become the crucial figure in the struggle for Cuban independence. Active in anti-colonial politics since his early youth, Martí was first deported from the island in 1871 for his clandestine activities as a journalist in favor of the Ten Years War (1868–1878). This was the beginning of his long life as a political exile. He would return to Cuba only for a brief interval in the late 1870s, and again in 1895, when he died fighting in one of the first battles of the revolutionary war he masterminded. Martí lived a significant part of his life in the United States (1882–1895). During his exile in New York City he worked as a translator and journalist for several Spanish-language and English-language newspapers. Known for his critical positions regarding U.S. imperialist policies toward Latin America, he was also asked to occupy distinguished diplomatic posts for the republics of Argentina and Uruguay. However, by the early 1890s, Martí would abandon these tasks to dedicate himself entirely to the resumption of Cuban insurgency. In 1892, he founded the Cuban Revolutionary Party and the newspaper *Patria*. Key to the success of Martí's plans was gaining the support of the many Cuban working-class émigré communities dispersed throughout the United States—most highly concentrated in the cigar-production centers of Florida. This was the audience to whom Martí delivered the following speech in Tampa, Florida, on November 26, 1891. Weary of divisions within the revolutionary movement—which he saw as a major reason for the defeat of the 1868 revolution—the speech was a call for patriotic unity beyond class, race, or national differences. (ALO)

Further reading: José Martí, *Inside the Monster: Writings on the United States and American Imperialism*, ed. Philip S. Foner (New York: Monthly Review Press, 1975); *Our America: Writings on Latin America and the Struggle for Cuban Independence*, ed. Philip S. Foner (New York/London: Monthly Review Press, 1977).

Cubans:

For suffering Cuba, the first word. Cuba must be considered an altar for the offering of our lives, not a pedestal for lifting us above it. And now, after calling forth its most cherished name, I shall lavish the tenderness of my soul upon these generous hands that come to give me strength—surely not inopportunely—for the agonizing task of building. Now, with our eyes placed higher than our heads, and my own heart torn out of my body, I shall not egoistically thank those who think they see in me the virtues they desire both from me and from every Cuban. Nor will I merely thank the genial Carbonell or the fearless Rivero for the magnificent hospitality of their words and the fervor of their generous affections. But I shall give all the gratitude in my soul to them, and through them in all those loving people who have stood up in the face of the ambitious landowner who spies upon us and divides us; to these virtuous people in whom the free strength of our industrious country is being tried; to these cultured people whose writing desks stand beside their work benches, and for whom the thunderings of Mirabeau stand beside the arts of Roland—answer enough for the contemptuous of this world; to this temple bedecked with heroes and built upon men's hearts. I embrace all those who know how to love. And I have within my heart the star and the dove.

Periodic respect for an idea that one cannot abjure without disgrace is not bringing us together here, reluctantly and through sheer effort. Nor is it the ever ready and at times too ready response of patriotic hearts to fame or a position of power, or to some hero who fails to crown his untimely longing for death with the higher heroism of repressing that longing, or to a beggar who under the cloak of the mother country goes about with his hand held out. The one who comes here will never be disfigured by flattery, nor is this noble people receiving him a servile and easily led people. My breast swells with pride, and at this moment I love my country even more than before, and I now have an even greater faith in its serene and well-ordered future—a future rescued from the serious danger of following blindly, in the name of freedom, those who make use of their yearning for it to bend it to their own purposes. Still more firmly do I believe in a Republic of open eyes, neither foolish nor timid, neither haughty nor professorial, neither over-cultured nor uncultured, for I can see—by the sacred affirmations of the heart when we are together on this night of brain and brawn, together for now and for later, together for as long as patriotism prevails—I can see those Cubans who put their free and frank opinions above all things, and one Cuban who respects them.

For if in my country's affairs I were permitted to offer one benefit to everyone—one fundamental benefit to be a basic principle of all my countrymen, and without which the other benefits would be faulty and insecure—this is the one I would choose: I want the first law of our Republic to be the Cuban cult of full dignity for man. Every true man must feel upon his own cheek the slap upon any other man's cheek. Nations are vilified from the cradle by the habit of resorting to personal cliques, fomented by notorious or fraudulent interests, in defense of freedoms. Set your souls afire and let them shine and crackle like lightning for the sake of truth, and follow it in freedom, you honest men. Put this tender consideration above all things, this manly tribute of each Cuban to the other. Neither mysteries, nor calumnies, nor willful injuring of reputations, nor long and crafty preparations for the baneful day of ambitions. Either the Republic is founded upon the integral character of every one of its sons—the habit of working with his hands and thinking for himself, the putting of his whole self into what he does, and respect, like family honor, for everyone's wholehearted effort; enthusiasm, in short, for a man's honor—or the Republic is not worth one of our mothers' tears or a single drop of our heroes' blood. We are striving for truth and not for dreams. We are striving to liberate Cubans and not to intimidate them. We are striving to peacefully and equitably adjust the rights and interests of Cuba's loyal inhabitants and not to establish, at the gateway of the continent, of the Republic, the frightful administration of Veintimilla, or the bloody possessions of Rosas, or the lamentable Paraguay of France! Better to fall under the excesses of our fellow countrymen's imperfect characters than to profit from the credit acquired with the guns of war or the words that defame character! This is my sole claim to these affections that have come in time to strengthen these hands of mine that never tire in the service of true freedom. Cut them off, those of you whom I passionately desired to lift higher, and—I do not lie!—I will cherish that violence because it comes to me out of the fury of my own land, and because for its sake I will see a Cuban heart show courage and rebellion! Above all, let us band together in this faith. Let us join hands, in avowal of this decision, where all may see them, and where there is no forgetting without punishment. Let us bar the way to a republic which fails to come through methods worthy of a man's integrity, for the benefit and prosperity of all Cubans!

Of all Cubans! I wonder what tender mystery there is in this sweetest of words, or what purest of pleasures in this very word of man. It is so beautiful already that if pronounced as it should be, the air would seem to be a golden halo and Nature a throne or a mountaintop! One says "Cuban" and a sweetness like a gentle brotherhood suffuses the heart, and the strongbox of our savings opens by itself, and we hasten to set another place at table, and the enamored heart stretches its wings to give shelter to anyone born in the same land as ourselves, even if misdeeds confuse him, or ignorance misleads him, or anger infuriates him, or he is bloodied by crime! It is as if some divine arms we cannot see were gathering all of us onto a breast in which the blood still flows and the heart still sobs! You must create, there in our country, in order to give us dedicated work later on. You must create, there where the corrupt proprietor rots whatever he looks upon, a new Cuban soul, hostile and bristling—a proud soul, different from that magnanimous and home-loving soul of our ancestors and illegitimate daughter of the misery that sees vice go unpunished, and of the useless culture that finds employment only in the dull contemplation of itself! Here where we keep watch for the absent ones, where we rebuild the house that topples upon our heads down there, where we create what must replace the things destroyed for us there—here, no word so closely resembles the light of dawn, no consolation enters our hearts with greater joy, than this ardent and ineffable word: Cuban!

For that is what this city is; it is the entire Cuban emigration; that is what we are accomplishing in these years of work without savings, families without pleasure, life without zest and a furtive death! To our fatherland crumbling to pieces down there, and blinded by corruption, we must take the devout and far seeing country being built here! To what is left of the country down there—everywhere being eaten away by gangrene beginning to gnaw at the heart—we must unite the friendly country to which we have come, here in our loneliness, accommodating our souls to all the realities with the firm hand that affection demands from within and without—realities so well concealed down there (in some because of despair and in others because of Babylonian pleasure) that although there are great certainties and great hopes and great risks, they are little less than unknown, even by experts! So what do they know down there about this glorious night of resurrection, about the methodical and resolute faith of our spirits? What do they know down there about the continuous and growing rapport of us Cubans away from the island whom the 10 years of mistakes and Cuba's natural fickleness and other malevolent causes have not succeeded in at last dividing? Indeed they have succeeded in becoming so intimate and affectionate a unifying force that all one can see is an eagle taking flight, a sun rising and an army advancing. What do they know down there about these subtle treaties, that nobody draws up or can terminate, between the despairing country and the waiting émigrés? What do they know about this character of ours, strengthened cautiously and by daily effort and cruel testing? What do they know about the brave and industrious and free people we are going to take to them? What does the man dying in the night know about the one awaiting him at dawn? Any stevedore can load a ship, and any artillery man can light a cannon fuse; but it has not been that lesser task, of mere opportunity and result, which is our duty; it has been the task of avoiding the harmful consequences, and hastening the happy ones, of the next and inevitable war, and of cleansing it of the naturally human neglect and indifference and envy that might needlessly and inexcusably put this war where they put the last one. It has been a task of disciplining our free souls in the knowledge and order of our country's genuine elements, and in this work which is the sun and air of freedom, so that, with the creative forces of a new situation, they may comprise without danger those inevitable remains of the difficult crises needed to produce those forces. And in this sublime task our hands will ache more than once. But the dead are commanding and counseling and keeping watch, and the living are listening to them and obeying; and in the wind there are sounds of adjutants passing by carrying orders, and the sound of flags unfurling! Let us band together, Cubans, in this other faith: with all, and for all: the inevitable war, so our country may respect and desire and support it, and the enemy not kill it for us at its height, because of location or staff or lack of men: the revolution of justice and reality for the recognition and unrestricted practice of the true freedoms.

Not even the brave men of war who are listening to me now agree with these scrupulous analyses of public affairs, because the enthusiast considers criminal even the delay of good sense in putting his enthusiasm to work. Nor do our wives, so attentively listening to us here, dream of anything but returning to tread their own land where their comrades will not be living bitterly and sullenly as they are living here. And the child, brother or son of heroes and martyrs, nourished by their legends, thinks of nothing but the beauty of dying in the saddle, fighting for his country, beside a palm tree!

This is my dream, the dream of us all. Palm trees are waiting brides, and we must establish justice as tall as the palms! This is what we wanted to say. The war of impulse, which collapsed in disorder, must at the insistence of national wrongs be followed by the war of necessity, feeble at first and with little chance of success without the encouragement of that strong and intelligent love of right whereby the souls most eager for it pick up from the grave the flag dropped upon it by those least in need of justice and weary of the first effort. Cubans in their independence are seeking their rights as men, and independence must be sought with man's entire soul. Let disconsolate Cuba turn her eyes to us! For with the logs in the road the children are testing the strength of their newfound arms! Wars break out, when there are reasons, because of the impatience of a brave man or a kernel of corn! For the Cuban spirit is forming ranks, and the confused masses are like the dawn! For the enemy, less surprised today and less concerned, does not have the wealth which he had to defend the last time. And we must not entertain ourselves with bickering about locality, or with vying for posts of command, or with national envies or insane hopes as much as we did then! Because outside of Cuba we have love in our hearts, our eyes upon the coast, our hands upon America, and a gun in our holsters! Then who can fail to read all this in the air in letters of light? And in letters of light it must be read that in this new sacrifice we are not seeking mere forms, or the perpetuation of the colonial spirit in our lives, with the latest in Yankee regimentals. What we are seeking is the essence and reality of a republican country of our own, without some people's sickly fear of a wholesome expression of all ideas and the honest use of all energies, and on the part of others the fear of that robbery of man which consists in the attempt to prevail in the name of freedom by means of ruthless actions in which the rights of others to freedom's methods and guarantees are set aside. Of course, the coxcomb politicians will be thrown out, for they forget how necessary it is to come to grips with what cannot be suppressed, and face-powder patriotism will start grumbling on the pretext that people, in the sweat of creating, do not always smell like garden pinks. And what are we to do about it? Without the worms that enrich the soil, no sumptuous palaces would be built! We have to enter truth with our shirt sleeves rolled up, the way a butcher enters a carcass of beef. All truth is sacred, even without the scent of garden pinks. Everything has ugly, bloody entrails. When the artist makes his wonderful jewelry, at first the gold in his crucible is muddy. It is from life's foulness that fruits derive their nectar and flowers their color. Man is born out of the pain and darkness of the maternal womb, out of the scream and the sublime rending, and from a distance and to human eyes, those magnificent forces and streams of fire leaping and fusing in the furnace of the sun only look like sunspots! Progress to those who do not fear the light; charity to those who tremble at its rays!

I would not regard that flag so fondly (resolved, as I am, to know that what is most sacred is taken as an instrument of interest by the world's bold victors) if I did not believe that out of its folds must come total freedom when the cordial recognition of every Cuban's integrity, and of a just means of resolving the conflicts in his affairs, robs of all reason those counselors of confused methods who deem terrible only that stubborn passion which refuses to recognize all there is in his just and equable demands. Drive a nail through the tongue of the popular flatterer, and hang it in the breeze like an ignominious flag where it may be a warning to those who further their own ambitions by vainly aggravating the pain of the sufferers, or hiding from them the essential truths of their problems, kindling their anger. And beside the tongue of the flatterer, nail the tongue of the one who withholds justice!

Let the flatterer's tongue be nailed there for all to see, as well as that of those who use as a pretext the exaggerations to which ignorance is entitled and whoever does not use every means to put a stop to ignorance, refusing to respect whatever of man's pain and sacred agony exists in the exaggerations: it is more comfortable to curse in judicial robes than to study, sympathetically, wholly immersed in human sorrow! Life's judges must be put into life's prisons if they wish to learn justice. Let the one who judges everything know everything. Let the one at the top judge neither hastily nor with bias. Let the one at the bottom judge neither with bias nor hastily. The jealous man must not censure the well-being which he secretly envies. The powerful must not disregard the moving poem and the bloody sacrifice of the man who has to dig the bread he eats, or the sacrifice of his long-suffering companion wearing her crown which the unjust cannot see, or the sacrifice of their children who do not have what belongs to other men's children around the world! Better never to have unfurled that flag from its staff if it were not to shelter all heads equally!

Little does he know of our country, little does he know of it—the man who is unaware of what it holds as spirit of the present and guarantee of the future, a powerful aggregate of that original freedom which man by himself creates out of the land's substance and the pain he sees and his own ideas and proud nature. Flesh-and-blood politicians must rely more upon this genuine and vigorous freedom, which can sin only through lack of the culture it is easy to place in it, than can paper politicians rely upon that freedom of dilettantes schooled in the catechisms of France or England. We are men, and we are not going to want paper-doll governments but intellectual effort cast in the mold of our country. A man knows little about our nation if he fails to observe that, together with this natural impulse that rouses it for war and will not allow it to sleep during peace, it has been reared by study and experience and a certain explicit knowledge that our lovely land affords. He knows little about it if he does not see the accumulation of human and cultivated forces of order—a phalanx of broad intelligence enriched by love for man without which intelligence is no more than scourge and crime. He is not well acquainted with our country if he overlooks the intimate harmony (a result of common sorrow) among Cubans of natural law, without history or books, and among Cubans who have put into their studies the passion they were unable to put into building their new country—so fervent a brotherhood among the abject slaves of life and those of an annihilating tyranny—that because of this unanimous and burning love of justice in those of one occupation and those of another; that due to this equally sincere human ardor of men who hold their necks erect because their heads are held high by nature, and men whose necks are bent because fashion demands the display of a handsome back; because of this vehement country where those whom various states of culture might drive apart are drawn together by the same dreams and honesty—due to all this our Cuba, free in the harmony of equality, will tie down the colonial hand which in its own time will not fail to fall upon us, disguised in the glove of the Republic. And beware, Cubans, for some gloves are so like the human hand that they cannot be distinguished from it! Of all who come demanding power, Cubans, you must ask them in broad daylight, where the hand can be clearly seen, "Hand or glove?" But there is really no reason to be afraid or to quarrel. The very thing we must combat, we need. What holds peoples in subjection is as necessary to them as what urges them ahead; in the family household the father, always active, is as necessary as the mother, always timid. There is a male policy and a female policy. A locomotive with a boiler to make it run and without brakes to stop it in time? In the affairs of nations it is necessary to man the brakes with one hand and stoke the boiler with the other. And from too much steam, and from too much braking, nations hereabouts are suffering.

Then what is there for us to fear? A lessening of our enthusiasm, the illusory quality of our faith, the small number of us with untiring spirits, our disorganized hopes? Well, I look around this hall and can feel the firmness and stability of the earth under my feet, and I say: "You lie." I look into my heart, which is only a Cuban heart, and I say: "You lie."

Are we to fear the habits of authority practiced in war and, in a certain sense, salved by a daily disdain for death? Well, then, I do not know the valiant Cuban soul, or the wisdom and experience in Cuban judgement, or to what extent the old authorities would have to rely upon the untried authorities, or the admirable agreement between republican thinking and the heroic action which honors, almost without exception, those Cubans who bear arms. But since I do recognize all this, to anyone who says we must expect from our veterans this criminal self-love, this disregard of homeland for their own interests, this iniquitous treason against their country, I tell him: "You lie!"

Or will we have to discard our fear of the trials and tribulations of war stirred up by corrupt people in the pay of the Spanish government, or our fear of walking barefoot, a common thing in Cuba because, amidst thieves and their accomplices, nobody in Cuba has shoes any more except those very thieves and their accomplices? Well, since I know that the very one who writes a book to stir up the fear of war has said in verse—very good verse, to be sure—that the *jutías* supply every need of the Cuban countryside—and I know that Cuba is full of *jutías*, I return to those who want to frighten us with the very sacrifice we desire so much, and I tell them: "You lie!"

Must we be afraid of the Cuban who has suffered most from being deprived of his freedom in the country where the blood he shed for it has made him love it too much to be a threat to it? Will we fear the Negro—the noble black man, our black brother—who for the sake of the Cubans who died for him has granted eternal pardon to the Cubans who are still mistreating him? Well, I know of black hands that are plunged further into virtue than those of any white man I have ever met. From the Negro's love for a reasonable freedom, I know that only in a greater natural and useful intensity does his differ from the white Cuban's love of freedom. I know that the black man has drawn his noble body to its full height and is becoming a solid column for his native liberties. Others may fear him; I love him. Anyone who speaks ill of him I disown, and I say to him openly: "You lie!"

Must we fear the Spaniard in Cuba? The armed Spaniard who could not defeat us by his bravery, only by our envy—for no other reason but our envy? Are we to be afraid of the Spaniard whose fortune is in El Sardinero or La Rambla and who will slip away with his fortune because it is the only country he has? Or shall we fear the Spaniard whose property is in Cuba because he is fond of the land and his children have roots there, and due to them and the fear and punishment will offer little resistance? Are we to fear the simple Spaniard who is as fond of freedom as are we ourselves, and who, together with us, is seeking a just country which is better than fondness for an incapable and unjust one? Or the Spaniard who with his Cuban wife suffers from irremediable desertion and the wretched future of the children born to them with the stigma of hunger and persecution, with the decree of exile within their own country, with the death sentence in life which is the Cuban's heritage? Should we be afraid of the good liberal Spaniard—my Valencian father, my bondsman from the North, the man from Cadiz who watched over my feverish sleep, the Catalonian who swore and cursed because he did not want the Creole to escape with his clothes, the man from Málaga who carried the feeble Cuban out of the hospital upon his back, the Galician who dies in alien snows returning from delivering the monthly bread ration to the home of the general acting as commander-in-chief of the Cuban war? In Cuba a man fights for his freedom, and there are many Spaniards who love freedom! Those Spaniards will be attacked by others, and I will help the former as long as I live! To the one who does not realize that those Spaniards are merely so many other Cubans, we say: "You lie!"

And must we fear the alien snows? Those who do not know how to fight with their fists in this life, or who measure other people's hearts by their own timid ones, or who believe that nations are merely chessboards, or who are so steeped in slavery that they need someone to hold their stirrup for them to extricate their foot—those people will seek in a nation of hostile and alien components the Republic which assures them of well-being only when it is administered for them in accord with their own character, and when it is bright and shining. To those who believe that Cubans lack the spirit and capacity to live for themselves in a land created by their own valor, I say: "You lie!"

And to the elegant young dandies who today sneer at this holy revolution whose foremost leaders and martyrs were men born to the marble and silk of fortune, this holy revolution which, in the shortest time and by the redemptive virtue of just wars, made brothers of the heroic first-born and the landless peasant, the master of men and his slaves; to those paperweight Olympians who step down from their slanderous tripods to ask, terrified and willing to submit, if this or that fighter has set foot upon the ground for the purpose of mollifying the soul with whom he can divide the power tomorrow; to the presumptuous who knowingly foment the deception of those who believe that this magnificent movement of souls, this burning idea of justified redemption, this sad but firm desire for the inevitable war, is only the stubbornness of an unruly tramp, or the escapade of an unemployed general, or the noisy chatter of persons who enjoy the wealth that can be kept only by collaborating with dishonor, or the threat of a mob of laborers with hate for a heart and waste paper for brains—a mob that can be led, as with a bridle, wherever the first ambitious man who flatters it, or the first despot who waves a flag before its eyes, cares to take it; to all the elegant dandies or Olympians, and to the presumptuous, I say: "You lie!" This is the mob of laborers, the coffer of our alliance, the baldric embroidered by a woman's hand where the sword of Cuba has been kept, the redemptive desert where one builds, forgives, foretells, and loves!

Enough, enough of mere words! We are not here for flattery, but to feel our hearts and see that they are sound and able; we are here to teach the despairing, the disbanded, the melancholic, the force of our idea and action, to teach them the proven virtue which assures them of happiness to come, to teach them our true stature, a stature having nothing of the presumptuous or the theorizer or the singsong chanter or the music fanatic or the chaser of clouds or the beggar. We are one, and we are able to march on to the end because we recognize the wrongs and will make certain that there is no backsliding. We have gathered together the scattered with absolute love and patience, and we have enthusiastically restored order to what was, after the catastrophe, distrustful confusion. We have brought about good faith, and we think we have succeeded in suppressing or repressing the wrongs that caused our defeat, and in gathering sincerely and for a lasting purpose the known or proposed elements whose unity will aid in carrying the imminent war to a successful conclusion. Now to form ranks!

Nations are not founded upon mere hopes in the depths of a man's soul! Again I see those flags before me, giving orders. And the sea seems to be coming to us from Cuba, surging with hopes and sorrows and tearing down the barrier of this alien land where we are living, its turbulent waves crashing against these gates. Down there is our Cuba, smothered in the arms that crush and corrupt it! There it is, wounded in heart and mind, tied to the torture chair, presiding over the banquet where gold-trimmed cuffs lift poisoned wine to the lips of sons who have forgotten their fathers! And the father died fighting the second lieutenant, and the son, arm in arm with the second lieutenant, goes to the orgy to rot! Enough of mere words! Out of torn entrails let us build an unquenchable love of country without which no man, good or bad, can live happily. There she is, calling to us. We can hear her moan; she is being raped and mocked and turned gangrenous before our eyes. Our dearest mother is being corrupted and torn into pieces! So let us rise up at once with a final burst of heartfelt energy. Let us rise up so that freedom will not be endangered in triumph, by confusion or clumsiness, or impatience in preparing it. Let us rise up for the true Republic, those of us who, with our passion for right and our habit of hard work, will know how to preserve it. Let us rise up to give graves to the heroes whose spirit roams the world, alone and ashamed. Let us rise up so that some day our children will have graves! And let us place around the star of our new flag this formula of love triumphant: "With all, and for the good of all."

CHAPTER 17

Hymn of the Exile

José María Heredia (1803–1839)

Hymn of the Exile (Himno del desterrado)

Wandering is the word that best describes the life and works of the Cuban poet José María Heredia. Born to Dominican parents, Heredia spent his childhood moving from one country to another: from Cuba to Florida, Santo Domingo, Venezuela, México, and eventually, although for a brief interval, back to Cuba. Books were his home, especially those of classical authors he studied and translated. Heredia's poetry is informed by ancient classical models such as the ode, the hymn, or the canto, but his language and themes, traversed by images of solitude, displacement, fear, death, ruins, dreams, or nightmares, are unquestionably romantic. Heredia studied law in Mexico and at the University of Havana. During his longest period of residency as an adult in Cuba (1821–1823), he became a visible member of liberal intellectual circles critical of the slave trade and of the absolutist policies of the Spanish government. In 1823 colonial authorities accused him of involvement in a revolutionary plan aimed at ending Spanish rule over the island (known as "Soles y Rayos de Bolívar/Bolívar's Sun and Rays"). Heredia managed to escape to the United States, where he spent a year, and in 1825 he established permanent residence in Mexico. During his brief exile in New York he compiled and published his first book of poems and wrote some of his most memorable texts. *Hymn of the Exile* was written in 1825, while en route to his final exile in Mexico. It has become the model for much of the exile poetry to follow him by Cuban and Puerto Rican authors in nineteenth-century New York. (ALO)

Further reading: José María Heredia, *Poesías completas* (Miami: Ediciones Universal, 1970), Anonymous, *El laúd del desterrado*, ed. Matías Montes-Huidobro (Houston: Arte Público Press, 1995).

Trans.: PP

The sun is shining and the serene waves
Are cut by the triumphant prow,

Reina el sol, y las olas serenas
corta en torno la prora triunfante,

and a deep trail of brilliant foam
the ship leaves in its wake.
Land-ho! is the cry; anxious, we look
at the border of the calm horizon
and in the distance discover a mountain . . .
I know it . . . Cry, my sad eyes!

It is the Pan . . . In its outskirts breathe
the kindest and most constant friend,
the beloved women of my life, my lover . . .
What treasures of love have I there!
And more distant, my sweet sisters
and my mother, my beloved mother,
by silence and sorrow surrounded,
consumes her life crying for me.

Cuba, Cuba, what life you gave me,
sweet land of light and beauty,
how many dreams of fate and glory
have I tied to your happy soil!
I look at you again . . . ! How heavily
the harshness of my luck weighs upon me!
Oppression threatens me with death
in the fields where to the world I was born.

What does it matter if the tyrant thunders?
Poor yes, but free am I,
only the soul of the soul is the center:
what is gold without glory or peace?
Although I am banished and forced to wander,
and severe destiny weighs upon me,
for the scepter of the Iberian despot
I would not trade my fate.

Since I lost the vision of joy,
give me, oh glory, your divine breath.
Dare I curse my destiny,
when I can still conquer or die?
There must still be hearts in Cuba
that envy my martyr's fate,
and prefer a splendid death
to their bitter, difficult life.

Surrounded by a sea of evils,

y hondo rastro de espuma brillante
va dejando la nave en el mar.
¡Tierra! claman; ansiosos miramos
al confín del sereno horizonte,
y a lo lejos descúbrese un monte . . .
Le conozco . . . ¡Ojos tristes, llorad!

Es el *Pan* . . . En su falda respiran
el amigo más fino y constante,
mis amigas preciosas, mi amante . . . .
¡Qué tesoros de amor tengo allí!
Y más lejos, mis dulces hermanas,
y mi madre, mi madre adorada,
de silencio y dolores cercada
se consume gimiendo por mí.

Cuba, Cuba, que vida me diste,
dulce tierra de luz y hermosura,
¡cuánto sueño de gloria y ventura
tengo unido a tu suelo feliz!
¡Y te vuelvo a mirar . . . . ! ¡Cuán severo,
hoy me oprime el rigor de mi suerte!
La opresión me amenaza con muerte
en los campos do al mundo nací.

Mas, ¿qué importa que truene el tirano?
Pobre sí, pero libre me encuentro,
sólo el alma del alma es el centro:
¿qué es el oro sin gloria ni paz?
Aunque errante y proscripto me miro
y me oprime el destino severo,
por el cetro del déspota ibero
no quisiera mi suerte trocar.

Pues perdí la ilusión de la dicha,
dame ¡oh gloria! tu aliento divino,
¿Osaré maldecir mi destino,
cuando puedo vencer o morir?
Aún habrá corazones en Cuba
que me envidien de mártir la suerte,
y prefieran espléndida muerte
a su amargo azaroso vivir.

De un tumulto de males cercado

the patriot is immutable and steadfast,
and either meditates upon the future,
or spends his time in contemplation of
the past.
Like the Andes, inundated with light,
serenity, in excelsis above the clouds.
listening to thunder and lightning
loudly resound at his feet.

Sweet Cuba! on your breast are seen
in the highest and most profound degree,
the beauties of the physical world,
the horrors of the moral world.
Heaven made you earth's fairest flower,
but you ignored your strength and destiny,
and by adoring the despot of Spain,
you learned to worship the blood-demon
of evil.

What does it matter now that, you reach
out to heaven
dressed in your verdure of perennial green,
or that you offer your palm-crowded
forehead
to the ardent kisses of the sea.
if the clamor of the insolent tyrant,
the pitiful groan of the slave,
and the crack of the terrible whip
only resound on your plains?

Opressed by the weight of insolent vice,
virtue falters and faints,
and the law is sold for gold,
and power is at the service of crime.
and a thousand fools, who believe
themselves great
because they have purchased honors
from the Crown
idolize the tyrant, and prostrate
themselves
before the sacrilegious throne.

Let life's very breath oppose the abuse
of power,
and death avenge death;

el patriota inmutable y seguro,
o medita en el tiempo futuro,
o contempla en el tiempo que fue.

Cual los Andes de luz inundados
a las nubes superan serenos,
escuchando a los rayos y truenos
retumbar hondamente a su pie.

¡Dulce Cuba!, en tu seno se miran
en el grado más alto y profundo,
las bellezas del físico mundo,
los horrores del mundo moral.
Te hizo el cielo la flor de la tierra,
mas tu fuerza y destino ignoras,
y de España en el déspota adoras
al demonio sangriento del mal.

¿Ya qué importa que al cielo te tiendas
de verdura perenne vestida,
y la frente de palmas ceñida
a los besos ofrezcas del mar,
si el clamor del tirano insolente,
del esclavo el gemir lastimoso,
y el crujir del azote horroroso
se oye sólo en tus campos sonar?

Bajo el peso del vicio insolente
la virtud desfallece oprimida,
y a los crímenes y oro vendida
de las leyes la fuerza se ve.
Y mil necios, que grandes se juzgan
con honores al peso comprados
al tirano idolatran, postrados
de su trono sacrílego al pie.

Al poder el aliento se oponga,
y a la muerte contraste la muerte:

constancy determines fate,
and he who knows how to die, conquers.
Let us weave a glorious name
for all the fleeing centuries:
let us raise our eyes to heaven,
and to the years that have yet to come.

It is worthier to present
a fearless chest to the enemy's sword,
than to languish in pain on our deathbed
and a thousand deaths suffer in dying.
May glory in battle foster
the ardor of the loyal patriot,
and circle with a brilliant halo
the happy moment of his death.

You shrink at blood . . . ? In battle
it is better spilt in torrents
than hauled in torpid canals
amid vices, agonies and horror.
What do you have . . . ? Not even a safe sepulcher
in that unhappy Cuban soil!
Doesn't our blood serve the tyrant
to fertilize the soil of Spain?

If it is true that people cannot
exist but in hardened chains,
and that a ferocious heaven condemns them
to ignominy and eternal oppression,
then my heart abjures the fatal truth,
the melancholy horror,
to pursue the sublime lunacy
of Washington and Brutus and Cato.

Cuba! At last you'll see yourself free and pure
like the air of light that you breathe,
like the boiling waves you watch
kiss the sand on your shores.
Although vile traitors serve
the tyrant, rage is useless;
it is not in vain that 'twixt Cuba and Spain
the broad sea tends its waves.

la constancia encadena la suerte,
siempre vence quien sabe morir.
Enlacemos un nombre glorioso
de los siglos al rápido vuelo:
elevemos los ojos al cielo,
y a los años que están por venir.

Vale más a la espada enemiga
presentar el impávido pecho
que yacer de dolor en el lecho
y mil muertes muriendo sufrir.
Que la gloria en las lides anima
el ardor del patriota constante,
y circunda con halo brillante
de su muerte el momento feliz.

¿A la sangre teméis . . . ? En las lides
vale más derramarla a raudales,
que arrastrarla en sus torpes canales
entre vicios, angustias y horror.
¿Qué tenéis? ¡Ni aun sepulcro seguro
en el suelo infelice cubano!
¿Nuestra sangre no sirve al tirano
para abono del suelo español?

Si es verdad que los pueblos no pueden
existir sino en dura cadena,
y que el cielo feroz los condena
a ignominia y eterna opresión:
de verdad tan funesta mi pecho
el horror melancólico abjura,
por seguir la sublime locura
de Washington y Bruto y Catón.

¡Cuba! al fin te verás libre y pura
como el aire de luz que respiras,
cual las ondas hirvientes que miras
de tus playas la arena besar.
Aunque viles traidores le sirvan
del tirano es inútil la saña,
que no en vano entre Cuba y España
tiende inmenso sus olas el mar.

Miguel Teurbe Tolón (1820–1857)

Always; Song of the Cuban Woman (Cantar de las cubanos)

Until recently it was believed that Miguel Teurbe Tol6n was born in Pensacola, Florida, but new data indicate that he was born in Matanzas, Cuba. As a youngster, he became fluent in English, French, Italian, and Latin and published his first poetry volume at the age of twenty-one. In 1847 he became the editor of *El Aguinaldo Matancero* and published his novel, *Lola Guara*. His anti-Spanish convictions forced him into exile in the United States in 1848. While living in New York, he was an editor for the *New York Herald* and was named Secretary of the Cuban Annexation Junta. Together with Cuban poets Juan Clemente Zenea and Pedro Santacilia, Teurbe Tol6n published *El laúd del desterrado* (*The Lute of the Exile*, 1856), a collection of exile poetry regarded as the first anthology of exile literature published in the United States. Taking advantage of an amnesty decree issued by Spanish authorities in Cuba, he returned to his native island, where he died of tuberculosis on October 16, 1857. Teurbe Tol6n was a romantic at heart. Unique in imagery and rich in rhetorical devices, the following selections are characterized by a feeling of nostalgia and solitude and a call for Cuban emancipation. (JBF)

Further reading: Anonymous, *El laúd del desterrado*, ed. Matías Montes Huidobro, (Houston: Arte Público Press, 1995).

Trans.: PP

Always *(Siempre)*

I suoi pensieri in lui dormir non ponno! (His innermost thoughts cannot sleep!)

—Tasso

I suoi pensieri in lui dormir non ponno!

—Tasso

To live in a foreign land
Rich and free, yet not mine,
And see in a gray sky
A sun that looks cold;
To recall dead joys
In my solitary confinement,
And to watch them pass
Wrapped in a shroud:
To raise, looking for God,
My sad eyes so often,
Crying for both of them,
And not see them, blind from weeping:
To dream that to the fatherland I return,
That the air of Cuba I breathe,
And then open my eyes... look around me,

Vivir en extraño suelo
rico y libre, mas no mío,
y ver en un pardo cielo
un sol que parece frío;
Muertas dichas recordar
en mi encierro solitario,
y verlas todas pasar
envueltas en un sudario:
Levantar, buscando a Dios,
mis tristes ojos en tanto,
y llorando ambos a dos,
no verles, ciegos de llanto:
Soñar que a la patria torno,
que aire de Cuba respiro,
y abrir los ojos . . . y en torno

Return to reality with a sigh:
To believe embraced in my arms
My loving and precious mother,
And see an iron arm
Reject me and separate us:
To see my past already dead,
My future cast in mourning
And farther away, in a desert,
An abandoned sepulcher . . .
All that, night and day,
And moment after moment,
Makes me think that a harpy
Has settled in my thoughts
And devours my soul.

volverlos con un suspiro:
Creer que en mis brazos cierro
la madre amorosa y cara,
y ver que un brazo de hierro
me rechaza y nos separa:
Ver mi pasado ya muerto,
mi porvenir enlutado,
y más allá, en un desierto,
un sepulcro abandonado . . .
Eso, eso noche y día,
y momento tras momento
es pensar que como harpía
se posa en mi pensamiento
y devora el alma mía.

Song of the Cuban Women (Cantar de las cubanas)

Then the foreigner asked that we should sing;
But no, never shall he have the pleasure of us.
Let my voice first be extinguished and my hand
Shrivelled before I pluck one single cord of
Israel's harp for its tyrants.
—*The Holy Bible* (A summary of Psalm 137,
or a conflation of many psalms)

Pidiónos entonces el extranjero que cantásemos; mas
no, jamás tendrá este placer. Antes se extinga mi voz;
séquese mi mano antes que pulsar, para que lo oigan
nuestros tiranos, una sola cuerda del arpa de Israel.
—*La Biblia*

Chorus

Untress your hair,
Silks and jewelry discard:
Let us cry while
The song of Freedom is unheard!

I
You are dressed in black,
The sweet heaven above our country:
Dressed also in mourning
Is our heart.

Coro

Destrenzad vuestros cabellos,
sedas y joyas dejad:
lloremos mientras no suene
¡el canto de Libertad!

I
Vestido está de tinieblas
nuestro patrio dulce Cielo:
vestido también de duelo
está nuestro corazón.

II
In the noisy dance,
We shall see appear
The ominous, wandering shade
Of the agonizing Fatherland,
And louder than the music
Of the party, a deep moan
Will come to stop the noise
Of the voices of pleasure.

II
Entre la danza ruidosa,
fatídica sombra errante
de la Patria agonizante
veremos aparecer,
y más alto que los sones
de la fiesta, hondo gemido
vendrá a apagar el ruido
de las voces del placer.

III
No, do not bathe our faces
In the flickering lights of the hall;
Let us not go like prisoners
To the Sultan's festival.
Let our eyes not meet
The eyes of the Tyrant,
And let our hand not be wounded
By his wrangling claw.

III
No, no bañen nuestras frentes
del salón las luces vivas;
no vayamos cual cautivas
a la zambra del Sultán.
Nuestros ojos no se encuentren
con los ojos del Tirano
no se hiera nuestra mano
con su garra al tropezar.

IV
Our souls should withhold
Their love from the vile slave:
Let our noble lovers
Grab iron! and fight!
Let there be no more in our breast
Than Fatherland and Hope:
Only one shout—Vengeance!
Only one song—Freedom!

IV
A un vil siervo nuestras almas
negar deben sus amores:
nuestros nobles amadores
hierro empuñen, ¡y a lidiar!
No haya más en nuestro pecho
que la Patria y la Esperanza:
Sólo un grito—¡de Venganza!
Sólo un canto—¡Libertad!

Pedro Santicilia (1826–1910)

To Spain (A España)

"To Spain" is one of the texts that appeared in *El laúd del desterrado*, an important collection of poetry published in New York City in 1858 by a group of Cuban exiles committed to ending Spanish colonialism in their country. Since childhood, Santicilia had tasted the bitterness of expatriation. In 1836, when he was barely ten years old, his whole family was deported to Spain amidst a repressive campaign conducted by the infamous Spanish Captain General Miguel Tacón against any Cuban who was suspected of liberal or abolitionist sympathies. Santicilia would return to Cuba in 1845 only to start a life of cultural/journalistic activism and conspiracy against Spanish rule. In 1852 he was again deported to Spain for his participation in Narciso López's separatist conspiracy of 1848, and shortly thereafter made his way to New York. There he continued his revolutionary activities as a journalist and writer in the vibrant Spanish-American exile community. Later, Santicilia established permanent residence in

Mexico, his adopted country, marrying Mexican president Benito Juárez's daughter, and becoming a seven-time deputy in the Mexican federal congress. *To Spain* deploys many of the conventions of what is known in Spanish-American literary history as the "poetry of emancipation." Such poetry attempted to do with words what the revolutionaries were doing with guns on the battlefield: to consummate in symbolic terms the most complete and profound rupture from the metropolis that ruled the continent for more than four centuries. (ALO)

Trans.: PP

Even when I was very small and they told me
That you were once great and powerful,
That your ships filled the ocean,
That your name filled the universe;
That your legions were triumphant everywhere,
And astonished the earth with their deeds,
And that the hidalgos of your land
Were all accomplished gentlemen;
That nations trembled with terror
When they heard your formidable accent,
And that the sun never set on your flag,
But shone forever on your nation's coat of arms.
That and even more that I can now remember
Of your power, Spain, they told me,
And I from Cuba's remote beaches
Cherished as a golden dream
The joyful hope of some day seeing
Your fertile soil, rich in remembrance.
Full of faith, with fervid enthusiasm,
Soaked in ardent patriotism,
A thousand times—oh!—from the green bank
Of my unhappy land, I searched in the distance,
With anxious gaze to the east,
For the shade of your expansive mountains,
And thousands of time imagined
I saw in the distance between sea and sky,
Through mists and space
The shade of your beautiful mountains.
Thus, intoxicated on sweet illusions,

Aún era yo muy niño y me contaban
Que fuiste grande y poderosa un tiempo,
Que tus naves llenaban el océano,
Que llenaba tu nombre el universo;
Que tus legiones por doquier triunfantes
Asombraban el mundo con sus hechos
Y que eran los hidalgos de tu tierra
Dechados de cumplidos caballeros;
Que temblaban de espanto las naciones
Al escuchar tu formidable acento,
Y que el sol sin cesar, en tu bandera
Alumbraba el escudo de tu pueblo.
Eso y aún más que guarda la memoria
De tu poder, España, me dijeron,
Y yo de Cuba en las remotas playas
Acariciaba cual dorado sueño,
La esperanza feliz de ver un día
Rico en recuerdos tu fecundo suelo.
Lleno de fe, con férvido entusiasmo,
Empapado en patriótico ardimiento,
Mil veces ¡ay! desde la verde orilla
De mi tierra infeliz, busqué a lo lejos,
Con ansiosa mirada hacia el oriente
La sombra de tus montes corpulentos,
Y mil veces y mil imaginaba
Mirar distante entre la mar y el cielo,
A través de las brumas y el espacio
La sombra aquella de tus montes bellos.
Así embriagado en dulces ilusiones,

Ignorant, happy, inexperienced child,
I dreamt about your brave captains,
I dreamt about your grand monuments,
About your beautiful women, about your bards,
About your feasts, combats and tournaments,
And always, Spain, in my memory
There was a cult consecrated to your remembrance . . .
—But time flew, and with it took wing
That age of magic reveries,
And no more through the prism of deceit
Could I look, Spain, upon your marvels.
I touched the idol that for so long
I had innocently admired from afar,
Opened the folds of its mantle
And beheld a body fashioned of squalid clay.
Then—la!—the beautiful illusions
That once excited my ardent thoughts,
Like leaves blown away by the north wind,
Disappeared, never to return.
I sensed the truth!—Disenchantment
Succeeded enthusiasm in my breast,
And instead of admiration, I felt in my soul
A sentiment, Spain, of contempt,
Because I saw your unpopulated cities,
Your fields transformed into deserts,
Your factories converted into ruins
And your ancient ports without ships;
And I saw also the fatherland of Viriato
Emancipated from the Iberian banner,
And the red flash of England
Dominating the waters of the straits of Gibraltar.
And I saw these brothers—if brothers
The Spanish ever were—
In civil discord divided,
Devouring one another like fierce tigers,
Staining thus their fertile land,
Which at one time so many laurels had produced.
In vain I asked—Where,

Ignorante, feliz, niño inexperto,
Soñaba con tus bravos capitanes,
Soñaba con tus grandes monumentos,
Con tus bellas mujeres, con tus bardos,
Con tus fiestas, combates y torneos,
Y sin cesar, España, en la memoria,
Un culto consagraba a tus recuerdos . . .
—Pero el tiempo voló, con él volaron
De aquella edad los mágicos ensueños,
Y no más por el prisma del engaño,
Pude mirar, España, tus portentos.
El ídolo toqué que tantas veces
Admiraba inocente desde lejos,
Aparté los girones de su manto
Y el barro inmundo contemplé del cuerpo,
Entonces ¡ay! las ilusiones bellas
Que agitaban mi ardiente pensamiento,
Cual hojas por el cierzo arrebatadas,
Para más no volver desaparecieron.
¡Palpé la realidad!—El desencanto
Al entusiasmo sucedió en mi pecho,
Y en vez de admiración, sentí en el alma
Un sentimiento, España, de desprecio,
Porque vi tus ciudades despobladas,
Transformados tus campos en desiertos,
Convertidas tus fábricas en ruinas
Y sin bajeles tus antiguos puertos;
Y vi también la patria de Viriato
Emancipada del pendón ibero,
Y la roja bandera de Inglaterra
Dominando las aguas del Estrecho;
Y los hermanos contemplé—si hermanos
Alguna vez los españoles fueron—
Que en discordias civiles divididos
Se devoraban como tigres fieros,
Manchando así la tierra, que fecunda
Tantos laureles produjera un tiempo.
En vano interrogué—¿Dónde, decía,

Is the Phoenician marvel?
Where are the rich Carthagenean
Mines and commerce hidden?
Why did I not detect the admired ancient
Splendors of Rome? Why did I not find

The walled gardens and canals
The Moors left behind?
Everything disappeared! Only ruins
Can the gaze of the traveler discover
As he surveys the lonely fertile
Fields everywhere, uncultivated;
And whoever dares to look in the moat
Of some castle where time has stood still,
Will find foul reptiles stirring
And hissing as they assemble in the mire;
So likewise around your rich, grand monuments
Can be seen swarming like reptiles in the mire,
Your backwards and barbaric people . . .
Wretched nation!—Yesterday your name
Filled the Universe with your glory,
Today . . . you have forgotten your own glorious deeds,
And history does not record them for scorn of you.
Oh, if those who fell at Lepanto and San Quintín
Were to raise their heads from their sepulchers
And contemplate the "glories" of their grandchildren
They would cover their faces in shame!
Balanguinguí! Joló! The Chafarinas!
Those are now the glories of the Iberian people!
After the giants that passed
There only remained . . . parodies of pygmies . . . !
To vanquish your invincible ships
The fury of heaven was once necessary,
But then came Trafalgar, and your fleets
Are now not even the shadow of what they once were.

Está de los fenicios el portento?
¿En qué lugar se ocultan de Cartago
Las riquísimas minas y el comercio?
¿Por qué no admiro de la antigua Roma
El pasado esplendor? ¿Por qué no encuentro

Los cármenes floridos y canales
Que dejara al partir el Agareno?
¡Todo despareció! Ruinas tan solo
Descubre la mirada del viajero
Al recorrer los solitarios campos
Fértiles por do quiera, pero yermos;
Y cual suele mirarse allá en el foso
De algún castillo que respeta el tiempo
Los reptiles inmundos que se agitan,
Y bullen, y se agrupan en el cieno;
Así también en derredor se miran
De tus ricos, grandiosos monumentos,
Bullir como reptiles en el fango,

Atrasados y bárbaros tus pueblos . . .
¡Desdichada nación!—Ayer tu nombre
Llenaba con su gloria el Universo,
Hoy . . . olvidada vives de la historia

Que menosprecia referir tus hechos.
¡Oh, si la frente alzaran del sepulcro
los que en Lepanto y San Quintín cayeron!
¡Cómo ruborizados la ocultaran,

Al contemplar las glorias de sus nietos!

¡Balanguinguí! ¡Joló! ¡Las Chafarinas!
¡Esas glorias son del pueblo ibero!

¡Después de los gigantes que pasaron
Sólo quedan . . . parodias de pigmeos . . . !

Para vencer tus invencibles naos
Fue preciso la cólera del cielo,
Mas vino Trafalgar, y tus escuadras
Una sombra no son de lo que fueron.

In Africa, Asia, and Europe,
Your warriors marched triumphant,
And when one world was not enough for
your power,
An even larger world did heaven grant you.
But your cruel and ferocious sons,
Thirsting for blood and gold and evil
Devoured like carnivorous vultures
The innocent tribes of that world,
And the thousand peoples who lived there
Descended to their tombs en masse.
The monarchy of Anahuac fell
And the Incan empire was toppled.
Atyahualpa, Caonaba, Montezuma,
Hateuy, Guatimozín . . . all fell!
And scarcely are their names recalled
Between the tears of their memory
inspire . . .
Bloodthirsty nation! Like Saturn
You devoured the children of your breast,
And then, like Cain, you sacrificed
Your brothers with fierce bitterness.
Like the tree of the American forest
Which poisons the ground it grows on,
Kills the birds that nest on it and the
neighboring plants,
In whose shadow flowers whither and
insects flee,
So, too, under the ill-omened shade
Of your bloodied fatalistic flag,
Freedom flees, industry ceases,
Learning declines, and progress dies.
Daughter of the African deserts,
It seems that the hand of Eternity,
To free Europe from contact with you,
Raised the Pyrenees in the ether.

What became, Spain, of your laurels?
What of your illustrious warriors?
Your conquests, your glories of other days,
Your matrons, your sages, what became of
them?
Your sons scarcely preserve
The memory of this immense power,
Even your ancient glory,

En la Africa, y en Asia, y en Europa,
Se paseaban triunfantes tus guerreros,
Y no bastando a tu poder un mundo,
Otro mundo más grande te dio el cielo;
Pero tus hijos crueles y feroces,
De sangre, y oro, y de maldad sedientos,
Las inocentes tribus de aquel mundo
Devoraron cual buitres carniceros,
Y mil pueblos, y mil que allí vivían,
En tropel a la tumba descendieron . . .
Cayó del Anahuac la monarquía
Y de los Incas sucumbió el imperio;
Atahualpa, Caonabo, Moctezuma,
Hatuey, Guatimozín . . . ¡todos cayeron!
Y apenas de sus nombres la memoria
Entre lágrimas guardan los recuerdos . . .
¡Sanguinaria nación! ¡Cómo Saturno
Devoraste los hijos de tu seno,
y después cual Caín, a tus hermanos
Sacrificaste con encono fiero.
Como el árbol del mundo americano
A cuya sombra que emponzoña el suelo,
Callan las aves y la planta muere,
Se marchita la flor y huye el insecto;
Así también a la funesta sombra
De tu pendón fatídico y sangriento,
Huye la libertad, cesa la industria,
Calla la ilustración, muere el progreso.
Hija de los desiertos africanos,
Parece que la mano del Eterno
Para librar de tu contacto a Europa
Hasta el éter alzó los Pirineos.

¿Qué se hicieron, España, tus laureles?
¿Qué se hicieron, tus ínclitos guerreros?
Tus conquistas, tus glorias de otros días,
Tus matronas, tus sabios, ¿qué se
hicieron?
Apenas de ese inmenso poderío
Conservan ya tus hijos el recuerdo,
Que hasta el recuerdo de tu antigua gloria

Your backward people, Spain, ignore it.
Stunted and bastardly generation
Of beggars, and friars, and bullfighters,
How could it understand the exploits
Of their illustrious grandsires?
How could the people who in abject servitude
Bow their necks calmly to oppression
Understand that there was a Padilla
Of noble audacity and a heart of fire?
How could these people who are energized
Only by pleasure, without Faith, mettle
Nor courage understand how big was
The soul of the Guzman called *the good*?
How could those men of servile
Spirit and weak breath admire
The sublime abnegation of Numancia,
Or Sagunto's outstanding deeds?
Illegitimate sons! Degraded race!
Degenerated lineage of pygmies!
Perhaps they mistake for a fable
The glorious exploits of other times?
Perhaps with a skeptical smile
They listen to the stories
Of the titanic deeds that one day
Gave renown to the Iberian banner!
Of your immense power, miserable Spain,
Only remains memories and reminiscences;
The nations that yesterday obeyed you
Today pronounce your name without respect:
And tomorrow the history in your annals
Will be written with tears,
And your sons . . . Perhaps at last ashamed!
Will curse their barbaric grandfathers
Because of this I saw your cities,
And studied your people, with bitter disenchantment,
And instead of admiration, I felt in my soul
A sentiment, Spain, of contempt.

Lo ignora, España, tu atrasado pueblo.
Generación raquítica y bastarda
De mendigos, y frailes, y toreros,
¿Cómo ha de comprender ¡ay! las proezas
Que acabaron sus ínclitos abuelos?
¿Cómo ha de comprender que hubo un Padilla
De noble audacia y corazón de fuego
El pueblo que en abyecta servidumbre
Dobla tranquilo a la opresión el cuello?
¿Cómo ha de comprender cuánto fue grande
El alma de Guzmán llamado *el bueno*,
La gente que enervada en los placeres
Ni tiene fe, ni fibra, ni denuedo?
¿Cómo admirar pudieran esos hombres
De espíritu servil y flaco aliento
La abnegación sublime de Numancia,
Ni de Sagunto los preclaros hechos?
¡Hijos espúreos! ¡Raza degradada!
¡Degenerada estirpe de pigmeos!
¡Acaso con la fábula confunda
Las gloriosas hazañas de otros tiempos!
¡Acaso con escéptica sonrisa
La relación escuche como un cuento
De los hechos titánicos que un día
Renombre dieran al pendón ibero!
De tu inmenso poder, mísera España,
Sólo quedan memorias y recuerdos;
Las naciones que ayer te obedecían
Hoy pronuncian tu nombre sin respeto:
Y mañana la historia en sus anales
Escribirá con lágrimas tus hechos,
Y tus hijos . . . ¡tal vez avergonzados!
Maldecirán sus bárbaros abuelos . . .
Por eso con amargo desencanto
Vi tus ciudades, y estudié tus pueblos,
Y en vez de admiración, sentí en el alma
Un sentimiento, España, de desprecio.

Juan Clemente Zenea (1832–1871)

In Greenwood (En Greenwood)

Journalist, poet, revolutionary, Juan Clemente Zenea is one of the most enigmatic and highly debated figures in nineteenth-century Cuban history. Born in the eastern provincial city of Bayamo, early in life (1845) Zenea moved to Havana to study with the distinguished educator José de la Luz y Caballero. Once in the Cuban capital, he became involved in the cultural and political restlessness of the time, attracting the attention of the colonial authorities for his clandestine publications against Spain. Like so many of his contemporaries, in 1852 he was forced into exile for his support of a failed separatist operation led by General Narciso López in 1848. He fled to New York City, where he joined the intellectually and politically active Spanish-American exile community. Zenea's life had a puzzling and tragic ending. In the midst of the first war of Cuban independence (known as the Ten Years War, 1868–1878), both the Spanish government and the New York Revolutionary Junta asked him to take messages to the commander of the rebel forces on the Cuban battlefields. Unable to arrange an interview with the military official, Zenea was attempting to return to the United States when he was captured and later shot by a Spanish squadron. Many questions surrounding these events still remain unanswered, and debate continues: Why did the Spanish government contact Zenea? Was he a double agent, a patriot, or traitor? His poetry, though, rises above these contentions, and in *In Greenwood*, one of his last poems, the romantic nostalgia for the homeland, wrapped in the shadow of death, is elaborated in the refined lyrical tone so characteristic of his style. (ALO)

Further Reading: Juan Clemente Zenea, *Poesías*, compiled by José Lezama Lima (La Habana: Academia de Ciencias de Cuba/Instituto de Literatura y Linguística, 1966), *El laúd del desterrado* [1858], ed. Matías Montes-Huidobro (Houston: Arte Público Press, 1995).

Trans.: MAT

Beside the waters of the silent brook,
Amid the forest, in this place of refuge,
Beneath the green grass and the rose
bushes
Is where I want to rest when my time
comes.

That time is nigh: my days have lost their
luster
And faded uniformly as life's snows
Begin to fall and gather on my head,
Announcing future happiness elsewhere.

But what shall happen if on quiet nights
I go wandering as shadows sometimes do,
And instead of finding my plaintive
palms,

Al lado de estas aguas silenciosas,
En medio de este bosque, en este asilo,
Debajo de estas gramas y estas rosas,
Es donde quiero reposar tranquilo.

Y pronto debo reposar! mis días
Se tiñen ya de pálidos destellos,
Y anuncian mis postreras alegrías
Las nieves de la vida en los cabellos.

Mas, ¿qué será si en las nocturnas clamas
Salgo á vagar como las sombras suelen,
Y en vez de hallar mis quejumbrosas
palmas,

The weeping willows alone should mourn me?	Los sauces sólo de mi afán se duelen?
Oh! What if racked by the deepest of sorrows,	Oh! qué será si en honda pesadumbre
I should sit me to meditate on my tomb,	Sentado á meditar sobre la losa,
And yearning still for my homeland in bondage,	Suspiro por mi pueblo en servidumbre
In vain I look for Cuba's beauteous sky?	Y el cielo busco de mi Cuba hermosa!
What torment that would be! But if, at some time,	Tormentosa será! Mas si tardío
The sun is born that I've long wished would shine,	Nace á brillar el sol de mis anhelos,
Then make for me a grave beside the family lake	Cabe la orilla del paterno río
And take me to rest among my grandsires.	Llevadme á descansar con mis abuelos.
There where my cradle in a bitter hour	Y allí donde mi cuna en hora amarga
Recklessly rocked me to a fickle fate,	Al capricho meció voluble suerte,
Let me at last lay down this heavy burden	Dejadme al fin depositar la carga
And in the bosom of death sleep serenely!	Y dormir en el seno de la muerte!

Bonifacio Byrne (1861–1936)

My Flag (Mi Bandera)

Known as the "Poet of Cuban Independence," Bonifacio Byrne was born in Matanzas, a city known as the "Athens of Cuba." A frequent contributor to the city's newspapers, Byrne published his first poetry volume in 1893. Due to his involvement in the war of independence, he was exiled to Tampa, Florida, where he worked as a reader in a cigar factory. A founding member of the Cuban Revolutionary Club of Tampa, Byrne was a commentator for the exile newspapers *Patria*, *El Porvenir*, and *El Expedicionario*. He returned to Cuba from his exile in 1899 and became a school superintendent in his native city. The author of five poetry volumes, Byrne is regarded by critics as an excellent modernist poet, but his fame rests in his patriotic poetry. In it, he lauds the heroes and martyrs of the Cuban struggle for independence as well as the symbols of Cuban nationalism. In *My Flag*, one of the most quoted poems in Cuban literature, Byrne demonstrates his patriotism and fiery nationalistic spirit as he disappointedly sees the American flag flying along with the Cuban flag upon his return to his native island. (JBF)

Further reading: Caroline Hospital and Jorge Cantera, eds., *A Century of Cuban Writers in Florida* (Sarasota: Pineapple Press, 1996).

Trans.: MAT

Upon returning from a distant shore, Weary of heart and somber, I searched for my flag anxiously And saw another flying beside her.	Al volver de distante ribera, con el alma enlutada, y sombría, afanoso busqué mi bandera ¡y otra he visto además de la mía!
With the faith of an austere soul, In this conviction I have grown That two flags should not be flown When one is enough: my own!	Con la fe de las almas austeras hoy sostengo con honda energía que no deben flotar dos banderas donde basta con una: ¡la mía!
In fields that have been turned to boneyards, She saw the struggles of the brave, And she has been the winding-sheet Of warriors who lie in the grave.	En los campos que hoy son un osario vio a los bravos batiéndose juntos, y ella ha sido el honroso sudario de los pobres guerreros difuntos.
She proudly held her own in battle, Without puerile or romantic praise: The Cuban who doesn't believe in her Should be branded a coward always!	Orgullosa lució en la pelea, sin pueril y romántico alarde: ¡al cubano que en ella no crea se le debe azotar por cobarde!
From the depths of the darkest prison, She heard not a word of woe; In other lands she was the beacon That led our footsteps in the snow . . .	En el fondo de obscuras prisiones no escuchó ni la queja más leve, y sus huellas en otras regiones son letreros de luz en la nieve . . .
Don't you see her! My flag is the one That ne'er has mercenary flown, In whose field there shines a star All more brightly for being alone.	¿No la veis? Mi bandera es aquélla que no ha sido jamás mercenaria, y en la cual resplandece una estrella con más luz, cuanto más solitaria.
I've brought her in my soul from exile Amongst my memories of home, And I have rendered her homage By raising her aloft in my poem.	Del destierro en el alma la traje entre tantos recuerdos dispersos y he sabido rendirle homenaje al hacerla flotar en mis versos.
Though listless now and sadly drooping, I hope some day the sun's pure light Will shine on her—on her alone!— On land and sea and mountain height.	Aunque lánguida y triste tremola, mi ambición es que el sol con su lumbre la ilumine a ella sola—¡a ella sola!— en el llano, en el mar y en la cumbre.
If my flag were torn to pieces Those who died to make her free Would raise their arms together And fight eternally! . . .	Si deshecha en menudos pedazos llega a ser mi bandera algún día . . . ¡nuestros muertos alzando los brazos la sabrán defender todavía! . . .

Lola Rodríguez de Tió (1843–1924)

Ode to October 10 (10 de Octubre)

Ode to October 10 is a patriotic poem written to commemorate the anniversary of the first Cuban war of independence (1868–1878). It was first read publicly in New York City in 1896 to an audience of Puerto Rican and Cuban expatriates committed to ending Spanish colonial rule over their islands. Many of those present had been forced into exile upon the resumption of Cuban insurgency in 1895. Rodríguez de Tió was well known at the time not only for her poetry, but also for her liberal convictions and the support she openly lent to a failed attempt for Puerto Rican independence in 1868, known as "El Grito de Lares" (The Shout at Lares). On that occasion she wrote the lyrics for a song that later became the revolutionary anthem of Puerto Rico, *La Borinqueña*. She was exiled from her country three times by an increasingly vigilant colonial government: 1877–1879 (to Caracas), 1889–1891 (to Havana), and again in 1896. This last time she was forced to leave for New York City due to her vocal support for the Cuban revolutionary cause. There she was an active participant in the exile community until 1899, when she finally established permanent residence in Cuba. Many of Rodríguez de Tió's poems exhibit the conventions of romantic patriotic love while conveying the desire for the political unity of the Greater Antilles. Perhaps her best-known verses—often mistakenly attributed to José Martí—are: "Cuba y Puerto Rico son/de un pájaro las dos alas/reciben flores o balas/en un mismo corazón" ("Cuba and Puerto Rico are/the two wings of one bird/they receive flowers or bullets/in a single heart"). In 1910 Cuba would reciprocate the love of this daughter of Puerto Rico by naming her to the Cuban Academy of Arts and Sciences. (ALO)

Further reading: Lola Rodríguez de Tió, *Obras completas* (San Juan: Instituto de Cultura Puertorriqueña, 1968).

Trans.: MAT

I
As on a noble monument,
I've come here to consecrate
My soul, my lyre, my thoughts
On the altar of the fatherland.
I've come to occupy my place,
And I do most fittingly
My song raise in memory
Of martyrs of yesterday,
Making the leaves again green
On their glorious laurel wreaths.

II
Blessed and solemn anniversary
Which is a poem incarnate,
Eloquent emblem of your fate
Which today fills our minds.

I
Aquí vengo a consagrar
como en noble monumento,
alma, lira y pensamiento,
de la patria en el altar.
Vengo mi puesto a ocupar,
y con voz propiciatoria
alzo mi canto en la memoria
de los mártires de ayer,
haciendo reverdecer
¡los laureles de su gloria!

II
Fecha solemne y bendita
Que encierra todo un poema,
Hoy como elocuente emblema
En nuestra mente palpita.

With tears and blood it is written
On the heart of every Cuban,
And despite the tyrant's wrath
It will never be forgotten.
For tears are never shed in vain,
Nor does crime forever prosper.

Con llanto y sangre está escrita
En cada pecho cubano,
Y aunque se ensañe el tirano
No la empañará el olvido;
¡que el llanto nunca es perdido
ni se hace el crimen en vano!

III

For you, my beloved Cuba,
Many martyrs their lives gave
And countless are all the graves
Opened in your blooddrenched earth . . .
No matter: you will be free
Of the tyrant's savagery,
And on your shores I will see
Floating above your royal palms,
On the same breeze as my song,
Your flag waving gloriously.

III

Por tí, Cuba idolatrada,
Muchos mártires cayeron,
Y muchas tumbas se abrieron
En tu tierra ensangrentada . . .
Mas ¿qué importa? Libertada
Serás de la garra fiera,
Y he de ver en tu ribera
Sobre tus palmas flotar,
Al eco de mi cantar
¡los pliegues de tu bandera!

IV

And when evoking the past,
Which, unlike men, never dies,
We see your dead leaders rise
From their cold graves at the last:
It's because your deathless name
Is pledged again in freedom's cause,
And your great people, which grows
Amid their own pain and sorrows,
Not even martyrdom fear
To win the supreme ideal!

IV

Al evocar el pasado
entre los despojos yertos,
se ven tus caudillos muertos
surgir del sepulcro helado:
y es que de nuevo empeñado
está su nombre inmortal,
con el pueblo colosal
que en el dolor se agiganta,
y ni el martirio le espanta
¡ante el supremo ideal!

V

Cespédes, Martí, Agramonte!
Moncada, Crombet, Maceo!
Well could such a panoply
Push the ends of the horizon!
Fame must soar beyond its limits
If it ever hopes to reach
The heroes that shine so bright
In the sun's resplendent light,
So that it can proudly claim them
And immortalize their triumph.

V

¡Céspedes, Martí, Agramonte!
¡Moncada, Crombet, Maceo!
¡bien puede tanto trofeo
ensanchar el horizonte!
¡Alto su vuelo remonte
la Fama, si ha de alcanzar
héroes en que ve brillar
del sol tan vivos destellos,
que puede orgullosa en ellos
el triunfo inmortalizar!

VI

They have not died, but are lighting

VI

¡Ellos no han muerto! Aún alumbran

With their dauntless warrior spirit
The glorious path to follow
By the heroes that are rising.
They can be seen in the distance,
Making all our hearts beat faster,
Fighting in heroic legions
Worthy of Spartan combats,
Following two liberators
Whose deeds are astonishing.

con su espíritu guerrero,
el glorioso derrotero
de otros héroes que se encumbran;
y vibran los corazones
agitándose en legiones
dignas de espartanas lides,
en pos de dos adalides
que asombran con sus acciones.

VII
Although each day there are tombs
Freshly opened in your soil,
Do not fear the energy
Which burns in your sons, will wane;
For none shall ever recoil,
And the cannon roars in vain
When on mountaintop or plain
Is heard this constant refrain:
"A Cuban knows how to die
His country to liberate!

VII
Aunque se abra una tumba
En tu suelo cada día,
No temas que la energía
Que arde en tus hijos, sucumba;
En vano el cañón retumba
Con ronco estruendo de guerra,
Si en el llano y en la sierra
Se oye al eco repetir
—¡Sabe el cubano morir
para libertar su tierra!—

VIII
With skill that all must admire,
Zayas has taken the field,
Such beautiful promise yields
Only to enemy fire.
My lips cannot tell the story
Without trembling with emotion
Of how in a blaze of glory
Without once resting his sword,
In the midst of a campaign,
This symbol of bravery fell.

VIII
Con esfuerzo que aún asombra,
Zayas al campo se lanza,
¡y a tan hermosa esperanza
hiere una bala en la sombra! . . .
¡Ni una vez mi labio nombra,
sin que se encienda en amor,
al que en su primer fulgor
cayó, sin cansar la espada,
en mitad de la jormada
simbolizando el valor!

IX
But, oh, his blood makes the earth seethe
And calls to heaven for justice,
So that humanity won't leave
Unpunished this crime of cowardice.
The sun's rays are shining brightly
On his cold lifeless remains,
And when the sun sees the rivers
With blood and tears overflowing,
Before this horrible spectacle
The sun sinks beneath the sea.

IX
Pero ¡ah! Que su sangre humea
Y clama al cielo piedad,
Porque ya la humanidad
Impune el crimen no vea.
La luz del sol centellea
Sobre sus despojos fríos,
Y al ver en hirvientes ríos
Correr la sangre y el llanto,
Ante el horror y el espanto
Se hunde en los mares sombríos.

X
Despite the bloodshed and violence,
The tyrant suffers the loss
If he doesn't raise a cross
On which to nail our conscience.
The cry of independence
Awakens us from darkness,
And the good fortune we bless
To fight in her defense.
Even if in the rude combat
Death is our sole recompense.

X
Es inútil la violencia
Del déspota sanguinario,
Si no levanta un calvario
Donde enclavar la conciencia;
Al grito de independencia
No hay pueblo que no despierte,
Y no bendiga la suerte
De luchar por su rescate,
Aunque en el rudo combate
¡halle por premio la muerte!

XI
There's another country . . . mine!
Which with an arduous effort
Awakens from the deep sleep
Too long imposed by tyranny.
Perhaps the day will come, I hope
—In the not too distant future—
When brave and pure she will dare
To follow Cuba's example,
Since by the great pain they share
God Himself has made them sisters!

XI
Hay otra tierra . . . ¡la mía!
Que con ardoroso empeño,
Despierta del torpe sueño
Que alargó la tiranía.
Tal vez, tal vez llegue el día,
—en época no muy lejana—
en que a la patria cubana
siga en virtud y en valor,
ya que en su inmenso dolor
¡el mismo Dios las hermana!

XII
Very soon, beautiful Cuba,
The blessed liberty you've won
A thousand sources of life
Will bring to your bounteous land!
Once your sword is again idle
When the tyrant is defeated,
You will forget how to hate,
And on your glorious shores
You will cover with your flag
Both the victor and the vanquished!

XII
¡Pronto será, Cuba hermosa,
Que la libertad querida,
Abra mil fuentes de vida
En tu tierra generosa!
¡Una vez espada ociosa
y el rudo opresor rendido,
darás el odio al olvido,
y en tu gloriosa ribera
cubrirás con tu bandera
al vencedor y al vencido!

Francisco Gonzalo "Pachín" Marín (1863–1897)

A Statistic (Estadistica); Fragments (Fragmentos)

"Pachín" Marín was born in Arecibo, Puerto Rico, on March 12, 1863, under the name of Francisco Gonzalo Marín Shaw. Early in his life, he showed an inclination for literature and music. Marín began his career as a journalist with the publication of a manuscript journal; later he contributed to local newspapers. In 1887, Marín founded *El Postillón*, a newspaper in which he criticized the Spanish regime. These activities produced his first exile to Santo Domingo, where he was exiled once again under the Ulises Hereaux dictatorship (1886–1889), thus beginning his career as an eternal exile. In 1892, he published *Romances* in New York, where he was named secretary of the "Club Borinquen," a revolutionary center that sought economic resources for the independence of Puerto Rico. In New York, he met and befriended José Martí, whom he helped to publish and distribute Cuban revolutionary propaganda. In 1896, Marín decided to join the Cuban Liberation Army and participated in the invasion of the island under General Máximo Gómez. On October 26, 1897, he died alone in a swamp where he fell victim to fever and malnutrition. "Pachín" Marín died at thirty-four without seeing the freedom of Puerto Rico or Cuba. *Romances* is composed of forty-nine poems, almost all of them written in his adolescence. Common themes in Marín's poetry are his homeland, exile, love, motherhood, death, and progress. (CV)

Further reading: Francisco Gonzalo Marín, *Romances* (New York, 1892), *En la arena* (Cuba, 1898).

Trans.: MAT

A Statistic

I
In a geography class
This exchange took place one day
Between a Puerto Rican child
And a schoolmaster from Spain.
"In this Universe, which country
Is populated most densely?"
"Puerto Rico, sir," he answered;
And the teacher further queried:
How many live on this island?"
He thought hard and quite unhurried;
The boy at last answered: "Two."
"Two strokes of the cane for you,
For such a stupid reply."
And putting his words in practice
The punishment he applied.

II
Today, as I am getting older
—For that boy was me—
I more than ever can see
The wisdom of that reply,
Ingenious for a boy
But quite obvious to a man.

Estadística

I
En la clase de patria geografía,
ved lo que aconteció
entre un niño nacido en Puerto Rico
y un maestro español:
—¿Cuál es del Universo el país que encierra
más densa población?
Y contestó el discípulo de pronto:
—Puerto Rico, señor.
—¿Dígame cuántos habitantes tiene?—
el dómine añadió;
y después de pensar un largo rato,
el rapaz dijo:—Dos.
—¡Dos palmetazos sufrirá el estúpido
alumno ignorantón!
Y uniendo a la palabra el hecho práctico
al niño castigó.

II
Hoy, a medida que me pongo viejo,
porque el niño era yo,
más me aferro a la ingénita respuesta
dada en esa ocasión.
Quien halló solitarios y sombríos,
sin amigos, sin sol,

For I have lived alone and somber,
Without friends and without sun,
In the lands where I have wandered
Since my exile first begun,
And can't conceive of another
Land with more people or sun
Than the place where I was born.
"How many live on this island?"
—My professor once asked me
When I was only a boy . . . —
If that unhappy apostle
Still lives who taught me to write
The name of you, my motherland,
Again I should answer: "Two."
For my country is in my heart
And the two of us can't part,
Even in the humble grave
That awaits me, there will be
Just two: my country and me.

Trans.: MAT

los extranjeros pueblos visitados
en larga expatriación,
no puede imaginar haya otra tierra
con más gente y más sol
que la tierra poblada de esperanzas,
la tierra en que nació.

"¿Dígame cuántos habitantes tiene?"
—me inquirió el profesor
ayer cuando era niño todavía . . . —
Hoy, que ya viejo soy,
si subsistiera el infeliz apóstol
que a escribir me enseñó
tu nombre, madre mía, le dijera
otra vez que eran dos,
porque a mi Patria me la tengo siempre
dentro del corazón,
y en el mezquino hueco que me resta
no caben más personas que tú y yo.

Fragments

I
To the unhappy land of my ancestors
—Today without pity denied this exile—
In the tragic ship of my own sorrows,
I arrived, not long ago, demanding entry.

My ship had sailed without rudder or compass,
With tattered sails and a demolished bridge,
Combating bravely a tempestuous ocean,
To conquer the violent storm that battered it . . .

II
How often did I do battle with myself,
Or with the wind in an unequal contest,
And standing at the edge of the abyss,
There came to me the flash of an ideal! . . .

How many times, in a delirious state,

Fragmentos

I
A la tierra infeliz de mis mayores
—hoy al proscripto sin piedad negada—
en el triste bajel de mis dolores
llegué, no ha mucho, demandando entrada.

Iba mi buque sin timón ni egida,
roto el velamen, destrozado el puente,
combatiendo á la mar embravecida,
venciendo el azotar de la rompiente . . . .

II
¡Cuántas veces en lid conmigo mismo,
ó con el viento en desigual pelea,
de pié, sobre la boca del abismo,
cruzó mi mente el rayo de una idea . . . . !

¡En cuántas ocasiones, delirante,

From this poor and feeble vantage point
Did I think of crashing 'gainst the distant rocks,
Or dashing myself at the craggy beachhead!

desde la pobre y débil atalaya,
pensé chocar con el peñón distante
ó estrellarme en la roca de la playa!

III

How beautiful that shipwreck would have seemed
By night, against the icebergs and sea mist:
The skiff left to its fate, the wounded man
Enveloped in a foamy shroud of sea spray! . . .

III

Qué hermoso aquel naufragio hubiera sido
de noche, entre los hielos y las brumas:
el esquife al azar, y un hombre herido
cubierto por un lábaro de espumas! . . .

How beautiful it would have been the next day
—As dawn awakened with uncertain splendor
Over the vast cold surface of the ocean—
To see the lifeless mariner float by! . . .

Qué hermoso hubiera sido al otro día,
de la alborada al resplandor incierto,
sobre la vasta superficie fría
ver que flotaba el marinero muerto . . . !

Francisco Sellén (1836–1907)

Hatuey

Poet, translator, dramatist, Francisco Sellén was deeply involved in the struggle for Cuban independence. Jailed for his revolutionary activities in Cuba, he escaped and went into exile in the United States in 1868. From that time on, his was a strong and frequent voice in the Hispanic exile press. He began publishing books of poetry and translations from English and German in New York in 1869. Sellén's play *Hatuey* is based on documents by the major promoter of the Spanish Black Legend, Fray Bartolomé de las Casas, who in his *Breve relación de la destrucción de las Indias* details the atrocities committed by the Spaniards during their Conquest of the Indies. Sellén chose the historical figure of Hatuey as a base for Cuban nationalism because the Cubans had a strong need to become less Spanish in their quest for developing a New World identity. They also identified with the plight of the Amerindians during the Conquest by the Spaniards. In *Hatuey*, Sellén sees the Amerindian as a noble savage, who inhabits a kind of Pre-Colombian paradise, which is destroyed violently by the Spaniards. In the play, the resistance to the conquerors and the interplay between traitors and loyals that ends with Hatuey's death are a perfect representation of the fights for independence, the internal problems of the revolutionaries, and the general martyrdom suffered by Cuban patriots. Sellén intended *Hatuey* to be the first national drama of Cuba. In the climactic scene below, Hatuey is martyred by the Spanish authorities despite the intervention of Las Casas, the protector of the natives. (MS)

Further reading: Francisco Sellén, *Hatuey, Poema Dramático* (New York: A. Da Costa Gómez, 1891).

Trans.: MAT

Act V

Velázquez's Tent
Velázquez, Grijalva

VELÁZQUEZ
Have you read the prisoner the sentence
Of death by fire pronounced against him?

GRIJALVA
With this charge I was headed to the prison,
But Father Las Casas who, with profound zeal,
Is moved to save the lives of these people,
Had already been there; and I thought it wise . . .

VELÁZQUEZ
Well, then, Grijalva, you may take your leave,
The sentence is suspended for the present.
(*Grijalva exits*)
To the ardent pleas and humane arguments
Of the good Father Las Casas, I have yielded,
And soon the rebel shall be here whose cause
He has defended so tenaciously:
His ardor misleads and his heart fools him.
It is one thing to win souls for heaven,
And quite another to rule conquered lands.
My authority suffers by consenting . . .
Well, he approaches; but what arrogance!
This surely cannot be a good portent.
(*Hatuey enters escorted by guards*)
Leave us alone.

HATUEY
Cacique of Christians, why have you sent for me?

VELÁZQUEZ
The law has condemned you to die at the stake:
Speak now in your defense.

HATUEY
What can I say? Why does the Christian take
My freedom, my land and sentence me to death?

VELÁZQUEZ
Because you are a traitor.

HATUEY
A traitor to whom?

VELÁZQUEZ
Against the king, who is your lord and mine,
And his authority did you conspire
And take up arms: a rebel and a traitor.

HATUEY
Neither rebel nor traitor am I: for free
As the wind or the waters, I was born,
And like the *guaraguao* that takes wing

And goes wither he lists, nesting in mountains,
I never had a master: and cannot live
Like the *guani*, when deprived of liberty.
I have fought for what is mine, and justice
Is on my side.

VELÁZQUEZ
What audacity! Are you a native of this land,
Or do you rule it as a usurper?
Were you not the cacique of Guanaja,
And did you not quit your realm and come here
To sow distrust and hatred against Christians?

HATUEY
I am no stranger here: this is my race.
When the land where I was born fell victim
To your savage fury and your avarice,
And I was not free to rule my people,
Who, now enslaved, did other gods worship
Than the ancient Semíes of Quisqueya,
I turned my back on the land of my forbears
And for the good of my people came here,
Unlike you, who came here to do them harm.

VELÁZQUEZ
By ¡blood, enough! My patience and kindness
You have abused. If I have deigned to hear you
'Twas not for your sake, but for Las Casas'.
You owe it to him; for I fain would speak

To traitors only with the stake or steel.

Hatuey
Take my life, then: for towards Christians, I feel
Only a deep and implacable hate;
And while the Spaniard rules the isle of Cuba
Hate will be my calling, vengeance my virtue.

Velázquez
Since such is your wish, I shall carry out
The sentence against you. Guards, present yourselves.
(*Guards enter*)

Hatuey
Death is for me naught but a welcome release;
For I fear Spaniards more than I fear death.

Velázquez
Shackle the prisoner and convey him
One more to jail, and have Grijalva come
Forthwith.
(*The guards take the prisoner away*)
My own anger is choking me!
I do not know how I could be so patient
And not let my sword punish such insolence
By cutting off his tongue.
(*Grijalva enters*)
Grijalva, the sentence must be carried out
In flames let him expatiate his treason.
Leave right away and don't waste any time.
Let the Franciscan priest accompany him.
You are in charge of everything; take care
Father Bartolomé learns nothing of this.
His love for these people is known to all,
And I would spare the good Las Casas this grief.

Grijalva
Your orders will be carried out forthwith,
As you've instructed.
(*Exits*)

Velázquez (*alone, paces the tent*)
His death is necessary and my duty;
And no less necessary is the warning
Implied in it, to establish the peace.

(*Pauses*)
What, is that not Las Casas? Yes . . . he comes
In this direction . . . A new campaign
Must I now wage . . . Does he already know?
Well, then: I must make him surrender all hope.
(*Las Casas enters*)

LAS CASAS
Can it be true that you are now resolved
To carry out immediately the sentence?
Is the prisoner to die?

VELÁZQUEZ
Yes, Father.

LAS CASAS
But why, my lord, do you proceed so quickly?
Wherefore this rush to judgment? I had hoped
Never again to see the horrid pyre
That lit the sky of Hispaniola burn here.

VELÁZQUEZ
Because I have no other choice, Father.
For rancor, vengeance and hatred sustain
This rebel: his influence among his people
Is great, and could be turned soon against us.

LAS CASAS
Consider, my lord, what a savage is,
Who can only express ever-changing thoughts,
Only mere sensations: theirs are children's souls
Who crave the very things that they discard,
And to punish a child would be a crime:
And what else but a child is a savage?

VELÁZQUEZ
A salutary example is needed.

LAS CASAS
No, cruelty is never necessary,
And in the end mercy always triumphs.
Is he not already in our power?
What can he do to conspire against us?
Alone, unarmed, his forces annihilated,
How can he oppose us? Let him voice in vain

His well-founded complaints, and pardon him.

VELÁZQUEZ
Clemency would be a show of weakness.

LAS CASAS
Mercy is the patrimony of the strong:
To be magnanimous is to be great.

VELÁZQUEZ
At times severity is a virtue.

LAS CASAS
A cursed virtue! Bloodshed demands more bloodshed;
And hatred, vengeance and rancor it sows.

VELÁZQUEZ
To shed a little blood in time will save
Great quantities of blood in later years.

LAS CASAS
Perhaps some would describe that as prudence,
Or an affair of State: I do not know;
But there's a virtue more exalted—charity.

VELÁZQUEZ
My worthy Las Casas: such seeming harshness
Is a dam to contain impending evils.
Sometimes a limb is ordered amputated
To save a life.

LAS CASAS
You are well-known for your humanity . . .
But time is flying, my lord: with each moment
The hour of execution fast approaches.
I do not ask that you should pardon him,
But only for a stay; justice must be
Always deliberate and in God's image,
Who corrects us calmly, never vengefully.
Behold me at your feet: I beg you, please,
Suspend the sentence now . . . My lord, I ask,
Have mercy . . . Else on my knees I shall remain.

VELÁZQUEZ
Arise, oh Father! For your sake, I grant

What you have asked of me. Arise, I say!

LAS CASAS
Thank-you, Velázquez, may the Lord reward you.
(*Exits*)

VELÁZQUEZ (*after a brief pause*)
Mere foolish pity! Though I do expect
That Lucifer has brought him to account.
(*He paces silently*)
But what is happening? Why all this noise?
(*Opens door and surveys the field*)
The soldiers are gathered round an object . . .
And Ordaz approaches.
(*Ordaz enters*)
Tell me what's happened
Upon the field, Ordaz? Is it a quarrel?

DIEGO DE ORDAZ
The young Indian maid to whom I owe my life
Has been found unconscious at the river's edge.

VELÁZQUEZ
Is she hurt, perchance? Does she need our help?

DIEGO DE ORDAZ
No: she is dead.

VELÁZQUEZ
Dead, you say? The guilty shall for this crime pay
With his own life, whoever he may be . . .

DIEGO DE ORDAZ
It was she, my lord, who put a violent end
To her own life.

VELÁZQUEZ
In what manner?

DIEGO DE ORDAZ
She visited this morning the prisoner:
What passed between them is a mystery.
She was in high esteem held by her people;
A lily she was called, their favorite jewel,
Beloved by all who knew her, and the sister

Of that Indian who was close friends with Hatuey.
They saw her leave in tears, her face downcast;
Alone, she wandered the length of the river,
And stopping at its banks, she did advance
Into the water, then retreat again;
When, suddenly, where the waters are roughest
And form whirlwinds, she flung herself with a will.
We all ran to her aid: a vain attempt;
She could swim like a fish, and had she wanted
Her own life could have saved; but her desire
Was to end her existence, and she did.
No trace of her did the current reveal,
And when at long last we caught sight of her,
She was floating in a pool made by the reeds,
Or, rather, her corpse was. Oh, the poor maid!

VELÁZQUEZ
Bring her remains to camp and bury her
As God ordains.

The Fields of Yara
Hatuey, Grijalva, a Franciscan friar, soldiers

HATUEY
These are the fields of Yara where I'll die:
And these the forests and the green meadows,
The sun, the sea, the sky, the hills. The rivers
Which as a free man I've long looked upon
And which so many times I've freely passed,
And which for one last time my eyes behold.
This earth that my ashes shall soon enrich,
Fields that I leave enslaved: Farewell forever!
But in this place, when many moons have passed,
These people also shall learn a harsh lesson.
Fortunate the man who sees the sun rise
More beautiful than ever on the great day
Of our longed-for redemption! That light
Bathes my face, and before my eyes there opens
The future. Now, Hatuey, you can die in peace.
A secret voice within me is proclaiming
That what was taken by the force of arms,
And rules by force and is by force maintained,
Can never have the sanction of the Semí
And must at last by force also perish.
Throw me into the pyre: I am ready.

THE FRANCISCAN FRIAR
You now must turn your mind to higher things.
Your soul shall not be lost: there is another life.
Once dead, the body's buried in the earth;
But the soul can enjoy eternal bliss,
Or else innumerable torments suffer.

HATUEY
What must be done to gain such happiness?

THE FRANCISCAN FRIAR
Renounce forever the Semíes you've worshipped
And render homage to our God, and then
Shall you in heaven find eternal bliss.
If you refuse, then you shall be condemned
To hell, whose horrors you'll never escape.

HATUEY
Do Spaniards go to heaven? And Christians
Do they also gain admittance to heaven?

THE FRANCISCAN FRIAR
The good may enter, but only the good.

HATUEY
If that is so, then I don't wish to go
Where even the good among them have gone.
For hell would be better, without their presence,
Than a heaven filled with such wicked people.
(*He mounts resolutely the pyre. There is a deep silence which lasts for a few moments; the Franciscan friar kneels*)

GRIJALVA
Praise God that the savage such courage shows
And dies like a hero of olden days!
(*Las Casas enters*)

LAS CASAS
In the King's name, halt the execution!

GRIJALVA
The reprieve comes too late.

LAS CASAS
Oh, dismal dispatch! . . . Perhaps there is yet time . . .

GRIJALVA (*pointing to the stake*)
It's too late: he belongs to another world
(*Pause for moments of solemn silence*)

LAS CASAS (*kneeling: many do likewise*)
Our Lord, who in human form was embodied
To save us from the scourge of death eternal;
Who knew the sorrow of becoming man
And who is moved to pity by man's errors;
Who can look into the abyss of our souls
And take compassion on our human frailties;
Who by divine unknown laws judges men's acts:
Open your heaven to this hapless savage
And grant his executioners your pardon.

José Marti (1853–1895)

Simple Verses (Versos sencillos)

Versos sencillos (*Simple Verses*), Martí's best-known work, was the second and final book of poems published during the author's lifetime. Popularized in the famous song *Guantanamera*, many of these verses are sung by heart all over the Hispanic world, forming an active part of the culture's poetic memory. Unlike his formally complex poems of the 1880s, in *Versos sencillos*, as the title suggests, Martí employed more basic poetic structures. Significantly, he recurred to highly codified forms of traditional Spanish popular poetry, such as the eight-syllable verse, the four-verse stanza, and a symmetrical rhyming pattern. Despite its apparently nonpolitical content, the poems may partly be read as Martí's subtle and personal reaction to a new colonial threat: the disruptive emergence of modern American imperialism. Here the hymn of the exile leaves behind the grievances against Spain to engage a new form of political culture. The book was written following Marti's participation in an 1891 international monetary conference that, to his dismay, resulted in an attempt to ensure U.S. economic predominance over Latin America. Once the conference was over, Martí, exhausted and sick, was ordered by his doctor to convalesce in the countryside. In peaceful proximity to nature, Martí wrote these exquisite and formally balanced verses run through not with conventional belligerence and heroism, but with a romantic longing for an equilibrium and harmony that is absent from the modern world. (ALO)

Further reading: José Martí, *José Martí: Major Poems, a Bilingual Edition*, ed. Philip S. Foner, trans. Elinor Randall (New York: Holmes and Meier Publishers, 1982); *Simple verses*, trans. Manuel A. Tellechea (Houston: Arte Público Press, 1997).

Trans.: MAT

I
A sincere man am I
From the land where palm trees grow,

I
Yo soy un hombre sincero
De donde crece la palma,

And I want before I die
My soul's verses to bestow.

Y antes de morirme quiero
Echar mis versos del alma.

I'm a traveler to all parts,
And a newcomer to none;
I am art among the arts,
With the mountains I am one.

Yo vengo de todas partes,
Y hacia todas partes voy:
Arte soy entre las artes,
En los montes, monte soy.

I know the strange names of willows,
And can tell flowers with skill:
I know of lies that can kill,
And I know of sublime sorrows.

Yo sé los nombres extraños
De las yerbas y las flores,
Y de mortales engaños,
Y de sublimes dolores.

. . .

I know that the word is weak
And must soon fall to the ground,
And, then, midst the quiet profound
The gentle brook will speak.

Yo sé bien que cuando el mundo
Cede, lívido, al descanso,
Sobre el silencio profundo
Murmura el arroyo manso.

. . .

All is beautiful and right,
All is as music and reason;
And as diamonds are their season
All is coal before it's light.

Todo es hermoso y constante,
Todo es música y razón,
Y todo, como el diamante,
Antes que luz es carbón.

. . .

V
If you've seen a mount of sea foam,
It is my verse you have seen:
My verse a mountain has been,
And a feathered fan become.

V
Si ves un monte de espumas
Es mi verso lo que ves:
Mi verso es un monte, y es
Un abanico de plumas.

My verse is like a dagger
At whose hilt a flower grows,
My verse is a fount which flows
With a sparkling coral water.

Mi verso es como un puñal
Que por el puño echa flor:
Mi verso es un surtidor
Que da un agua de coral.

My verse is a gentle green
And also a flaming red,
My verse is a deer wounded
Seeking forest cover unseen.

Mi verso es de un verde claro
Y de un carmín encendido:
Mi verso es un ciervo herido
Que busca en el monte amparo.

My verse is brief and sincere,
And to the brave will appeal:
With all the strength of the steel
With which the sword will appear.

XXXIX

I have a white rose to tend
In July as in January;
I give it to the true friend
Who offers his frank hand to me.
And to the cruel one whose blows
Break the heart by which I live:
Thistle nor thorn do I give:
For him, too, I have a white rose.

Mi verso al valiente agrada.
Mi verso, breve y sincero,
Es del vigor del acero
Con que se funde la espada.

XXXIX

Cultivo una rosa blanca,
En julio como en enero,
Para el amigo sincero
Que me da su mano franca.
Y para el cruel que me arranca
El corazón con que vivo,
Cardo ni oruga cultivo:
Cultivo una rosa blanca.

CHAPTER 18

Against Tyranny

Andrea Villarreal (1881–?) and Teresa Villarreal (dates unknown)

Why Are You Still Here, Mexican Men? Fly, to the Battlefield

Andrea and Teresa Villarreal were two firebrand revolutionaries, members of the Mexican Liberal Party founded in exile by their father, Antonio Villarreal, and the Flores Magón brothers, among others. From the site of their exile, San Antonio, Texas, the Villarreal sisters were in the vanguard of Mexican feminism as well as insurgents, who founded their own newspapers: *El Obrero* (1909), edited by Teresa; and *La Mujer Moderna* (1915–1919), edited by Andrea. They also wrote for an early feminist-insurgent periodical, *Vesper,* and for Flores Magon's famous periodical *Regeneración*, which was closed down various times by U.S. government agents for allegedly breaking neutrality laws. In the essay below, published on January 21, 1911, in *Regeneración*, the Villarreals postulate the exploitation of Mexican laborers in the United States as a basis for their call to them to become revolutionaries on their home soil. They end their plea for support of the revolution by quoting another famous revolutionary writer in exile, Santiago de la Hoz, who used Laredo, Texas, as his home base. The Villarreal family returned to Mexico after the Revolution, and in 1952 Andrea Villarreal applied for the Mexican Medal of the Revolution in recognition of her work on the insurgent newspapers. Antonio Villarreal made three unsuccessful bids for the presidency of Mexico. (NK)

Further reading: Nicolás Kanellos with Helvetia Martell, *Hispanic Periodicals in the United States: A Brief History and Comprehensive Bibliography* (Houston: Arte Público Press, 2000).

Trans.: TEW

Impotent misfortune has been unable to subdue the cold, sorrowful request that flows from our hearts.

Adversity, which debases and breaks fragile wills, is an infinite source of vigor and strength for those souls who, in the struggle, are happy to pursue high ideals.

We are women, yes, but we are not so weak as to abandon the fight. The more bitter the pain of our wounds, the greater the love we profess for freedom's cause. Why have we suffered without feeling the vertigo of cowardly regrets? Because we have the right to raise our voices and call for action; we have the right to demand integrity of those who are indecisive, to pick on the stragglers, to reprehend those who are indifferent, and to indict those who are vile.

Mexicans living in the United States, we are addressing you. In the mountains of Chihuahua, in Sonora, in Veracruz, and in ten other states, our brothers are fighting valiantly against the despotism that for a space of thirty years has confounded the progress of the Mexican people. Brave and destitute, they have sacrificed their well-being and risked their lives in the sacred duty of gaining freedom. They must contend with the unlimited resources of the Dictatorship; with the gold snatched by the Dictatorship from the Nation to be converted into machine guns and rifles that vomit death; with an army of criminals dulled by discipline, and through discipline, transformed into killing machines. And above all, they have to contend with the morbid apathy of millions of slaves who are reluctant to take up a rifle to free themselves; who, accustomed to disgraceful servitude, are unable to understand that they have the right to a better life and that such a right can easily be obtained by rebelling against those who have taken it from them.

There is another obstacle that the revolutionary movement faces: the difficulty of obtaining rifles and instruments of war in Mexican territory. There are so many valiant souls who do not get involved in the revolution because it is physically impossible for them to acquire fire arms in the dominions of Porfirio Díaz! The Mexican government has gathered the rifles that were in stores and arsenals and it has them warehoused in the large centers where federal detachments abound.

Mexicans who live in the United States, know that in that country weapons are in abundance and within reach of whoever wants to buy them. Arm yourselves and go to Mexico. We are not asking you to violate the laws of neutrality. No. To buy a fire arm in this country and to cross the border, individually, with the purpose of joining the insurgent forces operating on Mexican soil is not a crime in violation of American law.

Shake off your indolence and fly, fly to the battlefield where rebellious heroism attacks, fulminates and struggles, where it wins or dies. If it wins, the advent of freedom will draw near; if it dies, the agonizing act will be transformed into a symbol of glory.

Or what . . . . ? Are you afraid of Death? Don't covet the miserable existence you drag along, a heavy chain of infinite misfortunes. Could you possibly believe for a minute that it is dignified to live the life you live, or better said, the life you suffer? Listen to us. We are speaking to those who are deprived, to the censured, to the Mexican day workers, hungry nomads who wander this land searching for bread and work. The fruit of your labor is impudently stolen from you. Because you are Mexican, you are paid less than individuals of any other race; you are scorned, you are despised. What pleasures do you enjoy that can make your existence agreeable? Is it enjoyable to work, to work without end for the benefit of those who know how to become rich from the labor of others? Is it enjoyable to constantly spend your energy and vitality on unpleasant daily work, until you reach complete physical exhaustion or even come down with some illness making it impossible to earn enough to survive and you resort to begging? Is it pleasurable to always find in your home, upon arriving from work, the same somber images of hateful misery: the family crowded together in an infected hut without lights; the wife, old before her time from anguish and deprivation; the little ones in rags, deprived of food and education, getting close to the age in which, like the father, they are to be initiated into the yoke of servitude: the only inheritance this docile and disgraced generation leaves the workers of tomorrow. . . . !

What are you men doing here? Where ever possible, get hold of rifles, artillery and dynamite. Go, go to Mexico to execute the paid assassins and to conquer for yourselves and your children LAND AND LIBERTY.

Do not abandon your brothers who have raised up arms against despotism; nor think that only the Mexicans who live in Mexico are responsible for fighting for liberty. The same responsibility weighs upon you, and you have infinitely more ways of obtaining weapons than they do.

A rifle with a 200 cartridge supply turns a slave into a man. Do the work of men, Mexicans who live in the United States. Hurry to arm yourselves and quickly make up the distance that separates you from the battle fields.

But if you hesitate, if fear detains you, if the ghost of Death causes you to shake with fear and obliges you to remain distant from the danger, if you do not have the courage to fulfill your responsibilities, let us throw in your faces, bereft of dignity, the incandescent verses of Santiago de la Hoz.

People: raise your head with pride
And rush to the battle fields;
If you do not do so, if the Goddess Astrea
Implores in vain the assistance of your honor,
If you do not raise up the incendiary torch,
If the aura of vengeful fury
Does not shine in our eyes:
While justice clamors, humiliated,
While Caesar triumphs and Brutus sleeps,
While the beloved Country is in mourning:
Instead of with the caress
With which the cowardly orator would flatter you,
I will lash your fear and impudence
With explosive, fiery words!

Enrique Flores Magón (1877–1954)

Revolutionary Hymn (Himno revolucionario)

Among the many Mexican political figures who came to the United States as exiles before and during the 1910–1917 Mexican Revolution were the Flores Magón brothers—Jesús, Ricardo, and Enrique. As very outspoken members of Mexico's progressive movement, in 1900 they began publishing *Regeneración*, a Mexico City weekly newspaper. At first, they decried the excesses of the repressive government of Mexican President Porfirio Díaz and then later condemned the injustice of private land ownership. They were arrested and incarcerated several times for daring to openly challenge the President as well as local political leaders and influential landowners. The brothers finally left Mexico in 1903 and relocated in San Antonio and later Los Angeles and St. Louis, where they continued publishing *Regeneración* with the monetary support of Mexican liberals, including Francisco Madero, who in 1911 successfully challenged Díaz for the presidency. The following selection captures the brothers' radicalism. Enrique, its author, calls on the Mexican proletariat to rise against their oppressors by taking over the private land that is rightfully theirs. (ChT)

Further reading: Dirk W. Raat, *Revoltosos: Mexico's Rebels in the United States, 1903–1923* (College Station: Texas A&M Magón University Press, 1981).

Trans.: MAT

(To be sung to the music of the Mexican National Anthem)

(Cántese con la música del Himno Nacional Mexicano)

Chorus
Proletarians: At the cry of war
Fight bravely for your ideals;
And fearlessly expropiate the land
Which our exploiter took from us.

I
Proletarians: United we must topple
The vile construction
Of the bourgeois system that oppresses us
And subjects us to exploitation.
For it is time we should be free
And cease once and for all to suffer.
We are all equal and brothers,
With the same right to live.
Chorus

II
Let us show our awareness

And love for the Idea of truth,
Combatting tenaciously, face to face,
The wealthy, the friars and Authority.
If you wish to be free, brothers,
Some beautiful day in the future,

(Coro.)
Proletarios: al grito de guerra,
Por Ideales luchad con valor;
Y expropiad, atrevidos, la tierra
Que detenta nuestro explotador.

I
(Estrofa.) Proletarios: precisa que unidos
Derrumbemos la vil construcción
Del Sistema Burgués que oprimidos
Nos sujeta con la explotación;
Que ya es tiempo que libres seamos
Y dejemos también de sufrir.
Siendo todos iguales y hermanos,
Con el mismo derecho a vivir.
(Coro.) Proletarios: al grito de guerra, etc.

II
(Estrofa.) Demostremos que somos
conscientes,
Y que amamos la Idea de verdad,
Combatiendo tenaces de frente
Al rico, al fraile y a la Autoridad:
Pues si libres queremos, hermanos,
Encontrarnos algún bello día.

We need to squeeze our hands	Es preciso apretar nuestras manos
Around the necks of this trilogy.	En los cuellos de tal Trilogía.
Chorus	(Coro.) Proletarios: al grito de guerra, etc.
III	III
Those who suffer in the harshest prisons	(Estrofa.) Al que sufra en los duros presidios
For the Cause of Humanity,	Por la Causa de la Humanidad
Let us prove that we are their friends	Demos pruebas de ser sus amigos
By fighting for their freedom.	Y luchemos por su libertad.
It is our duty to wrest from the claws	Que es deber arrancar de las garras
Of the vultures of the God Capital	De los buitres del Dios Capital
The good men behind bars	A los buenos que, tras de las barras,
Who are threatened with capital punishment.	Amenaza una pena mortal.
Chorus	(Coro.) Proletarios: al grito de guerra, etc.
IV	IV
If in the struggle we've begun we wish	(Estrofa.) Si en la lucha emprendida queremos
To conquer our emancipation,	Conquistar nuestra emancipación,
We must not allow any chief to impose himself,	Ningún Jefe imponerse dejemos,
And so shall we evade betrayal	E impidamos así una traición.
For men who acquire any position	Pues los hombres que adquieren un puesto
From which to exercise power,	En el cual ejercer un poder.
Are quickly transformed into tyrants	Se transforman tiranos bien presto
Because the middle classes spoil them.	Porque el medio los echa a perder.
Chorus	(Coro.) Proletarios: al grito de guerra, etc.
V	V
Proletarians: Raise your heads high	(Estrofa.) Proletarios: alzad vuestras frentes,
And break the chains of slaves,	Las cadenas de esclavos romped.
Rid your minds of all prejudice	Despojaos de prejuicios las mentes
And the New Ideas Learn.	Y las Nuevas Ideas aprended.
And when the bugle summons us to war	Y al llamar del clarín a la guerra.
March bravely and decisively to combat	Con arrojo al combate marchad
To take back our land forever	A tomar para siempre la Tierra
And also to win liberty!	Y también a ganar Libertad!
Chorus	(Coro.) Proletarios: al grito de guerra, etc.

Ricardo Flores Magón (1873–1911)

Letter *(excerpt)*

Ricardo Flores Magón was the most influential ideologue of the Mexican Revolution. After being jailed and later expelled from Mexico in 1903 for his attacks on the dictatorship of Porfirio Díaz, Flores Magón led his brothers and band of revolutionaries into the United States to continue his radical journalism and political and labor organizing. A passionate orator, eloquent and fiery essayist and editorialist, Flores Magón inspired armed rebellion in Mexico and unity among all races of the working class in the United States. For his political activities, Flores Magón was persecuted by both the Mexican and American governments on U.S. soil. He was sentenced to twenty years at the federal penitentiary in Leavenworth, Kansas, where he died on November 21, 1922. In his letter to Winnie Branstetter, written from prison, Flores Magón reveals the utopic vision that had driven him throughout his life. In addition, the letter is a good example of the sincere and direct literary style that Flores Magón also employed in his poetry and drama. (NK)

Further reading: Ricardo Flores Magón, *Epistolario y textos de Ricardo Flores Magón* (Mexico City: Fondo de Cultura Económica, 1964).

Mrs. Winnie Branstetter March 24, 1921
Chicago, Illinois

My fate has been sealed. I have to die within prison walls, for I am not 42, but 47 years old, my good Comrade, and a 21-year sentence is a life-term for me. I do not complain against my fate, however, I am receiving what I have always gotten in my 30 years of struggling for justice—persecution. I knew since the first that my appeals to brotherhood, and love and peace would be answered by the blows of those interested in the preservation of conditions favorable to the enslaving of man by man. I never expected to succeed in my endeavor, but I felt it to be my duty to persevere, conscious that sooner or later humanity shall adopt a way of social intercourse with love as a basis. Now I have to die a prisoner, and under the sway of my growing infirmity. Before I be dead, darkness will have enshrouded me with a night without moons nor stars, but I do not regret it—it is my share in the great enterprise of hastening the advent of justice, the——— to unknown goddess. My present and my future are dark, but I am certain of the bright future which is opened to the human race, and this is my consolation, this certainly comforts me. There will not be babies whining for milk, there will not be women selling their charm for a crust of bread; competition and enmity will give way to cooperation and love among human beings. Will not this be great? As a lover of the beautiful I exult at this prospect. Hitherto man has wronged the beautiful. Being the most intelligent animal, the one most favored by nature, man has lived in moral and material filth. Deceit and treachery have been the key to success, and treachery and deceit are plied to by those on top of the social structure, alas!, and by those below, too, thus making of social life a pandemonium in which shrewdness and artfulness triumph upon honesty and decency. Who is he who, feeling like a human being, does not feel his dignity outraged at the sight of such a regression to animal ferocity and cunning? Are not his brothers those who wallow in the swamp? Is not their degradation his degradation as well? In the midst of the splendors of nature man cuts a sorrowful figure, man is a disgrace to her beauty. When all things and beings on earth honor the sun, displaying their beauty to its light, man has nothing to exhibit but his tatters and his mange. And I feel ashamed of this. A lover of beauty, I resent this jarring of man in the harmony of creation. . . .

Mariano Azuela (1873–1951)

The Underdogs (excerpt)

Azuela is one of many Mexican writers and other intellectuals who fled Mexico during the Mexican Revolution to seek temporary refuge in the United States, but he is arguably one of the most important. He was born in a town in the Mexican state of Jalisco, completed his medical degree in Guadalajara, the state's capital, and returned to his birthplace to practice medicine in 1909 on the eve of the eruption of the Mexican Revolution. He had already established himself as a writer, publishing his "Impressions of a Student" in 1896 in a Mexico City weekly, followed by many sketches and short stories; he published his first novel in 1911. *The Underdogs*, his most famous work and one thought to have initiated and perfected the genre known as the "novel of the Revolution," was published in 1915 in El Paso, Texas, where he spent time in exile after having served as a doctor in Pancho Villa's army. Azuela returned to Mexico after the Revolution and lived out his days writing and practicing medicine among the poor of Jalisco. *The Underdogs* was published in serialized form and as a book by El Paso's *El Paso del Norte* newspaper, later reprinted in its entirety in Mexico in 1924. In *The Underdogs*, Azuela reflects a deep cynicism and even bitterness about the Revolution, based on his firsthand participation in some of its fiercest battles. The idealism that had led him to join Villa's troops turned to dismay as he witnessed many acts of gratuitous brutality and he received news from Mexico City that the ideals of the Revolution had been betrayed even by those who were leading it. In the following selection, Solís, one of Azuela's characters—the one that comes closest to expressing the author's views of the Revolution—finds himself caught up in the furious vortex of a battle. He reflects on the aftermath once the revolutionary forces have defeated their enemies. (ChT)

Further reading: Mariano Azuela, *Andrés Pérez, maderista* (Mexico: Impr. de Blanco y Botas, 1911), *The Underdogs: A Novel of the Mexican Revolution* (New York and Scarborough, Ontario: Signet Classic, The New American Library, Inc., 1963).

Trans.: EM

XXI

The firing lessened, then slowly died out. Luis Cervantes, who had been hiding amid a heap of ruins at the fortification on the crest of the hill, made bold to show his face.

How he had managed to hang on, he did not know. Nor did he know when Demetrio and his men had disappeared. Suddenly he had found himself alone; then, hurled back by an avalanche of infantry, he fell from his saddle; a host of men trampled over him until he rose from the ground and a man on horseback hoisted him up behind him. After a few moments, horse and riders fell. Left without rifle, revolver, or arms of any kind, Cervantes found himself lost in the midst of white smoke and whistling bullets. A hole amid a debris of crumbling stone offered a refuge of safety.

"Hello, partner!"

"Luis, how are you!"

"The horse threw me. They fell upon me. Then they took my gun away. You see, they thought I was dead. There was nothing I could do!" Luis Cervantes explained apologetically. Then:

"Nobody threw me down," Solís said. "I'm here because I like to play safe."

The irony in Solís' voice brought a blush to Cervantes' cheek.

"By God, that chief of yours is a man!" Solís said. "What daring, what assurance! He left me gasping—and a hell of a lot of other men with more experience than me, too!"

Luis Cervantes vouchsafed no answer.

"What! Weren't you there? Oh, I see! You found a nice place for yourself at the right time. Come here, Luis, I'll explain; let's go behind that rock. From this meadow to the foot of the hill, there's no road save this path below. To the right, the incline is too sharp; you can't do anything there. And it's worse to the left; the ascent is so dangerous that a second's hesitation means a fall down those rocks and a broken neck at the end of it. All right! A number of men from Moya's brigade who went down to the meadow decided to attack the enemy's trenches the first chance they got. The bullets whizzed about us, the battle raged on all sides. For a time they stopped firing, so we thought they were being attacked from behind. We stormed their trenches—look, partner, look at that meadow! It's thick with corpses! Their machine guns did that for us. They mowed us down like wheat; only a handful escaped. Those Goddamned officers went white as a sheet; even though we had reinforcements they were afraid to order a new charge. That was when Demetrio Macías plunged in. Did he wait for orders? Not he! He just shouted:

"'Come on, boys! Let's go for them!'

"'Damn fool!' I thought. 'What the hell does he think he's doing!'

"The officers, surprised, said nothing. Demetrio's horse seemed to wear eagle's claws instead of hoofs, it soared so swiftly over the rocks. 'Come on! Come on!' his men shouted, following him like wild deer, horses and men welded into a mad stampede. Only one young fellow stepped wild and fell headlong into the pit. In a few seconds the others appeared at the top of the hill, storming the trenches and killing the Federals by the thousand. With his rope, Demetrio lassoed the machine guns and carried them off, like a bull herd throwing a steer. Yet his success could not last much longer, for the Federals were far stronger in numbers and could easily have destroyed Demetrio and his men. But we took advantage of their confusion, we rushed upon them and they soon cleared out of their position. That chief of yours is a wonderful soldier!"

Standing on the crest of the hill, they could easily sight one side of the Bufa peak. Its highest crag spread out like the feathered head of a proud Aztec king. The three-hundred-foot slope was literally covered with dead, their hair matted, their clothes clotted with grime and blood. A host of ragged women, vultures of prey, ranged over the tepid bodies of the dead, stripping one man bare, despoiling another, robbing from a third his dearest possessions.

Amid clouds of white rifle smoke and the dense black vapors of flaming buildings, houses with wide doors and windows bolted shone in the sunlight. The streets seemed to be piled upon one another, or wound picturesquely about fantastic corners, or set to scale the hills nearby. Above the graceful cluster of houses, rose the lithe columns of a warehouse and the towers and cupola of the church.

"How beautiful the revolution! *Even* in its most barbarous aspect it is beautiful," Solís said with deep feeling. Then a vague melancholy seized him, and speaking low:

"A pity what remains to do won't be as beautiful! We must wait a while, until there are no men left to fight on either side, until no sound of shot rings through the air save from the mob as carrion-like it falls upon the booty; we must wait until the psychology of our race, condensed into two words, shines clear and luminous as a drop of water: Robbery! Murder! What a colossal failure we would make of it, friend, if we, who offer our enthusiasm and lives to crush a wretched tyrant, became the builders of a monstrous edifice holding one hundred or two hundred thousand monsters of exactly the same sort. People without ideals! A tyrant folk! Vain bloodshed!"

Large groups of Federals pushed up the hill, fleeing from the "high hats." A bullet whistled past them, singing as it sped. After his speech, Alberto Solís stood lost in thought, his arms crossed. Suddenly, he took fright.

"I'll be damned if I like these plaguey mosquitoes!" he said. "Let's get away from here!"

So scornfully Luis Cervantes smiled that Solís sat down on a rock quite calm, bewildered. He smiled. His gaze roved as he watched the spirals of smoke from the rifles, the dust of roofs crumbling from houses as they fell before the artillery. He believed he discerned the symbol of the revolution in these clouds of dust and smoke that climbed upward together, met at the crest of the hill and, a moment after, were lost....

"By heaven, now I see what it all means!"

He sketched a vast gesture, pointing to the station. Locomotives belched huge clouds of black dense smoke rising in columns; the trains were overloaded with fugitives who had barely managed to escape from the captured town.

Suddenly he felt a sharp blow in the stomach. As though his legs were putty, he rolled off the rock. His ears buzzed.... Then darkness... silence... eternity....

Santiago Argüello (1871–1940)

The Aching Soul

Born in the Nicaraguan city of León, Santiago Argüello died in Managua, in 1940. Critics have described him as a romantic-modernist poet and essayist. The author of numerous poetry volumes, his poetry is characterized by its innovative language usage and nationalist affirmation. Although he lived in the United States for a number of years, Argüello was not one of its admirers. The myriad of American interventions in Central America and the Caribbean in the early decades of the twentieth century was the subject of condemnation. The occupation by American marines of his native Nicaragua in the 1920s prompted Argüello to write *The Fatherland's Aching Soul*. In it, he invokes Latin America's Amerindian-Hispanic heritage and pleads for Latin American solidarity against the United States' voracious imperialism. (JBF)

Further reading: Santiago Argüello, *El alma dolorida de la patria* (Nueva York: n.p., 1923), *Poesías escogidas y poesías nuevas* (Managua: n.p., 1935).

Trans.: MAT

Oh peoples of America! . . . My own America! . . .
Not the one which thinks and feels in gold.
But the America of fantasy and of hidalgos,
The America which carries the blood of the Moor,
The America of the noble Iberian blood,
The America of Spain, which is my America!
And God's America! . . . I speak to that America! . . .

Oh peoples of my Latin America,
Of the America which speaks Spanish,
Where the soul of a Byzantine icon
Beats in the vigor of the Indian stone!

Peoples with hard blackthorn hair,
With eyes like flames and a fraternal heart!
Oh peoples of my Latin America,
Of the America which speaks Spanish! . . .

Children of the Inca, essence of the sun!
Grandsons of the Cids Campeadores!
Oh peoples of my blondeless America,
Without Quakers, without Bibles, without ministers! . . .

I am told, oh my people, that the Goddess
Made you sit on the path along the shore's edge;
How on your skirts fell the arterial obolus;
And how before the Goddess of the somber countenance
The foreigner took your belt.

¡Oh pueblos de la América! . . . ¡La mía! . . .
No la que piensa y la que siente en oro.
¡La América de ensueño y de hidalguía,
la América en que puso sangre el moro,
la América de noble sangre ibérica,
la América de España, que es la mía!
¡La América de Dios! . . . ¡Le hablo a esa América! . . .

¡Oh pueblos de mi América Latina,
de esta América que habla castellano,
donde un alma de icono bizantina
palpita en el vigor del bloque indiano!

¡Pueblos de recia cabellera endrina,
de ojos de chispa y corazón de hermano!
¡Oh pueblos de mi América Latina,
de esta América que habla castellano! . . .

¡Hijos del Inca del solar efluvio!
¡Oh nietos de los Cides Campeadores!
¡Oh pueblos de mi América sin rubio,
sin cuakeros, sin biblias, sin pastores! . . .

Cuéntanme ¡oh Raza! que la Dea un día
te hizo sentar a orillas del sendero;
que en tu falda cayó el óbolo artero;
que ante la diosa de la faz sombría
cogió tu cinturón el extranjero.

They tell me of your impure breeding;
That there are women's tears in your
eyelashes;
That your wear the garments of women
And that you begin to spin yarns of
Spanish Herculeses!

I should not believe it. I don't believe it! . . .
The America which I now see, prostrate
in the earth,
Shall of its free-will rise!

Speak, Prophet, and tell it: "That which
should be will be!"
You who look at the wave and know
wither it goes!

Me dicen de tus yácigas impuras;
que hay llantos de mujer en tu pestaña;
que llevas femeniles vestiduras,
y has puesto a hilar los
Hércules de España

Yo no debe creerlo. ¡No lo creo! . . .
¡La América libérrima, que hoy veo
rodilla en tierra, se levantará!

¡Habla, Profeta, y dile: "Lo que
ha de ser será!"
¡Tú que miras la ola, y sabes dónde vá!

Gustavo Solano (1886–)

Blood

Salvadoran poet-playwright-journalist Gustavo Solano became persona non grata in various Central American countries and Mexico over a period of some twenty years of activism against dictatorships and pursuit of his dream of a united Central America. Solano first came to the United States as consul for El Salvador in New Orleans, where he founded and edited the bilingual newspaper *La Opinión* and published books of his own poetry. His involvement in politics took him throughout the United States, Cuba, Puerto Rico, and Mexico, and led to his imprisonment in Mexico City in 1916. He was declared persona non grata there and in Central American countries for insulting the government of Guatemala (1918) as well as for being a gunrunner (1924). Despite his adventurous life as a revolutionary, Solano was able to produce numerous comedies and social realist plays for the professional stage. Southern California was his home base throughout the 1920s, where he not only wrote for the stage, but also worked as a journalist for the Los Angeles daily *El Heraldo de México* and periodicals in San Diego and northern Mexico. *Blood*, Solano's four-act tragedy, depicts the crimes and finally the overthrow of Guatemala's bloody dictator Manuel Estrada Cabrera. In the excerpt below, Solano alludes to the Spanish classical drama of *Life Is a Dream*, in depicting the imprisonment of the dictator who Solano characterized as having indulged his unbridled passions and instincts, as had the protagonist of Calderón de la Barca's famous masterpiece. (NK)

Further reading: Gustavo Solano, *La Sangre: Crímenes de Manuel Estrada Cabrera* (Guatemala: n.p., 1919), *Composiciones escogidas* (Hermosillo, Mexico: Talleres Gráficos Cruz Gálvez, 1923).

Trans.: MAT

Meditations of Cabrera and the Apotheosis of the Fatherland

On raising the curtain will appear a set decorated in the manner of Calderón de la Barca's *Life is a Dream*, specifically, the scene which shows Segismund in his cave. In an appropriate ensemble will also be depicted the facade of the chapel and a belltower. In the cave, Estrada Cabrera will be confined by a long chain. Moments after the curtain is raised the tyrant will appear on stage dragging his long chain.

CABRERA (*sadly lamenting his fate*)
In my cave, consumed with sadness,
These cruel, somber, bitter hours
Of my confinement are endless;
I feel the loss of my powers,
And I know I well deserve it.
(*looks toward heaven*)
This is my punishment, Lord!
I was a traitor, a praetorian;
And although in chains, alone,
I still yearn for yesterday
And for my dictator's throne.

Twenty-two years did I rule
As a tyrant and a despot;
In my land I made my hand felt
By assassinating my foes,
Always killing, always killing.
While standing on my pedestal
I espoused but one ideal
And had but one rule of conduct,
Which for me was a religion—
The religion of the dagger.

I was a Nero, a Caesar;
I was a student of crime
And committed all I pleased.
My name astonished the world;
I was a psychotic criminal,
Striking fear in everyone.
I had a penchant for vengeance,
And in the midst of a massacre
I felt like an Emperor.

In the cold belfry of death,
I was the merciless bellman

CABRERA (*Entristecido, lamentándose.*)
En mi cueva, entristecido,
crueles, sombrías y amargas
se me hacen las horas largas,
Me siento desfallecido;
Lo tengo bien merecido
Viendo al cielo.
¡Esta es mi pena Señor!
Fui un pretoriano, un traidor;
Mas,no obstante, encadenado,
Aun añoro del pasado
Mi trono de dictador.

Veintidós años de mando
Hicieron sentir mi mano
De déspota y de tirano;
Fui al pueblo asesinando,
Siempre, siempre matando.
Erguido en mi pedestal,
Tuve como todo ideal,
Como norma en la jornada,
Como religión sagrada
La religión del puñal.

Fui un Nerón, César austero;
Del crimen émulo fuí,
Cuanto quise cometí.
Asombro del mundo entero
Fue mi nombre; verdadero
lombrosiano, mi terror
Infundió a todos pavor.
Conviví con la venganza
Me sentí un emperador.

En el frío campanario
De la muerte, siempre fiero,

Who tolled for the innocent;
Reckless as no other despot,
I wanted to turn the sea red
With the blood of those I governed,
And the more people I killed,
The greater my thirst for blood.

Me torné en el campanero,
Doblando por el calvario
De inocentes; temerario
Sin ejemplo quise ahogar
De la sangre en rojo mar
Al pueblo que gobernaba,
Por eso, cuando mataba,
Sentí más sed de matar.

I was great and powerful,
And enjoyed all of life's splendors;
I possessed riches and honors,
And my crimes did always prosper:
I thought myself a colossus.
The sun would never set on me,
I told myself, never thinking,
In my blind and foolish pride,
That one day I'd be defeated . . .
How painful to wake at last!

Fui grande, fui poderoso;
Sentí fruición de esplendores,
Tuve riquezas y honores,
Y en el crimen, victorioso,
Llegué a creerme coloso.
Mi sol no se ha de eclipsar
Me decía, sin pensar,
Con mi orgullo adormecido,
Pensé al fin iba a ser vencido . . .
¡Fue amargo es el despertar!

I've lost everything I loved!
The dream of power is over.
Today I feel like Segismund,
Chained to the wall of a cave;
The enchanted spell is broken! . . .
Or was it only a dream?
And my prison, is it real?
Or is it also a fiction?
I cannot figure it out,
And in the end it's all the same;
For as Calderón well said:
"Life is the stuff dreams are made of . . ."

¡Bien perdido! ¡Bien amado!
Me pasó el sueño profundo,
Hoy me siento Segismundo
En mi cueva, encadenado;
¡Pasó el brebaje encantado . . . !
¿Sueño acaso? Mi prisión
Es realidad o ficción
A descifrar no me empeño,
Porque al fin la vida es un sueño
Como dijo Calderón . . .

En esos momentos pasa un entierro. Gente con trajes de esqueletos, llevando velas encendidas en las manos descarnadas.

CABRERA

Al ver el entierro como asaltado por terribles elucubraciones.

Mis víctimas van pasando . . .
¡Las estoy reconociendo!
¿A quién llevan? No comprendo

Buscando aire.

Aire . . . ¡me estoy asfixiando!

CABRERA

A los muertos.

Lirón

Postcard (Postal)

Written by an as yet unidentified poet using the pseudonym Lirón (meaning probably Grand Lyre), the collection of poems *Bombas de mano* reflects the strong anti-Franco, antifascist sentiments of exiled Spaniards in New York during the time of the Spanish Civil War, in the mid- to late 1930s. Published by an immigrant patriotic organization, many of the book's pages, and even its cover, contain grotesque caricatures and bitingly satirical verses attacking Spanish dictator Francisco Franco, fascists, and the Church. The excerpt that follows, *Postcard*, serves to inform General Franco, "El Generalísimo," that the writer intends to "honor" him by erecting a statue of him hoisted upon a pedestal of refuse and scatological material. The drawing that accompanies it provides a comical glimpse at the author's conception of the monument. Crafted in perfect octosyllabic verse, the poem is highly creative and playful in its use of popular language and imagery. (KDM)

Further reading: Lirón, *Bombas de mano* (New York: Sociedades Hispanas Confederadas, 1938).

Trans.: MAT

To the biggest bastard lackey
And greatest warmongering traitor
Whom many call by the moniker
Of "Generalissimo."
I want you to know, Paco cretin*issimo*,
That in this neutral nation
I have opened a subscription
to erect a monument
of garbage and excrement
to commemorate your treason.

A colossal monument
at whose stinking base will rise
your offensive burlesque
of a general's size:
a grotesque corporal
dressed as a
Moroccan, Italian and German,
caudillo of shit;
But with the verve and dash
of a ruffian in trash.
Wait and see what great success
this monument will possess,
for it will never let fade

Al lacayo basterdísimo
y traidor militarote,
a quien, muchos, como mote,
llaman el Generalísimo.
Sabrás, Paco cretinísimo
que en esta neutral nación
he abierto una suscripción
para hacerte un monumento
de basura y excremento
que perpertúe tu traición.

Monumento colosal,
en cuya base apestosa
se levante tu afrentosa
figura de General:
Vestido de caporal
marroquí-italo-tudesco,
quedarás hecho un grotesco
caudillo de porquería;
pero con la bizarría
de un matachín rufianesco.
Ya verás tú qué exitazo
este monumento alcanza
pues cundirá la asechanza,

your treason and barracks coup,
You great big *mari*... I mean,
Field Marshal,
the servile jackasses will come
to adore your allegory,
and they'll say before they kiss you:
"Gentlemen, this is true Glory!"

la traición y el cuartelazo.
Y a ti, so ma... riscalazo,
de odiosa y triste memoria,
vendrán los "burros de noria,"
servilones a adorarte,
y exclamarán al besarte:
¡Caballeros, esto es GLORIA!

Juan Antonio Corretjer (1908–1985)

Emmaus (Emmaus); Stuck to the Wall (Pegaos a la Pared)

Many consider Juan Antonio Corretjer to be Puerto Rico's "national poet" not only because of the patriotic and epic sentiments that run through a significant part of his production, but also for his incisive reworking of the country's poetic traditions. Few contemporary poets have cultivated conventional metric forms such as the *décima* (the ten-line stanza) or the art of the *pie forzado* (forced rhyme) with the freshness, elegance, and technical mastery of Corretjer. A militant nationalist since his youth, U.S. colonial authorities condemned Corretjer to seven years in prison (1935–1942) during the most turbulent era of pro-independence activism on the island. Five of these years were spent in a federal prison in Atlanta, Georgia. Once liberated, he moved to New York City and cofounded with his second wife, Consuelo Lee Tapia, the anti-imperialist journal *Pueblos Hispanos*. During this period he also came into close contact with Marxist ideas and with the Communist Party of America. From then on, his nationalism was to be modified by a more articulated socialist perspective. Upon his return to Puerto Rico in 1946 (following four years of obligatory expatriation imposed by the U.S. federal government), he broke with the Puerto Rican Nationalist and Communist parties and eventually founded the Puerto Rican Socialist League (circa 1968). Convinced of the illegitimacy of U.S. rule over the island, he declared his nation existed in a state of war with the United States, and until the end of his life intransigently opposed any form of electoral participation in Puerto Rico. His is nationalist poetry and, to some extent, poetical nationalism. Both *Emmaus* and *Stuck to the Wall* were first published in *Pueblos Hispanos*. (ALO)

Further reading: Juan Antonio Corretjer, *Días antes: Cuarenta años de poesía (1927–1967)*, compiled by Ramón Felipe Medina (Río Piedras: Editorial Antillana, 1973); *Poesía y revolución* (Río Piedras: Editorial Qease, 1981), *Yerba bruja* (Ciales, Puerto Rico: Ediciones Casa Corretjer, 1992).

Trans.: PP

Emmaus

We were walking in a clear morning.
The sun, its rays
broken in the diffuse crystals of the earth.

The landscape exploded
in a deep palpitation of life. The tide

Emmaus

Íbamos en la limpia mañana.
El sol sus rayos
quebraba en los difusos cristales de la
tierra.
Estallaba el paisaje en una honda
palpitación de vida. La marea

of sudden color entered us
with stabbing hands through our restless
souls,
laid-out, like birds, to fly over the world

alone, terrified, amazed and beautiful.
What cold solitude! And the field was full

of sound, and embloomed by the
awakening magic.
And we were deaf, our sight darkened

moons without sun, ears without hearing.
Soft and straight, the road
was a propitious route for our soles.
And we went, vacillating, trembling,
like a new acrobat on the wire
when, quietly, at our shoulders
a mysterious wanderer joined us
without rich supplies and traveling
without passion.
The angel of music, her wings
opened, and unstrung pearls
her prodigious words. The gesture,
humble
touched by grace. Springtime
left a trace of roses at its passing
and the breeze, upon kissing him, turned
into silk.
And we could not see him. And we could
not see him! And we could
not see him!
My burned heart. My arid heart, a bonfire.

My pulse increased its painful lub-dub
and my mind shined like a volcano of stars.

Our eyes were shut to joy,
our souls were open to ignorance.
Our chests were wounded, and the
wound—
insensitive and dark like a closed door.

But we arrived at the inn together, and
together

del subido color se nos entraba
con mano de puñales por las almas
inquietas,
echadas, como pájaros, a volar sobre el
mundo,
solas, despavoridas, deslumbradas y bellas.
¡Que soledad tan fría! Y ¡el campo estaba
todo
sonoro, y florecido por la magia
despierta!
Y estábamos nosotros sordos y
anochecidos,
lunas sin sol, ¡oídos sin alertas!
Blando y recto, el camino,
ruta propicia a nuestras plantas era.
E íbamos vacilantes, temblorosos,
como novel acróbata en la cuerda.
Cuando, calladamente, a nuestros hombros
—ignorada la súbita presencia—
unióse un misterioso peregrino,
sin rica alforja y sin pasión viajera.
El ángel de la música sus alas
abría, y desgranaba perlas
su verbo prodigioso. El gesto, humilde,

tocado por la gracia. Primavera
una huella de rosas a su paso dejaba
y la brisa, al besarlo, se volvía de seda.

Y no podíamos verlo.
¡Y no podíamos verlo!
¡Y no podíamos verlo!
El corazón quemaba. El corazón ardía,
como hoguera.
El pulso agigantaba su tic-tac doloroso
y el cerebro brillaba como volcán de
estrellas.
Estaban nuestros ojos cerrados a la dicha,

estaban nuestras almas a la ignorancia
abiertas.
Estaban nuestros pechos heridos, y la
herida
insensible y oscura como cerrada puerta.

we went to the supreme unity of the table.
Bread, transubstantiated came from his fingers
while his revealed corporeality, undone,
as though a symphony vibrated in our nerves,
as though a smooth elixir ran through our veins.

Pero llegamos juntos a la posada, y juntos
fuimos a la suprema unidad de la mesa.
El pan transubstanciado salió de entre sus dedos,
mientras su revelada corporeidad deshecha,
como una sinfonía vibraba en nuestros nervios,
como un elixir suave corría en nuestras venas.

Stuck to the Wall

Why do you execute them? Don't you see they die
to live, dying in another life,
longer, more steady, without doubt or resignation?
Why do you execute them? They are offering you
their lives in a tray of holocausts,
if, for you, they also give their lives,
—they, the great, the sublime, the diaphanous!—
if your sons will build them statues
of lyric granite and eternal marble
in the same place that your hands
ferment with their redeeming blood.
If your sons will not know the name
of the victimizer, and, for loving the victim
without memory, they will give you scorn,
why do you execute them?

Outside, the people
are quiet, wounded, illuminated
by the secret light of internal wrath.
Their worker's hands strangle
yearning avengers restrained,
their hands, through the famous horrors,
their good, able, honored hands.
Hands of unexpected sweetness
in the haven of the blessed home,
hands of miraculous clarity
in the enclosure of workshop and kiln,
hands now contorted, like screws,
impious and cold, prepared

Pegaos a la pared

¿Por qué los fusiláis? ¿No veis que mueren
para vivir, muriendo en otra vida
más larga y firme, sin olvido o riesgo?
¿Por qué los fusiláis? Si os están dando
sus vidas en bandejas de holocausto,
si por vosotros dan también sus vidas,
ellos, los grandes, los sublimes, los diáfanos!
Si vuestros hijos le alzarán columnas
de lírico granito y eterno mármol
en el mismo lugar que vuestras manos
fecundan con su sangre redentora.
Si vuestros hijos no sabrán el nombre
del victimario, y, por amar la víctima
os darán al desprecio sin memoria,
¿por qué los fusiláis?

Afuera el pueblo
está callado, herido, iluminado
por la secreta luz de internas iras.
Sus manos laboriosas estrangulan
vengadores anhelos contenidos,
sus manos, por los callos prestigiadas,
sus manos buenas, hábiles, honradas.
Manos de insospechadas dulcedumbres
en el remanso del hogar bendito,
manos de claridades milagrosas
en el recinto del taller y el horno,
manos ahora crispadas, cual tornillos
impiadosas y frías, preparadas

to put the rope around your own necks.
They were your brothers, and now they
look at you
as if you were, in brutal form,
the hyenas that they see in our eyes.
Wretched! Redirect your rifles.
Aim away from the heroic chest
that is rich and mature country,
in all noble, bountiful, riped fruit.
Aim at the dark forehead
in which there is no idea that spills
one single drop of naked truth.
Aim at the horrid chest,
resort of ill-fated sentiments,
of impiety, of misery, of egoism.
Stuck to the wall. Stuck to the deed
of flesh and bone and pain without tears.
Stuck to the people that redeem and bleed.
You yourselves are stuck to the people!

a echar el lazo a vuestros cuellos mismos.
Eran vuestros hermanos, y, ahora os
miran
como si fueseis, en brutal materia,
las hienas que ellos ven en vuestros ojos.
¡Desgraciados! Cambiad vuestros fusiles.
Cambiad la mira del heróico pecho
que es campo frutecido y madurado
en todo fruto noble, bello, grato.
Cambiad la mira hacia la frente turbia
en la cual no hay idea que derrame
un solo rasgo de verdad desnuda.
Cambiad la mira hacia el horrendo pecho,
resorte de nefastos sentimientos,
de impiedad, de miseria, egoísmos.
Pegaos a la pared. Pegaos al hecho
de carne y hueso y de dolor sin llanto.
Pegaos al pueblo que redime y sangra.
Vosotros mismos sois ¡pegaos al pueblo!

Carmita Landestoy (dates unknown)

I Also Accuse! By Way of a Prologue

Carmita Landestoy belongs to a sizable middle-class migration of Dominicans who came to the United States fleeing the stifling compliance imposed by the dictatorship of General Rafael Leónidas Trujillo (1930–1961). The original Spanish title of her book, *¡Yo también acuso!*, intentionally resonates with the admonitory tone of "J'accuse," the title of Emile Zola's statement on the Dreyfus affair. Landestoy wished to differentiate herself from those who shunned overt "critique of tyrannies" and who chose "to write calmly about theory in an office full of light and peace." Portraying Trujillo as a selfish, power-thirsty ruler who would stop at nothing to advance his personal interest, Landestoy urges other rulers in the region to break diplomatic ties with him. The dictator was in the height of his power when Landestoy's book appeared in New York in 1946; but she defied the opposition, boasting she was "not afraid of death." (STS)

Further reading: Carmita Landestoy, *¡Yo también acuso!* (New York: Azteca Press, 1946); Silvio Torres-Saillant, "Before the Diaspora: Early Dominican Literature in the United States," in *Recovering the U.S. Hispanic Literary Heritage*, vol. 3, eds. Maria Herrera-Sobek and Virginia Sanchez Korrol (Houston: Arte Público Press, 2000), 250–267.

Trans.: TEW

Philosophy and the diverse sciences that have evolved from philosophy have effectively demonstrated that different types of people may be characterized by the distinct value that each one assigns to objects. In keeping with the discourse of the highest authorities, individuals may be reduced, thus far, to the following types: theoreticians, clerics and the exquisite, economical, social politicians.

Social types, those who love their neighbors, think only of others and never consider their own needs, are the most attractive in terms of the yield of tenderness and love that they impart and inspire during their lifetimes. The authentic politicians, in whom both political and social characteristics converge, are best suited to lead nations and are capable of exercising authority that is based upon a marriage of justice and love for their people.

For perspective, let us turn to the thoughts of the humanist Juan Roura Parella, who conveys to us, through uniquely simple and exquisite language, the experiences of Mercier, Wilhelm and Sprangler. He actually improves upon their wisdom with his own experiences and in doing so, reminds us of the critical need to view our current, desolating reality as a merciless threat to both "spiritual freedom and sacred respect for human rights."

In Roura Parella's words, the true politician is "the one who exercises power collectively—which is the most sophisticated kind of power—and who always is cognizant of the social ties of solidarity. A true ruler is invariably a leader, which signifies that by exercising power he seeks to contribute to the happiness of those he governs.

"We should be cautious in presuming that a real politician is arbitrary. His deepest motivation can be found in individual freedom, in the freedom to act responsibly, in autonomy. Consequently, the motivation of an authentic leader is based upon overcoming himself, so that the needs of others are elevated above all else, which is where they rightfully should be. The road to such heights is long and arduous, and many only achieve moral independence. Leaping from freedom of decision-making to an understanding of what one should be is the difficulty. It is not rare, for this reason, that true politicians are rare."

In referring to the one-dimensional politician—the one who has no characteristics of the socially oriented individual—Roura Parella says: "In these men everything is subordinate to their will to rule. The first thing neglected is knowledge of man, not in the abstract sense, but in terms of the discovery of the levers that can move men."

"In truth, the term knowledge is of no interest to this type of politician. Knowledge is insignificant to him as a mirror, however it does possess value in its potential strength. Thus, this man is an irremissible pragmatist and under him the political structure works incessantly to atrophy the instrument of objectivity and truth. The desire to dominate, to always be the first, to be in charge, does not combine well with the force of the truth, as it is known that truth is concealed or perverted in order to conserve or augment power.

"Power employs wealth to realize its own ends. It is well-known that one of the most efficient ways to influence someone is through material goods, through wealth. Dazzling clothes, insignias, military music, the grand pomp of residences and palaces, all combine to symbolize power.

"The ambitious man who wants to control everything does not seem very eager to assist others unselfishly. The one who wants to dominate cannot give of himself or make sacrifices. Scorn and contempt for man, not cordiality, flow from the political machine. The political individualist supposes he can maintain others at his disposal.

"For the political man, God is not the beneficent, omnipotent, almighty organizer of chaos in the cosmos; nor is he the supreme incarnation of love. He is the sovereign being that has begotten the world from nothing. He rules the world and is the king of creation. The politician, whose zeal for power knows no limits, is spared the limitations imposed upon him by the almighty, for he presumes himself to be the one chosen by God as his representative to administer his authority. This is the meaning of power, 'by the grace of God.'

"The instinct to control, the tendency to dominate, the will to power, all color the motivation behind the conduct of the politician. The end justifies the means. To prevail is essential."

From the preceding exposition, the conduct and behavior of tyrants is elucidated. Thus we understand, GOD and TRUJILLO, and other billboards that designate Trujillo as the only Dominican who can govern the country and as someone dispatched by God. We find Trujillo surrounded by splendor and pomp in order to dazzle and procure souls. He completely ignores the means used to achieve the ends he desires.

It is well-known that dictatorships and the establishment of a solitary political party in order to maintain power have their roots in Ancient Rome. The Latins perpetuated the system and the Spanish passed it on to Latin America. The Latin American tyrannies are a primordial evil. They harbor deep roots, and many and varied are the causes that spawn them. Identifying the sources and fighting them with education, environment, nutrition, hygiene, etc., is, or should be, the immediate job of the intellectuals, sociologists and pedagogues. While that unfolds in time, the first stage to ending the prevailing dictatorships, immediately, should be that all American nations break their diplomatic ties with the tyrants. Without that, the case of Bolivia will be repeated, or something even worse will ensue, and "the innocent will pay for the deeds of the sinners."

Dictatorships are an American problem and it would be a disloyalty to the American nations and humanity if their governments were to remain indifferent. Further, I think the second urgent step should be that all those who were elected by the people freely to office to govern, should be forced to do that which Grau San Martín and Romulo Bentacourt, the presidents of Cuba and Venezuela, have done. They should conduct an inventory of their goods prior to assuming control so that they do not have the opportunity to appropriate national funds and riches.

Trujillo has taken over the sources of the country's wealth. In the hands of this unscrupulous being, the resources are a very powerful weapon that make their way down every path as he subtly manages to buy or silence those who might otherwise go against him.

Trujillo, slowly but surely, has been able to infiltrate many sectors of the American continent by way of embassies, consulates and his spies, to the point where the number of people who openly critique tyrannies is minute; they prefer to write calmly about theory in an office full of light and peace. This has given way to Trujillo embracing the notion that he can run everything and everyone, to the point where he aims to destroy those who he cannot compensate in order to eulogize him, or silence to keep neutral. When gold fails, right away he directs his henchmen to hand out tabloids that he dispatches from Santo Domingo.

I feel that when we get to a certain place in the road, when "the need to express our thoughts" urges us in such a way that the distance we need to go to communicate our ideas in writing seems short, it is painful to waste time on polemics. They conceal the problems instead of highlight them, cloud your vision and make you feel cold to your soul. But as reality is something different, I beg the kind reader to forgive me for informing him or her of the following, which has obligated me to write this piece, "By Way of a Prologue."

With this book already at the printers, I received the first tabloid from Trujillo. It was different from others, as it was a pamphlet entitled "My involvements with President Trujillo," which was published in Santo Domingo under my name and that he has sent to New York and Washington, DC to be disbursed by his henchmen. The first page is not my work and does not carry my signature, following it is part of a letter I wrote and something about my journalistic work, and it finishes with his lampoon. Before doing this he should have thought about how the person "who lives in a glass house should not throw stones."

My letter to him, as well as my journalistic work are suitable to be published, as they are written in the censored language of the dictatorship. If Trujillo were to publish the correspondences from the highest ranking Dominican dignitaries, mine, in comparison, would be lacking in eulogies. I was not a politician, but worked in social assistance in support of the under classes of the country, and just because someone does a certain job, that does not mean you will sell your soul to a tyrant. That only happens in fairy tales, in which the devil demands the souls of good people by way of magic—like changing straw into gold.

I take responsibility for my actions. When I elected to fight in support of human rights in a broader sense, I began a series of articles, that, like all my writing, I have graced with my signature. When I have had to show, in particular, only some of the facets of the tyranny that my country endures, I decided to write this book, which I also grace with my signature. All the while, Trujillo shields himself in anonymity. Because I am a woman, and further more poor, he reasons that I am defenseless and maligns me with the most disgraceful weapons. He does not attack Mr. Robert C. Hicks, who has written about the crimes under Trujillo's dictatorship in the book Blood in the Streets. In the same way, he does not criticize the journalists or the newspapers that have not sold-out to him and instead have published innumerable articles about him and his relatives. Oh, it is because they are North Americans and he is fearful of them. Despite all of the military titles that he has granted himself, Trujillo has never fought fairly and openly with anyone, and has only taken aim against Dominicans—and this was behind their backs—supported by the invading forces.

I am the only woman from the Dominican Republic working as a journalist abroad in support of human rights, that is, against dictatorships, so I know well that Trujillo will use all of the instruments that money can buy to morally discredit me and to restrain my actions.

Trujillo can invent all of the propaganda that he wants, as well as try to frighten me with telephone calls and using my friends to slander me, which they already have done. I am not afraid of death, and in regards to the rest, time, and time alone, is the only judge.

It is an embarrassment for the people of the Dominican Republic and for the nations of the Continent, that a man, who resorts to the level of issuing tabloids, holds the highest public office in a free and sovereign nation that is part of America.

CHAPTER 19

Contemporary Exiles

Lino Novás Calvo (1905–1983)

The Cow on the Rooftop: A Story of the Cuban Revolution

Short story writer, novelist, and translator, Lino Novás Calvo was born in Galicia, Spain, and emigrated to Cuba with his family while he was still a child. Hoping to find a better life than the one he had left behind in Spain, the boy found his new island home to be just as difficult. The harshness of his childhood and adolescence left Novás Calvo with great animosity toward his father, which is reflected throughout many of his stories. While working as a taxi driver, he published his first poem. He pursued his career as a writer in Spain, where he lived until the collapse of the Spanish republic in 1939. He returned to Cuba, but he found himself an emigrant again, and he went into exile in New York in 1960, after the triumph of the Cuban Revolution. Novás Calvo, along with Alejo Carpenter and Entrique Labrador Ruiz, contributed greatly to the modern tradition in Cuban prose fiction, a trajectory he maintained even after entering exile. His use of everyday language helps his readers understand the problems of his many characters as they face their surroundings, uneasy because they do not quite fit into a particular situation or place. The following excerpt, from a story about the Cuban Revolution, consists of a letter that contains the insane ramblings of an actress who was abandoned by the letter's recipient after the Revolution. (KDM)

Further reading: Lino Novás Calvo, *Un experimento en el Barrio Chino* (Madrid: Reunidos, 1936), *La luna nono y otros cuentos* (Buenos Aires: Nuevos Romances, 1942), *Maneras de contar* (New York: Las Américas, 1970), *El Negrero* (Madrid: Espasa-Calpe, 1993).

Trans.: MIL

My More Than Forgotten Chucho Moquenque (wherever you may be):

Don't expect this letter to start off with a long complaint. Too late for that. Complaints, what for? What's done is done and the cow on the rooftop. The great Hurricane came and swept away the illustrious rubble, leaving the roots, some still embedded in the earth, others standing on end. Also some flowering but crushed branches, just like me, living on as though by a miracle. Because the Miracle exists in this Jungle, nobody can deny it. Or rather it is able to exist, which is the same thing.

I can't tell if your liking for all tales has rubbed off on me without my knowing it. At least it tempts me now. So many things have rubbed off on me, Chucho Moquenque, even your inclination for changing bed partners. Remember the dances at Luyano? You were always a scoundrel, Chucho. Just like the sparrow-hawk, always scampering off. Bite and run. So, as soon as you saw the conflagration come, you took flight.

"You stay here for a little while, my love," you said, "while I set up the hide-out over there."

People who know you told me about it; I can well imagine what that hide-out is like. That sort of thing isn't for you. You're always on the go. Everything in the safe and the bank you took with you to sell to the highest bidder. You left me the almost worthless house and lot, my job at the Ministry of Communications that would soon end, and a little boy who began to grow up too fast. Before running off, you told me:

"Rita, it's time to escape: a few months longer and you won't be able to." How right you were, Chucho Moquenque! Three months later the year ended, as did so many other things, including Chucho Moquenque for me and naturally Rita Fernandez for him. Period. Curtain comes down. The end. And now to another point.

I want to speak to you about it in this letter. I have my reasons. Thirteen years ago today you fled. You always said that was a lucky number. I wish it were. I don't even know if I have any ill feeling toward you; if I had, it would be like the ill feeling a person harbors toward the one he has killed. We are what we are and with you the situation might have been even worse. When I realized I was alone, I was relieved. You had made up your mind; there was no reason to be upset; the die was cast. I felt like telling you: "So long, Chucho, that's the last I'll ever see you." And I went my own way.

I didn't hesitate, because it was the only road I could take. I quickly took up with the new *Jefe*. The woman you abandoned, Chucho, was beautiful. You yourself used to tell her: "Rita, how pretty, how really pretty you are!" You at least left me that asset. The new *Jefe* didn't last long, and neither did my job at the Ministry. Everything began to change so fast. I won't tire you with all that since everyone knows it. But what I must tell you is that three men entered my life since then, that is, by official count. There were others too. To die, there is always time to die; the worst thing is to suffer. One resists this. I think we all have a cork in our soul to prevent us from sinking, especially if we are Cuban. But even cork, like the Island, gets soaked. We've gone only backwards since then: backwards, backwards. You should see what that means!

But that's not! what I want to talk to you about.

Your son—that's right, Chucho, he was yours, even though you doubted it—would be twenty now, if he were alive. He was seven when you fled. I noticed then he was looking more and more like you. Maybe for that reason I immediately gave him up to the *Juventudes*, if you know what that is. I doubt it, but it doesn't matter. I didn't see him again after that. A few messages, some letters (increasingly propagandistic) that became less and less frequent, and nothing else. I supposed they were educating him in their own special way out there in the countryside, from one military camp to another. In High School, he reached the top of the honor roll, or whatever they call it now. He had someone else tell me that. By then he was already a junior party leader. He seemed to be doing well, but things were going badly for me, as for everybody, if that's any consolation. When I saw him I was half frightened. In his uniform (a coarse, light colored khaki) he looked just like you when at his age you would put your jacket on to go to the beach. Those same watery, half-closed eyes that hid the evil in them, the same thick hair that came down to form an arrow in front, that same mouth forever in movement, saying what's on your mind and then contradicting it. For a moment I didn't know whether to run to embrace him or run away from him. Or maybe to look for something to hit him on the head with.

You remember, Chucho, that you always called me a born actress, perhaps because during those first years at the University I took part in some plays. What impressed you most was my role as a madwoman in the work by Novás-Calvo. You told me then: "But Rita, I bet you're really crazy. Impossible to pretend so well." We both laughed. The Revista de Avance thought you were right. Some student troublemakers began to call me the Madwoman. It was around 1931 and both of us then dropped out of school.

You're probably wondering what the point of all this is. I'll tell you. I've always suspected that because you thought I was an actress you distrusted me, in or out of bed. I even think that it was the accumulation of your doubts that drove you from me like a rocket once you had a good pretext. It must not have even bothered you leaving me alone in the vortex with a child in that flimsy house of ours in the Kholy development. If you could, you might have taken the house with you too. At that time I didn't believe you capable of that much. Resigned at last, I consoled myself saying: "At least he left me our son." That's right, Chucho, he was really ours. Yours and mine, however much you distrusted the actress who didn't exist or who remained submerged.

With you gone and the boy under their control, the actress reappeared when she saw herself alone in the house. You will never know, Chucho, how I felt seeing myself alone in that storm. I don't love you, I know, but I want to save you the details, though to tell you would be like summing up the endless misfortunes of an infinite number of other people. You can't imagine it: right in the midst of the foulest winds of land or heaven. What else was there to do then except put my head down, or rather try to raise it above the sea waves? Dying itself would be glory. But I've already said that one resists dying. I never could imagine itself it was so difficult to die . . . and so easy to kill.

You may understand this better if I go back a bit in my story. As I told you, at first I went from lover to lover. I was still pretty and the re-emerging actress in me helped a lot. Rehearsing before the wardrobe mirror—at least they never took that away from me—I was amazed at my own artistry. I also used the tape recorder you left me, the one you had used in your French classes at the Normal School. I coordinated gesture and voice just like a professional. The actress feigned being a partisan of the revolution, and very gracefully went from one bureau to the next, from one *Responsible* to another. It's good to talk to you a little about her, so what you will read won't be amiss.

You never really knew that actress, Chucho. She wasn't the one you had seen on stage, nor the one you later thought was feigning love for you off-stage. She was those two plus a third, all in one. I myself was surprised that it turned out so well, so naturally. With so much pretending I might have come to identify myself with the lie. First, so I could keep the house, just as soon as you escaped and they took our boy away. They wanted the entire house. Like hungry beasts they swarmed around. They promised to leave me a little corner, maybe the back room or the room on the rooftop. After that—the tenants were now ex-maids with their children and husbands—they could give me the front half or the rear half. I pretended. I armed myself with words and anger. I became a revolutionary. I went to see this one and that one. I got in touch with Diaz Aztarain, with Dr. Cabral . . . Do you remember Dr. Cabral? He's the son of the alienist who treated my deranged mother, and he is an alienist too. He had gone to the Sierra in his last year of medicine and when he returned they put him in charge of the insane. I finally managed to keep them from taking the house away from me. It was the only thing they didn't take away.

But everything here was collapsing. You gone, and everything else beginning to go; clothes, shoes, food, even water. Ay, Chucho, even though I have no love for you, may you never know such deprivation! Everything disappeared as if by magic. For some time we—and I'm including now neighbors and friends—stretched out the little there was, until everything was all threadbare. The ration lines went three times around each block. No need to tell you about that. It certainly came out in all the newspapers of the world. But one thing is to read about it and another to suffer through it. I was thrown around from one place to another, from one office to another, and I had to give part of my ration to the woman or women who stood in line for me. I had to go to the bureau even though there was nothing for me to do, and when I got back I was happy to find an egg or a cup of rice. Sometimes I ambled along Obispo, Galiano, and San Rafael, secretly afraid not to find anything, but these lingering walks through once well-stocked streets just increased my anguish. First, the store mirrors, high, wide, square, in all sizes, relentlessly shiny, reflecting my wasted, tired-eyed, overly made-up image, like that of a madwoman I was playing. And then those empty storewindows, the endless vacant storewindows, open mouths of corpses. Said like that, it no doubt smacks of literature to you. You should see it through my eyes. That image of mine in the mirrors kept on burning in my mind. I saw myself another person, and indeed I was.

But there was still a third person, which I would have to create. And soon.

It wasn't even hunger itself. I hardly felt it any more. I was getting adjusted to it, just like I was to the repetition of phrases and watchwords. You have no idea, my dear dead husband (and you'll soon see, you were the dead one) how willingly one can become just a machine. A dilapidated little machine like those that still operate around here coughing out their agony. A dark fear then begins to envelop us, as if made of crocodile shadows or perhaps vulture shadows that may draw near to devour us. Fear of staying on to the very end, without the little bit we still have left so that some blood may still circulate through our veins.

That was what my situation became. No strength was left in me even for those futile walks in front of the sarcastic mirrors and the empty storewindows. I returned home motivated only by the desire to exchange what I had—a month's salary, some old article of clothing or footwear—for something more to eat. At times, with considerable risk, it could be done. As more and more people risked such illegal traffic, it became less dangerous.

It was on one of those afternoons when one of those hucksters came to offer me a milk cow. He kept her for himself in a small house in the Orfilia district (do you remember Orfila, Chucho Moquenque?), and apparently it was his turn to leave the island on one of those flights reserved for anti-revolutionaries. This man (good luck to him!) found out that I still kept the new suit you forgot to take out of the cleaner's in your haste to leave. He also asked me for any gold, silver, and platinum jewelry I might still have. I gave him all I could, and one night (I'll never know how) he brought me the cow, and the two of us (I'll never know how either) took her up to the rooftop and put her in your room. At least that cubicle where you would go at night to write your poisonous articles was to serve some purpose.

It was a gift from San Lazaro, or perhaps from the *Viejo Touleño* from whom I sought some consolation.

The cow was young, gentle, and good. My greatest joy was to go to the bushes to find the finest grass for her in payment for the spurts of milk she gave me each day. It was like a return to glory. I've had some men in my life. I once loved you dearly, Chucho Moquenque. But I never loved anyone like I loved that cow.

You yourself would sometimes sing mockingly that the good things and the glories of life never come or reach us too late. Drunk as I was with my new happiness and my new love for the cow, I got to forget Bebo (your son, you know), who had never before been absent from my thoughts. The entire world reduced to a milk cow.

I became an expert. I read and inquired as if for a thesis. I knew how to take care of her. All I had was my precious cow. Now that you are in that land of abundance, Chucho Moquenque (that is, if you're still alive), you will never, never understand this. Because in that sense you are indeed dead.

Don't think this is just an image. You are really dead. Dead from a shot in the head, which is where it should be, because all evil comes to us from the head. Your ex-Rita Fernandez is the one who is telling you and she should know.

Because it was you, Chucho, who suddenly came one night to take the cow away from me. You, in the form of your son (or vice-versa) at the age of twenty-one. On seeing him come in, I walked forward three steps to throw my arms around his neck, but his face (those slanting eyes, that shined menacingly, that twisted grimace) stopped me. I embraced him just I used to embrace you even when I knew that you repelled me and that therefore deep down I repelled you.

Later I was to remember one of those many sardonic quotations you cited just like a typical pompous literature teacher: "You're not the one who deceives me; it's my dream that deceives me." That's right, Chucho, vile Chucho, because you were my dream, although you never believed it.

Our son returned, your Raulin (Bebo), and at once I began to shudder. Raulin was Chucho grown up. He was a man now, with a peach fuzz beard, rat-like eyes, and a twisted mouth. The first thing he did was to walk around the house and take a look at the backyard. He came back to the dining room (where I remained motionless) with a cruel smile and these words:

"Well, Mom, you've gotten along pretty well. There's room for more people here."

Without waiting for my answer, he leaped up the stairs. Halfway up he turned around to look back at me over his shoulder and again I saw those sharp murderous teeth, like those of a biting dog. I must have become transfigured, because that's how I felt inside. A minute later he would feel that way too looking at the cow. A whirlwind of thoughts passed through my head as I looked at the top of the stairs to see him reappear. He took quite a while. He must have been looking the cow over, feeling her as a buyer would. He reappeared and stopped at the top. I couldn't begin to describe his face to you. It was that of a young Satan I had seen on a religious engraving. His smile showed all his teeth now and his eyes told me first what his mouth—your mouth—would tell me seconds later halfway down the stairs.

"Mom, it's wrong what you're doing. It's against the law. That cow has to be turned over to the people."

Hand and heart and thought moved in unison. He had left his FN rifle (that's what they call it) on the table. I quickly grabbed it. I don't think he even had time to notice. He was just putting his foot down on the first step when I pulled the trigger. He fell flat.

I will need a sea of words to tell you what happened after that. Words like waves. Your son raised up his arms, opened his mouth, and hit his forehead against the tile floor. I don't think the neighbors heard anything; only one shot, short and abrupt like the breaking of a dry twig. Your twig, Chucho, your little twig, now under the earth.

But the neighbors answered my shouts. No, the shouts weren't mine any more, they belonged to the other me, the actress, who now took my place for good. Because the one who was your Rita ceased to exist right there, and it was the other one who replaced her.

Within an hour the news was on the radio. The actress went fluttering around the house like a wounded bird. At times she sang, at times she laughed. She sank into long silences and then spoke with those no longer there. When the militia came she was doing ballet steps around her dead son, your murdered son, you yourself.

No, don't think I really became insane. At least, not completely, but just enough to provide the actress with the stimulus and the naturalness to make her performance convincing. Even the radio announced (the set was turned on and I could hear it very well) that the criminal had lost her mind, for she had killed her son and had a cow on the rooftop.

I went to jail just like in a performance. I left my house singing the 26th of July hymn and speaking of incongruous matters to strangers, as if I knew them. I called one militiaman Chucho and reminded him of how much we loved each other in Puentes Grandes; and I called a militiawoman Mamita. Acting crazy was so natural for me.

The news soon spread and reached the ears of Dr. Cabral. I don't know if I told you that Dr. Cabral had an affair with me when he came down from the Sierra and before they put him in charge of the insane—both male and female. After that, on the way to Havana he would come by to spend a few hours with me. At that time I was an accomplished romantic actress and Dr. Cabral was thrilled with my performance. He went around saying:

"But, my angel, how luscious you are!"

The news of my crime must have intrigued him and he asked to examine me. Permission was probably rather easy to get. After a few days, I don't know how many, I was under his care, in the new sanitarium. There was no trial, as far as I knew. I didn't see Raulin's funeral either.

Since then I've been a celebrated figure among the patients. They let me move around freely, telling the crazy women lies they believe and truths they doubt. The more far-fetched the lies, the easier they are believed. I also teach them how to sing and dance, which Dr. Cabral tells me has great therapeutic value. I am the star of this permanent theatre of the absurd.

Time has not dimmed my talents as an actress. I think the role of a madwoman has become so much a part of me that even if I wanted to I could no longer act sane. Foreign doctors have often come here, and Dr. Cabral has explained my case to them and allowed them to examine me. They have subjected me to a lot of tests, from reflex actions to the most insidious questions. I have learned how to put on a good act. Not one of them appeared to have left with any doubts about me; they all think I'm a highly intelligent woman, but insane just the same.

The doubt is within me, and so I'm writing you this letter, which I'll send to Dr. Cabral—maybe if he wants to he can forward it to you. I'm well treated here, I have privileges, I keep entertained with the roles I play. To take me out of here, to send me away to pick tomatoes, would be like taking away my cow the second time. Dr. Cabral frequently has me brought to his office to examine me—a splendid place, with wide, soft sofas. We then make love as we did before. The woman is different, but our lovemaking is the same.

My doubt, Chucho, is this: Does Dr. Cabral really think I'm crazy? A thousand times I ask myself this question.

José Kozer (1940–)

It is dark, my sister, it is dark (Está oscuro, mi hermana, está oscura); This señor don Gringo is very academic today (Este señor don gringo está hoy muy académico)

Born in Havana of Jewish parents from Czechoslovakia and Poland, José Kozer lived in Cuba until he was twenty years old. He moved to New York in 1960, whereupon he pursued his career as a poet and professor at Queens College and the City University of New York. A prolific poet, much of his work strives to remember or, more accurately, not forget the many elements that defined his family as it was caught up in a double exile, an exile that would increase by yet another dimension for Kozer upon his departure from Cuba after the triumph of the Cuban Revolution in 1959. The poems below offer differing but compatible images of loss, frustration, and anger in their evocation of a family's displacement, life's complexities in an Hispanic barrio in New York, and one student's resistance to a Castilian-speaking, Anglo professor's attack on Caribbean Spanish. (KDM)

Further reading: José Kozer, *Las plagas* (New York: Exilio, 1971), *Antologia breve* (Santo Domingo: Luna Cabeza Caliente, 1981), *Réplicas* (Matanzas, Cuba: Vigìa, 1998).

Trans.: MAT

It is dark, my sister, it is dark

It is dark, my sister, it is dark
The room and our future:
Grandmother is stalking us,

Está oscuro, mi hermana, está oscuro

Está oscuro, mi hermana, está oscuro
el cuarto y el futuro:
abuela está rondando,

Her cadaver has one false tooth,
And a false skeleton.
Sylvia, we were born in Cuba.
Sylvia, we have been born,
But from mom and dad
We've received no news.
Sylvia, I don't remember the barrio.
You and I spoke so rarely of Martí.
I don't see you on the terrace,
I don't see you arriving at school at four,
I don't see you surrendering your virginity on the fifteenth of June.
Sylvita, grandmother is stalking.
Her eyes are filled with Czechoslovakian tears.
As she had an artificial hip
They are going to bury her in Israel.
Sister, sister, sister.

su cadáver tiene un diente artificial,
un esqueleto falso.
Sylvia, hemos nacido en Cuba.
Sylvia, hemos nacido,
y de mamá y papá
no ha llegado una sola noticia.
Sylvia, no recuerdo el barrio.
Tú y yo tan rara vez hablamos de Martí.
No te veo en la terraza,
no te veo llegar a las cuatro de la escuela,
no te veo el quince de junio entregar la virginidad.
Sylvita, abuela está rondando.
Tiene los ojos llenos de lágrimas checoeslovacas.
Como tiene la cadera apostillada
la van a enterrar en Israel.
Hermana, hermana, hermana.

This señor don Gringo is very academic today

This señor don Gringo is very academic today,
He is very much the professor today, this señor,
He declaims that there is an orbicular Spanish
To communicate sublime things of the university.
He is very much pinned to his tie, this señor,
With his "c" so pure it spits,
Telling us no to Caribbean Spanish,
Telling us no, it's not done that way,
That it's *hace* with an "h" and not an "s."
And the dressed-up señor is right.
I say that this señor who is today so very gringo
Must have profound and ocular motives

To ask that one speak with style,
In the name of education,
To ask that one pronounce with diction,
Phonology, avoiding the law of

Este señor don gringo está hoy muy académico

Este señor don gringo está hoy muy académico,
está hoy muy profesor este señor,
declama que hay un español orbicular,
para comunicar cosas sublimes de universidad.
Está muy enganchado a su corbata este señor,
con la "c" tan castiza que escupe,
diciéndonos que no al español caribe,
diciéndonos que no, que así no se hace,
y que es hace con "h" y no es con "s".
Y el señor acicalado tiene la razón.
Digo que el señor que está hoy muy gringo,
habrá de tener profundos y oculares motivos,
para pedir que se hable con estilo,
pro aras del estudio,
para pedir que se pronuncie con dicción,
fonología, evitando la ley de la ono matopeya,

Branding the cacophony	tildando de cacofonía,
Of the Antillean invasion of North America.	la invasión antillana de la América del Norte.
Let's not confuse the prisms:	No confundamos los prismas:
The vocabularies of man are very extensive,	son muy extensos los vocabularios del hombre,
And extremely extensive his dictions,	son extensísimas las dicciones,
They also say dick, prick, pole, cock and joystick.	también se dice polla, verga, tronco, palo y bicho.

Reinaldo Arenas (1943–1990)

Before Night Falls (excerpt)

A native of the province of Holguín, Reinaldo Arenas grew up in the countryside and moved to Havana as an adult only in order to pursue a writing career. His exile in the United States was not easy. In 1980 hundreds of Cubans occupied the Peruvian Embassy in Havana demanding political asylum. The Cuban government's response to the crisis was to open the nearby port of Mariel and allow thousands of Cubans to leave the island immediately. Reinaldo Arenas was one of the intellectuals who defected at that time. An outspoken critic of the revolutionary government as well as a homosexual persecuted and incarcerated under state-sponsored antigay policies, Arenas had started to find it increasingly difficult to publish his works in Cuba. The Mariel boatlift offered him an unexpected exit. He felt out of place in the Cuban communities of Miami and found himself disillusioned with what he felt was the banality of life in New York City. In the 1980s he contracted the AIDS virus, which prompted him to start writing his autobiography, *Antes que anochezca* (*Before Night Falls*, published posthumously in 1992). This extraordinary text displays the humorous and ironically lyrical inventiveness so characteristic of many of Arenas's writings. The following excerpt from the final pages of the text poetically depicts the feverishness of his final moments of life in the solitude of New York City. Upon finishing his autobiography, Arenas committed suicide. (ALO)

Further reading: Reinaldo Arenas, *Farewell to the Sea*, trans. Andrew Hurley (New York: Viking, 1986); *The Ill-Fated Peregrinations of Fray Servando* Trans. Andrew Hurley (New York: Avon, 1987); *Before Night Falls*, trans. Dolores Koch (New York: Viking, 1993).

Trans.: DK

The Eviction

It was also in 1983 that the owner of the building in which I lived at attempted to evict all the tenants; he wanted to empty the building in order to remodel it and raise the rents. During the war between the landlord and the tenants, the landlord managed to damage the roof of the building. Rain and snow were coming into my room. It is difficult to wage war against the powerful, especially for someone who is not living in his own country, does not know the language, and is not familiar with legal terms. I finally had to give up my one-room apartment. I was then transferred to an old building, not far from my previous one. In this country it is perfectly normal for people to move frequently, but a major problem I had to suffer in Cuba was having nowhere to live: having to be on the move all the time, having to live with the fear of being forced out at whim, never having a place I could call my own. Now in New York it was the same story. I had no choice but to take my belongings and move to the new hovel. I was later told that the people who had stuck it out in the building were paid by the owner up to twenty thousand dollars to move out. My new world was ruled not by political power but by another power, also sinister: the power of money. After having lived in this country for some years, I realized that it is a country without a soul: everything revolves around money.

New York has no tradition, no history; there can be no history where there are no memories to hold on to. The city is in constant flux, constant construction, constant tearing down and building up again; a supermarket yesterday is a produce store today, a movie house tomorrow, and a bank the day after. The city is a huge, soulless factory with no place for the pedestrian to rest, no place where one can simply be without dishing out dollars for a breath of air or a chair on which to sit down and relax.

The Announcement

In 1985 two of my great friends died: Emir Rodríguez Monegal, the person who had best understood my books, and Jorge Renut, with whom I had enjoyed wonderful nocturnal adventures. Emir died of a sudden cancer; Jorge died of AIDS, the plague that, until then, had been for me nothing but a distant though persistent rumor; now it had become something real, palpable, obvious: the body of my friend was proof that, very soon, I could be in the same condition.

Dreams

Dreams and nightmares have been an important part of my life. I always went to bed like someone getting ready for a long trip: books, pills, glasses of water, clocks, a light, pencils, notebooks. To go to bed and switch off the light has been for me to submit to a totally unknown world, full of delicious as well as sinister promises. Dreams have always had a great influence on me; the first image I remember from my childhood is a dream, a terrible dream. I was on a reddish esplanade and huge teeth were approaching from both sides; it was an enormous mouth that made a strange sound. The closer the teeth came, the more high-pitched their sound would become; at the point they were ready to devour me, I would wake up. In other dreams I would find myself playing on the eaves of our house in the country and all of a sudden, due to a wrong move, I would feel the most extraordinary shivers, my hands would sweat, and I would start to slide, falling into an immense dark void; the fall would become an endless agony and I would wake up right before smashing into the ground.

At other times my dreams were in full color and extraordinary people would approach me offering me their friendship, which I accepted gladly; they were gigantic creatures with smiling faces.

Later I often dreamed of Lezama, who was at a gathering in an enormous hall; music could be heard in the distance and Lezama pulled out a large pocket watch; facing him was his wife, María Luisa. I was a boy, and when I went up to him, he would open his legs and receive me smiling, while saying to María Luisa: "Look how well he is doing." But by then Lezama was already dead.

Occasionally I dreamed that although I had been in the United States, I was back in Cuba, I do not know why, perhaps because my plane was hijacked or because someone had deceived me by telling me I could return without any problem. I was in my hot room again, but now I could never leave; I was condemned to stay there forever. I needed to receive a special notification to go to the airport, someone had to pick me up in a car that never came; I knew I could never leave that place, and that the police would come any moment and arrest me. I had already traveled around the world and learned what freedom was, but due to some strange circumstance I was back in Cuba and could not escape. I would wake up and, seeing the deteriorating walls of my room in New York, feel an indescribable joy.

I had another dream. I want to get into my mother's house and there is a chicken-wire fence in front of the door. I repeatedly call for someone to open the door; my mother and my aunt are on the other side of the fence and I signal them. I move my hand toward my chest and birds start coming out, parrots of all colors, bigger and bigger insects and birds; I start yelling for them to open the gate, and they stare at me through the chicken wire; I continue to scream and all kinds of animals keep coming out of me, but I cannot get through the door.

In some dreams I am a painter; I have a huge loft, and create enormous paintings; I think the paintings I produce have to do with people dear to me; the color blue is predominant and people dissolve in it. Suddenly, Lázaro enters, young, slender; he greets me dejectedly, walks toward the large window facing the street, and jumps out. I scream and run down the stairs of my New York apartment, but as I am going down, I am back in Holguín; my grandmother is there, as well as several of my aunts. I tell them Lázaro has jumped out the window and they all run into the street; it is Tenth of October Street, where my mother lives. There, facedown in the mud, lies Lázaro, dead. I lift his head and look at his beautiful, muddy face; my grandmother comes, looks first at his face and then up at the heavens, saying: "My God, why?" I later tried to interpret this dream in various ways: it was not Lázaro who died but me; he is my double; the person I love most is the symbol of my destruction. For that reason it made sense that those rushing to see the body were my relatives, not Lázaro's.

I have dreamed that when I was a kid the sea came right up to my house; it came rushing over dozens of miles, and the whole yard would be flooded. It was great to let myself float on the water; I swam for a long time in my flooded house, looking at the ceiling, taking in the briny smell of the sea that continued rushing in a torrent.

In New York I once dreamed I could fly, a privilege not granted to humans, even though we gays are called *pájaros* [birds]. But I was in Cuba, flying over the palm trees; it was easy, you only had to believe you could do it. Soon I was flying over Fifth Avenue in Miramar, over the royal palms that line the street; the scenery was beautiful to behold while I, joyful and radiant, flew above it, over the crowns of the palm trees. I woke up here in New York still feeling that I was high in the air.

Once while I was on vacation at Miami Beach, I had a terrible dream. I was in a very large bathroom full of excrement and had to sleep there. Surrounding me were hundreds of rare birds that moved about with great difficulty. More and more of those awful birds kept coming, gradually closing all possibility of escape; the entire horizon was full of birds; they had something metallic about them, and made a dull noise; they sounded like buzzing alarms. Suddenly I realized that all those birds had managed to get into my head, and that my brain was swelling to accommodate them. As they entered my head, I grew old. This same nightmare occurred for several nights in a row while I was in Miami and I would wake up drenched in sweat. When I flew back to New York, I was getting ready as usual for my dream, taking with me all my things and a big glass of water. I always read for at least an hour or two before going to sleep, and I was finishing *A Thousand and One Nights*. This was already in 1986. I had been talking with Lázaro for a while and he had just left; he was still in the building when I heard a tremendous blast in the room; it sounded like a real explosion. I thought one of my jealous lovers or a burglar had broken the window facing the street; the sound was so loud that it seemed someone must have taken an iron bar and thrown it against the window. But the windowpane was undamaged. Something very strange had occurred in the room: the glass of water on my nightstand had exploded without my touching it; it was shattered. I ran to call Lázaro back before he left the building, and we carefully searched the whole apartment. I thought that someone had taken a shot at me and had hit the glass instead. On several occasions I had received death threats from the Cuban State Security; once in a while a person had broken into my apartment and gone through my papers; at times the window that I had left closed was open but nothing had been taken, so it could not have been a burglar. What really happened that night is still shrouded in mystery for me. How could a glass of water explode with such an infernal sound? A week later I understood that this was an omen, a premonition, a message from the gods of the underworld, a new and terrible message announcing that something truly different was about to happen to me, or was already happening. The glass full of water was perhaps a sort of guardian angel, a talisman; something had penetrated the glass that for years had protected me and shielded me from all dangers: terrible illnesses, falls from trees, persecutions, prison, shots in the middle of the night, being lost at sea, or attacked by gangs of armed delinquents in New York City on various occasions. Once I was attacked in the middle of Central Park; some young men searched my pockets, pointing a gun at my head, but they found only five dollars. They fondled me so much while they searched me that we ended up making love. Afterward I asked them for a dollar to get back home and they gave it to me.

Now, the state of grace that had saved me from so many misfortunes had come to an end. On another occasion, I had found an enormous black man inside my apartment in New York when I returned home. After breaking my window and stealing all my clothes, he was approaching me, threatening me with a gun. I was able to escape and yell that there was a thief in the building; several people came out into the hallway, among them a Puerto Rican neighbor with a double-barreled shotgun, which made the black man run away leaving all my belongings behind, and me unharmed.

One day I had asked a hoodlum who was carrying an umbrella what time it was and he gave me a rude reply. I think I said a few stupid things to him and finally gave him a shove. Clearly enraged, he removed a sort of ice pick or metallic tip from his umbrella and lunged at me with its sharp point. He cut my forehead several times, aiming his attacks at my eyes; evidently he wanted to blind me and failed. I returned to my apartment all bloody, and a week later I was completely healed. My guardian angel had again protected me.

But now, something much more powerful, more mysterious, more sinister than anything I had ever experienced seemed to be controlling my fate; I had fallen out of grace. The bursting of the glass was a symbol of my final destruction. Destruction: that was my interpretation a few weeks later and it seems that, unfortunately, I was right.

Lázaro and I were once in Puerto Rico at a secluded beach where I had taken him because it reminded me of our Cuban beaches. He had opened a book, and was starting to read when a gang of muggers came, more than six of them. One pointed a gun at us that he had hidden under a handkerchief. Another one said, "Lie down on the ground and give us all you have or we will kill you right now." I was ready to grab a stick and go after one of them, but Lázaro warned me not to; they were dangerous. We lay down on the ground while they searched us and took what little we had: swim fins, a diving mask. As the muggers were leaving I asked them to return the diving mask; one did not want to, but another decided they really had no use for it. They could have killed us, but my guardian angel had protected us: the same one who helped me survive El Morro, the one who warned me of the land mines as I was getting close to the Guantánamo naval base. Once again I had been saved.

But now the glass had burst, nothing could save me.

What was the glass that burst? It was the deity that protected me; it was the goddess that had always accompanied me, it was the Moon herself, my mother had turned into the Moon.

O Moon! You have always been at my side, offering your light in my most dreadful moments; since I was a child you were the mystery that watched over my terrors, you were the comfort of my most desperate nights, you were my very own mother, bathing me in a warmth that perhaps she never knew how to give me. In the midst of the forest, in the darkest places, in the sea, you were there with me, you were my comfort, you have always guided me in my most difficult moments. My great goddess, my true goddess, you who have protected me through so many calamities; I used to look up toward you and behold you; up to you rising above the sea, toward you at the shore, toward you among the rocks of my desolate Island, I would lift my gaze and behold you, always the same; in your face I saw an expression of pain, of suffering, of compassion for me, your son. And now, Moon, you suddenly burst into pieces right next to my bed. I am alone. It is night.

Luisa Valenzuela (1938–)

I'm Your Horse in the Night

In 1969, while she was attending the University of Iowa, Luisa Valenzuela realized her responsibility toward Latin America. In the United States, away from the nightmares of dictatorship, Valenzuela felt at liberty to write tales and novels concerning the harsh realities of Argentina during the late '70s and '80s. She positioned herself very strongly against the atrocities committed during the so-called dirty war, a war of the Argentine military against the "suspected" citizens. Tortures, disappearance of dissidents, censorship, forced exile of hundreds of thousands of people typified this war. Luisa Valenzuela's *I'm Your Horse in the Night* features great precision in the use of the language, the exploration of her character's psychology, the confrontation between fiction and reality, and sharp criticism of political power. (AB)

Further reading: Luisa Valenzuela, *The Censors* (Willimantic, Conn.: Curbstone Press, 1992), *Other Weapons*, 3rd ed. trans. Deborah Bonner (Hanover, N.H.: Ediciones del Norte, 1993).

Trans.: DBO

The doorbell rang: three short rings and one long one. That was the signal, and I got up, annoyed and a little frightened; it could be them, and then again, maybe not; at these ungodly hours of the night it could be a trap. I opened the door expecting anything except him, face to face, at last.

He came in quickly and locked the door behind him before embracing me. So much in character, so cautious, first and foremost checking his—our—rear guard. Then he took me in his arms without saying a word, not even holding me too tight but letting all the emotions of our new encounter overflow, telling me so much by merely holding me in his arms and kissing me slowly. I think he never had much faith in words, and there he was, as silent as ever, sending me messages in the form of caresses.

We finally stepped back to look at one another from head to foot, not eye to eye, out of focus. And I was able to say Hello showing scarcely any surprise despite all those months when I had no idea where he could have been, and I was able to say

I thought you were fighting up north
I thought you'd been caught
I thought you were in hiding
I thought you'd been tortured and killed
I thought you were theorizing about the revolution in another country

Just one of many ways to tell him I'd been thinking of him I hadn't stopped thinking of him or felt as if I'd been betrayed. And there he was, always so goddamn cautious, so much the master of his actions.

"Quiet, Chiquita. You're much better off not knowing what I've been up to."

Then he pulled out his treasures, potential clues that at the time eluded me: a bottle of cachaça and a Gal Costa record. What had he been up to in Brazil? What was he planning to do next? What had brought him back, risking his life, knowing they were after him? Then I stopped asking myself questions (quiet, Chiquita, he'd say). Come here, Chiquita, he was saying, and I chose to let myself sink into the joy of having him back again, trying not to worry. What would happen to us tomorrow, and the days that followed?

Cachaça's a good drink. It goes down and up and down all the right tracks, and then stops to warm up the corners that need it most. Gal Costa's voice is hot, she envelops us in its sound and half-dancing, half-floating, we reach the bed. We lie down and keep on staring deep into each other's eyes, continue caressing each other without allowing ourselves to give into the pure senses just yet. We continue recognizing, rediscovering each other.

Beto, I say, looking at him. I know that isn't his real name, but it's the only one I can call him out loud. He replies:

"We'll make it some day, Chiquita, but let's not talk now."

It's better that way. Better if he doesn't start talking about how we'll make it someday and ruin the wonder of what we're about to attain right now, the two of us, all alone.

"A noite eu so teu cavalo," Gal Costa suddenly sings from the record player.

"I'm your horse in the night," I translate slowly. And so as to bind him in a spell and stop him from thinking about other things:

"It's a saint's song, like in the *macumba.* Someone who's in a trance says she's the horse of the spirit who's riding her, she's his mount."

"Chiquita, you're always getting carried away with esoteric meanings and witchcraft. You know perfectly well that she isn't talking about spirits. If you're my horse in the night it's because I ride you, like this, see? . . . Like this . . . That's all."

It was so long, so deep and so insistent, so charged with affection that we ended up exhausted. I fell asleep with him still on top of me.

I'm your horse in the night.

The goddamn phone pulled me out in waves from a deep well. Making an enormous effort to wake up, I walked over to the receiver, thinking it could be Beto, sure, who was no longer by my side, sure, following his inveterate habit of running away while I'm asleep without a word about where he's gone. To protect me, he says.

From the other end of the line, a voice I thought belonged to Andrés—the one we call Andrés—began to tell me:

"They found Beto dead, floating down the river near the other bank. It looks as if they threw him alive out of a chopper. He's all bloated and decomposed after six days in the water, but I'm almost sure it's him."

"No, it can't be Beto," I shouted carelessly. Suddenly the voice no longer sounded like Andrés: it felt foreign, impersonal.

"You think so?"

"Who is this?" Only then did I think to ask. But that very moment they hung up.

Ten, fifteen minutes? How long must I have stayed there staring at the phone like an idiot until the police arrived? I didn't expect them. But, then again, how could I not? Their hands feeling me, their voices insulting and threatening, the house searched, turned inside out. But I already knew. So what did I care if they broke every breakable object and tore apart my dresser?

They wouldn't find a thing. My only real possession was a dream and they can't deprive me of my dreams just like that. My dream the night before, when Beto was there with me and we loved each other. I'd dreamed it, dreamed every bit of it, I was deeply convinced that I'd dreamed it all in the richest detail, even in full color. And dreams are none of the cops' business.

They want reality, tangible facts, the kind I couldn't even begin to give them.

Where is he, you saw him, he was here with you, where did he go? Speak up, or you'll be sorry. Let's hear you sing, bitch, we know he came to see you, where is he, where is he holed up? He's in the city, come on, spill it, we know he came to get you.

I haven't heard a word from him in months. He abandoned me, I haven't heard from him in months. He ran away, went underground. What do I know, he ran off with someone else, he's in another country. What do I know, he abandoned me, I hate him, I know nothing.

(Go ahead, burn me with your cigarettes, kick me all you wish, threaten, go ahead, stick a mouse in me so it'll eat my insides out, pull my nails out, do as you please. Would I make something up for that? Would I tell you he was here when a thousand years ago he left me forever?)

I'm not about to tell them my dreams. Why should they care? I haven't seen that so-called Beto in more than six months, and I loved him. The man simply vanished. I only run into him in my dreams, and they're bad dreams that often become nightmares.

Beto, you know now, if it's true that they killed you, or wherever you may be, Beto, I'm your horse in the night and you can inhabit me whenever you wish, even if I'm behind bars. Beto, now that I'm in jail I know that I dreamed you that night; it was just a dream. And if by some wild chance there's a Gal Costa record and a half-empty bottle of cachaça in my house, I hope they'll forgive me: I will them out of existence.

Emma Sepúlveda (1950–)

I Grew Accustomed (Me había acostumbrado); Here Am I Now (Aquí estoy ahora)

Born in Argentina and raised in Chile, Emma Sepúlveda came as an exile to the United States in 1974, two years after the military coup led by Augusto Pinochet imposed a military dictatorship on the country. After studying for her Ph.D., Sepúlveda became a professor at the University of Nevada, and has maintained a deep involvement in academic and community life, especially as an activist in Hispanic political issues, immigration policy, and the Holocaust. She has served as a founder, officer, and board member of organizations for Latino unity, and has been an activist for human rights, for which she received the Thornton Peace Prize in 1994. In 1979, Sepúlveda became a citizen of the United States and, in 1994, was the Democratic Party candidate for the Nevada State Senate. Despite her growing attachment and involvement in domestic political issues in the United States much of her poetry recalls the oppressive culture instituted by the dictatorship in Chile before she left. In *I Grew Accustomed*, from her collection, *Death to Silence*, Sepúlveda explores the more intimate aspects of self-censorship under a dictatorial regime. *In Here Am I Now*, she explores the indeterminate status of immigrants and exiles. (NK)

Further reading: Emma Sepúlveda, *A la muerte y otras dudas/To Death and Other Doubts* (Madrid, Spain: Ediciones Torremozas, 1996), *Death to Silence/Muerte al silencio*, trans. Shaun T. Griffin (Houston: Arte Público Press, 1997).

Trans.: STG

I Grew Accustomed

I grew accustomed
to not saying it,
storing it inside
as the blood
gorged through veins
but did not run away
I was made strong
with muteness
that concealed me
long enough to think
and think again
to give feeling
in this perpetual silence
I grew accustomed to being silent
drew dreams in memory
told stories
in the solitude of the mirror
made one shadow-voice
with darkness
I invented a proper world
with the hallucinations of breath
to drink in short sips
the threats of time
and wait
wait until someone or something
tells me I am allowed to talk.

Me habiá accustomtumbrado

A Jenny

Es que me había acostumbrado
a no decirlo
a guardarlo adentro
como la sangre
que galopa por las venas
sin desbocarse
me había hecho fuerte
con esta mudez
que se esconde sola
me bastaba pensarlo
y volverlo a pensar
para darle sentido
a este silencio perpetuo
me había acostumbrado a callar
a dibujar sueños en la memoria
a contarme cuentos
en la soledad del espejo
a hacerme una
con la voz de la sombra
me había inventado un mundo propio
me había inventado un mundo propio
para beberme con sorbos cortos
las amenazas del tiempo
y esperar
esperar hasta que alguien o algo
me dijera que podía hablar.

Here Am I Now

Here
am
I
now
Emma
laden
with
last names
with nothing from my past
a fine lot of nothing, waiting
for them to answer

Aquí estoy yo ahora

Para Ana María
Reno, Nevada, 1987

Aquí
estoy
yo
ahora
Emma
y
una
suerte de apellidos
sin nada de lo que traje
y bien poco de todo
esperando que me den respuesta

an exile who has endured much	a un exilio que tanto dura
and nothing cleanses, waiting	y nada borra
for them to give me a certificate	esperando que me den un certificado
that says I cannot return	que diga que no me voy
until my bones decide	y que no vuelvo hasta que los huesos decidan
if it's here	si es aquí
or there o es allá	
the place where the dead speak	el lugar en donde las cruces callan
and the crosses are silent.	y son los muertos los que hablan.

Matías Montes Huidobro (1931–)

Exile

Born and raised in Cuba, Matías Montes Huidobro was a young but seasoned playwright before he left his island home after the advent of the Castro regime in 1959. Yet he continued his writing while in exile, and has come to be perhaps one of the best-known Cuban playwrights in the United States and abroad. Upon beginning his residence in the United States, Montes Huidobro began a distinguished career as a university professor at the University of Hawaii at Manoa. A prolific playwright, prose writer, and poet, he has published numerous collections of stories, poems, and individual plays, the latter of which he has seen performed on stages both in the United States and abroad. His themes are universal and set in an indefinite time period, with few exceptions, such as *Las caretas (The Masks)*, which is about the carnival season in Cuba. The excerpt included here, which is taken from the second act, finds actors Victoria, Román, and Miguel caught up in the paranoia that is building among the Cuban intelligentsia and artists about free expression and possible censorship and retribution. It is only through theater that two of the friends discover their other friend's true political beliefs, beliefs that could cost him his life or imprisonment. (KDM)

Further reading: Matías Montes Huidobro, "The Guillotine," in *Selected Latin American One-Act Plays* (Pittsburgh: University of Pittsburgh Press, 1972); *Desterrados al fuego* (México: Fondo de Cultura Económica, 1975); *Obras en un acto* (Honolulu: Persona, 1991).

Trans.: KDM

MIGUEL: (*Opening his eyes, not quite joining in, with a hoarse voice.*) In a final, definitive version, in order to put an end to so many tales, Miguel Angel Fernández has decided, once and for all, to edit the text in question so that Victoria del Pueblo doesn't over do it so much. (*He stands and reconstructs his own entry into the scene.*) "Miguel Angel, drunk as a skunk, coming down from the Sierra Maestra and leaving the Plaza Cívica, emulates Fidel Castro and makes his entrance into the scene at the Teatro Nacional, which the damned lighting technician, by order of the playwright, has left darkened, on purpose, so that he might break his neck. Victim of a damned international conspiracy between Marxist-Leninism and Yankee Imperialism, all sweaty and smelly, and led by the nose like an ox, La Gorda del Pueblo has been exposed to the searing sun in the

Plaza Cívica, where she is finally redeemed by a torrential downpour decreed by the clergy, the Counterrevolution and Yankee Imperialism. Seeking refuge in the sacred Temple of Thalia, he enters, soaked to the skin, the Teatro Nacional, where he is finally subjected to the limitless lampooning of Roman and Victoria. Stumbling around, as would be expected, like Sigismund the Hunchback, he finds himself caught in the "life is but a dream" web, and seeks salvation in the soliloquy. (*He recites it, with a dress in hand, referring to the living room.*)

> Good Heavens! What do I make of it?
> Good Heavens! What do I discern?
> (*Looking at the dress.*)
> I see it with little concern
> And doubtfully, do I believe it.
> Don't tell me a dream is just fiction;
> My wits I have about me.
> No other but Miguel Angel could I be;
> Oh, Heavens, grant me conviction.
> (*Speaking to Roman.*)
> Tell me, what could this be?
> This fantasy-like happening
> That transpired while I was sleeping,
> And now behold before me.
> (*Declaiming, at center stage.*)
> But, regardless, I have to say,
> I have no need to keep speaking
> Let me be; I want to be serving,
> Come whatever may.

(*Pause. Thinking over what he has just said.*) Do you see now that Calderon was a communist? Look here, think about it. If "the Revolution is like a melon, green on the outside and red on the inside," the first line, "Come whatever may," fits it like a glove; and if it is true that "with the Revolution, everything, and without the Revolution, nothing," who is going to "need to keep speaking"? That is like saying you'd better shut your trap. "Let me be, I want to be serving . . ." (*Describing this in detail*): doing guard duty, doing volunteer work, joining the army . . . (*Concluding in animated fashion.*) "Motherland or death, we shall be victorious!" (*Transition.*) If La Gorda heard me I assure you that she'd nominate me for the Lenin Prize!

ROMAN: I thought you were in favor of all of this, Miguel Angel.

MIGUEL: Well, of course I am. I believe those Calderon lines to a tee and nobody can make me think otherwise. (*With an unexpected affectionate impulse, perhaps a little drunk, he gets close to embrace Roman, who tries to get out of it.*) Because, even if you don't believe it, Roman, deep down I really love you like a brother and it's impossible that you could be so wrong, dammit!

ROMAN: (*Getting loose.*) Leave me be, Miguel Angel. You're drunk.

MIGUEL: Either you learn those lines by Calderon or you'll have to go to hell.

ROMAN: I can't do that, Miguel Angel. I have to believe in the truth.

MIGUEL: You have to brainwash yourself, like everybody else. Don't you think it has been hard for me?

VICTORIA: It hasn't' been that hard for you.

MIGUEL: How do you know? Why do you think I've had to get drunk? I have spent all day at the Plaza Civica shouting out "Motherland or death! We shall be victorious!" Screaming my guts out . . . That gives me the right to drink all I want . . .

VICTORIA: Don't you forget that here nobody has a right to anything, and don't you go believing that you're better than anyone else. Ever since you left New York you were ready to play your hand and lose it all. You already knew those Calderon lines, "regardless" and "come whatever may." You had already sold your soul to the Devil.

MIGUEL: What right do you have to judge me? Who are you to cast the first stone?

VICTORIA: You don't have to go so far as to quote the New Testament. We've got enough with Calderon.

MIGUEL: But you're the one who brought up the Devil. After all, you signed up too. Or have you forgotten? Stop all this hypocrisy and chest beating. (*Pause.*) The only one here who didn't sign up was Roman. That's not counting that you also went out with Fidel to eat a spaghetti dinner.

VICTORIA: You are twisting the truth. All I did was have a coffee with milk.

MIGUEL: I'm going to give you a warning, Roman. You have to define yourself. Publicly. Or do you think it's fair that I have to go around interjecting lines from Fidel's speech to the metallurgists while you go around making metaphors with the guillotine?

ROMAN: What do I have to do with the guillotine?

MIGUEL: (*Pointing to the guillotine.*) And, what is this? The hammer and sickle?

ROMAN: I have nothing to do with that. I haven't ordered that a guillotine be put on the stage. I also have nothing to do with that mural of the Sierra Maestra. That's your affair.

MIGUEL: So, then, who the hell asked for it? Don't give me that. You're the playwright, aren't you?

VICTORIA: What are you up to? Are you trying to get Roman in trouble?

MIGUEL: That's a vile thing to say, Victoria. You know me all too well and know that I could never do that to Roman. Not Roman or anybody else. Because, if I am the Poet of the Revolution, you are Victoria del Pueblo. You and I can't fool each other. Because if I am the one who recites that poetry that Fidel writes to the metallurgists and the bus drivers, you are the one who, night after night, repeats it. If you suffer night after night for having to pretend to be someone you're not, how can you know what I'm going through? We know each other too well to fool each other, and I say this in front of Roman because Roman knows that there is nothing to hide . . . (*Furious.*) Dammit! You know that deep down I love you both . . . you . . . and Roman . . . And if there has been anything good about these last years it has been that certain things that existed between us . . . that separated us . . . have been erased forever . . . (*To Victoria, more directly.*) I know that that rejection you have always felt for me may remain . . . because . . . because it is inevitable. . . . Because, I, myself, at a particular moment, have . . . (*Furious.*) Dammit! Dammit! I hate to talk with my heart on my sleeve!

ROMAN: Why? Why can't we talk with our hearts on our sleeves? Wouldn't it be better for all of us?

VICTORIA: (*Getting close to Miguel Angel.*) Then . . . then you are the one in danger . . . the one who must save himself . . .

ROMAN: If we all spoke with our hearts on our sleeves . . .

MIGUEL: We can't talk with our hearts on our sleeves! We can't talk with our hearts! You have to talk with your head . . . With your stomach . . . With your mouth full of crap. . . But you can't talk with your heart on your sleeve because they'd bleed it and destroy it. . . . Do you remember when Fidel stuck us in the National Library and told us to talk to our hearts' delight, because here nobody paid attention to anybody?

ROMAN: Nobody did harm to anybody.

MIGUEL: No harm to anybody . . . And that there was freedom to say anything you wanted to, and all that crap . . . ? I didn't say a word, dammit! Those people who say everything and don't keep anything inside end up rehabilitated on agricultural farms . . . planting taro . . . in jails . . . before firing squads . . . with their mouths full of flies on roadside shoulders. Silence is golden, Roman, and it's better to shut you're mouth while you're alive . . . (*Next to the guillotine, referring to it.*) You'd better hurry up and get rid of this small detail, this guillotine, because if you are responsible . . .

ROMAN: But, I'm not.

MIGUEL: (*Handing him a libretto that had been left on a chair.*) Look at the margin notes. Maybe you put in a guillotine without realizing it . . . It's still better to get rid of that damned guillotine before it starts cutting heads off on its own . . . (*To Victoria.*) You are my witness that I've done everything that I could.

VICTORIA: Maybe it was Ruben's idea.

MIGUEL: No, Ruben doesn't have the balls to do that. He's really scared crapless.

ROMAN: Scared of what?

MIGUEL: Scared of everything, Roman. Just as scared as everybody else . . . Dammit! It's impossible to talk to you! I just can't believe that not even Victoria has managed to open your eyes . . . Even poor Ruben is scared, which I would say is a security measure . . . It's a survival instinct . . . And what's worse, in his case, is that he's afraid of everything and even something more. He was a nervous wreck today. He went off to the Beach trembling from head to toe.

VICTORIA: What do you mean, he's afraid of everything and . . . and even something more?

MIGUEL: He's queer.

VICTORIA: I didn't know that that was a different type of fear.

MIGUEL: Well, let me tell you something. If I were queer I'd also be 'that kind of' afraid. I don't know, but someone is spreading the rumor that a big queer roundup is in the making, that the revolution and homosexuality are incompatible, that one cannot be queer and a good revolutionary too . . . It may or may not be on account of the counter-revolution, Yankee imperialist campaigns, but if I were queer like Ruben, I'd be crapping in my pants . . . or wherever.

ROMAN: But, that doesn't make sense.

MIGUEL: It may not make sense to you but mostly everybody thinks just the opposite.

VICTORIA: Then, what are they going to do with Raul Castro?

MIGUEL: Ask his wife or Fidel Castro about that, because he is one of those guys who swings both ways... Anyway, Ruben is caught in a trap, in an existentialist alley that Sartre just forgot about... You have to imagine how difficult the decision is... Take it or leave it... To eat or not eat... The character has to choose between a rock and a hard place.

ROMAN: Dammit, it's amusing!

MIGUEL: No, there's nothing amusing about it. It's a goddamned difficult decision! Because, half jokingly and half seriously, it is a life-and-death decision. "With the Revolution everything, without the Revolution, nothing." Fasting and abstinence! It's really something else! We're not mystics, you know! It's what you call 'awareness,' and Ruben will have to decide what position to take, a vertical or supine one.

VICTORIA: I hope La Gorda doesn't suspect any of this.

MIGUEL: La Gorda knows more than you think. All eyes and ears, for everything. The other day she gave him a Marxist-Leninist lecture and just about put a chastity belt on him. She told him about the persecution of homosexuals during the Stalin era and made him all hysterical about the life, passion and death of Mayakowski, assuring him that Mayakowski had committed suicide because he was queer.

VICTORIA: But, how does she know what she's talking about?

MIGUEL: Do you remember how she used to arrive with overflowing shopping bags from the A&P?

ROMAN: (*Jocular tone.*) How could anyone forget? I can still see her. And she'd immediately start straightening up. Putting everything in its place.

VICTORIA: And then she'd get in the kitchen and start cooking.

MIGUEL: (*Quickly, jumping around the stage, counting.*) Pot roast, chicken and rice, fricasseed beef...!

VICTORIA: (*Laughing.*) Boy, could she cook!

ROMAN: (*Laughing.*) Boy, did we eat!

MIGUEL: (*Light-hearted crescendo.*) Cuban-style chopped beef, crunchy fried pork, Spanish-style codfish...!

ROMAN: She used to make it all without complaining, always in a good mood... she never protested despite whatever kind of day she might have had, working in the factory and doing overtime... Afterwards, when we were done, we'd all pitch in and help her clear off the table.

MIGUEL: (*Voice increasing in anger, with crescendo.*) Black beans, Asturian bean soup, chick pea soup...!

VICTORIA: That truly was volunteer work!

MIGUEL: (*Frenetic climactic, illogical, furious, shouting.*) Egg custard! Flan! French toast! Rice pudding! Holiday bread pudding!

VICTORIA: (*Thinking, not with the passion of Miguel Angel.*) Sometimes I used to think it was like theatre, you repeat a scene over and over... (*Absorbed in her own analysis.*) As if she were playing a role...

MIGUEL: (*Rapid transition, stopping suddenly.*) What made you think of that? Don't you think that's strange?

VICTORIA: Haven't you thought it?

MIGUEL: Not at that moment, but I have thought of it afterwards.

ROMAN: But it wasn't a scene from a play . . . It was . . . it was . . . altogether natural . . .

MIGUEL: But can't a scene from a play be totally natural?

ROMAN: Yes, it's possible . . . (*Thinking.*) Like with those actresses who act so well that you forget that they are play acting.

VICTORIA: But she's different now. When I see her, I no longer remember her arriving from the market and doing the things that she used to do in New York. Doesn't it seem strange to you?

MIGUEL: Ever since she got here she hasn't set foot in the kitchen.

ROMAN: We have all changed; maybe she has changed too.

VICTORIA: It's as if . . . they'd put another person in her place . . . (*To Miguel Angel.*) You must know it better than we do, Miguel Angel.

MIGUEL: It's just that La Gorda and I keep our distance.

ROMAN: And yet now, when you think about it, everything is too exact, too precise, maybe. Almost too natural. As if in reality, when she gets home, she were hiding something.

MIGUEL: Dammit! Maybe she was cheating on me!

ROMAN: It's just that she has changed so much. Even her sense of humor.

MIGUEL: I didn't know she had a sense of humor.

ROMAN: Well, because you didn't have much to do with her.

VICTORIA: Don't you think she's changed too much? Because, after all, we're not exactly the same as we were before and, on the other hand, we're not totally different either. We can . . . recognized ourselves. (*To Miguel Angel.*) Maybe you can remember some detail . . . something that would be significant.

MIGUEL: There isn't anything significant. La Gorda in the kitchen. La Gorda cleaning the house. La Gorda washing the dishes. And, if you will, La Gorda in bed. But there's nothing important to remember. It's just that I looked at her as little as possible. As if we had been together all the time and really not ever at all. As if I saw her on the outside, coming in, going out, but never really seeing her . . . (*Pause.*) But afterwards, when we came back, I began to realize that she existed. I don't know how to explain it. She was someone else. (*Pause.*) Then the business about the trip to Peking came up. When she told me that we were going to Peking, I was surprised. How was it possible for her to know that before me? Because I was the Poet of the Revolution, dammit, and she was nobody . . . (*Pause.*) Wasn't she just an ignoramus? When did she ever say anything that bore repeating? (*Pause.*) Then one day I began to fear her. La Gorda knew how I was. She knew my weaknesses, my frailties, my cynicism, if you want to call it that. I would get chicken skin. (*Pause.*) Later, during the trip to Peking, everyone in the Cuban delegation knew her . . . and she was treated with a kind of very subtle deference, that was sometimes mixed with fear . . . She was on a first name basis with Fidel. She spoke to high ranking Communist Party people as if they'd known each other forever. (*Furious, by the window.*) Even the Chinese knew La Gorda! I should have gotten rid of her while I still had a chance! What does La Gorda, who is in the Cuban Federation of Women, the Cultural Council, the Association of Professional Revolutionaries, the Journalism School, and even makes soup, have to do with any tamale and mash cook? It's just that I, just like Ruben, am between a rock and a hard place.

VICTORIA: (*After a brief pause.*) So she knows everything.

MIGUEL: Of course, she knows it all, because while we were speaking freely, she, I'm absolutely sure of this, was listening to our every word . . . because we've always said whatever we wanted to . . .

VICTORIA: Especially you, Miguel Angel, with your word games.

MIGUEL: She knows everything. And the worst of it is that she knows me like the back of her hand. Because I've told her. Because I, myself, have always made fun of Fidel's rantings that everybody swallows, like a gigantic sausage, in front of her. Do you follow me? I'm trapped. She's getting her revenge. She'll wind up twisting my balls.

VICTORIA: (*Moving away, towards the door. She turns around.*) We've got to get out of here.

MIGUEL: (*Confused, not understanding.*) Leave?

VICTORIA: To New York. Anywhere. The important thing is to get out of here. Go into exile how ever many times it takes.

PART V

Epilogue: *Sin Fronteras*, Beyond Boundaries

Guillermo Gómez-Peña (1955–)

Danger Zone: Cultural Relations between Chicanos and Mexicans at the End of the Century

Internationally renowned, Guillermo Gómez-Peña is at present one of the foremost Latino artists. A writer and performer born in Mexico City, he emigrated to the United States in 1978 and immediately became identified with the political and cultural concerns associated with the Chicano Movement. Few contemporary artists have undertaken such ideologically profound and aesthetically complex reflections on issues of colonialism and cultural otherness, (trans)border identities, and the political and ethical implications of the so-called processes of globalization as has Gómez-Peña. His defiant live performances not only are provocative challenges to views his audience often takes for granted, but these carefully elaborated yet spontaneous works also attempt to achieve the spiritual intensity of traditional rituals and shamanistic practices, at the same time formally engaging the full repertoire of postmodern electronic media. The boundaries between tradition and innovation, past and present, here and there, you and I are deeply problematized in his art, as well as in his writing. The following essay, *Danger Zone* (originally published in his book *The New World Border*, 1996), is an example of his meditations on the potential of "life on the border" as a political and ethical stand. Gómez-Peña has been the recipient of numerous awards, such as the Prix de la Parole and the New York Bessie Award, among others, and in 1991 he was honored with the prestigious MacArthur Fellowship. (ALO)

Further reading: Guillermo Gómez-Peña, *A Binational Performance Pilgrimage* (Manchester: Cornerhouse, 1993), *Warrior for Gringostroika: Essays, Performance Texts, and Poetry* (St. Paul, Minn.: Graywolf Press, 1993), *The New World Border: Prophecies, Poems, and Loqueras for the End of the Century* (San Francisco, Calif.: City Lights, 1996).

Trans.: CR

In February of 1995, the first stage of a binational performance project called "Terreno Peligroso/Danger Zone" was completed. For an entire month—two weeks in Los Angeles and two in Mexico City—eleven experimental artists whose work challenges stereotypical and/or official notions of identity, nationality, language, sexuality, and the creative process worked together daily. Representing Mexico were Lorena Wolffer, Felipe Ehrenberg, Eugenia Vargas, César Martínez, and Elvira Santamaría; from California were Elia Arce, Rubén Martínez, Nao Bustamante, Luis Alfaro, Roberto Sifuentes, and myself. Chosen by the curators and producers, Josefina Ramírez and Lorena Wolffer, this group was as eclectic and diverse as our two cultures (Chicano and Mexican). The performances were presented at the University of California at Los Angeles (UCLA) and in the Ex-Teresa Arte Alternativo (Mexico City).

The performance work we did covered a wide spectrum, ranging from the most intimate ritual actions to the most confrontational activist performance; including tableaux vivants, avant-cabaret, spoken word poetry, apocalyptic rituals, and street "interventions." Our goals (at least those we consciously expressed) were: to create art together (border art is collaborative by nature); to open the Pandora's box of North/South relations and unleash the border demons; to destroy taboos; and to replace simplistic views of cultural otherness with more complex visions. The following text attempts to outline some of the problems that the artists confronted during this binational encounter.

I

At the close of 1993, many artists of Latin American origin who were living in the United States ingenuously believed that NAFTA, or the "*Tratado de Libre Comer-se*"—despite its grave omissions in the areas of ecology, human and labor rights, culture, and education—would, at least indirectly, create the conditions for a rapprochement between Chicanos and Mexicans. But that idea completely backfired on us. Instead, ferocious nationalist movements began to arise in response to globalization of the economy and culture. Xenophobic proposals reminiscent of Nazi Germany—such as Operation Gatekeeper and California's chilling Proposition 187—were brandished to confront the increasing and inevitable Mexicanization of the United States. We watched, perplexed, as the sudden opening of markets occurred almost simultaneously with the militarization of the border and the construction of a huge metal wall to separate several border cities. Capital, hollow dreams, and assembly plants easily crossed from one side to the other, but human beings—along with critical art and ideas—were prohibited passage. It seemed that culturally, as well as economically, the *maquiladora* model had been perfected: Mexicans would provide the raw material and do the arduous, badly paid work; Anglos would run the show; and Chicanos would be left out of the picture.

We are like tiny, insignificant spectators at a great end-of-the-century wrestling match: "The Invisible Octopus of Pseudo-internationalization vs. the Hydra of Neonationalism." Round One: The neoliberal formula of a continent unified by free trade, tourism, and digital high-technology is confronted by indigenous, campesino, environmental, and human rights movements. *Coitus interruptus.* The Mexican peso plummets, foreign capital flees, and the Marlboro dreams of neoliberal elites vanish in a cloud of sulfurous smoke. *Cambio.*

The crises are also becoming globalized. In the topography of the end-of-the-century crisis, Bosnia is strangely connected to Los Angeles (L.A.—Herzegovina), just as Chiapas is connected to the Basque country and to Northern Ireland. Mexicans in California confront a dilemma similar to that faced by Palestinians and black South Africans, and the young people of Mexico City (members of Generation MEX) manifest the same existential and psychological illnesses that plague New Yorkers or Berliners.

The paradoxes multiply *loca*rhythmically. In the era of computers, faxes, virtual reality, World Beat, and "total television" (à la CNN), it has become increasingly difficult for us to communicate across the borders of culture and language. The smaller and more concentrated the world becomes, the more foreign and incomprehensible it seems to us. We are now exposed to many languages, but we lack the keys to translation. We have access to incredible amounts of information, but we don't have the codes to decipher it. The seductive virtual universe, with its unlimited options and multidirectional promises, confounds our ability to order information and to act in the world with ethical and political clarity.

If anything could be said to define "postmodernity," it is the steady increase in symptoms of border culture, the endless syncretisms with a complete lack of synchronicity, misencounters, and misunderstandings: "I am, as long as you (as the representative of racial, linguistic, or cultural otherness) no longer are"; "I cross, therefore you exist (or vice versa)"; "Fuck you, therefore I am"; and others that would be better left unsaid. Contemporary art—at its most critical, irreverent, and experimental—is an involuntary chronicle of the ontological and epistemological confusion that is affecting all of us equally.

Chicano rap, Mexican alternative rock, independent cinema, and performance art converge on these key points: the brave acceptance of our transborderized and denationalized condition; the *ars poetic* of vertigo; the metaphysics of fragmentation; and the total collapse of linear logic, dramatic time, and narrative aesthetics. (This book is hopefully an example of this.)

II

The myths that once grounded our identity have become bankrupt. Sixties-era pan-Latinamericanism, *la mexicanidad* (unique, monumental, undying), and Chicanismo (with thorns and a capital C) have all been eclipsed by processes of cultural borderization and social fragmentation. Like it or not, we are now denationalized, de-mexicanized, transchicanized, and pseudo-internationalized. And worse, in fear of falling into a new century we refuse to assume this new identity, roaming around instead in a Bermuda Triangle. We live in economic uncertainty, terrorized by the holocaust of AIDS, divided (better yet, trapped) by multiple borders, disconnected from ourselves and others by strange mass cultures and new technologies that appeal to our most mediocre desires for instant transformation and psychological expansion.

In this bizarre landscape, politics becomes pop culture, and technology turns into folklore. Mass culture, popular culture, and folklore are no longer distinguishable from one another: it seems that our only true community is television. Perhaps our only real nation is also television. Mexico is, and continues to be "one" by virtue of television;

without television perhaps it would cease to be. Televisa is Mexico's macro-Ministry of Communications, Culture, and Binational Tourism, all in one. In the United States of the '90s, the most famous Mexicans are TV personalities such as Gloria Trevi, Paco Stanley, "Verónica," and Raúl Velasco. Sadly, the main connection that Mexican immigrants maintain with that marvelous, imaginary country called Mexico is via soap operas. If we are familiar with "El Sup" (Subcomandante Marcos) and Superbarrio, it's because they are skillful manipulators of the symbolic (and performative) politics of the media. In this context, we "untelevisable" performance artists are asking ourselves what role will be left for us to perform in the immediate future. Maybe our only options will be to make conceptual commercials for MTV and/or appear in artsy rock videos. For the moment, I'm having a hard time imagining more dignified alternatives.

III

North Americans (in the United States) used to define their identity in direct opposition to the "Soviet threat." With the end of the Cold War, the United States fell into an unprecedented identity crisis. Today its place in the world is uncertain and its (fictitious) enemies are multiplying left and right. On the eclectic list of recent anti-American "others" one finds fundamentalist Muslims, Japanese businessmen, Latin American drug lords, black rap musicians, and more recently, "illegal aliens" in both senses of the word: cultural martians invading "our" institutions, and seditious laborers who are "stealing jobs from *real* Americans."

This identity crisis translates into an immense nostalgia for an (imaginary) era in which people of color didn't exist, or at least when we were invisible and silent. The political expression of this nostalgia is chilling: "Let's take our country back." The far right, like Pete Wilson, Newt Gingrich, Jesse Helms, and Pat Buchanan, along with many Democrats, are in agreement on the following: This country must be saved from chaos and collapse into Third-Worldization; "illegal" immigrants must be deported; the poor should be put in jail (three strikes, you're out); welfare, affirmative action, and bilingual education programs must be dismantled; and the cultural funding infrastructure that has been infiltrated by "liberals with leftist tendencies" (the National Endowment for the Arts and the Humanities and the Corporation for Public Broadcasting) must be decimated. In the euphemistic Contract with America, ethnic "minorities," independent artists and intellectuals, the homeless, the elderly, children, and especially immigrants from the South, are all under close watch.

In Mexico, ever since the implementation of NAFTA the border no longer functions as the great barrier of contention against which official Mexican identity is defined. This has created its own large-scale identity crisis. Without the continuous harassment from Washington's Power Rangers, the *yupitecas* and the *mariachis* have had no other alternative than to go off to a cantina and drown themselves in the depths of lost love and *neo-Porfirista* nostalgia. The social explosion in Chiapas has complicated things further and has literally torn the country in two. *Salinista* Mexico preferred to think of itself as *posmoderno* and international, desiring at all costs to look outward and northward, but the unfolding internal political crisis has forced the country's gaze back inward to confront its racism against indigenous peoples and its abysmal contradictions.

Although the roots of our crises are of a very different nature, both Califas (California) and Tenochtitlán (Mexico City) are living through unprecedented identity crises. And, for the first time in the twentieth century there is a growing consciousness on both sides of the border that the crises and dangers that we're undergoing are similar. This mutual recognition could be the basis for new, more profound cultural relations between Chicanos and Mexicans: If we recognize that we're all equally screwed, perhaps at the same time we are equally capable of greater compassion and mutual understanding.

IV

At present, the only thing that unites those who left Mexico and those who stayed is our inability to understand and accept our inevitable differences. We detect the existence of these invisible borders, but we are unable to articulate them, much less cross them with tact. This phenomenon is clearly evident in the area of cultural relations between Mexico and the United States, most especially, between Mexicans and Chicanos. It's here where the contradictions abound, where the wound opens and bleeds, and the poisoned subtext of mutual (and largely fictional) resentments rises to the surface.

We, the post-Mexican and Chicano artists from "over there/the other side" look to the South with a certain ingenuousness, a distorting nostalgia and admiration, always dreaming of our possible return. Meanwhile, the Mexicans who remain south of the border look at us with a combination of desire and repudiation, fear and condescension. The mirrors are always breaking. While we on the California coast—where the West literally ends—look toward the Pacific, those in Mexico City look attentively toward Europe and New York. (The paradox here is that Europe and New York—in spiritual and artistic bankruptcy—are carefully watching both Chicanos and Mexicans, searching for novelty, inspiration, and exoticism to decorate the blank walls of their nihilist crisis.)

The missed encounters continue. In the United States, Latino artists work in the flammable context of the multicultural wars and identity politics. We define ourselves as a culture of resistance, and in our eagerness to "resist the dominant culture" we frequently lose all sense of a continental perspective, and end up assuming ethnocentric and separatist positions. Meanwhile, the Mexican artistic communities—with some exceptions—are undergoing a stage of nonreflective extroversion and the rejection of textually political or politicized art, which they associate with "minor" art and with official Mexican cultural discourse. Although they are the protagonists and witnesses of their country's most serious crisis in modern history (perhaps comparable to that of Eastern Europe), many Mexican experimental artists have chosen not to "textually" use *la crisis* as subject matter in their work. Right now, they are more inclined to create a personal, intimate art of an existential or neoconceptual style.

When Mexican artists "go North," they do so with the intention of breaking into the commercial gallery circuit. They are prejudiced by the solemnity and virtual failure of official cultural exchange projects, and to them Chicano art appears didactic, reiterative, and poorly executed. Our themes—racism, immigration, the obsessive deconstruction of identities, and the subversion of media stereotypes of Mexicans—seem distant and irrelevant to their purely "Mexican" reality. They seem not to fully grasp the magnitude of their own crisis and refuse (not entirely without reason) to be seen as a "minority." Chicanos, hypersensitive to this fragile relationship, feel rejected by the Mexicans, and the gap between the two cultures grows wider.

The long and convoluted history of cultural exchange between Chicanos and Mexicans can be translated as a chronicle of missed encounters. For fifteen years Chicanos have tried, without success, to "return" through the great door and to reconcile themselves with Mexican relatives. With few exceptions, the reception to their art has been openly hostile or, at best, paternalistic. Despite the numerous and fashionable projects of binational interchange facilitated (or inspired) by NAFTA, Mexico's predominant vision of Chicano art is still antiquated. In 1995, most Mexicans still believe that all Chicano artists make barrio murals, write protest poetry, and erect neon altars to Frida Kahlo and the Virgin of Guadalupe; that they all speak like Edward Olmos in *American Me* and dance to Tex-Mex music; that they all drive low-riders. They ignore the actual diversity and complexity of our communities, and remain unaware of the influence of the Central American, Caribbean, and Asian communities that have moved into the Chicano neighborhoods. The influence of gay and lesbian communities of color, with their challenge to the excessive dose of testosterone from which Chicano culture has suffered for the last two decades, is also completely overlooked. The processes that have brought us to more fluid and interactive models of a Chicano/Latino multi-identity are still unheard of Mexico City, and two generations of young artists who have publicly questioned conventional, static notions of Chicanismo remain outside the realm of most Mexicans' consciousness.

V

In 1995, *la mexicanidad* and the Latino/Chicano experience are becoming completely superimposed. The 200,000 Mexicans who cross the border every month bring us fresh and constant reminders of our past (for Mexican Americans, the continual migratory flow functions as a sort of collective memory). And the opposite phenomenon also happens: the mythic North (which represents the future) also returns to the South, searching for its lost past. Many of the Mexicans who come to "the other side" become "chicanized" and return to Mexico—either on their own or by force of the immigration authorities. In the act of returning they contribute to the silent process of Chicanization which Mexico is currently undergoing.

This dual dynamic, as expressed in popular culture, functions as a sort of X-ray of the social psyche: the "northern" sounds of *quebradita* (a fusion of north Mexican banda and techno-pop) and rap can already be heard from Yucatán to Chihuahua; while the songs of Mexican bands such as Los Caifanes, La Lupita, Maldita Vecindad, and Los Tigres del Norte are being hummed from San Diego to New York. Selena, the "queen of Tex-Mex" (RIP), is venerated in both countries. The sounds of "tecno-banda" and quebradita (no one can deny that these are immigrant sounds) re-mexicanize Chicano music. The "cholos" and the "salvatruchos" (young Salvadorans in L.A.) are wearing Stetson hats and cowboy boots, while Aztec punk-rockers in Mexico City, Guadalajara, and Tijuana are expropriating Chicano iconography and fashion, and talking in Spanglish, ¿que no?

Mexican identity (or better said, the many Mexican identities) can no longer be explained without the experience of "the other side," and vice versa. As a socio-cultural phenomenon, Los Angeles simply cannot be understood without taking Mexico City—its southernmost neighborhood—into account. Between both cities runs the greatest migratory axis on the planet, and the conceptual freeway with the greatest number of accidents.

As transnationalized artists, our challenge is to recompose the fragmented chronicle of this strange end-of-the-century phenomenon. And so, the performance begins . . .

Luis Rafael Sánchez (1936–)

The Flying Bus

The Flying Bus (1987) is a joyful reflection on the ways in which migration has redefined the geography of Puerto Rico as a nation. Suspended in the air, the constant human flow between San Juan and New York dissolves conventional conceptions of national borders, making metropolitan New York an integral part of the fragmented Puerto Rican archipelago. Humorous in his tone and playful in his use of language, Luis Rafael Sánchez has distanced himself—in this and many of his works—from the solemnity that has characterized Puerto Rican meditations on national identity throughout much of the twentieth century. A permanent passenger on "la guagua aérea," "in recent years Sánchez has combined his pedagogical endeavors at the University of Puerto Rico in Río Piedras with many distinguished visiting professor appointments at diverse universities in the United States, especially at the City University of New York. He is a playwright, novelist, storywriter, and essayist. A significant part of his literary production is characterized by the unruly cadences of Puerto Rican Spanish language and by the reworking of selected icons and myths of popular and mass culture. (ALO)

Further reading: Luis Rafael Sánchez, *La guagua aérea*, 2nd ed. ([San Juan]: Editorial Cultural, 1994); *La pasión según Antígona Pérez*, 15th ed. (Río Piedras: Editorial Cultural, 1998); *Macho Comacho's Beat* (Normal, Ill.: Dalkey Archive Press, 2000).

Trans.: ELD

After the terrified scream, silences descend one by one. The stewardess, angelic and innocent like one of Horacio Quiroga's characters, a blonde with the sort of frozen intensity that would enliven the libido of any lovesick King Kong, begins to back away. The anxious faces of the passengers share the most bizarre premonitions as they search for the hand carrying the gun, the knife or a homemade bomb. For the terrified scream could easily be the hysterical and uncontrollable telltale sign of still one more skyjacker or any menacing madman. An *Our Father* bursts the catalytic silences one by one. The stewardess proceeds on her retreat, she has seen herself in the mirror of fear, and fear has stamped her with the lividity of a massive, overpowering fainting fit. But the skyjacker or frantic madman is nowhere in sight. Contrite, mumbled, the *Our Fathers* advance at different levels of faith and orality. Suddenly, light comes into being, and halogenous glare violates the retina and illumines the gallop of myriad heartbeats. The flying bus becomes a mammoth, autopsied by indiscreet fluorescences at thirty-one thousand feet above sea level. The Captain, or flying bus driver, and the Flight Engineer or mechanic, show up, and their studied inexpressivity incites an expression of cautiousness; the rest of the crew is alerted, the assault of general hysteria creeps in, grows, threatens, and the bleached stewardess is just half an inch from being consumed by terror. But the skyjacker or the menacing madman is nowhere to be seen.

Suddenly, unparalleled as a scandal or a surprise, a burst of laughter corrodes at once both the silences and the *Our Fathers* that in some lips were about to reach the first *a* of Amen. Pristine in its offensiveness, the clean-cut parentheses of laughter could have been collaged onto any page, were it not on account of its contagiousness which begins to contaminate the hundreds of passengers of the flying bus that ferries every night between the airports of San Juan and New York; an attractive laughter due to its inordinate and ferocious rashness, a disorderly laughter that underlines an almost automatic agreement, a ferocity that translates secret and unforgettable resentments. The timid of heart would immediately think that the flying bus is about to stall on account of the pitching and rolling generated by the mushrooming laughter. And low-flying angels with the curiosity of Peeping-Toms would gladly give away the gold of their curls just to know what the hell is the source of the laughter of that airbound crowd of mestizos who dare to trespass into their own turf. Only the flight crew, uniformly gringo this evening, seems immune to the plague of laughter, seems immune to the general ridicule of the terror that had distorted the innocent and angelic features of the blonde stewardess.

The general laughter now seems at the point of depressurizing the cabin and off-setting the angle-of-attack of the flying bus. No relief is in sight because, now, everyone can see the incredible culprits of their first terror. Down the carpeted aisle of the flying bus, walking defiantly into a "High Noon," bullying, snapping and squirming their way along, indifferent to the scandals and terrors their presence had provoked, a couple of self-conscious, proud and healthy mangrove crabs are making their way.—

Paradoxically, the notorious splendor of their health is the omen of their presumable fate—tomorrow, they will become crab gumbo in Prospect, or Alcapurria (Puerto Rican fried meat plantain pie) stuffing in the South Bronx, or marinated crab-in-the-shell in Sunset Park, or crab Asopao (mixture of rice and crabs) in the Lower East Side, or temporary tenants in the cultivated darkness of a basement, away from the surveillance of a super or a landlord. But tonight, their notable splendor and the surprising use of the flying bus as an improvised frontier, as a means of access, are the subject of imaginative commentaries, of loquacious witticisms which precipitate from the absolute anxiety which now reigns over the free expression of attitudes and even over the passengers' recourse to more agitated speech in that anarchical choreography of bodies bending, twisting and curling in the prisons of the planes seats. It is an absolute anxiety spurred on by speeches in favor of independence immediate attached by the prostatehood, by the avalanche of off-colored jokes and the winks of daring Don Juans and temporary floozies, by the detailed confessions—because autobiography seduces us. It was an absolute anxiety born in irate accounts of successive humiliation in crosstown buses, in the elevators and on the fucking job, at the liberal university and the Jew's corner junkshop store, an absolute disquiet that, suddenly, draws an invisible but tangible line between them, the gringos, and us, the Puerto Ricans; frontier of discourse that underlines the unsustainable assertion of the mulatto woman who presents her newborn child with a juicy and radiant breast: "the blonder they are, the more of an asshole," a disquiet that disquiets—or seems to disquiet—tonight's uniformly gringo flight crew. The crew, dumbfounded by this sudden collapse of electronic modernity, amazed at the fact that the rigorous security devices were unable to detect the infamous contraband, demands the POSITIVE IDENTIFICATION of the owner of the crabs with imposing gestures resembling a much too-German Expressionist comedy, toned-down by the pleasant and parodical memory of the antics of a Buster Keaton or a Charlie Chaplin. The insistent demands of a vigorous gesticulator and the insistent offering of a would-be crab executioner, are met with theatrical boastfulness by the half-asleep half-annoyed middle-aged man who stumbles his way to the first rows of seats of the flying bus and, with flashy manual dexterity (improperly termed "underdeveloped") grabs the fugitive couple of crabs and rebukes them "either you guys stay put or I'll shove a squirt of Valium up your joyholes, all included in today's shit-pay." Euphoria reigns, becomes collective. The laughter that decongests the reason of all fogged-up horizons, and the lungs of excessive mucosity, congests the thinking canals of the passengers of the flying bus. Someone who brooded over the belly-torn cadavers that illustrate the daily occurrences of the newspaper *El Vocero* excuses himself: "I choked"; a lady who was praising the Gallito de Manati's last show at Jefferson Theater declares "I almost pissed myself," another remarks that the evening is just cut out for enjoying a jug of something, a remark that elicits the approval of those within ear-range, while another poetic type sings in octosyllables the rationality of having a momentous chicken stew, out of the blue.

The flying bus fizzles, oscillates between a tumultuous atmosphere and the gravity of a chimera, between the aggressiveness of a will to succeed and an atavic burden of self-pity or charity, *Ay bendito*. A well poised woman who hides a multitude of hair rollers under a flowery turban informs us that she flies over *the pond* every month and that she has forgotten on which bank of it she really lives; an adolescent lady crisped by cosmetics and on the verge of desperation because Rene's voice changed and he was forced to retire from *Menudo*, listens uninterestedly to the adolescent gentleman, crisped by disorientation, who knows that he is going to Newark but cannot figure out why. A gregarious and outspoken lady stands up and unravels the folds of a kingsized bedspread forming a tent under whose artisanship an improvised quartet bleats the ballad *En mi viejo San Juan*; and a gentleman of educated and sober poise asks the mulatto woman of the juicy and radiant breast if they have not met before, perhaps, in the feast in honor of the Virgin of Monserrate in the town of Hormigueros. The virginal mulatto woman of the juicy and radiant breast tells him that she has never been to Hormigueros. He then asks the young lady stuffed in pumpkin-colored mechanic's jeans if, perhaps, they have not met before, possibly in the feast (in honor) of the Holy Guardian Angels in the city of Yabucoa. The young lady stuffed into the pumpkin-colored mechanic's jeans answers that she has never been to the city of Yabucoa, that she goes into *Bachelor, Bocaccio and Topaz* . . . or any other place as gay. From the makeshift kitchen of the flying bus a purposefully plaintiff Orpheon stridently nags to the chorus of *Si no me dan de beber, lloro* (popular Christmas song which repeats "If they don't give me something to drink, I'll cry"), another man obsessed with indignation narrates the imprisonment of a son who refused to testify to the Federal Grand Jury, while another categorizes that to be a nationalist in Puerto Rico carries with it a certain prestige but to be a nationalist in New York is received with public hostility.

And so, a chain of anecdotes is linked to a chain of resounding interjections; anguished and laughable anecdotes, some heart-breaking, others superficial, others dearly heroic in their formulation of resistance against insult, against open or concealed prejudice; an infinity of anecdotes where Puerto Ricans take a center stage in acts of roguishness, of witticism, of impudence, of craftiness: Delightful anecdotes on account of their intelligent narrative montage; moving anecdotes on account of their unbelievable events, anecdotes narrated with the most surprising circumlocutions of spiced rhetoric, and anecdotes narrated in the most rice-and-beans style. Anecdotes told by a waspish hick who is far from being docile and who speaks with a sharp tongue, and who speaks good English whenever need demands, a hick who speaks with smashing common sense; anecdotes of Puerto Ricans who have been guests of the same unemployment lines; who have been hosts to the same hunger and its allied hopes of a straight meal; pathetic anecdotes of the submissive who deny and excuse themselves for the involuntary error of being Puerto Ricans, and anecdotes of Puerto Ricans who raise hell and curse if anyone questions their being so; anecdotes of atrocious or shiftless lives, of life dealt with in the most willful and straight terms; anecdotes of tough-skinned survivors and debt-free hearts, anecdotes (sparkling) with a Puerto Rican Spanish, exact in its mumblings and in its brokenness, with a Puerto Rican Spanish stupendously vast and coarse, with a Puerto Rican Spanish vivificantly corrupt, just like Argentinian Spanish, just like Mexican Spanish, just like Venezuelan Spanish, and just like Spanish Spanish. A thousand anecdotes of travelers who come and go between the precarious and discredited paradise of New York and the eroded and uninhabitable paradise of Puerto Rico. . . .

The timid of heart—just like a Walter without Zodiac, without universal temple, without mystically-spangled gowns, like an underclass Walter Mercado—would now prophesize that tonight the flying bus will certainly explode because the sedicious laughter and the load of human energy it carries is a very dangerous kind of fuel. And low-flying angels with the curiosity of Peeping-Toms would gladly sacrifice the gold trimmings of one of their eucharistic and brief wings just to know about what the hell that crowd of airbound mestizos flying through their own turf, is yapping about. Only the uniformly gringo flight crew tonight seems to be immune to the laughter and is determined to stamp it out with a barrage of insipid turkey sandwiches, peanut shrapnel and Coke dispensed in hydrant-strong doses, with playing cards and the celluloid meditations of the Captain who risks himself to the pacification of the growing jokeful atmosphere with a few little jokes of his own, little jokes which do not catch on, do not cling, do not threaten anyone—*Ladies and Gentlemen, this is the Captain speaking, now that the dangerous skyjackers are back in their bags, now that we won't be taken to an unexpected meeting with that poso simpático* (not so likable) *señor Fidel Castro, I invite you all to look through the windows and catch the splash of the Milky Way. In a few minutes we will be showing, without charge tonight, a funny movie starring that funny man Richard Pryor.*

The lady sitting next to me asks me "*What did the man say?*" But the guy sitting in the front row, the one who boasts about travelling without luggage and who repeats over and over *"I live with one leg in New York and the other in Puerto Rico"* and who repeats over and again *"I make my dough in Manhattan but I spend it in Puerto Rico"* and who repeats every now and then *"I'm everybody's brother and nobody's friend. The only friends I have are my balls; they are always hanging around when I need them,"* takes a headstart on me in answering the lady and forces me to agree with his monotonous, serialized, sarcastic answer *"the Captain wants to kill us because he's high, he wants to spoil it for us so we let go and he can take over."* And he lowers and tones down his voice to a murmuring, orgasmic dialect with the most acid inferences about the Captain and the blond stewardess which, if written, would be published immediately by *Penthouse* or *Playboy.* My lady neighbor does not catch-on to the inferences for she has developed simultaneous conversations about the strike at an asylum for the insane in Puerto Rico where the patients are *"threatening to get sane if their demands are not met"* and about President Reagan's staunch stubbornness *"they say, that butcher is massacring El Salvador."*

The initial outburst which opened the door to the sedicious laughter, almost unanimously fertilizes the noisy cordiality that overwhelms the coach cabin of the flying bus; noisy cordiality which expresses itself in the noisy tolerance with which biting opinions are denied or agreed to, and in the noisy gratitude with which a compliment to the paper flowers someone brings as a present for an aunt who moved to a housing project in New Jersey is received; and in the noisy sharing typical of those who have suffered together and love the same things, a box of *guava* pastelillos (guava-filled pastries), a bag of *polvorones* (sugar cookies), a dozen *piononos* (baked sweet plantains), a string of *pirulies* (fruit-shaped candy bars), some slices of salami, a barrel of moonshine, rum cured with raisins . . . the one you can drink without any qualms of conscience . . . ; a noisy cordiality, passionate and indifferent to the sneers that their racket and indiscreet handlings, their coarse gastronomic delights and their proclivity to being friendly with just anyone because simply they are cut out that way, provokes in those who take refuge in the first class cabin and who, between sips of California champagne, establish a *tit-à-tête* with a stewardess of well-proportioned nose and subtle manners, venture a rationalized *"they are my people but . . ."* Or a resentful *"I wish they'd learn how to behave soon"* or an unexpected *"They'll never make it because they are trash"*; noisy and passionate cordiality that rises, fizzles and overruns when the fibrous middle-aged man recites his self-justifying postdata of *"I cannot live in Puerto Rico because there's no life for me there, then I'll bring it with me bit by bit; in this trip, four crabs from Vacía Talega, in the trip before, a fighting cock, in my next, all of Cortijo's records."* And he presses on with the inventory, defending it with the serial editing of amplified smiles, governing the relished memories of other cherished salvages, of other pretexts that efface any sense of distance, of other dear belongings that if seen with malice or judged by a myopic heart would amount to no more than folkloric junk, mediocre loyal color, light folk-lore . . . the *lelolai* syndrome.

But junk that, transcended from its not too impotent appearances or straightened-out from its crooked prestige as spendable triflings, become reiterated, useful, and necessary revelations of a temperament that, day after day gauges its diversity and underscores its permanence in spite of, even though and even if, although of course, perhaps or perchance, and other like dialectical stammerings or resources of enunciative discourse sprung from a catastrophic grammar which persists in conjugating into Spanish our inexorable and devastating *yankeezation*; a unique temperament, different, permanent, ours; a temperament which binds together our holiest dependence on the militant love of family and community . . . if you go to New York, you are seen off by four, if two return from New York, they are welcomed by eight; a temperament that keeps pure reserves of humor from drying up . . . for we like the kind of laughter which shakes and scandalizes, and the spicy jokes; temperament which upholds our affective empire, for we suffer and cry out, operatically, Mexican-cinema-like; this laughter of ours, this crying of ours, so indiscernable one from the other, just like the ones that now dispute among themselves the pressurized confines of the air bus. Because now, boasting of being outgoing and a helluva someone, unaware of the Chinese shadow that his body projects on the movie screen that a flight attendant is rolling out, the fibrous middle-aged man displays his gossip with one Cayo from Cayey who is travelling in order to hug his two grandsons whom he has not seen since September and with a Soledad Romero who jets down to Puerto Rico every time the energy cells of her soul run low, and with a certain Isidro from Juncos who had gone down to sell some land in order to get bail money for a son who fell in *trobol* and he does not want the boy to be ruined by jail, and with a Laura Serrano who cannot stand the winters but cannot miss her prefigured rendezvous with destiny in New York; and with a certain Yacoco Calderón from Loíza who moves for a few months to El Barrio so he can *"stuff himself with money,"* and with a certain Gloria Fragoso who is going to New York to prevent her dying son Vitín from dying, and with a certain Bob Márquez who greets him with a daring *"I'm Black and Puerto Rican, and to hell with it,"* and one other someone who mumbles his name and affirms that *"In New York, I'm strictly 'on loan'"*; all of them suddenly catapulted into the heated chatter in the aisles, sharing recently dusted hopes, repeating to each other *where are you from?* with the passion of a census taker, or meddling *if you are from Rio Grande you should know Mr. Pagán, who teaches Industrial Arts or if you are from Aguadilla, you must know for sure Tata Barradas. . . .* In the flying bus Puerto Ricans reconsider the adversity and the joy of the provincial fragrances of a country that became a huge town or the town that became a small country. Puerto Ricans who ritualize the difficult illusion of believing that they come to New York strictly "on loan," Puerto Ricans who swear by the revered memory of their dead make ends meet or only while things get better for Puerto Rico, or just so long as it takes them to raise enough money for a down payment on a house in the seventh section of Levittown; Puerto Ricans who any night of the week jump into the flying bus make sure they have the open return trip ticket that, in short notice, can cancel out the hunger to go back to that island, treasured in the limelight of a gentle and distorted memory, the *island "of the Palm trees and the swaying Sugar Cane flowers"* the island whose *"sandy waistline is gilded with foaming reefs"*; the open return trip ticket, the possession of which soothes the sudden urge to back-track your life over tropical mountains and beaches of the island, and waste your precious time strolling around the town plaza, and on the morning, noon and night to level out those streets—so beautiful because their so ugly town streets of an unique yesteryear, or to become an ineffable worker in some ineffable Idler's Company, and to recover your long lost friendships in a three-day talk-a-thon or in collective drunken frenzy with those who really know how to start it but ignore when to end it. And yes . . . return once again, momentarily, to what is left, to what remains, to what survives unaltered due to its constant erosion, its failure, or because of a fascinating inertia and which possesses not the glamour of any magical realism nor the lyricism of nostalgic repercussions; the open return trip ticket that certifies that in New York you are insured against the growth of roots that can only grow in your island, against the risk of being buried in an icy land unlike yours.

Puerto Ricans who cannot breathe in Puerto Rico but catch a lung-full in New York can achieve a ballpark average of four hundred; Puerto Ricans who are uneasy with the island's easy-going struggle and at home with the metropolitan sink-or-swim alternative; Puerto Ricans who wrest and tumble with their not being able to live in Puerto Rico and find themselves unnecessarily pissed and embarrassed when they have to verbalize their realities—*Listen, man, in the island the only thing you can do is drink and joke around, man, in Puerto Rico everything is a screwed-up complication, man, in Puerto Rico I feel amused and spaced-out by the verbal apotheosis and lack of discipline, man, in Puerto Rico people fail you and they keep their peace as if they would be eating yams, well, you know buddy, I've already cast my luck here, and there I feel lost, though maybe I'll give it a try there for a while and if things don't add up I'll scurry back to New York.* Puerto Ricans who want to be there but must remain here; Puerto Ricans who want to be there but cannot remain there; Puerto Ricans who live there and dream about being here; Puerto Ricans with their lives hanging from the hooks of the question marks *allá? acá?*, Hamletian disjunctives that ooze their lifeblood through both adverbs. Puerto Ricans installed in permanent errancy between "being there" and "being here" and who, because of it, deflate all the adventurous formality of the voyage until it becomes a mere "ride in a bus" . . . however aerial, so it may lift them filled with assurances over the blue pond . . . the *blue pond*, the Puerto Rican metaphor for the Atlantic Ocean.

A chauffered flight over the Atlantic and the plain fact of an arrival accomplished in order to be able to-go-out-again-and-come-back-again, a fact consecrated with the general applause that will follow the imminent touchdown of the flying bus.

The lady sitting next to me recollects now over the incident of the crabs which had unchained the three-hour-long accidents, and she hurls at me the unavoidable "*where are you from?*" at the very moment that the PA system says "*in a few minutes we will be landing at John F. Kennedy airport.*" And I answer: "*from Puerto Rico,*" in order that she should be able to retort, as a sort of medium in a rehearsed séance, "*one can tell THAT from your looks,*" adding immediately, "*I mean, from what town?*" "*From Humacao*" I answer. And anyone can tell that she is pleased because pleasantly, smilingly, she adds "*Oh, I was to Humacao once,*" while she looks at me as if I owed her. As if I were rudely avoiding the unavoidable ritual of asking her "*and you, where are you from?,*" as if, stupidly, I would be unaware that in the flying bus one must abide by the rules of the remnants of the tribal community and the unclogged flow of dialogue and the openness to everyone just for the asking, and to acknowledge the consciousness of an apparent yet presumed equality in risks and fate which binds together all the solidarity of the islanders who, after all, are "all aflame." "*Where are you from?*" I ask her although I do not even have to guess at the answer. Her playful, teasing glance and the shameless, divined blush under her bronze-skinned face underlines her answer, "*from Puerto Rico . . .*" forcing me to say, as a reasonable medium in a rehearsed séance "*even a blind man can see THAT,*" and, still, I add "*from what town, I mean.*" And she clearly specifies, "*from New York.*"

It all may seem, of course, either a smoothed-out commonplace or a pitiful geographical blunder, or a sarcastic joke out of a resounding box or a new category of the frontier or, perhaps, the sweet and swift revenge of the invaded who succeeded in invading the invader's domain. It is, of course, all that and a bit more. It is the other face of the political coin, the counter-flow of political rhetoric politicians fail to sound. It is the unstoried story not historicized in history books. It is the unrecorded datum of statistics. It is the transparent assertion that confirms the pragmatism of poetry. It is the belated justice that avenges the sorrows of those who once saw their beloved island blurred forever from the observation decks of the USSS *Borinquen* and the USSS *Coamo*; it is the vindication of those who crept, dazed, pioneering, into the fourteen hours of droned-in flight of the narrow, shaking, uncomfortable and silvered flying clippers of Pan American. It is the imposing flow of reality with its hallucinating proposal of newer, furiously conquered spaces. It is the relentless flow of a people who float between two ports, licensed for the smuggling of human hopes.

LIST OF EDITORS, CONTRIBUTORS, AND TRANSLATORS

Editors

NICOLÁS KANELLOS, the Brown Foundation Professor of Hispanic Literature at the University of Houston, is the director of a major national research program, Recovering the U.S. Hispanic Literary Heritage. Dr. Kanellos is the award-winning author of monographs, anthologies, and reference works on Hispanic literature and culture, including *A History of Hispanic Theater in the United States: Origins to 1940* (1990), *The Handbook of Hispanic Culture in the United States* (1993), and *Hispanic Periodicals in the United States: A Brief History and Comprehensive Bibliography* (2000). In 1994, President Bill Clinton appointed Dr. Kanellos to the National Council on the Humanities.

KENYA DWORKIN Y MÉNDEZ, Associate Professor of Spanish at Carnegie Mellon University, is an expert on Caribbean and U.S. Hispanic literature and theater. She has served as the editor of *Lucero: A Journal of Iberian and Latin American Studies* and is presently compiling the literary and theatrical works produced by the tobacco workers of Tampa in the late nineteenth and early twentieth centuries.

JOSÉ B. FERNÁNDEZ, Associate Dean of Arts and Sciences at the University of Central Florida, is a historian and literary critic who has published books and articles on Hispanic colonial literature as well as on writers of the Cuban Diaspora. He is also the coauthor and editor of various successful Spanish-language textbooks. Dr. Fernández's translation and critical edition, with Martin Favata, of *The Account*, by Alvar Núñez Cabeza de Vaca, has become the standard text of this foundational work.

ERLINDA GONZÁLES-BERRY, the Director of the Ethnic Studies Program at Oregon State University, has published books, anthologies, and articles on Chicano literature, women writers and the literature and culture of home her state, New Mexico. Included among her coedited anthologies are *Las Mujeres Hablan: An Anthology of Nuevo Mexicana Writers* (1988), *Pasó por Aquí: Critical Essays on New Mexico Literary Tradition, 1542–1988* (1989), and *Recovering the U.S. Hispanic Literary Heritage II* (1996).

AGNES LUGO-ORTIZ, Associate Professor of Spanish at Dartmouth College, is a specialist in Latin American and Caribbean Literature of the nineteenth century as well as in women's studies. Among her scholarly books and articles is *Identidades imaginadas: Biografía y nacionalidad en Cuba (1868–1898)*. Her current book project is *Paradoxes of Modern Identity: Biography, Portraiture and Nationality in Slaveholding Cuba (1760–1886)*.

CHARLES TATUM, Dean of Humanities at the University of Arizona, has published books, anthologies, and reference works on Chicano literature and culture and has served as the coeditor of *Studies in Latin American Popular Culture* since 1981. His *Chicano Literature* (1982) is a standard work in the field, as are his annual anthologies *New Chicana/Chicano Writing I, II, III* (1991–1993). He is also the coeditor of *Recovering the U.S. Hispanic Literary Heritage II* (1996).

Coordinator

ALEJANDRA BALESTRA is the coordinator of the national research program Recovering the U.S. Hispanic Literary Heritage at the University of Houston. She has Master's Degrees in Literature and Linguistics from the University of Buenos Aires and the University of Houston, and has published articles on Spanish American and U.S. Hispanic authors, as well as on linguistic topics.

Contributors

(EA) EMILIA ARCE, Department of Modern and Classical Languages, University of Houston

(GB) GABRIELA BAEZA VENTURA, Department of Modern and Classical Languages, University of Houston

(AB) ALEJANDRA BALESTRA, Project Coordinator, Recovering the U.S. Hispanic Literary Heritage Project, University of Houston

(EC) ELVIRA CASAMAYOR, Department of Modern and Classical Languages, University of Houston

(AC) ANTONIA CASTAÑEDA, Department of History, St. Mary's University, San Antonio

(KD) KENYA DWORKIN Y MÉNDEZ, Department of Modern Languages, Carnegie-Mellon University

(CS) CONSUELO STEBBINS, Department of Foreign Languages, University of Central Florida

(JBF) JOSÉ B. FERNÁNDEZ, History Department, University of Central Florida

(RF) RICHARD FLORES, Department of Anthropology, University of Texas at Austin

(MG) MARÍA GARCÍA, Department of Modern and Classical Languages, University of Houston

(EGB) ERLINDA GONZÁLEZ-BERRY, Department of Ethnic Studies, Oregon State University

(SH) SPENCER HERRERA, Department of Modern and Classical Languages, University of Houston

(NK) NICOLÁS KANELLOS, Department of Modern and Classical Languages, University of Houston

(TK) THOMAS KINNEY, Department of Rhetoric, University of Arizona

(EL) ENRIQUE LAMADRID, Spanish and Portuguese Department, University of New Mexico

(LL) LUIS LEAL, Chicano Studies Department, University of California at Santa Barbara

(HL) HUMBERTO LÓPEZ CRUZ, Department of Foreign Languages and Literatures, University of Central Florida

(ALO) AGNES LUGO-ORTIZ, Department of Spanish and Portuguese, Dartmouth College

(JM) JOY MEADOWS, Department of Modern and Classical Languages, University of Houston

(EO) EDNA OCHOA, Department of Modern and Classical Languages, University of Houston

(JO) JULIÁN OLIVARES, Department of Modern and Classical Languages, University of Houston

(EP) EDWIN PADILLA, Department of Arts and Humanities, University of Houston, Downtown

(SP) SONJA PÉREZ, English Department, University of Arizona

(BP) BEATRICE PITA, Department of Literature, University of California, San Diego

(GP) GERALD POYO, History Department, St. Mary's University, San Antonio

(TDR) TEY DIANA REBOLLEDO, Department of Spanish and Portuguese, University of New Mexico

(SR) SERGIO REYNA, Department of Modern and Classical Languages, University of Houston

(JMR) JOHN-MICHAEL RIVERA, Department of English, University of Colorado, Boulder

(MS) MARCELA SALAS, Spanish Department, Rice University

(VSK) VIRGINIA SÁNCHEZ KORROL, Department of Puerto Rican and Latino Studies, Brooklyn College, City University of New York

(AS) ALEXANDRA SUNUNU

(ChT) CHARLES TATUM, University of Arizona

(STS) SILVIO TORRES-SAILLANT, English Department, Syracuse University

(CV) CAROLINA VILLARROEL, Department of Modern and Classical Languages, University of Houston

(KW) KARINA WIGOZKI, Department of Modern and Classical Languages, University of Houston

(TEW) TONYA E. WOLFORD, Department of Modern and Classical Languages, University of Houston

Translators

(FA) Francisco Amy
(MA) María Arrillaga
(HA) Harold Augerbraun
(DB) Daniel Balderston
(PMB) Percy M. Baldwin
(HEB) Herbert Eugene Bolton
(DBO) Deborah Bonner
(GICF) Guillermo I. Castillo-Feliú
(ECB) Ethriam Cash Brammer
(KD) Kenya Dworkin y Méndez
(WHE) William H. Ellison
(ME) Miguel Encinias
(MES) Martín Espada
(JME) José Manuel Espinosa
(AFF) A. F. Falcones
(JBF) José B. Fernández
(JF) Juan Flores
(DWF) David William Foster
(STG) Shawn T. Griffen
(SGR) Susan Giersbach Rascón
(ALO) Agnes Lugo-Ortiz
(MFO) Margarite Fernández Olmos
(EGB) Erlinda González-Berry
(NK) Nicolás Kanellos
(DK) Dolores Koch
(ELD) Elpidio Laguna-Díaz
(EL) Enrique R. Lamadrid
(HL) Helen Lane
(MIL) Myron I. Lichtblau
(CLM) Carmen Lilian Marín
(EM) E. Munguía, Jr.
(TCN) Thelma Campbell Nason
(CRN) Catherine Rodríguez-Nieto
(VO) Victoria Ortiz
(LPG) Lizabeth Paravisini-Gebert
(CPB) Camilo Pérez-Bustillo
(PP) Pablo Peschiera
(ChP) Charles Pilditch
(FP) Francis Price
(CR) Clifton Ross
(ER) Elinor Randall
(DJR) Dick J. Reavis
(AR) Alfred Rodríguez
(JPS) Joseph P. Sanchez
(MSP) Margaret Sayers Peden
(FS) Florence Sender
(AS) Alexandra Sununu
(MAT) Manuel A. Tellechea
(LT) Larry Torres
(IHT) Inés Hernández Tovar
(EVP) Evangelina Vigil-Piñón
(KW) Karl Wagenheim
(TEW) Tonya E. Wolford

SOURCE NOTES

Algarín, Miguel. "Saliendo" and "Light After Blackout" from *On Call.* Copyright © 1980 by Arte Público Press. Reprinted by permission of Arte Público Press.
Allende, Isabel. "The Argonauts" from *Daughter of Fortune.* Copyright © 1999 by Isabel Allende. Reprinted by permission of HarperCollins Publishers, Inc., HarperCollins Publishers Ltd. (UK) and the author.
Alurista. "must be the season of the witch" and "mis ojos hinchados" from *Floricanto en Aztlán.* Creative Series, No. 1 (1971), UCLA Chicano Studies Research Center. Reprinted by permission of The Regents of the University of California. Not for further reproduction.
Anonymous. "The Contest of Coffee and Corn Gruel" originally published as "Trovo Del Cafe y Atole" from Embudo, New Mexico. Collected by Tomás Atencio and Estevan Arellano from Dwight Durán. Copyright © 1988 by Enrique R. Lamadrid. Reprinted by permission of Tomás Atencio, Estevan Arellano, Dwight Durán and Enrique R. Lamadrid.
Anonymous. "Little Indian Ballad of Plácido Romero" originally published as "La Indita de Plácida Romero/Indita Ballad of Plácido Romero" from *Tesoros del Espiritu: A Portrait in Sound of Hispanic New Mexico.* Collected by Herman Bustamante. Sung by Margaret Johnson. Copyright © 1988 by Enrique R. Lamadrid. Reprinted by permission of Herman Bustamante, Margaret Johnson and Enrique R. Lamadrid.
Anzaldúa, Gloria. "How to Tame a Wild Tongue" from *Borderlands/La Frontera: The New Mestiza.* Copyright © 1987, 1999 by Gloria Anzaldúa. Reprinted by permission of Aunt Lute Books.
Arenas, Reinaldo. "The Eviction," "The Announcement" and "Dreams" from *Before Night Falls: A Memoir* by Reinaldo Arenas, translated by Dolores M. Koch. Copyright © 1993 by the Estate of Reinaldo Arenas and Dolores M. Koch, English translation. Used by permission of Viking Penguin, a division of Penguin Putnam, Inc.
Azuela, Mariano. Excerpt from *The Underdogs.* Translation by E. Munguía, Jr. Reprinted by permission of Arte Público Press.
Bencastro, Mario. Excerpt from *Odyssey to the North.* Copyright © 1998 by Mario Bencastro. Reprinted by permission of Arte Público Press.
Braschi, Wilfredo. "A Prayer in the Snow." Translation by Tonya E. Wolford. Reprinted by permission of Arte Público Press.
Cabeza de Vaca, Alvar Núñez. Excerpt from *The Account.* Copyright © 1993 by Arte Público Press. Reprinted by permission of Arte Público Press.
Calvo, Lino Novás. "The Cow on the Rooftop." Reprinted by permission of Latin American Literary Review.
Cervantes, Lorna Dee. "Beneath the Shadowy Freeway" from *Emplumada.* Reprinted by permission of University of Pittsburgh Press.
Chavez, Fray Angelico. "The Fiddler and the Angelito" from *The Short Stories of Fray Angelico Chavez.* Edited by Genaro M. Padilla. Reprinted by permission of Genaro M. Padilla.
Cofer, Judith Ortiz. "Volar" from *The Year of Our Revolution.* Copyright © 1998 by Judith Ortiz Cofer. Reprinted by permission of Arte Público Press. "Exile" from *Terms of Survival.* Copyright © 1987 by Judith Ortiz Cofer. "Maria Elena." Permission held by author.
Colón, Jesús. "Kipling and I." Copyright © 1982 by International Publishers. Reprinted by permission of International Publishers.
Corpi, Lucha. "Mexico," "Dark Romance" and "Marina Mother." Reprinted by permission of Arte Público Press.
Cruz, Victor Hernandez. "Loisada" and "Energy" from *Rhythm, Content & Flavor.* Copyright © 1989 by Victor Hernández Cruz. Reprinted by permission of Arte Público Press. "The Latest Latin Dance Craze" and "today is a day of great joy." Permission held by author.
de Burgos, Julia. "I Was My Own Route" and "Farewell in Welfare Island" from *Song of Simple Truth* by Julia de Burgos. Edited and translated by Jack Agüeros. Reprinted by permission of Curbstone Press.
de la Guerra Ord, María de las Angustias. "Occurrences in Hispanic California." Copyright © 1956 by The Academy of American Franciscan History. Reprinted by permission of The Academy of American Franciscan History.
de la Selva, Salamón. "A Song for Wall Street" and "The Secret" from *Tropical Town and Other Poems.* Edited by Silvio Sirias. Reprinted by permission of Arte Público Press.
de Zavala, Adina. "The Courteous and Kindly Child and the 'Good People' on the Underground Passageway" from *History and Legends of the Alamo and Other Missions in and around San Antonio.* Edited and introduced by Richard R. Flores. Copyright © 1996 by Arte Público Press. Reprinted by permission of Arte Público Press.
Diaz, Junot. "No Face" from *Drown.* Copyright © 1996 by Junot Diaz. Used by permission of Riverhead Books, a division of Penguin Putnam, Inc. and Watkins/Loomis Agency.
Esteves, Sandra María. "My Name is María Cristina." Excerpted from *Yerba Buena*: Greenfield Review. Copyright © 1981 by Sandra María Esteves. Reprinted by permission of the author. "Anonymous Apartheid" from *Bluestown Mockingbird Mambo.* Copyright © 1990 by Sandra María Esteves. Reprinted by permission of Arte Público Press.
Fernández, Roberta. "Amanda" from *Intaglio: A Novel in Six Stories.* Copyright © 1990 by Roberta Fernández. Reprinted by permission of Arte Público Press.
Fernández, Roberto. "Miracle on Eighth and Twelfth" from *Raining Backwards.* 2nd Edition. Copyright © 1988 by Roberto Fernández. Reprinted by permission of Arte Público Press.
Firmat, Gustavo Pérez. Excerpt from *Anything but Love.* Copyright © 2000 by Gustavo Pérez Firmat. Reprinted by permission of Arte Público Press.
Galarza, Ernesto. Excerpt from *Barrio Boy.* Reprinted by permission of University of Notre Dame Press, 1971.
García, Cristina. "A Matrix Light" from *Dreaming in Cuban.* Copyright © 1992 by Christina García. Used by permission of Alfred A. Knopf, a division of Random House, Inc. and Ellen Levine Literary Agency.
Goldemberg, Isaac. "Chronicles" and "Self-Portrait." Copyright © 1989 by Isaac Goldemberg. Reprinted by permission of the author.
González, José Luis. "The Night We Became People Again" from *Cuentos: An Anthology of Short Stories from Puerto Rico.* New York: Schocken Books, 1978. Courtesy of Kal Wagenheim, translator.
González, Rodolfo "Corky." "I am Joaquín" from *Message to Aztlín: Selected Writings.* Copyright © 2001 by Rodolfo "Corky" González. Reprinted by permission of Arte Público Press.
Gregorio de Escobedo, Alonso. "Florida" from *Pirates, Indians and Spaniards.* Edited by James W. Covington and A.F. Falcones. Reprinted by permission of James W. Covington.
Grillo, Evelio. "Going Up North" reprinted from *Black Cuban, Black American* with permission of Arte Público Press.
Guerra, Alirio Díaz. Excerpt from *Lucas Guevara.* Translation by Ethrian Cash Brammer. Copyright © 2001 by Arte Público Press. Reprinted by permission of Arte Público Press.
Hijuelos, Oscar. Excerpt from "The Cuban Illness: 1954–1955" from *Our House in the Last World.* Copyright © 1983 by Oscar Hijuelos. Reprinted by permission of Persea Books, Inc. (New York).
Hinojosa, Rolando. Excerpt from *Dear Rafe.* Copyright © 1985 by Rolando Hinojosa. Reprinted by permission of Arte Público Press.
Huidobro, Matías Montes. *Exile.* Translation by Kenya Dworkin y Mendez. Reprinted by permission of Arte Público Press.
Kozer, Jose. "It is dark, my sister, it is dark" and "This señor don Gringo is very academic today" from *Por La Libre.* Edited by Bayú Menoráh. Copyright © 1973 by José Kozer. Reprinted by permission of the author.
Laviera, Tato. "my graduation speech" and "the africa in pedro morejón" from *La carreta made a U-turn.* Copyright © 1992 by Tato Laviera. Reprinted by permission of Arte Público Press.
Limón, Graciela. Excerpt from *The Day of the Moon.* Copyright © 2000 by Graciela Limón. Reprinted by permission of Arte Público Press.
Marqués, René. Excerpt from *The Oxcart.* Reprinted by permission of Charles Scriber's Sons.
Martí, José. Excerpt from *Simple Verses.* Spanish copyright © 1997 by Arte Público Press. Translation copyright © 1997 by Manuel A. Tellecha. "Two Views of Coney Island" from *Inside the Monster.* Reprinted by permission of Monthly Review Press. "With All, for the Good of All" from *Jose Martí Reader:*

Writings on the Americas. Copyright © 1999 by Ocean Press. Copyright © 1999 by Editorial Jose Martí and Centro de Estudios Martianos. Reprinted by permission of Ocean Press.
Méndez, Miguel. Excerpt from *Pilgrims in Aztlán*. Copyright © 1992 by Bilingual Press/Editorial Bilingüe. Reprinted by permission of Bilingual Press/Editorial Bilingüe (Arizona State University, Tempe, AZ).
Mohr, Nicholasa. "Uncle Claudio" from *El Bronx Remembered*. Copyright © 1986 by Nicholasa Mohr. Reprinted by permission of author.
Mora, Pat. "Curandera" and "Legal Alien" from *Chants*. Copyright © 1985 by Pat Mora. Reprinted by permission of Arte Público Press.
Moraga, Cherríe. "La Güera" from *Loving in the War Years: lo que nunca pasó por sus labios*. Reprinted by permission of South End Press and the author.
Morales, Aurora Levins and Rosario Morales. "Ending Poem." Reprinted by permission of the authors.
Muñoz, Miguel Elías. *The Greatest Performance*. Copyright © 1991 by Elías Miguel Muñoz. Reprinted by permission of Arte Público Press.
Obejas, Alicia Achy. Excerpt from "Above All, a Family Man" from *We Came all the way from Cuba*. Copyright © 1994 by Alicia Achy Obejas. Reprinted by permission of Cleis Press and the author.
Peña, Guillermo Gómez. Excerpt from "Danger Zone: Cultural Relations between Chicanos and Mexicans at the End of the Century" from *The New World Border*. Copyright © 1996 by Guillermo Gómez Peña. Reprinted by permission of City Lights Bookstore.
Pérez, Luis. Excerpt from *El Coyote/The Rebel*. Copyright © 1947, 2000 by Luis Pérez. Reprinted by permission of Arte Público Press.
Pérez de Villagrá, Gaspar. Excerpt from *The History of New Mexico*. Translated and edited by Miguel Encinas, Alfred Rodríquez, and Joseph P. Sánchez. Reprinted by permission of University of New Mexico Press.
Pietri, Pedro. "Puerto Rican Obituary" from *Puerto Rican Obituary*. Copyright © 1973 by Pedro Pietri. Reprinted by permission of Monthly Review Press.
Piñero, Miguel. "A Lower East Side Poem" from *La Bodega Sold Dreams*. Copyright © 1985 by the estate of Miguel Piñero. Reprinted by permission of Arte Público Press.
Prida, Dolores. "The Herb Shop" from *Beautiful Señoritas and Other Plays* (1994). Reprinted by permission of Arte Público Press.
Ramírez, Sandra Estela. "Speech Read by the Author on the Evening That the 'Society of Workers' Celebrated the Twenty-Fourth Anniversary of Its Founding" from *Sara Estela Ramirez: The Early Twentieth Century* Texas-Mexican Poet. Ph.D. dissertation, University of Houston. Translation copyright © 1984 by Inés Hernández Tovar. Reprinted by permission of the Translator.
Ríos, Alberto Alvaro. "Mi abuelo," "Wet Camp" and "Nani." Copyright © 1982 by Alberto Alvaro Ríos. Reprinted by permission of the author.
Rivera, Tomás. "First Communion" from *... y no se lo tragí la tierra/...And the Earth did Not Devour Him*. Translated by Evangelina Vigil Piñón. English translation copyright © 1987 by Evangelina Vigil- Piñón. Reprinted by permission of Arte Público Press.
Ruiz de Burton, María Amparo. Excerpt from *The Squatter and the Don*. Edited and Introduced by Rosaura Sánchez and Beatrice Pita. Copyright © 1992 by Arte Público Press. Reprinted by permission of Arte Público Press.
Sánchez, Luis Rafael. "The Flying Bus" from *Images and Identities: The Puerto Rican in Two World Contexts*. Copyright © 1987 by Luis Rafael Sánchez. Reprinted by permission of Transaction Books.
Santicilia, Pedro. "To Spain" from *El laúd del desterrado*. Edited by Matías Montes Huidubro. Reprinted by permission of Arte Público Press.
Sepúlveda, Emma. "I Grew Accustomed" and "Here Am I Now" from *Death to Silence/Muerte al silencio*. English translation copyright © 1997 by Shaun T. Griffin. Reprinted by permission of Arte Público Press.
Soto, Pedro Juan. "Scribbles" from *Spiks: Stories by Pedro Juan Soto*. Reprinted by permission of Monthly Review Press.
Suárez, Virgil. "Spared Angola" from *Spared Angola: Memories From A Cuban American Childhood*. Copyright © 1997 by Virgil Suárez. Excerpt from *Going Under*. Copyright © 1996 by Virgil Suárez. Reprinted by permission of Arte Público Press.
Thomas, Piri. Excerpt from *Down These Mean Streets* by Piri Thomas. Copyright © 1967 by Piri Thomas. Used by permission of Alfred A. Knopf, a division of Random House, Inc. and Peter Basch.
Tolón, Miguel Teurbe. "Always" and "Song of the Cuban Woman" from *El laúd del desterrado*. Edited by Matías Montes Huidobro. Copyright © 1995 by Matías Montes Huidobro. Reprinted by permission of Arte Público Press.
Ulibarrí, Sabine. "My Wonder Horse" from *Tierra Amarilla: Stories of New Mexico/Cuentos de Nuevo México*. Reprinted by permission of University of New Mexico Press.
Valdez, Luis. "Los Vendidos" from *Luiz Valdez—Early Works*. Copyright © 1971 by Luis Valdez for El Teatro Campesino. Reprinted by permission of Arte Público Press.
Valenzuela, Luisa. "I'm Your Horse in the Night" from *Other Weapons* by Luisa Valenzuela. Translated by Deborah Bonner. First edition in Spanish, 1982. First edition in English 1985. Copyright © Luisa Valenzuela. Translation copyright © Deborah Bonner. Copyright © 1985 by Ediciones del Norte. Reprinted by permission of Ediociones del Norte
Vega, Bernardo. "Memoirs" from *Memoirs of Bernardo Vega: A Contribution to the history of the Puerto Rican Community in New York*. Reprinted by permission of Monthly Review Press.
Vélez, Clemente Soto. "Horizons" and "Five Points Stars" from *La Sangre que sigue cantando/The Blood That Keeps Singing* by Clemente Soto Velez. Copyright © 1997 by Curbstone Press. Reprinted with permission of Curbstone Press.
Venegas, Daniel. Excerpt from *The Adventures of Don Chipote or, When Parrots Breast Feed*. Translation copyright © 2000 by Ethriam Cash Brammer. Reprinted by permission of Arte Público Press.
Villarreal, Andrea and Teresa. "Why Are You Still Here, Mexican Men? Fly, Fly to the Battlefield." Translation by Tonya E. Wolford. Reprinted by permission of Arte Público Press.
Villegas de Magnón, Leonor. "The Rebel is a Girl" from *The Rebel*. Copyright © 1994 Leonor Smith. Reprinted by permission of Arte Público Press.
Viramontes, Helena María. "The Moths" from *Moths and Other Stories*. Copyright © 1985 by Helena María Viramontes. Reprinted by permission of Arte Público Press.
Yglesias, José. Excerpt from *The Truth About Them*. Copyright © 1971 by José Yglesias. Reprinted by permission of Arte Público Press.

Works in translation by the following authors reprinted by permission of Arte Público Press, University of Houston: Gustavo Alemán Bolaños, Santiago Argüello, Julia de Burgos, Bonifacio Byrne, Anonymous "A Jíbaro in New York," Anonymous "Joaquín Murieta," Anonymous "Deportees," Anonymous "The Dishwasher," Anonymous "Gregorio Cortez," José Alvarez de Toledo y Dubois, Julio G. Arce, Nicanor Bolet Peraza, Luisa Capetillo, Adolfo Carrillo, Herminia Chacón, Jesús Colón ("The Flapper"), Joaquín Colón, Juan Nepomuceno Cortina, Juan Antonio Corretjer, Guillermo Cotto-Thorner, Richard Valle "La Defensa," Alirio Díaz Guerra, Miguel Angel Figueroa, Enrique Flores Magón, "The Friend of Men," "P.G.," Wen Gálvez, Tomás Gares, Isaac Goldenberg, Pablo de la Guerra, Conrado Espinosa, María Luisa Garza, José María Heredia, Jovita Idar, Carmita Landestoy, Lirón, Francisco Marín, Américo Meana, Alberto O'Farrill, Gonzalo O'Neill, A. Ortiz Vargas, José F. Palomares, Alonso Perales, E. Pérez Díaz, Lorenzo Piñero Riveiro, Francisco Ramírez, Vicente Rocafuerte, Jesús y Netty Rodríguez, Gustavo Solano, Lola Rodríguez de Tió, Pablo Santicilia, Francico Sellén, Consuelo Lee Tapia, Miguel Teurbe Tolón, Rodolfo Uranga, Erasmo Vando, Félix Varela, Enrique José Varona, Daniel Venegas, Andrea & Teresa Villarreal, Juan Clemente Zenea.

CPSIA information can be obtained at www.ICGtesting.com
Printed in the USA
LVOW09s0709021214

416538LV00006B/88/P

9 780195 138252